Building a Future on Peace and Justice

Kai Ambos · Judith Large · Marieke Wierda
Editors

Building a Future on Peace and Justice

Studies on Transitional Justice, Peace and Development
The Nuremberg Declaration on Peace and Justice

Springer

Editors

Kai Ambos

University of Göttingen
Head Department for Foreign
and International Criminal Law
Chair for Criminal Law, Criminal Procedure
Comparative Law and International
Criminal Law
Judge at the State Court
Platz der Göttinger Sieben 5
37073 Göttingen
Germany
kambos@gwdg.de

Judith Large

Lancaster University
The Richardson Institute
Bailrigg
Lancaster LA1 4YD
United Kingdom
Special Advisor, Berghof Peace Support
Berlin
judith.large@berghof-peacesupport.org

Marieke Wierda

Director, Prosecutions Program
International Center of Transitional Justice
5 Hanover Square, Floor 24
New York, NY 10004
USA
MWierda@ictj.org

ISBN: 978-3-540-85753-2 e-ISBN: 978-3-540-85754-9

Library of Congress Control Number: 2008935033

Printed on acid-free paper

springer.com

Preface

I.

Tensions between Peace and Justice have long been debated by scholars, practitioners and agencies, including those of the United Nations, and both theory and policy must be refined for very practical application in situations of emergence from violent conflict or political repression. Specific contexts demand concrete decisions and approaches aimed at the redress of grievance and creation of conditions for social justice and non-violent futures. Within the United Nations, discourse on 'post-conflict' justice originally grew out of the Nuremberg trials and focused on prosecutions for serious international crimes committed by an accused individual, placing accountability at the individual level and not on an entire nation. In international law, the responsibility lies with states to ensure individuals are held accountable, and also with the international community as a whole. This view holds that support for the rule of law and human rights norms cannot be established in a society while the perpetrators of crime enjoy impunity. This has been confirmed by the establishment of the International Criminal Court, whose jurisdiction extends to ongoing conflicts and whose work has given particular impetus to the peace and justice debate.

Opposing voices point out that prosecutions can make it impossible to achieve a negotiated settlement to conflict, may divide and even threaten the affected population, if they open old wounds or prompt re-mobilization for war or criminal intent. Alternative justice approaches thus emerged from the 1970s onwards in countries where conflicts were deeply rooted in the structure of society. Rather than focusing only on individual perpetrators, transitional justice shifted attention to broader issues which related needs for reconciliation and social justice, on the basis that too narrow a definition of justice in legalistic and judicial terms was preventing countries from addressing the root causes of poverty and violent conflict. In some situations, including El Salvador, Peru and South Africa, transitional justice mechanisms such as truth commissions were pursued in lieu of criminal prosecutions. Now, in post-conflict settings, it is generally accepted that an integrated approach of measures such as criminal justice, truth seeking, reparations and institutional reforms are necessary to reflect the complexity of the demands of justice.

But what does this mean in situations in which there is still no peace? The cry for 'no peace without justice' resonates in many bitterly divided settings throughout the world. International responses have included diverse institutions such as the already mentioned International Criminal Court and more recently the Peace Building Commission, with a consistent message from the United Nations that peace and justice can and must be pursued in tandem. As recently stated by the Secretary General in a statement on 5 June 2008: "The Secretary-General is convinced that there can be no sustainable peace without justice. Peace and justice go hand in hand."

II.

For the purpose of addressing these tensions between peace and justice, 60 years after the famous judgment of the International Military Tribunal at Nuremberg, a distinguished gathering in the same courtroom opened a conference entitled *Building a Future on Peace and Justice*. The large international conference held at Nuremberg from 25 to 27 June was co-hosted by the Governments of Germany, Jordan and Finland, as well as two non-governmental organizations with experience in these issues (Crisis Management Initiative (CMI) and the International Center for Transitional Justice, (ICTJ). Participants included numerous international dignitaries, government representatives from nearly 40 governments, and almost 300 academics, practitioners and experts from settings which face dilemmas in achieving a balance between peace and justice (for the list of participants see the annex at the end of this book). The conference unfolded in plenary sessions on the first and last days, and ten workshops on the second day. These workshops were prepared by some thirty studies and abstracts that the conference organizers had commissioned especially for the conference.

Some key aspects of the relationship between peace and justice were addressed in the opening speeches by the German Foreign Minister, *Frank-Walter Steinmeier*, Jordanian Minister of Justice *Sharif Al-Zubi*, ICC Prosecutor *Luis Moreno Ocampo*, and *Sonia Picado* speaking as Personal Representative of the Costa Rican President Oscar Arias. UN Secretary General Ban Ki-moon sent a written message (see page 3). The former Finnish Foreign Minister *Erkki Tuomioja* summarized several aspects in his concluding speech and paved the way for the elaboration of the Nuremberg Declaration on Peace and Justice. In his opening speech, Steinmeier highlighted the importance of dealing with the past and cautioned against simplistic dichotomies between peace and justice (full speech begins on page 5). Moreno Ocampo noted that the entry into force of, and the adherence by more than half of all countries to the Rome Statute of the ICC had changed the parameters for peace (full speech begins page 9).

Sonia Picado highlighted the specific experiences of Latin America in these dilemmas, including the "Esquipulas Agreement" signed by the Presidents of Central America to end the long wars afflicting the area, and the recent developments in Argentina and Chile in the aftermath of the decision of the Inter-American Court of Human Rights in the case of *Barrios-Alto v. Peru* which confirmed the incompatibility of amnesty laws with the Convention. In her suggestions for initiatives to meet these challenges, including addressing some of the root causes of conflict, she mentioned the Japanese initiative on human security launched at the 2000 UN Millennium Summit; the concept of an "arms trade treaty" now with the First Committee of the United Nations, and a "Costa Rica Consensus" promoted by President Arias, aiming to create mechanisms to forgive the debt of developing nations that invest less in soldiers and weapons and more in education, health and environmental protection. She quoted President Arias to say: "It is time that the international financial community reward not only those who use resources efficiently, but also those who use resources morally."

Jordanian Justice Minister *Sharif Al-Zubi* spoke as a representative of the Middle East which he called "one of the most troubled regions in the world today." He stressed the fact that peace must include justice if it is to hold, including a settlement of the Israeli-Palestinian conflict or the situation in Iraq. Even if justice is postponed as negotiators try to hammer out a cessation of hostilities or try to negotiate interim peace accords, justice must ultimately be addressed to fortify the peace. He mentioned that today's reality has forced populations to accept delayed justice or barely any justice at all in the interim or even final peace accords. He remarked that reconciliation is not a dictate handed down when hostilities cease. Mr. Zubi said it was time to develop a broad framework to address these issues, and that he was particularly interested in how the promotion of justice influences the course of the conflict, including in places such as Afghanistan and Lebanon, with the creation of the Hariri Tribunal. He remarked that:

> "Current circumstances in the region, and a sense that the rest of the world does not understand or care, through a selective approach of implementing international resolutions, has raised the voices and influence of a militant minority. The majority undoubtedly want peace, but not any peace. [...] For it to last, it has to be a just peace, and the world community must demonstrate neutrality, even-handedness, superior ethics and morality in dealing with the conflict."

He mentioned that Jordan is particularly aware of the need to educate people to confront extremist aberrations, thriving on the region's instability and the world's complacency, and issued the Amman Message in November 2004, to clarify the true nature of Islam. It articulates Islam's social values: compassion, respect for others, tolerance, acceptance and freedom of religion, equal dignity of all people, and the pursuit of peace. The most stable foundation for security in a region is improved quality of life for its people.

The closing speech was given by the former Minister of Foreign Affairs from Finland, *Erkki Tuomioja*, who commented that the dilemmas of peace and justice yield no quick and self-evident solutions, but that there are a number of assertions that can be drawn from past exercises in peace negotiations and post-conflict peace-building. For instance, it should be clear that decisions on peace and justice need the support of the local population. This poses great challenges for outreach within society and for international institutions engaged in the provision of justice, maintenance of peace and assistance in the reconstruction of society. Post-conflict societies must have the necessary capacity to cater to peace and justice, and may require international assistance. An example given by former Minister Tuomioja is the Justice Rapid Response initiative, supported by Germany and Finland, among other states. Justice Rapid Response is intended to be an international cooperative mechanism for the supply of voluntary assistance at the request of a State or international institution, where the identification, collection and preservation of information would assist at any stage a wide range of international and transitional justice options. Criminal justice is an indispensable part of any reconciliation after horrendous crimes have been committed, but justice is more than criminal justice and must include victim-centered mechanisms such as reparations, truth commissions whose recommendations are implemented, gender-sensitive approaches, and vetting programs that improve the integrity of state institutions. The responsibility to protect is another important development. Finally, Mr. Tuomioja stressed once more that peace and justice are not contradictory forces or mutually exclusive objectives, but rather mutually reinforcing imperatives. The question is not about the inclusion or exclusion of justice and accountability, but as the Secretary-General of the United Nations pointed out in his report in 2004, about strategic planning, careful integration and sensible sequencing of activities. Tensions between peace and justice are most pronounced when people expect simple and straightforward solutions to very complex situations.

III.

The complexities of these questions were revealed during the conference. Deliberations and presentations on the second and third days touched on changes in the nature of modern war; the relationship between internationally brokered political settlements (peace agreements) and emerging norms and practices in the field of transitional justice; and the need for creating conditions for sound human development.

There has been definitive progress from a world in which blanket amnesties were granted at times with little hesitation, or accompanied with generous power-sharing arrangements, as was the case with the Lome Agreement in Sierra Leone in 1999. There is a growing understanding that accountability has pragmatic as well as principled arguments in its favor. Peace agreements can no longer be seen as an end in themselves. It is increasingly evident that 'just' conflict resolution is as critical to the successful implementation as to the negotiation of a settlement. In this sense, it may no longer be appropriate to view 'peace' and 'justice' in opposition to each other. The conference sought to identify ways in which both can be simultaneously pursued.

The UN has stated that nearly half of all peace agreements collapse within five years. Increasingly, difficulties of implementing the rule of law are being seen as one key to that failure. As international actors are confronted increasingly with a role in implementing and sustaining the ‘peace’ they have helped to negotiate, questions of rule of law, accountable political and legal institutions, and the social meanings and symbolism of justice become increasingly important. Indeed it is cumbersome, if not contradictory, to build a culture based on the rule of law when the political arrangement underlying it is founded in impunity. Practical arguments as much as shifts in the norms have created a situation in which the choice is increasingly seen as ‘which forms of accountability’, rather than a stark choice between peace and justice. In other words, it is socio-political transformation, not just an end to violence, that is needed to build sustainable peace and resolution to conflict. It is increasingly evident that conflict resolution is as critical to the implementation as to the negotiation of a settlement.

IV.

The book offers the most important speeches delivered at the Nuremberg Conference and the updated version of the studies prepared for the Conference. This main part of the book is divided into four parts.

Part I seeks to give a thorough overview of the current state of legal obligations in relation to peace and justice. If offers new and comprehensive studies on the laws relevant for transitional justice, in particular the concept of amnesties and the role of the International Criminal Court. *Part II* gives an overview of some of the dilemmas faced by practitioners engaged in conflict mediation and peace building. The papers argue for a holistic approach to justice in building a sustainable peace. This increasingly implies socio-economic justice and the vital parameters of development for visible peace dividends and human security to guarantee better futures for the affected population. *Part III* discusses the specific challenges pursuing justice during or after conflict, taking into account the new problems arising from the coming into force of the International Criminal Court. While this Part looks at these challenges from a rather general perspective *Part IV* includes a selection of case studies, many of which may be described as “hard cases” in which internationalized and local approaches were devised to navigate the tensions between peace and justice. Lessons are drawn from these cases for future scenarios.

The tensions between peace and justice are increasingly topical and have been written about from various perspectives. However, to our knowledge, this is the first volume that seeks to provide an interdisciplinary approach to this issue, viewing the dilemmas from the perspectives of those with experience in conflict mediation, transitional justice, and development. The interdisciplinary approach reflects the competing demands which converge in transition settings. Also unique are the contributions by policy-makers in the form of speeches delivered at the conference, which help to frame the issue in a political context. The book touches on cases and themes that are very recent and currently much under discussion in the field, including the implications of the coming into force of the International Criminal Court, the legality of amnesties, the relevance and contribution of traditional forms of justice, and the effectiveness of international assistance.

Finally and importantly, this collection is the first one to publish one of the main legacies of the conference: *The Nuremberg Declaration on Peace and Justice*. Quite foreseeably, conference participants would have been overwhelmed with negotiating and agreeing upon an outcome document on such complicated issues in such limited time. Therefore, the outcome document was only drafted after the completion of the conference, but drawing on the workshop conclusions that HRH Prince Zeid, chairperson of the concluding plenary session of the conference, had presented (see page 533). The Nuremberg Declaration on Peace and Justice was elaborated by a group of international experts designated by the conference organizers, working under the auspices of H.E. President Oscar Arias of Costa Rica. After several consultations with interested practitioners and civil society organizations, the Declaration was distributed at the United Nations in June 2008 (UN Doc. A/62/885 of 19 June 2008, see annex in this volume). It contains definitions, principles and recommendations on issues of peace, justice and impunity, dealing with the past and future developments. Although it is not a legal document, it aspires to "guide those involved at the local, national and international levels in all phases of conflict transformation, including mediation, post-conflict peace-building, development, and the promotion of transitional justice and the rule of law" and thus to influence the future practice of making and building "just and lasting peace".

It is our hope that this entire compilation will contribute to such guidance, and that learning from the experiences and knowledge reflected in its pages, will assist those who both contemplate and act for peace, justice and transformative development now and in the future.

V.

Last but not least, we would like to pay a special tribute to the *Robert Bosch Stiftung* in Stuttgart, Germany, and the *Dräger Foundation* in Lübeck, Germany, for the very substantial financial and moral support that they have lent to the conference. Both foundations have thus set a remarkable example of a public-private partnership aimed at furthering two of humanity's noblest aspirations: peace and justice. Furthermore, the Robert Bosch Stiftung deserves special credit for contributing towards most of the costs of the expert meetings that led to the drafting of the Nuremberg Declaration on Peace and Justice, and to some of the cost of publishing this book.

Very importantly, one individual has played a central role in the inception, implementation and follow-up to the Nuremberg Conference initiative, working steadily and calmly at the vortex of fast-paced and pressured activities, and offering leadership in the best sense of trust, guidance and inspiration. *Christian Much*, (2005–2008 Head of the German Foreign Ministry's Division for Conceptual UN Affairs) chose the topic of the conference, brought together its various actors, steered the conference preparations and also the drafting of the Nuremberg Declaration, and enabled the realization of this publication. To Christian, with appreciation for his patience, attention to detail and sense of humour, go our very particular, personal thanks and recognition.

Germany *Kai Ambos*
UK *Judith Large*
USA *Marieke Wierda*
November 2008

Contents

Conclusions

Annex

About the Editors

Kai Ambos is Professor of Criminal Law, Criminal Procedure, Comparative Law & International Criminal Law at the Georg-August-Universität Göttingen; Germany. He is also Judge at the State Court (*Landgericht*) in Göttingen. He served as a member of the German delegation to the Rome Conference on the ICC and was a member of the German Völkerstrafgesetzbuch Drafting Commission. He is currently member of various editorial boards of international journals and of scientific selection committees of the German Academic Exchange Service (DAAD) and the Alexander von Humboldt Foundation. He has completed various assignments and guest professorships in Europe, Latin America and Africa and has a wide variety of publications on criminal law, criminal procedure, comparative law and international criminal law.

Judith Large is Honorary Research Fellow at the Richardson Institute for Peace and Conflict Studies, Lancaster University, UK and Special Advisor to the Berghof Foundation for Peace Support, Berlin. Previously she served as Director for Conflict Resolution with CMI (Brussels), Senior Advisor for Democracy and Conflict Management at International IDEA (Stockholm), and as Consultant to UN, national and non-governmental agencies. She has been Visiting Lecturer at universities in the Netherlands, Austria and the UK on conflict analysis and mediation. As a practitioner of post-war recovery and strategies for multi-level peacebuilding, her regional experience and expertise include the Balkans (1992–1999) and South/Southeast Asia (1999–current). She has published widely on conflict transformation and human security.

Marieke Wierda is Director of the Prosecutions Program at the International Center for Transitional Justice, where she has worked on a variety of current and post-conflict situations, including, in particular, Sierra Leone, Iraq, Afghanistan, Lebanon and Uganda (in the last she has been involved directly in the peace talks to advise on justice issues). Prior to joining ICTJ, Marieke Wierda worked as a lawyer at the International Criminal Tribunal for the former Yugoslavia. She has published widely on issues of international criminal law, including a book on international criminal evidence and publications and reports on Sierra Leone, Iraq, Lebanon, and the International Criminal Court. She also advised the German government on the Nuremberg Conference.

Contributors

Paloma Aguilar Universidad Nacional de Educación a Distancia, Madrid, Spain, paguilar@poli.uned.es

Kai Ambos Department for Foreign and International Criminal Law, Institute of Criminal Law and Criminal Justice, University of Göttingen, Platz der Göttinger Sieben 5, 37073 Göttingen, Germany, kambos@gwdg.de

Christine Bell Transitional Justice Institute University of Ulster Northern Ireland, UK, c.bell@ulster.ac.uk

Karen Brounéus Department of Peace and Conflict Research, Uppsala University, P.O. Box 514, 75120 Uppsala, Sweden, Karen.brouneus@pcr.uu.se

Catalina Díaz Reparations ICTJ, Colombia Bogotá, Colombia, cdiaz@ictj.org

Pablo de Greiff International Center for Transitional Justice, 5 Hanover Square, 24th Fl NY 10004, USA, pdegreiff@ictj.org

Victor Igreja Royal Netherlands Academy of Arts and Sciences (NIAS), Wassenaar, The Netherlands, vigreja@yahoo.com

Lars Kirchhoff Institute for Conflict Management, Center for Peace Mediation, Berlin, European University Viadrina, Große Scharrnstr. 59, 15230 Frankfurt/Oder, Germany, Kirchhoff@euv-frankfurt-o.de

Louis Mallinder Law School, Queen's University Belfast, 28 University Square, Belfast BT 7 1 NN, UK, l.mallinder@qub.ac.uk

Barbara Oomen Roosevelt Academy/Utrecht University, Lange Noordstraat 1 4330 CB, Middelburg, The Netherlands, B.Oomen@roac.nl

Stina Petersen Chr. Michelsen Institute (CMI), POB 6033 Postterminalen, 5892 Bergen, Norway, Stina.petersen@cmi.no

Iavor Rangelov Centre for the Study of Global Governance, London School of Economics and Political Science, Houghton Street, London WC1A 2AE UK, i.p.rangelov@lse.ac.uk

Ingrid Samset Chr. Michelsen Institute (CMI), POB 6033 Postterminalen, 5892 Bergen, Norway, Ingrid.samset@cmi.no

Chandra Lekha Sriram University of East London School of Law, Duncan House, Stratford High Street, London E15 2JB, UK, c.sriram@uel.ac.uk

Marika Theros Crimes of War Project, London, mtheros@crimesofwar.org

Thomas Unger ICTJ Brussels, Blvd. Bischoffsheim 11, 8th Floor, 1000 Brussels, Belgium, TUnger@ictj.org

Nahla Valji Centre for the Study of Violence and Reconciliation, Cape Town, South Africa, nvalji@csvr.org.za

Stef Vandeginste Institute of Development Policy and Management, University of Antwerp, Prinsstraat 13, 2000 Antwerp, Belgium, stef.vandeginste@ua.ac.be

Vibeke Wang Department of Comparative Politics, University of Bergen, Christiesgt 15, 5007 Bergen, Norway, Vibeke.wang@isp.uib.no

Marieke Wierda International Center for Transitional Justice, MWierda@ictj.org

Introductory Speeches

Message from Mr. Ban Ki-moon, Secretary-General of the United Nations, for the Meeting on "Building a Future on Peace and Justice"

I am delighted to send greetings to the distinguished participants in this conference on "Building a Future on Peace and Justice."

One of the most fundamental challenges of peacemaking and peacebuilding is confronting the past while building a just foundation for the future. Fighting impunity and pursuing peace are not incompatible objectives – they *can* work in tandem, even in an ongoing conflict situation. This requires us to address very real dilemmas, and the international community must seize every opportunity to do so. This conference represents an important occasion for exchanging ideas and experience in this complex and vital area, and I wish you a most stimulating session.

25 June 2007 Ban Ki-moon

B. Ki-moon
Secretary General of the United Nations

K. Ambos et al. (eds.), *Building a Future on Peace and Justice: Studies on Transitional Justice, Peace and Development.*

Opening Speech by Federal Foreign Minister Dr. Frank-Walter Steinmeier (slightly abridged)

Excellencies, Ladies and Gentlemen,

Historical truth is hard to come by. It is sought wherever violence, war and civil war have rent societies asunder. It is an essential requirement for any rapprochement or reconciliation in society; without it, it would be unimaginable, impossible to build up a joint future in Somalia or Afghanistan, not to mention in Iraq.

After the dark chapter of the Nazi past, a peacebuilding milestone was set and legal history written here, in Courtroom 600 of the Nuremberg Palace of Justice.

It was here that the principle was first applied whereby those at the top levels of the State could be brought to justice, as persons, for war crimes, for crimes against humanity, for genocide and for wars of aggression.

This was the start of a development which reached its culmination 5 years ago when the International Criminal Court began its work. The Court has become a pillar of hope in ensuring that crimes do not go unpunished. It has also become an influential – though not uncontroversial – international player in conflict and post-conflict situations.

In this very room in 1947 – when the Nazi reign of terror had been defeated – the prosecutor in the IG Farben Trial said these visionary words: "It will not be possible to re-establish a healthy and peaceful European community by simply covering the dead with a shroud without any investigation".

And indeed, uncovering the truth has become a leitmotiv in conflict management: as a legally established truth in the war crimes tribunals for Yugoslavia, Rwanda and Sierra Leone; as an impartially documented truth in Guatemala and Morocco; as a repentantly well-known truth in South Africa; as the "right to truth"; as the supporting pillar for the collective national memory. Some 125 years ago, Ernest Renan said that there were two things which constituted a nation: one is the possession in common of a rich legacy of memories – including painful ones in particular – and the other is present-day consent, the desire to live together.

In the past 60 years, Germany has returned to the fold of respected nations. We are very glad that this is so because we know that it is by no means a matter

F.-W. Steinmeier
Foreign Minister of Germany

K. Ambos et al. (eds.), *Building a Future on Peace and Justice: Studies on Transitional Justice, Peace and Development.*

of course. Perhaps it has something to do with the way in which we processed and came to terms with the barbaric acts of the Nazis. The nuances of the words "Vergangenheitsbewältigung" ("coming to terms with the past") and "Trauerarbeit" ("mourning"; "grieving") are very specific to the German language. Criminal prosecution, the documentation and remembering of historical truth, compensation for the victims and public gestures of asking forgiveness (I recall the historical picture of Willy Brandt falling to his knees in Warsaw): each of these elements from the repertoire of transitional justice was and is a part of the way we come to terms with the past. The city of Nuremberg is symbolic as a model for dealing openly with our difficult history.

The search for truth comes to haunt societies – sooner or later. Here in Germany, it took more than 20 years before a young generation broke the collective silence of their fathers in 1968. There is no reason for us to be self-satisfied. For the thorough, painful coming to terms with our past started too timidly and too late. It should be mentioned here – and this brings me to the subject of this conference – that in one specific regard we had it easier than others. In Germany, post-1945 and also post-1990, it was clear that the legal proceedings, compensation, imminent staffing decisions and public debate on guilt and forgiveness would not jeopardize peace either within Germany's borders or abroad.

In many parts of the world, the reality is more complex and complicated. Many regions are populated by warlords who do not come to the negotiating table until they are threatened with criminal prosecution, and even then only to demand that prosecution be suspended – warlords who, all the same, are needed to broker peace. Many conflicts cannot be resolved against the will or without the involvement of partisan representatives of a former regime who, in the post-conflict period, still have sufficient influence to spoil things by sabotaging or even preventing the search for justice.

We all know that peace, justice and development are interdependent. But we also know that there is no master plan showing us how to help societies damaged by conflict find their own path, to link together "peace and security", "justice", "reliable institution-building" and "the re-establishment of trust within a society", and to lay the foundations for this early on, during peace negotiations.

The aim of this conference is to identify and map out such paths. Over the coming days, that will be in the hands of the politicians, the renowned scientists and the numerous representatives from areas directly affected by crises whom we have invited here to Nuremberg.

To the representatives of non-governmental organizations sitting today here in the courtroom in what used to be the dock, I would say this:

You come from various different countries: Afghanistan, Bosnia, Iraq, Sierra Leone and Colombia, to name but a few. With your presence here today, you give this historic place a new meaning. For you remind us of injustice – and this is the difference – not because you are criminals, like those who sat in your place 60 years ago, but because you serve to represent victims. You represent societies in which people have been permanently marked, indeed traumatized, by war, persecution and massive violations of human rights; societies which have, in many cases, lost faith in the protective function of the state and the international community, and, as a result, hope even more strongly for peace, the reestablishment of legal certainty, the acknowledgment of past events and the success of a reconciliation process between perpetrators and victims. We must not disappoint you here today. We have invited you as guests of honour in the hope that you will contribute to our discussions as eye witnesses and living testimonies. For you have experienced and endured the topic of our conference in all its aspects.

With your experience, the studies drawn up in preparation for the conference and the discussions in tomorrow's workshops, we have recourse to a wealth of knowledge never before gathered on this topic. This gives us all the more reason to make a concerted effort to ensure that as many as possible of those who could not be here in Nuremberg today also benefit from this wealth. We are not just looking for conclusions, but conclusions which make a difference. What can we learn from each other? Which lessons apply outside the scope of the event, outside the immediate context? We intend to lay down the answers to these questions in a "Nuremberg Declaration on Peace and Justice".

Of course, it will be difficult to feed our conclusions into one single approach, applicable in every case. Peace talks and political processes of reconstruction and transformation represent unique situations which cannot be compared.

Moreover, there are widely differing opinions and practices when it comes to rebuilding states.

"Security first" is an approach which acknowledges, first and foremost, the overwhelming desire of conflict victims to see an end to bloodshed and tyranny. But "security first" must not mean "security alone" – to the detriment of goals such as justice, truth and the dismantling of structures at the heart of the conflict. Indeed, in the very interests of peace and security, the door to justice must never be closed for good.

The approach of "rule of law first" rightly assumes that it is only through respect for human rights and the institutions which guarantee them that people are truly free to realize their potential. Only the observance of human rights can give rise to the trust needed for population groups formerly in conflict to live side by side and for the economy to flourish. But we all know of cases where hastily imposed liberalization has had a destabilizing effect. And the promise of justice can turn out to be hollow, indeed counter-productive, as long as the institutions intended to guarantee justice are unable to carry out their duty, and as long as the society in question has not reached an understanding on the aims and scope of justice.

The approach "civil society first" rightly assumes that the quality and acceptance of political decisions depends on the active participation of the people. The key jurisprudential issue of how much punishment and how much forgiveness the society wants requires broad discussion and feedback from civil society. But the strengthening of civil society cannot replace the vital development of a legitimate state order. This applies particularly to states where structures have been devastated by conflicts.

Lasting peace in Darfur, Somalia, Afghanistan, Colombia and other regions can only be brought about if we take into account the complexities I have mentioned. Peace and reconciliation cannot be achieved by thinking in black and white. I see this as one of the most difficult political and moral challenges of my daily work. Simple "either/or" models do not help. Addressing the dilemma of peace and justice effectively means bringing together a variety of approaches in a thoughtful combination – in terms of substance and sequence.

We must not let ourselves be discouraged by the complexity of this issue. We know that there is no magic formula. But we suspect, and this is the good news, that our pool of options is larger than is generally thought. In this sense, our conference is the ideal opportunity to map out the course, examine options, compare experiences and learn lessons. This conference is taking place in the belief that difficult decisions, the kind of which we will face for many years to come, can in future be taken on a more differentiated, creative and informed basis.

25 June 2007 Frank-Walter Steinmeier

Building a Future on Peace and Justice: The International Criminal Court

By Chief Prosecutor of the ICC Luis Moreno Ocampo*

Excellencies, Ladies and Gentlemen,

It is an honour to be here today and I wish to thank the foreign Ministers of Finland, Germany and Jordan for their invitation to address this Conference.

60 years ago with the Nuremberg Trials, for the first time, those who committed massive crimes were held accountable before the international community. For the first time, the victors of a conflict chose the law to define responsibilities. In the words of the Nuremberg Prosecutor Justice Robert H. Jackson:

"That four great nations, flushed with victory and stung with injure stay the hand of vengeance and voluntarily submit their captive enemies to the judgement of law is one of the most significant tributes that power has ever paid to reason."

Nuremberg was a landmark. However the world was not ready to transform such a landmark into a lasting institution. The Cold War produced massive crimes in Europe, Latin America, and Asia; Africa was still under the rule of colonialism and apartheid.

In the end, the world would wait for almost half a century after Nuremberg, and would again witness two genocides – first in the Former Yugoslavia, and then in Rwanda – before the Security Council decided to create the ICTY and the ICTR, thus connecting peace and international justice again.

The contribution of the *ad hoc* Tribunals is yet to be fully recognized and measured. They developed the law, prosecuted the worst perpetrators, Generals, members of Governments. They contributed to restore lasting peace in conflict-torn regions.

The *ad hoc* tribunals for Yugoslavia and Rwanda paved the way for the decision to establish a permanent criminal court.

Ladies and Gentlemen,

For centuries, conflicts were resolved through negotiations without legal constraints. In Rome in 1998, a new and entirely different approach was adopted. Lasting peace requires justice – this was the decision taken in Rome by 120 States.

L.M. Ocampo
Chief Prosecutor of the International Criminal Court

*This speech was originally published in Zeitschrift für Internationale Strafrechtsdogmatik ZIS 13/2007, p. 491–493.

K. Ambos et al. (eds.), *Building a Future on Peace and Justice: Studies on Transitional Justice, Peace and Development.*

They committed to put an end to impunity for the most serious crimes of concern to the international community and to contribute to the prevention of such crimes.

They created an International Criminal Court, a permanent court, with jurisdiction over genocide, crimes against humanity and war crimes. International Justice was not a moment in time any longer, neither an *ad hoc* post conflict solution: it became an institution.

The Rome Statute created a comprehensive and global criminal justice system:

Substantial law has been codified in one detailed text; the content of different international conventions such as the Genocide Convention and the Geneva Conventions have been incorporated; elements of crimes have been meticulously defined; based on the jurisprudence by the *ad hoc* tribunals the definition of sexual violence has been further elaborated; special emphasis has been put on crimes against children.

Different legal and procedural traditions have been integrated into a new international model; victims have been given the right to participate in proceedings; their voices and interests formally included at different stages of the process; a trust fund has been created for reparations or compensation in their favour.

The scope of ICC jurisdiction reaches beyond any national or regional boundary; where as its predecessors were each limited in scope to a particular territory, the ICC is a worldwide criminal justice system. Its jurisdiction extends over crimes committed on the territory or by the nationals of more than a 100 States Parties; it could extend to the entire world as the United Nations Security Council can refer any situations to the Court.

Even more important, and the object of strong debate in Rome was the decision of States to give the Prosecutor the ability to trigger the Jurisdiction of the Court. By establishing the *proprio motu* powers of the Prosecutor to open an investigation, the treaty creates a new autonomous actor on the international scene. Such a provision, which allows the Court to act without an additional trigger from States or the UN Security Council, ensures that the requirements of justice will prevail over any political decision. This is a key defining provision for the new legal framework.

Ladies and Gentlemen,

Again let me emphasize the Rome Treaty was not drafted overnight. It is a strong and consistent body of law; the drafters were well aware that rendering justice in the context of conflict or peace negotiations would present particular difficulties and they prepared our institution well to meet those challenges. Careful decisions were made: a high threshold of gravity for the jurisdiction of the Court was established; a system of complementarity was designed whereby the Court intervenes as a last resort, when States are unable or unwilling to act; the UN Security Council was given a role in cases of threats to peace and security.

States demonstrated their understanding and firm support to this new design by the tremendous speed of the ratification process; less than 4 years after its adoption in Rome, the Statute entered into force.

It is the new law.

The issue is no longer about whether we agree or disagree with the pursuit of justice in moral or practical terms.

It is the law.

Ladies and Gentlemen,

The next challenge was to make this body of law operational, to transform ideas and concepts into a working system. This has been my objective during those first 4 years, as the Prosecutor of the ICC.

How to select the gravest situations to investigate? How to trigger the jurisdiction of the Court? How to protect witnesses and investigate in ongoing conflict situations?

These were the main issues to address.

As you know, over these 4 years, we have opened investigations in four situations – the Democratic Republic of Congo, Northern Uganda, Darfur and Central African Republic – all countries still engulfed at various degrees in conflict. We also analyzed the situation in Venezuela and the activities of nationals of 25 States Parties involved in Iraq. We are currently monitoring other situations in three different continents.

In each case, we collected evidence. The Court protected the witnesses. Victims started participating in the proceedings.

As of today, the Judges have issued eight arrest warrants.

Thomas Lubanga Dyilo, the leader of the most dangerous militia in Ituri, in the DRC, is in the custody of the Court, awaiting trial.

In Darfur, our evidence has unveiled an organised system of attacks against the civilian population coordinated by Ahmed Harun, then Minister of State for Interior.

In Northern Uganda, we proved that the top Commanders of the Lord's Resistance Army were personally responsible for conscripting and enslaving children, slaughtering their families, forcing the displacement of millions.

After 4 years, the Rome system is in motion.

And we are faced now with a new and even more complex challenge, that all of you are familiar with in a domestic context – the enforcement of the law.

How to ensure the enforcement of the Court's decisions? How to ensure, in particular, the arrest and surrender of individuals sought by the Court?

How to ensure the enforcement of the Court's decisions in situations where the international community is trying to achieve in parallel many objectives; re-establishing security, providing humanitarian assistance, promoting political dialogue between the parties to the conflict, and preparing for reconstruction and development.

As the Prosecutor of the ICC, I was given a clear judicial mandate. My duty is to apply the law without political considerations. I will present evidence to the Judges and they will decide on the merits of such evidence.

And yet, for each situation in which the ICC is exercising jurisdiction, we can hear voices challenging judicial decisions, their timing, their timeliness, asking the Prosecution to use its discretionary powers to adjust to the situations on the ground, to indict or withdraw indictments according to short term political goals. We also hear officials of States Parties calling for amnesties, granting of immunities and other ways to avoid prosecutions, supposedly in the name of peace; we can hear voices portraying the ICC as an impediment to progressing further with Peace processes.

These proposals are not consistent with the Rome Statute. They undermine the law States Parties committed to. It is essential on the contrary to ensure that any conflict resolution initiative be compatible with the Rome Statute, so that peace and justice work effectively together. Arrest warrants are decisions taken by the judges in accordance with the law, they must be implemented. I call upon States Parties and other stakeholders to remain in all circumstances aware of the mandate given to the Court; there can be *no* political compromise on legality and accountability.

The challenges are immense for political leaders. In this new system, global standards have been established without a global police or enforcement apparatus; enforcement of Court's decisions is the responsibility of national states.

Dealing with the new legal reality is not easy. It needs political commitment; it needs hard and costly operational decisions: arresting criminals in the context of ongoing conflicts is a difficult endeavour. Individuals sought by the Court are often enjoying the protection of armies or militias, some of them are members of governments eager to shield them from justice.

Those difficulties are real. They can however not lead us to change the content of the law and our commitment to implement it. In all situations, more State cooperation in terms of securing arrests is needed. For the ultimate efficiency and credibility of the Court you created, arrests are required. The Court can contribute to galvanize international efforts, and support coalitions of those willing to proceed with such arrest. But ultimately, the decision to uphold the law will be the decision of States Parties. If States Parties do not actively support the Court, in this area as in others, then they are actively undermining it.

Ladies and gentlemen,

International justice, national justice, search for the truth, peace negotiations can and must work together; they are not alternative ways to achieve a goal; they can be integrated into one comprehensive solution. The Court, as I emphasized earlier, was created to investigate and prosecute the worst perpetrators, responsible for the worst crimes, those bearing the greatest responsibility, the organizers, the planners, the commanders; national proceedings and other accountability mechanisms remain essential for the purpose of achieving comprehensive solutions; they are not alternative but complementary processes; in Uganda, the Court has issued arrest warrants against four individuals; other national mechanisms can be useful for the other combatants, those who want to give up arms and rejoin their families, those who did not bear the greatest responsibility.

The tension I see in Uganda or Darfur is not between Peace and Justice. It is not the decisions of the International Criminal Court which undermine peace processes and conflict resolution initiatives.

On the contrary, the beneficial impact of the ICC, the value of the law to prevent recurring violence is clear: deterrence has started to show its effect as in the case of Cote d'Ivoire, where the prospect of prosecution of those using hate speech is deemed to have kept the main actors under some level of control; in Colombia, legislation and proceedings against paramilitary were influenced by the Rome provisions; we also have examples of military officials incorporating the constraints of the Rome Statute in their operational planning; arrest warrants have brought parties to the negotiating table; have contributed to focus national debates on accountability and to reducing crimes; exposing the criminals and their horrendous crimes has contributed to weaken the support they were enjoying, to de-legitimizing them and their practices such as conscription of children; on the longer term, the Court will contribute to harmony or at least peaceful co-existence between former enemies as a sense of justice and reparation is achieved.

It is the lack of enforcement of the Court's decisions which is the real threat to enduring Peace. Allowed to remain at large, the criminals exposed are continuing to threaten the victims, those who took tremendous risks to tell their stories; allowed to remain at large, the criminals ask immunity under one form or another as a condition to stopping the violence. They threaten to attack more victims. I call this extortion, I call it blackmail. We cannot yield.

Ladies and Gentlemen,

The decisions taken in Rome must be respected.

Because it is the law.

Because this law was built upon the lessons of decades of massive violence and atrocities, when the international community failed, failed to protect the Jewish, Russians, members of different communities in Europe and the Balkans, Tutsis, Arabs.

Because experience has taught us that such a law is the only efficient way to prevent recurrent violence and atrocities.

Because in the real world, it is respect for the law that will protect our citizens.

Because in the real world of 2007, no State has sufficient power to guarantee the life and freedom of its citizens, if the international community is not upholding the rule of law.

We must learn at last: there is no safe haven for life and freedom if we fail to protect the rights of any citizen in any country of the world. To protect each of them we have to protect all of them.

Thank you.

25 June 2007 Luis Moreno Ocampo

Studies

Part I
Transitional Justice: The Legal Perspective

The Legal Framework of Transitional Justice: A Systematic Study with a Special Focus on the Role of the ICC

Kai Ambos

Abstract 1. Transitional Justice (hereafter: "TJ") has been the object of great attention in conflict and post-conflict societies. The *concept* deals with justice in societies in transition, either post-conflict or during an ongoing conflict; it entails a series of measures which could be judicial and/or non-judicial in nature. Its success depends on to what extent it contributes to true reconciliation and the consolidation of democracy and the domestic judicial system (para. 1). Experience shows that the quest for *justice* often conflicts with the mostly official efforts towards *peace*. Indeed, TJ aims at ensuring justice and peace at the same time but refraining from criminal prosecution and/or punishment seems sometimes necessary to facilitate a peaceful transition (para. 3), the issuing of an *amnesty* being the most important technique of exemption from criminal prosecution (para. 5). In any case, whether the absence of criminal prosecution contributes to *reconciliation* depends on the framing of this concept and the circumstances of each case (para. 4).

2. To develop the legal framework of TJ and, ultimately, to establish some more or less precise *guidelines* for peace negotiations within the framework of transition, necessary to "judicialize" the politics of TJ (para. 6), one must first determine the contents of the *justice element* in TJ. Justice in this sense is to be understood broadly, going beyond mere criminal justice and including certain key elements such as accountability, fairness in the protection and vindication of rights and the prevention and punishment of wrongs (para. 2).

3. The *legal substance* of the justice element or interest has as a starting point the *duty to prosecute* the international core crimes as defined in Art. 6–8 of the ICC Statute (para. 8). While this duty would almost logically lead to a prohibition of amnesties or other exemption measures regarding these crimes (para. 9) the broad concept of justice applicable in TJ calls for a more sophisticated approach. On the one hand, the justice interest is to be complemented by the *rights of victims* of

K. Ambos
Department for Foreign and International Criminal Law, Institute of Criminal Law and Criminal Justice, University of Göttingen, Platz der Göttinger Sieben 5, 37073 Göttingen, Germany
e-mail: kambos@gwdg.de

K. Ambos et al. (eds.), *Building a Future on Peace and Justice: Studies on Transitional Justice, Peace and Development.*

international core crimes (para. 10-11); these rights go well beyond criminal prosecution and include, besides a right to justice, the rights to truth and reparation in a broad sense (para. 11). On the other hand, as another consequence of a broad concept of justice, *alternatives to criminal prosecution* must be developed and applied (para. 12 et seq.), in particular (*effective*) Truth Commissions (para. 13 et seq.). In general, though, alternative measures can only complement, not substitute criminal justice (para. 10). To do so, they must offer a serious alternative way of dealing with the past and as such effectively take into account the interest of victims (para. 12). Ultimately, the admissibility of limitations of the justice interest depends on the result of a complex process of *balancing of the conflicting interests* which is carried out by a threefold proportionality test (para. 19 et seq.). This test leads, on the third stage of the *proportionality stricto sensu*, to some important limitations (*ratione materiae* and *personae*) and requirements (esp. some form of accountability) to be taken into account to assess the admissibility of exemption measures (para. 21). From the above analysis follows a *bifurcated approach* as to the admissibility of *amnesties* (para. 23 et seq.): On the one hand, blanket amnesties are generally inadmissible (strict approach) since their primary goal is to completely conceal past crimes by prohibiting any investigation (para. 24 et seq.); on the other, conditional ("accountable") amnesties are, in principle, admissible (flexible approach) since they do not – unlike blanket amnesties – automatically exempt perpetrators from punishment but make the exemption conditional on certain acts or concessions by the benefiting person(s), e.g., unreserved promise to lay down arms, satisfaction of the victim's legitimate demands, in particular by a full disclosure of the facts, acknowledgment of responsibility and repentance (para. 30 et seq.).

4. With the *ICC* a *permanent accountability mechanism* has been established (para. 34). It is part of the TJ project in that it may interfere in processes of transition and thus come into conflict with the parties on the ground. The Ugandan situation where the ICC has issued arrest warrants against leading members of the LRA is a vivid example of such a possible conflict. Yet, it must not be overlooked that the Prosecutor's strategy only to prosecute the most responsible perpetrators and the most serious crimes (para. 36) limits the ICC's "interventionist" or "monitoring" role considerably and leaves the bulk of the prosecutions to the *domestic judicial systems* which therefore still have an important role to play in bringing less important perpetrators and/or crimes to justice (para. 34). In any case, as to the most important cases, the question arises whether and, if so, to what extent national peace deals, including amnesties or other exemptions, may bar the ICC from exercising its jurisdiction. While this issue was not explicitly dealt with in the ICC Statute, the Statute is a *flexible instrument* which enables the Prosecutor and the Court to take transitional situations on the ground into account (para. 35). This follows from the broad discretion of the Prosecutor during the preliminary investigation (para. 35), the ICC's judicial autonomy (para. 34, 36) and in particular three provisions of the ICC Statute, namely Art. 17 on complementarity, Art. 16 on the intervention by the Security Council and Art. 53 (1) (c), (2) (c) on the interest of justice.

5. *Art. 17* tries to strike an adequate balance between the states' sovereign exercise of (criminal) jurisdiction and the international community's interest in preventing impunity for international core crimes by according prevalence to the

State Parties if they are willing and able to investigate and prosecute the international core crimes (para. 37). The detailed analysis of the provision (para. 37 et seq.) shows that a national exemption measure (esp. an amnesty) as such does not make a case inadmissible; rather, the admissibility depends on the *specific content* and *conditions* of the measure (para. 44). If one applies this conclusion to certain scenarios (para. 44 et seq.) it follows that, as to full exemptions, only a *conditional amnesty with a TRC* may render a case inadmissible if an effective TRC grants an amnesty on an individual basis under certain strict conditions (para. 46); other full exemptions (blanket self-amnesty, conditional amnesty *without* a TRC) will not pass the complementarity test (para. 45, 47). In the case of *partial exemptions*, e.g., a considerable mitigation of punishment in exchange of demobilisation and full cooperation, the admissibility in the sense of Art. 17 depends on the extent to which the respective process satisfies the justice interest, e.g., by employing alternative mechanisms of justice, in particular an effective TRC and/or non-punitive sanctions (para. 48). In the case of *ex post exemptions*, the admissibility depends exclusively on the criterion of "genuine" willingness to prosecute in the sense of Art. 17 (1) (a), (b) or/and (2) (para. 49). *Art. 16* gives the Security Council the faculty to suspend proceedings but leaves ICC's competence to indirectly review the Council's decision unaffected (para. 50). The *interests of justice clause* of Art. 53 (para. 51 et seq.) gives the Prosecutor an additional instrument to exercise his discretion going beyond the rather "technical" Art. 17 (para. 51). Yet, this discretion does not convert the clause to a mere policy instrument irrespective of the legal criteria provided by it (gravity of the crime, interests of victims, age or infirmity of the alleged offender and the role of the perpetrator in the alleged crime); rather the Prosecutor has to take a legally substantiated decision in each individual case (para. 52).

1 Introduction

1. In recent years the issue of *Transitional Justice* (hereinafter "TJ") has received increased attention in conflict and post-conflict societies.[1] TJ, as understood in this study, "comprises the full range of processes and mechanisms associated with a society's attempts to come to terms with a legacy of large-scale past abuses, in order to ensure accountability, serve justice and achieve reconciliation".[2] While regime change is not at all a new phenomenon the concept of TJ is recent and innovative in that it recognizes the importance of "justice" in processes of transition; in short, TJ deals with justice in transition.[3] However, TJ is not limited to situations of post-conflict and/or regime change, in particular transition from dictatorship to

[1] See the three volume study of the Institute of Peace (Kritz [ed.], *Transitional justice*, US Institute of Peace Press, Washington D.C., 1995) which is, however, essentially a reprint of articles and materials already published.

[2] Report Secretary General transitional justice, para. 8; for a similar broad definition Bickford in Shelton (ed.) 2005, at 1,045.

[3] See also Uprimny/Saffon in Rettberg (ed.) 2005, 211 at 214 et seq. with a good definition: "forma específica de justicia, caracterizada por aparecer en contextos excepcionales de transición ..."

democracy, but also encompasses situations of peace processes within ongoing conflict and/or formal democracy.[4] The measures applied in such situations may be of a judicial and/or non-judicial nature "with differing levels of international involvement (or none at all) and individual prosecutions, reparations, truth-seeking, institutional reform, vetting and dismissals, or a combination thereof".[5] The kind of transition and the role of the (former) elite(s) in the process affect the kind of TJ and its success in that the possibilities of TJ increase with the decreasing influence of the (former) elite(s).[6] The success of TJ may be measured by the quality of the political reforms achieved,[7] in particular whether and to what extent TJ contributes to the reconstruction and consolidation of democracy[8] and the domestic judicial system.[9] The period of time over which the transition takes place varies according to the circumstances of each case and may pass through different phases.[10] While TJ structurally faces similar problems as ordinary justice, e.g., the question of selective prosecutions, court congestion and changes in the civil service,[11] it is distinct from the latter in that it has to deal with large-scale and particularly serious abuses committed or tolerated by a past, normally authoritarian regime within the framework of a military or at least violent socio-political conflict.

2. The *justice* element in TJ must be understood broadly. Accordingly, justice is "an ideal of accountability and fairness in the protection and vindication of rights and the prevention and punishment of wrongs. Justice implies regard for the rights of the accused, for the interests of victims and for the well-being of society at large. It is a concept rooted in all national cultures and traditions and, while its administration

(at 217). Von Braun (2008) at 7 describes TJ as "Mechanismen und Strategien, die die neu etablierte Staatsführung entwickelt, um mit den begangenen Verbrechen umzugehen".

[4] Colombia is maybe the most important case at hand, see for the "Ley de Justicia y Paz" (No. 975) note 203 and corresponding text. While Rettberg in Rettberg (ed.) 2005, 1 at 2 considers that Colombia is not "propiamente un caso de transición" she recognizes that "las preguntas y los debates en torno a la justicia transicional son de gran relevancia para este país". In any case, the attitudes of victims living in a post-conflict or still conflict scenario differ, see Kiza/Rathgeber/Rohne (2006) at 148 et seq., 161.

[5] Report Secretary General transitional justice, para. 8.

[6] Cf. Posner/Vermeule (2004) 117 Harv. L. Rev. 761, at 769–70; see also Sooka (2006) 88 ICRC Int. Rev. 311, 316–7.

[7] Cf. Posner/Vermeule (n 6) at 768; see also Filippini/Magarrell in Rettberg (ed.) 2005, 143, at 149.

[8] Cf. Filippini/Magarrell (n 7) at 158 et seq.; for a "shift to democracy" Sooka (n 6) at 315.

[9] On the desirability of this effect see Kritz in Bassiouni (ed.) 2002, 55, at 84.

[10] See Hazan (2006) 88 ICRC Int. Rev. 11, at 28 distinguishing four phases: armed conflict/repression phase, immediate post-conflict phase (first 5 years), medium term (5–20 years), long term.

[11] See Posner/Vermeule (n 6) at 761 arguing that transitional justice is "continuous with ordinary justice" (at 764) and the respective issues are "at most overblown versions of ordinary legal problems" (at 765). Yet, apart from the difference I see between transitional and ordinary justice (see text), I have a difficulty to share Posner and Vermeule's assumption that "the dominant view in the academic literature is that transitional justice is counterproductive ...". The literature I know does not take this view but rather considers transitional justice as a necessary form of exceptional justice for situations of transition. Equally, my reading of the literature does not lead to the conclusion that "writers generally understand transitional justice as backward-looking" (ibid. at 766).

usually implies formal judicial mechanisms, traditional dispute resolution mechanisms are equally relevant".[12] Thus, justice in TJ reaches well beyond retributive, criminal justice – assuming, in fact, that criminal justice cannot be fully enforced[13] – and encompasses restorative justice in that it aims to restore or even to reconstruct the community (in the sense of "creative" justice).[14] Ultimately, TJ is a justice of exception, which aims to change the conflict and post-conflict situation "from a worse to a better condition".[15]

3. Recent experience shows that the victims' demand for accountability and justice often, if not always, conflicts with the mostly official efforts towards peace and reconciliation. Indeed, refraining from criminal prosecution and/or punishment is sometimes necessary to facilitate peace and reconciliation.[16] To put it bluntly, the price for peace is often justice[17] or a "trade off between peace and justice".[18] A victim-centred definition of TJ does not take this tension sufficiently into account.[19] It is a common argument that a policy of consequent criminal prosecution could trigger more and worse abuses and endanger a peaceful transition from dictatorial to democratic rule or ultimately even destroy an emergent and still fragile democracy. It is said that the dilemma of peace negotiations is that one cannot exclude the most responsible for international crimes without endangering the peace itself; yet, if one includes them one may give them an undeserved legitimacy.[20] The underlying argument may be called *"worse abuses" or "risk transition" argument.* Latin American scholars (based on their experiences in their own painful transitions) have probably articulated it most forcefully.[21] Also, the South African Con-

---

[12] Report Secretary General transitional justice, para. 7.

[13] Teitel (2000) at 55; see for the post-dictatorial Argentinean case Malamud-Goti in Kritz (ed.) 1995, 189 at 190.

[14] Cassin (2006) 88 ICRC Int. Rev. 235, at 238; Tutu (2007) 1 IJTJ 7: "reconstruction of our country", "merciful justice", "moral justice". See for the different forms of justice also Opotow, in Bassiouni (n 9) 207 et seq., in particular focusing on the long-term social reconstruction (at 212 et seq.). See also Meintjes, in Joyner (ed.) 1998 at 463 "reforming the law enforcement and judicial system".

[15] Cf. Cassin (n 14) at 238 referring to Protagoras as quoted in Plato, Theaetetus, 167 a.

[16] See Werle (2005) at 66 (mn 190): "As a matter of fact, refraining from punishing crimes under international law can be necessary in individual cases to restore domestic peace and make national reconciliation possible". For a good discussion of the arguments against criminal prosecution see Osiel (2000) 22 HRQ 118, 119 et seq., 128 et seq., 147.

[17] See, e.g., Opotow (n 14) 210; Werle (2007) mn 204.

[18] BBC World News, 27.2.2007, 9 p.m.

[19] See for such a definition, e.g., Durán Puentes, 54 Facetas Penales (Leyer, Colombia) 33. For a victim-centered critique of TJ see Mani in de Feyter/Parmentier et al. (eds.) 2005 at 62 et seq.

[20] Cf. Williams in Bassiouni (n 9) at 117.

[21] See Nino (1999) 100 YLJ 2,619, at 2,620; Zalaquett (1992) 43 Hastings Law Journal 1,425, at 1,425, 1,432; Malamud-Goti (n 13) at 191; Villa-Vicencio (2000) 49 Emory Law Journal 205, at 212; Fuchs (2007) 16 Lateinamerika Analysen 35, at 54 (on the discussion in Uruguay); García Ramírez, separate vote in the *Barrios Altos vs. Perú Case* (n 95) para. 11 (referring to his separate vote in the Castillo Páez Case) recognizing, in principle, "la alta conveniencia de alentar la concordia civil a través de normas de amnistía que contribuyan al restablecimiento de la paz y a la apertura de nuevas etapas constructivas en la vida de una nación". See also Arsanjani (1999)

stitutional Court, in its historic decision on the amnesty provision in the epilogue to the interim Constitution of 1994,[22] recalls that a successful transition does not only require "the agreement of those victimized by abuse but also those threatened by the transition to a democratic society ...".[23] The Sierra Leonean TRC acknowledged the credibility of the government's position that without an offer of amnesty and pardon the Lomé Peace Agreement[24] would not have come into existence.[25]

4. Yet, while all these arguments may be correct in the situations they refer to, they do not necessarily apply to other situations, often lack empirical support,[26] may be exaggerated[27] and are rarely accompanied by a precise definition of the decisive concepts – peace, reconciliation and justice – employed. In particular, whether a renunciation of criminal prosecution really contributes to *reconciliation* obviously depends on the meaning of this concept. While a minimalist concept of reconciliation in the sense of "nonlethal coexistence" is less demanding than a more substantive understanding in the sense of "democratic reciprocity" or even social harmony[28] as

---

Proceedings of the Ninety-Third Annual Meeting of the American Society of International Law 65, at 66: "sometimes (...) only feasible option for stopping bloodshed". In the same vein Joyner in Joyner (ed.) 1998, 37, at 38; Scharf/Rodley in Bassiouni (n 9) at 89–90; Morris, in ibid, 135, at 135; Goldstone/Fritz (2000) 13 LJIL 655, at 659–60; Seibert-Fohr (2003) 7 Max Planck Yearbook of United Nations Law 553, at 571; Kemp (2004) 15 CLF 67, 69–70; Brubacher (2004) 2 JICJ 71, 82; Seils/Wierda, ICTJ Report 2005 at 12–3; Kreicker in Eser/Sieber/Kreicker (eds.) 2006, at 306; Schabas (2008) 19 CLF, 5 at 22. For the background of the discussion in the 1980s Orentlicher (2007) 1 IJTJ 10, 12–3.

[22] The title of the epilogue is "national unity and reconciliation". The Constitution aims to provide for "a historic bridge between the past of a deeply divided society characterised by strife, conflict, untold suffering and injustice, and a future founded on the recognition of human rights, democracy and peaceful co-existence and development opportunities for all South Africans, irrespective of colour, race, class, belief or sex" (epilogue, para. 1). For that purpose, para. 5 cl. 1 of the epilogue states: "In order to advance such reconciliation and reconstruction, amnesty shall be granted in respect of acts, omissions and offences associated with political objectives and committed in the course of the conflicts of the past". The Constitution of 18 December 1996 omits the epilogue and thus this phrase.

[23] *AZAPO et al. vs. The President et al.* [25 July 1996] Case CCT 17/96 (Constitutional Court of South Africa), para. 19. See also Boraine (2001) at 285 recalling the threat by the security forces.

[24] See n 224.

[25] 3B Witness to Truth: Report of the Sierra Leone Truth and Reconciliation Commission (GPL Press, Ghana: 2004) ch. 6, p. 365, para. 10 (hereinafter: "Sierra Leone TRC Report").

[26] Hazan (n 10) at 22 correctly criticizes the lack of empirical analysis of the effects of TJ and pretends to fill this gap (at 19, 27 et seq.); yet, he offers only some hypotheses based on a journalistic account of some cases and experiences and concedes that further research would be necessary (e.g., at 35). See also Pham/Vinck (2007) 1 IJTJ 231, at 234 for general challenges and methods of empirical research in Transitional Justice Societies.

[27] See, e.g., as to the apparently exaggerated argument of an institutional crisis in post-dictatorial Uruguay Fuchs (n 21), at 63.

[28] On these forms of reconciliation, see Crocker (2002) 5 Buff. Crim. L. Rev. 509, at 525 et seq.; following Mallinder, published in this volume, para. 56 et seq. See also Méndez (2001) 15 Ethics and International Affairs 25, 28 giving reconciliation also a more substantive meaning ("long-term setting aside of disputes ... that have divided a society"); on the different meanings also Sooka (n 6) at 320 et seq. (calling herself for a "holistic set of objectives"); Pfanner (2006) 88 ICRC Int. Rev. 363, 373; Brounéus, published in this volume, at 205.

expressed in the African concept of *Ubuntu*,[29] only the latter would justify measures of clemency. Consequently, if one adopts such a – more meaningful – concept of reconciliation it is by no means certain that the appeasement of the greatest violators through impunity does lead to reconciliation or even a sustainable peace;[30] rather, in many cases, prosecution may be more promising to facilitate reconciliation and nation-building[31] and may even be a prerequisite for true reconciliation.[32] In any case, empirical data shows that the overwhelming majority of victims demand accountability in form of criminal prosecutions, trials and punishment[33] and reject amnesty;[34] the higher the degree of victimization the more criminal prosecution and punishment is demanded.[35] In addition, justice as understood by TJ theory is not necessarily the one experienced by the people on the ground.[36] In light of these findings it is not surprising that in South Africa it was recognized that an "amnesty per se cannot (...) have a reconciliatory effect and could in fact lead to the perpetuation of existing divisions, unless it is granted with due regard to certain requirements and principles".[37] Nor is it surprising that it was found for Uganda that, while the amnesty of 2000 was considered "a vital tool" for reconciliation, at

---

[29] On Ubuntu see Boraine (n 23) at 362.

[30] Cf. Schlunck (2000) at 129, 130–31, 262 referring especially to the El Salvadorian peace process; Joyner (n 21) at 40 ("Peace without justice is not durable"); Šimonović (2004) 2 JICJ 701, at 702; Olson (2006) 88 ICRC Int. Rev. 275, at 284. Also recently Ban Ki-moon in a statement concerning the lack of cooperation with the ICC, UN Doc. SG/SM/11617, AFR/1709 (5 June 2008): "The Secretary-General is convinced that there can be no sustainable peace without justice. Peace and justice go hand in hand".

[31] Robinson (2003) 14 EJIL 481, at 489; Olásolo (2003) 3 ICLR 87, at 139.

[32] Uprimny/Saffon (n 3) at 211, 224, 229 (with special reference to Colombia at 227 et seq.).

[33] According to Kiza/Rathgeber/Rohne (n 4) at 97, Table 18, 79% of the victims interviewed in Afghanistan, Bosnia and Herzegovina, Cambodia, Croatia, DRC, Israel, Kosovo, Former Yugoslav Republic of Macedonia, Palestinian Territories, Philippines and Sudan expressed their wish to have the perpetrators prosecuted. 68% of the interviewed wanted that the perpetrators be put on trial with the death penalty (4%), a prison (36%) or monetary sanction (45%) be imposed (at 111 et seq., Table 28); for a summary see ibid. at 121, 156, 158. These findings correspond to the ones regarding the attitude of the Acholi people in Northern Uganda (ICTJ/Human Rights Center, 2005, 28 et seq.). On this and other studies Kiza/Rathgeber/Rohne (n 4) at 50 et seq. Conc. also Orentlicher (n 21) at 22. According to OHCHR, however, especially the people from Acholiland are not in favour of prosecutions, not for reasons of principle but very specific ones (OHCHR, "Making peace our own – Victims' Perception of Accountability, Reconciliation and Transitional Justice in Northern Uganda", at 49 et seq.).

[34] Kiza/Rathgeber/Rohne (n 4) at 112, 114, 121 with Table 28; OHCHR (n 33) at 48 et seq. for a "more varied and complicated than usually portrayed" victims' view in Northern Uganda. Amnesty is not an automatic response to crimes for them, but rather motivated by various pragmatic considerations as to reintegrate rebels quickly into the community.

[35] Kiza/Rathgeber/Rohne (n 4) at 140 (Table 39), 141 (Table 40).

[36] See the very helpful research by Theidon (2007) 1 IJTJ 66, 78–9 finding that justice for demobilised fighters in Colombia is essentially revenge. See also the selective quotes in the Editorial Note (2007) 1 IJTJ 1, indicating that victims' interests range from public trials to jobs and schooling.

[37] Memorandum on the "Promotion of National Unity and Reconciliation Bill" of 1995, http://www.doj.gov.za/ (last visited 23 October 2008), also quoted in Schlunck (n 30) at 230.

the same time the lack of parallel mechanisms for truth-telling and the admission of guilt hindered the process of reconciliation.[38] Thus, it is clear that an amnesty alone does not satisfy the demands of true reconciliation; it must be accompanied by alternative mechanisms allowing for the full and public establishment of the truth and the acknowledgement of those responsible of their criminal acts.[39] This again is confirmed by victims' research according to which the prevalent purpose of taking action against the perpetrators is to reveal the truth about the past.[40] The risk transition argument ultimately blackmails a "new" state and its judiciary[41] and this may be a bad start for the establishment of a true democracy and rule of law.[42] Even the argument of the necessity of an amnesty to end hostilities is disputed.[43] From all this it follows that neither the restorative effect of amnesty and forgiveness should be overestimated nor the reconciling power of (criminal) justice underestimated.[44] The issue of how to come to terms with the crimes and perpetrators of a former regime is too difficult and complex as to lend itself to quick and easy solutions.[45] Every transition is different and requires taking into account the specific circumstances of its context;[46] a purely legal analysis loses sight of these mostly socio-political

[38] Cf. Refugee Law Working Paper 2005: "The findings suggest that, despite a number of challenges in its implementation, the Amnesty Law is perceived as a vital tool for conflict resolution, and for longer-term reconciliation and peace within the specific context in which it is operating. Furthermore, numerous respondents emphasised the fact that it resonates with specific cultural understandings of justice: amnesty is taking place within societies in which the possibility of legal and social pardon is seen to better address the requirements for long-term reconciliation than more tangible forms of punishment meted out within the legal structures. However, the findings also indicate that lack of formal mechanisms for the process of truth-telling, or the admittance of guilt on the part of former combatants, is currently hindering the process of reconciliation. According to Baines (2007) 1 IJTJ 91, 101 the "Acholi are one of the first victim populations in the world to lobby their government for the creation of a blanket amnesty".

[39] Memorandum (n 37); on the necessity of acknowledgement and recognition also Sooka (n 6) 318.

[40] See Kiza/Rathgeber/Rohne (n 4) at 123 (Table 34), 126: 66% of the victims consider "truth-telling" as the most important purpose of taking action, 27% to enable people to live together, 20% revenge, etc.; in the same vein OHCHR (n 33) at 47: "Truth about past atrocities is the most expected result transitional justice mechanisms could provide".

[41] See also Méndez (n 28) at 31; Robinson (n 31) at 497.

[42] See also Méndez (n 28) at 33.

[43] See Méndez (n 28) at 35 "by no means a certainty (...)".

[44] Cf. Crocker (n 28) at 511, 544 critically discussing the arguments in favour of reconciliation put forward by Tutu. In the same vein Blewitt in Blumenthal/McCormack (eds.) 2008, at 39 et seq., highlighting at 46 that the retributive and the restorative approach are complementary. See also Darcy (2007) 20 LJIL 377, at 402 pointing out, that international courts or tribunals are no "panacea" for the complex problems in a transition process. Crit. with regard to reconciliation through international courts, Diggelmann (2007) 45 AVR 382, at 396 et seq., seeing the mischief of a perpetrators interchange of roles with the victim (at 398).

[45] Cf. Frankel (1989) at 103–4: "A nation divided during a repressive regime does not emerge suddenly united when the time of repression has passed".

[46] Cf. Méndez (n 28) at 29, 33; Posner/Vermeule (n 6) at 767; see also Cárdenas (2005) at 166, 167; Stahn (2005) 18 LJIL 425, at 428; Seils/Wierda (n 21) at 13, 14; Botero M./Restrepo S., in Rettberg (ed.) 2005, 19, 20; Durán (n 19) at 34; Olson (n 30) at 294; Orentlicher (n 21) at 18.

circumstances[47] and the moral dimension of TJ.[48] It is crucial to strike a right balance between the countervailing values of peace and justice taking into account all the interests at stake[49] (see on this balancing exercise in more detail below para. 19 et seq.).

5. The most important technique to exempt perpetrators from criminal prosecution is the issuing of an *amnesty* in the form of a political or post-conflict amnesty; other, maybe less polemical types of amnesties, such as amnesties favouring ordinary criminals, amnesties at the occasion of certain festivities[50] or so-called corrective amnesties used to reverse an injustice,[51] are not relevant in our context.[52] Interestingly, Immanuel Kant, the great proponent of retribution, wrote in his "Metaphysic of Morals" that "the very concept of peace entails the idea of amnesty".[53] Thus, it is not surprising that in modern peace processes examples of amnesty proposals and the concomitant conflicts with the quest for justice abound. Take for example the case of El Salvador where the peace treaty of 16 January 1992 expressed the parties' compromise decision to end impunity, explicitly stating that the serious crimes "must be the object of exemplary action by the law courts (...)";[54]

---

[47] See also Kemp (n 21) at 69: "purely legal analysis (...) unrealistic"; equally as to the fight against impunity Meintjes (n 14) at 459; on the importance of the political context also Filippini/Magarrell (n 7) 149 et seq.; Sriram/Ross (2007) 1 IJTJ 45, at 54 identifying "zones of impunity" especially in African countries.

[48] From a moral or ethical perspective one may dissociate the moral from the legal, i.e., the renunciation of criminal prosecution from moral forgiveness: "That is why pardon and amnesty do not necessarily go together. A crime can be legally amnestied without being morally forgiven. In André Van In's fine film The Truth Commission, the lawyer Bheki's widow testifies to what she saw (pieces of Bheki's body strewn all over the garage). 'How could I ever forgive that cruel murderer?' she asks (or words to that effect). And Yasmin Sooka, who was conducting the proceedings, replies very gently with something like this: 'It is true that these people are requesting amnesty, but you are not obliged to forgive them'. You are not obliged to forgive them, but we are going to grant amnesty. The dissociation of the ethical from the politico-legal was essential to the mechanism" (quoted according to Cassin [n 14] at 239; see also Osiel (n 16) referring to Jaspers).

[49] Cf. Crocker (n 28) at 546, 549; Méndez (n 28) 28 rejecting "extremes in both postures"; Duggan in Rettberg (ed.) 2005, at viii arguing that today "la decisión es entre cuánta justicia y cuánta paz"; Uprimny/Saffon (n 3) at 216 ("resolver la tensión entre los imperativos jurídicos internacionales de castigo [...] y las exigencias prácticas de amnistía [...]"), 217 ("encontrar un punto medio entre [...] justicia retributiva plena [...] y de impunidad absoluta [...]") and 229.

[50] See ICTJ-guidelines, p. 4.

[51] Cf. Slye (2002) 43 Virgina Journal of International Law 173, at 243–4; on his distinction see n 88.

[52] For an empirical analysis of state motivations for the introduction of amnesties see Mallinder study (n 28) para. 6 et seq. with Fig. 1 finding that the most common reason is internal pressure, followed by peace and reconciliation, cultural or legal traditions, international pressure, favouring the regime itself, reparations and favouring exiles. Mallinder further shows how amnesties are introduced (para. 19 et seq. with Fig. 2: mostly by executive degree or parliamentary laws) and who they benefit (para. 26 et seq. with Fig. 3: mostly political opponents). The other findings will be referred to in the following text.

[53] Kant (1797) § 58.

[54] Quoted in Schlunck (n 30) at 116; Cassel (1996) 59 Law and Contemporary Problems 196, at 224; Popkin (2004) 15 CLF 105, at 108–9.

yet, a few days later the Legislative Assembly approved a "National Reconciliation Law" providing for a delayed amnesty and in March 1993 – after the TRC's report had been published – a blanket amnesty for "political crimes, crimes with political ramifications, or common crimes committed by no less than twenty people, before January 1st 1992" was enacted.[55]

6. Notwithstanding the enormous practical importance of exemptions from criminal prosecution within the framework of TJ, the current practice and debate suffers from a *lack of clear rules and criteria*, which help to reconcile peace and justice in situations of transition. The absence of such rules leaves it completely to the unfettered discretion of the negotiators whether they accept exemptions from criminal prosecution or not.[56] Policy arguments prevail over legal considerations, the outcome mostly depends on the power structure between the negotiating parties. Thus, it is necessary to develop "a common basis in international norms and standards"[57] in order to "judicialize" the politics of TJ.[58] This study attempts to make a modest contribution in this regard by, in the first part (Sect. 2), analysing and identifying the concrete legal substance and contents of the justice interest in TJ. As a result of this analysis one can distinguish between admissible and inadmissible amnesties and other exemption measures. The increasing importance of the ICC makes it then necessary, in the second part (Sect. 3), to examine its law with regard to peace processes.

2 Part I. The Legal Substance of the Justice Interest: Guidelines for Exemptions from Criminal Responsibility, in Particular Amnesties

7. A broad concept of justice, as defined in para. 2, allows for a full range of judicial measures to comply with a minimum standard of justice and is not limited to measures of criminal justice such as criminal investigation, prosecution and eventual punishment.[59] Nevertheless, the criminal prosecution of international crimes has always been and still is at the forefront of the global fight against impunity. It suffices

[55] Quoted according to Cassel (n 54) at 225; see also Popkin (n 54) at 109, 115; Schlunck (n 30) at 116. For a detailed analysis of El Salvador's process see Buergenthal in Kritz (ed.) 1995, 292, at 295 et seq.; Schlunck (n 30) at 87 et seq.; Cassel, op. cit., 224 et seq.

[56] For the standard policy arguments see Scharf (1999) 32 Cornell Int'l. L. J. 507, at 508 et seq.; for a policy-oriented approach also Cassel (n 54) at 228 referring to the New Haven School ("[...] legal criteria serve not as mechanical limits, but as explicitly postulated public order goals [...]").

[57] Report Secretary General transitional justice, p. 1; calling for guidelines also Cassel (n 54) at 204 et seq. who, however, softens them considerably by his policy approach (n 56).

[58] The idea of a "judicialización de la política de la justicia transicional" stems from Orozco, in Rettberg (ed.) 2005, 117 at 187 who recognizes such a "judicialización" because of the increasing judicial treatment of TJ situations.

[59] See also Kemp (n 21) at 69. Mani (n 19) at 57 correctly states that prosecutions "may not in themselves provide a comprehensive and adequate response to the needs of victims and survivors for justice in transition". According to Freemann (2006) at 10 "if criminal trials were alone sufficient, the field of transitional justice would never have emerged".

to refer to arguably the most important instrument of this fight, the Rome Statute of the ICC, which in its preamble (para. 4) affirms that the prosecution of "the most serious crimes of concern to the international community" "must not go unpunished" and that the "effective prosecution" of these crimes "must be ensured". Thus, the first element of the justice interest to be defined is a possible legal duty to prosecute international crimes (para. 8–9); such a duty, obviously, may severely limit the discretion of the negotiators with regard to exemptions from criminal prosecution. Thereafter we have to examine and identify the victims' rights derived from the justice interest (para. 10 et seq.) and alternatives to criminal prosecution (para. 12 et seq.) in order to propose, on this basis, a proportionality test for the balancing of the interests involved (para. 19 et seq.). Finally, the appropriate treatment of amnesties can be suggested (para. 23 et seq.).

2.1 The Duty to Prosecute Core Crimes

8. Before the adoption and entry into force of the ICC Statute it was controversial whether and in particular to what extent a duty to prosecute international crimes existed in international law.[60] While such a duty may convincingly be inferred from treaty obligations, e.g., under the Genocide,[61] Geneva[62] or Torture Conventions,[63]

---

[60] See for a detailed discussion before the ICC Statute Ambos (1999) at 37 AVR 318 et seq. and id, Impunidad (1999) at 66 et seq. with references to the doctrine to this date. The subsequent literature overwhelmingly recognizes a duty to prosecute: Dugard in Cassese/Gaeta/Jones (eds.) 2002, 693, at 696–97; Botero/Restrepo (n 46) at 26 et seq.; HRW, 2005, at 9 et seq.; identifying a "trend" towards such a duty Van der Voort/Zwanenburg (2001) 1 ICLR 315, at 316, 324; for a partial duty depending on the crime Gropengießer/Meißner (2005) 5 ICLR 267, at 272 et seq.; Office of the UN High Commissioner for Human Rights Report, p. 21; crit. on an enforceable right to punishment Teitel (n 13) at 55.

[61] Convention on the Prevention and Punishment of the Crime of Genocide, Adopted by Resolution 260 (III) A of the U.N. GA, 9.12.1948, <www.preventgenocide.org> (last visited 23 October 2008).

[62] First Geneva Convention "for the Amelioration of the Condition of the Wounded and Sick in Armed Forces in the Field" (first adopted in 1864, last revision in 1949); Second Geneva Convention "for the Amelioration of the Condition of Wounded, Sick and Shipwrecked Members of Armed Forces at Sea" (first adopted in 1949, successor of the 1907 Hague Convention X); Third Geneva Convention "relative to the Treatment of Prisoners of War" (first adopted in 1929, last revision in 1949); Fourth Geneva Convention "relative to the Protection of Civilian Persons in Time of War" (first adopted in 1949, based on parts of the 1907 Hague Convention IV). See also the three additional protocols, Protocol I (1977): Protocol Additional to the Geneva Conventions of 12.8.1949, and relating to the Protection of Victims of International Armed Conflicts; Protocol II (1977): Protocol Additional to the Geneva Conventions of 12.8.1949, and relating to the Protection of Victims of Non-International Armed Conflicts; Protocol III (2005): Protocol Additional to the Geneva Conventions of 12.8.1949, and relating to the Adoption of an Additional Distinctive Emblem. See <www.icrc.org/web/eng/siteeng0.nsf/htmlall/genevaconventions?opendocument> (last visited 23 October 2008).

[63] United Nations Convention against Torture and Other Cruel, Inhuman or Degrading Treatment or Punishment, Adopted by Resolution 39/46 of the U.N. GA, 10.12.1984, <www2.ohchr.org/english/law/> (last visited 23 October 2008).

for the respective crimes of genocide, grave breaches and torture[64] this duty is limited to the State Parties of these treaties. Beyond that, it is controversial to what extent such a duty may flow from customary international law (Art. 38 [b] ICJ Statute) or general principles of law (Art. 38 [c] ICJ Statute). As to the former, it is difficult to adduce a state practice to that effect,[65] and the latter meets with criticism since it apparently intends to overcome the lacking or even contrary state practice by just ignoring it.[66] On the other hand, the duty to respect and ensure and the right to remedy provisions of general human rights treaties (e.g., Art. 2 [1] and [3] Int. Covenant on Civil and Political Rights) do *not necessarily* – contrary to the dominant opinion in the doctrine[67] and the case law of the Inter-American Court of Human Rights[68] – entail an obligation of *criminal* prosecution since the rights may also be "ensured" through other mechanisms and such mechanisms may constitute "remedies" within the meaning of these provisions.[69] In addition, it is controversial whether the general

---

64 Cf. Scharf (n 54) 526; Dugard (1999) 12 LJIL 1003, at 1004; Schlunck (n 30) at 30 et seq. (32), 33 et seq. (35); Gavron (2002) 51 ICLQ 91, 92; Benzing in König/Stoll/Röben/Matz-Lück (eds.) 2008, 17, 40; Scharf/Rodley (n 21) at 92–3; Robinson (n 31) at 490–1; Van der Voort/Zwanenburg (n 60) at 317–18; Gropengießer/Meißner (n 60) at 273, 274; Stahn (2005) 3 JICJ 695, 703; O'Shea in du Plessis/Peté (eds.) 2008, 179, 195; Clark (2005) 4 Washington University Global Studies Law Review 389, at 399; Office of the UN High Commissioner for Human Rights Report, p. 21; HRW, 2005, at 10; Kreicker (n 21) at 9 et seq.; Principles combating impunity, principle 1 A. As to grave breaches Salomón (2006) 88 ICRC Int. Rev. 327, at 328, 337; for a general duty to exercise jurisdiction for all war crimes Olson (n 30) at 279–80.

65 See, e.g., Schlunck (n 30) at 49 concluding that such a state practice can only be identified with regard to genocide; for a "developing obligation" to prosecute crimes against humanity Mallinder (2007) 1 IJTJ 208, at 214. For an earlier critique see already Ambos (n 60) at 328 et seq.

66 Ambos (n 60) at 332 et seq.

67 See Ambos (n 60) at 319 et seq. with further references. See more recently on Art. 2 (3) ICCPR Bassiouni in Bassiouni (ed.) 2005, 3, at 43 et seq.; Principles combating impunity, principle 1 B; Van der Voort/Zwanenburg (n 60) at 322; Olson (n 30) at 282–3.

68 From *Velásquez-Rodríguez* [29 July 1988] Judgement, para. 162 et seq., 166, 174 to *Almonacid Arellano et al. vs. Chile* [26 September 2006] Judgement, Series C No. 154, para. 110: "La obligación conforme al derecho internacional de enjuiciar y, si se les declara culpables, castigar a los perpetradores de determinados crímenes internacionales, entre los que se cuentan los crímenes de lesa humanidad, se desprende de la obligación de garantía consagrada en el artículo 1.1 de la Convención Americana. (...) Como consecuencia de esta obligación los Estados deben prevenir, investigar y sancionar toda violación (...)". In the same vein most recently HRC, General Comment 31, identifying "positive obligations" in Art. 2 (1) ICCPR and calling for "appropriate measures or (...) due diligence to prevent, punish, investigate or redress the harm caused" violations of the ICCPR committed by state organs and as well "private persons or entities" (para. 8); as to Art. 2 (3) ICCPR the HRC demands "effective remedies", "judicial and administrative mechanisms for addressing claims of rights violations" thereby giving effect "to the general obligation to investigate allegations of violations promptly" (para. 15); further, "States Parties must ensure that those responsible are brought to justice", notably in case of serious violations such as torture, arbitrary killing and enforced disappearance (para. 18). For an earlier, practically identical position of the HRC with regard to Uruguay see Cassel (n 54) 214. See also Basic Principles Victims, Sect. II and n 103.

69 As to the argument that an effective remedy need not necessarily be a criminal prosecution see Schlunck (n 30) at 44–45; Gavron (n 64) at 99 with note 42 referring to decisions of the ICPR's Human Rights Committee. Also, the Basic Principles Victims, Sect. VII, para. 11 include in the

obligation to effectively protect human rights entails the active prosecution of the perpetrators given that human rights treaties also pretend to protect these same perpetrators by way of fair trial provisions and other substantive rights.[70] Be that as it may, the ICC Statute advanced the debate considerably because with its entry into force it can now safely be said – on the basis of para. 4-6 of its preamble[71] – that a state party to this treaty is, at least, obliged to prosecute the crimes covered by the Statute.[72] Non State Parties may be bound either by a specific treaty obligation or by the combined effect of the pre-ICC Statute instruments and the ICC Statute. Indeed, the Statute has reinforced the customary law duty in that it expresses – as a kind of "Verbalpraxis"[73] – the general acceptance of such a duty with regard to the ICC crimes (genocide, crimes against humanity and war crimes).[74] This duty will be further strengthened and consolidated with the increasing number of ICC State Parties.

9. If a state has the duty to prosecute certain crimes it follows from sheer logic that it cannot exempt these crimes from punishment, e.g., by granting an amnesty.[75] The same result follows from a rule of law argument: if the law provides for a duty to prosecute then the rule of law entails a prohibition of amnesty[76] and as such constitutes a limit to politics;[77] otherwise the very legal and social order to be protected by the rule of law would be undermined and, instead, a culture of impunity

right to a remedy the rights to "access justice", "reparation", and "access the factual information concerning the violations".

[70] See on this contradiction also Werle (n 16) mn 187.

[71] On para. 4 of the preamble see already supra para. 7. Para. 5 and 6 read: *Determined* to put an end to impunity for the perpetrators of these crimes and thus to contribute to the prevention of such crimes, *Recalling* that it is the duty of every State to exercise its criminal jurisdiction over those responsible for international crimes, [...].

[72] See also Schlunck (n 30) at 30; in the same vein El Zeidy (2002) 32 Michigan Journal of International Law 869, at 947–8 who even considers these crimes as ius cogens norms. For a general (emerging) duty to prosecute the ICC crimes Robinson (n 31) at 491–3.

[73] See also Kreicker (n 21) at 12–3, 305.

[74] See also Bassiouni (n 67) at 26 and Kritz (n 9) at 56 extending this duty to torture; for a duty to prosecute "crimes under international law" Basic Principles Victims, Sect. III, para. 4 and Principles combating impunity, principle 1; in favour also, albeit imprecise Méndez (n 28) at 26–7, 39; for a "much clearer and stronger presumption in favor of accountability and against impunity" in light of the developments of the last 10 years Seils/Wierda (n 21) at 2; for a customary duty to prosecute crimes committed in non-international conflicts also Salmón (2006) 88 ICRC Int. Rev. 327, at 337; von Braun (n 3) at 12 – With regard to the crime of aggression (Art. 5 [1] [d] ICC Statute) this duty may arise with its final definition and effective incorporation in the Statute.

[75] See for a discussion Ambos (1997) at 209 et seq.; id., Impunidad (n 60) at 126 et seq.; in favour of such an inference argue many writers, e.g., Cassel (n 54) at 210; Kritz (n 9) at 56; Botero/Restrepo (n 46) at 27 et seq. (with special reference to Colombia); Kreicker (n 21) at 305–6; indirectly Principles combating impunity, principle 2; with regard to grave breaches Pfanner (n 28) at 371, see also HRW, 2005, at 11; Cryer/Friman/Robinson/Wilmshurst (2007) at 32.

[76] Generally on the rule of law argument in this context Schlunck (n 30) at 24 et seq., 62; see also the statement of Badinter, rapporteur of the French Senate's Commission on Constitutional Law, stressing that an amnesty for international core crimes could simply not be envisaged in a state that respected the rule of law (quoted in Van der Voort/Zwanenburg [n 60] at 337).

[77] Teitel (n 13) at 21–2, 59; see also Olson (n 30) at 278–9.

created or promoted.[78] In fact, the rule of law argument entails a host of other arguments in favour of prosecution typically known from the debate of the purposes of punishment:[79] non-prosecution would undermine the effectiveness of criminal law deterrence,[80] prosecution reinstates the victims' status as fellow citizens,[81] sends the right message to the perpetrators but also the society in general (negative special and general prevention) and reasserts the values of a given society (positive general prevention).[82] The reinforcement of values such as the right to life, bodily integrity and liberty has a stabilizing effect for the new democratic system[83] and shows the moral dimension of the question.[84] Despite all these forceful arguments in favour of prosecution the duty to prosecute is generally considered a rule or principle[85] and as such permits – strictly defined – exceptions. From a policy perspective, the practical need of a bargaining chip – albeit of last resort[86] – in domestic

---

[78] See Meintjes (n 14) at 462; Crocker (n 28) at 538 and Slye (n 51) at 197–8 referring to Aryeh Neier (2002); see also Olásolo (n 31) at 144–5.

[79] Cf. Ambos/Steiner (2001) JuS 9, 12–3. See also Crocker (n 28) at 512; Clark (n 64) at 402–3; crit. Zolo (2004) 2 JICJ 727 lamenting (at 728) the "poverty of theoretical reflection on the key issues of the meaning and quality of punishment (...)".

[80] Crocker (n 28) at 536–7; Robinson (n 31) at 489; Uprimny/Saffon (n 3) at 225–6; Olson (n 30) at 291; crit. of this argument Malamud-Goti (n 13) at 196; Méndez (n 28) at 30–1; also Zolo (n 79) at 732: "little or no deterrent power"; Hazan (n 25) at 35 finds that "warring parties take the risk of prosecution into account" but the "deterrent effect soon diminishes without prompt indictments and arrests". Burke-White (2005) 18 LJIL 559, 587–7 affirms that the ICC investigation provides some deterrent effect on rebel leaders in the DRC; similarly Seils/Wierda (n 21) at 19 and Wierda/Unger, published in this volume, at 269 fn 15, explaining, that the ICC has a deterrent effect by the likelihood "that there will be consequences" just like in national criminal law. According to Cryer et al. (n 75) at 30, "deterrence is unlikely to be possible if potential offenders take the view that they may be able to obtain exemption from prosecution". Blewitt (n 44) at 45 et seq. admits, that "the mere existence of courts (...), will never bring a complete end to widespread atrocities" but still believes that courts do act as a deterrent and prevent the commission of crime. On the other hand, Grono/O'Brien in Waddel/Clark (eds.) 2008, 13, at 17 emphasize the negative effects of the deterrent power, i.e., that government officials "cling to power at all costs".

[81] Similarly Malamud-Goti (n 13) at 199 et seq.; Méndez (n 28) at 31; Seils/Wierda (n 21) at 3; on a possible therapeutic effect Hazan (n 25) at 39–40.

[82] See also Scharf/Rodley (n 21) at 90–1; Teitel (n 13) at 28, 67; Méndez (n 28) at 31–2; Kemp (n 21) at 71; Gropengießer/Meißner (n 60) at 279; Uprimny/Saffon (n 3) at 225–6; Orentlicher (n 21) at 15; crit. Zolo (n 79) at 734: "retributive conception of criminal punishment can hardly be reconciled with any project of social peace making".

[83] Teitel (n 13) at 67; Boraine (n 23) at 280–81; Seils/Wierda (n 21) at 3; Uprimny/Saffon (n 3) at 226.

[84] Robinson (n 31) at 489–90.

[85] See also Gropengießer/Meißner (n 60) at 276: "in principle"; Stahn (n 64) at 701, 703: "generally incompatible" (701).

[86] Scharf (n 54) at 512; see also Kemp (n 21) at 71; Clark (n 64) at 404, 409; similarly Arsanjani (n 21) at 67, considering amnesty as a "contract" which is "valid only to the extent that the parties (...) comply with its terms".

peace or reconciliation processes dictates a more flexible approach.[87] With regard to amnesties, a two-pronged or bifurcated approach is called for to distinguish between general, blanket amnesties, on the one hand, and limited, conditional amnesties on the other (see below para. 23 et seq.).[88]

2.2 Victims' Rights

10. Justice in TJ is foremost and predominantly justice for victims. However, victims have not only interests, as part of a broad notion of justice (para. 2); they have also rights, namely a right to justice[89] and other rights directly inferred from the notion of justice as a legal concept. These rights have been elaborated in great detail by the Human Rights case law, especially the Inter-American Court of Human Rights. They are also explicitly recognized in the ICC Statute (cf. Art. 68 (3), 75).[90] While

---

[87] See, e.g., Sierra Leone TRC Report (n 25) ch. 6, p. 365, para. 11 ("amnesties should not be excluded entirely"), p. 367–8, para. 20 ("trade of peace for amnesty represents the least bad of the available alternatives"). The same position is taken by the ICRC, see Pfanner (n 28) at 372 ("balancing competing interests"). See also Kemp (n 21) at 67 ("automatic assumption that truth-seeking and/or criminal prosecution are necessary [...] to be avoided"), 71.

[88] For the same distinction Dugard (n 64) 1005, 1009; id., in Cassese/Gaeta/Jones (n 60), 693 at 699–700; Goldstone/Fritz (n 21) at 663–4; Vandermeersch in Cassese/Delmas-Marty (eds.) 2002, 89, at 108; Office of the UN High Commissioner for Human Rights Report, p. 23; Van der Voort/Zwanenburg (n 60) 325; Cassese (2003) at 316 (regarding Third State jurisdiction); Méndez (n 28) at 39–40; Mallinder (n 65) at 214; Young (2002) 35 U.C. Davis L. Rev. 427, at 456–7; Robinson (n 31) at 484; Seibert-Fohr (n 21) at 588, 590; Salomón (n 64) at 331 et seq.; Slye (n 51) at 240 et seq. further distinguishes between amnesic, compromise, corrective and accountable amnesties. See also Ramirez, separate vote (n 229) para. 10 (distinguishing between "autoamnistías", which are "expedidas a favor de quienes ejercen la autoridad y por éstos mismos", and amnesties "que resultan de un proceso de pacificación con sustento democrático y alcances razonables, que excluyen la persecución de conductas realizadas por miembros de los diversos grupos en contienda, pero dejan abierta la posibilidad de sancionar hechos gravísimos, que ninguno de aquéllos aprueba o reconoce como adecuados").

[89] See Slye (n 51) at 192–3. For the different needs and expectations of victims, see Mallinder (2008) at 356 et seq. and Schotsmans in de Feyter/Parmentier et al. (eds.) 2005, 105, at 107 et seq. naming physical security, recognition of suffering, some kind of justice, truth and some kind of reparation.

[90] According to Stahn/Olásolo/Gibson (2006) 4 JICJ 219 victims have broad rights of participation under the ICC-Statute pursuant to Art. 15 (3), 19 (3), 53 (3), 61, 68 (3) ICC-Statute and Rules 89–93 of the Rules of Procedure and Evidence. See also Calvo-Goller (2006) at 244 et seq.; WCRO, November 2007 at 18 et seq.; Guhr (2008) 8 ICLR 109, 111 et seq.; Goetz in Waddell/Clark (eds.) 2008, 65, at 68 et seq. and Bock (2007) 119 ZStW, 664, 670 et seq. On victims' rights to reparation under the ICC-Statute see most recently O'Shea (n 64) at 186 et seq. and De Brouwer (2007) 20 LJIL 207 et seq. Wierda/Unger (n 80) at 275 et seq. wonder who speaks on behalf of victims and find that victims' perspectives on their rights are diverse, in the same vein Simpson in Waddel/Clark (eds.) 2008, 73, at 76.

these rights are not limited to criminal justice *stricto sensu*, i.e., to criminal prosecution of the perpetrators, available empirical data indicates that victims have strong criminal justice interests with regard to the prosecution and punishment of the perpetrators[91] and their own active participation (*partie civile*) in criminal prosecution and trials.[92] This does not preclude alternative justice mechanisms (para. 12 et seq.) but they can only *complement not substitute* criminal justice.[93]

11. In sum, victims have a right[94] to:

- *Truth*, i.e., "the clarification of the illegal facts and the corresponding responsibilities";[95] this is both "a collective right that ensures society access to information

[91] See Kiza/Rathgeber/Rohne (n 4) and OHCHR (n 33) both as quoted n 33. In the same vein *Prosecutor v. Katanga/Chui*, Decision on the set of procedural rights attached to procedural status of victim at the Pre-Trial Stage of the Case, 13 May 2008 (ICC-01/04–01/07) (ICC), para. 37 with fn 40 quoting additional reports. Otim/Wiedra in Waddell/Clark (eds.) 2008, 21 at 26 point out that victims' views can change over time, as shown by victims studies in Uganda indicating that the number of victims that support options such as forgiveness, reconciliation and reintegration instead of trials and punishment increased dramatically.

[92] Cf. Kiza/Rathgeber/Rohne (n 4) at 102 et seq. with Tables 23, 24 finding that victims have a "dual role" as a witness contributing to judicial fact-finding and a "narrator" contributing to the historical truth (at 104, 157). Diggelmann (n 44) at 393 points out, that justice from a victims perspective means, in the first place, atonement for the crimes, truth and the perpetrators' acknowledgment of guilt. See for the participation of victims in the trial proceedings of the ICC: *Prosecutor v. Thomas Lubanga Dylo*, Decision on victims' participation 18 January 2008 (ICC-01/04-01/06-1119), para. 84 et seq. and Decision on the Defence and Prosecution Requests to Leave to Appeal the Decion on Victims' Participation of 18 January 2008, 26 February 2008 (ICC-01/04-01/06-1191), para. 20 et seq., regarding the participation modalities, recently approved by the Appeals Chamber, Judgment on the appeals of the Prosecutor and the Defence against TC I's Decision on Victims' Participation of 18 January 2008, 11 July 2008 (ICC-01/04-01/06 OA 9 OA 10), para. 17 et seq.

[93] Cf. IACHR, *Rochela Massacre v. Colombia* [11 May 2007] Judgement, Series C No. 163, para. 187 et seq. This is also confirmed by the study of Kiza/Rathgeber/Rohne (n 4), see for example at 139 ("reparative and punitive notions are complementary") and passim. Thus, Clark's view (n 64, at 405) that alternative mechanisms may be preferable since they are more comfortable and comprehensive is not supported by empirical evidence.

[94] See also *Gustavo Gallón y otros* [18 May 2006] Sentencia C-370/2006, Expediente D-6032 (Colombian Constitutional Court) para. 48–9; Méndez in Joyner (ed.) 1998, 255, at 263.

[95] *Bámaca-Velásquez v. Guatemala* [25 November 2000] Judgement, Series C No. 70 (IACHR) para. 201; *Barrios Altos vs. Perú Case* [14 March 2001] Judgment, Series C No. 75 (IACHR) para. 48; *Carpio Nicolle y otros vs. Guatemala Case* [22 November 2004] Judgement, Series C No. 117 (IACHR) para. 128; *Moiwana Community v. Suriname* [15 June 2005] Judgement Series C No. 124 (IACHR) para. 203 et seq.; *"Mapiripán Massacre" v. Colombia* [15 September 2005] Judgement, Series C No. 134 (IACHR), para. 297; *Gómez-Palomino v. Perú* [22 November 2005] Judgement, Series C No. 136 (IACHR) para. 76 et seq.; *Blanco-Romero et al v. Venezuela* [28 November 2005] Judgement, Series C No. 138 (IACHR) para. 95 et seq.; *Pueblo Bello Massacre v. Colombia* [31 January 2006] Judgment, Series C No. 140 (IACHR) para. 219, 266;

that is essential for the workings of democratic systems, and (...) a private right for relatives of the victims, which affords a form of compensation, in particular, in cases where amnesty laws are adopted".[96] The right to truth can be traced back to Art. 32, 33 of AP I of 1977 to the GC I-IV of 1949;[97] subsequently, it has been recognized, in particular with regard to the fate of missing or disappeared persons,[98] by (international and national) case law, human rights bodies and state practice,[99] the latter in particular evidenced by the establishment of

Baldeón-García v. Perú [6 April 2006] Judgement, Series C No. 147 (IACHR) para. 196; *Ituango Massacre v. Colombia* [1 July 2006] Judgement, Series C (IACHR) para. 399; *Ximenes-Lopes v. Brasil* [4 July 2006] Judgment, Series C No. 149 (IACHR) para. 245; *Servellón-García et al. v. Honduras* [21 September 2006] Judgement, Series C No. 152 (IACHR) para. 193; *Almonacid-Arellano et al. v. Chile* (n 68) para. 148 et seq.; *Miguel Castro-Castro Prison v. Perú* [25 November 2006] Judgement, Series C No. 160 (IACHR) para. 440. See also *Hugh Jordan v. UK* [4 May 2001] Judgement, 24746/94 [2001] ECHR 327 (European Court of Human Rights) para. 93 ("the broad purpose of an inquiry is to discover the truth about the events leading to the suspicious death of a victim"). See also *Gustavo Gallón y otros* (n 94) para. 4.9.11.4. ("la posibilidad de conocer lo que sucedió y de buscar una coincidencia entre la verdad procesal y la verdad real"). For the doctrine see Slye (n 51) at 193-4. Recently approved by the International Criminal Court, *Prosecutor v. Katanga/Chui* (n 91), para. 32 et seq.

[96] *Ignacio Ellacuría et al. case* [22 December 1999] Report 136/99 (Inter-American Commission on Human Rights) para. 224. See also the judgement of the Peruvian Constitutional Court in *Villegas Namuche* [9 December 2004] Expediente 2488-2002-HC/TC, para. 9: "Al lado de la dimensión colectiva, el derecho a la verdad tiene una dimensión individual (...)"; Abrams/Morris in Joyner (ed.) 1998, 345, at 347 ("also a collective right").

[97] Art. 32, 33 pertain to the section referring to "missing and dead persons". Art. 32 provides for "the right of families to know the fate of their relatives", Art. 33 obliges the State Parties to "search for the persons who have been reported missing" (para. 1).

[98] On the national and international mechanisms to clarify the fate of the missing Crettol/La Rosa (2006) 88 ICRC Int. Rev. at 355 et seq.; on the cooperation of the ICRC with a TRC Pfanner (n 28) 368 et seq.

[99] The most explicit recognition can be found in the Joinet report where "the inalienable right to the truth" is defined, as part of a broader right to know (containing as further "general principles" the duty to remember, the victims' right to know and guarantees for the implementation), as follows: "Every people has the inalienable right to know the truth about past events and about the circumstances and reasons which led, through systematic, gross violations of human rights, to the perpetration of heinous crimes. Full and effective exercise of the right to the truth is essential to avoid any recurrence of violations in the future". (Annex 1 principle 1). See also Res. 2005/66 of the Commission on Human Rights (20 April 2005). For a detailed analysis of the applicable (international) law and practice see Naqvi (2006) 88 ICRC Int. Rev. 245, at 254 et seq.; also Botero/Restrepo (n 46) at 40 et seq. On the not fully consistent state practice see Naqvi, see above, at 261–2, 265–6. For an "emerging" right to truth which is part of a "greater right to justice" Méndez (n 94) at 257 et seq. (260, 263); similarly Hayner in Joyner (ed.) 1998, 215; for Abrams/Morris (n 96) at 347 the right to know "stems from the notion that states have a duty to acknowledge and remember human rights abuses". Many writers, however, take the right to truth for granted, see for example Odio Benito in Joyner (ed.) 1998, 149, at 151.

TRCs. Against this background, it can safely be concluded that it is an emerging customary norm and a general principle of law.[100]

- *Justice*,[101] i.e., some form of judicial protection either by access to the legal system of the violator state[102] (which – according to human rights case law[103] – has an obligation to investigate, prosecute and sanction the responsible)[104] or by way of an alternative (public) forum where the victims can confront and challenge the perpetrators.[105]

---

[100] See Naqvi (n 99) at 267–8 whose conclusion, however, that it stands "somewhere above a good argument and somewhere below a clear legal rule" (at 273) appears too cautious and contradicts her preceding legal analysis (at 254 et seq.). *Prosecutor v. Katanga/Chui* (n 91) para. 32. Daly (2008) 2 IJTJ 23, at 30 questions whether the truth and truth telling has a measurable benefit for victims.

[101] The Colombian CC in *Gustavo Gallón y otros* (n 94) para. 4.9.11.4., defines the right to justice "como aquel que en cada caso concreto proscribe la impunidad". See also *Prosecutor v. Katanga/Chui* (n 91), para. 39: "(...) identification, prosecution and punishment (...) are at the root of the well-established right to justice".

[102] See Basic Principles Victims, Sect. VIII, para. 12 referring to "all available judicial, administrative, or other public processes under existing domestic laws as well as under international law" (similarly Principles combating impunity, principle 8); see also *Hugh Jordan v. UK* (n 95) para. 16 (family members of the victims "shall be informed of, and have access to, any hearing as well as all information relevant to the investigation and shall be entitled to present other evidence (...)"), para. 23 ("Persons affected by the use of force and firearms (...) shall have access to an independent process, including a judicial process"); see also Chicago Principles at 16, Principle 3: "States shall acknowledge the special status of victims, ensure access to justice, and develop remedies and reparations." for the doctrine see Slye (n 51) at 195–6, 197; Young (n 88) at 477, 479; also Arsanjani (n 21) at 66; Robinson (n 31) at 498.

[103] See already n 68 and IACHR: *Carpio Nicolle y otros vs. Guatemala Case* (n 95) at 128; *Moiwana Community v. Suriname* (n 95) para. 204; *"Mapiripán Massacre" v. Colombia* (n 95) para. 295; *Blanco-Romero et al v. Venezuela* (n 95) para. 95; *Pueblo Bello Massacre v. Colombia* (n 95) para. 266; *López-Álvarez v. Honduras* [1 February 2006] Judgment, Series C No. 141, 207; *Baldeón-García v. Perú* (n 95) para. 168, 195; *Ituango Massacre v. Colombia* (n 95) para. 399; *Ximenes-Lopes v. Brasil* (n 95) para. 245; *Montero-Aranguren et al. (Detention Center of Catia) v. Venezuela* [5 July 2006] Judgment, Series C No. 150, para. 137 et seq.; *Servellón-García et al. v. Honduras* (n 95) para. 192 et seq.; *Goiburú et al. v. Paraguay* [22 September 2006] Judgement, Series C No. 153, para. 164; *Vargas-Areco v. Paraguay* [26 September 2006] Judgement, Series C No. 155, para. 153 et seq.; *Almonacid-Arellano et al. vs. Chile* (n 68) para. 148; *Miguel Castro-Castro Prison v. Perú* (n 95) para. 436; *La Cantuta v. Perú* [29 November 2006] Judgment, Series C No. 162, para. 222. See also ECHR: *Aksoy v. Turkey* [18 December 1996] Judgement, 21,987/93 [1996] ECHR 68, para. 98 ("obligation on States to carry out a thorough and effective investigation of incidents of torture (...)", "identification and punishment of those responsible and including effective access for the complainant to the investigatory procedure"); conc. *Aydin v. Turkey* [25 September 1997] Judgment, 23,178/94 [1997] ECHR 75, para. 103; *Selçuk and Asker v. Turkey* [24 April 1998] Judgement, 23,184/94, 23,185/94 [1998] ECHR 36, para. 96; *Kurt v. Turkey* 825 May 1998] Judgement, 24,276/94 [1998] ECHR 44, para. 140; *Selmouni v. France* [28 July 1999] Judgement, 25,803/94 [1999] ECHR 66, para. 79; *Hugh Jordan v. UK* (n 95) para. 157, 160 with further references. For a restrictive interpretation of the ECHR case law Benzing (2003) 7 Max Planck Yearbook of United Nations Law, 591, 608.

[104] See for a discussion already supra para. 8.

[105] See *Hugh Jordan v. UK* (n 95) para. 11 referring to an "independent commission of inquiry or similar procedure"; see also Slye (n 51) at 245; Clark (n 64) at 409.

- *Reparation*, used as an umbrella term[106] and encompassing full restitution (*restitutio in integrum*),[107] compensation[108] (Art. 75 ICC Statute),

---

[106] For this usage see, e.g., HRC, General Comment 31, para. 16 (defining reparation as "restitution, rehabilitation and measures of satisfaction, such as public apologies, public memorials, guarantees of non-repetition and changes in relevant laws and practices, as well as bringing to justice the perpetrators of human rights violations"); in the same vein ICTJ Reparation Report at 9; Peté/du Plessis in du Plessis/Peté (eds.) 2007, 3, at 15; de Greiff, published in this volume, at 338; see also Basic Principles Victims, Sect. X, para. 21 and Principles combating impunity, principle 10 A referring to "restitution, compensation, rehabilitation, and satisfaction and guarantees of non-repetition" as forms of reparation; see also Chicago Principles at 45 et seq.; Teitel (n 13) at 119; Bassiouni (n 67) at 37 et seq.; Mallinder (2008) at 171 et seq; Botero/Restrepo (n 46) at 44 et seq.; Sooka (n 6) at 319–20; Kiza/Rathgeber/Rohne (n 4) at 118 with Table 32; von Braun (n 3) at 20 et seq.; for a comprehensive historical account Torpey in Bassiouni (ed.) 2002, at 217 et seq. Also Ludi in du Plessis/Peté (eds.) 2007, 119, at 122 et seq.; especially for reparations concerning slavery cf. du Plessis in du Plessis/Peté (eds.) 2007, 147, at 167. For a survey of the Basic Principles Victims see Tomuschat in Kohen (ed.) 2007, at 569 et seq. (at 581 et seq. for the practice of selected international bodies) and Shelton in de Feyter/Parmentier et al. (eds.) 2005, 11, at 19 et seq. For the different meaning of "reparations" see Torpey in de Feyter/Parmentier et al. (eds.) 2005, 35, at 36 et seq.; for general obstacles to reparation see Schotsmans (n 89) at 125 et seq.; for the importance of active involvement of victims in the reparation process Hamber in de Feyter/Parmentier et al. (eds.) 2005, 135, at 141 et seq.; for general recommendations concerning the process and different types of reparation measures Rombouts/Sardaro/Vandeginste in de Feyter/Parmentier et al. (eds.) 2005, 345 at para. 146 et seq. – For a detailed summary of reparations and remedies ordered by the IACHR from 1989–2004 see Cassel in de Feyter/Parmentier et al. (eds.) 2005, 191, at 193 et seq.; for reparations by the Human Rights Chamber for Bosnia and Herzegovina cf. Nowak in de Feyter/Parmentier et al. (eds.) 2005 at 245 et seq. The German reparations for Nazi victims amounted by the end of 2006 to more than 64 billion € (see Bundesfinanzministerium – Referat VB4 "Leistungen der öffentlichen Hand auf dem Gebiet der Wiedergutmachung – Stand 31. Dezember 2006" [2007/0122828] at 1).

[107] See IACHR: *Palamara-Iribarne v. Chile* [22 November 2005] Judgment, Series C No. 135, para. 234; *Gómez Palomino vs. Perú* (n 95) para.113; *García-Asto and Ramírez-Rojas v. Perú* [25 November 2005] Judgment, Series C No. 137, para. 248; *Blanco-Romero et al v. Venezuela* (n 95) para. 69; *Pueblo Bello Massacre v. Colombia* (n 95) para. 228; *López-Álvarez v. Honduras* (n 103) para. 182; *Acevedo-Jaramillo et al. v. Perú* [7 February 2006] Judgment, Series C No. 144, para. 296; *Sawhoyamaxa Indigenous Community v. Paraguay* [29 March 2006] Judgment, Series C No. 146, para. 197; *Baldeón-García v. Perú* (n 95) para. 176; *Ituango Massacre v. Colombia* (n 95) para. 347; *Ximenes-Lopes v. Brasil* (n 95) para. 209; *Montero-Aranguren et al. (Detention Center of Catia) v. Venezuela* (n 103) para. 117; *Servellón-García et al. v. Honduras* (n 95) para. 162; *Goiburú et al. v. Paraguay* (n 103) para. 142; *Vargas-Areco v. Paraguay* (n 103) para. 141; *Almonacid-Arellano et al. vs. Chile* (n 68) para. 136; *Aguado-Alfaro et al. v. Perú (Case of Dismissed Congressional Employees)* [24 November 2006] Judgment (only in Spanish), Series C No. 158, para. 143; *Miguel Castro-Castro Prison v. Perú* (n 95) para. 415; *La Cantuta v. Perú* (n 103) para. 201. See also Basic Principles Victims, Sect. X, para. 22 and Principles combating impunity, principle 10 B ("restore the victim to the original situation before the violations"; "restitution includes: restoration of liberty, legal rights, social status, family life and citizenship; return to one's place of residence; and restoration of employment and return of property"). Crit. du Plessis (n 106) at 169 and de Greiff, published in this volume, at 340 emphasizing that, "there is no massive reparations program that has even approached the satisfaction of this criterion".

[108] See for "pecuniary damage" IACHR: *Sawhoyamaxa Indigenous Community v. Paraguay* (n 107) para. 216; *Rochela Massacre v. Colombia* (n 93) para. 248; *Baldeón-García v. Perú* (n 95) para. 183; *Pueblo Bello Massacre v. Colombia* (n 95) para. 246; *Ximenes-Lopes v. Brasil* (n 95) para. 220; *Montero-Aranguren et al. (Detention Center of Catia) v. Venezuela* (n 103) para. 126;

rehabilitation,[109] satisfaction and guarantees of non-repetition[110] and other measures,[111] i.e., in sum, measures which aim at a full recognition of the victims'

Servellón-García et al. v. Honduras (n 95) para. 173; *Goiburú et al. v. Paraguay* (n 103) para. 150; *Vargas-Areco v. Paraguay* (n 103) para. 146; *Almonacid-Arellano et al. vs. Chile* (n 68) para. 158; *Miguel Castro-Castro Prison v. Perú* (n 95) para. 423; for "non-pecuniary damage": *Rochela Massacre v. Colombia* (n 93) para. 273; *"Mapiripán Massacre" v. Colombia* (n 95) para. 282; *Palamara-Iribarne v. Chile* (n 107) para. 234; *Gómez Palomino vs. Perú* (n 95) para. 130; *García-Asto and Ramírez-Rojas v. Perú* (n 103) para. 276; *Blanco-Romero et al v. Venezuela* (n 95) para. 86; *Pueblo Bello Massacre v. Colombia* (n 95) para. 254; *López-Álvarez v. Honduras* (n 103) para. 199; *Acevedo-Jaramillo et al. v. Perú* (n 107) para. 308; *Sawhoyamaxa Indigenous Community v. Paraguay* (n 107) para. 219; *Baldeón-García v. Perú* (n 95) para. 188; *Ituango Massacre v. Colombia* (n 95) para. 383; *Ximenes-Lopes v. Brasil* (n 95) para. 227; *Montero-Aranguren et al. (Detention Center of Catia) v. Venezuela* (n 103) para. 130 et seq.; *Servellón-García et al. v. Honduras* (n 95) para. 179 et seq.; *Goiburú et al. v. Paraguay* (n 103) para. 156; *Vargas-Areco v. Paraguay* (n 103) para. 149 et seq.; *Almonacid-Arellano et al. v. Chile* (n 68) para. 158; *Miguel Castro-Castro Prison v. Perú* (n 95) para. 430; *La Cantuta v. Perú* (n 103) para. 201, para. 216. See also ECHR: *Hugh Jordan v. UK* (n 95) para. 166 et seq.; *Aksoy v. Turkey* (n 103) para. 110 et seq.; *Aydin v. Turkey* (n 103) para. 131; *Selçuk and Asker v. Turkey* (n 103) para. 104 et seq.; *Kurt v. Turkey* (n 103) para. 174–5; *Selmouni v. France* (n 103) para. 123. According to Basic Principles Victims, Sect. X, para. 23 and Principles combating impunity, principle 10 C: "[C]ompensation should be provided for any economically assessable damage (...)". For a critical view of victim reparations in Peru see Garcia-Godos (2008) 2 IJTJ 63, at 77 et seq. According to Du Plessis (n 106) at 169 this form of reparation is politically the most controversial and easily approaches excessive amounts; he refers (at 171, fn 98) to a group (called "The African World Reparations and Repatriation Truth Commission") which recently demanded $ 777 billion to be paid within 5 years by western governments as compensation for slavery. Mani (n 19) at 62 et seq. criticizes the failures especially of trials and TRC's to fulfil victims' rights to reparation. She further argues (at 76) that reparations have a bigger deterrent effect than penal sanctions. For advantages and disadvantages of obtaining reparation through either criminal or civil proceedings see Sarkin in de Feyter/Parmentier et al. (eds.) 2005, 151, at 155 et seq. Arsanjani/Reisman in Sadat/Scharf (eds.) 2008, 325, at 344, wonder where the money for the ICC's Trust Fund for Victims should come from "in a world of increasing donor fatigue".

[109] For "medical and psychological assistance" see IACHR: *Rochela Massacre v. Colombia* (n 93) para. 302; *"Mapiripán Massacre" v. Colombia* (n 95) para. 312; *Gómez Palomino v. Perú* (n 95) para.143; *García-Asto and Ramírez-Rojas v. Perú* (n 103) para. 280; *Pueblo Bello Massacre v. Colombia* (n 95) para. 274; *Baldeón-García v. Perú* (n 95) para. 206; *Ituango Massacre v. Colombia* (n 95) para. 403; *Vargas-Areco v. Paraguay* (n 103) para. 159; *Miguel Castro-Castro Prison v. Perú* (n 95) para. 448; *La Cantuta v. Perú* (n 103) para. 238. According to Basic Principles Victims, Sect. X, para. 24 and Principles combating impunity, principle 10 D "[R]ehabilitation should include medical and psychological care as well as legal and social services".

[110] According to Basic Principles Victims, Sect. X, para. 25 and Principles combating impunity, principle 10 E satisfaction and guarantees of non-repetition should include, inter alia, cessation of violations, verification of the facts, search for the bodies of the killed or disappeared, apology, judicial or administrative sanctions against the responsible, commemorations to the victims, prevention of the recurrence of violations. Thus, this right is in part mixed up with the rights to truth and justice. Therto also du Plessis (n 106) at 174 et seq. On public apologies see also Hazan (n 25) at 42–3; IACHR *Rochela Massacre v. Colombia* (n 93) para. 295; Jenkins in du Plessis/Peté (eds.) 2007, 53, at 57 et seq.

[111] For example "search and identification of persons" disappeared or killed, delivery of the body: *Juan Humberto Sánchez v. Honduras* [7 June 2003] Judgment, Series C No. 187 (IACHR), para. 127 et seq.; *19 Tradesmen v. Colombia* [5 July 2004] Judgment, Series C No. 109 (IACHR) para. 265; *"Mapiripán Massacre" v. Colombia* (n 95) para. 305 et seq.; *Pueblo Bello Massacre v. Colom-*

status[112] and, to the extent possible, the re-establishment of their rights.[113] However, a state's duty to provide reparation for violations of international law, especially of human rights obligations, is controversial[114] and the kind of reparation required depends very much on context of the conflict.[115]

---

bia (n 95) at 270–273; *Acevedo-Jaramillo et al. v. Perú* (n 107) para. 315; *Baldeón-García v. Perú* (n 95) para. 208; *Goiburú et al. v. Paraguay* (n 103) para. 171; *La Cantuta v. Perú* (n 103) para. 231; or "educational measures": *Rochela Massacre v. Colombia* (n 93) para. 303; *"Mapiripán Massacre" v. Colombia* (n 95) para. 316 et seq.; *Ituango Massacre v. Colombia* (n 95) para. 409; *Vargas-Areco v. Paraguay* (n 103) para. 161; *López-Álvarez v. Honduras* (n 103) para. 210; *Servellón-García et al. v. Honduras* (n 95) para. 200; *Montero-Aranguren et al. (Detention Center of Catia) v. Venezuela* (n 103) para. 147; *Miguel Castro-Castro Prison v. Perú* (n 95) para. 451; "monuments and other memorial sites": *"Mapiripán Massacre" v. Colombia* (n 95) para. 315; *Pueblo Bello Massacre v. Colombia* (n 95) at 278; Case of *Baldeón-García v. Perú* (n 95) para. 205; *Ituango Massacre v. Colombia* (n 95) para. 408; *Vargas-Areco v. Paraguay* (n 103) para. 158; *Servellón-García et al. v. Honduras* (n 95) para. 199; *Miguel Castro-Castro Prison v. Perú* (n 95) para. 454). On public memorialization with regard to the Cono Sur in South America see Elizabeth Jelin (2007) 1 IJTJ 138 et seq.

[112] Public act of *acknowledgment of responsibility*: IACHR, *Indigenous Community Yakye Axa v. Paraguay* [17 June 2005] Judgment, Series C No. 125, para. 226; *Moiwana Community v. Suriname* (n 95) para. 216; *Jean and Bosico v. República Dominicana* [8 September 2005] Judgment, Series C No. 130, para. 235; *"Mapiripán Massacre" v. Colombia* (n 95) para. 314; *Pueblo Bello Massacre v. Colombia* (n 95) para. 277; *Baldeón-García v. Perú* (n 95) para. 204; *Ituango Massacre v. Colombia* (n 95) para. 406; Case of *Servellón-García et al. v. Honduras* (n 95) para. 198; *Goiburú et al. v. Paraguay* (n 103) para. 173; *Vargas-Areco v. Paraguay* (n 103) para. 158; *Miguel Castro-Castro Prison v. Perú* (n 95) para. 445; *La Cantuta v. Perú* (n 103) para. 235. See also Sooka (n 6) at 318.

[113] The Colombian CC (*Gustavo Gallón y otros* [n 94]), para. 4.9.11.4., defines the right to reparation "como aquel que comprende obtener una compensación económica, pero que no se limita a ello sino que abarca medidas individuales y colectivas tendientes, en su conjunto, a restablecer la situación de las víctimas". See also ICTJ-guidelines, p. 5; see also Schlunck (n 30) at 71–72; Slye (n 51) at 196–7, 245; Young (n 88) at 477, 479; Robinson (n 31) at 498.

[114] See for a critical discussion Tomuschat (2002) 10 Tul. J. Int'l. Comp. L. at 158 et seq. concluding at 184, that "there exist no general rule of customary international law to the effect that any grave violation of human rights creates an individual reparation claim". In favour of such a duty Res. 2002/44 of the Commission on Human Rights (23 April 2002), Basic Principles Victims, Sect. IX (in particular para. 16 referring to the "international legal obligations") and Principles combating impunity, principle 9 B. See also Bassiouni (n 67) at 48 et seq. with further references of the case law. For a detailed study of the relevant international law and practice see Rombouts/Sardaro/Vandeginste (n 106) at para. 36 et seq., concluding (para. 135) that "every human rights violation entails a duty for the responsible state to provide reparation and a correlative right of victims to obtain reparation". As to an inter-state duty of reparation arising out of State responsibility see Bosnia and Herzegovina v. Serbia and Montenegro (Case concerning the application of the Convention on the Prevention and Punishment of the Crime of Genocide) [26 February 2007] Judgement (ICJ) para. 459 et seq. stating at para. 460 (with further references) that where a restitutio in integrum is not possible "an injured State is entitled to obtain compensation from the State which has committed an internationally wrongful act for the damage caused by it" (for the same result with regard to human rights violations Méndez (n 94) at 263).

[115] According to Kiza/Rathgeber/Rohne (n 4) at 118 (Table 32), 122 the majority of the victims (42%) demand monetary compensation, 41% an apology (by the offender or an official), 29% a memorial, etc. On a discussion with regard to international crimes see Teitel (n 13) at 124 et seq. For an overview of symbolic and material reparation policies in Spain, Argentina and Chile see Aguilar, published in this volume, at 510 et seq. For the challenges of designing a reparation

2.3 Alternatives to Criminal Prosecution

12. The renunciation of criminal prosecution in exchange for peace and reconciliation begs the question of adequate alternatives to criminal justice and prosecution. While these alternatives need not be an equivalent to criminal prosecution – they do not substitute but only complement it (para. 10) – they must offer a *serious alternative way of dealing with the past* and as such effectively take into account the interests of victims. This presupposes, firstly, the full participation of victims in the design and execution of these measures.[116] For a *peace process*, especially the negotiations regarding the treatment of the crimes committed, this means that the voice of the victims must be heard. Their participation is indispensable to lend legitimacy to this process and make it socially acceptable.[117] The level and degree of participation is decisive in the contribution that the alternative measure(s) can make to national reconciliation. A real and positive contribution to reconciliation is, in turn, a prerequisite for the democratic and international legitimacy of the measure(s): Did a process of consultation with the society at large take place? Have the measures been discussed publicly and/or in democratic organs, such as a democratically-elected parliament? Is an open and free discussion, including a critique of the measures possible? Did a referendum take place? Did international (UN) negotiators and/or experts take part?[118]

13. The most important alternative to (pure) criminal prosecution is the establishment of a *Truth and Reconciliation Commission* (TRC). According to an authoritative definition TRCs:

> are official, temporary, non-judicial fact finding bodies that investigate a pattern of abuses of human rights or humanitarian law committed over a number of years. These bodies take a victim-centred approach and conclude their work with a final report of findings of fact and recommendations. (...) Truth commissions have the potential to be of great benefit in helping post-conflict societies establish the facts about past human rights violations, foster accountability, preserve evidence, identify perpetrators and recommend reparations and

---

policy especially in Darfur see ICTJ Reparation Report at 26; for Sierra Leone see Schabas in de Feyter/Parmentier et al. (eds.) 2005, 289, at 290 et seq.; for Rwanda see Rombouts/Vandeginste in de Feyter/Parmentier et al. (eds.) 2005, at 309 et seq. For the question of the necessary seriousness of violations to entitle victims to reparations see Peté/du Plessis (n 106) at 17 et seq.; for a possible time limit at 20 et seq. For a special gender reparation program and its benefits Rubio-Marin/de Greiff (2007) 1 IJTJ 318, at 321 et seq.

[116] See UN-ECOSOC, Impunity, 27 February 2004, para. 11; Report Secretary General transitional justice, para. 18; see also Duggan (n 49) xi referring to the (official) recognition of the suffering of the victims. For a "central role" also Mallinder (n 65) at 220.

[117] See UN-ECOSOC, Impunity, 27 February 2004, para. 11; Report Secretary General transitional justice, para. 18.

[118] Cf. Slye (n 51) at 245; Robinson (n 31) at 497; Seibert-Fohr (n 21) at 571–2; Gropengießer/Meißner (n 60) at 278; Clark (n 64) at 409–10; Duggan (n 49) xi; also Arsanjani (n 21) at 66. In Sudan, the UN Security Council encourages the creation of institutions such as truth and/or reconciliation commissions, cf. S/RES1593 (2005), adopted 31 March 2005, para. 5.

> institutional reforms. They can also provide a public platform for victims to address the nation directly with their personal stories and can facilitate public debate about how to come to terms with the past.[119]

Thus, TRCs try to cope with the past by establishing a truth which, on the one hand, goes far beyond the judicial, narrative truth of the courtroom (whose limitations are most clearly manifested by the use of guilty pleas and other bargaining mechanisms)[120] but, on the other hand, always remains incomplete in that it only opens the door to further inquiry and truth establishment.[121] TRCs may establish what some have termed a "global truth",[122] "macro-truth",[123] "moral truth",[124] "overall truth",[125] "objective truth"[126] or "historical truth"[127] – as opposed to mere judicial or factual truth[128] – i.e., a truth taking into account all facets of past crimes and

[119] Report Secretary General transitional justice, para. 50. See generally also Bassiouni (n 67) at 32; from a practical perspective Sooka (n 6) at 315 et seq. See for a positive assessment of the Latin American TRCs Salmón (n 74) at 352: "(...) the work of the truth commissions in the region has had the irreversible effect of bringing victims of violence into the spotlight and ensuring that their voices are heard. (...) the reports document a conscious state policy of using human rights violations to achieve governmental objectives".

[120] See Damaška (2004) 2 JICJ 1018; see also Naqvi (n 99) at 271–2 and Bell, published in this volume, at 112 et seq.; crit. also Pastor (2007) 59 Jueces para la democracia at 106 et seq.

[121] Cf. Imbleau (2004) 15 CLF 159, at 188 ("opening [...] for further truth establishment"); see also the interview with Salomón Lerner (2006) 88 ICRC Int. Rev. 225, at 227. ("The truth thus exposed is open and susceptible to later enrichment [...] we are not making an incontrovertible, dogmatic statement [...] It starts from an open reading of scientifically established facts and interpretations that can complement this sort of endless search for a truth, which, as we know, will never be complete".) On different memories see also Jelin (n 111) at 141 et seq.

[122] Hayner (2001) at 85.

[123] Imbleau (n 121) 177.

[124] Hunt (2004) 15 CLF 193, at 195.

[125] Mattarollo in Bassiouni (ed.) 2002, 295, at 300.

[126] Boraine (n 23) at 287.

[127] González (2004) 15 CLF 55, at 61; von Braun (n 3) at 22; see also Zalaquett in Aspen Institute (ed.) 1989, 3, at 31: "The important thing is that the truth is established in an officially sanctioned way, in a manner that allows the findings to form part of the historical record (...) and that establishes an authoritative version of the events, over and above partisan considerations". Crit. Hunt (n 124) at 198 asking for caution as to the truth value of TRCs and regarding them as "historical events" rather than "sources"; on this point see also Cole (2007) 1 IJTJ 115, at 119–20 who herself calls for a linking of TRCs to history education; on the educational effect also Boraine (n 23) at 294. According to Elberling (2008) 21 LJIL at 529 et seq., international tribunals engage in the process of writing history and therefore have been accused of being "partial in their coverage of the conflict and of writing the history that some other party wanted them to write" (at 530). Diggelmann (n 44) at 394 argues that for most victims, the historical truth is more important than the mere factual truth.

[128] For Diggelmann (n 44) at 394 the judicial truth often ignores emotions, general impressions and atmosphere and focuses on the external, visible facts; further (at 395) the logic of due process is often opposed to victims justice. On the different objectives of criminal trials and TRCs see also *Prosecutor v. Norman*, Decision on the request by the TRC of Sierra Leone to Conduct a Public Hearing with Samuel Hinga Norman [29 October 2003] Case No. SCSL-2003-08-PT (Special Court for Sierra Leone) para. 12. See also Boraine (n 23) at 292 et seq.; Cárdenas (n 46) at 172–3.

conflicts;[129] however, this is not necessarily the case.[130] Thus, TRCs are the expression of the integrated approach necessary to face the multiple problems in post-conflict societies.[131] However, TRCs may also examine individual cases[132] and may operate with different concepts of truth.[133]

14. With the increasing importance of TRCs,[134] especially the relatively successful South African model,[135] the research has also increased considerably.[136]

---

[129] See on this complex concept of truth in more detail Imbleau (n 121) 160, 162, 167 (truth "in the context of transition"), 177–8, 187 et seq.; see also the interview with Lerner (n 121) at 225–6 ("[...] phenomenological concept of truth, if that is how we understand a process of discovery, of drawing aside a veil and therefore of exploring the sense, the meanings of human actions"); Chaparro in Rettberg (ed.) 2005, 233, at 246 et seq. refers to "memoria"; Orentlicher (n 21) at 16. See also Daly (n 100) at 26: "(...) it is impossible to say which is the 'truest' truth".

[130] On partial truth see Osiel (n 16) at 134; see also the crit. discussion by Teitel (n 13) at 81 et seq.; according to Daly (n 100) at 23 "the problem is that the truth neither *is* or *does* all that we expect of it".

[131] Calling for such an approach, e.g., Kritz (n 9) at 58–9, 66; Roht-Arriaza in Bassiouni (ed.) 2002, at 97; id. in Joyner (ed.) 1998, at 279; for a holistic approach Stahn (n 46) at 458; Sooka (n 6) at 320; for "multiple instruments" Kiza/Rathgeber/Rohne (n 4) at 111, 162; Orentlicher (n 21) 16; Jelin (n 111) at 156.

[132] See Mattarollo (n 125) at 300 ("individual truth").

[133] See Cassin (n 14) at 240 referring to the South African TRC ("According to the report itself, the TRC did in fact work with four intermeshed, explicitly rhetorical concepts of truth, each defined by the situation in which it was voiced. The first was 'factual' or 'forensic' truth, a court truth, referring to the reasoned decisions of the Amnesty Committee. The second was 'personal and narrative' truth, the truth expressed in practical terms by each person during the hearings and individual testimony. The third was referred to as 'social' truth, a truth of dialogue obtained through the process of confrontation or verbal exchange between victims and tormentors. And finally, the fourth truth was 'healing' and 'restorative' truth, the truth where it was decided to draw the line, the truth that was enough to bring about a consensus upon what and with what the rainbow nation could be built. These were the stages in the discursive construction that put in place an effective truth by suspending the difference between the real truth, which is objective, and false truths, which are subjective"); on these kinds of truth see also Boraine (n 23) at 288 et seq. On the concepts of truth from a philosophical perspective Naqvi (n 99) at 249 et seq. Daly (n 100) at 27 argues that, "the biggest problem with the truth is not that there are too many truths but rather that there is not enough truth. Often the truth that victims and others most want to hear is not the forensic truth, nor the historical or dialogic truth, but the psychological truth. Why did the perpetrator do this? Why did the government try to erase my people? How could the world stand by and let it happen? To these questions there are no answers".

[134] Cf. Mallinder study (n 28) para. 51 with Fig. 6 showing the increase from 1985 to 2005.

[135] Cf. Boraine (n 23) at 258 et seq. indicating as reasons for the "degree of success" (258) of the South African TRC six: support from the ruling party (ANC) and the government (espec. President Nelson Mandela), the successful political negotiations preceding the TRC, a very strong civil society, interest of the international community, the religious character of the TRC, the personality of its chairman Desmond Tutu; on the benefits of a TRC compared to criminal prosecutions ibid., at 286 et seq.

[136] See for the most detailed study Hayner (n 122) Chart 1, Appendix 1, p. 291 et seq., analyzing 21 truth commissions since 1974; for an update see id. (2006) 88 ICRC Int. Rev. 295 et seq. An overview over Latin American TRC provides Salmón (n 74) at 344 et seq. referring to Argentina, Chile, Ecuador, El Salvador, Guatemala, Panama and Peru. See also Schlunck (n 30) at 64 et seq., 260–61 focusing on El Salvador and South Africa. On the Peruvian TRC see González (n 127)

It shows that one must analyse each and every TRC on its own merits since their competences and powers as well as the socio-political framework of their functioning vary widely.[137] From a simplified structural perspective one may distinguish between TRCs with a limited mandate and no judicial powers which therefore tend to primarily legitimize and/or prepare the impunity of the most responsible (here so-called "impunity TRCs") and others which possess a broad mandate with quasi judicial powers,[138] sufficient resources and the necessary independence to decide on the basis of rationale criteria ("effective TRCs").[139] TRCs ideally complement or prepare criminal prosecution.[140] In this case, complex issues of delimitation between the (national or international) court(s) and the respective TRCs arise,[141] especially whether and to what extent confessions or testimonies before a TRC can be used in subsequent criminal trials.[142] If a TRC is thought to be a substitute for criminal

at 55 et seq. and the interview with its president, Salomón Lerner (n 121) at 225 et seq.; also Garcia-Godos (n 118) at 77 et seq.; on the Guatemalan "Commission for Historical Clarification" see Seils in Bassiouni (ed.) 2002, 775, at 785 et seq.; on the El Salvadorean TRC ibid., at 779 et seq.; Buergenthal (n 55) at 292 et seq.; Kemp (n 21) at 77 et seq.; Popkin (n 54) at 107 et seq.; on the Sierra Leone TRC see Shaw (2007) 1 IJTJ 183 et seq.; Schabas (2004) 15 CLF 3 et seq.; Kritz (n 9) at 66 et seq. and Poole in Bassiouni (ed.) 2002, 563, at 577 et seq.; on Ghana's "National Reconciliation Commission" Agyemang (2004) 15 CLF 125 et seq.; on East Timor's "Commission for Reception, Truth and Reconciliation" (the respective Regulation 2001/10 of UNTAET is reprinted in Bassiouni [n 9] at 546 et seq.) Burgess (2004) 15 CLF 135 et seq.; Devereux/Kent in Blumenthal/McCormack (eds.) 2008, 171, at 172 et seq.; Kritz (n 9) at 78–9; on the TRCs in Bosnia-Hercegovina, Kritz (n 9) at 60 et seq.; for the Nigerian "Human Rights Violations Investigation Commission, called "Oputa Panel" see Yusuf (2007) 1 IJTJ 268 et seq., for the TRC in Burundi cf. Vandeginste, published in this volume, at 406 et seq. The Colombian "Ley de Justicia y Paz" (n 203) provides for a "Comisión Nacional de Reparación y Reconciliación" (Art. 50–52) but its competences are very limited, in particular it is not authorized to recommend criminal prosecutions (crit. also Durán [n 19] at 34–5).

[137] Hayner (n 99) at 216; Abrams/Hayner in Bassiouni (ed.) 2002, 283, at 284; Werle (n 17) mn 205; von Braun (n 3) at 22.

[138] Normally not judicial powers stricto sensu, i.e., the powers of a criminal court, see Mattarollo (n 125) at 295–6; exceptionally the South African TRC possessed even search and seizure as well as subpoena powers, see Boraine (n 23) at 272–3.

[139] See for a comparison of the Chilean and South African Truth commissions in this sense Dugard (n 64) at 1,009 et seq.; see also Dugard (n 60) at 703; for a comparison of the Chilean and South African amnesty processes see Gavron (n 64) at 112 et seq. For a structural comparison along the lines of international vs. domestic, selective vs. general inquiry, quasi-judicial vs. fact-finding, enquiry vs. reintegration see Stahn (n 46) at 428 et seq.

[140] Hayner (n 99) at 215; Abrams/Hayner (n 137) at 286; see also Méndez (n 28) 29–30, 33; Crocker (n 28) at 546–7 et seq.; Robinson (n 31) 484; Cárdenas (n 46) at 172; Naqvi (n 99) at 270; Kiza/Rathgeber/Rohne (n 4) at 106; von Braun (n 3) at 24. Similarly, restorative justice cannot substitute but only complement criminal prosecutions, see Uprimny/Saffon (n 3) at 219, 220 et seq.

[141] In general on this issue Abrams/Hayner (n 137) at 287; Kemp (n 21) at 74 et seq.; on the relationship between the ICTY and the TRC in Bosnia-Hercegovina Kritz (n 9) at 62 et seq.; on the relationship between the SCSL and the Sierra Leone TRC Schabas (n 136) 25 et seq.; Kritz (n 9) at 68 et seq. and Poole (n 136) at 589 et seq.; on the relationship between the East Timorese TRC and the UN Serious Crimes Investigation Unit Burgess (n 136) 144 et seq.

[142] On the "immunity for testimony" mechanism see Naqvi (n 99) at 270–1. According to Mallinder (n 65) at 226 this could prevent perpetrators from participating in a TRC for fear of having to incriminate themselves.

prosecutions, the ability of the respective criminal justice system to deal with the crimes of the past must be questioned. Given the fact that a TRC cannot be considered an equivalent to criminal prosecution[143] the renunciation of the latter in favour of the former smacks of a political deal, which does not strengthen the rule of law and separation of powers but indicates inability within the meaning of Art. 17 (3) ICC Statute (see para. 42) on the part of the criminal justice system concerned.[144] In any event, if a TRC operates as a (partial) substitute for justice the truth to be discovered by this TRC must, in qualitative and quantitative terms, compensate for the loss or deficit of justice.

15. TRCs are as effective as the main political actors are prepared to make them; they depend on their willingness and cooperation.[145] If the most responsible perpetrators do not come forward to tell the truth without certain guarantees, e.g., that their declarations may not be used against them in a subsequent criminal trial, these guarantees may have to be given.[146] An effective TRC may certainly constitute a serious alternative way of dealing with the past in that it establishes a "global truth" going beyond the mere judicial truth (para. 13);[147] thereby it may contribute to national reconciliation[148] and constitute an integral part of a society's restora-

---

[143] IACHR, *Almonacid-Arellano et al. vs. Chile* (n 68) para. 150 ("'verdad histórica' contenida en los informes de las citadas Comisiones no puede sustituir la obligación del Estado de lograr la verdad a través de los procesos judiciales"); *La Cantuta v. Perú* (n 103) para. 224; *Rochela Massacre v. Colombia* (n 93) para. 187 et seq. see also IAComHR, *Chanfeau et al. v. Chile* [7 April 1998] Report No. 25/98, para. 68 ("No puede considerarse a la Comisión de verdad como un sustituto adecuado de un proceso judicial". Similarly *Ellacuría et al. v. El Salvador* [22 December 1999] Report No. 136/99 (IAComHR) para. 229 et seq.; *Romero y Galdámez v. El Salvador* [13 April 2000] Report No. 37/00 (IAComHR) para. 149–50; HRW Memorandum 2007 at 6 et seq; see also Freemann (n 120) at 83 ("never [...] adequate substitute").

[144] For this reason against a substitution of criminal prosecution by a TRC Principles combating impunity, principle 12 A; similarly Joyner (n 21) at 39 criticizing that TRCs "cannot (...) call a specific criminal to account for his crimes"; it is too simplistic and polemical, however, to characterize TRCs as "modern-day Spanish Inquisitions" (ibid. at 37); also Kiza/Rathgeber/Rohne (n 4) at 107 referring to the risk of a trade-off implying a non-prosecution for political reasons. Crit. also Méndez (n 94) at 275; Seils (n 136) at 794; Cárdenas (n 46) at 180. A good summary of the pros and cons is offered by Kiza/Rathgeber/Rohne (n 4) at 107.

[145] Cf. Seils (n 136) at 793. See for a positive example the support of the South African TRC by the ANC and President Nelson Mandela (Boraine, as quoted in n 135).

[146] For a discussion with regard to Sierra Leone see Schabas (n 136) at 29–30, 41–2 for whom the willingness to cooperate with a TRC "may have far less to do with promises of amnesty or threats of prosecution than many may think" (at 42). See generally Cárdenas (n 46) at 174.

[147] For the better "truth effect" see also Dugard (n 64) 1,006 quoting the decision of the South African CC's decision in *AZAPO et al. vs. The President et al.* (n 23); see also Dugard (n 60) at 695; Havel in Bassiouni (ed.) 2002, 383, at 389 et seq.

[148] Hayner (n 99) at 216; Abrams/Hayner (n 137) at 290. Apart from contributing to reconciliation the establishment of the truth may contribute to restoring and maintaining peace, erradicating impunity, reconstruction national identities, setting straight the historial record (cf. Naqvi [n 99] at 247) and bring about institutional change (Šimonović [n 30] at 703). See also Pfanner (n 28) at 363–4.

tion process[149] containing an important transformative potential.[150] In this sense, a TRC may claim international recognition, especially *vis-à-vis* the international criminal justice system.[151] This recognition, however, depends on the treatment of exemptions from punishment by a TRC, especially amnesties. Mallinder finds that amnesties have been introduced independently of a TRC, before or after its establishment (e.g., in Chile and El Salvador respectively), or in conjunction with a TRC,[152] the most direct relationship being the South African case where the TRC had the power to grant the amnesty individually.[153] Clearly, if the amnesty decision is taken by the government without considering the findings of the TRC, its credibility is severely weakened. On the other hand, the faculty to grant an amnesty begs the question whether any limitations *ratione materiae* or *personae* (below para. 21) have been respected. Thus, for example, the South African TRC's amnesty faculty even extended to the most serious (political) crimes, while this possibility was ruled out in the case of the East Timorese Commission for Reception, Truth and Reconciliation (CAVR).[154] In any event, in most cases amnesty for war crimes, crimes against humanity, and genocide has been excluded.[155]

16. Taking into account the experiences from various TRCs certain best practices can be deduced and guidelines developed.[156] If they are followed we may speak of an *effective TRC* in the sense mentioned above (para. 14) and the ultimate goals of peace, justice (in the broad sense) and reconciliation will most probably be achieved. The relevant criteria can be summarized as follows:

---

[149] Boraine (n 23) at 295–6; Meintjes (n 14) at 460. According to Kiza/Rathgeber/Rohne (n 4) at 143, Table 42 the usefulness of a TRC increases, from a victims' perspective, with the degree of victimization.

[150] Kiza/Rathgeber/Rohne (n 4) at 126.

[151] See in this regard the legitimate claim made by the South African TRC with regard to the international criminal responsibility for the crime of apartheid: "The Commission believes that international recognition should be given to the fact that the Promotion of National Unity and Reconciliation Act, and the processes of this Commission itself, have sought to deal appropriately with the matter of responsibility for such policies" (TRC Report, vol. 5, at. 349 [1998], quoted according to Dugard [n 64] at 1,009.)

[152] Mallinder study (n 28) para. 46.

[153] This was one of the unique features of the South African TRC (cf. Boraine [n 23] at 269), see more detailed below para. 31 with n 272 et seq.

[154] Cf. UN-Ecosoc, Impunity, 27 February 2004, para. 12.

[155] See, e.g., the Guatemalan Law of National Reconciliation, excluding an amnesty for genocide, torture, forced disappearance or crimes without a statute of limitations (Méndez [n 28] at 36; Kemp [n 21] at 82; see generally ICTJ-guidelines, p. 5).

[156] See in particular UN-ECOSOC, Impunity, 27 February 2004, para. 19; Abrams/Hayner (n 137) at 283 et seq. (293); Mattarollo (n 125) at 295 et seq.; Cassese (n 88) at 451–2; Mallinder (n 65) at 224 et seq.; see also ICTJ-guidelines, p. 5; Principles combating impunity, principles 11, 13; Joyner (n 21) at 40; Roht-Arriaza (n 131) at 281 et seq.; Dugard (n 64) at 1012; Schiff in Bassiouni (ed.) 2002, at 325 et seq.; Robinson (n 31) at 497; Cárdenas in Kleffner/Kor (eds.) 2006, 115, at 135; Salmón (n 74) at 343; Sooka (n 6) at 317 et seq.; on the quite unique features of the relatively successful South African TRC Boraine (n 23) at 269 et seq. See also the accountability principles proposed by Bassiouni (n 67) at 40. Mani (n 19) at 61 argues that "a truth commission badly done can be worse than none at all".

- A TRC should be composed of recognized and independent *personalities* from all relevant social groups and sectors to be selected in a consultative and representative process.
- On the operational level, a publicly identified contact point for victims and witnesses should be set up.
- A TRC must dispose of adequate *resources* and have sufficient *independence* from the state and other interested groups;[157] it must possess sufficient investigative powers and receive national and international support.
- The *mandate* of a TRC should not be limited to the establishment of individual responsibilities but also shed light on the *causes of the conflict* in order to prevent the recurrence of future violations. At a minimum, the crimes codified in the ICC Statute (genocide, crimes against humanity and war crimes)[158] should be within the mandate. Representative cases illustrating patterns of criminality should be investigated and special attention should be given to gender-related violence.[159]
- The mandate should be time-bound,[160] but there should be a *follow-up* process eventually allowing for a continuation of the investigation if clarification of past atrocities has not been satisfactorily achieved by the first TRC.
- A TRC should identify the *victims* and recommend reparations to the competent state organs.[161]
- There should be full *cooperation* with other state organs involved in TJ, including providing information to the prosecution authorities.
- The suspected *perpetrators*[162] should be brought before the TRC to publicly confess their crimes and give evidence on other crimes; victims should be present;[163]

[157] See ECHR, *Hugh Jordan v. UK* (n 95) para. 11. ("Members of such a commission [of inquiry] shall be chosen for their recognised impartiality, competence and independence as individuals. In particular, they shall be independent of any institution, agency or person that may be the subject of the inquiry".)

[158] For Cassese (n 88) at 451 genocide must be dealt with exclusively by the criminal justice system.

[159] See for example on this issue Roht-Arriaza (n 131) at 284; Sooka (n 6) at 322–3.

[160] According to UN-ECOSOC, Impunity, 27 February 2004, para. 19 (h) it should generally last no more than two fully-operational years; according to Abrams/Hayner (n 137) at 288 the Commissions have mostly operated for less than 2 years; according to Hayner (n 136) at 295 "one to three years on average", see also the examples given by Mattarollo (n 125) at 313; for a limited mandate also Roht-Arriaza (n 131) at 283.

[161] According to UN-ECOSOC, Impunity, 27 February 2004, para. 19 (b) a TRC should not directly grant reparations since this would skew their truth seeking role; according to Cassese (n 88) at 451 a TRC may determine reparations; Boraine (n 23) at 294–5 sees this even as a an important function. Devereux/Kent (n 136) at 195 et seq., point to the possible disparity between victims and perpetrators and argue (at 201), that "in the absence of attention to issues of reparations, truth and reconciliation commissions may risk having little impact on the everyday lives and attitudes". For Daly (n 100) at 33 at least the findings of a report should be directed to the courts.

[162] For Cassese (n 88) at 451 the top-level perpetrators should be prosecuted either by the national or international criminal justice system.

[163] Cf. Cassese (n 88) at 451; more restrictive UN-ECOSOC, Impunity, 27 February 2004, para. 19 (d) ("If a truth commission has authority to identify suspected perpetrators [...]").

in case of the identification of the perpetrators ("name names") their due process rights must be respected.[164]

- The possible granting of *amnesties* or pardons should be conditional, i.e., depend on the nature and gravity of the crimes and the extent to which the suspects have cooperated in the discovery of the truth and the compensation of the victims; if these conditions are not fulfilled the TRC must have the authority to reject the application and turn the case over to the criminal justice system.
- There should be *broad participation* of the society concerned in the design and operation of the TRC, in particular of the victims and/or their representatives.[165]
  The final *report* should be published and made *widely available* to the general public through media that are technically and culturally accessible. "The closer a commission's work can be brought physically and psychologically to the victims and the public at large, the more potent the commission's cathartic and educational effects will be".[166]
- All state organs are required to consider in good faith the *recommendations* of a TRC and implement them to the greatest extent possible; a *monitoring* body should be established for that purpose.[167]

---

[164] The naming of the perpetrators is for the due process issue controversial, the Orentlicher impunity principles provide some guidance in principle 9: "Before a commission identifies perpetrators in its report, the individuals concerned shall be entitled to the following guarantees: (a) The commission must try to corroborate information implicating individuals before they are named publicly; (b) The individuals implicated shall be afforded an opportunity to provide a statement setting forth their version of the facts either at a hearing convened by the commission while conducting its investigation or through submission of a document equivalent to a right of reply for inclusion in the commission's file". For a discussion see Osiel (n 16); Hayner (n 122) at 114–5 et seq.; Hayner (n 136) at 296; Naqvi (n 99) at 272; in favour Abrams/Hayner (n 137) at 286, but recalling due process rights of the suspects; in the same vein Freemann (n 120) at 268 et seq.; Mallinder (n 65) at 225; Imbleau (121) at 186–7; in favour only if no prosecution will follow Méndez (n 94) at 267–8; recalling due process rights also Pfanner (n 28) at 370. This competence had, for example, the South African TRC (Boraine [n 23] at 275) and the Salvadorean TRC (cf. Popkin [n 54] at 109, 111). The problem is apparently ignored by Posner/Vermeule (n 6) at 767 if they argue, without more, that the purpose of TRCs "is to reveal the identities of perpetrators".

[165] On the importance of public participation and the civil society's integration in accountability processes see Meintjes (n 14) at 460; Roht-Arriaza (n 131) at 98 et seq.; Mattarollo (n 125) at 306–7; Filippini/Magarrell (n 7) at 160 et seq.; Chaparro (n 129) at 234; Sooka (n 6) at 314; on the South African experience Boraine (n 23) at 270 et seq.; Bell (n 120) at 119; Chicago Principles at 38; on participation in East Timor see Devereux/Kent (n 136) at 182 et seq., 190 et seq.

[166] Abrams/Hayner (n 137) at 288; Hazan (n 25) at 37. Generally crit. of TRC Reports Daly (n 100) at 28 et seq.; with regard to South Africa Mamdani in du Plessis/Peté (eds.) 2007, 83, at 85 et seq.

[167] Article 18 of the Sierra Leonian TRC Act 2000 stipulates that the Government must establish a body to monitor implementation of the Commission's recommendations and facilitate their implementation. The Government must provide to this body quarterly reports which will be published and assessed by it (UN-ECOSOC, Impunity, 27 February 2004, para. 19 [e]). According to Abrams/Hayner (n 137) at 286 and Mattarollo (n 125) at 322 greater attention should be given to the implementation of the recommendations. For Sooka (n 6) at 324 the often lacking implementation of the recommendations leads to a crisis of the legitimacy of TRCs. Generally on the reform impact Daly (n 100) at 33 et seq.

17. Apart from a TRC there are *other alternative justice mechanisms*,[168] which may be organized in four groups:

- Restitution, reparation/compensation, rehabilitation and non-repetition are all aimed at victims and as such a direct consequence of victims' rights.[169]
- Lustration,[170] vetting and purges are screening and administrative procedures aimed at the exclusion of a certain group of persons linked to the former regime from public office and/or other socially important posts in order to facilitate institutional reform.[171] Examples include the de-nazification by the Allies after WW II, the inquiry into former informers with the State Security policy ("Stasi") in the Ex-GDR, the exclusion of Baath party members from the army and other public offices by the U.S. occupation authority in Iraq and a new, very controversial Polish Law.[172]
- Disarmament, demobilization, reintegration (DDR) is a collective process aimed at the reintegration of the former armed groups into the (new) society.[173]
- Forms of traditional (non-western) justice, e.g., *Gacaca* in Rwanda, *Ubuntu* in South Africa or the Acholi rites of reconciliation (especially *mato oput*) in Uganda, are often a reaction to the western inspired systems of national or international criminal justice and may appear to offer a more promising approach since they take into account the local traditions and culture.[174] Indeed, the imposition of western style criminal justice may impede victims from asserting control

[168] See ICTJ-guidelines, p. 5.

[169] See supra para. 10 with n 113.

[170] From latin *lustratio*: "purification by sacrifice", see definition in Smith (1875) at 719.

[171] See for a critical study Boed in Bassiouni (ed.) 2002, at 345 et seq. concluding that (at 379 et seq.) lustration may lead to unjust discriminations, not target the most responsible and not further reconciliation; in a similar vein Posner/Vermeule (n 6) 802 et seq.; crit. on the lack of procedural guarantees also Joyner (n 21) at 37; Williams in Joyner (ed.) 1998, 287, at 289–90; Šimonović (n 30) at 704; see also Schwartz in Kritz (ed.) 1995, at 461 et seq.; Schlunck (n 30) at 70–1; ICTJ-guidelines, p. 5; Teitel (n 13) at 163 et seq.; Bassiouni (n 67) at 34–5; Kritz (n 9) at 80 et seq.; Durán (n 19) at 37; Cryer et al. (n 75) at 35. Daly (n 100) considers lustration as a form of "administrative accountability". According to von Braun (n 3) at 20 the restructuring of the political system takes centre state in the case of lustration. See also Principles combating impunity, principles 14, 15 and 17–19.

[172] The new Law of 15 March 2007 obliges individuals born before 1 August 1972 to submit so-called "Lustration statements" to the authorities regarding their relationship with the Polish security services during the period of communist rule. It has received strong criticism and was declared unconstitutional by the Polish Constitutional Court on 12 May 2007 (see BBC News, "Polish court strikes down spy law" 11 may 2007, <news.bbc.co.uk/2/hi/europe/6648435.stm> last visited 23 October 2008).

[173] ICTJ-guidelines, p. 5; UN Department of Peace Keeping Operations, 1999; Debiel/Terlinden, GTZ Discussion Paper 2005, at 10 et seq.; for a concrete GTZ project in the Ivory Coast, see: <www.gtz.de/de/weltweit/afrika/cote-d-ivoire/16849.htm> (last visited 23 October 2008); for a critical evaluation of DDR in Colombia Theidon (n 36) at 66 et seq. finding, inter alia, that DDR traditionally focused too much on military and security objectives and ignored the TJ aspects of historical clarification, justice, reparation and reconciliation. See de Greiff, published in this volume, at 324 et seq. for a comparison of DDR and reparation programs.

[174] Chicago Principles at 17, Principle 6: "States should support and respect traditional, indigenous, and religious approaches regarding past violations." See for example with regard to Gacaca

over their own victimization and lead to an "externalization of justice".[175] Traditional processes may, however, conflict with the – admittedly: western – concept of due process.[176]

18. The measures included in the first two groups constitute predominantly non-criminal or non-punitive sanctions,[177] while the third group entails benefits for the individuals concerned and the fourth group may consist of both criminal and non-criminal sanctions. Non-criminal sanctions should, in principle, not substitute but rather complement criminal sanctions.[178] The applicability of the individual measures depends on the circumstances of each case. A system of variables referring to the characteristics of the conflict, the players (structure and context variables), the intervention process (process variables) and the possible results (outcome variables) helps to select the adequate measures.[179] The most probable scenario is a combined application given the fact that the measures are "complementary, each playing a distinctly important role".[180] The application of alternative forms of justice may be considered as a mitigating factor in normal criminal proceedings.[181]

2.4 Balancing of Interests by Way of a Proportionality Test

19. Ultimately, the admissibility of limitations of the justice interest, in particular by refraining from criminal prosecution, depends on the result of a sophisticated balancing of the conflicting interests – peace and justice – at stake. This bal-

Uvin/Mirenko (2003) 9 Global Governance 219, at 228 et seq. arguing that the western inspired systems of justice (ICTR, domestic prosecution) have failed and Gacaca offers a promising alternative; on Ubuntu see Boraine (n 23) at 362; on the Acholi rites see Baines (n 38) at 103 et seq. finding, however, that "there are many outstanding questions that would need to be answered" (114). See also Kritz (n 9) at 77–8; Simon in Albrecht/Simon/Rezaei/Rohne/Kiza (eds.) 2006, 99, at 104 et seq.; Schilling (2005) at 270 et seq.; Wierda/Unger (n 80) at 288 et seq.; Ssenyonjo (2007) 7 ICLR 361, at 373 et seq.; Allen in Waddell/Clark (eds.) 2008 at 47 et seq. For the different views of victims about the possible use of Acholi practices see OHCHR (n 33) at 52 et seq. For the *Magamba* spirits practices in Mozambique see Igreja, published in this volume, at 423 et seq. For *Bashingantahe* in Burundi cf. Vandeginste, published in this volume, at 423.

[175] Cf. Kiza/Rathgeber/Rohne (n 4) at 95; in a similar vein Darcy (n 44) at 394: "international courts and trials involve a typically Western concept of retributive justice that may have little resonance with many of the communities in whose favour they are supposed to operate(...)".

[176] Stahn (n 64) at 713; id., (n 46) at 454; Baines (n 38) at 108 and HRW Memorandum 2007 at 7, insisting on "internationally recognized fair trials standards (...) in any national alternative to ICC prosecutions"; see as well the case example by Clark (n 64) at 411–2. This also generates problems with regard to Art. 17 (2) ICC Statute, see para. 42 with n 377.

[177] On the use and meaning of this term see also Williams (n 171) at 287; Kritz (n 9) at 80 et seq.; Meyer (2006) 6 ICLR 549, at 552.

[178] See also Principles combating impunity, principle 16 A and HRW Memorandum 2007 at 6 et seq.

[179] See for more details Schlunck (n 30) at 79 et seq.

[180] UN-ECOSOC, Impunity, 27 February 2004, para. 10.

[181] Cf. Stahn (n 64) at 704.

ancing exercise consists methodologically of a threefold *proportionality test*[182] as developed by the German Constitutional Court[183] and theoretically further elaborated by the German scholar Robert Alexy with his famous "Rule of Balancing" (*Abwägungsgesetz*).[184] Applying this threefold test to our case goes as follows: First, the respective measure, for example, an amnesty, must be examined to determine whether it is *appropriate* to achieve the alleged objective, i.e., a peaceful transition or peace for the society concerned.[185] This implies an analysis of the seriousness and legitimacy of the alleged objective, i.e., if the respective authority (normally the government) which offers the exemption measure, really and seriously pursues this objective and not other political plans, for example, the legalization of an armed group sympathetic to it. The criterion of appropriateness particularly begs the question whether the measure is part of an overall scheme to break with the former regime or, on the contrary, rather guarantees continuity.[186] In addition, it is essential whether the new system created on the basis of the amnesty supports human rights and respects the rule of law.[187]

20. Secondly, the measure must also be *necessary* or *indispensable* to achieve the said objective,[188] i.e., there must not exist other measures, which would be less intrusive with regard to the justice interest. For example, amnesty offers for irregular armed groups raise the question whether the peace or peaceful transition could not be achieved by less, i.e., either by a less comprehensive amnesty (e.g., excluding the most serious crimes and the most responsible perpetrators) or by a different measure, e.g., a substantial mitigation of punishment. In the sense of a necessity exception or principle, as proposed by Robinson,[189] one may ask whether the measure is due to the political, social and economic realities.

21. Last but not least the *proportionality stricto sensu* must be examined. At this stage, all the different elements and criteria favouring either the peace or justice interest come into play. In sum, a balancing of the quantity and quality (gravity)

---

[182] See also Gropengießer/Meißner (n 60) at 278–9; Uprimny/Saffon (n 3) at 229–30.

[183] See the fundamental decision in *Erdölbevorratung* [16 March 1971] BVerfGE 30, 292 (German Constitutional Court) at 316.

[184] See Alexy's fundamental work *Theorie der Grundrechte* (1985) at 146 where he explains this Rule in the following words: "Nach dem Abwägungsgesetz hängt das zulässige Maß der Nichterfüllung oder Beeinträchtigung des einen Prinzips vom Wichtigkeitsgrad der Erfüllung des anderen ab. Bereits in der Definition des Begriffs des Prinzips wurde mit der Klausel 'relativ auf die rechtlichen Möglichkeiten' das, was durch das jeweilige Prinzip geboten wird, in eine Relation zu dem, was durch gegenläufige Prinzipien geboten wird, gesetzt. Das Abwägungsgesetz sagt, worin diese Relation besteht. Es macht deutlich, dass das Gewicht von Prinzipien nicht an sich oder absolut bestimmbar ist, sondern daß stets nur von relativen Gewichten die Rede sein kann." (see also Brenner/Klein/v.Mangoldt/Starck (2005) Band 2, Art. 20 bis 82, mn 314).

[185] Slye (n 51) 246; Gropengießer/Meißner (n 60) at 278–9.

[186] See also Clark (n 64) at 409.

[187] See also Arsanjani (n 21) at 66–7.

[188] Gropengießer/Meißner (n 60) at 279.

[189] Robinson (n 31) at 497. For a similar limitation taking into account a state's real possibilities to investigate and prosecute international crimes and calling for a "good faith" prosecution Méndez (n 94) at 264, 270.

of the acts to be covered by the measure (justice aspect) and the objective(s) to be achieved (peace aspect) must be undertaken;[190] in other words, a "balance between the extent of the departure from full prosecution, i.e., the quality of the measures taken, and the severity of the factors necessitating a deviation".[191] There are some particularly important criteria, which follow from the above discussion and tend to limit the scope of the measures that may be offered for the sake of peace:

- *Limitation ratione materiae* with regard to international core crimes:[192] given the general duty to prosecute the ICC crimes (para. 8) it is, in principle, inadmissible to exempt these crimes from criminal prosecution and punishment.
- *Limitation ratione personae* with regard to the most responsible:[193] given the particular and decisive responsibility of political and military leaders, they must not benefit from an exemption, especially if they granted it themselves (the most practical case being the so-called self-amnesty).[194] Indeed, victims research shows that the political and military elite are identified as the most responsible and therefore should be held responsible.[195] Further, the exclusion and/or separation of those criminal elites from the victimized community benefits this community directly and the political system as a whole and thus holds positive transformative potential.[196]
- Importance of the *procedural stage* at which the exemption takes effect:[197] the more advanced an investigation or criminal proceedings, the more acceptable it becomes to exempt the responsible from punishment given that with the advancement of the investigation at least a part of the truth has been established and full impunity has been avoided.

[190] Gropengießer/Meißner (n 60) at 279; Uprimny/Saffon (n 3) at 229–30.

[191] Robinson (n 31) at 497.

[192] See already Ambos (n 75) at 210 et seq.; id., Impunidad (n 60), at 126 et seq.; Cassel (n 54) at 219, 220, 228–9; Joyner (n 21) at 40, 42–3; Méndez (n 94) at 274; more recently Young (n 88) at 476, 477–8; Bassiouni (n 67) at 41, 42; Stahn (n 46) at 458; Clark (n 64) at 408–9; Seils/Wierda (n 21) at 19; Uprimny/Saffon (n 3) at 230; Meyer (n 177) at 576–8; Olson (n 30) at 284; Werle (n 17) mn 212. See also Joinet report, principle 25; Orentlicher impunity principles, principle 24 (a) and Expert paper complementarity, para. 73; on the international criminal tribunals in this regard see n 335 and main text. An example for such a limited amnesty is the Ugandan 2003 amnesty law, exempting the former warlord Mathieu Ngudjolo Chui from internal prosecution from crimes committed in Ituri but excluding crimes against humanity and war crimes (on his subsequent arrest see Hemedi (2008) Issue No. 36 ICC Monitor at 10).

[193] Slye (n 51) at 245, 246; Bassiouni (n 67) at 41; Scharf/Rodley (n 21) at 95–6; Robinson (n 31) at 493 et seq.; Stahn (n 46) at 458; Clark (n 64) at 409; Meyer (n 177) at 577; Murphy (2006) 3 Eyes on the ICC 33, at 52. See also Expert paper complementarity, para. 73; on the international criminal tribunals in this regard see n 336 and main text.

[194] See already Ambos (n 75) at 213 et seq.; id., Impunidad (n 60) at 129 et seq.; Cassel (n 54) at 219, 228; more recently Young (n 88) at 477; Clark (n 64) at 409, 410. See also Expert paper complementarity, para. 73.

[195] See Kiza/Rathgeber/Rohne (n 4) at 115 (Table 30), 122, 158, 161 demonstrating that 71% of the victims considered "political leaders" and 42 "military leaders" responsible (Table 30).

[196] Ibid. at 127. See also HRW, 2005, at 15: "The stigmatizing effect of criminal prosecutions helps isolate disruptive actors from the political scene and strengthen political stability".

[197] Gropengießer/Meißner (n 60) at 279.

- Some form of *accountability*[198] and/or a public procedure (where the victims can confront the suspected perpetrators), which results in the disclosure of the facts (right to truth)[199] and identifies the responsible, i.e., eventual benefits for the responsible (partial pardons, mitigation of punishment, etc.) presuppose their effective cooperation (benefits for cooperation);[200] otherwise the measure constitutes an autonomous violation of the right to a remedy (para. 8).[201] To assess the quality of the alternative form of justice the victims' rights (para. 10–11) and the criteria developed for an effective TRC must be taken into account (para. 16).
- The *overall* political, social and economic *effects* of the measure(s) must be assessed.[202] Do they contribute to a lasting and stable peace, to a true reconciliation? Do they contribute to the consolidation of democracy and rule of law?

22. In practice, the balancing exercise has been applied by the Colombian Constitutional Court with regard to the compatibility of the Colombian Justice and Peace Act (*Ley de Justicia y Paz*)[203] with the Constitution.[204] In the Court's view, to achieve a stable and lasting peace the legislator may, on the one hand, transcend certain restrictions derived from the justice interest since otherwise peace may be unattainable; on the other hand, the peace interest is not absolute, it cannot be converted into a kind of "reason of State" ("*razón del Estado*") and the justice interest and the victims' rights must also be respected. It is the Court's task to determine, by balancing the interests involved ("*método de ponderación*"), whether the challenged Act respects the minimum standards protected by the Constitution.[205] Distinguishing between three possible options of balancing the Court applies the most comprehensive one requiring a balancing between the peace, on the one hand, and the justice, on the other, including in the latter not only justice as an abstract and objective value but also the particular victims' rights.[206] In practice, the limitations imposed by the Act on the right to justice must be balanced against the right to peace.[207] Yet, as the limitations on the right to justice do not only constitute limitations of a

---

198 Accountability in this sense is to be understood broadly; it is not limited, as suggested by Joyner (n 21) at 37, to a criminal process, i.e., denunciation, accusation and punishment. Daly (n 100) at 34 convincingly argues that "without accountability, truth produces only injustice". Similarly Grono/O'Brien (n 80) at 18 et seq. argue, while recognizing that past amnesties (in Liberia, Mozambique, South Africa) helped to bring about peace, that, "peace deals that sacrifice justice often fail to produce peace".

199 Cassel (n 54) at 219, 228; Slye (n 51) at 239, 245; Robinson (n 31) at 498; Kemp (n 21) at 69.

200 Uprimny/Saffon (n 3) at 211, 229–30 speak of pardons "responsabilizantes", i.e., the granting of pardons presupposes the recognition of responsibilities and effective cooperation by the responsible.

201 Cf. Ambos (n 75) at 218 et seq.; id., Impunidad (n 60) at 135 et seq.

202 Expert paper complementarity, para. 73.

203 Ley 975 de 2005.

204 Gustavo Gallón y otros (n 94); see also on the Colombian process Diaz, published in this volume, at 469 et seq.

205 Ibid. para. 5.5., 5.9., 5.10. and passim.

206 Ibid. para. 5.6.

207 Ibid. para. 5.7.

right but, at the same time, an instrument to achieve the peace they also contribute to the realization of the victims' rights of non-repetition, truth and reparation. On the one hand, peace is a fundamental prerequisite to satisfy these rights, on the other hand, the specific measures provided for in the Act, e.g., to confess the crimes and compensate the victims, contribute to the realization of the said victims' rights.[208] Given this ambivalence and complex interdependence of the measures provided for in the Act, the Court opts for an integral approach ("vision integral"), i.e., it analyses each measure in the context of the other and with regard to all its effects.[209] As to the considerable mitigation of punishment ("*pena alternativa*") for the persons covered by the Act, the Court affirms that this "alternative" sanction does not affect the original sanction to be imposed according to the Penal Code; rather, the original sanction can always be applied if the person concerned does not comply with the conditions linked to the alternative sanction. Given the existence of the original sanction and its possible application, the possible mitigation is, in the view of the Court, not (reversed) disproportionate.[210] Equally, the right to truth is not unduly restricted since the benefits of the Act, especially the alternative sanction, only apply if the person concerned provides a full and true confession.[211] In the result the Court considers the Act as compatible with the Constitution but demands some specific improvements with regard to the victims' rights.[212] This is not the place to critically assess the Colombian process of demobilization[213] and the Constitutional Court's decision, but it is clear that the Colombian legislator could have given more legitimacy to the process if the available alternative mechanisms to criminal prosecution (para. 12 et seq.), in particular an effective TRC[214] and measure of lustration,[215] were used in a more extensive way.

---

[208] Ibid, para. 5.12.

[209] Ibid. para. 5.15.

[210] Ibid. para. 6.2.1.4. Anyway, there are good reasons to contend that there can be proportional sentences for mass atrocities, see the discussion of Arendt's position by Osiel (n 16) at 128–9; see also Osiel (1997) at 118 with fn 122.

[211] Ibid. para. 6.2.2., esp. 6.2.2.1.7.29–30.

[212] Ibid. part. VII (decisión). The changes have been made by way of Executive Decree 3391 of 29 September 2006 but subsequent legislation and practice indicates a roll back of the CC's decision.

[213] For a crit. account of the negotiations with the paramilitary groups see Orozco (n 58) at 195 et seq.; Chaparro (n 129) at 233 et seq.; for a crit. account on the basis of empirical research in Bogotá, Medellín and Turbo-Apartadó see Theidon (n 36) at 70 et seq. finding, inter alia, that paramilitary groups continue to exist and reintegration has not been sufficiently addressed.

[214] See for a crit. assessment of the "Comisión Nacional de Reparación y Reconciliación" already n 136.

[215] To the contrary, with the recognition of the persons object of the "Ley 975" as political offenders they are fully entitled to political activity (crit. also Durán [n 19] at 37). In the meantime, however, the Colombian Supreme Court has declared that acts committed by paramilitary groups cannot be considered as "delitos políticos" (Proceso No. 26945, c/Orlando César Caballero Montalvo, Judgement of 11 July 2007).

2.5 Consequences for Amnesties: Two Approaches

23. Given the particular importance of amnesties as a bargaining chip in peace processes, the question arises whether and, if so, under which conditions, amnesties can be offered to combatant groups within conflicts. At the outset it is clear from the above that "[J]ustice and peace are not contradictory forces"[216] if, on the one hand, justice is understood broadly, i.e., not limited to criminal justice (para. 2), and, on the other, criminal prosecutions are carried out in a fair and complementary (not exclusive) manner to reinforce peace.[217] Indeed, a broad concept of justice reveals that the slogan "no peace without justice" must be read – overcoming a too narrow concept of justice – as referring to "global truth" (para. 13) as a (minimum) prerequisite for real reconciliation and peace.[218] The UN itself refers to cases where "a failure to address justice through *formal prosecution* has not undermined long term peace".[219] Yet, clearly, some form of accountability must be offered in exchange. Thus, while it is clear that respect for the justice interest is indispensable to achieve a lasting peace, the hard question is how much justice can be sacrificed on the altar of peace negotiations without unduly restricting a state's duty *vis-à-vis* international crimes (para. 8) and demolishing the foundations of true reconciliation. As for amnesties, it has already been pointed out that a bifurcated approach is called for to distinguish between blanket and conditional amnesties,[220] the former ones being generally inadmissible and the latter ones admissible in principle.

2.5.1 Blanket Amnesties are Generally Inadmissible (Strict Approach)

24. This type of amnesties may in their most extreme form be characterized as "amnesic amnesties" (from amnesia, Greek, referring to an act of oblivion) since their primary goal is to completely conceal past crimes by prohibiting any investigation.[221] If these amnesties are the result of a political compromise to end a violent conflict or facilitate a process of transition they may be called "compromise amnesties"; yet, the underlying compromise does not change their substantive deficiency in terms of international obligations and victims' rights.[222] A classical example of such an amnesty is the Chilean decree 2.191 of April 1978 which extended the amnesty to "perpetrators, accomplices or beneficiaries" (*autores, complices o*

[216] Report Secretary General transitional justice, para. 21; see also *Gustavo Gallón y otros* (n 94) para. 5.10. ("[...] la justicia no se opone necesariamente a la paz"); Joyner (n 21) at 42. This also follows from Art. 1 (1) of the Statute of the UN Charta according to which the purpose of the UN is to achieve peace "in conformity with the principles of justice".

[217] Cf. Crocker (n 28) at 533, 543, 545–6; on the importance of fairness see also Méndez (n 28) at 33.

[218] For a similar reading Bassiouni (n 67) at 41.

[219] ICTJ-guidelines, p. 4 (emphasis added).

[220] Supra para. 8 with n 88.

[221] Cf. Slye (n 51) at 240–1.

[222] Cf. Slye (n 51) 241 et seq.

encubridores) regarding all crimes committed between 11 September 1973 (the day of the *coup d'état* by General Augusto Pinochet) and 10 March 1978.[223] A more recent example is Art. IX (2) of the Lomé peace agreement of 7 July 1999 between the Sierra Leonean government and the Revolutionary United Front (RUF) which provides that the government "shall (...) grant *absolute* and free pardon and reprieve to all combatants and collaborators in respect of *anything* done by them in pursuit of their objectives (...)".[224]

25. International law quite unequivocally prohibits this type of amnesty. There are various recent *instruments* taking this position, most notably – and contrary to the just mentioned Lomé Agreement – the Statute of the Special Court of Sierra Leone (SCSL).[225] *International* criminal and human rights *courts* have commented on amnesties at various times. The ICTY has prohibited an amnesty for torture,[226] the SCSL has considered the Lomé amnesty as without effect since it is, inter alia, "contrary to the direction in which customary international law is developing and (...) to the obligations in certain treaties and conventions the purpose of which is to protect humanity".[227] On a regional level, the case law of the Inter-American Court of Human Rights (IACHR) is of particular importance since the Court had to examine the compatibility of a classical blanket amnesty, namely the Peruvian amnesty Act No. 26.479 (and its interpretative Act No. 26.492),[228] with

223 Decreto Ley no. 2,191, published in Diario Oficial no. 30.042 of 19 April 1978. For an analysis of these and other Latin American impunity norms see Ambos (n 75) at 83 et seq. (101–2), 227 et seq.; id., Impunidad (n 60) at 147 et seq.

224 See <www.sc-sl.org/documents.html> (last visited 23 October 2008); reprinted in Bassiouni (n 9) at 593 et seq. (emphasis added).

225 Its Art. 10 reads: "An amnesty(...) shall not be a bar to prosecution"; see also S/RES/1315 (2000) of 14 August 2000 stating that "the amnesty provisions of the Agreement [Lome Agreement] shall not apply to international crimes of genocide, crimes against humanity, war crimes and other serious violations of international humanitarian law"; Art. 40 of the Law of the Cambodian Extraordinary Chambers (reprinted in Ambos/Othman (eds.) 2003 at 267): "Government of Cambodia shall not request an amnesty or pardon (...)".

226 *Prosecutor v. Furundzija* [10 December 1998] Judgement, IT-95–17/1-T (ICTY) para. 155 (n. omitted): "The fact that torture is prohibited by a peremptory norm of international law (...) serves to internationally de-legitimise any legislative, administrative or judicial act authorising torture. It would be senseless to argue, on the one hand, that on account of the *jus cogens* value of the prohibition against torture, treaties or customary rules providing for torture would be null and void *ab initio*, and then be unmindful of a State say, taking national measures authorising or condoning torture or absolving its perpetrators through an amnesty law".

227 *Prosecutor v. Kallon and Kamara* [13 March 2004) App. Decision, SCSL-2004–15AR72(E) and CSCSL-2004 – 16 AR72(E) (SCSL) para. 84 and para. 71, 73, 88; conc. *Prosecutor v. Kondewa* [25 May 2004] App. Decision, SCSL – 2004 – 14 AR72 (E) (SCSL) with separate opinion by Judge *Robinson*; for a commentary see Ambos in Klip/Sluiter (eds.) 2006, at 103 et seq.

228 The Law 26.479 of 14 June 1995 (reprinted in Normas Legales No. 229, at 143–4) was a blanket amnesty in favour of military, police and civilian personnel for crimes committed in the fight against terrorism between may 1980 and the promulgation of this law; Law 26.492 was a law to "interpret" the scope of that amnesty law (see Ambos [n 75] at 95–6; id., Impunidad [n 60] at 140–1).

the American Convention on Human Rights (ACHR).[229] The Court considered that all amnesty provisions, statutes of limitation and measures designed to eliminate responsibility are inadmissible because they are intended to prevent the investigation and punishment of those responsible for serious human rights violations such as torture, extrajudicial, summary or arbitrary executions and forced disappearances; acts which all violate non-derogable rights recognized by international human rights law.[230] In adopting self-amnesty laws Peru failed to comply with the obligation to implement internal legislation to make the Convention rights effective as provided for in Art. 2 ACHR.[231] Such laws violate Art. 8 and 25, in relation to Art. 1 (1) and 2 ACHR.[232] Self-amnesty laws lead to the defencelessness of victims and perpetuate impunity; they preclude the identification of the perpetrators by obstructing the investigation and access to justice; they prevent the victims and their relatives from knowing the truth and receiving the corresponding reparation. Consequently, such laws are manifestly incompatible with the aims and spirit of the Convention.[233] These considerations have been confirmed by a subsequent judgement against Peru.[234] In another judgement against Chile, referring to the infamous *Decreto Ley* 2.191 of 1978 (para. 24), the Court affirmed the *Barrios Altos* judgement and held that crimes against humanity cannot be amnestied[235] and therefore the said amnesty must remain without legal effect.[236] The European Court of Human

[229] *Barrios Altos vs. Perú Case* (n 95) para. 41 et seq. For the similar earlier position of the Inter-American Commission with regard to the amnesties in Argentina, Chile, El Salvador and Uruguay see Cassel (n 54) 208 et seq. with further references. In *Velásquez-Rodríguez* (n 68) the Court did not refer to the amnesty issue although Honduras passed an amnesty during the proceedings (cf. Cassel, op. cit., at 210). See generally on the IACHR's case law Kourabas (n 243) 86–90, concluding (at 89) that the "jurisprudence on the issue has become more concrete and potentially more expansive".

[230] *Barrios Altos vs. Perú Case* (n 95) para. 41.

[231] Ibid. para. 42. Art. 2 ACHR ("Domestic legal effects") reads: "Where the exercise of any of the rights or freedoms referred to in Article 1 is not already ensured by legislative or other provisions, the States Parties undertake to adopt, in accordance with their constitutional processes and the provisions of this Convention, such legislative or other measures as may be necessary to give effect to those rights or freedoms".

[232] Art. 8 (1) ACHR contains the right to a hearing before and independent and impartial tribunal; Art. 25 (1) provides for "a right to simple and prompt recourse, or any other effective recourse, to a competent court or tribunal for protection against acts that violate his fundamental rights recognized by the constitution or laws of the state concerned or by this Convention (...)"; Art. 1 (1) establishes the States' obligation to respect the rights and freedoms of the ACHR.

[233] *Barrios Altos vs. Perú Case* (n 95) para. 43 (where the Court even helds that such laws are incompatible with the letter of the Convention).

[234] *La Cantuta v. Perú* (n 103) para. 62, 80, 174.

[235] *Almonacid-Arellano et al. vs. Chile* (n 68) para. 114. See also the separate opinion by Judge Cançado Trindade where he affirms, inter alia, that self-amnesties "no son verdaderas leyes, por cuanto desprovistas del necesario carácter genérico de éstas, de la *idea del Derecho* que las inspira (esencial inclusive para la seguridad jurídica), y de su búsqueda del bien común". (para. 7, n. omitted). Rather they are "la propia negación del Derecho" and violate ius cogens (para. 10, n. omitted; see also para. 17 et seq.).

[236] *Almonacid-Arellano et al. vs. Chile* (n 68) para. 118: "(...) el Decreto Ley n. 2191 carece de efectos jurídicos y no puede seguir representando un obstáculo para la investigación de los hechos

Rights (ECHR) affirmed in a case against Turkey that for "crimes involving torture or ill-treatment" criminal proceedings must neither be time-barred nor impeded by an amnesty or pardon.[237]

26. While *UN human rights bodies* had previously rejected amnesties for serious human rights violations,[238] in particular torture, in their case law, the position of the *UNO* itself is not free from doubt. To be sure, the organization, while "recognizing that amnesty is an accepted legal concept and a gesture of peace and reconciliation at the end of a civil war or an internal armed conflict", has several times made clear that it does not accept amnesty clauses in peace treaties for international core crimes "such as genocide, crimes against humanity or other serious violations of international humanitarian law".[239] Yet, the UNO has taken part in peace negotiations with an amnesty on the table (e.g., El Salvador, Guatemala, Haiti, Sierra Leone)[240]

---

que constituyen este caso, ni para la identificación y el castigo de los responsables, ni puede tener igual o similar impacto respecto de otros casos de violación de los derechos consagrados en la Convención Americana acontecidos en Chile." Highly crit. also Cançado Trindade, (n 235) para. 11 et seq.

[237] *Abdülsamet Yaman v. Turkey* [2 November 2004] Judgement, Application No. 32446/96 [2004] ECHR 572, para. 55.

[238] Cf. Commission of Human Rights, Question of enforced disappearance, E/CN.4/RES/1994/39, 4 March 1994, stating that individuals "should not benefit from any special amnesty law or other similar measures having the effect of exonerating them from any prosecution or penal sanction". More recently, any impediments to the establishment of legal responsibility have been considered incompatible with Art. 2 (3) ICCPR (HRC, General Comment 31, para. 18: "[...] where public officials or State agents have committed violations of the Covenant rights [...], the States Parties concerned may not relieve perpetrators from personal responsibility, as has occurred with certain amnesties [...] and prior legal immunities and indemnities. [...]. Other impediments to the establishment of legal responsibility should also be removed [...]"). As to torture, the HRC already stated earlier the following: "The Committee has noted that some States have granted amnesty in respect of acts of torture. Amnesties are generally incompatible with the duty of States to investigate such acts; to guarantee freedom from such acts within their jurisdiction; and to ensure that they do not occur in the future. States may not deprive individuals of the right to an effective remedy, including compensation and such full rehabilitation as may be possible". (HRC General Comment 20, para. 15). See also Joinet report, para. 32 affirming that "amnesty cannot be accorded to perpetrators of violations before the victims have obtained justice by means of an effective remedy". Against a statute of limitations for "crimes under international law" Basic Principles Victims, Sect. IV and Principles combating impunity, principle 3.

[239] Report of the Secretary General on the Establishment of the Special Court for Sierra Leone, S/2000/915, 4 October 2000, p. 22 (n. omitted). In the same vein, in a later report it was recognized that "carefully crafted amnesties can help in the return and reintegration" of armed groups (Report Secretary General transitional justice, para. 32) but at the same time confirmed that the UN "can never promise amnesties for genocide, war crimes, crimes against humanity or gross violations of human rights (...)" (Ibid. para. 10, 32, 64). See also ICTJ-guidelines, p. 1, 2 ("prohibition on UN personnel approving an amnesty for grave human rights violations") and Guidelines Negotiations, para. 13 ("necessary and proper for immunity from prosecution to be granted (...); however, the UN cannot condone amnesties regarding war crimes, crimes against humanity and genocide or foster those that violate relevant treaty obligations of the parties in this field").

[240] Crit. on the UN-involvement in El Salvador, Guatemala and Haiti Cassel (n 54) 221 et seq.; crit. on the changing position towards an amnesty in Sierra Leone the Sierra Leone TRC Report (n 25) ch. 6, at 365, para. 10 ("inconsistency in UN practice") and at 369, para. 25 ("By repudiating the amnesty in the Lomé Peace Agreement, the United Nations and the Government of Sierra Leone

and thus given such amnesties a kind of international legitimacy.[241] In probably the most dramatic case, the Lomé Agreement, this tightrope walk forced the Special Representative to attach an "interpretative declaration" to the Agreement stating that "[T]he UN interprets that the amnesty and pardons in Art. 9 of the Agreement shall not apply to international crimes of genocide, crimes against humanity, war crimes, and other serious violations of international humanitarian law".[242] In the Ugandan process (former) UN humanitarian coordinator Jan Egeland was in the difficult situation where he, on the one hand, had to mediate between the government and the Lord's Resistance Army (LRA), and on the other hand, refuse to talk with the rebel leaders about lifting the ICC arrest warrants against them and/or a possible amnesty blocking the ICC investigation.[243] To avoid these problems the UN should make clear at the outset that a blanket amnesty is not on the negotiating table.[244]

27. The *national practice* on blanket amnesties is, on a worldwide scale, quite rare since most countries do not issue such amnesties and therefore do not have to legally deal with them. The Mallinder study finds that while "international crimes" are covered by amnesties these amnesties are not necessarily blanket amnesties and, in any case, "political crimes" and "crimes against individuals" are more often covered than international crimes.[245] According to a recent study on the national

---

have inadvertently undermined future peace negotiations where amnesty is contemplated"); on Haiti see Gavron (n 64) 106-7 and Mattarollo in Bassiouni (ed.) 2002, at 763 et seq. In Guatemala, the U.N. deserves credit for the ratione materiae limitation already mentioned, n 155.

[241] On this risk see also Scharf/Rodley (n 21) at 91.

[242] Quoted according to Cassese (n 88) at 315; see also UN-Ecosoc, Impunity, 27 February 2004, para. 31; Van der Voort/Zwanenburg (n 60) at 321 referring to the 7th Progress Report of the Secretary General of the UN Observer Mission in Sierra Leone of 30 July 1999, UN Doc. S/1999/836, para. 7.

[243] See Reuters, "UN humanitarian chief willing to meet Uganda's LRA", 10 November 2006 <www.alertnet.org/thenews/newsdesk/L10722529.htm> (last visited 23 October 2008). On the conflict between the ICC and some local Acholi leaders see Baines (n 38) at 102–3 and Ssenyonjo (n 174) at 365 et seq. The Ugandan government recently argued that its referral of the LRA situation to the ICC was due to the inability to arrest the LRA's leadership but not to the inability of its judicial system; thus, the ICC indictees can be prosecuted in Uganda after signing a peace deal with the LRA (see Ministry of Justice and constitutional affairs of Uganda, Answer to "Request for information from the Republic of Uganda on the status of execution of the warrants of arrest", 23 March 2008, ICC-02/04-01/05-286-Anx2, at 3; see also Otim/Wierda in Waddell/Clark [eds.] 2008 at 25 and Allen [n 174] at 51 et seq.). However, Uganda has not yet incorporated the ICC core crimes into its domestic law and this will make it difficult to prosecute suspects of these crimes (cf. Nakayi [2008] Issue No. 36 ICC Monitor at 4). On the conflict and negotiations in Uganda see Kourabas (2007) 14 Davis J. Int'l L. & Pol'y 60, at 62 et seq. and Otim/Wierda in Waddell/Clark (eds.) 2008 at 21 et seq.

[244] See also Méndez (n 28) 37. The documents, quoted above supra note 239, are not clear in this respect. In particular the Guidelines Negotiations only call for "[E]arly commitments to respect human rights and humanitarian principles (...)" (para. 7). For obstacles in regional conflict mediation with regard to the ICC see Sriram, published in this volume, at 311 et seq.

[245] Mallinder study (n 28) para. 34 et seq. with Fig. 4 (but recognizing the "elastic" definition of political crimes, para. 36, and that crimes against individuals may also be international crimes, para. 39).

prosecution of international crimes, covering 33 countries,[246] only the Venezuelan (written) law[247] contains an amnesty prohibition for international crimes while the law of the other (32) countries is silent on the matter.[248] While this may be true for the law of other countries too, one certainly finds judicial pronouncements in countries where the courts have been confronted with amnesties and similar exemptions in the course of the prosecution of crimes committed during a totalitarian past. The recent case law of some Latin American courts is of particular importance in this regard.[249] Probably the most explicit judgement against (procedural) exemptions was delivered by the Argentinean Supreme Court in *Simon* where the Court, on the basis of the ICHR's affirmation of a duty to prosecute and a prohibition of amnesties (*Barrios Altos*, para. 25), held that the "Full Stop" (*Punto Final*) and "Due Obedience" (*Obediencia Debida*) Laws[250] are null and void.[251] The situ-

---

[246] Eser/Sieber/Kreicker, *Nationale Strafverfolgung völkerrechtlicher Verbrechen/National Prosecution of International Crimes, vol. I–VII* (Max Planck Institute for Foreign and International Criminal Law, Freiburg 2003–2006).

[247] Art. 29 of the Constitution provides for a duty to prosecute "crimes against human rights" and prohibits a statute of limitations and any exemption, in particular amnesties and pardons, for "crimes against humanity, grave human rights violations and war crimes". But see also the *ratione materiae* limitation in the Guatemalan Law of National Reconciliation, supra note 155.

[248] Kreicker (n 21) at 306–7. But see the recent Algerian amnesty of February 2006 by a Presidential decree (Ordonnance n 06-01 du 28 Moharran 1,427 correspondant au 27 février 2006 portant mise en oeuvre de la Charte pour la paix et la réconciliation nationale, in Journal Officiel de la Republique Algerienne Democratique et Populaire, n 11, http://www.joradp.dz/JO2000/2006/011/F_Pag.htm last visited 23 October 2008); see Olson (n 30) at 288 and the amnesty discussions in Somalia and Afghanistan (on Afghanistan see especially the not yet implemented "Action Plan of the Islamic Republic of Afghanistan for peace, justice and reconciliation adopted December 2005" and Nader Nadery [2007] 1 IJTJ 173 et seq.) – There are also historical examples, e.g., the Italian "Amnistia Togliatti" from 22 June 1946 (reprinted in Mimmo Franzinelli, Amnistia Togliatti (2006) at 313 et seq.) which covered political offences (Art. 2, 3) and excluded certain especially serious crimes, for example torture (Art. 3).

[249] For a recent analysis of this case law Ambos/Malarino, (eds.) 2008; for an overview of Latin American amnesties (in eleven countries) see Cassel (n 54) 200–1.

[250] On these laws (Ley 23.492 of 29 December 1986 and Ley 23.521 of 9 June 1987) see Ambos (n 75) at 109 et seq.; id., Impunidad (n 60) at 158 et seq. A Chilean-like earlier blanket amnesty law (DL 22.924 of 22 September 1983) has been derogated by Congress three months after its entry into force (see Ambos, Impunidad [n 60], at 107–8 and 156).

[251] Recurso de hecho deducido por la defensa de Julio Héctor Simón en la causa Simón, Julio Héctor s/privación ilegítima de la libertad, etc., causa N 17.768 [14 June 2005] Judgment of 14 June 2005 (Argentinean Supreme Court) reprinted in Fallos de la Corte Suprema de Justicia de la Nación, vol. 328, pp. 2056 et seq. The judgement consists of the individual votes of the seven judges which, taken together, show a clear tendency in favour of a duty to prosecute and a prohibition of amnesties and similar norms (see inter alia, the Votes of Judge Petracchi, para. 19, 20 et seq., 31; Judge Maqueda, para. 19, 21, 76, 81, 82; Judge Zaffaroni, para. 14–16, 26 and Judge Argibay, para. 14). However, Judge Fayt dissents in the characterization of the two laws as amnesties and considers that they are not prohibited. In two earlier judgements the Supreme Court hold that crimes against humanity, e.g., a qualified murder (homicidio calificado) committed in the course of the military dictatorship's fight against the "subversions", have no statute of limitations (Recurso de hecho deducido por el Estado y el Gobierno de Chile en la causa Arancibia Clavel, Enrique Lautaro s/homicidio calificado y asociación ilícita y otros causa N 259 [24 August 2004] Judgment (Argentinean Supreme Court) reprinted in Fallos de la Corte Suprema de Justicia de la

ation is much more complex in Chile where the Supreme Court for a long time took the view that the amnesty decree 2.191 (para. 24) impeded any investigation of the crimes covered;[252] only after two judgements by the Santiago Appeals Court did the position of the Supreme Court become a little bit more flexible and finally in 1998 it held that the amnesty is "inapplicable" – not "invalid" – as long as the perpetrator(s) or the victim(s) have not been identified;[253] later this position was confirmed but also rejected[254] so that it is fair to say that the Court is ambiguous at least. Last but not least, in Uruguay the "Law on the Extinction of Public Penal Action" (*Ley de Caducidad de la Pretension Punitiva del Estado*)[255] was upheld by the Supreme Court treating this law as an amnesty.[256]

28. On the other hand, the courts of *third states* had to deal, on the basis of universal jurisdiction or other extraterritorial links, with amnesties or similar exemptions issued in the territorial states, and normally declared these measures invalid or irrelevant for the national prosecutions. Thus, the Spanish *Audiencia Nacional* held that the Argentinean *Punto Final* and *Obediencia Debida* Laws are – notwithstanding their violation of international law – irrelevant for the Spanish prosecution of these cases since these laws do not establish pardons but only decriminalize the respective

---

Nación, vol. 327, pp. 3312 et seq.). This has also been affirmed with regard to mere violations of the ACHR (Espósito, Miguel Angel s/incidente de prescripción de la acción penal promovido por la defensa [23 December 2004] Judgement (Argentinean Supreme Court) reprinted in Fallos de la Corte Suprema de Justicia de la Nación, vol. 327, pp. 5668 et seq.). See also Malarino in Ambos/Malarino (eds.) 2003, at 69–70; Parenti in Ambos/Malarino/Woischnik (eds.) 2006, at 77–8, 84; Parenti in Ambos/Malarino (eds.) 2008, at 22 et seq. Recently, the Cámara Federal of Buenos Aires declared the pardons decreed in favour of the (convicted) Generals Videla and Admiral Massera invalid (causa 13/84 "Incidente de inconstitucionalidad de los indultos dictados por el decreto 2,741/90 del Poder Ejecutivo Nacional". Registro de la Secretaría General n°02/07/P, Sentencia del 25 de abril de 2007); the decision of the Supreme Court is pending.

252 See on this case law Ambos (n 75) at 239 et seq.; id., Impunidad (n 60) at 163 et seq.

253 *Pedro Enrique Poblete Córdova* [9 September 1998] Judgement, rol no. 895–96 del Segundo Juzgado Militar de Santiago (Chilean Supreme Court), reprinted in Gaceta Jurídica 219, pp. 122 et seq. The Court invoked the Geneva Conventions (which earlier had been considered inapplicable) and some procedural provisions (see Ambos, Impunidad [n 60] at 165 et seq.; Guzmán Dalbora in Ambos/Malarino (eds.) 2003, at 175, 187).

254 See on the one hand *Miguel Ángel Cotreras Sandoval* [17 November 2004] Judgement (Chilean Supreme Court) where the Court held that an amnesty for war crimes is prohibited (para. 34 and 35), and, on the other, *Secuestro de Ricardo Rioseco Montoya y Luis Cotal Älvarez* [4 August 2005] Judgement (Chilean Supreme Court) where the Court (again) rejects the application of the Geneva Conventions and applies the amnesty. On the recent Chilean case law Guzmán Dalbora in Ambos/Malarino (eds.) 2008, at 131 et seq.

255 Ley No. 15.848 del 22 December 1986. This law was a consequence of earlier blanket amnesties (see González in Ambos/Malarino (eds.) 2003, at 519–20; on the *genesis* of the law see Fuchs [n 21] at 48 et seq.).

256 *Detta Josefina/Menotti Noris/Martínez Federico/Muso Osiris/Burgell Jorge – Denuncia – Inconstitucionalidad de la Ley 15.848, art. 1,2,3 y 4* (Ficha 112/87) [2 Mayo 1988] Sentencia No. 184 (Uruguayan Supreme Court) and *González José Luis en Representación de Juan Gelman – Inconstitucionalidad* (Ficha 90-10462/2002) [15 Noviember 2004] Sentencia No 332 (Uruguayan Supreme Court). On the recent Uruguayan case law see González/Galain in Ambos/Malarino (eds.) 2008, at 307 et seq.

acts.[257] This practice is supported by the general consideration that the prosecuting third state is exercising its own jurisdiction and therefore is not bound by procedural obstacles existing in another jurisdiction.[258] The underlying substantive or normative argument is that a third state cannot breach international law, especially the sovereignty of the accused's state, if it does what international law requires, i.e., to prosecute international core crimes while the territorial state – contrary to this duty – amnesties these crimes instead of prosecuting them.[259]

29. The vast *literature* on amnesties overwhelmingly adopts the position described in the preceding para. 25–28 and normally refers to the same normative sources.[260] Often it is argued, from a *ratione materiae* perspective, that amnesties for international core crimes are inadmissible.[261] The same argument is made invoking the duty to prosecute these crimes.[262] The ICC Statute's clear commitment against impunity (para. 4–6 of the preamble) is considered an expression of *opinio iuris* that amnesties for the ICC crimes are prohibited.[263] Even more pragmatic and policy oriented scholars do not accept amnesties which would be an equivalent of

[257] Auto AN (Sala de lo Penal, Sección 3ª), 4 noviembre 1998, Recurso de Apelación núm. 84/1998 (ARP 1998\5943). Fundamento jurídico "OCTAVO". Cosa juzgada. See also Gil Gil in Ambos/Malarino (eds.) 2003, at 357; id., in Ambos/Malarino (eds.), 2008, at 471 et seq. See also the German prosecution of the disappearances of German nationals during the Argentinean military regime which was not barred by the Argentinean punto final and obediencia debida laws (cf. Ambos/Ruegenberg/Woischnik [1998] 25 EuGRZ 468, at 474 et seq.).

[258] Cf. Cryer et al. (n 75) at 33. See for a discussion Ambos (2008) § 3 mn 53 et seq.

[259] Cf. Cassese (n 88) at 316; similarly Pfanner (n 28) at 371–2; Werle (n 17) mn 212.

[260] See Ambos (n 75) at 209 et seq. with further references in n. 214; id. (n 258) § 7 mn. 114; see also Teitel (n 13) at 58; Bassiouni (1999) at 10–14, 22; Goldstone/Fritz (n 21) at 663; Méndez (n 28) at 33; O'Shea (2002) 195–6; Möller (2003) at 614–5, 619; Cassese (2004) 2 JICJ 1130 et seq.; Sánchez (2004) at 372 et seq.; Behrendt (2005) at 308; Menzel/Pierlings/Hoffmann (2005) at 795; Stahn (n 64) at 704; id. (n 46) at 461; Bell (n 120) at 106 et seq.; Burke-White (n 80) at 582; Seils/Wierda (n 21) at 14; Olson (n 30) at 283–4; Salmón (n 74) at 332 et seq. (339–40); Sriram, published in this volume, at 315; Chicago Principles at 35; HRW, 2005, at 12 et seq. does not distinguish between blanket and conditional amnesties but generally holds that an amnesty for the "most serious crimes" is inadmissible. For a philosophical position see Matwijkiw in Bassiouni (n 9) 155, at 193 et seq.

[261] Werle (n 16) at 65: "across-the-board exemption (...) unacceptable", "general amnesties for crimes under international law are impermissible under customary international law"; Meyer (n 177) at 556–7: "The prevailing school of thought (...) excludes at least general amnesties as legitimate accountability mechanisms for crimes against international law"; Kourabas (n 243) at 91: "crystallizing norm of international law prohibiting amnesties", "domestic amnesty laws (...) are *ipso facto* illegal"; Simpson in Waddell/Clark (eds.) 2008 at 75: "global consensus that blanket amnesties are both unacceptable and unenforceable"; Olson (n 30) at 284; Boraine (n 23) at 278; Wouters et al. (2008) 8 ICLR at 293 (refering to the original www version of this study); Kirchhoff, published in this volume, at 255.

[262] See *Princeton Principles,* Principle 7: "Amnesties are generally inconsistent with the obligation of states to provide accountability (...)" <www1.umn.edu/humanrts/instree/princeton.html> (last visited 23 October 2008) and Werle (n 17) mn 212; Ssenyonjo (n 174) at 386.

[263] Gropengießer/Meißner (n 60) at 300; see also Scharf (n 54) at 522; Stahn (n 64) at 702.

impunity.[264] The sovereignty argument brought forward by the French *Conseil Constitutionnel*,[265] i.e., that the effective exercise of sovereignty entails the right to take a sovereign decision on amnesty, is not convincing since it is based on a Grotian concept of sovereignty irrespective of international obligations, i.e., the duty to prosecute international core crimes.[266]

2.5.2 A Conditional Amnesty May Be Admissible Under Certain Circumstances (Flexible Approach)

30. A conditional amnesty is an amnesty which – unlike a blanket amnesty – does not automatically exempt from punishment for acts committed during a certain period of time but makes the benefit of an amnesty conditional on certain acts or concessions by the benefited person(s). The first and minimum condition is the armed groups' unreserved promise to lay down their arms and thus facilitate the end of hostilities. This condition is the consequence of the worse abuses or risk transition arguments mentioned above (para. 3). More concretely, the (former) perpetrators must undertake certain acts with a view to comply with the core of the justice element, i.e., especially satisfy the legitimate victims' demands (para. 10–11), in particular a full disclosure of the facts, acknowledgement of responsibility, repentance, etc.[267] As an important side effect, this process of coming to terms with their own past will help the former perpetrators in their own rehabilitation and reintegration into the new society. Given that a conditional amnesty is normally accompanied by a TRC, the criteria developed for an effective TRC (para. 16) also apply. As in the case of a TRC the legitimacy of an amnesty depends on the procedure employed in its creation:[268] The broader the participation, the more democratic and transparent this process has been, the more legitimacy will the amnesty enjoy. Equally important is the democratic quality of the procedure by which the beneficiaries of the amnesty were selected. Having said all this, it is clear that from the victims' perspective the gist of a conditional amnesty is that it provides for *some form of accountability*, if

---

[264] See Scharf (n 54) at 512 arguing that amnesties are not an equivalent to impunity but rather often tied to accountability mechanisms; against amnesties for "true" international crimes also Joyner (n 21) at 40, 42–3.

[265] Décision 98–408, 22 January 1999, Journal officiel de la République Francaise du 24 Janvier 1999, 1317, at 1320. See also Young (n 88) at 479 et seq.

[266] See also Van der Voort/Zwanenburg (n 60) at 333–34.

[267] Cf. Cryer et al. (n 75) at 33, affirming, that "an amnesty is less likely to be unlawful if other mechanisms are put in place for victim compensation and the like". For possible conditions attached to amnesties see Mallinder study (n 28) para. 42 et seq. with Fig. 5 finding that in most cases reparation measures have been provided for, followed by surrender/disarm, time limits for application, repentance and cooperation, TRCs, lustration and community based justice.

[268] See also IACHR, Annual Report, 192–3 (1986); Slye (n 51) at 239, 245, 246; see also Young (n 88) at 476; on the democratic procedure see also Teitel (n 13) at 58; Goldstone/Fritz (n 21) at 664; Mallinder (n 65) at 226–27 and 228–29 ("democratic legitimacy"); as further criteria she proposes: genuine desire to promote peace and reconciliation, limited scope, conditional and accompanied by reparations.

not within the framework of a criminal trial then through an alternative mechanism, especially a TRC. Only this type of amnesty, which could be called "accountable amnesty",[269] may, depending on the conditions and circumstances of the concrete case, contribute to true reconciliation.[270] The enforcement of all the conditions may be facilitated by an *amnesty revocation clause* as part of a peace treaty establishing that the amnesty will be revoked if the parties to the treaty violate the agreed conditions.[271]

31. The most famous example of such an accountable amnesty is the South African one[272] provided for in the epilogue to the Constitution[273] and regulated in detail in the Truth and Reconciliation Act.[274] Accordingly, an individual amnesty could be granted upon application to a specific Amnesty Committee[275] within the framework of a trial-like procedure that exposed the applicant to public scrutiny. In South Africa, the conditions were, inter alia, that the applicant fully disclosed all committed acts ("acknowledgment-for-amnesty-scheme",[276] "amnesty in exchange for truth"[277]) and that these acts could be considered political offences.[278] Of the

---

[269] Slye (n 51) at 245–6.

[270] For a similar conclusion and a helpful, albeit not completely satisfactory intent to develop criteria for assessing the possible contribution of an amnesty to reconciliation Mallinder study (n 28) para. 54 et seq. stating in para. 66 that the effect on reconciliation "is dependent upon the wider political conditions with a state (...)".

[271] Cf. Sierra Leone TRC Report (n 25) ch. 6, p. 369, para. 26; Bell (n 120) at 119 et seq.

[272] See the fundamental study of Sarkin (2004); an insider's perspective provides Boraine (n 23); see also Dugard (n 64) at 1,011–12; Schlunck (n 30) at 186 et seq., 226 et seq.; Gavron (n 64) at 113 et seq.; Schiff (n 156) at 328 et seq.; van Zyl in Bassiouni (n 9) 745 et seq.; Cassin (n 14) esp. 238 et seq.; Sarkin in Werle (ed.) 2006, 43 et seq.; Nerlich in ibid. 55 et seq.; for post-TRC prosecutions see Fernandez in ibid. at 65 et seq.

[273] See supra para. 3 with n 22.

[274] Its full name is "Promotion of National Unity and Reconciliation Act 34 of 1995". See also Sarkin (n 272) at 234 et seq.

[275] The TRC Act (sect. 3 [3]) establishes three committees (Committee on Human Rights Violations, Committee on Reparation and Rehabilitation, Amnesty Committee). The Amnesty Committee has the power to grant amnesty in respect of any act, omission or offence to which the particular application for amnesty relates, provided that the applicant concerned has made a full disclosure of all relevant facts and provided further that the relevant act, omission or offence is associated with a political objective committed in the course of the conflicts of the past (sect. 20 [1], [2], [3] TRC Act).

[276] Abrams/Hayner (n 137) at 287.

[277] Boraine (n 23) at 275 et seq. (276: "full disclosure").

[278] See sect. 3 (1) of the TRC Act according to which the TRC is required to facilitate "(...) the granting of amnesty to persons who make full disclosure of all the relevant facts relating to acts associated with a political objective(...)". Sect. 20 (3) defines an act "associated with a political objective" by taking recourse to the following criteria:

(a) The motive of the person who committed the act, omission or offence.
(b) The context in which the act, omission or offence took place, and in particular whether the act, omission or offence was committed in the course of or as part of a political uprising, disturbance or event, or in reaction thereto.
(c) The legal and factual nature of the act, omission or offence, including the gravity of the act, omission or offence.

7,116 individual applications, 1,167 were granted amnesty and in 145 cases the applicant was partially successful.[279] Given these conditions the South African amnesty must be clearly distinguished from a blanket amnesty as defined above (para. 24).[280] Thus, it is not surprising, that it has been approved by the Constitutional Court, basically arguing that it was necessary in order to cross the "historic bridge" on the way to national reconciliation and unity.[281] Yet, it has been criticized that the South African amnesty, apart from the political offence requirement, had no *ratione materiae* or *personae* limitations[282] and it is indeed questionable whether

---

(d) The object or objective of the act, omission or offence, and in particular whether the act, omission or offence was primarily directed at a political opponent or State property or personnel or against private property or individuals.
(e) Whether the act, omission or offence was committed in the execution of an order of, or on behalf of, or with the approval of, the organisation, institution, liberation movement or body of which the person who committed the act was a member, an agent or a supporter.
(f) The relationship between the act, omission or offence and the political objective pursued, and in particular the directness and proximity of the relationship and the proportionality of the act, omission or offence to the objective pursued, but does not include any act, omission or offence committed by any person referred to in subsection (2) who acted:
    (i) For personal gain Provided that an act, omission or offence by any person who acted and received money or anything of value as an informer of the State or a former state, political organisation or liberation movement, shall not be excluded only on the grounds of that person having received money or anything of value for his or her information.
    (ii) Out of personal malice, ill-will or spite, directed against the victim of the acts committed.

For a critical analysis of the disclosure and political offence requirements see Sarkin (n 272) at 249 et seq., 278 et seq.; on the political nature of the acts see also Boraine (n 23) at 276–7.

[279] See for a detailed analysis Sarkin (n 272) at 107 et seq.

[280] See also Constitutional Court, n 23, para. 32: "The amnesty contemplated is not a blanket amnesty against criminal prosecution for all and sundry, granted automatically as a uniform act of compulsory statutory amnesia. It is specifically authorised for the purposes of effecting a constructive transition towards a democratic order. It is available only where there is a full disclosure of all facts to the Amnesty Committee and where it is clear that the particular transgression was perpetrated during the prescribed period and with a political objective committed in the course of the conflicts of the past". For a defence in this regard also Boraine (n 23) at 297–8.

[281] The Constitutional Court, n 23, basically approved the epilogue to the Constitution (n 22) which uses the metaphor of a "historic bridge". Mahomed DP concluded, followed by all other nine judges (Didcott J. dissenting only as to the reasoning with regard to the exclusion of civil liability): "In the result, I am satisfied that the epilogue to the Constitution authorised and contemplated an 'amnesty' in its most comprehensive and generous meaning so as to enhance and optimise the prospects of facilitating the constitutional journey from the shame of the past to the promise of the future" (Constitutional Court, n 23, para. 50).

[282] For a general account of the criticism see Sarkin (n 272) at 6 et seq.; crit. also Imbleau (n 121) at 170; Hunt (n 124) at 196; Orozco (n 58) at 186–7; Sooka (n 6) at 316–7. According to Schiff (n 156) at 331, 339, 341 the widespread impunity in South Africa is rather due to the weaknesses of the domestic judicial system than to the work of the TRC. Similarly, van Zyl (n 272) at 745 et seq., argues that the TRC had no authority over prosecutions and reparations (at 760); in any case, it was "extraordinarily successful as a *process of truth-telling*" (at 759); for a positive evaluation also Boraine (n 23) at 258 et seq. (see already n 135 and 280), 340 et seq. (with regard to reconciliation). According to Fernandez (n 272) there is little doubt that "the choice of granting amnesties to persons who have committed gross human rights violations is not in accordance with international law" (at 79). For a recent defence, Tutu (2007) 1 IJTJ 6–7.

these generally recognized limitations (para. 15, 21, 25 et seq.) may be ignored without a second thought. While it follows, on an abstract level, from the proportionality test (para. 19 et seq.) that international core crimes must not be the object of an exemption and less so if the exemption also extends – for lack of a *ratione personae* limitations – to the most responsible (para. 21), this rule is a principle and as such is not written in stone but open to – albeit very strict – exceptions. While the admissibility of these exceptions depends on the circumstance of the concrete case – as in South Africa where it is important to take into account that most amnesty applications have been dismissed – it is clear that such exceptions may, on an abstract level, only be justified by extreme circumstances which leave virtually, with a view to a peaceful transition, no other option than to ultimately accept impunity for international core crimes (on this "worse abuses argument" see already para. 3). To be sure, to accept this argument means to give in to the power of the arms – "*auctoritas, non veritas facit legem*" – and it is hardly possible to prove in a given situation that the concessions were really necessary since the alternative – sticking to the *ratione materiae* and *personae* limitations – has not been put to practice.

32. Probably the most forceful legal argument for a flexible approach is provided for in *Art. 6 (5) Additional Protocol II* (AP II) to the Four Geneva Conventions.[283] The provision has always been interpreted – in accordance with the travaux based view of the ICRC[284] – as only referring to legal acts in combat and to those mutual breaches of IHL which have been committed as a necessary consequence of the armed conflict, i.e., as not covering violations of IHL.[285] Indeed, the provision applies only to non-international armed conflicts and thus cannot undermine the duty to prosecute grave breaches. As for amnesties for crimes committed in non-international conflicts the recent criminalization of these acts by the *Tadić* case law[286] and Art. 8 (2) (c) and (e) of the ICC Statute makes it necessary to either follow the restrictive ICRC interpretation or reject amnesties for war crimes from the perspective of the principle of the unity of the (international) legal order: If this order establishes a duty to prosecute war crimes (in particular the grave breaches of the Geneva Conventions, para. 7) it cannot at the same time (and even by an instrument of the same legal area, namely IHL) allow that these crimes be exempted from

[283] The provision reads: "At the end of hostilities, the authorities in power shall endeavour to grant the broadest possible amnesty to persons who have participated in the armed conflict, or those deprived of their liberty for reasons related to the armed conflict, whether they are interned or detained".

[284] Cf. Sandoz/Swinarski/Zimmermann (1987) mn. 4618: "L'objet de cet alinéa est d'encourager un geste de réconciliation qui contribue à rétablir le cours normal de la vie dans un peuple qui a été divisé." See also Pfanner (n 28) at 371.

[285] Conc. Inter-American Commission on Human Rights, case 10.480, report no. 1/99, para. 116; UN-ECOSOC, Impunity, 27 February 2004, para. 27. See also Cassel (n 54) at 218; Méndez (n 28) at 35; Gavron (n 64) at 101–2 and Slye (n 51) at 178 all referring to the ICRC position; also Young (n 88) at 446–7; Seils/Wierda (n 21) at 14; Olson (n 30) at 286; Salmón (n 74) at 338; ICRC 2007, at 61.

[286] *Prosecutor v. Tadic* [2 October 1995] App. Decision, IT-94–1-AR 72 (ICTY) para. 71 et seq.

punishment.[287] Be that as it may, the mere existence of Art. 6 (5) AP II with its explicit reference to an amnesty calls for a certain flexibility; consequently, an amnesty after an armed conflict within the meaning of Art. 6 (5) AP II must remain possible if it is an appropriate and necessary tool to achieve national reconciliation[288] and if it does not undermine the respective state's duty to prosecute.

33. The overwhelming *doctrine* follows the two-pronged approach to distinguishing between blanket and conditional amnesties[289] and, consequently, allows for the latter under certain, exceptional circumstances. Some scholars argue that, from a legal perspective, a general prohibition does not yet exist,[290] others that, for policy reasons, it cannot exist.[291] Still others emphasize the criteria for allowing conditional or limited amnesties, for example, that the whole truth be told and that the amnesty be necessary for the peaceful transition[292] or that it only be applied to collective crimes.[293] In some cases, the argumentative dilemma becomes manifest in the attempt to reconcile both – the prohibitive and permissive – views. The studies carried out by Orentlicher[294] and Dugard[295] serve as good examples in this regard. The former proposes, on the one hand, a principle (no. 22) according to which states "should adopt safeguards against any abuse of rules such as those pertaining to prescription, amnesty (...)", and, on the other, a specific principle (no. 24) according to which amnesties and other measures of clemency shall be, in general, possible but be kept within certain bounds, namely, that either an independent and impartial investigation was undertaken by the state concerned[296] or the person concerned was prosecuted by national or international courts[297] and that the amnesty has no effect on the victim's right to reparation.[298] In interpreting these contradictory principles (22 and 24) in this way, she states that she sought:

[287] See already Ambos (n 75) at 210–11; see also Tomuschat in Cremer (ed.) 2002, 315; Werle (n 16) mn 191 with n. 366; Sánchez (n 260) at 371; Gropengießer/Meißner (n 60) at 272; Hafner/Boon/Rubesame/Huston (1999) 10 EJIL 108, 111; Gavron (n 64) at 103.

[288] See also Arsanjani (n 21) at 65 and Bell (n 120) at 110 et seq.

[289] See the references in supra n 88.

[290] See, e.g., Cassese (n 88) at 315: "There is not yet any general obligation to refrain from enacting amnesty laws on these crimes". For a stricter view apparently Olson (n 30) at 289 et seq. generally against amnesty for international core crimes.

[291] See, e.g., Werle (n 16) at 66 (mn 190): "(...) international (criminal) law cannot completely block an amnesty that is necessary to restore peace"; Gropengießer/Meißner (n 60) at 278–79: "relative ban"; Ferdinandusse (2006) at 205 et seq. (207: "presumption" for prohibition); Kreicker (n 21) at 17–8, 306. See also the crit. analysis of the justice element in the Dayton Peace Process by Williams (n 20) at 115, concluding, at 133, that "the current prevailing perspective appears to be that it is better to negotiate a peace deal with those responsible for atrocities than to insist on the inclusion of norms of justice which may derail the peace process (...)".

[292] Van der Voort/Zwanenburg (n 60) at 324 et seq. (326).

[293] May (2005) at 243 et seq., 251–2.

[294] Orentlicher impunity principles.

[295] Dugard (n 60) at 693 et seq.

[296] Orentlicher impunity principles, Principle 24 (a) with reference to Principle 19.

[297] Ibid., Principle 24 (a).

[298] Ibid., Principle 24 (b).

> to avoid any possible implication that a perpetrator of serious crimes under international law may be exempted from criminal punishment *altogether* by disclosing his or her violations during a period of persecution.[299]

Dugard derives, on the one hand, a prohibition of amnesty for international crimes from the duty to prosecute these crimes,[300] but on the other, rejects, in the light of state practice, the existence of such a duty and, consequently, an amnesty prohibition[301] leaving it ultimately to the discretion of the states concerned to grant amnesties as long as they do not cover genocide, grave breaches and torture.[302] In fact, while Dugard does not clearly distinguish between the duty to prosecute and the granting of amnesties, he does distinguish between blanket and conditional amnesties, concretely the Chilean and South African ones.[303] For the latter one he requires a judicial approval or a quasi-judicial inquiry[304] and accepts them – following the South African example – if they have "been granted as part of a truth and reconciliation inquiry and each person (...) has been obliged to make full disclosure of his or her criminal acts as a precondition for amnesty and the acts were politically motivated".[305]

3 Part II. Peace Processes and the ICC

3.1 Preliminary Remarks

34. While peace processes have not been under scrutiny by a *permanent accountability mechanism* for a long time – at best ad hoc mechanisms like international and internationalized courts have been established *ex post facto*[306] – the situation has radically changed with the establishment of the ICC.[307] Indeed, the ICC is "part of

---

[299] Orentlicher Impunity principles commentary, para. 56 (emphasis added). More recently Orentlicher confirmed her support for criminal accountability, but stresses the importance of local agency which may make a temporal suspension of criminal prosecution necessary (Orentlicher [n 21] 21–2).

[300] Dugard (n 60) at 697.

[301] Ibid. at 698.

[302] Ibid. at 699. Similarly already Dugard (n 64) 1,003-1,004 expressing doubts whether international law – given the opposite state practice – prohibits amnesties albeit recognizing that it is "moving in this direction". As to the crimes in particular he argues that genocide and war crimes ("grave breaches") cannot be covered by an amnesty the law being unclear for the other international crimes (at 1,015).

[303] Dugard (n 60) at 699-700.

[304] Dugard (n 60) at 703.

[305] Dugard (n 60) at 700. Similarly already Dugard (n 64) at 1,005, 1,015 considering that a blanket, unconditional amnesty without a truth commission "is no longer an acceptable option".

[306] On "hybrid" courts in this context see Kritz (n 9) at 70 et seq.

[307] Schlunck (n 30) at 251-52, 254; Goldstone/Fritz (n 21) at 665-6; for a positive assessment Seils/Wierda (n 21) at 18.

the transitional justice project"[308] and the parties to conflicts may take the "threat" by the ICC seriously well before the actual negotiations start, and some most responsible may even be excluded from these negotiations.[309] This effect is not limited to the State Parties since, as the Sudanese situation shows, even a Non State Party can be made the object of ICC investigations by a Security Council referral (Art. 13 [b] ICC Statute).[310] Interestingly, empirical research shows that the majority of victims support the idea of an universalized and international criminal justice.[311] In addition, as the ICC is an independent treaty body (Art. 1, 4 ICC Statute) other actors, especially the UNO, cannot, with the exception of the Security Council (on Art. 16 ICC Statute see para. 50), interfere with its investigations. As the situation in Northern Uganda shows, the UN as a peace broker is not in a position to decide on the continuation of an investigation or the lifting of arrest warrants.[312] The ICC has judicial autonomy *vis-à-vis* other international organizations and courts as well as *vis-à-vis* the parties to a conflict. This follows from its organizational position just described and various provisions of its Statute.[313] At the same time, in situations of ongoing conflict the ICC, especially the OTP, must keep the parties to the conflict at equal distance in order to preserve its impartiality and neutrality.[314] On the other hand, the Court's decisions have no limiting effect on third states, i.e., they decide autonomously on their jurisdiction and interest to prosecute international crimes.[315] On the contrary, the Court's *ratione personae* and *materiae* limitations (see below para. 36) mean that domestic jurisdictions still have an important role to play in bringing less important perpetrators for less serious crimes to justice.[316] In turn, the ICC Statute may have a limiting effect on national amnesties insofar as the State

---

[308] Moreno-Ocampo (2007) 1 IJTJ 8.

[309] Seils/Wierda (n 21) at 19. On the exclusionary effect of criminal prosecution see already supra para. 21 with n 196.

[310] This jurisdictional expansion has been called the "sledgehammer" of the ICC by Cassese (1999) 10 EJIL 144, at 161.

[311] According to Kiza/Rathgeber/Rohne (n 4) at 100 et seq. (Table 21), 110, 156 53% of the victims interviewed wanted to have an international court to prosecute the perpetrators. Cf. for a non-uniform Ugandan victims' view OHCHR (n 33) at 50 et seq.

[312] See supra para. 25 with n 243.

[313] See for example Art. 19 (1) according to which the ICC shall "satisfy itself" and determine the admissibility "on its own motion" (cf. Stahn [n 64] 700).

[314] See OTP Activities Report, p. 16-17 where it is stated, referring to peace initiatives in Northern Uganda, that "(...) in order to preserve its impartiality, the Office cannot be a component of these initiatives. The Office policy is to maintain its own independence and pursue its mandate to investigate and prosecute, and do so in a manner that respects the mandates of others and attempts to maximise the positive impact of the joint efforts to all actors. (...) the Office maintained a low public profile during the investigation (...). At no time, however, did the Office stop its investigation". Crit. about the situation in Uganda and the one-sided prosecution strategy Schabas (n 21) at 18 et seq.

[315] Cf. Robinson (n 31) at 503-4; Seibert-Fohr (n 21) at 576 et seq. See also supra para. 25.

[316] See also OTP Policy Paper, p. 3 and 7 calling for a two-tiered approach leaving the prosecution of "lower-ranking perpetrators" to domestic jurisdictions.

Parties are obliged to cooperate, e.g., by surrendering a person who is protected by a national (unconditional) amnesty.[317]

35. The *amnesty* issue was raised during the Preparatory Committee but not seriously considered[318] and deliberately evaded during the Rome conference.[319] In fact, a general agreement on the issue was not feasible and therefore it was left, as many other issues, to the Court.[320] Equally, the issue of alternative accountability mechanisms was not specifically addressed.[321] In any case, the ICC Statute is a flexible instrument and the ICC a flexible accountability mechanism.[322] From a legal perspective, this follows, on the one hand, from the Prosecutor's relatively broad discretion with regard to the preliminary investigation and the taking of certain investigative measures[323] and, on the other, from Art. 16, 17 and 53 of the ICC Statute, to be analysed in more detail below (para. 37 et seq.). One may even interpret the said provisions as an indirect recognition of measures refraining from criminal prosecution for the sake of a peaceful transition or the achievement of peace.[324]

---

[317] In more detail Seibert-Fohr (n 21) at 584 et seq.

[318] Report of the PrepCom on the Establishment of the ICC (1996), UN-GAOR, 51st session, suppl. No. 22 (A/51/22), vol. I., p. 40 (para. 174): "The view was also expressed that the 'exception' to the principle *non bis in idem* as set out in article 42 (b) should extend beyond the trial proceedings to embrace parole, pardon, amnesty, etc." Scharf (n 54) 507, 508; Gavron (n 64) at 108 and Seibert-Fohr (n 21) at 562 refer to an U.S. "non-paper"; in addition, Seibert-Fohr (n 21) at 556 suggests that one of the reasons of the Bush administration to "unsign" the ICC Statute was the absence of a provision on amnesties. See also Arsanjani (n 21) at 67: "never seriously discussed"; Robinson (n 31) at 483; Cárdenas (n 46) at 155–6.

[319] Hafner/Boon/Rübesame/Huston (n 287) at 109–113; see also Dugard (n 64) 1013; Dugard (n 60) at 700–01 with further references.

[320] The history of the negotiations is misread by Young (n 88) at 459 et seq. who criticizes the absence of an explicit provision and precise guidelines on amnesty in the Statute and the RPE (470–1, 475–6, 482). He does not only ignore that the question was deliberately left open by the drafters since an agreement was just impossible (see also Robinson [n 31] 483; Seibert-Fohr [n 21] at 561, 589; Cárdenas [n 46] at 156) but also – on a more general level – erroneously converts the ILC into the drafters of the Statute (at 459: "[...] the ILC simply drafted provisions [...") and the Statute into an UN-treaty (at 464: "The UN adopted the Rome Statute ...]"). These are grave errors and one wonders how the paper could have been published without correcting them.

[321] Cf. Bassiouni (2005) at 133–4.

[322] Cf. Ntanda Nsereko (1999) 10 CLF 87, at 120; Arsanjani (n 21) at 65, at 66, 68; Robinson (n 31) at 483–4, 502, 505; Seibert-Fohr (n 21) at 557–8, 573–4; Clark (n 64) at 407, 414; Meyer (n 177) at 564 et seq., at 576 stating "as long as national decisions (...) comport with complexity of societal convictions and dynamics the ICC should be deferential". Schlunck (n 30) at 259 argues that it would be short-sighted to put the ICC above the political will of national decision makers, this would go against flexible conflict management.

[323] The "reasonable basis" standard in Art. 15 (3) and Art. 53 as such leaves a broad discretion; the application for an arrest warrant according to Art. 58 may be delayed if the suspect participates in peace negotiations (see also Seils/Wierda [n 21] at 2, 7). Even HRW, 2005, at 21 admits that there is some prosecutorial discretion regarding "timing", e.g., with regard to the application of an arrest warrant; yet, the prosecutor should not publicly acknowledge that the delay is due to a peace process and the delay should not be indefinite (ibid. at 22). On the "extremely complex and daunting task" of prosecutorial discretion see also Ralston/Finnin (n 333) at 49 et seq.

[324] See also Scharf (n 54) at 508 even arguing that the formally rejected U.S. "nonpaper" (n 318) was indirectly codified; crit. Cárdenas (n 46) at 156.

In practice, the Prosecutor takes the risk transition argument (para. 3) into account and seeks to evaluate the real and concrete risk through detailed discussions with sources on the ground.[325] As a result, the ICC Statute leaves room for amnesties or other exemptions if they are conditional and accompanied by alternative forms of justice, which ultimately may lead to prosecution and criminal sanction.[326] Indeed, it is inconceivable that the ICC pretends to substitute a policy judgement of a whole nation that seeks peace and justice by alternative means.[327] It goes too far, however, to justify this flexibility with the ICC's "overall goal (...) to protect peace and security".[328] On the one hand, this is an overstatement: Although the Preamble (para. 3) refers to peace and security in connection with the ICC crimes, as a *criminal* court concerned with individual responsibility the ICC has a much more concrete and modest objective, namely to prosecute and punish the perpetrators of international crimes (Preamble, para. 4) and thereby "put an end to impunity" of these crimes (Preamble, para. 5). If, as a side effect, this also contributes to peace and security it is to be welcomed[329] but cannot be construed as the main or "overall" goal of the ICC. On the other hand, if the continuing impunity of these crimes really threatens international peace and security, as suggested by para. 3 of the Preamble, it is contradictory to justify exemptions from punishment, i.e., the impunity of these crimes, with the protection of these very same values. At best, the non-prosecution facilitates the achievement of peace and security but it does not protect or consolidate it. In fact, it is difficult to explain that an institution created to avoid impunity, should promote it by accepting amnesty;[330] indeed, this would go against the *telos* of the ICC.[331]

36. The ICC's judicial autonomy (para. 34) means that it has broad discretion on deciding how to deal with amnesties. It could even reject amnesties covering crimes for which no clear-cut duty to prosecute exists.[332] On the other hand, the *ratione materiae* and *personae* limitations mentioned above (para. 21) operate for the ICC in the opposite direction: As the ICC – as well as the Ad Hoc Tribunals[333] – pursues

---

[325] Seils/Wierda (n 21) at 13.

[326] Goldstone/Fritz (n 21) at 656, 667; Stahn (n 64) at 719.

[327] Goldstone/Fritz (n 21) at 667.

[328] Seibert-Fohr (n 21) at 574.

[329] See, e.g., OTP Activities Report, p. 18 (referring to the importance of justice and accountability for peace in Darfur): "This clear acknowledgement of the important links between justice, peace and security (...) is a great achievement in the evolution of the role of international justice".

[330] The issue came up before the ICTY in *Prosecutor v. Deronic* [30 March 2004] Sentencing Judgement, Case No. IT-02-61-S (ICTY), dissenting opinion Judge Schomburg, para. 11: "a) Promises (...) cannot result in de facto granting partial amnesty/impunity by the Prosecutor, particularly not in an institution established to avoid impunity".

[331] Young (n 88) at 471; Robinson (n 31) at 497; Stahn (n 64) at 703; Ssenyonjo (n 174) at 377.

[332] Stahn (n 64) at 705.

[333] See, e.g., UN SC Res. 1534 (26 March 2004) para. 5 calling on the ICTY and ICTR to ensure that the indictments concentrate on the most senior leaders and Rule 28 (A) ICTY RPE providing that the Bureau shall determine whether the indictment "concentrates on one or more of the most senior leaders suspected of being the most responsible"; otherwise and if the crimes are not of sufficient gravity the case should be referred to the local courts (Rule *11bis* (C)); see also Art.

a prosecutorial strategy[334] focusing on the most serious crimes[335] and the most responsible perpetrators[336] amnesties or other exemptions for mid- or low-level perpetrators and/or for less serious crimes are of no concern to it.[337] For the crimes, the Court may pursue a crime-specific approach, i.e., decide on a case by case basis with regard to each crime concerned if it is barred by an amnesty; for forced disappearance, for example, it could opt for a retroactive rejection of an earlier amnesty since it is a continuous crime.[338] In any event, given the exclusion of large groups of minor perpetrators and less serious crimes by the current prosecutorial strategy, targeted prosecutions by a national judiciary focusing on the most serious crimes and the most responsible perpetrators would generally pass the complementarity test and therefore render the ICC's intervention inadmissible.[339]

3.2 *Analysis of Relevant Provisions*

3.2.1 Complementarity (Art. 17 ICC Statute)

Analysis of the Provision

37. Art. 17, for some the "most delicate" provision in the context of TJ,[340] concerns the relationship between the ICC and domestic jurisdictions and as such consti-

1 SCSL Statute ("persons who bear the greatest responsibility [...]"). For the prosecution strategies of ICTY, ICTR, SCSL, the courts in East Timor and Kosovo see Ralston/Finnin in Blumenthal/McCormack (eds.) 2008, 47, at 52 et seq.

334 The Chief Prosecutor, Luis Moreno-Ocampo distinguishes in this regard – taking into account the budget concerns of the Donor countries – between a very limited "resource driven approach" and a less selective "case driven approach" (Moreno-Ocampo Statement 2005, p. 8–9).

335 This already follows from the Preamble (e.g., para. 4: "most serious crimes") and Art. 17 (1) (d) referring to "sufficient gravity", on this requirement see below para. 38 with n 353 et seq. See also OTP Activities Report, p. 7–8, 23; OTP Report on Prosecutorial Strategy, 14.9.2006, p. 5; OTP Fourth Report, p. 4; Moreno-Ocampo Statement 2006b, p. 2.

336 Cf. OTP Policy Paper, p. 3, 7 ("focus [...] on those who bear the greatest responsibility [...]); conc. OTP Activities Report, p. 7–8, 16, 23; OTP Report on Prosecutorial Strategy, 14.9.2006, p. 5; OTP Fourth Report, p. 4; Moreno-Ocampo Statement 2006b, p. 2. See also Schlunck (n 30) at 260; El Zeidy (n 72) at 905; Olásolo (n 31) at 146; Stahn (n 64) at 707–8; Ralston/Finnin (n 333) at 65, 68; Meyer (n 177) at 577 arguing that for low-level perpetrators non-criminal sanctions suffice. For PTC I, Situation in the DRC in the case of *Prosecutor v. Thomas Lubanga Dyilo*, Decision concerning PTC I's Decision of 10 February 2006 and the Incorporation of Documents into the Record of the Case against Mr. Thomas Lubanga Dyilo, 24 February 2006 (ICC-01/04–01/06) (ICC) para. 50, this is also ensured by the gravity threshold of Art. 17 (1) (d). This ratione personae limitation is confirmed by research on victims' attitudes, see supra notes 195, 196.

337 On this "impunity gap" Seils/Wierda (n 21) at 14; see also Mallinder (n 65) at 223.

338 Cf. Stahn (n 64) at 706.

339 For the same result Robinson (n 31) at 500–1.

340 Stahn (n 64) at 719; for the historical development see Williams/Schabas in Triffterer (ed.) 2008, Art. 17 mn 3–20.

tutes the most fundamental provision of the ICC Statute with regard to the State Parties.[341] The provision tries to strike an adequate balance between the states' sovereign exercise of (criminal) jurisdiction and the international community's interest in preventing impunity for international core crimes[342] by according prevalence to the State Parties if they are willing and able to investigate and prosecute the international core crimes. Art. 17 provides rules on the *admissibility* of ICC proceedings *vis-à-vis* domestic jurisdictions. Thus, it is not a jurisdictional provision *stricto sensu* but *presupposes* the existence of jurisdiction (as provided for in Art. 11, 12 ICC Statute) which may be *exercised* when the case is admissible.[343] The determination of inadmissibility by the ICC according to para. 1 of Art. 17 presupposes that national proceedings with regard to the same incidents and conduct[344] – Art. 17 refers to the specific case, not the overall situation[345] – take place at all; if this is not the case, i.e., if the national system is absolutely inactive, the case is to be considered admissible without more.[346] In this sense, state sovereignty is restricted since State Parties are not allowed to remain inactive in the face of international core crimes.[347] It is important to note, though, that a state's duty to act in the face of these crimes, in particular to prosecute them (para. 8), did not come only into existence with the establishment of the ICC but existed already before it. While the question of inactivity is of an *empirical* nature, the actual examination of Art. 17 – in case of the existence of national proceedings – is essentially *normative* focusing on the quality of the proceedings and – intimately linked to this – the unwillingness and inability of the domestic system concerned.[348] Thus, summarizing, one

[341] Cf. Benzing (n 103) at 593; Williams/Schabas in Triffterer (ed.) 2008, Art. 17 mn 1 ("cornerstone"); on "positive" complementarity, i.e., the ICC's contribution to the effective functioning of national justice systems see Burke-White (2008) 19 CLF 59, at 61 et seq.; Stahn (2008) CLF 87, at 100 et seq.; with regard to DRC Mattioli/van Woudenberg in Waddell/Clark (eds.) 2008, 55, at 57 et seq.

[342] Cf. Benzing (n 103) at 595 et seq., 600; Pichon (2008) 8 ICLR 185, at 187; according to Stahn (n 341) at 88, complementarity must be "primarily viewed as an instrument to overcome sovereignty fears".

[343] See also Benzing (n 103) at 594; unclear Seibert-Fohr (n 21) 561 dealing with the issue as a jurisdictional one.

[344] See the recent Art. 58 (7) application of the ICC Prosecutor in the Darfur case: "Although investigations in the Sudan do involve Ali Kushayb, they are not in respect of the *same incidents or conduct* that are the subject of the case now before the Court. Therefore, the case is admissible." (ICC Prosecutor Presents Evidence on Darfur Crimes, The Hague, 27 February 2007, ICC-OTP-20070227-206-En, emphasis added).

[345] See also Benzing (n 103) at 603. Yet, a situation, consisting of various cases, is referred to the Court (Art. 13); also, in the case of "inability" (Art. 17 [3]) the effect of a collapse of the national justice system may go well beyond the specific case and extend to the situation as a whole (cf. Bergsmo [1998] 6 Eur. J. Cr., Cr. L. & Cr. J. 29, at 43; Cárdenas [n 46] at 130–1).

[346] Benzing (n 103) 601; contrary to Benzing, this also applies for inactivity due to a procedural obstacle since then an investigation does not take place at all, see also below n 371 and text. See also Seils/Wierda (n 21) at 6.

[347] Benzing (n 103) at 600.

[348] For the same empirical and normative distinction Robinson in Kleffner/Kor (eds.) 2006, 141, at 142.

can say that the "ICC only acts when States do not undertake proceedings or do not do it properly".[349] Procedurally, claims of inadmissibility may be brought by the State concerned (Art. 18 [2], 19 [2] [b], [c] ICC Statute) or the accused (Art. 19 [2] [a]).[350]

38. A closer look at Art. 17 reveals various distinguishing features. On the one hand, the provision distinguishes between investigation and prosecution (Art. 17 [1] [a] and [b]) and a trial by a court (Art. 17 [1] [c] referring to Art. 20 [3]). On the other hand, there is a temporal distinction as to the *procedural stage* of the investigation: Either the investigation (or the prosecution) is currently taking place (Art. 17 [1] [a]) or it is already completed and the corresponding decision not to prosecute has been taken (Art. 17 [1] [b]). If, in turn, a decision to prosecute has been taken and the person has already been tried the procedural stage is even more advanced and Art. 17 (1) (c) applicable. Independent of these temporal criteria, the crimes concerned must be of sufficient *gravity* "to justify further action by the Court" (Art. 17 [1] [d]),[351] i.e., notwithstanding the gravity of ICC crimes as such, Art. 17 (1) (d) establishes an *additional* gravity threshold.[352] In any case, the gravity in the sense of Art. 17 (1) (d) is relevant at two different stages of the proceedings[353] and must be determined on a case by case basis[354] invoking as criteria the nature and social impact ("social alarm") of the crimes (systematic or large-scale?), the manner of commission (e.g., particular brutality or cruelty) and the status and role of the suspected perpetrators (are they the most responsible as mentioned above?).[355] Given

349 Ibid. at 142; Cárdenas (n 156) at 115.

350 See also Stahn (n 64) 698; for a detailed analysis El Zeidy (n 72) at 906 et seq.

351 See also Art. 53 (1) (b) and (2) (b).

352 Cf. PTC I (n 336), para. 41: "(...) this gravity threshold is in addition to (...) the crimes included in articles 6 to 8 of the Statute (...)." See also OTP Activities Report, p. 6: "Although any crime falling within the jurisdiction of the Court is a serious matter, the Rome Statute (...) clearly foresees and requires an additional consideration of 'gravity' (...)"; Moreno-Ocampo Statement 2005, p. 8–9: "(...) gravity in our Statute is not only a characteristic of the crime, but also an admissibility factor, which seems to reflect the wish of our founders that the ICC should focus on the gravest situations in the world". See also Benzing (n 103) at 619–20; Cárdenas (n 46) at 90 et seq.; id., (n 156) at 119–20; El Zeidy (2008) 19 CLF 35, at 39; Williams/Schabas in Triffterer (ed.) 2008, Art. 17 mn 28; for a narrow interpretation Seibert-Fohr (n 21) at 565 et seq.; for a more detailed approach see WCRO (March 2008) at 12 et seq., El Zeidy at 36 et seq.

353 Regarding the initiation of the investigation of a situation and of the case(s) arising from this situation (PTC I, n 336, para. 44). See also WCRO (n 352) at 21, 25 et seq.; at 29 et seq.; El Zeidy (n 352) at 39.

354 Cf. Cárdenas (n 46) at 158, 176. For the selection criteria in the first individual cases see WCRO (n 352) at 25 et seq., 29 et seq.

355 PTC I, n 336, para. 42 et seq. (46, 50–4, 63). See also OTP Activities Report, p. 6 and OTP Report on Prosecutorial Strategy, 14.9.2006, p. 5, referring to the scale and nature of the crimes, the manner of commission and the impact of the crimes. Crit. On the "social alarm" criterion El Zeidy (n 352) at 45 ("weird novelty"), in addition pointing out (at 44) that these factors are illustrative and not exclusive. Crit. as to the quantitative approach Schabas (n 21) at 28 et seq.; Williams/Schabas in Triffterer (ed.) 2008, Art. 17 mn 28. See also El Zeidy (n 72) 905; Cárdenas (n 46) at 93 et seq. focusing on the international concern ("internationaler Belang", at 98, 100) of the matter. For the gravity analysis of the ad-hoc Tribunals see WCRO (n 352) at 37 et seq., recommending a "sufficiently flexible" analysis (at 42) taking into account exceptional circumstances as "the impact

the particular gravity of the genocide offence and its specific *mens rea* requirement one may argue that a genocide case always fullfills the gravity threshold of Art. 17 (1) (d).[356]

39. Regarding the precise application of Art. 17 to exemptions from criminal prosecution one may draw a distinction as to the procedural stage affected by these exemptions. If one takes for example an *amnesty* as the most important exemption subparas. (a) and (b) of Art. 17 (1) seem to be the only applicable provisions. As an amnesty either impedes a (criminal) investigation or a criminal prosecution,[357] subpara. (c) of Art. 17 (1) is not applicable since it presupposes more, namely that a trial by a Court has taken place.[358] In fact, subpara. (c) is only applicable to exemptions or suspensions of punishment after conviction, in particular pardons.[359] Then the (empirical) question arises whether the earlier proceedings "were for the purpose of shielding the person concerned from criminal responsibility" (Art. 17 [1] [c] with Art. 20 [3] [a]).[360] Art. 17 (1) (a) presupposes that the case is "being investigated or prosecuted", i.e., for the inadmissibility it is sufficient that either an investigation or prosecution is taking place. While these requirements are in the alternative, it does not make much sense to separate the investigation from the prosecution, i.e., to examine an investigation in isolation, since, in any case, once an investigation is finished a decision to prosecute or not to prosecute must be taken. In other words, while an investigation in the sense of subpara. (a) may block the intervention of the ICC for a certain period of time (namely, as long as the case is "being investigated"), afterwards a prosecution decision must be taken and in this precise moment Art. 17 (1) (b) becomes applicable.[361] In any case, in both subpara. (a) and (b) the decisive criteria are unwillingness and inability as defined in Art. 17 (2) and (3). Therefore, for the investigation and prosecution requirements the distinction between subpara. (a) and (b) is merely of temporal nature. In sum, in practice, if a state "in its sovereign wisdom"[362] decides not to investigate and/or

---

on victims, the manner in which the crimes were carried out, and the vulnerability of the victim population". On the difficult relation between OTP and Chambers in this matter see El Zeidy (n 352) at 51 et seq.

[356] Cf. Cárdenas (n 46) at 99; id., in Werle (ed.) 2006, 239, at 244; id., in Hankel (ed.) 2008, 127, at 138. For higher gravity of genocide and crimes against humanity vis á vis war crimes Schabas (n 21) at 25 et seq. In this respect crit. with regard to the selection of the DRC situation and rejection of the Iraqi communication El Zeidy (n 352) at 40.

[357] Garner (2004) at 93 on "amnesty".

[358] Cf. Robinson (n 31) 499; Cárdenas (n 46) at 160.

[359] Garner (n 357) "pardon", at 1144. While an "amnesty after a conviction" (Van den Wyngaert/Ongena in Cassese/Gaeta/Jones [n 60] 705, at 726–7; Seibert-Fohr [n 21] at 565; Cárdenas [n 46] at 162) may be possible in practice, conceptually it mixes up amnesties and pardons and is therefore to be avoided.

[360] Cf. Cárdenas (n 46) at 162–3; on Art. 20 (3) generally see also Cárdenas (n 46) at 134 et seq.; Scharf (n 54) at 525; Gavron (n 64) at 109; Benzing (n 103) at 616 et seq.

[361] This temporal aspect has apparently been overlooked by Cárdenas (n 46) at 159 et seq. who distinguishes too artificially between investigation and prosecution and therefore applies Art. 17 (1) (a) too formalistic to an amnesty.

[362] Nsereko (n 322) at 119; crit. El Zeidy (n 72) at 942–3.

prosecute by granting an amnesty, Art. 17 (1) (b) applies and three conditions must be fulfilled to make the ICC's intervention inadmissible:

- The respective state must have "investigated" the case.
- It must have taken the decision "not to prosecute".
- This decision must not result from unwillingness or inability.[363]

40. For the *investigation requirement*, the core issue is whether a criminal investigation by the respective criminal justice organs is necessary or alternative, even non-judicial forms of investigation mentioned above (para. 12 et seq.), in particular a (effective) TRC, would suffice.[364] Clearly, as a minimum, a systematic inquiry into the facts and circumstances of the case is required.[365] This investigation must be carried out by state organs, i.e., non judicial organs like a TRC must be set up and supported by the state,[366] since the duty to investigate and prosecute rests upon the state (see para. 7). Apart from that, the wording and *telos* of Art. 17 indicate that the *objective* of any "investigation" is criminal prosecution or adjudication, namely "to bring the person concerned to justice" (Art. 17 [2] [b] and [c]).[367] While this does not exclude a *preliminary* investigation by a TRC with respective powers and indeed the wording of Art. 17 (1) (a) ("being investigated") leaves room for such alternative investigations,[368] their ultimate objective must always be a criminal prosecution *stricto sensu*[369] where the legal and factual prerequisites of such a prosecution are fulfilled.[370] In turn, this means that investigations of a general nature about past events which do not individualize responsibility and therefore can not serve as basis for a criminal prosecution or adjudication do not satisfy the investigation requirement of Art. 17. Equally, if a subsequent prosecution is blocked *a limine* by a (blanket) amnesty – unacceptable anyway (para. 24 et seq.) – the investigation

---

[363] Robinson (n 31) at 499; Stahn (n 64) at 710. See also Gropengießer/Meißner (n 60) at 283–284.

[364] The question is left open by Robinson (n 31) at 499–500 but his general flexible approach indicates that he takes the "slightly broader approach" discussed by himself; undecided also Benzing (n 103) at 602.

[365] Cárdenas (n 46) at 58; id. (n 156) at 117, 119; Murphy (n 193), 44.

[366] See also Cárdenas (n 46) at 177, 183.

[367] In this sense also Gavron (n 64) 111 arguing that "to bring someone to justice" is to be interpreted in the legal, not wider moral sense. Stricter even Holmes in Lee (ed.) 1999. 41, at 77: "Statute's provisions on complementarity are intended to refer to criminal investigations".

[368] See also Seibert-Fohr (n 21) at 569 and Stahn (n 64) at 697, 711 arguing against the requirement of a criminal investigation since it is not expressly contained in Art. 17. For the same result Cárdenas (n 46) at 58–9, 101; id. (n 156) at 129. Too restrictive Meißner (2003) at 76 requiring investigations within the framework of criminal proceedings; also Schomburg/Nemitz in Schomburg/Lagodny/Gleß/Hackner (eds.) 2006 at 1,730 against an upward *ne bis in idem* effect (towards international courts).

[369] In this sense also Seibert-Fohr (n 21) at 569 linking the investigation to the prosecution requirement; also Gropengießer/Meißner (n 60) at 287 arguing that "proceedings which do not have the *quality of a criminal proceeding* cannot rule out prosecution by the Court" (emphasis added); similarly Cárdenas (n 156) 137 stressing the need of criminal prosecutions after the TRC's work has been finished; conc. (modifying his earlier position) Robinson (n 348) at 144–5 (possibility of a criminal prosecution after investigation).

[370] See also Stahn (n 64) at 711–2.

requirement is not fulfilled and thus it would not make sense to hold the ICC at bay under complementarity.[371]

41. This interpretation is confirmed by the second requirement, the *decision to prosecute*. Such a decision can only be taken if a substantial investigation of concrete acts and individual suspects has been carried out. In other words, a decision to prosecute presupposes a criminal or at least individualized investigation, which precedes and prepares it.[372] Clearly, prosecution refers to criminal prosecution[373] but not the prosecution itself, only the "decision" to prosecute is required. This presupposes that the organ that takes this decision must at least have two options, namely either to prosecute or not to prosecute.[374]

42. As to the third requirement – no *unwillingness* or *inability* to *genuinely* prosecute – the criteria are laid down in Art. 17 (2) and (3). From a policy perspective, these concepts are intended, in the words of former UN Secretary General Kofi Annan, "to ensure that mass-murderers and other archcriminals cannot shelter behind a State run by themselves or their cronies, or take advantage of a general breakdown of law and order".[375] While this may provide general guidance as to the overall goal of this requirement, a more precise and technical analysis begs some intricate questions. According to Art. 17 (2) the Court "shall consider" whether "one or more" of the "following" criteria exist; a literal and teleological interpretation indicates that this is a closed list.[376] While these criteria must be interpreted strictly, taking into account "the principles of due process",[377] they are highly normative and as such open to value judgment. In any event, the structural distinction between unwillingness and inability consists of the following: While in the former case, in principle a functioning judicial system is politically manipulated to generate impunity for powerful and influential perpetrators, in the latter case such a system does not exist, is substantially collapsed or unavailable.[378] Consequently, exemption provisions

[371] Cf. Robinson (n 348) at 145; Cárdenas (n 46) at 159; apparently overlooked by Benzing, as quoted in n 346; Mallinder (n 65) at 212.

[372] See also Stahn (n 64) at 712.

[373] Cf. Cárdenas (n 46) at 58, 101.

[374] Robinson (n 31) at 500; see also Stahn (n 46) at 463.

[375] Speech at the University of Witwatersrand (South Africa), as quoted in Villa-Vicencio (n 21) at 222.

[376] Holmes in Cassese/Gaeta/Jones (n 60) 667, 675; Meißner (n 368) at 72–3; Benzing (n 103) at 606; Cárdenas (n 46) at 133; Cárdenas (n 356) at 139; diss. Robinson (n 31) at 500 arguing that the term "consider" implies that the Court may take into account other factors; this is not convincing since the drafters employed an unambigous wording when they wanted to leave the criteria open, e.g., "in addition to other grounds" (Art. 31 ICC Statute), "inter alia" (Art. 97) or "including but not limited to" (Art. 90 [6]). In the same vein Pichon (n 342) at 191; Williams/Schabas in Triffterer (ed.) 2008, Art. 17 mn 29.

[377] These principles cannot be interpreted, *in the context of Art. 17*, as to refer to the rights of the accused or the victim since the rationale of Art. 17, as explained above (para. 37), is not to protect these rights but to avoid that impunity is created by reason of unwillingness or inability (for a good discussion see Benzing [n 103] at 606 et seq.).

[378] For a general analysis see Benzing (n 103) at 613 et seq.; for a similar distinction Seils/Wierda (n 21) at 6; see also Cárdenas (n 365) at 138 et seq.; for a concrete proposal and analysis of

conceded in processes of transition are more a problem of unwillingness than inability,[379] at least if one construes "inability" strictly in the sense of a lack of the physical or substantial capacity.[380]

43. *Unwillingness* is demonstrated, for example, if the proceedings are undertaken "for the purpose of shielding the person concerned from criminal responsibility" (para. 2 [a]). The notion "purpose" suggests a subjective interpretation in the sense of the specific state intention or objective to protect the individual responsible from (criminal) justice.[381] This intention constitutes, at the same time, an expression of bad faith of the state concerned with regard to the intention to bring the responsible to justice. Indeed, *mala fide* lies at the core of the unwillingness test.[382] While an amnesty may demonstrate such bad faith, this is not always and necessarily the case.[383] Imagine a situation where a state pursues the higher objective of peace and it grants, in good faith, an amnesty as a necessary means to achieve this higher end; then such a "bad faith purpose" cannot be assumed.[384] Similarly, if one recognizes the right to a peaceful transition it would be contradictory to argue that the unwillingness to jeopardize this transition demonstrates unwillingness in the sense of Art. 17.[385] In sum, the fact that impunity will be a certain side effect of an exemption measure is not *per se* sufficient to qualify this measure as pursuing the overall negative purpose.[386] In any case, while subpara. (a) of Art. 17 (2) clearly

inability criteria with regard to the DRC see Burke-White (n 80) at 576 et seq. who suggests (at 576) four criteria "to judge the effectiveness of judicial systems in states recovering from a total or substantial judicial collapse", namely availability of experienced and unbiased judicial personnel, a viable legal infrastructure, adequate operative law and a sufficient police capability. For Arsanjani/Reisman (n 108) at 329, inability exists if "the judical system (...) is unable to obtain the accused or the necessary evidence and testimony or (is) otherwise unable to carry out its proceedings".

379 Cf. Gropengießer/Meißner (n 60) at 282 et seq.; Werle (n 16) mn 193; Kreicker (n 21) at 305. For a different view Pichon (n 342) at 195 arguing that "amnesties have to be subsumed in general under the notion of unavailability, since it would contradict the whole purpose of an amnesty if it could easily be lifted in a concrete case".

380 If, on the other hand, inability is interpreted to include also unavailability in the human rights sense, i.e., a lack of an effective judicial remedy (for this broader interpretation for example Meißner [n 368] at 87 arguing that a functioning judiciary exists but it cannot deal with the particular case for normative or factual reasons; also Benzing [n 103] at 614: "capacity overload") an exemption measure within the framework of transitional justice may be considered as an indicator of unavailability (in this sense O'Shea [n 260] at 126 arguing that a failure to prosecute based on amnesty would amount to an inablility to prosecute owing to the unavailability of the state's national judicial system; for inability due to a blanket amnesty also Burke-White [n 80] at 582). Against this broad interpretation, however, runs the Spanish version of the Statute referring, regarding inability, to the lack of a national judiciary ("carece de ella").

381 Cárdenas (n 46) at 115–6. For Schabas (n 21) at 18 et seq. the Ugandan self-referral has been an unwillingness issue from the outset "self-referral will only work" (for states) "if it can be followed by self-deferral" (at 22).

382 Cárdenas (n 46) at 113.

383 For this strict view however Cárdenas (n 46) at 117, 164, 183, 184; id. (n 156) 130.

384 Seibert-Fohr (n 21) at 570.

385 But see Gavron (n 64) at 111–2.

386 Stricter Cárdenas (n 156) at 131 arguing that impunity as certain "collateral damage" must be considered part of the purpose.

calls for a subjective interpretation, subparas. (b) and (c) must be interpreted more objectively.[387] Although the notion of "intent", present in both subparas., normally carries a subjective meaning it must be read in context and this context, referring to such objective criteria like "unjustified delay",[388] independence and impartiality[389] and the "circumstances", implies an overall objective interpretation. Also, the term "*genuinely*" (para. [1] [a], [b]) – "the least objectionable word" – was inserted to give the unwillingness/inability test a more concrete and objective meaning[390] and implies good faith and seriousness on the part of the state concerned with regard to investigation and prosecution.[391] It would be difficult to argue, for example, that a state, which opts for an effective TRC with the ultimate goal of peace in mind, is "genuinely" unwilling.[392] If the TRC, being an "effective" one, is independent and impartial the assumption of unwillingness would even contradict para. (2) (c) since unwillingness presupposes a lack of independence and impartiality. Also, if one defends a broad concept of justice, as does this author (para. 2), a quasi-judicial procedure with a possibility of a criminal sanction would suffice to "bring the person concerned to justice" within the meaning of para. (2) (b) and (c).[393]

Possible Scenarios

44. The preceding analysis shows that a national exemption measure (esp. an amnesty) as such does not make a case inadmissible;[394] rather, the admissibility depends on the specific content and conditions of the measure. Five *scenarios* may be distinguished:

- A blanket self-amnesty
- A conditional amnesty with a TRC

---

[387] Benzing (n 103) at 610.

[388] For an objective interpretation insofar El Zeidy (n 72) at 901. An "unjustified" delay requires more than an "undue" delay and for this very reason the former term was preferred (Benzing [n 103] at 610–1). The general standard may be taken from the due process rules of human rights instruments (ibid.), a delay may be "unjustified" in particular if it could have been avoided if the respective state organs had employed the adequate care (cf. Cárdenas [n 46] at 119–20). Pichon (n 342) at 195 determines a delay with a view to similiar national proceedings.

[389] Here, again (supra n 377), it must be observed that subpara. (c) only refers to cases where the lack of independence and impartiality plays in favour of the accused and thus would lead to impunity (cf. Benzing [n 103] at 612–3 and Pichon [n 342] at 193–4, 196).

[390] Cf. Holmes (n 367) at 50; id (n 376) at 674; see also El Zeidy (n 72) at 900; Cárdenas (n 46) at 110.

[391] Holmes (n 376) at 674; Benzing (n 103) 605; Cárdenas (n 46) at 110.

[392] Seibert-Fohr (n 21) at 570.

[393] Stahn (n 64) at 716, 719; see also Expert paper complementarity, para. 73: "some form of punishment".

[394] French Conseil Constitutionnel, supra note 265; conc. Gropengießer/Meißner (n 60) at 282; for the same result also Seibert-Fohr (n 21) at 571, 573, 586; Stahn (n 64) at 709–10. See also Schlunck (n 30) at 260 arguing that complementarity is to be interpreted to allow national conflict settlement structures. For a stricter view Cárdenas (n 156) at 129 et seq.

- A conditional amnesty without a TRC
- Measures not amounting to full exemptions
- Ex post exemptions, in particular pardons

45. A *blanket self-amnesty* ("Chilean model") would be *a limine* against the spirit and *raison d'être* of the ICC Statute.[395] It would not fulfil any of the requirements of Art. 17 (1) (a) or (b):[396] There would be neither an investigation[397] nor a decision to prosecute, since the amnesty would bar any investigation and, consequently, the possibility of a prosecution. In addition, as such a measure would constitute "prima facie evidence of unwillingness or inability",[398] it may be interpreted as a "decision (...) for the purpose of shielding" the beneficiaries of the amnesty within the meaning of Art. 17 (2) (a).[399]

46. A *conditional amnesty with a TRC* ("South African model") is a more difficult case.[400] If one follows the broad interpretation of *investigation* suggested here (para. 40) a quasi-judicial investigation by an effective TRC, which fulfils the criteria set out above (para. 16), can be considered an investigation in the sense of the first requirement of Art. 17 (1) (b).[401] If, in addition, the TRC has the option to decide in favour or against *prosecution*, i.e., if it possesses the power to deny an amnesty (para. 40), be it that the crimes committed by the person concerned are too serious, be it that his/her performance before the Commission and in front of the victims is not considered satisfactory or that for any other reasonable and independent assessment he/she does not deserve the exemption measure, the second requirement is also fulfilled.[402] As to the third requirement, the matter is more complicated and the ultimate decision depends on the circumstances of each case[403]

[395] Robinson (n 31) at 505; Seibert-Fohr (n 21) at 557–8.

[396] Robinson (n 31) at 501; Seibert-Fohr (n 21) at 563 et seq., 588; Stahn (n 46) at 461; Cárdenas (n 46) at 73, 159; id. (n 156) at 129; Werle (n 17) mn 215; Wierda/Unger (n 80) at 278 et seq.; Cárdenas (n 356) at 148.

[397] El Zeidy (n 72) at 940, 942; Robinson (n 31) at 503; Seibert-Fohr (n 21) at 565; Gropengießer/Meißner (n 60) at 283. See also supra note 371 and text.

[398] Dugard (n 64) 1014; Dugard (n 60) at 702; Nsereko (n 322) at 119; Expert paper complementarity, para. 73 and annex 4; for the same result regarding Chile Gavron (n 64) at 113.

[399] Gavron (n 64) at 111; Robinson (n 31) at 501; Cárdenas (n 46) at 159 et seq.; Gropengießer/Meißner (n 60) at 285.

[400] Unclear Scharf (n 54) at 525 and Van der Voort/Zwanenburg (n 60) at 330 arguing, on the one hand, that a truth commission constitutes "a genuine investigation" and, on the other, that the obligation to bring a person to justice may require "criminal proceedings". Against an ICC intervention the former UN Secretary General Kofi Annan, stating that "No one should imagine that it [the ICC Statute] would apply to a case like South Africa's, where the regime and the conflict which caused the crimes have come to an end, and the victims have inherited power (speech at the University of Witwatersrand, as quoted in Villa-Vicencio [n 21] at 222). Murphy (n 193) at 49 calls for a "well-tailored truth commission with similar characteristics to a criminal trial". For Cárdenas (n 356) at 155 the case may still be admissible before the ICC.

[401] Robinson (n 31) at 501; Cárdenas (n 156) at 135; Wouters et al. (n 261) at 293 (refering to the original electronic version of this study).

[402] Robinson (n 31) at 501.

[403] Similarly Werle (n 16) at 66 (mn 192); Cárdenas (n 46) at 179; id. (n 156) at 135–6; conc. Robinson (n 348) at 146.

with due consideration to the proportionality test (para. 19 et seq.) and the criteria regarding conditional amnesties (para. 28) and an effective TRC (para. 16).[404] If, for example, a TRC is independent and impartial this can be considered – based on Art. 17 (2) (c) *a contrario* – as an indicium of willingness and, therefore, an argument against admissibility.[405] Further, one may differentiate according to the nature of the amnesty decision:[406] If it is decided on an individual basis, like in the South African case, each individual decision must be examined in the light of Art. 17 (2) and (3); if it is decided generally with regard to a number of persons and crimes the decision is comparable to a (general) amnesty and as such indicates unwillingness, although the final assessment depends, as always, on the circumstances of the concrete case. In sum, one may conclude that a conditional amnesty with a TRC results in inadmissibility only in exceptional cases, namely only if an effective TRC grants an amnesty on an individual basis under certain strict conditions.

47. From the preceding conclusion follows, *a fortiori*, with regard to a *conditional amnesty without a TRC* that it will hardly ever meet the requirements of Art. 17 (1) (b). First, it is difficult to imagine an effective enforcement of conditions attached to an amnesty without an effective TRC. To be sure, it is perfectly possible to attach conditions to an amnesty independent of the existence of a TRC, for example, a full confession of the crimes committed. However, it is more difficult to enforce these conditions for individual state organs, for example, a prosecutor or an investigating judge, without the public support, resources and legitimacy of an effective TRC. While the investigation and decision to prosecute requirements may be complied with even by the said individual organs if they are able to carry out an investigation in order to, for example, verify a confession, and to take a decision to prosecute in case of non-compliance with the condition(s) (for example, only partial or/and false confession), the absence of an effective TRC deprives the process of the most important alternative justice element and cannot be compensated by other alternative mechanisms (para. 17), at least as far as these are only consequentialist as, e.g., non-criminal sanctions. In fact, only alternative forms of traditional (non-western) justice may be compared to an effective TRC if they enjoy broad legitimacy and guarantee adequate participation and publicity.

48. Other (collective) *measures not amounting to full exemptions*, e.g., a considerable (conditional) mitigation of punishment in the course of a peace deal, do, in principle, meet the requirements of Art. 17 (1) (b). If we take the "Colombian model" (supra para. 22) as an example both the investigation and the prosecution requirements are certainly met since the mitigation of punishment does neither preclude an investigation nor a prosecution. On the contrary, sticking to the letter of the law, the benefits contained therein are dependent on the cooperation (*versión libre*) of the members of the armed groups; if they do not meet their cooperation obligations they may be subjected, at least theoretically, to a normal criminal process. As to the unwillingness or inability test, the outcome depends on the

[404] See also Robinson (n 31) at 501–2.

[405] See also Cárdenas (n 46) at 179.

[406] See Cárdenas (n 46) at 179.

seriousness of the government's commitment to, on the one hand, peace as the ultimate goal of the process and, on the other, justice for the victims as far as is possible without seriously endangering the former. The government's commitment may be measured, inter alia, by the comprehensiveness of the measure, i.e., whether it is designed to reach out to all groups involved in the conflict or whether it privileges one group in particular and, therefore, implies unwillingness with regard to this group.[407] As to the proportionality test, the Colombian Constitutional Court has considered the law as proportional and therefore compatible with the constitution provided that certain improvements with regard to victims rights are made (supra para. 22). From a purely normative perspective this verdict can hardly be criticized, yet it does not relieve the government from taking recourse with more determination to alternative mechanisms of justice, in particular an effective TRC and non-punitive sanctions.[408] Without such mechanisms it is difficult to reconcile such a demobilization process with the justice interest. In addition, it is difficult to imagine that, especially without an effective TRC, the practice of such a process can live up to the normative pretensions following from international and/or national law.

49. It is also conceivable that an investigation and prosecution takes place, i.e., the two first requirements of Art. 17 (1) (a) and (b) are met, but the *case* will subsequently be closed; or the person will be accused but then acquitted or he/she will even be convicted and sentenced but then (immediately) pardoned or the execution of the sentence will be suspended. In all these cases of *ex post exemptions*, the admissibility would depend on the third requirement, i.e., either the trial was not "genuine" in the sense of Art. 17 (1) (a), (b) and/or the proceedings have been undertaken to shield the person from criminal responsibility (Art. 17 [2] [a]), and/or the proceedings were not conducted with the intent / in a manner to bring the person to justice (Art. 17 [2] [b], [c]). In the case of a full court trial, in addition, Art. 17 (1) (c) in connection with Art. 20 (3) would be applicable but that would only lead – by way of Art. 20 (3) – to the same unwillingness criteria contained in Art. 17 (2) (a), (c),[409] albeit from a different ("after trial") perspective.[410] In any event, in all these cases it is difficult to assume the admissibility of the proceedings before the ICC since this would presuppose a quite harsh value judgement about the respective national system, namely that it is acting in bad faith to save the perpetrators from real punishment.[411] The more advanced the proceedings are the more difficult will it be to make such a bad faith argument. In any event, it can only convincingly be made if a clear "impunity intention" on the part of the responsible state organs can be demonstrated; this would, for example, not be possible if there was a regime change and the regime granting the exemption is completely different from the one in power during trial.[412]

---

407 See also Stahn (n 64) at 714–5.

408 See supra para. 20 with n 214 and 215.

409 Gropengießer/Meißner (n 60) at 285–86.

410 See on Art. 20 (3) (a) and (b) in particular Cárdenas (n 46) at 138 et seq.

411 See Holmes (n 390) at 50, 77; El Zeidy (n 72) at 901.

412 See also Schabas (2008) at 184; El Zeidy (n 72) at 944–5.

3.3 Intervention by the Security Council (Art. 16)

50. Art. 16 allows the Security Council to hold an investigation or prosecution on the basis of a resolution under Chapter VII of the UN Charter, i.e., in order to prevent a situation identified as a threat to or breach of the peace (Art. 39, 40 UN Charta). Thus, the Council may, by such a decision, lend international validity to a national peace process with an amnesty or other exemption measure for a limited period of time;[413] it could also stay proceedings which under Art. 17 would be considered admissible.[414] It must not be overlooked, however, that the decision remains a decision to *suspend* the proceedings and as such cannot be interpreted as a deference to the national exemption measure.[415] In addition, the ICC would not necessarily be bound by such a decision for it is not part of the UN system[416] and decides autonomously about its jurisdiction, i.e., it possesses *Kompetenz-Kompetenz*[417] (para. 34). More importantly, the Court cannot be forced to accept a measure which would eventually go against its duty to prosecute the international crimes which are part of its subject-matter jurisdiction.[418] For all these reasons, it can be said that the Court has the power to *indirectly* review the Council's decision.[419]

3.4 Interests of Justice, Art. 53 (1) (C), (2) (C)

51. There is a strong strand in the doctrine which argues that the interests of justice clause in Art. 53 (1) (c) and (2) (c) is the most explicit gateway of the ICC Statute

---

[413] See Scharf (n 54) at 523–24; Seibert-Fohr (n 21) at 583; Van der Voort/Zwanenburg (n 60) at 329; Robinson (n 31) at 503; Ssenyonjo (n 174) at 378 seq.; Gropengießer/Meissner (n 60) at 288–89 even admitting direct Security Council amnesties under chapter VII of the Charter which would be binding for the Court (289 et seq.). Crit. Dugard (n 64) at 1014 arguing that "it is difficult to contemplate a situation in which refusal to recognize a national amnesty could constitute a threat to international peace". HRW, 2005, at 7 et seq. wants to reserve the right to let "concerns about a peace process (...) trump prosecutorial efforts" exclusively to the SC. HRW Memorandum 2007 at 10 "believes" that "an article 16 deferral of the ICC's investigation or prosecution of LRA suspects would be inappropriate".

[414] Seibert-Fohr (n 21) at 589; see also Bergsmo/Pejić in Triffterer (ed.) 2008, Art. 16 mn 11 et seq.

[415] But see Scharf (n 54) at 522; convincingly against this view Gavron (n 64) 109; Stahn (n 64) at 698–9, 717. See also Seils/Wierda (n 21) at 8–9: only stay of proceedings, no de facto amnesty.

[416] Cf. Art. 4 (1) ICC Statute and Art. 48 (2), 103 UN Charta according to which the obligations arising out of SC resolutions are to UN members addressed only (see also Stahn [n 64] at 701 with note 19).

[417] See also Scharf (n 54) at 523; Stahn (n 64) at 700–01 with further references; against this view Seibert-Fohr (n 21) at 584 conceding the Security Council a "margin of appreciation"; for a more Security Council friendly view also Benzing (n 103) at 626–7 but admitting that it must not ignore the ICC's competence with regard to complementarity.

[418] See also Scharf (n 54) at 523–24; Seils/Wierda (n 21) at 9; Gropengießer/Meissner (n 60) at 291–92 conceding that the Security Council itself is bound by an eventual duty to prosecute international crimes; similarly Stahn (n 64) at 717.

[419] See also Schabas (n 412) at 84; conc. El Zeidy (n 72) at 966.

for the recognition of alternative processes of national reconciliation, including the granting of an amnesty or other exemption measures.[420] Another view doubts that Art. 53 is the appropriate legal basis for this scenario and argues that the interests of justice clause does not provide for additional criteria which would go beyond Art. 17. Consequently, it is affirmed that "it can hardly be argued that the prosecution is not in the interests of justice" if the case is admissible under Art. 17.[421] Another, even more restrictive view argues that the object and purpose of the ICC Statute (the fight against impunity) and the use of "interests of justice" in other provisions of the ICC and other Statutes[422] indicate that the non-investigation/prosecution cannot be based on considerations of TJ.[423] While these latter views deserve much credit in trying to overcome the broad prosecutorial discretion built into the interests of justice clause (below para. 52) and a possible political interference by limiting the legal analysis to the more precise criteria of Art. 17, they are difficult to reconcile with the wording of Art. 53 and the sheer existence of the interests of justice clause. It would appear that the drafters of the ICC Statute wanted to give the Prosecutor – admittedly without having a unanimous definition of "interests of justice"[424] – an additional instrument to exercise his discretion going beyond the rather "technical" Art. 17.[425] Indeed, there could be situations, which would be considered admissible under Art. 17 and therefore could only be taken away from the ICC, if at all, by recourse to the interests of justice clause. Take for example the scenario that a TRC undertakes an investigation which can never lead to a prosecution since this possibility is precluded by an amnesty. Such a TRC investigation would not correspond to the investigation requirement of Art. 17 (1) (b) because there is no true option for the TRC to decide in favour of a prosecution (para. 40–41), i.e., the case would be admissible and the only way to avoid an interference with the TRC's ongoing work would be – apart from an intervention of the Security Council (Art. 16) – a recourse to the interests of justice clause.[426]

---

[420] Dugard (n 64) at 1014; Dugard (n 60) at 702; Wouters et al. (n 261) at 292; Goldstone/Fritz (n 21) at 656, 662; Mallinder (n 65) at 218 et seq., Robinson (n 31) at 486; Olásolo (n 31) at 111 referring to a TRC; Brubacher (n 21) at 81–2 referring to post-conflict reconciliation processes; Seils/Wierda (n 21) at 12 ("most direct significance to mediators"); Meyer (n 177) at 579; less emphatic Scharf (n 54) at 524.

[421] Seibert-Fohr (n 21) at 578 et seq.

[422] See HRW, 2005, at 6 referring to Art. 55 (2) (c), 61, 65, 67 ICC Statute and (in n 17) to Statutes of earlier International Criminal Tribunals where the notion was always understood in the sense of a fair administration of justice.

[423] See HRW, 2005, at 4 et seq. stating at 4–5 that "the prosecutor may not fail to initiate an investigation or decide not to proceed with the investigation because of national efforts, such as truth commissions, national amnesties, or traditional reconciliation methods, or because of concerns regarding an ongoing peace process (...)". Similarly Kourabas (n 243) 69–79 (at 79) argues that "prosecution is required without an exception for amnestys".

[424] Cf. HRW, 2005, at 3–4 with further references.

[425] Olásolo (n 31) at 135 et seq. even argues that the drafters of the ICC Statute have with the interests of justice clause granted unlimited political discretion to the Prosecutor "through the back-door", unmaking the core policy choices against impunity of the Preamble (at 149).

[426] See also Robinson (n 348) at 145.

52. Clearly, whether one likes it or not, there is no other clause in the ICC Statute allowing so explicitly for policy considerations.[427] In particular Art. 15 only provides for an evidentiary test ("reasonable basis to proceed") but does not imply a value judgement as to the appropriateness of an amnesty.[428] In any case, it would go too far to construe the interests of justice clause as granting an "unlimited political discretion"[429] as to a possible amnesty exception.[430] While Art. 53 para. 1 (c) may be distinguished from para. 2 (c) in that the former construes "interests of justice" as an autonomous criterion separate to the other criteria (e.g., gravity of the offence), i.e., as an element which may "nonetheless" (para. 1 [c]) lead to a non-investigation decision, and para. 2 (c) construes "interests of justice" as an element of the "circumstances of the case",[431] this distinction does not convert "interests of justice" in a fully free-standing element but it still refers – extrinsically or intrinsically – to the legal criteria mentioned, i.e., the gravity of the crime, the interests of victims, the age or infirmity of the alleged offender and the role of the perpetrator in the alleged crime (cf. para. [1] [c] and [2] [c]).[432] These criteria, in turn, make clear that the Prosecutor has to take a legally substantiated decision in each individual case and cannot just invoke general policy considerations in their own right; otherwise, he could indeed "risk being mired in making political judgements that would ultimately undermine his work" (or more exactly: his authority) and be subjected "to enormous political pressures and attempted manipulations by governments and rebel groups".[433] Also, the Prosecutor has to take into account the legal situation and debate on the admissibility of amnesties or other exempting measures in the course

[427] Cf. Arsanjani (n 21) at 67: "broad range of possibilities". See also Goldstone/Fritz (n 21) at 662–3; Brubacher (n 21) at 80 et seq. (at 81: "broader interests of the international community"); Meyer (n 177) at 580; Murphy (n 193) 43. Gallavin (2003) 14 KCLJ 179, at 195, 197 draws a comparison to the "public interest" criterion in English and Welsh law and arguing that while the Prosecutor must be independent she must at the same time be aware of the political realities (on this parallel see also Brubacher [n 21] at 80 arguing at 95 that prosecutorial "discretion must exclude partisan politics, but not the more statesmanlike politics of persuading state compliance"; Seils/Wierda [n 21] at 12).

[428] Cf. Seibert-Fohr (n 21) at 581–2 convincingly against Dugard (n 64) at 1,014 who argues that the Prosecutor can decline to proceed under Art. 15 because of the existence of a national amnesty. Only the reconsideration of a case by the Prosecutor according to Art. 15 (5) (see also Art. 53 [4]) implicitly confers upon him political discretion (cf. Olásolo [n 31] 128 et seq.).

[429] See Olásolo (n 31) at 110–11, 135 et seq., esp. 141 distinguishing (at 110–11) between a limited discretion regarding the goals to be achieved with the prosecutorial decision and an unlimited discretion regarding the convenience of a prosecution with a view to these goals; Olásolo critically concludes that the combination gives "the broadest possible scope of political discretion".

[430] In the same vein Stahn (n 64) at 717–8.

[431] Cf. Gallavin (n 427) at 185 et seq. distinguishing between an external/extrinsic and internal/intrinsic interpretation with regard to para. 1 (c) and para. 2 (c) of Art. 53 and giving para. 1 (c) precedence over para. 2 (c) (at 187). For HRW, 2005, at 19 para. 2 (c) gives a broader discretion than para. 1 (c).

[432] For a very helpful elaboration of these criteria on the basis of the case law of the ICTY and ICTR see HRW, 2005, at 16 et seq., 23–4; OTP, Policy paper interests of justice, September 2007, at 4 et seq.; Bergsmo/Kruger in Triffterer (ed.) 2008, Art. 53 mn 29–30 with 19–23.

[433] HRW, 2005, at 14. See also Bergsmo/Kruger in Triffterer (ed.) 2008, Art. 53 mn 22–23.

of peace processes (para. 7 et seq., 23 et seq.) for he is bound by the international *lex lata* by way of Art. 21 ICC Statute.[434] Last but not least, the possibility[435] of a *proprio motu* judicial review by the PTC of a non-prosecution decision based on a lack of interests of justice (Art. 53 [3] [b])[436] clearly shows that the Prosecutor has no *unfettered* discretion; indeed, while the PTC must not replace the prosecutorial discretion by its own, it is entrusted to review the legality of the Prosecutor's decision.[437]

53. The notion of *justice* in the interests of justice clause is the same broad one defended throughout this paper (para. 2). Thus, "justice" does not focus only on the case itself[438] or is limited to criminal justice but encompasses alternative forms of justice (para. 12 et seq.) and entails an overall assessment of the situation taking into account peace and reconciliation as the ultimate goals of every process of transition.[439] Most scholars, therefore, stress the Prosecutor's discretion in striking the right balance, he shall decide on a case by case basis whether the formal initiation of an investigation (Art. 53 [1]) or prosecution (Art. 53 [2]), independent of the admissibility of the case, would jeopardize higher justice interests in the broad sense.[440] Yet, it must not be overlooked that taking into account the possible (negative) consequences of criminal prosecution implies speculating about hypothetical, future events and therefore is fraught with insecurity. In addition, as in the similar worse abuses argument, the state is vulnerable to blackmail (para. 3). Apart from that, the notion of justice, even in its broad sense, is difficult to reconcile with the total absence of justice, e.g., by deference to a national exemption measure without mechanisms of compensation. In other words, the interests of justice clause can only be invoked if the reason(s) which cause the Prosecutor to abstain from investigation

---

434 See also Gropengießer/Meißner (n 60) at 297; OTP (n 432) at 8 et seq.

435 The PTC is not obliged but "may" review the prosecutorial decision (Art. 53 [3] [b], see also Rule 109 RPE granting the PTC a period of 180 days to decide on the review).

436 See also Robinson (n 31) at 487–8; Brubacher (n 21) 86–7; Seils/Wierda (n 21) at 5; HRW, 2005, at 4; Gropengießer/Meißner (n 60) at 297–8; Schabas (n 21) at 31; very critical on the judicial review mechanisms Olásolo (n 31) at 142–3.

437 Cf. Gropengießer/Meißner (n 60) at 299; Wouters et al. (n 261) at 292; OTP (n 432) at 3; Bergsmo/Kruger in Triffterer (ed.) 2008, Art. 53 mn 38.

438 Gavron (n 64) at 110.

439 See also Goldstone/Fritz (n 21) at 662; Robinson (n 31) at 488; Meyer (n 177) at 579.

440 See for example Stahn (n 64) at 698 arguing that abstinence from (immediate) prosecution may be allowed if otherwise reconciliation would be seriously put a risk; or Gropengießer/Meißner (n 60) at 296, arguing that it is "possible to suspend the punishment even of serious offences in favour of higher-priority-interests" (similarly Van der Voort/Zwanenburg [n 60] at 329–30) or, at 297 that the Prosecutor makes "his *own* decision on prognosis and balance" (emphasis in the original). See also OTP (n 432) stating, on the one hand, that "the broader matter of international peace and security is not the responsibility of the Prosecutor; it falls within the mandate of other institutions" (at 9) and, on the other, "fully" endorsing "the complementary role that can be played by domestic prosecutions, truth seeking, reparations programs, institutional reform and traditional justice mechanisms in the pursuit of a broader justice" and ensuring "that all efforts are as complementary as possible in developing a comprehensive approach" (at 8). For considerations governing the timing of indictments see Wierda/Unger (n 80) at 266 et seq.

and prosecution can really be traced back or are linked to justice interests, i.e., if the abstention really serves these (broad) justice interests.[441]

Acknowledgements I thank my research assistants Ignaz Stegmiller and Ousman Njikam as well as my student research assistant Katrin Isabel Müller for helping in the preparation of this study. I also thank Miguel Lamadrid for helping in the research of the case law of the IACHR and Ms. Lydia Löhner for updating the study. I finally thank Dr. Louise Mallinder and Judith Large for a final language revision.

List of Literature and Other Materials Used

Books

Alexy R (1985) *Theorie der Grundrechte*. Nomos, Baden-Baden

Ambos K (1997) *Straflosigkeit von Menschenrechtsverletzungen*. Edition iuscrim, Freiburg i. Br. (available at www.mpicc. de/ww/de/pub/forschung/publikationen/straf/s60.htm accessed 23 October 2008)

Ambos K (1999) *Impunidad y derecho penal internacional*. 2nd edn. Ad Hoc, Buenos Aires

Ambos K (2008) *Internationales Strafrecht*. 2nd edn. Beck, München

Ambos K, Othman M (eds) (2003) *New approaches in international criminal justice: Kosovo, East Timor, Sierra Leone and Cambodia*. Edition iuscrim, Freiburg i. Br

Ambos K, Malarino E (eds) (2003) *Persecución Penal Nacional de Crímenes Internacionales en América Latina y España*. Konrad-Adenauer-Stiftung, Montevideo

Ambos K, Malarino E, Woischnik J (eds) (2006) *Dificultades jurídicas y políticas para la ratificación o implementación del Estatuto de Roma de la Corte Penal Internacional*. Konrad-Adenauer-Stiftung, Montevideo

Ambos K, Malarino E (eds) (2008) *Juriprudencia Latinoamericana sobre derecho penal internacional*. Konrad Adenauer Stiftung/Temis, Montevideo/Bogotá

Bassiouni C (1999) *International criminal law*. Transnational, Ardsley

Bassiouni C (2005) *The legislative history of the international criminal court, vol. 1*. Transnational, New York

Bassiouni C (ed) (2002) *Post-conflict justice*. Transnational, Ardsley

Behrendt U (2005) *Die Verfolgung des Völkermords in Ruanda durch internationale und nationale Gerichte*. BWV, Berlin

Boraine A (2001) *A country unmasked, inside South Africa's truth and reconciliation commission*. Oxford University Press, Oxford

von Braun L (2008) *Internationalisierte Strafgerichte*. BWV, Berlin

Brenner M, Klein F, Mangoldt H, Starck C (2005) *Kommentar zum Grundgesetz*. 5th edn. Vahlen, München

Cassese A (2003) *International criminal law*. Oxford University Press, Oxford

Calvo-Goller KN (2006) *The trial proceedings of the international criminal court*. Martinus Nijhoff, Leiden

---

441 Contrary to HRW, 2005, at 19–20 the victims' justice interests cannot be limited to the interests of a criminal prosecution excluding *a limine* their possible interests in peace, traditional reconciliation, etc. It is equally unconvincing to adduce as an additional factor in favour of criminal prosecution the victims' interest in the memory since this can normally be better preserved by a TRC.

Cárdenas C (2005) *Die Zulässigkeitsprüfung vor dem Internationalen Strafgerichtshof.* BWV, Berlin
Cryer R, Friman H, Robinson D, Wilmshurst E (2007) *International criminal law and procedure.* Cambridge University Press, Cambridge
Eser, Sieber, Kreicker (eds) (2003–2006) *Nationale Strafverfolgung völkerrechtlicher Verbrechen/ National prosecution of international crimes*, vols. *I–VII.* Max Planck Institute for Foreign and International Criminal Law, Freiburg i. B.
Ferdinandusse W (2006) *Direct application of international criminal law in national courts.* TMC Asser, The Hague
Frankel M (1989) *Out of the shadows of the night: the struggle for international human rights.* Delacorte, New York
Franzinelli M (2006) *L'Amnistia Togliatti.* Mondadori, Milano
Freeman M (2006) *Truth commissions and procedural fairness.* Cambridge University Press, Cambridge
Garner B (2004) Black's Law Dictionary. 8th edn. West, St. Paul
Hayner PB (2001) *Unspeakable truths.* Routledge, New York
Kant (1797) *Metaphysik der Sitten.* Rechtslehre
Klip A, Sluiter G (eds) (2006) *Annotated leading cases Vol. IX. The special court for Sierra Leone 2003–2004.* Intersentia, Antwerp
Kreicker H (2006) *Völkerstrafrecht im Ländervergleich.* In: Eser/Sieber/Kreicker (eds) *Nationale Strafverfolgung völkerrechtlicher Verbrechen/National Prosecution of International Crimes, vol. 7.* Duncker & Humblot, Berlin
Kritz NJ (ed) (1995) *Transitional justice. vol. I General considerations. vol. II Country studies. vol. III Laws, rulings and reports.* US Institute of Peace Press, Washington DC
Kiza E, Rathgeber C, Rohne H-C (2006) *Victims of war. An empirical study on war-victimization and victims' attitudes towards adressing atrocities.* Hamburger edition online, Hamburg (available at www. his-online.de accessed 23 October 2008)
Mallinder L (2008) *Amnesty, Human Rights and Political Transition.* Hart, Portland
May L (2005) *Crimes against humanity.* Cambridge University Press, Cambridge
Meißner J (2003) *Die Zusammenarbeit mit dem Internationalen Strafgerichtshof nach dem Römischen Statut.* Beck, München
Menzel J, Pierlings T, Hoffmann J (2005) *Völkerrechtsprechung.* Mohr Siebeck, Tübingen
Möller C (2003) *Völkerstrafrecht und IStGH – kriminologische, straftheoretische und rechtspolitische Aspekte.* LitV, Münster
Sánchez A (2004) *Jurisdicción universal penal y derecho internacional.* Tirant lo Blanch, Valencia
O'Shea A (2002) *Amnesty for crime in international law and practice.* Kluwer, The Hague
Sandoz Y, Swinarski C, Zimmermann B (1987) *Commentary on the Additional Protocols of 8 June 1977 to the Geneva Conventions of 12 August 1949.* Martinus Nijhoff, Geneva
Sarkin J (2004) *Carrots and sticks: TRC and the South African amnesty process.* Intersentia, Antwerp, Oxford
Schabas WA (2008) *An introduction to the international criminal court*, 3rd edn. Cambridge University Press, Cambridge
Schilling S (2005) *Gegen das Vergessen.* Peter Lang Verlag, Bern
Schlunck A (2000) *Amnesty versus accountability: third party intervention dealing with gross human rights violations in internal and international conflicts.* Berlin Verlag Spitz, Berlin
Schomburg W, Lagodny O, Gleß S, Hackner T (2006) *Internationale Rechtshilfe in Strafsachen.* Beck, München
Smith W (1875) *Dictionary of Greek and Roman antiquities.* John Murray, London; for the scanned version by the University of Michigan's project see http://www.digital-librarian.com/classics.html (accessed 23 October 2008)
Triffterer O (ed.) (2008) *Commentary on the Rome statute of the international criminal court. observers' notes, article by article.* 2nd edn. Beck, Hart, Nomos, München
Osiel M (1997) *Mass atrocity, collective memory, and the law.* Transaction, New Brunswick
Teitel RG (2000) *Transitional justice.* Oxford University Press, Oxford

Werle G (2005) *Principles of international criminal law*. TMC Asser, The Hague
Werle G (2006) *Justice in transition – prosecution and amnesty in Germany and South Africa*. BWV, Berlin
Werle G (2007) *Völkerstrafrecht*, 2nd edn. Mohr Siebeck Verlag, Tübingen

Articles

Abrams JS, Hayner P (2002) Documenting, acknowledging and publicizing the truth. In: C Bassiouni (ed) *Post-conflict justice*. Transnational, Ardsley, pp 283–293
Abrams J, Morris M (1998) Assessing the efforts to develop international principles or guidelines on accountability. Report of the Rapporteurs' In: Joyner Ch (ed) *Reining in impunity for international crimes and serious violations of fundamental human rights: proceedings of the Siracusa conference 17–21 September 1998*, érès, Toulouse pp 345–348
Aguilar P The timing and the scope of reparation, truth and justice measures: A comparison of the spanish, argentinian and chilean cases. Published in this volume 503–533
Agyemang KA (2004) An overview of Ghana's National Reconciliation Commission and its relationship with the courts. CLF 15:125–134
Allen T (2008) Ritual (ab)use? Problems with traditional justice in northern Uganda. In: Waddell N, Clark P (eds) *Courting conflict? Justice, Peace and the ICC in Africa*. Royal African Society (available at http://www.royalafricansociety.org/index.php?option=com_ content&task=view&id=415, accessed 23 October 2008) pp 47–54
Ambos K (1999) Völkerrechtliche Bestrafungspflichten bei schweren Menschenrechtsverletzungen. AVR 37:318–356
Ambos K, Ruegenberg G, Woischnik J (1998) Straflosigkeit in Argentinien für während der Militärdiktatur (1976–1983) begangene Taten des "Verschwindenlassens"? / Rechtslage für Opfer mit deutscher oder anderer Staatsangehörigkeit. EuGRZ 25:468–479
Ambos K, Steiner C (2001) Vom Sinn des Strafens auf innerstaatlicher und supranationaler Ebene. JuS 9–13
Arsanjani MH (1999) The international criminal court and national amnesty laws. In: *Proceedings of the Ninety-Third Annual Meeting of the American Society of International Law*, pp 65–68
Arsanjani MH, Reisman M (2008) The international criminal court and the Congo: From theory to reality. In: Sadat LN, Scharf MP (eds) *The theory and practice of International Criminal Law – Essays in honor of M. Cherif Bassiouni*. Martinus Nijhoff, Leiden, pp 325–347
Baines EK (2007) The haunting of alice: local approaches to justice and reconciliation in Northern Uganda. IJTJ 1:91–114
Bassiouni C (2002) Accountability for Violations of International Humanitarian Law and Other Serious Violations of Human Rights' In: Bassiouni (ed) *Post-Conflict Justice*. Transnational Publishers, Ardsley, pp 3–54
Bell C The "new law" of transitional justice. Published in this volume 105–127
Benzing M (2003) The complementarity regime of the ICC: International criminal justice between state sovereignity and the fight against impunity. Max Planck Yearbook of United Nations Law 7: 591–632
Benzing M (2008) Sovereignty and the responsibility to protect in international criminal law. In: König D, Stoll PT, Röben V, Matz-Lück N (eds) *International law today: new challenges and the need for reform?* Springer, Heidelberg, pp 17–50
Bergsmo M (1998) The jurisdictional regime of the international criminal court, Part II, Art. 11–19. Eur J Cr, Cr L Cr J 6:29–47
Bickford L (2005) Transitional Justice. In: Shelton D (ed) *The encyclopedia of genocide and crimes against humanity, vol. 3*. Macmillan Reference, New York, pp 1045–1047

Blewitt GT (2008) The importance of a retributive approach to justice. In: Blumenthal D, McCormack T (eds) *The legacy of nuremberg: civilising influence or institutionalised venegance?* Martinus Nijhoff, Leiden, Boston, pp 39–46

Bock S (2007) Das Opfer vor dem Internationalen Strafgerichtshof. ZStW 119:664–680

Boed R (2002) An evaluation of the legality and efficacy of lustration as a tool of transitional justice. In: Bassiouni C (ed) *Post-conflict justice*. Transnational, Ardsley, pp 345–382

Botero C, Restrepo E (2005) Estándares internacionales y procesos de transición en Colombia. In: Rettberg A (ed) *Entre el perdón y el paredón. Preguntas y dilemas de la Justicia Transicional.* Ediciones Uniandes, Bogotá, pp 19–65

Brounéus K Reconciliation and Development. Published in this volume 203–217

Brubacher MR (2004) Prosecutorial discretion within the international criminal court. JICJ 2: 71–95

Buergenthal T (1995) The United Nations Truth Commission for El Salvador. In: Kritz N (ed) *Transitional justice, vol 1*. U.S. Institute of Peace Press, Washington D C, pp 292–325

Burgess P (2004) Justice and reconciliation in East Timor. The relationship between the commission for reception, truth and reconciliation and the courts. CLF 15:135–158

Burke-White WW (2005) Complementarity in practice: The international criminal court as part of a system of multi-level global governance in the Democratic Republic of Congo. LJIL 18: 557–590

Burke-White WW (2008) Implementing a policy of positive complementarity in the Rome System of justice. CLF 19:59–85

Cárdenas C (2006) The admissibility test before the ICC under special considerations of amnesties and truth commissions. In: Kleffner J, Kor G (eds) *Complementary views on complementarity*. Asser, The Hague, pp 115–139

Cárdenas C (2006) The admissibility test before the international criminal court. In: Werle G (ed) *Justice in transition – prosecution and amnesty in Germany and South Africa*. BWV, Berlin, pp 239–255

Cárdenas C (2008) Wann darf der Internationale Strafgerichtshof ermitteln oder verfolgen? Das Verhältnis der internationalen Strafgerichtsbarkeit zu nationalen Gerichten. In: Hankel G (ed) *Die Macht und das Recht. Beiträge zum Völkerrecht und Völkerstrafrecht am Beginn des 21. Jahrhunderts*. HIS Verlagsges, Hamburg, pp 127–156

Cassel D (2005) The expanding scope and impact of reparations awarded by the Inter-American court of human rights. In: de Feyter K, Parmentier S et al (eds) *Out of the ashes*. Intersentia, Antwerpen, pp 191–223

Cassel D (1996) Lessons from the Americas: guidelines for international response to amnesties for atrocities. Law Contemp Probl 59:196–230

Cassese A (1999) The statute of the international criminal court: some preliminary reflections. EJIL 10:144–171

Cassese A (2004) The special court and international law: the decision concerning the lomé agreement amnesty. JICJ 2:1130–1140

Cassin B (2006) Removing the perpetuity of hatred: on South Africa as a model example. ICRC Int Rev 88:235–244

Chaparro A (2005) La función crítica del 'perdón sin soberanía' en procesos de justicia transicional. In: Rettberg A (ed) *Entre el perdón y el paredón. Preguntas y dilemas de la Justicia Transicional*. Ediciones Uniandes, Bogotá, pp 233–257

Clark TH (2005) The prosecutor of the international criminal court, amnesties, and the "interests of justice": striking a delicate balance. Washington Univ Glob Stud Law Rev 4:389–414

Cole EA (2007) Transitional justice and the reform of history education. IJTJ 1:115–137

Crettol M, La Rosa A-M (2006) The missing and transitional justice: the right to know and the fight against impunity. ICRC Int Rev 88:355–362

Crocker DA (2002) Punishment, reconciliation, and democratic deliberation. Buff Crim L Rev 5:509–549

Daly E (2008) Truth skepticism: an inquiry into the value of truth in times of transition. IJTJ 2: 23–41

Damaška M (2004) Negotiating justice in international criminal courts. JICJ 2:1018–1039
Darcy S (2007) Imputed criminal liability and the goals of international justice. LJIL 20:377–404
De Brouwer A-M (2007) Reparation to victims of sexual violence: possibilities at the international criminal court and at the trust fund for victims and their families. LJIL 20:207–237
De Greiff P DDR and Reparations: Establishing links between peace and justice instruments. Published in this volume 321–357
Devereux A, Kent L (2008) Evaluating timor leste's reception, truth and reconciliation comission. In: Blumenthal D, McCormack T (eds) *The legacy of Nuremberg: civilising influence or institutionalised venegance?*. Martinus Nijhoff, Leiden, pp 171–203
Diaz C Colombia's bid for justice and peace. Published in this volume 469–503
Diggelmann O (2007) Staatsverbrechen und internationale Justiz. AVR 45:382–399
Dugard J (2002) Possible conflicts of jurisdiction with truth commissions. In: Cassese A, Geata P, Jones J (eds) *The Rome statute of the international criminal court: a commentary, vol 1.* Oxford University Press, Oxford pp 693–704
Dugard J (1999) Dealing with crimes of a past regime. Is amnesty still an option? LJIL 12: 1001–1015
Duggan C (2005) Prólogo. In: Rettberg A (ed) *Entre el perdón y el paredón. Preguntas y dilemas de la Justicia Transicional.* Ediciones Uniandes, Bogotá, pp 7–12
du Plessis M (2007) Reparations and international law: how are reparations to be determined (past wrong or current effects), against whom, and what form should they take? In: Max du P, Stephen P (eds) *Repairing the past? International perspectives on reparations for gross human rights abuses.* Intersentia, Antewerpen, pp 147–177
Durán Puentes JA La importancia de una ley de lustración para el proceso de justicia transicional. Facetas Penales (Leyer, Colombia) 54:33–38
Elberling B (2008) The next step in history-writing through criminal law: Exactly how tailor-made is the special tribunal for Lebanon? LJIL 21:529–538
El Zeidy MM (2008) The gravity threshold under the statute of the international criminal court. CLF 19:35–57
El Zeidy MM (2002) The principle of complementarity: a new machinery to implement international criminal law. Michigan J Int Law 32:869–975
Fernandez L (2006) Post TRC Prosecutions in South Africa. In: Werle G (ed) *Justice in transition – prosecution and amnesty in Germany and South Africa.* BWV, Berlin, pp 65–81
Filippini L, Magarrell L (2005) Instituciones de la justicia en transición y contexto politico. In: Rettberg A (ed) *Entre el perdón y el paredón. Preguntas y dilemas de la Justicia Transicional.* Ediciones Uniandes, Bogotá, pp 143–168
Fuchs R (2007) A grandes odios, grandes perdones: Vergangenheitspolitik in Uruguay 1985–1986. Lateinamerika Analysen 16:35–67
Gallavin C (2003) Article 53 of the Rome Statute of the International Criminal Court: In the interests of justice? KCLJ 14:179–198
Garcia-Godos (2008) Victim reparations in the peruvian truth commission and the challenge of historical interpretation. IJTJ 2:63–82
Gavron J (2002) Amnesties in the light of developments in international law and the establishment of the international criminal court. ICLQ 51:91–117
Gil Gil A (2003) España. In: Ambos K, Malarino E (eds) *Persecución penal Nacional de Crímenes Internacionales en América Latina y España.* Konrad-Adenauer-Stiftung, Montevideo, pp 335–402
Gil Gil A (2008) España. In: Ambos K, Malarino E (eds) *Juriprudencia Latinoamericana sobre derecho penal internacional.* Konrad Adenauer Stiftung, Temis, Montevideo, Bogotá, pp 471–501
Goetz M (2008) The international criminal court and its relevance to affected communities. In: Waddell N, Clark P (eds) *Courting conflict? Justice, Peace and the ICC in Africa.* Royal African Society. (available at http://www.royalafricansociety.org/index.php?option=com_content&task= view&id=415, accessed 23 October 2008) pp 65–72

Goldstone RJ, Fritz N (2000) In the interests of justice and independent referral: The ICC Prosecutor's unprecedented powers. LJIL 13:655–667

González JL (2003) Uruguay. In: Ambos K, Malarino E (eds) *Persecución penal Nacional de Crímenes Internacionales en América Latina y España*. Konrad-Adenauer-Stiftung, Montevideo, pp 495–534

González JL, Galain P (2008) Uruguay. In: Ambos K, Malarino E (eds) *Juriprudencia Latinoamericana sobre derecho penal internacional*. Konrad Adenauer Stiftung/Temis, Montevideo,Bogotá, pp 307–334

González Cueva E (2004) The contribution of the Peruvian truth and reconciliation commission to prosecutions. CLF 15:55–66

Grono N, O'Brien A (2008) Justice in conflict? The ICC and peace processes. In: Waddell N, Clark P (eds) Courting conflict? Justice, peace and the ICC in Africa. Royal African Society. (available at http://www.royalafricansociety.org/index.php?option=com_content&task=view&id=415, accessed 23 October 2008) pp 13–20

Gropengießer H, Meißner J (2005) Amnesties and the Rome Statute of the international criminal court. ICLR 5:267–300

Guhr AH (2008) Victim participation during the pre-trial stage at the international criminal court. ICLR 8:109–140

Guzmán Dalbora JL (2003) Chile. In: Ambos K, Malarino E (eds) *Persecución penal Nacional de Crímenes Internacionales en América Latina y España*. Konrad-Adenauer-Stiftung, Montevideo, pp 163–200

Guzmán Dalbora JL (2008) Chile. In: Ambos K, Malarino E (eds) *Juriprudencia Latinoamericana sobre derecho penal internacional*. Konrad Adenauer Stiftung, Temis, Montevideo, Bogotá, pp 131–158

Hafner G, Boon K, Rübesame A, Huston J (1999) A response to the American view as presented by Ruth Wedgwood. EJIL 10:108, 109–113

Hamber B (2005) The dilemmas of reparations: In search of a process-driven approach. In: de Feyter K, Parmentier S et al (eds) Out of the ashes. Intersentia, Antwerpen, pp 135–149

Havel BF (2002) Public law and the construction of collective memory. In: Bassiouni (ed) *Post-conflict justice*. Transnational, Ardsley, pp 383–397

Hayner PB (1998) Recording the facts and the truth. Report of the Rapporteur. In: Joyner Ch (ed) *Reining in impunity for international crimes and serious violations of fundamental human rights. Proceedings of the Siracusa conference, érès, Toulouse, 17–21 September 1998*, pp 215–219

Hayner PB (2006) Truth commissions: a schematic overview. ICRC Int Rev 88:295–310

Hazan P (2006) Measuring the impact of punishment and forgiveness: a framework for evaluating transitional justice. ICRC Int Rev 88:19–47

Hemedi C (2008) Unfinished business in Ituri. The Monitor (36):10

Holmes JT (1999) The principle of complementarity. In: Lee RS (ed) The international criminal court: the making of the Rome Statute, Issues, Negotiations, Results. Kluwer Law International, The Hague, pp 41–78

Holmes JT (2002) Complementarity: National courts *versus* the ICC. In: Cassese A, Geata P, Jones J (eds) The Rome Statute of the international criminal court: a commentary, Vol 1. Oxford University Press, Oxford, pp 667–686

Hunt T (2004) Whose truth? objective truth and a challenge for history. CLF 15:193–198

Igreja V Justice and Reconciliation in the aftermath of the civil war in Gorongosa, Mazambique Central. Published in this volume 423–439

Imbleau M (2004) Initial truth establishment by transitional bodies and the fight against denial. CLF 15:159–192

Jelin E (2007) Public memorialization in perspective: truth, justice and memory of past repression in the Southern cone of South America. IJTJ 1:138–156

Jenkins C (2007) Taking apology seriously. In: Max du Plessis, Stephen Peté (eds) *Repairing the past? International perspectives on reparations for gross human rights abuses*. Intersentia, Antwerpen, pp 53–81

Joyner CC (1998) Policy considerations on accountability, peace and justice. Report of the Rapporteur. In Joyner (ed) *Reining in impunity for international crimes and serious violations of fundamental human rights: proceedings of the Siracusa conference, érès, Toulouse, 17–21 September 1998*, pp 37–43

Kemp S (2004) The inter-relationship between the Guatemalan commission for historical clarification and the search for justice in national courts. CLF 15:67–103

Kirchhoff L Linking mediation and Transitional Justice: The use of interest-based-mediation and transitional justice. Published in this volume 237–263

Kourabas M (2007) A Vienna convention interpretation of the "Interest of Justice" provision of the Rome Statute, the legality of domestic amnesty agreements, and the situation in northern Uganda: A "great qualitative step forward", or a normative retreat? Davis J Int L Policy 14: 60–94

Kritz NJ (2002) Progress and humility: the ongoing search for post-conflict justice. In: Bassiouni (ed) Post-conflict justice. Transnational, Ardsley, pp 55–87

Lerner S (2006) Interview with Salomón lerner. ICRC Int Rev 88:225–233

Ludi R (2007) Historical reflections on Holocaust reparations: unfinished business or an example for other reparations campaigns? In: Max du Plessis, Stephen Peté (eds) Repairing the past? International perspectives on reparations for gross human rights abuses. Intersentia, Antwerpen, pp 119–144

Malamud-Goti J (1995) Transitional government in the breach: why punish state criminals? In: Kritz N (ed) *Transitional justice, vol 1.* U.S. Institute of Peace Press, Washington DC, pp 189–202

Malarino E (2003) Argentina. In: Ambos K, Malarino E (eds) Persecución Penal Nacional de Crímenes Internacionales en América Latina y España. Konrad-Adenauer-Stiftung, Montevideo, pp 35–81

Mallinder L Exploring the practice of states in introducing amnesties. Published in this volume 127–175

Mallinder L (2007) Can amnesties and international justice be reconciled? IJTJ 1:208–230

Mamdani M (2007) Amnesty or impunity? a preliminary critique of the report of the truth and reconciliation commission of South Africa. In: Max du Plessis, Stephen Peté (eds) *Repairing the past? International perspectives on reparations for gross human rights abuses*. Intersentia, Antewerpen, pp 83–118

Mani R (2005) Reparation as a component of transitional justice: Pursuing 'reparative justice' in the aftermath of violent conflict. In: de Feyter K, Parmentier S et al (eds) *Out of the ashes*. Intersentia, Antwerpen, pp 53–82

Mattarollo R (2002) Definition and primary objectives: to search for the truth and safeguard the evidence. In: Bassiouni (ed) *Post-conflict justice*. Transnational, Ardsley, pp 295–324

Mattarollo R (2002) The transition to democracy and institution building: the case of Haiti. In: Bassiouni (ed) *Post-conflict justice*. Transnational, Ardsley, pp 763–774

Mattioli G, van Woudenberg A (2008) Global catalyst for national prosecutions? The ICC in the Democratic Republic of Congo. In: Waddell N, Clark P (eds) *Courting conflict? Justice, peace and the ICC in Africa*. Royal African Society. (available at http://www.royalafricansociety.org/index.php?option=com_content&task=view&id=415, accessed 23 October 2008) pp 55–64

Matwijkiw A (2002) A philosophical perspective on rights, accountability and post-conflict justice: setting up the premises. In: Bassiouni (ed) *Post-conflict justice*. Transnational, Ardsley, pp 155–199

Meintjes G (1998) Post-conflict justice issues: restoring order and justice. Report of the Rapporteur. In: Joyner (ed) *Reining in impunity for international crimes and serious violations of fundamental human rights. Proceedings of the Siracusa conference, érès, Toulouse, 17–21 September 1998*, pp 459–463

Méndez JE (1998) The right to truth. In: Joyner Ch (ed) *Reining in impunity for international crimes and serious violations of fundamental human rights. Proceedings of the Siracusa conference, érès, Toulouse, 17–21 September 1998*, pp 255–278

Méndez JE (2001) National reconciliation, transnational justice and the international criminal court. Ethics Int Affairs 15:25–44
Meyer F (2006) Complementing complementarity. ICLR 6:549–583
Moreno-Ocampo L (2007) Transitional justice in ongoing conflicts. IJTJ 1:8–9
Morris M (2002) Lacking a Leviathan: the quandaries of peace and accountability. In: Bassiouni (ed) *Post-conflict justice*. Transnational, Ardsley, 135–153
Murphy R (2006) Establishing a precedent in Uganda: the legitimacy of national amnesties under the ICC. Eyes ICC 3:33–55
Nadery AN (2007) Peace and jusitce? Transitional Justice in Afghanistan.IJTJ 1:173–179
Nakayi R (2008) Is Uganda ready for national trials? The Monitor (36):4
Naqvi Y (2006) The right to the truth in international law: fact or fiction? ICRC Int Rev 88:245–273
Nerlich V (2006) Lessons for the international criminal court: the impact of criminal proceedings on the South African amnesty process. In: Werle G (ed) *Justice in transition – prosecution and amnesty in Germany and South Africa*. BWV, Berlin, pp 55–63
Nino CS (1999) The duty to punish past human rights abuses put into context: The case of Argentina. YLJ 100:2619–2640
Nowak M (2005) Reparation by the human rights chamber for Bosnia and Herzegovina. In: de Feyter K, Parmentier S et al (eds) Out of the ashes. Intersentia, Antwerpen, pp 245–288
Nsereko D, Ntanda D (1999) The ICC: jurisdictional and related issues. CLF 10:87–120
Odio Benito E (1998) Justice for peace: no to impunity. In: Joyner Ch (ed) *Reining in impunity for international crimes and serious violations of fundamental human rights. Proceedings of the Siracusa conference, érès, Toulouse, 17–21 September 1998*, pp 149–153
Olásolo H (2003) The prosecutor of the ICC before the initiation of investigations: A quasi-judicial or a political body? ICLR 3:87–150
Olson LM (2006) Provoking the dragon on the patio. Matters of transitional justice: penal repression vs. Amnesties. ICRC Int Rev 88:275–294
Opotow S (2002) Psychology of impunity and injustice: implications for social reconstruction. In: Bassiouni (ed) Post-conflict justice. Transnational, Ardsley, pp 201–216
Orentlicher DF (2007) Settling accounts revisited: Reconciling global norms with local agency. IJTJ 1:10–22
Orozco I (2005) Reflexiones impertinentes: Sobre la memoria y el olvido, sobre el castigo y la clemencia. In: Rettberg A (ed) *Entre el perdón y el paredón. Preguntas y dilemas de la Justicia Transicional*. Ediciones Uniandes, Bogotá, pp 171–209
O'Shea A (2007) Reparations under international criminal law. In: Max du Plessis, Stephen Peté (eds) *Repairing the past? International perspectives on reparations for gross human rights abuses*. Intersentia, Antewerpen, pp 179–196
Osiel MJ (2000) Why prosecute? Critics of punishment for mass atrocity. HRQ 22:118–147
Otim M, Wierda M (2008) Justice at Juba: international obligations and local demands in northern Uganda. In: Waddell N, Clark P (eds) *Courting conflict? Justice, Peace and the ICC in Africa*. Royal African Society. (available at http://www.royalafricansociety.org/index.php?option=com_content&task=view&id=415, accessed 23 October 2008) pp 21–28
Parenti P (2006) Argentina. In: Ambos K, Malarino E, Woischnik J (eds) *Dificultades jurídicas y políticas para la ratificación o implementación del Estatuto de Roma de la Corte Penal Internacional*. Konrad-Adenauer-Stiftung, Montevideo, pp 49–98
Parenti P (2008) Argentina. In: Ambos K, Malarino E (eds) *Juriprudencia Latinoamericana sobre derecho penal internacional*. Konrad Adenauer Stiftung, Temis, Montevideo, Bogotá, pp 21–66
Pastor DR (2007) Procesos penales sólo para conocer la verdad? Jueces para la democracia 59: 95–126
Peté S, du Plessis M (2007) Reparations for gross violations of human rights in context. In: M du Plessis, S Peté (eds), *Repairing the past? International perspectives on reparations for gross human rights abuses*. Intersentia, Antewerpen, pp 3–28
Pfanner T (2006) Cooperation between truth commissions and the International Committee of the Red Cross. ICRC Int Rev 88:363–373

Pham P, Vinck P (2007) Empirical research and the development and assessment of Transitional Justice mechanisms. IJTJ 1:231–248
Pichon J (2008) The principle of complementarity in the case of the sudanese nationals *Ahmad Harun* and *Ali Kushayb* before the International Criminal Court. ICLR 8:185–228
Poole JL (2002) Post-conflict justice in Sierra Leone. In: Bassiouni C (ed) *Post-conflict justice*. Transnational, Ardsley, pp 563–592
Popkin M (2004) The Salvadorean truth commission and the search for justice. CLF 15:105–124
Posner EA, Vermeule A (2004) Transitional justice as ordinary justice. Harv L Rev 117:761–825
Ralston JH, Finnin S (2008) Investigating international crimes: a review of international law enforcement strategies. In: Blumenthal D, McCormack T (eds) *The legacy of Nuremberg: civilising influence or institutionalised venegance?*. Martinus Nijhoff, Leiden, Boston, pp 47–68
Rettberg A (2005) Reflexiones sobre la relación entre construcción de paz y justicia transicional. In: Rettberg A (ed) *Entre el perdón y el paredón. Preguntas y dilemas de la Justicia Transicional*. Ediciones Uniandes, Bogotá, pp 1–15
Robinson D (2003) Serving the interests of justice: amnesties, truth commissions and the international criminal court. EJIL 14:481–505
Robinson D (2006) Comments on chapter 4 of Claudia Cárdenas Aravena. In: Kleffner J, Kor G (eds) *Complementary views on complementarity*. Asser, The Hague, pp 141–146
Roht-Arriaza N (1998) Truth commissions as part of a social process: possible guidelines. In: Joyner Ch (ed) *Reining in impunity for international crimes and serious violations of fundamental human rights. Proceedings of the Siracusa conference*, érès, Toulouse, 17–21 September 1998, pp 279–284
Roht-Arriaza N (2002) Civil society in processes of accountability. In: Bassiouni C (ed) *Post-conflict justice*. Transnational, Ardsley, pp 97–114
Rombouts H, Vandeginste S (2005) Reparation for victims in Rwanda: caught between theory and practice. In: de Feyter K, Parmentier S et al (eds) *Out of the ashes*. Intersentia, Antwerpen, pp 309–341
Rombouts H, Sardaro P, Vandeginste S (2005) The right to reparation for victims of gross and systematic violations of human rights. In: de Feyter K, Parmentier S et al (eds) *Out of the ashes*. Intersentia, Antwerpen, pp 345–503
Rubio-Marin R, de Greiff P (2007) Women and reparations. IJTJ 1:318–337
Salmón EG (2006) Reflections on international humanitarian law and transitional justice: lessons to be learnt from the Latin American experience. ICRC Int Rev 88:327–353
Sarkin J (2005) Reparations for gross human rights violations as an outcome of criminal versus civil court proceedings. In: de Feyter K, Parmentier S et al (eds) *Out of the ashes*. Intersentia, Antwerpen, pp 151–188
Sarkin J (2006) The amnesty hearings in South Africa revisited. In: Werle G (ed) *Justice in transition – prosecution and amnesty in Germany and South Africa*. BWV, Berlin, pp 43–53
Schabas W (2004) A synergistic relationship: the Sierra Leone truth and reconciliation commission and the special court for Sierra Leone. CLF 15:3–54
Schabas W (2005) Reparation practices in Sierra Leone and the truth and reconciliation commission. In: de Feyter K, Parmentier S et al (eds) *Out of the ashes*. Intersentia, Antwerpen, pp 289–307
Schabas W (2008) Complementarity in Practice: some uncomplimentary thoughts. CLF 19:5–33
Scharf M (1999) The amnesty exception to the jurisdiction of the international criminal court. Cornell Int L J 32:507–527
Scharf M, Rodley N (2002) International law principles on accountability. In: Bassiouni C (ed) *Post-conflict justice*. Transnational, Ardsley, pp 91–96
Schiff BN (2002) Do truth commissions promote accountability or impunity? the case of the South African truth and reconcialition commission. In: Bassiouni C (ed) *Post-conflict justice*. Transnational, Ardsley, pp 325–343
Schotsmans M (2005) 'Victims' expectations, needs and perspectives after gross and systematic human rights violations. In: de Feyter K, Parmentier S et al (eds) *Out of the ashes*. Intersentia, Antwerpen, pp 105–133

Schwartz H (1995) Lustration in Eastern Europe. In: Neil Kritz (ed) *Transitional justice*, vol 1. U.S. Institute of Peace Press, Washington DC, pp 461–483
Seibert-Fohr A (2003) The relevance of the Rome Statute of the ICC for amnesties and truth commissions. Max Planck Yearbook of United Nations Law 7:553–590
Seils P (2002) The limits of truth commissions in the search for justice: an analysis of the truth commissions of El Salvador and Guatemala and their effect in achieving post-conflict justice. In: Bassiouni C (ed) *Post-conflict justice*. Transnational, Ardsley, pp 775–795
Shaw R (2007) Memory frictions: localizing the truth and reconciliation commission in Sierra Leone. IJTJ 1:183–207
Shelton D (2005) The United Nations principles and guidelines on reparations: Context and contents. In: de Feyter K, Parmentier S et al (eds) *Out of the ashes*. Intersentia, Antwerpen, pp 11–32
Simon J-M (2006) Criminal accountability and reconciliation. In: Albrecht H-J, Simon J–M, Rezaei H, Rohne H, Kiza E (eds) Conflicts and conflict resolution in middle eastern societies – between tradition and modernity. Duncker & Humblot, Berlin, pp 99–116
Šimonović I (2004) Dealing with the legacy of past war crimes and human rights abuses. JICJ 2:701–710
Simpson G (2008) One among many: The ICC as a tool of justice during transition. In: Waddell N, Clark P (eds) *Courting conflict? Justice, peace and the ICC in Africa*. Royal African Society (available at http://www.royalafricansociety.org/index.php?option=com_content&task=view&id=415, accessed 23 October 2008) pp 73–80
Sriram CL, Ross A (2007) Geographies of crime and justice: contemporary transitional justice and the creation of zones of impunity. IJTJ 1:45–65
Sriram CL Conflict Mediation and the ICC: challenges and options for pursuing peace with justice at the regional level. Published in this volume 303–321
Stahn C (2008) Complementarity: a tale of two notions. CLF 19:87–113
Slye RC (2002) The legitimacy of amnesties under international law and general principles of Anglo-American law: is a legitimate amnesty possible? Virgina J Int Law 43:173–247
Sooka Y (2006) Dealing with the past and transitional justice: building peace through accountability. ICRC Int Rev 88:311–325
Ssenyonjo M (2007) The international criminal court and the lord's resistance army leaders: prosecution or amnesty? ICLR 7:361–389
Stahn C (2005) Complementarity, amnesties and alternative forms of justice: some interpretative guidelines for the international criminal court. JICJ 3:695–720
Stahn C (2005) The geometry of transitional justice: choices of institutional design. LJIL 18: 425–466
Stahn C, Olásolo H, Gibson K (2006) Participation of victims in the pre-trial proceedings of the ICC. JICJ 4:219–238
Theidon K (2007) Transitional subjects: the disarmament, demobilization and reintegration of former combatants in Colombia. IJTJ 1:66–90
Tomuschat C (2002) The duty to prosecute international crimes committed by individuals. In: Cremer HJ (ed) *Tradition und Weltoffenheit des Rechts, Festschrift für Steinberger*. Springer, Berlin, pp 315–329
Tomuschat C (2007) Reparation in favour of individual victims of gross violations of human rights and international humanitarian law. In: Kohen MG (ed) *Promoting justice, human rights and conflict resolution through international law. Liber Amicorum Lucius Caflisch*. Martinus Nijhoff, Leiden, pp 569–590
Tomuschat C (2002) Reparation for victims of grave human rights violations. Tul J Int Comp L 10:157–184
Torpey J (2002) Making whole what has been smashed: reflections on reparations. In: Bassiouni C (ed) *Post-conflict justice*. Transnational, Ardsley, pp 217–242
Torpey J (2005) Victims and citizens: the discourse of reparation(s) at the dawn of the new millennium. In: de Feyter K, Parmentier S et al (eds) *Out of the ashes*. Intersentia, Antwerpen, pp 35–52

Tutu DM (2007) Reflections on moral accountability. IJTJ 1:6–7
Uprimny R, Saffon MP (2005) Justicia transicional y justicia restaurativa: tensiones y complementariedades. In: Rettberg A (ed) *Entre el perdón y el paredón. Preguntas y dilemas de la Justicia Transicional*. Ediciones Uniandes, Bogotá, pp 211–232
Uvin P, Mirenko C (2003) Western and local approaches to justice in Rwanda. Glob Govern 9: 219–231
Vandeginste S Transitional justice for Burundi: a long and winding road. Published in this volume 393–423
Vandermeersch D (2002) Droit belge. In: Cassese A, Delmas-Marty M (eds) *Juridictions nationales et crimes internationaux*. PUF, Paris, pp 89–97
Van der Voort K, Zwanenburg M (2001) From 'raison d'État' to'état de droit international – Amnesties and the French implementation of the Rome Statute ICLR 1:315–342
Van den Wyngaert C, Ongena T (2002) *Ne bis in idem* principle, including the issue of amnesty. In: Cassese A, Gaeta P, Jones J (eds) *The Rome Statute of the international criminal court: a commentary, vol. 1*. Oxford University Press, Oxford, pp 705–729
Van Zyl P (2002) Unfinished business: the truth and reconciliation commission's contribution to justice in post-apartheid South Africa. In: Bassiouni C (ed) *Post-conflict justice*. Transnational, Ardsley, pp 745–762
Villa-Vincencio C (2000) Why perpetrators should not always be prosecuted: where the international criminal court and truth commissions meet. Emory Law J 49:205–222
Wierda M, Unger T Pursuing justice in ongoing conflict: a discussion of current practice. Published in this volume 263–303
Williams P (1998) Non-criminal civil and political measures for combating impunity for international crimes. Report of the Rapporteur. In: Joyner Ch (ed) *Reining in impunity for international crimes and serious violations of fundamental human rights. Proceedings of the Siracusa conference, érès, Toulouse, 17–21 September 1998*, pp 287–294
Williams P (2002) The role of justice in peace negotiations. In: Bassiouni C (ed) *Post-conflict justice*. Transnational, Ardsley, pp 115–133
Wouters J, Verhoeben S, Demeyere B (2008) The international criminal court's office of the prosecutor: navigating between independence and accountability. ICLR 8:273–318
Young GK (2002) Amnesty and accountability. UC Davis L Rev 35:427–482
Yusuf HO (2007) Travails of truth: achieving justice for victims of impunity in Nigeria. IJTJ 1: 268–286
Zalaquett J (1992) Balancing ethical imperatives and political constraints: the dilemma of new democracies confronting past human rights violations. Hastings Law J 43:1425–1438
Zalaquett J (1989) Confronting human rights violations committed by former governments: Principles applicable and political constraints. In: Aspen Institute (ed) States crimes: punishment or pardon? Aspen Institue, Wye Center, Colorado pp 3–31
Zolo D (2004) Peace through Criminal Law? JICJ 2:727–734

UN Documents[1]

Commission of Human Rights, Question of enforced disappearance, E/CN.4/RES/1994/39, 4.3.1994.
Guidelines for United Nations Representatives on Certain Aspects of Negotiations for Conflict Resolution. Internal Document, without date (quoted as "Guidelines Negotiations").
Human Rights Committee, General Comment No. 20: Replaces general comment 7 concerning prohibition of torture and cruel treatment or punishment (Article 7) (Forty-fourth session, 1992), 10 March 1992 (quoted as "HRC, General Comment 20").

[1] A useful compilation of UN Doc. on TJ can be found in Bassiouni (n 9) at 399–424.

Human Rights Committee, General Comment No. 31 [80], The Nature of the General Legal Obligation Imposed on States Parties to the Covenant, adopted on 29 March 2004 (2,187th meeting), CCPR/C/21/Rev.1/Add.13, 26.5.2004 (quoted as "HRC, General Comment 31").

International Centre for Transitional Justice, UN guidelines meeting, June 9–10, 2005 (quoted as "ICTJ-guidelines").

Office of the United Nations High Commissioner for Human Rights, Making Peace our own – Victims' Perceptions of Accountability, Reconciliation and Transitional Justice in Northern Uganda, 2007 http://www.ohchr.org/english/docs/northern_Uganda_august2007.pdf (last visited 23 October 2008 quoted as "Making Peace our own").

Office of the United Nations High Commissioner for Human Rights, Rule-of-law tools for post-conflict states. Prosecution initiatives, New York & Geneva 2006 (quoted as "Office of the UN High Commissioner for Human Rights Report").

Report of the Secretary General on the Establishment of the Special Court for Sierra Leone, S/2000/915, 4 October 2000.

UN-ECOSOC-Commission on Human Rights, The administration of justice and the human rights of detainees: The question of impunity for perpetrators of human rights violations, Revised final report prepared by Mr. Joinet pursuant to Sub-Commission decision 1996/119, E/CN.4/Sub.2/1997/20/Rev.1, 2 October 1997 (quoted as "Joinet report").

Basic Principles and Guidelines on the Right to a Remedy and Reparation for Victims of Violations of International Human Rights and Humanitarian Law, Annex to UN-ECOSOC-Commission on Human Rights, Civil and Political Rights Including the Question of Independence of the Judiciary, Administration of Justice, Impunity. The Right to Restitution, Compensation and Rehabilitation for Victims of Gross Violations of Human Rights and Fundamental Freedoms. Final Report of the Special Rapporteur, Mr. M. Cherif Bassiouni, submitted in accordance with Commission resolution 1999/33 (quoted as "Basic Principles Victims").

UN Departement of Peace Keeping Operations, Principles and Guidelines, Disarmement, Demobilization and Reintegration of Ex-Combatants in a Peacekeeping Environment, New York: 1999 (quoted as "UN Departement of Peace Keeping Operations").

UN-ECOSOC-Commission on Human Rights, Promotion and Protection of Human Rights. Impunity. Note by the Secretary General, Commission on Human Rights, 60th session, E/CN.4/2004/88, 27 February 2004 (quoted as "UN-ECOSOC, Impunity, 27 February 2004").

UN-ECOSOC-Commission on Human Rights, Promotion and Protection of Human Rights – Impunity, Report of the independent expert to update the Set of principles to combat impunity, Diane Orentlicher, United Nations Economic and Social Council, Commission on Human Rights, 61st session, E/CN.4/2005/102/18 February 2005 (quoted as "Orentlicher impunity principles").

UN Security Council, The rule of law and transitional justice in conflict and post-conflict societies. Report of the Secretary-General, S/2004/616, 23 August 2004 (quoted as "Report Secretary General transitional justice").

ICC Documents

Ministry of Justice and constitutional affairs of Uganda, Answer to "Request for information from the Republic of Uganda on the status of execution of the warrants of arrest", 23 March 2008, (ICC-02/04–01/05–286-Anx2).

Office of the Prosecutor, Policy Paper on the Interests of Justice, September 2007, <www.icc-cpi.int/otp/otp_docs.html> (last visited 23 October 2008 quoted as "policy paper interests of justice").

Office of the Prosecutor, Informal expert paper: the principle of complementarity in practice, 2003 (quoted as "expert paper complementarity").

Office of the Prosecutor, Report on Prosecutorial Strategy, The Hague, 14.09.2006. <www.icc-cpi.int/library/organs/otp/OTP_Prosecutorial-Strategy-20060914_English.pdf> (last visited 23 October 2008; quoted as "Report on Prosecutorial Strategy").

Office of the Prosecutor, Report on the activities performed during the first three years (June 2003–June 2006), The Hague, 12 September 2006. <www.icc-cpi.int/library/organs/otp/OTP_3-year-report-20060914_English.pdf> (last visited 23 October 2008 quoted as "OTP Activities Report").

Office of the Prosecutor, Paper on some policy issues before the Office of the Prosecutor, The Hague, ICC-OTP 2003, September 2003. <www.icc-cpi.int/otp/otp_docs.html> (last visited 23 October 2008; quoted as "OTP Policy paper").

Office of the Prosecutor, Fourth Report of the Prosecutor of the International Criminal Court, to the Security Council pursuant to UNSC 1593 (2005), The Hague, 14.12.2006. <www.icc-cpi.int/otp/otp_events.html> (last visited 23 October 2008; quoted as "OTP Fourth Report").

Report of the PrepCom on the Establishment of the ICC (1996), UN-GAOR, 51st session, Supplement No. 22 (A/51/22), vol. I.

Statement by Luis Moreno-Ocampo, Prosecutor of the International Criminal Court: Informal meeting of Legal Advisors of Ministries of Foreign Affairs, New York, 24.10.2005. <www.icc-cpi.int/otp/otp_events.html> (last visited 23 October 2008; quoted as "Moreno-Ocampo Statement 2005").

Statement by Luis Moreno-Ocampo, Prosecutor of the International Criminal Court: Fifth session of the Assembly of States Parties, Opening Remarks, The Hague, 24.11.2006 <www.icc-cpi.int/otp/otp_events.html> (last visited 23 October 2008; quoted as "Moreno-Ocampo Statement 2006a").

Statement of the Prosecutor of the International Criminal Court, Mr. Luis Moreno Ocampo, to the UN Security Council pursuant to UNSCR 1593 (2005), Office of the Prosecutor, The Hague, 14.12.2006. <www.icc-cpi.int/otp/otp_events.html> (last visited 23 October 2008; quoted as "Moreno-Ocampo Statement 2006b").

Other Documents and Reports

3B Witness to Truth: Report of the Sierra Leone Truth and Reconciliation Commission (GPL Press, Ghana: 2004) 1–520 (quoted as "Sierra Leone TRC Report").

Baldo, Suliman/Magarrell, Lisa, ICTJ Reparative Justice Series, 'Reparation and the Darfur peace process: Ensuring victims'rights' November 2007, www.ictj.org/en/news/pubs/index.html (last visited 23 October 2008, quoted as ICTJ Reparation Report).

Bassiouni et al., 'Proposed guiding principles for combating impunity for international crimes' reprinted in Bassiouni (ed.), *Post-Conflict Justice* (Tansnational Publishers, Ardsley 2002) 255–282 (quoted as "Principles combating impunity").

Bassiouni Cherif et al., 'The Chicago principles on post-conflict justice', International Human Rights Law Institute 2007 (quoted as "Chicago Principles").

Bundesfinanzministerium- Referat VB4 'Leistungen der öffentlichen Hand auf dem Gebiet der Wiedergutmachung- Stand 31. Dezember 2006' (2007/0122828).

Debiel, Tobias/Terlinden, Ulf, 'Promoting Good Governance in Post-Conflict Societies', Discussion Paper (GTZ, Eschborn 2005) 1–54.

Human Rights Watch, Memorandum: Benchmarks for assessing possible national alternatives to International Criminal Court cases against LRA leaders, May 2007 http://hrw.org/backgrounder/ij/icc0507/ (last visited 23 October 2008; quoted as "HRW Memorandum 2007").

Human Rights Watch, Policy paper: The meaning of "the interests of justice" in Art. 53 of the Rome Statute, June 2005 (quoted as: "HRW 2005").

ICRC, International Humanitarian Law and the challenges of contemporary armed conflicts, 2007 (30IC/07/8.4.)

ICTJ and Human Rights Center, University of Berkeley, California 'Forgotten voices: A population-based survey on attitudes about peace and justice in Northern Uganda' (2005) (quoted as "ICTJ/Human Rights Center, 2005").

Ministry of Foreign Affairs Sweden, Stockholm Initiative on Demobilisation, Disarmement and Reintegration. Final Report. March 2006, available at <www.sweden.gov.se/sb/d/4890> (last visited 23 October 2008).

Refugee Law Project Working Paper No. 15, 'Whose Justice? Perceptions of Uganda's amnesty act 2000: the potential for conflict resolution and long term reconciliation' February 2005 (quoted as "Refugee Law Working Paper 2005").

Seils, Paul/Wierda, Marieka, 'The International Criminal Court and conflict mediation' (International Center for Transitional Justice, New York 2005) <www.ictj.org/en/news/pubs/index.html> (last visited 23 October 2008).

War Crimes Research Office, 'Victim participation before the International Criminal Court' November 2007, <www.wcl.american.edu/warcrimes/icc/icc_reports.cfm> (last visited 23 October 2008).

War Crimes Research Office, 'The gravity threshold of the International Criminal Court', March 2008, <www.wcl.american.edu/warcrimes/icc/icc_reports.cfm> (last visited 23 October 2008).

Table of Cases

Abdülsamet Yaman v. Turkey [2 November 2004] Judgement, Application No. 32446/96 [2004] ECHR 572 (European Court of Human Rights).

Acevedo-Jaramillo et al. v. Perú [7 February 2006] Judgment, Series C No. 144 (Inter-American Court of Human Rights).

Aguado - Alfaro et al. v. Perú (Case of Dismissed Congressional Employees) [24 November 2006] Judgment (only in Spanish), Series C No. 158 (Inter-American Court of Human Rights).

Aksoy v. Turkey [18 December 1996] Judgement, 21987/93 [1996] ECHR 68 (European Court of Human Rights).

Almonacid-Arellano et al. v. Chile, [26 September 2006] Judgment, Series C No. 154 Inter-American Court of Human Rights).

Aydin v. Turkey [25 September 1997] Judgment, 23178/94 [1997] ECHR 75 (European Court of Human Rights).

AZAPO et al. vs. The President et al. [25 July 1996] Case CCT 17/96 (Constitutional Court of South Africa).

Baldeón-García v. Perú [6 April 2006] Judgement, Series C No. 147 (Inter-American Court of Human Rights).

Bámaca-Velásquez v. Guatemala [25 November 2000] Judgement, Series C No. 70 (Inter-American Court of Human Rights).

Barrios Altos vs. Perú Case [14 March 2001] Judgment, C Series No. 75 (Inter-American Court of Human Rights).

Blanco-Romero et al. v. Venezuela [28 November 2005] Judgement, Series C No. 138 (Inter-American Court of Human Rights).

Bosnia and Herzegovina v. Serbia and Montenegro (Case concerning the application of the Convention on the Prevention and Punishment of the Crime of Genocide) [26 February 2007] Judgement (ICJ).

Carpio Nicolle y otros vs. Guatemala Case [22 November 2004] Judgement, C Series No. 117 (Inter-American Court of Human Rights).

Chanfeau et al. v. Chile [7 April 1998] Report No. 25/98 (Inter-American Commission of Human Rights).

Detta Josefina, MENOTTI Noris, MARTINEZ Federico, MUSO Osiris, BURGELL Jorge - Denuncia – Inconstitucionalidad de la Ley 15.848, art. 1,2,3 y 4 (Ficha 112/87) [2 Mayo 1988] Sentencia No. 184 (Chilean Supreme Court).

Ellacuría et al. v. El Salvador [22 December 1999] Report No. 136/99 (Inter-American Commission of Human Rights).

Erdölbevorratung [16 March 1971] BVerfGE 30, 292 (German Constitutional Court).

Espósito, Miguel Angel s/incidente de prescripción de la acción penal promovido por la defensa [23 December 2004] Judgement (Argentinean Supreme Court) reprinted in Fallos de la Corte Suprema de Justicia de la Nación, vol. 327, 5668.

García-Asto and Ramírez-Rojas v. Perú [25 November 2005] Judgment, Series C No. 137 (Inter-American Court of Human Rights).

Goiburú et al. v. Paraguay [22 September 2006] Judgement, Series C No. 153 (Inter-American Court of Human Rights).

Gómez-Palomino v. Perú [22 November 2005] Judgement, Series C No. 136 (Inter-American Court of Human Rights).

González José Luis en Representación de Juan Gelman - Inconstitucionalidad (Ficha 90–10462/2002) [15 Noviember 2004] Sentencia No 332 (Urugayan Supreme Court).

Gustavo Gallón Giraldo y otros [18 May 2006] Sentencia C-370/2006, Expediente D-6032 (Colombian Constitutional Court).

Hugh Jordan v. UK [4 May 2001] Judgement, 24746/94 [2001] ECHR 327 (European Court of Human Rights).

Indigenous Community Yakye Axa v. Paraguay [17 June 2005] Judgment, Series C No. 125 (Inter-American Court of Human Rights).

Ituango Massacre v. Colombia [1 July 2006] Judgement, Series C (Inter-American Court of Human Rights).

Jean and Bosico v. República Dominicana [8 September 2005] Judgment, Series C No. 130 (Inter-American Court of Human Rights).

Juan Humberto Sánchez v. Honduras [7 June 2003] Judgment, Series C No. 187 (Inter-American Court of Human Rights).

Kurt v. Turkey [825 May 1998] Judgement, 24276/94 [1998] ECHR 44 (European Court of Human Rights).

La Cantuta v. Perú [29 November 2006] Judgment, Series C No. 162 (Inter-American Court of Human Rights).

López-Álvarez v. Honduras [1 February 2006] Judgment, Series C No. 141, 207 (Inter-American Court of Human Rights).

"Mapiripán Massacre" v. Colombia [15 September 2005] Judgement, Series C No. 134 (Inter-American Court of Human Rights).

Miguel Ángel Cotreras Sandoval [17 November 2004] Judgement (Chilean Supreme Court).

Miguel Castro-Castro Prison v. Perú [25 November 2006] Judgement, Series C No. 160 (Inter-American Court of Human Rights).

Moiwana Community v. Suriname [15 June 2005] Judgement Series C No. 124 (Inter-American Court of Human Rights).

Montero-Aranguren et al. (Detention Center of Catia) v. Venezuela [5 July 2006] Judgment, Series C No. 150, (Inter-American Court of Human Rights).

Palamara-Iribarne v. Chile [22 November 2005] Judgment, Series C No. 135 (Inter-American Court of Human Rights).

Pedro Enrique Poblete Córdova [9 September 1998] Judgement, rol no. 895–96 del Segundo Juzgado Militar de Santiago (Chilean Supreme Court) reprinted in Gaceta Jurídica 219, 122.

Prosecutor v. Deronic [30 March 2004] Sentencing Judgement, Case No. IT-02–61-S (ICTY).

Prosecutor v. Furundzija [10 December 1998] Judgement, IT-95–17/1-T (ICTY).

Prosecutor v. Kallon and Kamara [13 March 2004) App. Decision, SCSL-2004–15AR72(E) and CSCSL-2004 – 16 AR72(E) (SCSL).

Prosecutor v. Norman, Decision on the request by the TRC of Sierra Leone to Conduct a Public Hearing with Samuel Hinga Norman [29 October 2003] Case No. SCSL-2003–08-PT (SCSL).

Prosecutor v. Tadic [2 October 1995] App. Decision, IT-94–1-AR 72 (ICTY).

Prosecutor v. Thomas Lubanga Dyilo, Decision concerning PTC I's Decision of 10 February 2006 and the Incorporation of Documents into the Record of the Case against Mr. Thomas Lubanga Dyilo, 24 February 2006, (ICC-01/04–01/06) (ICC).

Prosecutor v. Thomas Lubanga Dylo, Decision on victims' participation, 18 January 2008, (ICC-01/04–01/06–1119) (ICC)

Prosecutor v. Thomas Lubanga Dylo, Decision on the Defence and Prosecution Requests to Leave to Appeal the Decion on Victims' Participation of 18 January 2008, 26 February 2008, (ICC-01/04–01/06–1191) (ICC).

Prosecutor v. Thomas Lubanga Dylo, Judgment on the appeals of the Prosecutor and the Defence against TC I's Decision on Victims' Participation of 18 January 2008, 11 July 2008 (ICC-01/04–01/06 OA 9 OA 10) (ICC).

Prosecutor v. Germain Katanga and M. Ngudjolo Chui, Decision on the set of procedural rights attached to procedural status of victim at the Pre-Trial Stage of the Case, 13.05.2008 (ICC-01/04–01/07).

Pueblo Bello Massacre v. Colombia [31 January 2006] Judgment, Series C No. 140 (Inter-American Court of Human Rights).

Recurso de hecho deducido por la defensa de Julio Héctor Simón en la causa Simón, Julio Héctor s/ privación ilegítima de la libertad, etc., causa N 17.768 [14 June 2005] (Argentinean Supreme Court) reprinted in: Fallos de la Corte Suprema de Justicia de la Nación, vol. 328, 2056.

Recurso de hecho deducido por el Estado y el Gobierno de Chile en la causa Arancibia Clavel, Enrique Lautaro s/ homicidio calificado y asociación ilícita y otros causa N 259 [24 August 2004] Judgment (Argentinean Supreme Court) reprinted in Fallos de la Corte Suprema de Justicia de la Nación, vol. 327, 3312.

Rochela Massacre v. Colombia [11 May 2007] Judgement, Series C No. 163 (Inter-American Court of Human Rights).

Romero y Galdámez v. El Salvador [13 April 2000] Report No. 37/00 (Inter-American Commission of Human Rights).

Sawhoyamaxa Indigenous Community v. Paraguay [29 March 2006] Judgment, Series C No. 146 (Inter-American Court of Human Rights).

Secuestro de Ricardo Rioseco Montoya y Luis Cotal Älvarez [4 August 2005] Judgement (Chilean Supreme Court).

Selçuk and Asker v. Turkey [24 April 1998] Judgement, 23184/94, 23185/94 [1998] ECHR 36 (European Court of Human Rights).

Selmouni v. France [28 July 1999] Judgement, 25803/94 [1999] ECHR 66 (European Court of Human Rights).

Servellón-García et al. v. Honduras [21 September 2006] Judgement, Series C No. 152 (Inter-American Court of Human Rights).

Vargas-Areco v. Paraguay [26 September 2006] Judgement, Series C No. 155 (Inter-American Court of Human Rights).

Velásquez-Rodríguez v. Honduras [29 July 1988] Judgement (Inter-American Court of Human Rights).

Villegas Namuche [9 December 2004] Expediente 2488–2002-HC/TC (Peruvian Constitutional Court).

Ximenes-Lopes v. Brasil [4 July 2006] Judgment, Series C No. 149 (Inter-American Court of Human Rights).

19 Tradesmen v. Colombia [5 July 2004] Judgment, Series C No. 109 (Inter-American Court of Human Rights).

Abbreviations

ACHR	American Convention of Human Rights
ALC	Annotated Leading Cases of International Criminal Tribunals (André Klip Göran Sluiter, eds.)
AN	*Audiencia Nacional* (Spanish National Court)

ANC	African National Congress
AP	Additional Protocol to the Geneva Conventions
AVR	Archiv des Völkerrechts
Buff. Crim. L. Rev	Buffallo Criminal Law Review
BWV	Berliner Wissenschaftsverlag
CC	*Corte Constitucional* (Constitutional Court)
CLF	Criminal Law Forum
Cornell Int'l L. J.	Cornell International Law Journal
CRP	Community Reconciliation Procedures
DL	*Decreto Legislativo* (Executive Decree)
Davis J. Int'l L. & Pol'y U.C.	Davis Journal of International Law & Policy
DRC	Democratic Republic of Congo
ECCC	Extraordinary Chambers in the Courts of Cambodia
ECHR	European Court of Human Rights
EJIL	European Journal of International Law
Eur. J. Cr., Cr. L. & Cr. J.	European Journal of Crime, Criminal Law and Criminal Justice
EuGRZ	Europäische Grundrechte Zeitschrift
GAOR	General Assembly Official Records
GC	Geneva Conventions
Harv.L.Rev.	Harvard Law Review
HRQ	Human Rights Quarterly
IACHR	Inter-American Court of Human Rights
IAComHR	Inter-American Commission of Human Rights
ICC	International Criminal Court
ICJ	International Court of Justice
ICLQ	International and Comparative Law Quarterly
ICLR	International Criminal Law Review
ICRC	International Committee of the Red Cross
ICRC Int. Rev.	International Review of the Red Cross
ICTJ	International Center for Transitional Justice
ICTY	International Tribunal for the Former Yugoslavia
IHL	International Humanitarian Law
ILC	International Law Commission
IJTJ	International Journal of Transitional Justice
JICJ	Journal of International Criminal Justice
JuS	Juristische Schulung
KCLJ	The King's College Law Journal
LJIL	Leiden Journal of International Law
OHCHR	Office of the United Nations High Commissioner for Human Rights
OTP	Office of the Prosecutor
PrepCom	Preparatory Committee ICC
Res.	Resolution

SCSL	Special Court for Sierra Leone
SPSC	Special Panels for Serious Crimes (East Timor)
TJ	Transitional Justice
TRC	Truth and Reconciliation Commission
U.C. Davis L. Rev.	University of California Davis Law Review
WCRO	War Crimes Research Office
WW II	World War II
YLJ	Yale Law Journal
ZStW	Zeitschrift für die gesamte Strafrechtswissenschaft

The "New Law" of Transitional Justice*

Christine Bell

Abstract This paper asserts that the combination of peace agreement practice and legal developments have given rise to a "new law" of transitional justice. This "new law" draws on human rights law, humanitarian law, international criminal law and ordinary criminal law, but cannot be justified in terms of any one of these regimes on their own (and therefore remains controversial). The "new law" can be viewed as a new developing practice rather than a new law, but finds some basis in soft law standards that are emerging with reference to transitional justice, and in the practice of states and international organisations.

I open the chapter by "stating" this new law, and then examine where the "new law" can be backed up with reference to law and practice, illustrating its ambiguities and controversies. I then point to the difficulties of obtaining any further clarity, or resolution to these ambiguities and controversies, by recourse to the normative frameworks of human rights or humanitarian law. The chapter provides an assessment of the advantages and disadvantages of the "new law", and considers whether it is advisable to try to clarify the new law's ambiguities through further legal standards.

Finally, the chapter concludes by suggesting somewhat provocatively that there is a certain attractiveness to the current state of legal uncertainty around transitional justice, in enabling both the assertion of an obligation to combat impunity, while leaving some scope for flexibility in peace negotiations.

C. Bell
Transitional Justice Institute University of Ulster Northern Ireland, UK
e-mail: c.bell@ulster.ac.uk

*This paper draws on and extends Chap. V, of Bell (2006) which drew on a research paper commissioned by the project, Roht-Arriaza (2006). Both are available on www.ichrp.org. The ideas in the chapter are further extended and discussed in Bell (2008, Chap. 12).

K. Ambos et al. (eds.), *Building a Future on Peace and Justice: Studies on Transitional Justice, Peace and Development.*

1 The New Law of Transitional Justice

The new "law" of transitional justice can be stated as follows:

1. Blanket amnesties that cover serious international crimes are not permitted.
2. Some amnesty, however, is required as conflict-related prisoners and detainees must be released, demilitarised, demobilised, and enabled to reintegrate.
3. Mechanisms should be creatively designed aimed at marrying the normative commitment to accountability, to the goal of sustaining the ceasefire and developing the constitutional commitments at the heart of the peace agreement. The following approaches may be used:

   (a) Quasi-legal mechanisms which deliver forms of accountability other than criminal law processes with prosecution, such as truth commissions.
   (b) A bifurcated approach whereby international criminal processes for the most serious offenders, coupled with creatively designed local mechanisms aimed at a range of goals such as accountability and reconciliation, for those further down the chain of responsibility, and general amnesty at the lowest level.

4. Where new mechanisms are innovated, they should be designed with as much consultation with affected communities as is possible.
5. Should any party evidence lack of commitment to the peace agreement, and in particular return to violence, any compromise on criminal justice is void and reversible through the use of international criminal justice.

2 Sources of the New Law, and its Ambiguities

2.1 Blanket Amnesties that Cover Serious Crimes are not Permitted

International law outlaws blanket amnesties, for "serious crimes under international law". This prohibition has found articulation in Principles 19 of the Updated Principles to Combat Impunity which provides that:

> States shall undertake prompt, thorough, independent and impartial investigations of violations of human rights and international humanitarian law and take appropriate measures in respect of the perpetrators, particularly in the area of criminal justice, by ensuring that those responsible for serious crimes under international law are prosecuted, tried and duly punished.

These principles define serious crimes under international law as:

> Grave breaches of the 1949 Geneva Conventions and of 1977 Additional Protocol I thereto and other violations of international humanitarian law that are crimes under international law, genocide, crimes against humanity and other violations of internationally protected human rights that are crimes under international law and/or which international law requires states to penalise, such as torture, enforced disappearance, extrajudicial execution, and slavery.

Similarly, the United Nations Secretary General’s Report on The Rule of Law and Justice in Conflict and Post-Conflict Societies August 2004, provides in recommendation 64 that

Peace agreements and Security Council resolutions and mandates should:

(a) Reject any endorsement of amnesty for genocide, war crimes, or crimes against humanity, including those relating to ethnic, gender and sexually based international crimes, ensure that no such amnesty previously granted is a bar to prosecution before any United Nations-created or assisted court
(b) Ensure that the United Nations does not establish or directly participate in any tribunal for which capital punishment is included among possible sanctions

The prohibition on blanket amnesty for these crimes also finds a “hard law” basis in a number of treaties that specifically require prosecution of violations. These legal sources would seem to proscribe amnesty for at least the following sub-set of crimes: torture, genocide, and grave breaches of the Geneva Conventions, which include the following, if committed against protected persons (such as medical and religious personnel and prisoners) and property protected by the Convention (clearly civilian property): wilful killing, torture or inhuman treatment, including biological experiments, wilfully causing great suffering or serious injury to body or health, and extensive destruction and appropriation of property, not justified by military necessity and carried out unlawfully and wantonly. The main treaty obligations are:

(1) Genocide Convention: Persons committing genocide are required to be punished.
(2) Convention Against Torture: alleged torture must be investigated and, if the state has jurisdiction under any of the enumerate bases, it must either extradite the offender, or “submit the case to it competent authorities for the purpose of prosecution”.
(3) The Inter-American Convention on Forced Disappearance of Persons and the Inter-American Convention on Torture have similar provisions.
(4) 1949 Geneva Conventions: require that persons accused of grave breaches be sought and prosecuted, or extradited to a state that will do so. This requirement, however, only applies in international conflicts, which under Protocol I to the Geneva Conventions includes conflicts involving “national liberation movements” – a term that is currently viewed as somewhat anachronistic with states resisting its use with reference to armed actors. Where Protocol I does apply, it also adds to the list of “grave breaches” matters such as: attacking a person who is hors de combat; perfidious use of the distinctive emblems of the International Committee of the Red Cross and other signs protected by the Convention; and practices of apartheid and other inhuman and degrading practices involving outrages upon personal dignity, based on racial discrimination.
(5) The Convention on Non-Applicability of Statutory Limitations to War Crimes and Crimes Against Humanity: holds that the passage of time cannot bar prosecutions for war crimes, crimes against humanity and genocide.
(6) The other major source of treaty-based obligation affecting the scope of amnesty is found in general human rights treaties at the international and regional level, including the International Covenant on Civil and Political Rights (ICCPR),

American Convention on Human Rights and European Convention on Human Rights. These treaties clearly outlaw deprivation of the right to life, including arbitrary disappearances and extra-judicial executions and torture. While the treaties, contain no explicit references to prosecution or amnesty, they prohibit the underlying violations, and provide for a right to a remedy (in general terms), and to a hearing before a competent tribunal for violations of rights. This might seem to leave open whether prosecution and punishment are required, or whether other "restorative justice" type approaches might fulfil human rights obligations. Increasingly, jurisprudence relating to torture and the right to life in particular requires adequate investigation capable of leading to a determination of guilt or innocence. In some cases the treaties and international bodies talk of prosecution and/or punishment. These obligations apply to successor regimes as regards the human rights abuses of the previous regime, provided that the state has been a party to the Conventions throughout.

(7) Crimes against humanity and gross human rights abuses. In addition to these treaty provisions, there are strong arguments that some fundamental rights are protected as a matter of customary law and apply even where key treaties have not been ratified. These arguments have been bolstered by the notion of "crimes against humanity" as crimes which cannot be amnestied. Crimes Against Humanity are defined by the statutes establishing the international criminal tribunals for Rwanda, the former Yugoslavia, the Sierra Leone Special Criminal Court and the Rome Statute of the International Criminal Court (ICC). They include crimes such as murder, extermination, enslavement, deportation, imprisonment, torture and rape. The crimes have to be part of widespread or systematic attack, and directed against a civilian population. As regards gross human rights violations, the violations need to be of a serious scale. While it has for a long time been the case that states have permission to prosecute for these crimes, a view that there a duty on states to prosecute crimes against humanity is beginning to emerge. Indeed, there have been increasing assertions of universal jurisdiction (the ability of states anywhere) to prosecute these offences regardless of where they occurred.

2.2 *Some Amnesty, However, is Required as Conflict-Related Prisoners and Detainees must be Released, Demilitarised, Demobilised, and Enabled to Reintegrate*

Some level of amnesty would seem to be allowed by international law and even required. Article 6(5) of Protocol II of the Geneva Conventions provides:

> At the end of hostilities, the authorities in power shall endeavour to grant the broadest possible amnesty to persons who have participated in the armed conflict, or those deprived of their liberty for reasons related to the armed conflict, whether they are interned or detained.

The International Committee of the Red Cross (ICRC) view, however, is that this provision does not apply for those who have committed any crimes under international law.[1] The UN SG recommendations and the Updated Principles on Impunity also seem to contemplate that the use of amnesty is lawful on occasion.

It is also important to note that human rights standards require the release of those imprisoned for matters such as freedom of speech or association, where prescription of such activities as a crime itself violates human rights standards. However, it is problematic to achieve this through an "amnesty" which, by its very definition, suggests that a crime was still committed (see Principle 24 Impunity).

The notion of some scope for amnesty can also be argued to find a basis in human rights law itself. Orentlicher has argued that:

> states operating under constraints commonly associated with political transition could satisfy their treaty obligations through exemplary prosecutions – focusing, for example, on those who appear to bear principle responsibility for systemic atrocities or on individuals believed to have committed notorious crimes that were emblematic of a regime's depredations. (Orentlicher 2007, p. 14; see also Orentlicher 1991, p. 2548; Roht-Arriaza 1990, p. 505–511)

This suggests some residual role for amnesty.

2.3 *Remaining Ambiguities*

These first two statements of the "new law" however, have ambiguities. In particular, they do not clearly delimit where the prohibition on amnesty ends, or the scope of possible compromise between crimes that can, and crimes that cannot be amnestied. There is no easy "list" to hand to negotiators, and this means that clear instruction - the easiest way to ensure that mediators play a normative role – is not possible. The law as currently developed does not enable this.

2.3.1 What is the Precise List of Crimes that cannot be Amnestied?

The definition of serious crimes under international law as set out above, also talks of "other violations of international humanitarian law", in a definition that has a circular quality – crimes are serious crimes when they are considered serious crimes. Exploring what these crimes might be exposes a grey area in international law. Common Article 3 of the Geneva Conventions and Protocol II apply to non-international armed conflicts. They do not explicitly impose an obligation to prosecute and punish. It is widely accepted that they permit individual responsibility and prosecutions and punishment and, as noted, international law seems to be moving to a position whereby "serious violations" require prosecution and punishment, and even enable

[1] Letter of the ICRC Legal Division to the ICTY Prosecutor of 24 November 1975 and to the Department of Law at the University of California of 15 April 1997 (referring to CDDH, Official Records, 1977, Vol. IX, p. 319, as cited in Roht-Arriaza (2002, p. 97, n. 15).

universal jurisdiction. The notion of compulsory prosecution and punishment finds some support in the fact that the crimes in question have been included in the Rome Statute of the ICC, and in the statutes for the International Criminal Tribunals in Former Yugoslavia (ICTFY) and Rwanda (ICTR), which have added impetus to the idea that prosecution and punishment are compulsory. The list of crimes is a broad one, including: violence to life, health, and physical or mental well-being of persons, in particular murder, as well as cruel treatment such as torture, mutilation, or any form of corporal punishment. However, given lack of clarity as to whether prosecution and punishment are permitted or required, it is unclear what can be amnestied. A second grey area arises over the nature of the link between these crimes and the level of conflict prevailing: what the level of conflict is required to trigger these crimes; and what link is required between crime and conflict?

2.3.2 What is the Permissible Scope of Amnesty?

What then is the permissible scope of amnesty? Again, the answer is a little unclear (see further Roht-Arriaza 2006). First, perhaps individual war crimes that were neither grave breaches nor, in the cases of non-international conflict, violations of Article 3 of the 1949 Conventions and Protocol II, might be able to be amnestied so long as they did not at the same time constitute crimes against humanity due to the fact that they were part of a widespread and systematic attack. However, where it applies, this composite list of crimes is already quite extensive.

At a minimum it is possible to amnesty crimes such as treason or rebellion committed by insurgent forces (although interestingly certain peace agreements take a strong stand on coup d'état) (Roht-Arriaza 2006). In Côte D'Ivoire the Linas-Marcoussis Agreement (2003) for example holds that "the Government of National Reconciliation will take the necessary steps to ensure the release and amnesty for all military personnel being held on charges of threatening State security and will extend this measure to soldiers living in exile" (Article 3(i)).[2] To the extent that such an amnesty might include serious international crimes, a separate clause could exclude these, as the Côte D'Ivoire agreement went on to do ("The amnesty law will under no circumstances mean that those having committed serious economic violations and serious violations of human rights and international humanitarian law will go unpunished". Article 3(i)). In summary, the list of possible crimes which can be amnestied seems fairly minor, short, and not particularly helpful in terms of giving mediators some room to manoeuvre.

Secondly, crimes that breach only domestic law might be amnestied. Some conflicts, for example Northern Ireland (see below), can be argued not to trigger humanitarian law at all (although some argue that certain periods of the conflict did fall within its ambit). These crimes might include minor related crimes such as mayhem, arson and the like if not committed by state-related forces, or during armed conflict, or are widespread or systematic enough to be considered a crime against humanity.

[2] Agreement available at http://www.usip.org/library/pa/cote_divoire/cote_divoire_01242003en.html.

However, the current direction of human rights jurisprudence on the right to life and torture, particularly at the regional level, seem to indicate that murder and serious assault may have to be taken out of the equation altogether as this would violate the state's positive obligation under international human rights conventions to pro-actively protect life and prevent torture, inhuman and degrading treatment, through adequate criminal laws, investigation and prosecution procedures.[3] This could catch offences committed in conflicts even where humanitarian law was not triggered. Commentators arguing that human rights law requires prosecution and trial, have often contemplated this requirement as discharged by dealing with the most serious offenders and offences (see Orentlicher 1991, 2007; Roht-Arriaza 1990). The difficulty is that human rights jurisprudence is developed through individual complaints to which it is addressed: human rights bodies, in their complain mechanisms, do not make abstract decisions. Thus legal reasoning allows little to no consideration of how victims and society as a whole have been served by a selective approach, but requires adjudicating on whether an individual rights have been violated or not, within a framework that was not designed to deal with accountability of acts committed in the course of large scale violent conflict. As a result, judicial mechanisms are required to adjudicate on the individual's rights meaning that any trade off between the individual's rights and social goals directed at group benefits are likely to be found to violate human rights law.

2.4 Permissible Trade-offs

The scope and requirements of permissible "trade-offs" between blanket amnesty and full accountability, are also unclear. The "new law" stated two possibilities. The first possibility involved making an amnesty less "blanket" by having some process of accounting, short of criminal trials. The second suggestion was the possibility of having trials for the top end of crimes and offenders, and alternative forms of accountability and even amnesty for those further down. However, while both these options frequently appear in practice, neither of these options entirely squares with existing international law requiring accountability.

2.5 Quasi-Legal Mechanisms which Deliver Forms of Accountability Other than Criminal Law Processes Culminating in Punishment, such as Truth Commissions

Academic literature has begun to suggest that there are different types of amnesties, some of which offer comply with "justice" standards, and possibly international law, and most of which do not, depending on the extent to which the amnesty is coupled

[3] See, e.g., *Jordan v. United Kingdom* 2003, 37 E.H.R.R. 2.

with some provision for accountability, and a rationale for sustainable peace (see, e.g., Slye 2002, pp. 172–247).[4]

Truth for amnesty/investigation without prosecution? One of key issues with impunity, particularly with relation to peace processes, is its denial of information or "truth" to victims and relatives. The Updated Principles on Impunity begin with a section detailing a "right to know", that stresses the "inalienable right to truth". Many of the instrumental goals of accountability listed above, such as reconciliation or institutional reform or even vetting, can be facilitated in part at least by full and accurate information about the type of abuses that occurred, what institutions or mechanisms facilitated them, what individuals perpetrated them, and what happened to victims. A practice of truth commissions is now fairly widespread (Hayner 2001; Freeman 2007). Although powers, remits, and effectiveness vary dramatically, all claim to offer some form of accounting for the past, usually in a social rather than an individual sense. At the least, truth commissions aim to establish some sort of record of the violations and abuses that were perpetrated.

Investigation or inquiry short of prosecution would seem to deliver a "right to truth". Does investigation falling short of prosecution or punishment then, form a possible compromise between full accountability and blanket amnesty? Most famously, the South African Truth and Reconciliation Commission effectively traded truth against amnesty: amnesty was exchanged for full disclosure.[5] Proponents of the South African Truth and Reconciliation Commission (TRC) did not justify this merely as a pragmatic trade-off between truth and justice. They argued that there were goals which could be accomplished by the Truth Commission mechanism that could not be accomplished by trials. Trials by their nature are concerned with high standards of proof to evaluate individual guilt or innocence. Victims are reduced to the standing of "mere witnesses", with the state and the accused as the main parties. In contrast, a well-run commission, it is argued, can focus on overall patterns of violations, keep the focus on victims and design victim-friendly procedures, examine institutional responsibility as well as individual responsibility, and in general deal with the many "shades of grey" in terms of guilt and accountability that conflicts tend to produce. Furthermore, in offering a clear incentive for giving information (instead of a disincentive), truth commissions might be more effective than trials in delivering information and "truth". The TRC in its final report argued that "justice" had not been denied, but that a concept of "restorative justice" had in fact been delivered – that is, justice as a process between victim, perpetrator and community, rather than justice as retributive punishment. When challenged in court in human rights terms, the Constitutional Court upheld the legislation, albeit with fairly scant attention to international law (they relied in part on Article 6(5) of Protocol II to the Geneva Conventions).[6]

---

[4] In fact Slye finds that only one amnesty – that of South Africa – comes close to satisfying the conditions he identifies for legitimate amnesty.

[5] Promotion of National Reconciliation Act, No. 34 of 1995, provided for "the granting of amnesty to persons who make full disclosure of all the relevant facts relating to acts associated with a political objective committed in the course of the conflicts of the past during the said period".

[6] *Azapo v. President of the Republic of South Africa* 1996 (4) SA 562 (CC).

So are there occasions in which investigation alone can satisfy international standards requiring accountability? While standards on torture, genocide, and Geneva Conventions talk of "prosecution", the main human rights standards do not mention a need for prosecution, and this seems to leave the investigation-only route open. The status of the Updated Principles on Impunity as principles rather than "law", with their emphasis on the right to know, might also seem to suggest that "hard law" leaves negotiators able to work with a "spectrum of accountability" running from investigation through prosecution to punishment.

However, national and international courts and quasi-judicial bodies that have considered this issue have often not taken this view (see Roht-Arriaza 2006). Furthermore, the existence of a truth commission, or even administrative sanctions, has not been found to modify the state's obligations to investigate, and if warranted, criminally prosecute. In the words of the Inter-American Court of Human Rights in the Barrios Altos case, 2001:

> all amnesty provisions, provisions on prescription and the establishment of measures designed to eliminate responsibility are inadmissible, because they are intended to prevent the investigation and punishment of those responsible for serious human rights violations such as torture, extrajudicial, summary or arbitrary execution and forced disappearance, all of them prohibited because they violate non-derogable rights recognized by international human rights law [emphasis added].[7]

National jurisprudence and legislation in the Americas has increasingly affirmed this view, as has the UN Human Rights Committee in addressing the requirements of the ICCPR. Furthermore, the Updated Principles on Impunity assert clearly that: "[t]he fact that a perpetrator discloses the violations that he, she or others have committed in order to benefit from the favourable provisions of legislation on disclosure or repentance cannot exempt him or her from criminal or other responsibility" (Principle 28).

Forgoing punishment? What then about investigating, prosecuting, and then failing to punish, either by use of pardon, or other measure? The South African invocation of restorative justice and confession as itself "punishment" further opens up the possibility of defining "punishment" as meaning something different from prison. Vetting, for example, could also be considered punitive.

The Updated Principles on Impunity do not rule this out as an amnesty "compromise". Principle 24 suggests that "even when intended to establish conditions conducive to a peace agreement or to foster national reconciliation, amnesty and other measures of clemency shall be kept within... bounds". One of these bounds is that perpetrators of serious crimes under international law may not benefit from such measures until such time as the State has met its obligations to prosecute, try and punish such offenders (Principle 24 together with Principle 19). Although Principle 19 talks of "criminal justice", it leaves open the meaning of the term "punishment", what constitutes punishment, and if imprisonment, what length of sentence is appropriate. Although it is unclear that the South African TRC, which had one of the

---

[7] Inter-American Court of Human Rights, *Case of Barrio Altos v. Peru* Judgement of March 14, 2001, para 41.

most nuanced and "accountable" amnesties, could have presented itself as "criminal justice". Principle 28 seems to indicate that reduction of sentence is at least appropriate; it provides that "[t]he disclosure may only provide grounds for a reduction of sentence in order to encourage revelation of the truth". However, some doubt on the appropriateness of forgoing punishment is raised by the pronouncements of international human rights bodies which seem to be moving towards the notion that accountability requires punishment in a traditional sense under requirements of adequacy, effectiveness and proportionality.[8] Against this, it is worth noting that restorative justice mechanisms are now a part of domestic criminal justice in many non-conflict situations. In the domestic context, restorative justice is viewed as a progressive form of criminal accountability, rather than denial of accountability or exception to criminal justice, but often does not apply to the most serious offences.

The case of Northern Ireland provides an interesting example of sentence shortening as a compromise. Here, a "sentence review" process set out in the Belfast Agreement set in train a process which resulted in nearly all of the prisoners imprisoned as a result of the conflict being released.[9] However, technically the process was one of "sentence review" and sentence shortening, rather than amnesty or lifting of punishment altogether (life sentence prisoners remained subject to recall). The compromise preserved the accountability effected by the criminal law, while meeting the demands of paramilitary groups for "normalisation" – demands which were crucial to reaching a peace agreement. There are, however, some limitations to the application of this example elsewhere. Firstly, in Northern Ireland the level of conflict was low with the government insisting throughout the conflict that humanitarian law did not apply, and refusing to ratify Protocols I and II to the Geneva Conventions 1949. Therefore, the crimes for which shortened sentences were given did not amount to "grave breaches" of the Geneva Conventions of 1949 (under the Protocol I definition of international armed conflict), or a violation of Protocol II, or (more arguably) Common Article 3 of the Geneva Conventions. It is also difficult to argue that the conflict saw any crimes against humanity or gross human rights violations. Secondly, and even more pertinently, the only persons in prison were members of armed opposition groups (state actors seldom being prosecuted or imprisoned). Given that the only requirements as regards accountability came from human rights conventions, the duty with regard to these non-state actors was only that of a relatively loosely defined positive duty on the state to have in place criminal processes capable providing a safeguard for the right to life and the right not to be tortured. It is therefore easier to argue that the state responsibility as regards non-state actions had been satisfied by adequate investigation, a full trial and partial punishment.

[8] The UN Human Rights Committee, addressing the requirements of the ICCPR, has found that disciplinary and administrative remedies were not "adequate and effective" under Art. 2(3) of the Covenant in the face of serious violations, and that criminal prosecution was required for such violations. General Comment No. 20 (Compilation of General Comments and General Recommendations Adopted by Human Rights Treaty Bodies, U.N. Doc. HRI\GEN\1\Rev. 1 at 30 (1994)).

[9] Northern Ireland Sentences Act 1998.

2.6 A Bifurcated Approach Whereby International Criminal Processes for the Most Serious Offenders, Coupled with Creatively Designed Local Mechanisms Aimed at a Range of Goals such as Accountability and Reconciliation, for those Further Down the Chain of Responsibility, and General Amnesty at the Lowest Level

The provision for the Sierra Leone Special Court to prosecute "persons who bear the greatest responsibility" for perpetration of "crimes against humanity, war crimes and other gross abuses of international humanitarian and Sierra Leonean law" (UN SC Res. 1315, 2000), also raises the question of whether prosecutions can be explicitly limited to "those most responsible" or conversely, whether an amnesty law can be valid if it excludes from its terms the top leaders and organizers, while encompassing lower- and mid-level fighters.

Peace processes indicate an emerging practice along these lines, even though neither the treaty instruments nor general human rights obligations make these types of distinctions (indeed humanitarian law expressly provides that being a foot soldier acting under superior orders does not remove individual responsibility, nor does lack of knowledge apparently absolve commanders of responsibility for serious crimes committed by those under their command). A number of recent peace agreement in Africa (for example Côte D'Ivoire 2003 Democratic Republic of Congo 2002) have all included amnesties or provision for release of prisoners but excepted serious crimes under international law (see also Georgia-Abkhazia 1994).[10] In most cases, however, the agreement has not specified a mechanism to achieve accountability for these cases. While open to the charge of de facto impunity, these peace agreements at least formally comply with the international legal position by leaving open the possibility of future trials.

In Sierra Leone the bifurcation approach was unplanned. The Lomé Accord (2000) (like the earlier Abidjan Accord of 1996) had included a broad amnesty. Unlike the earlier accord it also provided for a Truth and Reconciliation Commission to be established. This Commission did not have a focus on individual accountability. However, after renewed fighting, the government appealed to the UN who through Security Council Resolution 1315 of 2000 established the Special Criminal Court for Sierra Leone. Although there were some tensions, both mechanisms were established and undertook their different mandates during overlapping time periods.

The Arusha Peace and Reconciliation Agreement for Burundi (2000) provided for the bifurcated approach in its design in a multi-faceted and overlapping approach to the past.[11] The agreement provided for prisoner release, and established amnesty for all combatants other than for acts of genocide, crimes against humanity or war crimes, or participation in coups d'état. It also established a National Truth and Reconciliation Commission (TRC) with powers of investigation, arbitration and

[10] All agreements available at http://www.usip.org/library/pa.html.

[11] For text of agreement see http://www.usip.org/library/pa/burundi/pa_burundi_08282000_toc.html.

reconciliation and clarification of history, and requested the UN Security Council to establish an International Judicial Commission of Inquiry and an International Criminal Tribunal. The Agreement also sets out as a political principle, the "establishment of a national observatory for the prevention and eradication of genocide, war crimes and other crimes against humanity", and noted the need for a regional observatory to do the same.[12]

One way of interpreting this practice is that, rather than indicating scope for amnesty, it reflects a division of labour as between national and international courts or tribunals (Roth-Arriaza 2006). The Security Council, since at least 2000, has supported the idea that the International Criminal Tribunals for the Former Yugoslavia and Rwanda should focus on civilian, military and paramilitary leaders and should, as part of their completing strategy "concentrate on the prosecution and trial of the most senior leaders suspected of being most responsible for crimes" while transferring cases involving lesser offenders to the national courts.[13] The Prosecutor for the ICC has similarly expressed his office's intention to focus on the leaders who bear most responsibility, leaving the rest to national courts or other (unspecified) means.[14] However, this is not an absolute bar on moving further down a chain of command if necessary for the whole case to be properly considered. The Sierra Leone Special Court found that its mandate to prosecute those who bear the "greatest responsibility" could include not just leaders but mid-level commanders who by their acts encouraged others. The notion of "most responsibility" can be interpreted on a rank or level of responsibility basis, or on an "actual responsibility" basis that cuts across ranks. To a certain extent prosecutorial discretion will often focus on leaders and organisers. This also happens due to the nature of at least some international crimes, such as genocide, which require proof of elements, such as "intent to destroy a certain type of group, in whole or in part" which require a certain degree of command.[15]

Is it legitimate, therefore, for a peace agreement to amnesty all but the leaders and organisers – or those "bearing the greatest responsibility" – while specifying prosecution for these persons to the extent that they have committed international crimes? This might be permissible provided that there was a credible prosecution mechanism in place for the leaders, and an alternative form of accountability for those lower down. These alternatives might include national court prosecutions, a truth for amnesty scheme like South Africa's, a gacaca-type process as used in Rwanda resulting in community service or some other sanction, or a new variant rooted in a country's culture and community conflict resolution traditions.

[12] Arusha Peace and Reconciliation Agreement for Burundi, 28 August 2000, Protocol I "Nature of the Burundi Conflict: Problems of Genocide, Exclusion and their Solutions", Article 6.

[13] Security Council Res. 1329, U.N. Doc. S/RES/1329, 30 Nov. 2000; Security Council Res. 1503, U.N. Doc. S/RES/1503, 28 Aug. 2003; also S/RES/1534 (2004).

[14] Paper on some policy issues before the Office of the Prosecutor, Sept. 2003, available at http://icc-cpi.int/library/organs/otp/030905_policy_paper.pdf.

[15] Ibid.

It is, however, worth pointing out that this compromise does may do little to address any tensions between "human rights" and "conflict resolution", as those at the negotiating table are likely to be the very leaders and organisers who remain vulnerable to prosecution under the scheme.

2.7 The Development of the ICC

As the International Criminal Court has begun its task, a new dimension has been added to the bifurcated approach. The threat of the ICC can potentially be used to toughen up the restorative justice mechanism at the domestic level, in an attempt to square the amnesty/accountability circle. States signing peace agreements can attempt to avoid international criminal jurisdiction by fashioning domestic mechanisms in the shadow of prosecution, so as to enable Prosecutor and Court to decide that accountability has taken place at the domestic level. This brings Article 17(a) and (b) of the Rome Statute 1998 into play, which provides that a case is inadmissible if the case is or has been "investigated or prosecuted by a state which has jurisdiction over it, unless the state is unwilling or unable genuinely to carry out the investigation or prosecution". If the state can come up with a satisfactory form of criminal justice it can displace the jurisdiction of the ICC.

The dynamic is illustrated by the AUC law in Colombia, and appears to characterise current attempts to reach agreement on amnesty in Uganda. In Colombia, the "Justice and Peace" law (Law 975) dealing with the demobilisation and reintegration of the United Self-Defence Forces of Colombia (AUC) seems designed so as not to appear an illegitimate amnesty, in order to satisfy the requirement for domestic investigation and prosecution and evade the ICC's jurisdiction. The law links demobilisation to procedural benefits such as pardon and significantly reduced prison sentences, with little formal investigation.[16] Similar dynamics are at work in Uganda. Here indictments were issued by the prosecutor of the International

---

16 While accepted by some international and regional organisations, the Office of the High Commissioner on Human Rights and human rights non-governmental organisations view it as a troubling example of impunity, given the self-amnesty dimension (the groups amnestied have links with the state), the lack of distinction between levels of responsibility, and the lack of any clear link to a coherent peace process capable of ending the conflict as a whole, and have called for it to be revoked, Amnesty International (2007) Colombia: the justice and peace law will benefit human rights abusers. Press Release, 13 September 2007. http://news.amnesty.org/index/ENGAMR 230302005. See further International Crisis Group (2005) and International Center for Transitional Justice (2005). The law has been criticised by the Inter-American Court, and portions have been struck down by the Colombian Constitutional Court. *Caso de la "Masacre de la Mapiripán" v Colombia,* 15 September 2005, Inter-American Human Rights Court (found that the law did not provide sufficient incentive for exhaustive confessions, and that the multiple perpetrators who were part of demobilised paramilitary blocks could deny the full truth. The Court declared that the state must remove all actual and juridical obstacles to an exhaustive judicial examination of the violations, prosecution of those responsible, and reparations for the victim). See also, *Gustavo Gallon Giraldo y otros v. Colombia*, Constitutional Court Judgement No. C-370/2006, Expediente D-6032 (18 May 2006) available (in Spanish) at, http://www.constitucional.gov.co/corte/.

Criminal Court (ICC), against the Lord's Resistance Army (LRA), during the conflict.[17] A peace process subsequently developed to which the indictments were argued to be an obstacle.[18] At time of writing, this peace process has seen a peace agreement on accountability signed between the LRA and the government.[19] The agreement appears to be attempting to creatively discharge the state obligation to investigate and prosecute, so as to displace the ICC's jurisdiction under Article 17 Rome Statute 1998. The agreement's preamble notes "the principle of complementarity" and its text provides a blueprint involving broad commitments to combine conventional criminal justice with more restorative elements aimed at "reconciliation".

The shadow of international criminal law in Colombia and Uganda can be argued to be capable of forcing greater domestic accountability than would otherwise be contemplated. However, Uganda and Colombia also show the capacity for hard cases to soften the court's hard criminal justice edge. The political demand for compromise delivers criminal justice sufficient to displace the court's jurisdiction, but in the process may well redefine criminal justice as a softer mechanism than normally envisaged.

2.8 Where New Mechanisms are Innovated, they should be Designed with as much Consultation with Affected Communities as is Possible

A number of soft law standards require consultation with affected groups, and woman before peace agreements and/or transitional justice mechanisms are designed and implemented. These standards include various victims' rights standards, the Updated Principles on Impunity, UN SC Res 1325 of 2000, on women, peace and security, and the UN SG 2004 report recommendations. Furthermore, international criminal law mechanisms have increasingly involved constituencies, in particular women, to enable them to effectively input to their design and mandate. Peace agreements also have provided for broader input into transitional justice issues; for

[17] In December 2003, President Museveni referred the situation in Northern Uganda to the International Criminal Court (ICC). In October 2005, the ICC made public its first arrest warrants since it was established in 2002, indicting LRA leaders Joseph Kony and Vincent Otti, as well as three other LRA commanders, Raska Lukwiya, Okot Odiambo, and Dominic Ongwen, see http://www.icc-cpi.int/cases/UGD.html.

[18] Note, however, Statement by the Chief Prosecutor Luis Moreno-Ocampo, The Hague, 12 July 2006, noting that the prosecutor was updated on the peace process and that "It is the view of the Office of the Prosecutor and the Government of Uganda that justice and peace have worked together thus far and can continue to work together". Available at http://www.icc-cpi.int/pressrelease_details&id=167&l=en.html.

[19] Agreement on Accountability and Reconciliation between the Government of the Republic of Uganda and the Lord's Resistance Army/Movement, 29 June 2007, UN Doc S/2007/435 [hereafter Ugandan Agreement on Accountability], at http://www.fides.org/eng/documents/uganda_agreement_290607.doc.

example, Guatemala's 1996 Agreement on the Strengthening of Civilian Power and on the Role of the Armed Forces in Democratic Society (III.16(i)) provides for the active involvement of bodies outside the state system of justice in the legal reform process, and the Arusha Accord in 2000 (Protocol 1, Art. 8.2) provided for civil society organizations to put forward candidates for membership of the Burundian Truth and Reconciliation Commission. In El Salvador, the Mexico Agreement (1991) provided for the restructuring of National Council of the Judiciary to include sectors of society not directly connected with the administration of justice.

2.9 Should any Party Evidence Lack of Commitment to the Peace Agreement, and in Particular Return to Violence, any Compromise on Criminal Justice is Void and Reversible through the Use of International Criminal Justice

This requirement has been "stated" somewhat boldly. It does not appear in any soft law standards, nor find articulation in any peace agreement. However, if one looks at the cases where explicit and implicit amnesty deals have been overruled within a relatively short time period, then this return to violence would seem to provide some level of explanation. In Sierra Leone, as noted, the UN Security Council was established explicitly because of renewed fighting by the RUF who were benefiting from the amnesty. Indeed, in one of the challenges before the court where defendants used the peace agreement amnesty to argue that prosecution was an "abuse of process", one of the judges in one of the cases found that the amnesty ceased to have any effect once the fighting resumed (the other judges and other cases found the amnesty to be irrelevant because they found the Lomé Agreement to be a domestic agreement).[20] It can also be more argued that Milošević's indictment and prosecution were enabled politically because of his role in the conflict in Kosovo. Finally, Charles Taylor's indictment before the Sierra Leone Criminal Court, even though amnestied by the peace accord in Liberia, was arguably accepted more easily because of his on-going military role. There is some commonality between the notion of a "wait and see" approach, and the notion of temporary stays of prosecution to take account of the political situation in the ICC's Rome Statute, article 16, which permits the UN Security Council to ask for such a stay of prosecution for a period of up to 12 months. Furthermore, the notion that some amnesties may be more justifiable than others is also asserted by academic writers who suggest that "justifiable" amnesties must be linked to the goal of peace (see further Slye 2002). Logically, this suggests that should those amnestied be involved in fighting should have their amnesty revoked if they subsequently return to violence. Domestic "prisoner release" provisions often condition prisoner release on a commitment to peace, and the Northern Irish provi-

[20] For a good review of the cases see William (2005, p. 271).

sions explicitly provided for "recall" to prison in the event of new offences being committed (although this raised some fair trial issues).[21]

3 The Advantages of the New Law

The new law can be argued to evidence an increased commitment to accountability for serious violations of human rights and humanitarian law. While the law's coverage may be unclear and impartial, it can be argued that unclear and impartial is better than no normative impact at all. We should not forget that as recently as 1990 requirements of accountability were not widely viewed as applicable, and amnesty was seen by mediators and parties to conflict as a tool that could readily be used with few international consequences. In fact, until the UN's dissent in the Lomé Accord in 2000, human rights standards on accountability held little sway outside peace agreements in Central and South America. Controversial as the UN's Lomé Accord dissent was and is, it played a key awareness raising role that norms mattered in peace negotiations.

The normative consensus that has emerged has underlined amnesty as an exception to a norm of accountability, rather than an option of first resort. This has arguably changed the emphasis of public debate – international and local - in peace negotiations. Rather than needing to justify measures aimed at accountability, acceptance of the relevance of international law means that it is now the use of amnesty that must be justified. The argument still persists that issues of accountability should not constrain negotiations (see below). However, the position is asserted in less absolute terms than before, with detractors fewer and quieter, and where a counter-practice of innovative forms of accountability can now be pointed to.

Accountability is now seen as having a pragmatic as well as principled arguments in its favour. The period in which human rights norms were viewed as marginal to a peace process was the period when peace agreements briefly seemed to be an end in themselves, and the point at which international actors could walk away. That is no longer the case. Increasingly, the crucial conflict resolution difficulty seems to be implementing the deal rather than "cutting it". The UN has stated that nearly half of all peace agreements collapse within 5 years (see United Nations 2004). Increasingly, difficulties of implementing the rule of law are being seen as key to that failure. The more that mediators and international actors are faced with a role in implementing and sustaining the peace they have negotiated, the more questions of the rule of law, accountable political and legal institutions, and the symbolism of justice, matter. It is difficult to build a culture based on the rule of law, when the deal is founded in impunity. It can be argued that these practical arguments as much as shifts in the norms, have created a situation in which the choice is increasingly seen as "how much accountability when" rather than a choice between some and none.

[21] On the issue of "risk" see Dwyer (2007, pp. 779–797).

The “new law” has the second advantage that it retains some scope for compromise, even if this is through lack of clarity in what standards require, as much as by design.

Finally, the new law is usefully beginning to set standards of participation in transitional justice design, which can be argued to be important not just to those mechanisms, but to requiring the participation of a broader range of actors than military elites in peace processes more generally.[22] This is important not only to democratic practice, but to enabling creative locally tailored approaches and broad public debate over the connections between the means and the end of transitional justice mechanisms.

4 The Disadvantages of the New Law

As noted, some criticise normative constraints on amnesties. These critics cannot all be dismissed as committed “pragmatists” who have no commitment to human rights. Just as principled arguments can appeal to pragmatism, so pragmatic arguments can appeal to principle. The Truth Commission in Sierra Leone, for example, recognised the principle that it is generally desirable to prosecute perpetrators of serious human rights abuses, particularly when they rise to the level of gravity of crimes against humanity. However stated that it was “unable to condemn the sort to amnesty by those who negotiated the Lomé Peace Agreement” as too high a price for peace (Truth Commission in Sierra Leone 2004, Chap. 6, p. 4). This statement has been defended by Commission member, Professor William Schabas. Professor Schabas (2004, p. 163–164) argues that “those who argue that peace cannot be bartered in exchange for justice, under any circumstances must be prepared to justify the likely prolongation of an armed conflict”. For those who thought that the tension between peace and justice was resolved, current developments in Uganda where International Criminal Court indictments stand in tension with a developing peace process, point to the on-going relevance of the debate.

The new law’s ambiguities can conversely be criticised for being too soft on accountability (to the point of being unable to be reconciled with human rights standards), and open to manipulation. The suggestion that responses other than criminal justice in the sense of prosecution and punishment are permissible, can be argued not to comply with developing jurisprudence, particularly at the regional level in the Americas, but lately also in Europe. From a more pragmatic point of view, the “new law” can be argued to enable new more devious forms of impunity. The “Justice and Peace” law dealing with demobilisation and reintegration of the United Self-Defence Forces of Colombia (AUC), seems designed so as not to appear as an illegitimate amnesty –it links demobilisation to procedural benefits such as pardon and significantly reduced prison sentences, with little formal investigation (see further Laplante and Theidon 2007, pp. 49–108; International Crisis

[22] See Freeman (2007) (setting out procedural standards which should apply to Truth Commissions).

Group (2005). While apparently accepted by international and regional organisations, it has been condemned by human rights NGOs who view it as a troubling example of impunity, given the self-amnesty dimension (the groups amnestied are pro-state), the lack of distinction between levels of responsibility, and the lack of any clear link to coherent process capable of ending the conflict as a whole. The law has now been criticised by the Inter-American Court of Human Rights, and elements struck down by the Colombian Constitutional Court.[23]

Finally, it can be argued that an unclear law is a bad law that brings the concept of normativity as something that aims to guiding conduct, into disrepute. Liberal proceduralists, for example would reject any advance in ends (such as increased accountability), if the means are inconsistent with those ends. They would reject any notion that the rule of law in a substantive sense can be promoted by processes that themselves violate the rule of law in a procedural sense.

5 Developing the New Law

The new law will be developed whether anyone "develops" it or not. Peace agreements cannot but deal with the past – at the very least prisoners need released and so something about the past has to be said. More often achieving a deal requires some more substantial agreement on a process for dealing with the past. Human rights bodies and international organisations are then required to take a position. The post 1990 practice has shown just how rapidly the interpretive interaction between peace process and normative assertion can produce shifts in what the norms are understood to require, and even produce new norms and mechanisms. There are on-going attempts to further codify the law in the form of statements, UN resolutions, and various soft law standards. These can have just as much effect as "hard" law in effecting compliance.

The question remains, however: to what extent is it possible to develop the law so as to resolve its ambiguities? It is assumed that this would lead to further consolidation and extension of what seems like a trend towards an emphasis on accountability. A note of caution should perhaps be sounded, at least for sake of discussion.

The idea of an international consensus on a prohibition on amnesty should not be assumed. There is a great danger that in trying to tie down this consensus further, it would be tested. Moreover, the need to preserve some flexibility to enable negotiated ends to conflict is a real one. While the law can be charged as being incoherent and inconsistent, this is at present the main way that flexibility for negotiations is enabled. Reducing this flexibility further could again lead to normative frameworks being rejected more easily. Any attempt to articulate more clearly within normative frameworks the permissible scope of exceptions or alternative approaches to accountability, would start to be very prescriptive, and it is unclear that it is a project

[23] Op cit.

that has any coherent possibilities at all. There is further the possibility that in articulating any exceptional regime, human rights framework as they apply in more normal situations would be weakened. Transitional justice discourses have a contemporary purchase well beyond transitions from violent conflict. Exceptionalism in the name of the difficulties of transition could lead to a broad exceptionalism as more and more situations are defined as transitional.[24]

Increased normativity also can have some unintended side effects. In particular, it stands to implicate mediators as well as parties to conflicts. Viewing mediators as themselves "caught" by amnesty norms (as logically should happen) can lead to two unintended side effects:

(a) *Norm-dodging mediators*. There are several possible norm-dodging techniques, such as fashioning meaningless exceptions to blanket amnesties which will never see a mechanism for accountability implemented. More subtly, normative restrictions on mediators could lead to those mediators defining the mediation role in terms of a "client-lawyer" or disconnected "facilitator" in which the mediator has no tangible connection with the agreement (and therefore is not "tainted" with its amnesty). This would be a pity. At present mediators and international actors often sign peace agreements as witnesses, guarantors or observers, or sometimes with no specific nomenclature. While signature can be viewed as a paper commitment only, it can also be viewed as important to the status of the peace agreement, the parties sense of obligation, and, pertinently, the norm promotion role that third parties, groups of "friends" and international organisations can bring.
(b) *Normative-mediator dodging parties*. The field of mediation is a "sexy" and crowded one. Parties are astute at choosing mediators who will serve them. There have been suggestions that in adopting a normative stance the UN ruled itself out of mediation business. In the case of the UN this may not matter; it can be argued that it will always be in peace processes in some shape or form, it was unclear that this was part of its business in any case, and that given that the key norms at stake are UN norms, its own normative commitment had to be beyond doubt. However, it would be clearly undesirable if all those who took their normative commitments seriously were ruled out of business.

These possibilities should not, however, be overstated.

6 Conclusions: In Defence of Mess

The prohibition on blanket amnesty has been important. It has particularly been important in conflicts where the nature of the conflict has been closely tied to impunity. To some extent, this explains why the jurisprudence from central America most clearly articulates the need for accountability in the form of prosecution, trial and

[24] Posner and Vermule argue in any case, that transitional justice is ordinary justice, see Posner and Vermule (2004, pp. 761–825).

even punishment. (More controversially, it suggests that this jurisprudence should not be read automatically into all contexts.)

In other conflicts, silence on the past, or even explicit amnesties, have been important to achieving an end to fighting and human rights abuses. Two types of conflicts have seen this approach as prevalent: first, conflicts in Africa where both state and non-state actors often have the appearance of private rather than public actors, and second, in conflicts that only arguably triggered humanitarian law at all and where prosecution and punishment were let-go but this was seen as a purely domestic process of demobilisation.

At present international law emphasises the need for clear accountability for the most serious abuses and violations, and points in the direction of a need for accountability more generally. A presumption of the legality of amnesties has been replaced with a presumption of their illegality. However, the new law has ambiguities, gaps and incoherencies that leave some room for negotiation, sequencing, and creative approaches.

The question is, does the law need to be more coherent than this? It can be argued that the current position points away from a direct choice between accountability or no accountability, towards its reframing in terms of how much accountability can be achieved when. If one follows up what happens peace agreement provisions, the following observations can be made:

(a) Not all blanket amnesties last. Arguments for accountability persist, internationally and locally, seldom without effect. The early transitions of Chile and Argentina where amnesties continue to be "undone" by counts serve as an example.
(b) Often reasonable and effective accountability mechanisms are followed by effective broad amnesty though inaction, as in El Salvador and Guatemala (although here again the picture is not static with new trials emerging).
(c) "Strong" accountability mechanisms such as trials often deliver "weak" results. The numbers and calibre of military figures dealt with by ad hoc international criminal tribunals, and sometimes the outcome, are often disappointing.
(d) Weak mechanisms can deliver strong results, where they mobilise constituencies and rule of law arguments that the powerful cannot resist, as (a) and (b) indicate.

This might leave one to argue that the symbolism and the "idea of law" is as important as what the law actually says at any one point in time. If this is the case, then the question becomes: how do we best create a common consensus as to the "idea of law". The answer might be – we establish a notion of best practice, and encourage people to comply through processes that include democratic dialogue on how international standards are best implemented in any one context. Is this not the best that international law can offer in any case?

I leave with Sierra Leone as an analogy. Disagreement continues on whether the UN "disclaimer" to the Lome accords (accent on Lome) fuelled renewed conflict, or enabled its root causes to eventually be addressed. Disagreement continues on whether the Special Criminal Court's rejection of the amnesty's validity completed the peace process (and even assisted one in Liberia), or was unfair and unhelpfully removed amnesty from the mediation tool kit.

However, there seems to be broad agreement that while the Lomé Accord was not perfect, in the words of Schabas (2004, p. 164): "it provided a framework for a process that pacified the combatants and, 5 years later, has returned Sierra Leoneans to a country in which they need not fear daily violence and atrocity".

In hindsight, is it just possible that both Truth and Reconciliation Commission and Special Criminal Court played a role? The TRC through acknowledgement (still rooted in a concept of truth as accountability) of the political relationship between both the promulgation of the amnesty and its rejection and mutations in the violent conflict. The Special Criminal Court by articulating objective justice standards capable of underwriting the democracy. Could it be that the very inconsistencies between the two mechanisms were important in reflecting a complex conflict, and in acknowledging the difficulties of right answers? Could it be, that what is prescribed on paper is less important than what the mechanisms and those who interact with them are able to articulate and acknowledge through them?

The existence of both the Truth Commission and the Special Criminal Court brought inconsistencies, complications and a certain degree of mess. But in conflicts and peace processes in which easy right answers are seldom to be found, and dilemmas and inconsistencies to be managed rather than wished away, perhaps this should be embraced rather than sorted out.

References

Bell C (2006) Negotiating Justice? Human Rights and Peace Agreements. International Council on Human Right Policy, Geneva

Bell C (2008) On the law of peace: peace agreements and the Lex Pacificatoria. Oxford University Press, Oxford

Dwyer C (2007) Risk, politics and the 'scientification' of political judgment: prisoner release and conflict transformation in Northern Ireland. Br J Criminol 47:779–797

Freeman M (2007) Truth commissions and procedural fairness. Cambridge University Press, Cambridge

Hayner P (2001) Unspeakable truths: confronting state terror and atrocity. Routledge, New York

International Crisis Group (2005) Colombia: presidential politics and peace prospects, Latin America Report No. 14. ICG, Dakar

Laplante LJ, Theidon K (2007) Transitional justice in times of conflict: Colombia's *Ley de Justicia y Paz*. Michigan J Int Law 28(49):49–108

Orentlicher D (1991) Settling accounts: the duty to prosecute human rights violations of a prior regime. Yale Law J 100:2537–2615

Orentlicher D (2007) 'Settling accounts' revisited: reconciling global norms with local agency. Int J Transitional Justice 1:10–22

Posner E, Vermule A (2004) Transitional justice as ordinary justice. Harvard Law Rev 117:761–825

Roht-Arriaza N (1990) State responsibility to prosecute grave human rights obligations in international law. Cal Law Rev 78:449–513

Roht-Arriaza N (2002) Combating impunity: some thoughts on the way forward. Law Contemp Probl 59:93–102

Roht-Arriaza N (2006) Transitional justice. International Council on Human Rights Policy

Schabas W (2004) Amnesty, the Sierra Leone Truth and Reconciliation Commission and the Special Court for Sierra Leone. U C Davis J Int Law Policy 11(1):145

Slye RC (2002) The legitimacy of amnesties under international law and general principles of Anglo-American Law. Is a legitimate amnesty possible? Virginia J Int Law 43:172–247

Truth Commission in Sierra Leone (2004) Witness to Truth: Report of the Sierra Leone Truth and Reconciliation Commission

William S (2005) Amnesties in international law: the experience of the special court for Sierra Leone. Hum Rights Law Rev 5:271

Exploring the Practice of States in Introducing Amnesties

Louise Mallinder

Abstract Although amnesty laws have ancient origins, today their use as political tools increasingly triggers protest from human rights activists, who argue that amnesties for serious violations of human rights are prohibited under customary international law. These claims will be assessed in this chapter through a systematic cross-country analysis of amnesties since the Second World War. This chapter will use the Amnesty Law Database, which was created by the author, to explore state practice and place considerations of the legal framework against impunity within a factual context. It will highlight patterns in state practice such as the relationship between amnesties and truth commissions, and explore whether states are moving away from granting amnesty for crimes under international law. This chapter will argue that there is a wide disparity in state practice relating to the types of amnesty laws introduced, with some aiming to provide victims with a remedy, whereas others aim to create complete impunity for perpetrators. The chapter will argue that this disparity indicates that amnesties can be tailored to meet specific strategic and legal objectives. It will conclude by assessing the impact of the relationship between the different forms of amnesty and reconciliation.

1 Executive Summary

Amnesty laws are of fundamental importance in transitional justice and conflict resolution: they go to the heart of difficulties in managing political transitions as they speak directly to notions of justice, accountability and peace. However, despite their central role in such transitions, amnesties can inspire much opposition from stakeholders, particularly victims' groups, and from international human rights activists, who argue that some forms of amnesty can violate international law and deny victims their rights. This view can contradict the approach of political negotiators, and

---

L. Mallinder
Law School, Queen's University Belfast, 28 University Square, Belfast BT 7 1 NN, UK
e-mail: l.mallinder@qub.ac.uk

K. Ambos et al. (eds.), *Building a Future on Peace and Justice: Studies on Transitional Justice, Peace and Development.*

sometimes the wider populace, who often view amnesties as the necessary price to pay for ending violent conflict and political oppression.

As amnesties are introduced within the context of conflicts and political transitions, they are generally tailored to meet the specific needs of the state, and consequently, there is considerable diversity in state practice in the introduction of amnesties. This chapter was commissioned to examine how states approach and design amnesties. This is an important area of study as it can provide insights into the innovative approaches taken by states in addressing past crimes, and how such measures can be balanced with efforts to move transitional societies towards a peaceful and equitable future. The study of state practice can also contribute to delimiting the scope of state's obligations under international law.[1]

The Amnesty Law Database, developed by the author, provides the basis for exploring state practice in this chapter. At the time of writing, this database contained information on 506 amnesties in 130 countries. By comparing the practice in such a large number of cases, it is possible to highlight trends in the introduction of amnesties, such as why and how they were introduced, and in the nature of amnesties, such as which individuals or crimes benefit. The database can also be used to explore how states have chosen to combine amnesties with other transitional justice mechanisms. Each of the characteristics of amnesty laws represents the different options available to transitional governments and reflects how an amnesty can be tailored to address the unique conditions within a transitional state. Furthermore, each adaptation can affect the amnesty's potential to contribute to reconciliation.

The chapter begins by exploring the definition of the term "amnesty" and argues that amnesties have moved from traditional understandings of the term, which entailed casting the crime into oblivion, to more flexible notions of amnesty as a tool to complement other transitional justice mechanisms and to facilitate investigation of past crimes. The chapter then begins to deconstruct this more flexible approach to amnesty by investigating the motives behind the introduction of amnesties. It finds that they can be introduced to meet a wide range of objectives, which can be overlapping, and are often deliberately obscured by governments. It further finds that in introducing amnesties, governments can have several methods available to them, each of which can have a varying impact on reconciliation depending on how much involvement is permitted for all sectors of the population, either directly or through their representatives. This chapter finds that formal enactment procedures through executive decrees or statutes are the most common ways of introducing amnesties, but in a limited number of cases amnesties result from direct public engagement through referenda.

---

[1] As will be explored below, amnesties are, however, inherently political tools and can be introduced by states on the basis of political, economic, legal and social factors. The impact of non-legal issues on decisions to introduce amnesties for crimes under international law inhibits the identification of state practice in a technical legal sense as for a recognized state practice to constitute convincing evidence of a rule of customary international law, there must be (1) the actual behaviour by states; and (2) a belief that such behaviour is law. The influence of non-legal concerns within decision-making of states makes it difficult to identify such a belief. However, as this study aims to provide a detailed picture of the different forms of amnesty that are introduced in order to illustrate trends, a less restrictive understanding of state practice has been used which looks at the behaviour of states regardless of whether they have publicly expressed views on the legality of their actions.

Following this contextual analysis of why and how amnesties are introduced, the report assesses the scope of amnesties. It begins by considering governmental decisions on which individuals or groups will receive amnesty. Most commonly, this involves distinguishing between state agents and opponents of the state. It can also involve efforts to distinguish between offenders who are perceived to bear different levels of responsibility for human rights violations. The research finds that amnesties are most commonly introduced for those who oppose (or are perceived to oppose) the state, through a range of actions ranging from peaceful protest to armed conflict. Despite this willingness to amnesty opponents, the chapter further finds that 9% of the amnesty laws for opponents of the state exclude the leaders of rebel forces or political movements.

In addition to who receives amnesty, governments much also decide which crimes to amnesty: whether to grant amnesty for crimes under international law, or whether to focus their efforts on more purely political crimes. Here, the chapter finds that the vast majority of amnesties are offered to perpetrators of political crimes, but that crimes under international law have been amnestied in 19% of the laws that have been examined (although crimes under international law would not have arisen in all contexts), and that states have continued to amnesty crimes under international law despite the growth of the human rights movement and the change in the UN's approach to amnesties following the signing of the Lomé Accords on 7 July 1999.[2]

The third decision on the scope of the amnesty that governments face is whether to make the amnesty conditional upon potential beneficiaries performing specific actions, each of which can affect the amnesty's potential to promote reconciliation. These conditions can be practical, such as having to apply for amnesty within prescribed time limits, or they could involve participation in complementary transitional justice processes, such as truth-recovery mechanisms. The chapter finds that it is most common for amnesty processes to be accompanied by reparations programmes, which can range from symbolic gestures to memorialize the suffering of the victims, to institutional reform to prevent a repetition of the crimes, to financial compensation for victims. The chapter further finds that since the Human Rights Violations Committee of the South African Truth and Reconciliation Commission submitted its report in October 1998, the popularity of truth commissions accompanying amnesties has increased.

These findings illustrate trends in state practice relating to amnesty laws, which can provide insights into the potential of amnesties to contribute to reconciliation. This potential is explored in the final section, which argues that there is no clear and easy relationship between amnesty and reconciliation. It begins by analysing what is meant by the term "reconciliation" and investigates how amnesty can relate to the various understandings of the term. It addresses reconciliation as a continuum between "thinner" understandings of reconciliation as simply as an end to the violence, to "thicker" understandings where reconciliation entails repairing relationships on individual, inter-personal, communal and national levels. The chapter

[2] For a discussion of this change in position see fn 51.

argues that amnesty can clearly contribute to achieving "thinner" conceptions of reconciliation by encouraging former combatants to surrender and disarm without fear of retribution. For longer-term goals of achieving "thicker" understandings of reconciliation, the role of amnesty can be more complex. For amnesty to contribute to restoring relationships and promoting national reconciliation, it must be accompanied by restorative justice and truth-recovery mechanisms, which can contribute to breaking cycles of violence by pursuing policies of forgiveness and compromise, rather than vengeance. Using broader conceptions of justice to encompass restorative approaches can contribute to individual and inter-personal reconciliation by creating space for victims and offenders to recognize each other's humanity.

2 Introduction

Amnesty laws are long-standing political tools that are used by states wishing to quell dissent, introduce reforms or achieve peaceful relationships with their enemies. Indeed, political negotiators often argue that amnesty is a necessary price to pay in order to achieve a stable, peaceful, and equitable system of government. In recent years, however, they have elicited much criticism from human rights non-governmental organizations (NGOs) and inter-governmental bodies, particularly the Office of the High Commissioner for Human Rights (OHCHR). These organizations have argued strongly that amnesties for serious human rights violations are now prohibited under customary international law. Despite this opposition, and the concurrent growth of international criminal justice institutions, amnesty laws continue to be introduced, even for the most serious crimes. Indeed, as shown in Fig. 1, amnesties have in fact increased in frequency since the end of the Second World War. As illustrated, this trend remains true when the number of amnesties introduced in each 5-year period is looked at against the total number of states in existence during that time. This chapter will investigate this trend, by exploring why and how amnesty laws are introduced, and by assessing the diversity among existing

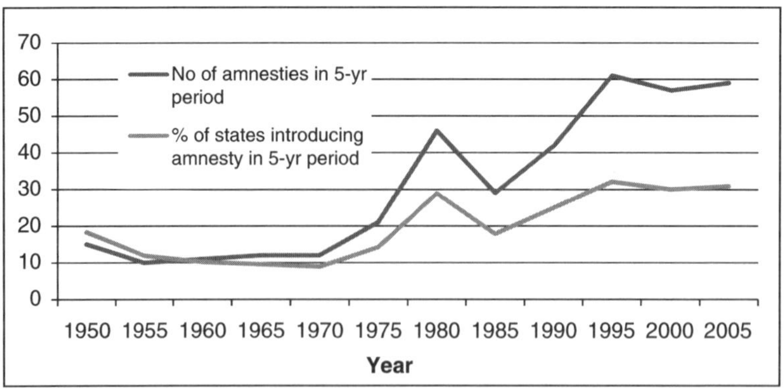

Fig. 1 Amnesties by 5-year intervals (1945–2005)

amnesty laws. This exploration of the approach of states to amnesties is designed to provide a factual background to the legal framework explored elsewhere in this book. Exploring the diverse array of amnesty laws is an important area of study as it can provide insights into the innovative approaches taken by states in addressing past crimes, and how such measures can be balanced with efforts to move a transitional society towards a peaceful and equitable future. Analysing the forms of amnesty that are introduced can also contribute to delimiting the scope of states' obligations under customary international law.

This chapter will use the Amnesty Law Database,[3] developed by the author, to conduct a systematic cross-country analysis of amnesties. The database contains information on amnesties that have occurred since the end of the Second World War in all regions of the world relating to societies enduring international or internal conflict or authoritarian government, or making a transition to democracy. At the time of writing, it contained information on 506 amnesty processes in 130 countries.[4] The profiles of the amnesty processes were compiled using a wide range of sources including domestic legislation; academic writing; jurisprudence from national and international courts; international treaties; opinions given by treaty-monitoring bodies; statements by intergovernmental organizations; reports by states and NGOs; and newspaper articles. These materials influenced the development of the categories explored throughout this chapter. For each amnesty process, data was gathered on the characteristics of the amnesty, the political and social context in which it was introduced and, where appropriate, on complementary transitional justice mechanisms that accompanied the amnesty, such as truth commissions, lustration programmes and reparations.

This chapter will begin by exploring what the term "amnesty" denotes. It will then use the database to map trends in the introduction of amnesties, such as why and how they are introduced, and in the nature of the amnesties, such as which individuals or crimes benefit or are excluded. It will also explore how states have chosen to combine amnesties with other transitional justice mechanisms. In this analysis, the chapter will briefly explore the potential consequences of each approach to the pursuit of reconciliation within the transitional state. It will not evaluate, however, whether the different forms of amnesty comply with states' international obligations, as this is explored more fully in Ambos's chapter; nor will it evaluate the merits of alternative transitional justice mechanisms as these are discussed elsewhere in this book.[5] Finally, the chapter will investigate whether amnesty can be used as a tool to promote reconciliation. This chapter will argue that there is a wide disparity in state practice relating to the types of amnesty laws introduced, with some aiming to provide victims with a remedy, and others aiming to create complete impunity for perpetrators. Consequently, the author contends that there is no clear and

[3] This database is in the process of being updated and will be available online during 2009. summer 2008.

[4] This comprises amnesty laws identified in all parts of the world, which were enacted between August 1945 and December 2007.

[5] The author does, however, tackle these issues in depth in her book: Mallinder (2008). See also Mallinder (2007, p. 208).

easy relationship between amnesty and reconciliation, but rather the contribution amnesties can make to restoring relationships within transitional states can depend on the objectives of the amnesties, how they are designed, and whether they are part of wider reform packages.

3 Defining "Amnesty"

Although "amnesty" is often popularly used to describe a range of measures to tackle such diverse issues as illegal immigrants[6] or unreturned library books (BBC 2006b), this chapter is only concerned with amnesties that are introduced in specific political contexts including: coups, civil unrest, conflicts, peace agreements, dictatorial regimes, or democratic transitions.[7] Within each of these contexts, amnesties can have a range of characteristics, and consequently, the definition of amnesty can differ substantially between jurisdictions. Therefore, before progressing with this study, the meaning of the term "amnesty" must be clarified. This word, like "amnesia" comes from the Greek word "*amnēstia*", meaning "forgetfulness" or "oblivion" (Chigara 2002, p. 8). It has traditionally been understood in a legal sense to denote efforts by governments to eliminate any record of crimes occurring by barring criminal prosecutions and/or civil suits (Bull 2001). In extinguishing liability for a crime, amnesty assumes that a crime has been committed (O'Shea 2002, p. 2). In this way, amnesties are retroactive; applying only to acts committed before the laws were passed (Bourdon 1999). Furthermore, amnesties are always exceptional, and can be limited in a variety of ways: they could exclude certain categories of crimes, such as serious human rights violations; or certain individuals, such as the leaders and intellectual authors of the policies of oppression and violence. In addition, an amnesty process could be conditional, requiring applicants to perform tasks such as surrendering weapons, providing information on former comrades, admitting the truth about their actions, or showing remorse, to benefit from amnesty. These conditional amnesties could be individualized, so that applicants can only benefit from an amnesty upon successful compliance with its conditions. Where the amnesty is linked to truth-recovery mechanisms, particularly by granting amnesty in exchange for truth, it differs from the traditional understandings of the term, as rather than casting the crime into oblivion, it is investigated and the events are publicized in public hearings and official reports, which can play a significant role in promoting reconciliation. This chapter will discuss both more traditional blanket amnesties and the newer more flexible approaches.

[6] See, for example, the recent debates in the United States on the temporary worker programme for illegal immigrants.

[7] For a discussion of the motives for amnesty laws, see s 4.1.

4 Introducing Amnesty in Transitional Contexts

This section will explore why and how states introduce amnesties. It will consider the range of motivations that trigger amnesties and discuss how they can influence the method by which the amnesty is introduced. The potential impact of the motivations and methods on reconciliation will also be explored.

4.1 Why do States Introduce Amnesties?

The political triggers of amnesty laws in each state are unique and therefore, the goals that amnesties are designed to achieve can be diverse. However, during the process of designing the Amnesty Law Database, the motivations behind amnesty laws were allocated to the following overarching categories: alleviating internal pressure; promoting peace and reconciliation; responding to international pressure; adhering to cultural or religious traditions; providing reparations; encouraging exiles to return; and protecting state agents from prosecution.

Within each of these categories, the amnesty can be introduced in response to a range of stimuli. For example, amnesties in the first category, *alleviating internal pressure*, can occur across a continuum from stability to conflict. Amnesties for political prisoners can represent an attempt to bolster support for the government within an already comparatively stable (although not necessarily democratic) society. In such societies, governments usually have a monopoly over political, economic and military power, and consequently, might choose to introduce an amnesty as a show of strength, to demonstrate clearly that any opposition does not pose a threat to its rule. This idea was often vocalized, usually disingenuously, in the amnesty laws of the former communist bloc countries. For example, in its 1989 amnesty decree providing for the release of political prisoners, the Albanian government proclaimed amnesty "taking into consideration the constant consolidation of our socialist order, the sound moral and political state of the country, the steel-like unity of the people around the party ...".[8] Indeed, amnesty could provide a means for governments to undermine support for the opposition by appearing benevolent whilst eliminating the opposition's ability to rely on the detention of political prisoners as a rallying cry.

Alternatively, governments could proclaim amnesties as part of internal reform programmes. Their reason for doing this could perhaps be a genuine desire to transfer power peacefully from a dictatorial regime to a democratically-elected one. This seems to have been the case in Benin in 1990, where, following a wave of internal political protests, the president amnestied all his political opponents in exile and convened a national conference to discuss establishing democratic rule (BBC 1989).

More commonly, amnesty is introduced in response to severe internal pressure, such as widespread rioting or anti-government protests; minor armed incursions

[8] Decree No. 7338, 1989 (Albania), Preamble.

across a border; serious unrest focused solely on one small region of the country; or threatened military coups, where the government faces serious threats to its power. Amnesties can also be introduced in the wake of failed military coups to pacify the military, encourage their cooperation with the government, and stabilize the regime.

Finally, the most common form of internal pressure that can inspire amnesty is a desire to end violent conflict, either national or international. From the above, it seems clear that the potential for amnesties introduced in response to internal pressure to contribute to reconciliation will very much depend upon the political context in which they are introduced, with some governments genuinely working towards reconciliation, and others simply using an amnesty as a means to reinforce their own hold on power.

In addition to amnesties introduced as a political response to internal pressure, the second category of motivation highlights amnesties that are, or are at least allege to be, introduced *to promote peace and reconciliation*. This objective particularly characterizes amnesties in conflict situations, where the amnesty is part of a wide-ranging package of reforms to address the root causes of the violence and establish representative government. For example, the 1997 Bangladeshi amnesty was part of a peace process to encourage insurgents to stop fighting. It was accompanied by other measures to ensure greater autonomy for the peoples of the Chittagong Hill Tracts.[9] Such amnesties can be the starting point to enable other aspects of the agreement to occur, such as demobilization, integration of combatants into the armed forces, or the transformation of insurgent groups into political parties that could perhaps participate in governments of national unity. In these instances, the amnesty could be a tool for trust building between the parties and creating a climate in which the leaders can focus on the redevelopment of the country and the promotion of reconciliation. The relationship between amnesty and reconciliation will be discussed in more detail below.

In addition to internal catalysts, amnesty can also be introduced *to respond to international pressure*. International actors are clearly involved in amnesties following international conflicts, and even in the majority of internal conflicts, there are often international mediators, either from states or international organizations. Their involvement is often based on political motives, for example, advocating amnesty to increase the strength of their chosen allies. Furthermore, support for national amnesties by international actors can provide examples of state practice and contribute to the development of customary international law.[10] In addition to direct mediation, international actors can influence decisions on amnesties indirectly by contributing to the conditions that make amnesty necessary, for example, by imposing sanctions or conditioning military or economic aid on the release of political prisoners or by providing military support to a party to the conflict to bring about a particular political settlement. For example, during the 1980s, several countries in Latin America introduced amnesties for their political opponents to secure funding and military support from a United States Congress that was critical of

[9] Chittagong Hill Tracts Peace Treaty 1997 (Bangladesh).

[10] For a detailed overview of international involvement in national amnesty processes, see Mallinder (2008, Chap. 8).

human rights violations (see, e.g., Trumbull 2007, p. 283; Moore Jr 1991, p. 733; Cassel 1996, p. 197). International actors have also occasionally played a role in encouraging states to introduce amnesty laws without a deliberate policy to intervene in the transition. For example, external events, such as the fall of the Berlin Wall, can contribute to pressure for reform in other countries, including the release of political prisoners, through the diffusion of liberal norms.[11] Furthermore, amnesties could result from what Jones and Newburn term "policy transfer".[12] For example, the experience of the South African Truth and Reconciliation Commission (TRC) has sparked considerable interest in other states, with delegations often travelling to and from South Africa to exchange experiences. In any transitional context, international actors are able to exert considerable pressure using a variety of diplomatic, economic, legal or military tools. This pressure can be used to either encourage or deter transitional governments from introducing amnesty laws. However, international actors should seek not to dictate policy, but to complement and support national decisions. If transitional justice mechanisms are viewed as externally imposed their legitimacy will be reduced, and consequently, their potential to contribute to reconciliation will be lessened.

The fourth category of motivation to be identified covers amnesties that are introduced *to adhere to cultural or religious traditions*, which encourage the head of state to grant amnesty to individuals on national or religious holidays. Under normal circumstances, these amnesties would usually apply to certain categories of offenders, such as minor criminals, veterans, elderly or unhealthy prisoners, first-time offenders, or female prisoners. However, in many dictatorial regimes they can be used as occasions to appear benevolent by releasing opponents of the state. The occasions employed will differ depending on the country, for example, in many Arab countries, it is usual to introduce amnesties on religious holidays, whereas in former Soviet bloc countries, amnesties are introduced to celebrate national holidays, such as the anniversary of the founding of the country.

In political transitions, amnesties are sometimes introduced *to repair the harm* inflicted upon those who are deemed opponents of the state due to their ethnicity, or supposed religious or political views. These prisoners are often known as "prisoners of conscience" and are generally associated with non-violent opposition to repression (McEvoy et al. 2007). Alternatively, they are also often described as "political prisoners", but as Vanderginste highlights in his chapter on Burundi, this term is often political divisive, and consequently, it is understood here to describe only individuals who are imprisoned for non-violent crimes or who are falsely imprisoned. Reparative amnesties can be granted by oppressive regimes to reduce tensions or mitigate dissent, as shown by the amnesties to release political prisoners used by the Polish communist government in 1983 and 1984; or alternatively, as discussed above, to gain international goodwill. Often when political prisoners are amnestied,

[11] For a discussion of the formation of these norms, see Sikkink and Walling (2007, p. 427). Cf. Subotic (2005).

[12] Jones and Newburn (2005, p. 58, 74). The authors use the term "policy transfer" to describe the convergence in penal policies between Britain and the United States in both initial ideas and the "substantive manifestations of policy".

they have already been convicted. Such amnesties resemble pardons where there has been a conviction and merely the punishment is withdrawn. A distinction remains, however, as many amnesties for political prisoners, particularly those following the collapse of an oppressive regime, aim to rehabilitate the prisoners and declare their innocence, thereby eliminating the conviction from their record. Such amnesties can imply that the criminal proceedings by which the accused was sentenced were unfair and can rehabilitate those individuals who lost their jobs, pensions, property, or political rights due to their perceived political views or identity. In this context, amnesty is a reparative instrument that can contribute positively to national reconciliation, whilst restoring the dignity and status of those who have been oppressed.

In addition to amnesties to benefit political prisoners, amnesty can also be introduced for exiles and refugees. It is common practice to encourage refugees to return home after a conflict and this is encouraged by the international community, as illustrated by the amnesty provisions in Annex 7 of the Dayton Peace Accords 1995 for the conflict in Bosnia-Herzegovina. However, amnesties to encourage dissidents to return, if introduced by the dictatorial regime from which they fled, can represent an effort by the government to bolster its position domestically by introducing a populist policy. Furthermore, the leaders of opposition groups are often amnestied when a transition is occurring to enable them to participate in negotiations on new constitutional arrangements. For example, the 1993 Malawian amnesty introduced during the transition from dictatorship enabled Malawian exiles to return home to participate in the political process, including the formation of new political parties prior to the holding of general elections (Xiaoyi 1993; US Department of State 1994). In the past, there have been amnesties designed solely to encourage exiles to return to their countries of origin, but today, amnesties that provide protection for the other groups usually include some provisions for exiles. For example, Article 1 of 1990 Law on General Amnesty and National Reconciliation in Nicaragua was applicable to "all Nicaraguans, *whether or not currently residing in the country...*" (emphasis added).

The final category of motivation covers amnesties introduced specifically *to benefit state agents.*[13] Governments may introduce such laws when they wish to reward the military for its role in establishing the government's power or eliminating political threats. This motivation is occasionally expressed in the law by declaring that the state agents, when they committed crimes, were performing their duty. For example, the 1982 Guatemalan amnesty law for "political crimes" committed during the civil war includes immunity for "members of the state security forces that, in carrying out their duties, have participated in actions against subversion".[14] On occasion, governments claim such "self-amnesties" are necessary to ensure national security. For example, the 1986 Israeli amnesty was introduced to protect members of Shin Bet, Israel's counter-intelligence agency, and possibly Israeli politicians, from an investigation into the deaths of two Palestinian bus hijackers in 1984. The government justified the amnesty by arguing that any investigation could risk revealing

[13] For a discussion of who is a state agent, see s 5.1.

[14] Decreto-Ley No 33–82, Diario Oficial No 84, tomo 218, 1982 (Guatemala) art 1.

information crucial to state security.[15] However, as this example indicates, amnesty could also be a response to a particular event in which the state is implicated and for which it wants to avoid any investigations. This appears to have been the motivation behind the 2002 Kyrgyz amnesty. The amnesty was introduced following clashes in the Aksy district on 17–18 March 2002 between supporters of leading opposition deputy Azimbek Beknazarov and the police in which five people were killed and 90 injured, sparking a wave of protests which destabilized the country for months. The amnesty was designed to protect the police officers responsible for killing civilians and maybe higher-ranking police and politicians who were named in the 18 May 2002 inquiry into the events (see, e.g., BBC 2001). Amnesties have also often been issued at the end of a conflict, including conflicts that occurred abroad, to shield the soldiers who participated from prosecution. For example, France has issued a succession of amnesty laws for the actions of its military in Indochina and Algeria.[16] Finally, self-amnesties could also be introduced by outgoing dictatorial regimes wishing to protect themselves from future prosecutions. This form of amnesty has been particularly common in Latin American transitions. The idea of governments amnestying themselves is of course troubling, particularly where the government bears responsibility for the human rights violations and the amnesty is used to reinforce existing propaganda by applauding the actions of the armed forces. In such cases, the amnesty would contribute little to reconciliation.

Allocating individual amnesties to the above categories can be problematic as states often have multiple objectives for introducing an amnesty law. These objectives may be inter-related, such as demobilizing combatants, encouraging the surrender of weapons, obtaining a ceasefire, and creating conditions for economic development. They could also be disparate, particularly where the state is responding to both exogenous and endogenous factors. For example, a state by releasing its political opponents from prison may simultaneously be trying to appear benevolent before the international community and to undermine its domestic opponents. Furthermore, as will be discussed below, states can introduce amnesty to satisfy both short-term and long-term goals, such as ending the violence, and building a climate of trust that could provide the basis for reconciliation. Where a state has multiple objectives, it may deliberately obscure some of its motives (Sarkin and Daly 2004, p. 661, 689). For example, a government may publicly pronounce certain reasons, usually to promote reconciliation, which may even be highlighted in the name it chooses to give the law.[17] But these public reasons may not have been its sole motives. In certain circumstances, the government may even try to conceal the fact that

[15] Murray (1986); Barzilai v Government of Israel, ("Shin Bet Affair") Case HCJ 428/86, [1986].

[16] Décret N° 62–328 du 22 Mar 1962 portant amnistie de faits commis dans le cadre des opérations de maintien de l'ordre dirigées contre l'insurrection algérienne; Loi portant amnistie d'infractions contre la sûreté de l'Etat ou commises en relation avec les événements d'Algérie, 1966; Loi N° 68–697 du 31 juillet 1968 portant amnistie, Journal officiel, 2 Aug 1968, at 77521; Loi N° 74–643 portant amnistie; Loi n° 81–736 Loi Portant Amnistie, 1981; Loi no 82–1021 (3 Dec 1982) relative au règlement de certaines situations résultant de évènements d'Afrique du Nord, de la guerre d'Indochine ou de la seconde guerre mondiale.

[17] Amnesty laws are frequently given titles involving words such as peace, reconciliation, and harmony.

it is introducing an amnesty, by describing the legislation in other terms, such as the Due Obedience Law 1987 in Argentina.[18]

Where the motives behind amnesty laws are not be fully apparent in the text of the legislation, they may be revealed only through implementation. This can become complicated where governments alter the terms of their amnesties in response to changing political circumstances. For example, following the introduction of amnesty for all members of insurgent groups in Uganda in 2000,[19] President Museveni requested in December 2003 that the International Criminal Court (ICC) investigate the situation in northern Uganda where the rebel group, the Lord's Resistance Army (LRA), had been fighting the Ugandan army.[20] Arrest warrants were issued in 2005 for five members of the LRA leadership: Vincent Otti, Okot Odhiambo, Dominic Ongwen and Raska Lukwiya, three of whom are now believed to be dead.[21] Following the launching of the ICC investigation, the Ugandan president repeatedly asserted that the LRA leaders would be excluded from the amnesty (although he often made contradictory statements) and on 20 April 2006, the Ugandan parliament passed the Amnesty (Amendment) Act. This legislation grants the Minister of Internal Affairs the power to exclude named individuals from the amnesty. These exclusions have not been implemented, and instead, as the peace negotiations progressed, the Ugandan president repeatedly publicly stated that Kony himself would benefit from amnesty if he surrendered (BBC 2006a). However, at the time of writing, it appears that these peace talks have collapsed and both the Amnesty Act and the ICC arrest warrants remain in place.[22]

Despite these difficulties, information has been compiled on the motivations underlying 464[23] amnesty processes, and their distribution across the categories can be seen in Fig. 2. As discussed previously, each amnesty process may fall within one or several of these categories. This figure shows that amnesties resulting from internal pressure are, perhaps unsurprisingly, the most common, but overall amnesties are introduced for a diverse array of reasons. Each of these motivations has been influential throughout the period since the Second World War. Furthermore, every motivation has been present in amnesty laws in each region of the world.

---

[18] Ley de Obedencia Debida, No. 23.521 (4 June 1987) (Arg.).

[19] Amnesty Act 2000 (Uganda) s 3.

[20] The ICC Prosecutor, Luis Moreno Ocampo announced the investigation in a joint press conference with President Museveni on 29 January 2004. The Office of the Prosecutor began investigations in July 2004 and issued arrest warrants under seal on 8 July 2005, which were unsealed on 13 October 2005.

[21] On 11 July 2007, Pre-Trial Chamber II decided to terminate the proceedings against Raska Lukwiya following confirmation of Lukwiya's death. See ICC, "Decision to Terminate Proceedings against Lukwiya", Case N° ICC-02/04–01/05–248 of 11 July 2007. Vincent Otti was reportedly killed on Joseph Kony's ordered on or around 8 October 2007. His death was initially denied by the LRA and then confirmed by Kony on 22 January 2008. Finally, Okot Odhiambo was reportedly killed on 14 April 2008 as a result of "rebel infighting".

[22] For a discussion of the difficulties faced by the ICC in its investigation into the northern Ugandan situation, see the ICTJ Prosecutorial Program's chapter on "Pursuing Justice in Ongoing Conflict".

[23] Motivations could not be clearly identified for all the amnesties in the Amnesty Law Database. This could be due to the problems discussed above such as a lack of transparency in governmental decision-making.

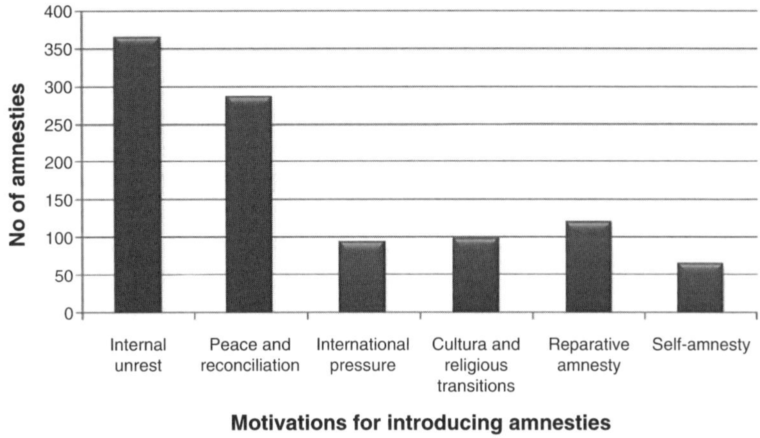

Fig. 2 Motivations of states that introduce amnesty laws

The wide range of motivations for amnesties indicates that they may help governments to attain a variety of goals. These goals can be positive such as attempts to repair the suffering inflicted on opponents of the former regime, or negative, such as providing impunity for state agents. The potential for an amnesty to promote reconciliation is dependent on the amnesty being introduced in good faith by a government committed to reform, and the goals of the amnesty being clearly communicated to the population in order to reduce the risk of false expectations and reduce fears. Where possible, the contribution of amnesty to reconciliation would be further strengthened by such communication strategies being two-way processes, with the views of all sectors of society, including vulnerable groups such as women and minorities being taken into account by the state when designing the amnesty.

4.2 How are Amnesty Laws Introduced?

Depending on the political context and domestic legal framework, there are four methods by which a formal amnesty process can be introduced: (1) exercises of executive discretion; (2) negotiated peace agreements; (3) promulgated amnesty laws; and (4) referendums. The choice of each method can affect the role of the amnesty in promoting reconciliation.

"*Exercises of executive discretion*" refers to amnesties that are introduced by presidential decrees or proclamations. For many amnesty processes, these decrees emanate from undemocratic rulers, such as military *juntas*. For example, the 2005 amnesty law for supporters of the former regime in Mauritania was introduced by Col. Ely Ould Mohamed Vall, the Head of the governing Military Council for Justice and Democracy, which seized power 3 August 2005 (IRIN 2005). This means that the legitimacy of the law is undermined, as representatives of the people did not approve it.[24] However, according to the constitutions of some democratic states, the president has the power to declare any amnesties or pardons.[25] Where this occurs, the amnesty can have more legitimacy than those of dictators, as the ruler declaring it has been democratically elected. Furthermore, s/he would probably consult the government, the Attorney General, or possibly a specially appointed commission. For example, before the Northern Irish Prime Minister enacted an amnesty in 1969 for offences relating to political demonstrations, he consulted his cabinet and the provincial Attorney General (Bell 2003, p. 1095; Bowyer Bell 1993). Executive decrees also include amnesties that are promulgated by transitional administrations before the establishment of a parliament, or by occupying powers. For example, President Karzai of Afghanistan declared an amnesty for former Taliban fighters in 2003 during the transitional administration (Rubin 2003, p. 567), and amnesties were sanctioned by the Allied occupying powers in Germany after the Second World War for lower-level individuals who had worked with the Nazi regime (Larsen and Hagtvet 1998; Elster 2004; Frei 2002). Although presidential decrees can have the advantage of being introduced rapidly in reponse to a delicate political situation, O'Shea highlights that executive amnesty decrees risk being "arbitrary exercises of presidential discretion", and suggests that "properly introduced laws" are preferable (O'Shea 2002, p. 22), as they provide a greater opportunity for the terms of the law to be debated and negotiated, where the process of debate could strengthen the rule of law and contribute to establishing a consensus on the amnesty.

In contrast to exercises of executive discretion, which can be introduced unilaterally by the government, many amnesty processes result from the more participative circumstances of peace talks. *Negotiated peace agreements* can be either international or national depending on the nature of the conflict. But as warfare has changed since the Second World War, there are far fewer international peace treaties today than in earlier times, and many that have occurred resulted from decolonization conflicts, rather than wars that were fought solely between sovereign states. For example, the Evian Accord 1962 which marked the end of Algeria's battle for independence from France, offered amnesty to combatants on both sides. Today, however, the vast majority of amnesties emanating from peace agreements are the result of internal conflicts, although representatives of the international community mediate many of the peace agreements. These agreements can grant amnesty, either in response to demands from insurgents who require safeguards from prosecution before surrendering their weapons, or when the leaders of both state and non-state actors wish to immunize themselves from prosecution.[26] Negotiated peace agreements can potentially be more democratically legitimate than presidential decrees as they involve representatives of the parties to the conflict or transition process, and

[24] This is the view that has been taken by the Inter-American Commission, see Garay Hermosilla et al v Chile, Case 10.843, Inter-Am. C. H. R., Report 36/96, OEA/Ser.L/V/II/95 [1996] [30]. For a discussion of the importance of legitimacy see Oomen's chapter on "Justice Mechanisms and the Question of Legitimacy: The Example of Rwanda's Multi-layered Justice Mechanism".

[25] For more information on the presidential power to pardon, see Sebba (1977, p. 83).

[26] For a detailed discussion of the relationship between amnesty and peace agreements, see Vinjamuri and Boesenecker (2007).

international observers. If none of the representatives are elected, however, the democratic legitimacy can be reduced, as although the spokespersons of all the main communities can participate, it may be unclear whether those individuals have a legitimate right to speak on behalf of others.

The democratic legitimacy of an amnesty can, however, be enhanced where it is adopted in the form of a parliamentary statute. Formally enacted amnesty laws can be introduced to ratify the provisions of negotiated peace agreements or to respond to demands from civil society. Within a peaceful, democratic society amnesties passed by democratically-elected legislatures would normally be perceived as legitimate due to their approval by the chosen representatives of the people. This legitimacy would be reduced, however, for those who do not support the regime, when the politicians are not elected, or have achieved their positions following rigged elections, or where the executive dominates parliament to such an extent that opposition opinions are disregarded, particularly where opposition parties represent oppressed minorities. Similarly, the legitimacy of an amnesty could be undermined where it is approved by a bare majority in a divided legislature. In such cases, the author believes that consultation is desirable and that attempts should be made to address the concerns of those who are against the amnesty. Such consultation could perhaps entail direct public involvement in the enactment of the law.

Direct public involvement could take many forms including an orchestrated consultation programme such as the consultation in South Africa that preceded the adoption of the Promotion of National Unity and Reconciliation Act 1995 (Boraine 2000; Sarkin 2004). Alternatively, election campaign promises could give voters the opportunity to express their views on the amnesty. Such promises were made in Greece in 1973, where the political party offering an amnesty for coup plotters and legal professionals who cooperated with the military *junta* received the support of the electorate. Amnesties could also be induced following a referendum, either specifically on the amnesty law or on a new constitution that contains amnesty provisions. The complex question of the timing and methods of consultation will clearly depend on the conditions within each transitional state, including the quality of the communication infrastructure and the extent of security concerns, particularly where public involvement during delicate negotiations could destabilize the process by undermining the mandate of the negotiators. However, in principle, consultations should be as full and inclusive as circumstances permit.

Even where an amnesty law is approved by referendum, difficulties could arise. For example, simple majority support will not be appropriate where minority groups were the victims of the oppression (Sarkin and Daly 2004, p. 703). Furthermore, after a referendum, it may be unclear whether the result truly reflects the will of the populace. For example, the 1989 Uruguayan referendum on the 1986 Expiry Law,[27] where the population voted in favour of the amnesty, is often lauded as an example of democratic approval. But it has been contended that the democratic politicians were intimidated by the still powerful army, the Supreme Court disqualified many signatures from the petition that led to the referendum, and there were allegations

[27] Ley de Caducidad de la Pretensión Punitiva del Estado, No. 15.848 (1986) (Uru.).

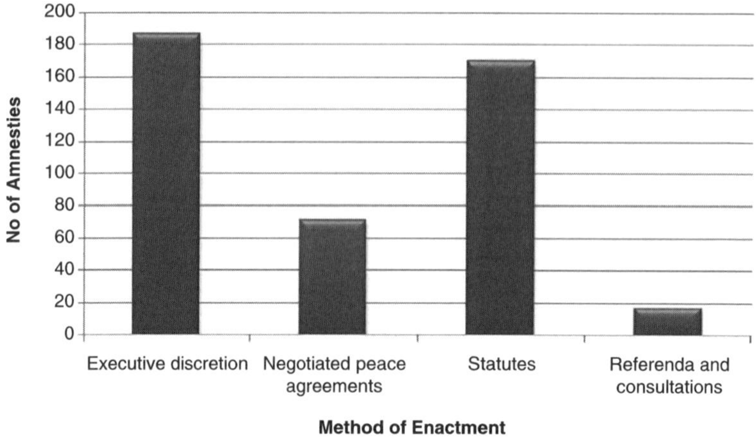

Fig. 3 How amnesty laws are introduced

of intimidation of voters by the police.[28] If these allegations were true, they would undermine the extent of true democratic approval that the amnesty law received. This does not devalue the referendum process entirely, however, as referendums, by inspiring public debate on an amnesty law, can help it to achieve the aim of fostering reconciliation.

These methods of introducing amnesty laws are not mutually exclusive and individual amnesties can employ multiple methods. For example, amnesties that are approved by referenda are usually subsequently enacted by the legislature. Based on the information obtained for 372[29] amnesty processes, the occurrence of the different methods is shown in Fig. 3. This illustrates that the most popular means of introducing amnesty laws are through executive decrees and legislation. In contrast, few amnesties have resulted from public consultation. These differences are significant as the extent to which an amnesty can be viewed as democratically legitimate within the state where it has been introduced may depend upon whether it was approved directly by the populace or by their elected representatives. Where amnesty is introduced unilaterally by an oppressive regime, or where the views of oppressed populations are overlooked, it seems likely that the amnesty will have less legitimacy, and consequently, its potential to contribute to peace and reconciliation could be undermined, as rather than the amnesty contributing to trust building between stakeholder groups within society, it could be viewed as merely a reward for those who perpetrated human rights abuses. In contrast, amnesties which are introduced

[28] For a study of the referendum process in Uruguay, see Weschler (1998); Americas Watch (1989). It should also be noted that Uruguayan civil society launched a campaign in September 2007 to trigger a second referendum on the 1986 Expiry Law. For information on this campaign see http://nulidadleycaducidad.blogspot.com/ (accessed 10 June 2008).

[29] It has not been possible to obtain clear data on the enactment processes for all amnesties in the Amnesty Law Database, due to the paucity of information on some amnesty processes, particularly those introduced during the earlier years under consideration or by a dictatorial regime.

following widespread public involvement and which result from the establishment of a consensus among the main groups have a greater chance at encouraging targeted groups and individuals to participate, and in contributing to the promotion of reconciliation.

5 Characteristics of Amnesties

Every transition is unique in terms of the nature of the violations that occurred, the duration of the repression, the resources available, the balance of power between parties to the transition, the ability of their leaders, the level of international involvement and the existence of a sense of national unity. Each amnesty should therefore be tailored to address the specific needs of the transitional state. This tailoring is commonly done by designing amnesties to target specific groups or levels of offenders, who can be identified by their organizational membership and their position within the organizational hierarchy. Such targeting is significant for any analysis of the legality of amnesty under international and domestic law. For example, during conflicts, members of the armed forces are frequently acting under different domestic legal obligations to insurgents whose organizations are usually banned under domestic law. In contrast, the actions of state agents may be legal domestically, but criminalized under international law that holds states accountable for the actions of its agents. For example, according to the 1984 Convention Against Torture, torture can only be committed "by or at the instigation of or with the consent or acquiescence of a public official or other person acting in an official capacity".[30] Therefore, the criminality of similar actions may depend on the status of the perpetrator.

Amnesties can also be targeted to certain groups of offenders by granting immunity to specific categories of crimes. This approach can, however, breach the state's obligations under international law where amnesty is granted to perpetrators of crimes under international law, such as genocide or grave breaches of the Geneva Conventions.[31] Less contentiously, amnesty laws can also be introduced that do not conflict with international law, where their scope extends only to less serious or purely political crimes.

The characteristics of amnesties can be shaped further by attaching conditions to the grant of amnesty. These conditions, which can aim inter alia to disarm combatants, to reveal the truth about events and the suffering of victims, or to purify a state by removing individuals who are responsible for human rights violations,

[30] Convention against Torture and Other Cruel, Inhuman or Degrading Treatment (adopted 10 December 1984, entered into force 26 June 1987) 1465 UNTS 85 (CAT), art 1(1). This understanding of torture as a discrete crime applies in peacetime. In contrast, when torture occurs during a conflict and can be treated as a war crime, or where it is sufficiently systematic and widespread to be considered a crime against humanity, private individuals can be held accountable. See Cassese (2003, p. 118).

[31] For a discussion of the duty to prosecute crimes under international law, see Christine Bell, "The 'New Law' of Transitional Justice"; Orentlicher (2007, p. 10); Trumbull (2007); Sadat (2006, p. 955); O'Shea (2002); Gavron (2002, p. 91).

can, if properly applied, serve to make the amnesty more acceptable within the territorial state and internationally by seeking to fulfil the victims' rights to truth and reparations, whilst working to (re-)establish peace and stability. The nature of each characteristic of amnesty (recipients, crimes, and conditions) will be described below.

5.1 Who Benefits from Amnesty Laws?

In analysing the recipients of amnesty laws, the following categorizations have been used: state agents, opponents of the state, convicts, exiles and refugees, and foreign nationals.

The category of *state agents* comprises a broad group covering those who worked for the state in an official capacity when they committed their crimes, such as soldiers, police officers, prison guards, intelligence agents, civil servants, and politicians. It can also cover retired personnel. For this study, these individuals continue to be regarded as state agents even when the amnesty law is introduced by a successor regime that has removed them from power. The category of state agents can also be extended to individuals who acted on behalf of the state without officially being state employees, such as pro-government militias or paramilitary organizations that are armed, trained and supported by the state. Often, such non-state actors commit crimes according to state policy, without the government officially recognizing any links to them.[32] This study also regards collaborators as state agents when their criminal activities were perpetrated in support of the de facto regime. This group can include business people who traded with an enemy regime, or individuals who enlisted in an enemy army. As discussed above, the contribution of amnesties for state agents to reconciliation is constrained where the amnesty is a "self-amnesty" enacted by a dictatorial regime to protect its agents. However, where this group are amnestied by a successor regime or as part of a negotiated political settlement that grants a mutual amnesty, it can potentially contribute more to reconciliation, particularly if accompanied by alternative accountability mechanisms.

"*Opponents of the state*" applies to those who, at the time of committing their (supposed) crimes, were acting in opposition to the state, or whom the state had chosen to label as opponents. This category can range from armed insurgents who are fighting to overthrow a central government, to non-political individuals who are interned by repressive regimes. Between these two extremes, groups such as resistance fighters, members of opposition political parties, draft dodgers and deserters,

[32] Jamieson and McEvoy (2005, p. 504). Jamieson and McEvoy outline four "strategies through which states seek to 'other' the actors who carry out state actors: perfidy, special forces, collusion and privatization". Perfidy refers to the concealment of the affiliation of state forces to gain a tactical advantage. Special forces refers to the establishment of dedicated counter-insurgency units who receive special training and are usually subject to less oversight than other units of the security forces. Collusion refers to ignoring or even cooperating with non-state forces to achieve a political objective. Finally, privatization refers to the increased reliance by states on private military companies.

and even members of the military who participated in *coups d'état* can be situated. Participants in coups are included in this category, as it would often be impossible to determine definitively whether an attempted military coup had the support of some state officials and as military coups are actions against the government, at the moment the crimes were committed the members of the armed forces involved were acting as opponents of the state. Similarly, this category can also cover those who initially campaigned against a regime before forming part of a new government following a transition, and then introducing an amnesty to cover their previous actions. Within this category, there is a great disparity between warlords fighting a central government who commit heinous abuses against civilians, and peaceful protesters who are interned for campaigning for their civil liberties. Therefore, the label of "opponents of the state" is not meant to be any reflection of the legitimacy or otherwise of the actions of these individuals. As amnesties within this category range from those introduced in the midst of a civil war to end the violence, to amnesties that are used as tool to rehabilitate those who were oppressed by the former regime, their potential to contribute to reconciliation will vary considerably depending on the levels of violence involved and whether the amnesty is a part of a wider reform and truth-seeking programme.

Using the classification system of *political prisoners* proposed by McEvoy et al. (2007),[33] as discussed above, this study views political prisoners as prisoners of conscience who are imprisoned for expressing their religious or political beliefs through non-violent means (McEvoy et al. 2007). Often such individuals are imprisoned under repressive laws that would be regarded as unjust within liberal societies. Similarly, "conscientious objectors" who are interned for refusing to participate in the armed forces due to their ideological or religious beliefs are treated as political prisoners. Amnesties for such individuals can be viewed as a form of reparations and as discussed above, they can be introduced for an array of tactical reasons.

Amnesties that are granted to *exiles* can benefit refugees who escaped violent conflict or dissidents who escaped tyranny and oppression. They could also cover individuals whose political or religious beliefs inspired them to become "conscientious objectors" and to flee across borders to evade military service. Finally, amnesties for exiles could also include members of insurgency groups that organize or have facilities outside the borders of their state. As discussed previously, such groups may be offered amnesty when a transition is already occurring to encourage them to return home and participate in the peace negotiations.

Finally, amnesty may be granted to *foreign nationals*, where they become involved in a conflict as mercenaries, or ideological supporters who often share an ethnic or religious identity with one of the belligerent groups. When granting amnesty, states have taken a variety of approaches to foreign nationals within their borders. In some cases, amnesty is granted for foreign fighters to encourage them to leave the country. For example, the 2004 Pakistani amnesty targeted foreign nationals fighting with al-Qaeda and pledged to repatriate those who surrendered to Pakistani forces to their homelands, rather than extraditing them to the United States (AFP 2004).

[33] The approach used in this study is narrower that the approach followed by McEvoy et al.

In contrast, many amnesties frequently exclude foreigners from their provisions. For example, the amnesty resulting from the Linas-Marcoussis Agreement 2003 that aimed to end the civil conflict in Côte d'Ivoire excluded mercenaries and other foreigners who fought in the unofficial militia groups that were used by both sides during the conflict.[34]

Individual amnesty laws can apply to either one or several of these categories, and these categories can overlap. For example, opponents of a dictatorial regime may have gone into exile to escape political repression, and hence an amnesty to encourage them to return would be categorized as both for opponents and for exiles. Furthermore, the categorization of amnesties can be problematic where an amnesty is implemented differently to its stated objectives, for example, by claiming on paper to apply to both state and non-state actors, but in practice only benefiting state agents. In these instances, the categorization used has relied on the provisions outlined in the law itself, although additional data has been added to the database to describe the law's implementation. Based on the information gained for 501[35] amnesties, the distribution of the protection received by each group is shown in Fig. 4. This shows quite clearly that the most common beneficiaries of amnesty laws are the opponents of the state with protection explicitly granted to this group in almost three times the number of amnesty laws than for state agents. This pattern is common to each region under consideration although the ratio between the groups of recipients does vary.

The categories of state agents and opponents of the state were further subdivided in the database to isolate provisions for those who are deemed "most responsible" for the policies of violence and repression. States have attempted to distinguish levels of responsibility between beneficiaries in the minority of cases, with only

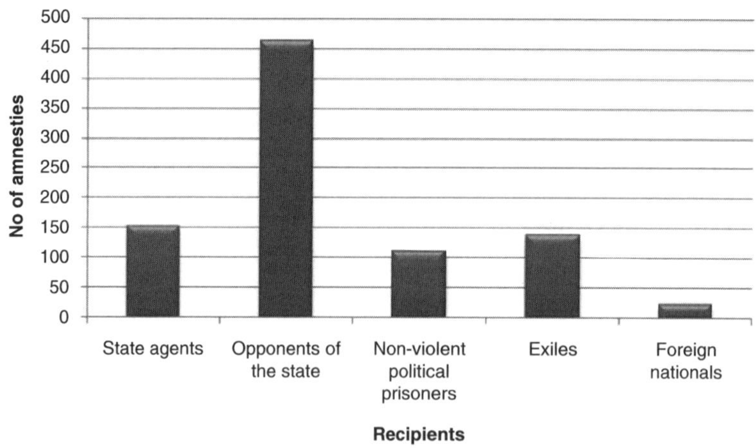

Fig. 4 Beneficiaries of amnesty laws

[34] Loi portant amnistie, 2003 (Côte d'Ivoire).

[35] Recipients could not be clearly ascribed to a category for five amnesties of the 506 in the Database, due to a paucity of data on the amnesty processes concerned.

11% of the amnesty laws that provide immunity for state agents excluding higher-ranking officials, and 9% of the amnesty laws for opponents of the state excluding the leaders of rebel forces or political movements. By distinguishing between the varying levels of culpability between offenders, amnesties can recognize that individuals who commit human rights violations are not a monolithic group and that in some instances, victims and perpetrators may overlap, particularly where individuals commit crimes under duress. Furthermore, by pursuing prosecutions only for those who are deemed "most responsible", whilst creating alternative justice mechanisms for lower-level offenders, states could potentially be argued to fulfil their international obligations, where it is unrealistic to expect the state to pursue formal prosecutions for all offenders, due to the lack of resources and volume of crimes that occurred. Indeed, amnesties that are coupled with truth-recovery mechanisms could help rival communities within a transitional society accept that their opponents also suffered, and that not every member of the rival community represents a dangerous threat. Such understanding could pave the way for reconciliation.

5.2 Which Crimes are Granted Amnesty?

To analyse which crimes states choose to amnesty, for the purposes of this study, the crimes were divided into the following categories: crimes under international law, political crimes, economic crimes, and crimes against individuals. For each of these categories, information was compiled on whether the amnesty included or excluded the relevant crimes, and whether the crimes must have occurred within specific regions or between specific dates.

"*Crimes under international law*", as discussed in elsewhere in this book,[36] are those which are of the most serious concern to policy makers and human rights activists, and place the most restrictions on those who wish to introduce amnesty laws. For the purpose of this research, this category comprises genocide, war crimes, crimes against humanity, torture and disappearances. For each of these crimes, the extent of obligations upon states varies according to each state's treaty ratifications, the status of the crime under customary international law, the nature of the violence, and the context in which it occurs. Amnesties for crimes under international law are commonly formulated as benefiting "all persons and parties engaged or involved in military activities" during the conflict.[37] This approach generally provides a blanket amnesty that covers all crimes, unless any are specifically excluded, and means that states can avoid explicitly declaring that they are amnestying *génocidaires* or torturers. Alternatively, a state could develop an exclusive list of crimes which are included or excluded from the amnesty.

[36] As discussed above, this chapter does not engage with the duty to prosecute as it is addressed in the other studies in this book, see Kai Ambos, "The Legal Framework of Transitional Justice" and Christine Bell, "The 'New Law' of Transitional Justice". See also Ambos (2004, p. 219–282).

[37] See, e.g., Comprehensive Peace Agreement between the Government of Liberia and the Liberians United for Reconciliation and Democracy (LURD) and the Movement for Democracy in Liberia (MODEL) and Political Parties ("Accra Peace Accord") 2003, art XXXIV.

Whether a state includes or excludes crimes under international law from an amnesty often seems to be influenced by political concerns, rather than legal absolutes. For example, the 1972 Simla Agreement between India and Pakistan provided inter alia amnesty for 195 Pakistani soldiers who had been accused of crimes against humanity and genocide. This amnesty was used as a trade off to obtain Pakistan's recognition of Bangladesh's independence and to persuade Pakistan to drop its case against India at the International Court of Justice (Scharf 1996, fn 100). Here it is clear that the perpetrators of crimes under international law were used as pawns in a wider political dispute, and that consequently, the states concerned felt that they did not have to prosecute these individuals, if doing so conflicted with their other goals. Similarly, where a regime chooses to exclude crimes under international law from an amnesty, it is not always possible to tell whether it is doing so to comply with its international obligations, or simply to respond to domestic or international pressure.[38] A further difficulty with the exclusion of crimes under international law is that many amnesties exclude crimes that resulted in the death of the victim, but allow amnesty for torturers where the victim survived.

Even where crimes under international law are clearly excluded from the provisions of an amnesty, the process can be further complicated during implementation. For example, the excluded crimes under international law are often not fully incorporated into domestic law, which may permit individuals to benefit from an amnesty under national law, when it would have been denied using the broader definitions recognized in international law. Furthermore, where the judiciary remain loyal to the former regime, they may interpret amnesty laws in as wide a manner as possible to benefit more perpetrators than was intended. Even where the screening process of those eligible for amnesty is conducted by an independent commission, there can be difficulties when dealing with the complex definitions of crimes under international law, particularly where the commissioners are not appropriately trained legal professionals. More often, serious crimes that are excluded from the formal amnesty process are often granted de facto impunity due to a lack of political will to pursue prosecutions.

In contrast, to the contentious nature of amnesties for serious human rights violations, *political crimes* are frequently included in amnesty laws; indeed, offering protection to political offenders is often the purpose of an amnesty. The concept of political offence has been described as "elastic", as it can encompass a wide range of behaviours and offences that stretch across a "spectrum" from "extreme purely passive offences such as political dissidence" to more violent actions "against the prevailing social order" (Van den Wyngaert 1980, p. 95). Amnesties for purely political crimes include activities such as treason, sedition, rebellion, using false documents, anti-government propaganda, possessing illegal weapons, espionage, membership of banned political or religious organizations, desertion, and defamation. A political amnesty may only cover the less serious of these offences, whilst permitting criminal prosecutions of individuals accused of espionage. Defining political crimes becomes more complicated, however, for common offences which

[38] The issue of international pressure, particularly emanating from the ICC, on domestic actors is explored in the chapter by Chandra Lekha Sriram.

are related to political crimes, as most common crimes "can, as a matter of fact, be considered as political crimes under certain circumstances, namely when they are committed with a political purpose or when they have political consequences" (Van den Wyngaert 1980, p. 95). Furthermore, as Valji argues elsewhere in this book, attempting to distinguish between "criminal" and "political" acts may offer a false dichotomy from the perspective of victims by failing to "account for the common impact of violations and insecurity".[39]

The approach of states to this issue has often been influenced by extradition law which distinguishes between common crimes and political offences using either subjective,[40] objective[41] or mixed[42] approaches, although the level of detail in describing "related common crimes" has varied considerably in different amnesty laws. To date, the most thorough consideration of political crimes relating to amnesty laws occurred in South Africa. In the constituent legislation of the Truth and Reconciliation Commission, the criteria for determining political crimes are outlined as follows:

Whether a particular act, omission or offence contemplated in subsection (2) is an act associated with a political objective, shall be decided with reference to the following criteria:

1. The motive of the person who committed the act, omission or offence.
2. The context in which the act, omission or offence took place, and in particular whether the act, omission or offence was committed in the course of or as part of a political uprising, disturbance or event, or in reaction thereto.
3. The legal and factual nature of the act, omission or offence, including the gravity of the act, omission or offence.
4. The object or objective of the act, omission or offence, and in particular whether the act, omission or offence was primarily directed at a political opponent or State property or personnel or against private property or individuals.
5. Whether the act, omission or offence was committed in the execution of an order of, or on behalf of, or with the approval of, the organisation, institution, liberation movement or body of which the person who committed the act was a member, an agent or a supporter.
6. The relationship between the act, omission or offence and the political objective pursued, and in particular the directness and proximity of the relationship and the

[39] Nalha Valji, "Gender Justice and Reconciliation".

[40] The "subjective approach" which "emphasizes the intentions of the perpetrator" to determine whether he or she was politically motivated, "regardless of whether the act had a political outcome". Also known as the "predominant motive test". See Van den Wyngaert (1980, p. 109) and Bhargava (2002, p. 1304, 1229).

[41] The "objective approach", which focuses instead on the "political context of the act and its actual outcome or consequences". In this instance, if there is a political outcome, the act is considered a political crime, "regardless of the intentions of the perpetrator". See Van den Wyngaert (1980, p. 109).

[42] The "mixed approach" combines the other two approaches "requiring that in order to be political, the offence should be at the same time subjectively and objectively a political crime". See Van den Wyngaert (1980, p. 109).

proportionality of the act, omission or offence to the objective pursued, but does not include any act, omission or offence committed by any person referred to in subsection (2) who acted:

(a) For personal gain: Provided that an act, omission or offence by any person who acted and received money or anything of value as an informer of the State or a former state, political organisation or liberation movement, shall not be excluded only on the grounds of that person having received money or anything of value for his or her information.
(b) Out of personal malice, ill-will or spite, directed against the victim of the acts committed.[43]

However, despite such detailed criteria, the implementation of the legislation by the TRC's Amnesty Committee was inconsistent. Some criteria were not uniformly applied, with provisions such as the target of the attack[44] often being ignored in favour of other criteria, such as whether "an authorized superior in a recognized political organization ordered the act, or whether the act was closely related to an explicit programmatic statement of an established political organization" (Slye 2000, pp. 179–180). This can be problematic as it can distort the truth that is revealed. For example, as Slye argues focusing on the existence of orders grants power to "the state, political parties and other political organizations in decisions concerning amnesty" as an individual's application for amnesty may depend on whether the organization admits to having ordered the act in question (Slye 2000, p. 180). In practice, many superiors would be reluctant to admit ordering acts if doing so would make them liable to prosecution (Gallagher 2000, p. 149, 163). Despite these difficulties in implementation, amnesties for political crimes are often argued to be necessary for reconciliation, as many political offenders do not perceive their acts as criminal, but rather as part of an armed struggle to protect their way of life or gain equality with their compatriots. Furthermore, as such individuals are responding to specific political conditions, it can be argued that where peace settlements address the root causes of a conflict, their motivations to re-offend will be diminished (Slye 2000, p. 181–182).

Economic crimes often reach epidemic proportions during situations of mass human rights violations, whether in terms of members of the ruling elite using their power to enrich themselves; foreign corporations exploiting (or perhaps even instigating) political instability for profit; corruption by state officials, usually by extracting bribes or expropriating property; collaboration with enemies by business people; or simply engagement in black market trade by ordinary civilians. These crimes are commonly excluded from amnesty laws as the exposure of extensive greed and plunder by a dictatorial regime can contribute to undermining any support that it might have, as a dictator can usually claim that human rights abuses result from a selfless desire to eradicate the dangers to the state; but there can be no such defence for corruption (Freeman 2001, p. 3). Furthermore, "with crimes of corruption, the public

[43] Promotion of National Unity and Reconciliation Act, 1995, s 20.3 (S. Afr.).

[44] Sarkin (2004, pp. 288–298). For further discussion of the approach of the Amnesty Committee, see Slye (2000).

may collectively feel that they are the victims of theft", whereas "human rights violations generally lack this sense of collective victimization because in most cases the violations have not affected the majority of the public" (Freeman 2001, p. 3). The exclusion of economic crimes can also apply to the criminal fund-raising activities of armed opposition groups or to economic activities that were subverting the political (usually socialist) order, where governments viewed economic control as fundamental to the entire social system. For example, the 1989 Albanian amnesty excluded:

> ... illicit appropriation of socialist property according to arts 61–68 of the Penal Code; appropriation of private property according to arts 101–102 of the Penal Code; as well as those persons who have been given uncommutable sentences for various repeated penal offences.[45]

Finally, serious offences for personal enrichment such as drug trafficking seem to be consistently barred from national amnesty laws. Nonetheless, in many transitional contexts, amnesties have been granted for economic crimes, often recognizing that under the previous regime, obtaining necessities was hard and individuals were forced to engage in smuggling, black market purchasing, or breaking rationing rules. Even where the crimes are more serious, such as business people trading with the enemy, amnesty is sometimes granted as the support of the business community is necessary for national reconstruction. This occurred in several countries in Europe after 1945. For example, the 1953 French amnesty covered "those convicted of trading with the enemy, if their sentences did not exceed 5 years of prison and a 20,000 franc fine".[46]

"*Crimes against individuals*" is an extremely broad category of crimes, which applies, in this study, to crimes committed against individuals who were not belligerents, such as civilians or former combatants who were *hors de combat* due to "sickness, wounds, detention, or any other cause" and hence entitled to "be treated humanely" according to common Article 3 of the Geneva Conventions. The category covers all crimes against these persons, including common crimes that are not political but occur within a period of dictatorial rule or conflict. This category could therefore include a range of activities from damage to property to serious acts of physical or sexual violence. As crimes against individuals always occur during dictatorial or conflict situations, they frequently benefit from amnesty. However, it is common for amnesty laws that prevent prosecution for crimes against individuals to make exceptions for certain crimes, particularly rape, murder, kidnapping and theft.

Each amnesty law can apply to either one or several of the four categories of crimes, and these categories can overlap. For example, crimes against individuals can, when particularly severe, also be crimes under international law, although distinguishing when the threshold of severity for crimes under international law has been reached can be difficult. For example, if several civilian deaths occur, should they be treated as murder or crimes against humanity? Where crimes under international law did occur, but are classified in the amnesty as domestic crimes such as

---

[45] Decree No. 7338 (n 8).

[46] Loi N° 53–681 portant amnistie, 1953 (France).

murder, perpetrators of crimes under international law can benefit from the amnesty, without the nature of the crimes that they committed being recognized by the state. States can also create ambiguity in the terms of the amnesty by using phrases such as "ferocious and barbarous acts",[47] "atrocious" acts,[48] or "blood crimes", but failing to define these terms. This ambiguity contributes to concealing the truth about events and denies acknowledgement to the victims. For the purposes of this study, amnesties have been described as including crimes under international law only where conflicts that were characterized by crimes under international law resulted in blanket amnesties for all crimes that occurred;[49] or where there is specific evidence, such as court proceedings, to demonstrate that the amnesty was applied to crimes under international law. For this reason, the proportion of amnesty laws granting amnesty for crimes under international law is probably under-represented in the data.

The distribution of the inclusion and exclusion of each category of crimes in 494[50] amnesty laws is shown in Fig. 5. This figure shows that the vast majority of amnesty laws were offered for political crimes, although 22% of amnesties excluded all or some political crimes. Immunity for crimes against individuals, including crimes that did not have a political objective, was granted in 24% of amnesties.

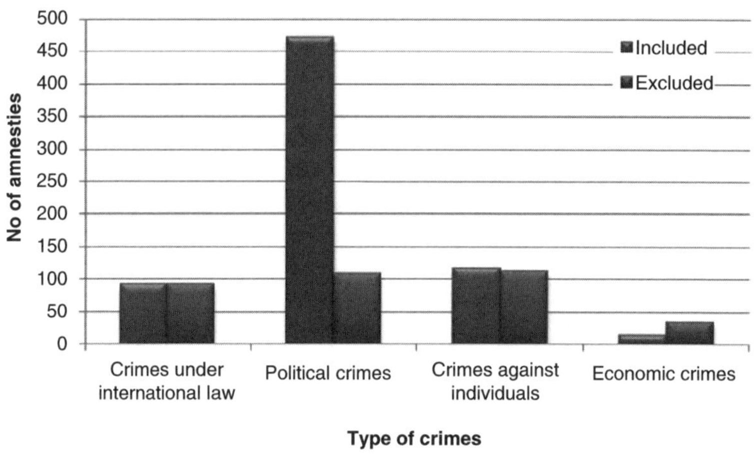

Fig. 5 Treatment of categories of crimes in amnesty laws

[47] Ley 37 de 1981 por la cual se declara una amnistía conditional, Diario Official No. 35760, 14 May 1981, p. 442 (Colom.).

[48] Ley 35, Diario Official N° 36133 bis, p. 529 "por la cual se decreta una amnistía y se dictan normas tendientes al restablecimiento y preservación de la paz", 19 November 1982 (Colom.) This amnesty provided immunity to torturers, despite exempting "atrocious crimes", for further information see Ambos (1999, pp. 126–141).

[49] See, e.g., Peace Agreement between the Government of Sierra Leone and the Revolutionary United Front of Sierra Leone ("Lomé Accord") 1999 (Sierra Leone) art IX(2).

[50] Crimes could not be clearly ascribed to a category for 12 amnesties of the 506 in the database, due to a paucity of data on the amnesty processes concerned.

In contrast, an almost equal number of amnesties excluded some form of crimes against individuals, this meant usually amnestying lower-level offences against individuals, but denying immunity for serious crimes such as murder or sexual violence. Only 19% of the amnesties included in the database have explicitly included protection for some or all of the crimes under international law, although, for many amnesties the crimes occurring, although serious, did not reach the threshold of crimes under international law. This means that, of the amnesties where crimes under international law were a factor, the proportion granting amnesty for crimes under international law would be higher.

When the patterns relating to amnestying crimes under international law are looked at over time, it becomes apparent that the number of amnesties both including protection for crimes under international law and excluding immunity for them has increased since the Second World War, particularly during the 1990s. Perhaps the most significant period relating to amnesties for crimes under international law is after the UN changed its approach to amnesty laws with the signing of the Lomé Accord on 7 July 1999.[51] From this date until December 2007, 34 amnesty laws excluded some form of crimes under international law. This development has inspired human rights activists to point to a growing trend to prohibit impunity for these crimes (Sikkink and Walling 2007). This research has found, however, that during the same period, 28 amnesty laws granted immunity to perpetrators of crimes under international law, and that consequently, it is too early to suggest that an international custom is developing.[52]

This section has argued that amnesties can grant immunity for many types of crimes and that not all amnesties violate the provisions of international law. For example, amnesties for political crimes have traditionally been viewed as a purely domestic matter that are not of concern to the international community. Problems arise, however, where amnesties are granted for crimes under international law which violate a state's international obligations. Despite the growth of international law during the post-war period, states continue to amnesty such crimes, although some states are now pursuing more nuanced approaches, by, for example, combining amnesty with alternative justice procedures such as lustration or restorative justice programmes. If a state relies upon a broader conception of justice by using traditional or community-based justice processes rather than formal prosecutions, such processes, as will be discussed below, could also be argued to fulfil the state's obligations and contribute to reconciliation.

---

[51] At the signing of the Lomé Accords, the Special Representative of the Secretary-General of the UN, Francis Okelo, appended "a hand-written disclaimer to the agreement", stating "the UN holds the understanding that the amnesty provisions of the Agreement shall not apply to crimes under international law of genocide, crimes against humanity, war crimes and other serious violations of international humanitarian law". For more information see UNSC (1999); Schabas (2004, p. 145).

[52] For a detailed analysis of whether amnesties violate the duty to prosecute under customary international law, see Trumbull (2007).

5.3 Which Conditions are Attached to Amnesties?

In researching conditional amnesties, the following classifications were identified: surrendering and disarming; repenting and providing information on comrades; fulfilling the conditions within prescribed time limits; telling the truth; repairing the harm; participating in community-based justice mechanisms; and submitting to lustration and vetting procedures. These conditions can either be an integral part of the amnesty process, such as surrendering, or they can be independent yet complementary mechanisms that are introduced before, at the same time as the amnesty, or possibly some time afterwards to lessen its negative impact on victims and society. On occasion, this distinction can become muddled. For example, although truth commissions are usually independent yet complementary mechanisms, in the case of the South African TRC, telling the truth to the Amnesty Committee was an integral part of the amnesty process.

The first category, the obligation *to surrender and hand over weapons* to the authorities, is a long-standing condition of peace initiatives following conflicts or internal unrest, and is increasingly formalized in Disarmament, Demobilization and Reintegration (DDR) programmes which can be outlined in negotiated peace agreements.[53] Amnesties and DDR programmes can be mutually reinforcing, as even where an amnesty is conditional on surrendering weapons, the other measures within the DDR programme to reintegrate former combatants into society could help to allay the combatants' fears of retaliation or destitution. Indeed, on occasion, DDR programmes have been administered jointly with amnesties. For example, the Ugandan Amnesty Commission is responsible for overseeing the DDR programme for surrendering combatants.[54] Where former combatants are required to surrender, the amnesty often stipulates that combatants must do so voluntarily to benefit from the amnesty,[55] although it can be accompanied by threats of further legal or military action against those who refuse to turn themselves in. For example, on 20 May 1997 in Afghanistan, the Taliban chief asked all opposition forces to surrender and offered them amnesty, warning that those who did not would be tried by Islamic courts (AFP 1997). The process of surrendering can vary between different conflicts. For example, in some conflicts, combatants could be required to surrender to civilian authorities, whereas in others they may have to present themselves to the security forces. Occasionally, insurgents can surrender to more neutral institutions, for example, under the 1983 Bangladeshi amnesty for insurgents in the Chittagong Hill Tracts, individuals could surrender to inter alia leading members of their locality, and in the Indo-Sri Lanka Accord 1987 for the conflict between the Sri Lankan government and the Tamil Tigers, it was agreed that "Tamil militants shall surrender their arms to authorities … The surrender shall take place in the presence of one

---

[53] For a discussion of a state currently undergoing a DDR programme, see Diaz's chapter on Colombia, Catalina Diaz, "Colombia's Bid for Justice and Peace". See also Vinjamuri and Boesenecker (2007).

[54] Amnesty Act 2000 (n 19) s 9.

[55] See, e.g., Loi relative au rétablissement de la Concorde civile, Loi No 98–08, 1999 (Algeria), art 41.

senior representative each of the Sri Lanka Red Cross and the Indian Red Cross".[56] Most often, they can surrender to a range of government bodies, depending on their preference and location. For example, the 1999 Algerian amnesty for Islamic militants permitted insurgents to surrender to military, civilian, administrative, or judicial authorities.[57]

In addition to surrendering, former combatants are often required to disarm. Sometimes, cash incentives, known as "buy back" programmes, are introduced. These offer payments usually on a varying scale depending on the type of weaponry that is surrendered. In addition to contributing to disarmament, such programmes can provide financial resources to insurgents to help them establish their new lives, although as De Greiff explores in his chapter offering financial support to former combatants can be problematic.[58] In addition to handing over weaponry, in some conflicts, amnesty is also conditional on the surrender of hostages. For example, following the attempted coup in Fiji in May 2000 in which Prime Minister Chaudhry and his cabinet were taken hostage, the negotiated Maunikau Accord 2000 required George Speight and his followers to release the hostages before benefiting from the amnesty.[59] This seems to reflect a military tradition of exchanging prisoners at the end of a conflict, particularly where the release of hostages is timed to coincide with the release of detained insurgents. Amnesties that require beneficiaries to surrender can contribute positively to attempts to achieve stability by providing a symbol that the violence is finished; reducing the potential of rebel forces to cause disruption; facilitating trust-building initiatives to enable different stakeholder groups to work together in rebuilding the country; contributing to a general demilitarization of society; and boosting "the local community's confidence that progress could be made in restoring law and order" (Watson 2005, p. 11).

The idea of *repentance* being a necessary prerequisite for amnesty has been employed in many countries, usually for opponents of the state. Repentance requirements can make amnesties conditional on the beneficiaries signing written documents or making public statements in which they renounce their political or violent activities and swear loyalty to the state and its laws. For example, the 1981 Colombian amnesty required each beneficiary to "make an express and individual statement to cease his participation in the punishable acts that the foregoing rule applies to".[60] Where individuals have promised to obey these conditions, there can be stiff penalties for recidivism, such as having to serve the punishment for the actions that were amnestied, in conjunction with the punishment for the subsequent crimes.[61] For example, the 1991 Lebanese amnesty stated that "that those committing crimes covered by the amnesty, after the date of its promulgation, will be

[56] Indo-Sri Lanka Accord (1987), annex 7.

[57] Loi relative au rétablissement de la Concorde civile, (n 55), art 30.

[58] Pablo De Greiff, "DDR and Reparations: Establishing Links Between Peace and Justice Instruments". See also, UNSC (2000) and Isima (2004).

[59] Maunikau Accord (2000) (Fiji).

[60] Ley 37 (n 47) art 3.

[61] In her chapter on "The 'New Law' of Transitional Justice", Christine Bell discusses the possibility that if any parties to the conflict return to violence, the amnesty will be "void and reversible".

liable for prosecution and will also be liable for all the offences they committed during the war".[62] It has been suggested that amnesty should not be exchanged for a "pre-existing duty (such as the duty to obey the law)" (Sarkin and Daly 2004, p. 722). But for insurgents who were willing to risk their life and liberty to fight the central government, any public statement of recognition of the legitimacy of the state can be of major symbolic importance. Alternatively, amnesty processes may require applicants to admit their guilt. For example, Sarkin highlights that the Amnesty Committee of the South African TRC "deemed denial of guilt to be an obstacle to the granting of amnesty" (Sarkin 2004, p. 237). He comments that this can be problematic where "people might be guilty, but believe that they are not, since they view the acts they admittedly performed as legitimate" (Sarkin 2004, p. 238). Amnesty applicants in other processes have been required to show remorse. For example, in Timor-Leste, individuals who participated in the Community Reconciliation Process were often required to perform an act of reconciliation, such as a public apology (UNTAET 2001, s 27.7). Amnesty applicants may also be required to demonstrate that they have turned their back on their former organizations by providing information on their former comrades. For example, under a series of "Repentance Laws" in Turkey, those who surrendered were required to provide information on the identities and whereabouts of fellow fighters who had not surrendered (Zaman 2003). Finally, some states have decided to try to ensure that repentance is genuine by requiring that beneficiaries of the amnesty participate in re-education programmes. For example, Eritrean secessionist guerrillas who received amnesty in Ethiopia in 1978 and 1980 were required to attend briefings on "Ethiopia's long-recorded unity, the theory of Marxism–Leninism and the process of the Ethiopian revolution" (BBC 1980). Where states encourage amnesty beneficiaries to show their repentance for their previous actions by, for example, apologizing directly to their victims within the context of a truth commission or community-based justice mechanism it could be viewed as pre-dominantly of benefit to individual victims and their families. However, the symbolism of public displays of repentance from belligerent institutions or individual amnesty applicants can contribute to repudiating the crimes of the past and demonstrating an intention to adhere to the rule of law. Where this occurs, such proclamations although symbolic, may be necessary to build trust in the fledging institutions of a transitional state and reduce enmity between previously warring factions.

The third category relates to the common practice within amnesties of requiring potential beneficiaries to apply and adhere to the conditions within a specified *time limit*, which is often integrated into overall time frames to establish democratic rule. The limits that are imposed have ranged from 15 days in the Central African Republic in 1997, to 8 years in Uganda.[63] The limits have frequently been lengthened either by an extension as provided for in the text of the amnesty, an amendment to the original law, or by the introduction of a subsequent amnesty law. However, problems may arise where an amnesty is frequently extended or renewed, as such

[62] Loi d'amnistie générale n° 84/91 (1991) Lebanon), art 2.

[63] The Ugandan amnesty came into force in 2000 and is still in operation at the time of writing (June 2008).

activity may create an expectation among insurgents that they can benefit from an amnesty at any time, and can therefore take a "wait and see" approach rather than engage with the process. In contrast, imposing time limits on amnesty applicants can increase pressure on the targeted groups to participate in an amnesty process while the option is available to them, which may help the peace process to progress.

The fourth category concerns the relationship between amnesties and *truth commissions*. This relationship can take many forms.[64] Firstly, an amnesty can be introduced before the establishment of the truth commission. This was the case in Chile, where the military *junta* had promulgated an amnesty law in 1978 to shield members of the armed forces from prosecution for serious crimes that they had committed during the "dirty war". When the democratic government subsequently came to power in 1990, it found for a number of reasons that the amnesty law was impossible to repeal, which led the president, Patricio Aylwin, to inaugurate a truth commission to achieve "justice inasmuch as was possible" (cited in Coonan 1996, p. 512, 539). Secondly, an amnesty can be introduced following a truth commission, as occurred in El Salvador. Here, the truth commission in its report named individual perpetrators who were linked to the government, causing the government to respond by enacting an amnesty to protect those who had been named (Hayner 2001, p. 91). Finally, an amnesty can be introduced in conjunction with a truth commission. This could mean either two independent mechanisms that are introduced simultaneously, as, for example, under the 1999 Lomé Accord that aimed to end the conflict in Sierra Leone; or a truth commission that has the power to grant amnesty. It is this latter relationship between the two forms of transitional justice that has sparked the most debate in recent years, following the establishment of the South African TRC. Its appeal is based on the belief that providing amnesty encourages the involvement of perpetrators in revealing the truth, thereby contributing to the establishment of a more balanced historical account than would be the case if only the stories of the victims were heard.

"*Community-based justice*" refers to informal mechanisms that employ a more restorative approach to justice than the retributive approach typified by trials.[65] As explored more fully elsewhere in this volume,[66] restorative approaches can be suitable where formal Western-style retributive prosecutions are not possible due to practical and political constraints, or where restorative mechanisms are the preferred approach to justice among the general population, which is the case in many societies in Africa and elsewhere. To date, there have been several situations where amnesty laws have been introduced in conjunction with community-based justice

[64] For a discussion of the impact of the amnesty in exchange for truth model, see literature on the South African TRC, such as Cobban (2007); Dugard (2005); Sarkin (2004). See also McEvoy (2008).

[65] For a discussion of restorative approaches, see Minow (1998); Orentlicher (2007); Alley (2005); Harper (2005, p. 149), See also Llewellyn and Howse (1999, pp. 355, 374–375) and Sarkin and Daly (2004, p. 693).

[66] For an exploration of various forms of informal justice mechanisms, see Stef Vandeginste, "Transitional Justice for Burundi: A Long and Winding Road"; Dexter and Ntahombaye (2005); Victor Igreja, "Justice and Reconciliation in the Aftermath of the Civil War in Gorongosa, Mozambique Central"; and Le Sage (2005).

processes. For example, the Acholi people of northern Uganda, who have suffered greatly from the acts of the LRA, use their traditional dispute resolution mechanisms, known as *nyouo tong gweno* and *mato oput* as a means of reintegrating into society former combatants who have been amnestied.[67] In addition to traditional conflict resolution processes, restorative justice in transitional states may also be incorporated into the work of a truth commission or take the form of a hybrid between truth commissions and community-based justice mechanisms, as illustrated by the work of the Community Reconciliation Process of the East Timorese Commission for Reception, Truth and Reconciliation (Harper 2005). The flexibility of the restorative justice approach to punishment offers the opportunity for an amnesty to be reconciled with a legitimate justice process in which the needs of the victims are acknowledged. Perpetrators might also have to perform appropriate cultural or religious rituals to show their desire to change and become reintegrated into society (Bassiouni 1996b, p. 9, 21). This could enable the amnesty to be granted in a context of societal forgiveness and reconciliation. Furthermore, where the community-based justice initiatives impose "punishment" on offenders, such as participating in community service or making reparations to their victims, the amnesty could be conditional on the offenders complying with the penalties imposed by the restorative justice mechanism and could therefore work as an enforcement mechanism, and act to reassure the victims of the genuineness of the process. Furthermore, it is argued by restorative justice advocates that this more integrative approach to justice can contribute to breaking the cycles of power and oppression which frequently exist in transitional societies.

Amnesty laws can be related to *lustration or vetting* policies that aim to remove those implicated in the former regime from office or to bar them from certain public sector posts in a number of ways.[68] Firstly, a few amnesty laws have followed purges to undo their perceived excesses. For example, immediately following World War Two, there were purges (also known as *épuration*) in several European countries of Nazi and Fascist operatives and collaborators. As time passed, these measures became viewed as too severe, and consequently, amnesties were introduced to reverse them (see, e.g., Elster 2004; Frei 2002; Larsen and Hagtvet 1998; Herz 1982; Deák et al. 2000). More commonly, however, lustration policies are implemented in conjunction with amnesty, or soon afterwards, to create some form of accountability. Although there can be risks associated with lustration (see, e.g., Kritz 2004, p. 25; Diamond 2004; Theissen 2005, p. 5), combining amnesties with programmes to remove those associated with abusive policies from office can provide a form of accountability for perpetrators, can meet the needs of victims that their former oppressors do not continue to benefit from their crimes and can help to restore faith in government institutions. Furthermore, immunity from prosecution through an amnesty process can make removal from office more palatable for former elites who might otherwise violently resist institutional reforms.

---

[67] OHCHR (2007); Clark (2008); Justice and Reconciliation Project (2007); Hanlon (2007, p. 295); Baines (2005, 2007, p. 97); Harlacher et al. (2006).

[68] For a discussion of lustration, see Boed (1999, p. 357, 358).

Amnesty laws raise various issues relating to the final category: *reparations*.[69] According to the UN's *Basic Principles and Guidelines on the Right to a Remedy*,[70] this category can be divided in the following sub-categories: restitution, compensation, rehabilitation, satisfaction and guarantees of non-repetition. Furthermore, although the right of individuals to regain property that was confiscated or that they had been forced to abandon whilst fleeing violence could be regarded as a form of restitution, it has been treated as a separate category in the database, due to the complex issues related to it.

The relationship between amnesty and reparations can have diverse implications on reconciliation within transitional states. Firstly, as discussed above, an amnesty could be a form of reparation to individuals who have been penalized or imprisoned by the state for their alleged political or religious beliefs. In contrast, amnesty laws that are issued to perpetrators of crimes under international law could constitute a violation of the victims' right to a remedy, which should then itself be remedied. An amnesty law could, however, include provision for reparations, or could be accompanied by legislation to provide financial compensation for victims and their families, to facilitate the victims' right to file a civil suit, and to memorialize the suffering of the victims and prevent such violations re-occurring.[71] Such measures could result in the amnesty being regarded as satisfying a state's obligation to provide a remedy.

Within the seven categories of conditional amnesties outlined here, in practice, many of the categories can overlap. For example, a requirement to repent for past crimes could be a stand-alone obligation to be made before a state official in exchange for amnesty, or it could form part of a truth commission or community-based justice mechanism, where applicants will confess their actions as a sign of repentance. Similarly, the existence of time limits for amnesty applications are frequently tied to requirements that combatants seeking amnesty surrender to designated institutions.

The conditions that are attached to amnesties can vary between extremes with some amnesties such as those in Cameroon, Chad (1983) and Sierra Leone (1996) explicitly stating that they were unconditional; others imposing very few conditions; and finally, others introducing nearly all possible measures by, for example, combining amnesty with truth commissions and reparations programmes. Often, however, conditions are simply not described in the amnesty law, although they may be created by subsequent implementing regulations. Due to this disparity to practice, information has only been gathered on the conditions attached to 278 amnesty

[69] For a more detailed discussion of the nature of reparations, see Pablo De Greiff, "DDR and Reparations: Establishing Links Between Peace and Justice Instruments".

[70] UNGA (2005, Princs 19–23). These guidelines are not binding on states but are intended to reflect international standards on the right to a remedy.

[71] For a discussion of memorialisation processes, see Paloma Aguilar, "The Timing and the Scope of Reparation, Truth and Justice Measures: A Comparison of the Spanish, Argentinian and Chilean Cases".

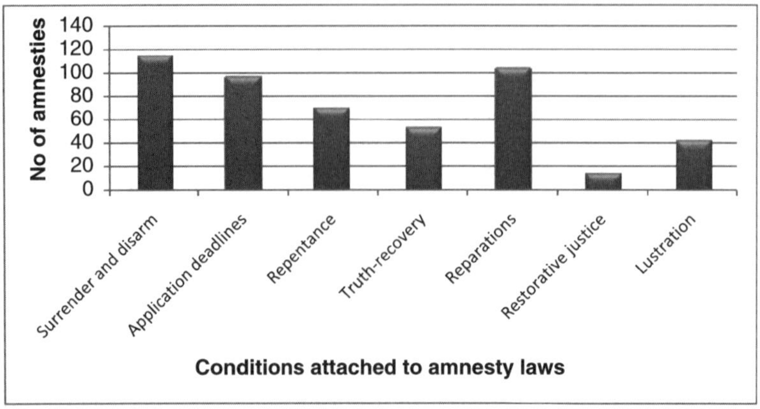

Fig. 6 Distribution of conditions attached to amnesty laws

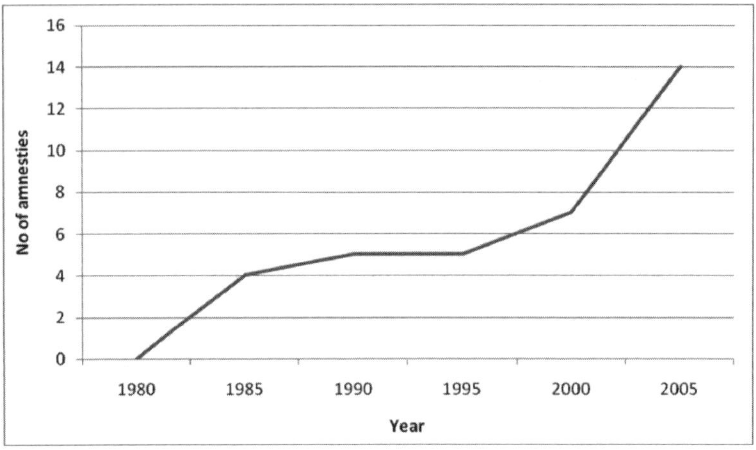

Fig. 7 Truth commissions coinciding with amnesties between 1985 and 2005

laws.[72] The distribution of these conditions is shown in Fig. 6. The most striking result in this figure is the number of amnesties with reparations measures attached. This pattern could be argued to reflect the wide array of measures which can fall under financial and symbolic forms of reparations.

Perhaps the most discussed development has occurred in the area of truth recovery. Although truth commissions and commissions of inquiry were used before the fall of apartheid in South Africa in the early 1990s, the South African Truth and Reconciliation Commission became highly influential and has contributed to a rise in the number of amnesties that are related to truth-seeking processes, as shown in Fig. 7. From this chart, it is clear that in the period after the Human Rights

[72] Reparative amnesties for non-violent political prisoners and refugees were excluded as the figure is intended to illustrate the frequency with which non-reparative amnesties have conditions attached.

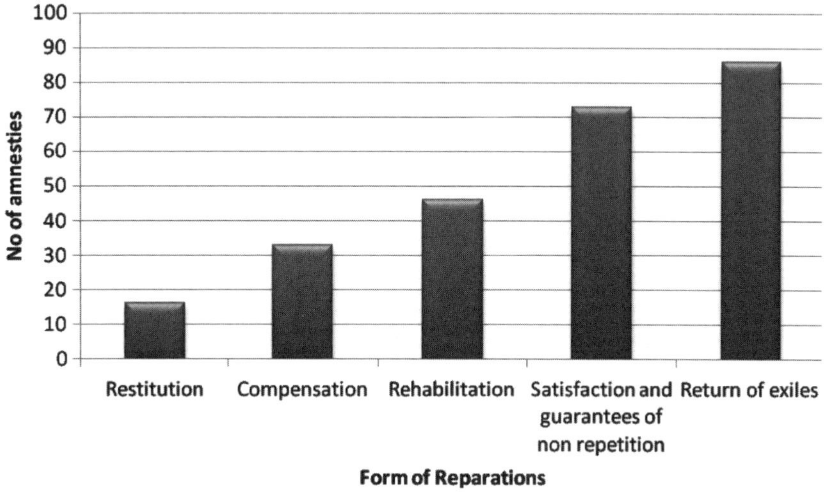

Fig. 8 Amnesties and reparations programmes.

Violations Committee of the South African TRC submitted its report in October 1998, the popularity of truth commissions accompanying amnesty processes increased substantially. Between January 2005 and December 2007, 41 amnesty processes were introduced, of which four have been accompanied by truth-recovery mechanisms. This appears to indicate that although the figures are small as yet, a trend is developing.

The distribution of each form of reparations accompanying amnesty measures is shown in Fig. 8. The differences in the distribution of each form of reparation perhaps reflect their differing natures, with measures introduced to provide satisfaction and guarantees of non-repetition often corresponding to other provisions in the peace agreement, such as institutional reform, and being beneficial to more individuals than rehabilitation. The introduction of reparation measures has grown in popularity during the period since the Second World War with 97 amnesty laws having complementary reparation measures since 1990. Although some of the reparation measures can be expensive for the state to provide, others can occur without any financial burden, for example, an official apology. This could perhaps explain why, when comparing the regions that most frequently rely on amnesty laws, there is little difference in the number of amnesties that are related to reparations, despite the wide disparities in wealth between these regions: related reparations and amnesties were introduced in 50 countries in Europe and Central Asia, and in 64 countries in Sub-Saharan Africa. All forms of reparations have increased in popularity during the period with the most dramatic growth in recent years occurring in the category of satisfaction and guarantees of non-repetition.

This section has explored the conditions that can be attached to an amnesty, including practical conditions to improve the law's efficacy, and more reparative conditions that aim to fulfil the state's obligations to ensure the victims' rights to truth and reparations. This section has argued that states are often willing to impose practical conditions such as requiring combatants to surrender and lay down their weapons within a specified period before being considered eligible for amnesty. Where an amnesty aims to promote peace and stability within a war-torn society, such conditions can create an incentive for former combatants to engage promptly with a peace process, and can contribute to the gradual demilitarization of the society and a reduction in violence. The Amnesty Law Database has also revealed that states are becoming increasingly willing to attach more reparative conditions to the grant of amnesty. Such conditions can result in investigations of human rights abuses and provide victims with appropriate reparations, including compensation and restitution, whilst working towards establishing a society in which the suffering of the victims is memorialized and measures are taken to prevent a repetition of the crimes that they endured. The relationship of these more nuanced forms of amnesty to reconciliation will be explored below.

6 Amnesty as a Tool to Promote Reconciliation

Many amnesties have been, or are at least claimed by governments to have been, introduced to promote reconciliation, as either the sole objective, or more usually, in conjunction with other considerations, such as unsuccessful military campaigns. These governments proclaim that amnesties are needed to "create a climate of détente, confidence and assurance"[73] in which all parties can come together in an atmosphere of acceptance and tolerance to establish democracy.[74] Indeed, experiences to date in countries such as Spain,[75] Mozambique and South Africa indicate that amnesties, even for the most serious crimes, can have a positive impact on reconciliation (Daly and Sarkin 2007, p. 178), although there are numerous counter examples where amnesties were introduced repeatedly during ongoing conflicts but did not stem the violence. This indicates that the ability of amnesties to contribute to promoting reconciliation will often depend on the conditions within the state in which they are introduced. Amnesties are only one measure within often complex transitional arrangements and their contribution could be undermined by a failure to improve the standard of living of those individuals who were previously oppressed; by a failure to implement measures to integrate former combatants causing them to return to armed conflict or criminality; by an insincere government effort to introduce real reform; or by the failure of a peace agreement between elites to trickle down to stem grassroots violence. This section will therefore argue that the potential of amnesty to contribute to reconciliation is multifaceted and depend on how the amnesty relates to other transitional justice initiatives and wider reform measures.

[73] Wording is taken from the 1989 announcement of amnesty by the Beninese government, see BBC (1989).

[74] This wording is taken from expressions used in a number of amnesty processes.

[75] Paloma Aguilar, "The Timing and the Scope of Reparation, Truth and Justice Measures: A Comparison of the Spanish, Argentinian and Chilean Cases". See also, Aguilar (2001).

Before attempting to evaluate the contribution that amnesty can make to promoting reconciliation within transitional states, the term "reconciliation" must first be explored. This term is often highly disputed,[76] with different stakeholder groups, or individuals, holding differing interpretations on its meaning, how it can be achieved or even its objectives. The term can even be appropriated to justify competing political goals. For example, calls for retribution through widespread prosecutions for past crimes are often based on arguments that without justice there can be no reconciliation (UNCHR 2005, Preamble), whereas advocates of blanket impunity can also describe their goal as to reconcile society by looking towards the future, rather than reliving the pain and suffering of the past.

In describing the objectives of reconciliation, Crocker has suggested that understandings can range from thinner conceptions that aim at ending the violence and establishing "simple coexistence" between previously warring factions, to thicker conceptions where former enemies "must not only live together non-violently but also respect each other as fellow citizens". This could entail encouraging individuals to engage in processes of "forgiveness and mercy", such as truth commissions or community-based justice initiatives (Crocker 1999, p. 43). Adopting a thicker conception of reconciliation entails recognizing that reconciliation can occur at different levels within society. Daly and Sarkin have broken down these levels as follows: (1) individual; (2) inter-personal; (3) communal; (4) national; and (5) international (Daly and Sarkin 2007, p. 41–42). They further highlight that the emphasis placed by individual governments on each level of reconciliation may be influenced by the nature of the human rights violations, particularly whether they were predominantly committed by state agents. Furthermore, as Brounéus explains, the government's choice of transitional justice mechanisms could correspond with how the government prioritizes each level of reconciliation ranging from "top-level" mechanisms such as trials to more grassroots approaches.[77] In conceptualizing an end goal for reconciliation, Daly and Sarkin have suggested that, although it is a continual process, the objective of reconciliation policies is to reach a point "when the nation's politics become normalized, conducted in deliberate and peaceful ways, and the predominant issues are not transitional". They continue that "this does not mean that everyone in the country has become friends, but it does mean that the country functions with acceptably low levels of division because the population is generally committed to resolving disputes peaceably" (Daly and Sarkin 2007, p. 254).

In assessing the impact of amnesty on reconciliation, Crocker's approach to reconciliation as a continuum between thinner and thicker forms will be explored. Firstly, if a thinner conception of reconciliation, namely simply ending the violence, is adopted, it seems clear that amnesty can play a positive role in encouraging combatants to surrender and hand over their weapons. Here, it is argued that amnesties can potentially contribute to reducing human rights violations when a conflict is ongoing by creating conditions to enable peace negotiations to occur, particularly where some of the interlocutors would be at risk of prosecution (Hadden 2004,

[76] For discussion of the meaning of "reconciliation", see Daly and Sarkin (2007); Graybill and Lanegran (2004, p. 1); Fletcher and Weinstein (2002, p. 573); Daly (2001, p. 73).

[77] Karen Brounéus, "Reconciliation and Development".

p. 212). In this context, amnesty is often considered "the realistic price one has to pay for ending a destructive war or removing a government that has committed gross violations of human rights in the past" (Slye 2002, p. 173, 198), and that without it, the human rights violations would continue. Slye describes this scenario as a "trade-off ... not between victims of past abuses and accountability for perpetrators, but between victims of past abuses and yet to be identified victims of future abuses" (Slye 2002, p. 198). The utility of amnesty in this context was recognized by the Sierra Leonean Truth and Reconciliation Commission, which described the amnesty provisions of the Lomé Peace Accord "as necessary in the circumstances that prevailed at the time" (Truth and Reconciliation Commission of Sierra Leone 2004, Vol. 2, Chap. 3.4). In a later passage, the commission asserted:

Those who argue that peace cannot be bartered in exchange for justice, under any circumstances, must be prepared to justify the likely prolongation of armed conflict. Amnesties may be undesirable in many cases. ... However, amnesties should not be excluded entirely from the mechanisms available to those attempting to negotiate a cessation of hostilities after periods of brutal armed conflict. Disallowing amnesty in all cases would be to deny the reality of violent conflict and the urgent need to bring such strife and suffering to an end (Truth and Reconciliation Commission of Sierra Leone 2004, Vol. 3b, Chap. 6).

In addition to the short-term objective of simply ending the violence, a number of potentially positive, long-term outcomes of amnesty processes can be identified. Firstly, amnesties can be argued "to quell the need for vengeance" among those who have been defeated, where the amnesty entails policies of compromise and leniency on behalf of the victors (O'Shea 2002, pp. 24–25). Such leniency can be particularly important where there is no clear victor in a conflict, and consequently, any political settlement has to be a compromise between the different parties, as an attempt by one side to punish their opponents could reignite the violence (Sarkin 2004, pp. 2–3). Where amnesty is granted in these circumstances, it is generally part of a negotiated peace agreement or reform package introduced by a transitional government to reduce the justification for further violence by addressing the root causes of the conflict and to strengthen a human rights culture through the establishment of human rights institutions and complementary transitional justice initiatives. This reconciliatory approach to amnesty was the justification for the South African amnesty process as expressed in the 1994 Interim Constitution: "there is a need for understanding but not for vengeance, a need for reparation but not for retaliation, a need for *ubuntu* but not for victimization".[78] In contrast, where more retributive policies are pursued, Hadden has asserted that "strict punishment of all violators may serve to maintain rather than reconcile the differing recollections and attitudes of the various communal or political groups from which the conflict arose" (Hadden 2004).

Furthermore, attempts to pursue formal prosecutions could undermine reconciliation where there is a risk of acquittal of individuals widely believed to be guilty due to a lack of evidence or where the legal proceedings are viewed as biased (Daly

[78] Interim Constitution of South Africa 1994, Postamble.

and Sarkin 2007, p. 27). It has also been argued by some commentators that adversarial trials, due to inter alia the limited participation they afford victims may not always meet the needs of transitional societies.[79] In such circumstances, it can be argued that amnesties which are offered in exchange for truth recovery or participation in traditional justice programmes could further meet the needs of victims and their societies than trials.

Amnesties can also contribute to rebuilding transitional societies by enabling collaborators, such as bureaucrats from the former regimes, to participate in the reconstruction, as they are often the only people with the necessary knowledge and experience (Adam and Adam 2001, p. 34). It has been argued that without the certainty of amnesty, these individuals, even when they keep their jobs, may resort to corruption to supplement their income, due to the precariousness of their employment (Call and Stanley 2001, p. 151). This could contribute to undermining support for the new regime by making it appear as tainted as its predecessor. An amnesty for such individuals could also be beneficial following long periods of dictatorial rule in which large segments of the population were implicated in the oppression due to their role as state employees, party members, or informers. Such widespread involvement often makes it difficult to distinguish between victims and perpetrators as individuals can fall into different categories at different points in their lives. Any programme to allow members of the former regime to continue in public office should in principle, however, be coordinated with individualized measures to remove those responsible for serious human rights violations from office, as a failure to do so could cause disillusionment among victims' groups and inhibit institutional reform.

If it is assumed that amnesty laws can contribute positively to reconciliation as part of wider reform measures, efforts should be made to assess with the impact on different levels of society. Individual reconciliation is perhaps the hardest for an amnesty to address, as national policies can often do little to "heal the physical and psychological wounds of trauma" (Daly and Sarkin 2007, p. 45). However, where an amnesty contributes to reducing or ending the violence, plus saving the expense of costly prosecutions for large numbers of offenders, this could help to create conditions where investment can go into the health infrastructure to provide services for those who have been physically or psychologically injured. The end of the violence would also enhance the physical security of the population, which is a necessary prerequisite for healing to occur. Furthermore, as restorative justice literature indicates individual victims may benefit from the opportunity to interact directly with *their* perpetrator, to ask questions and to receive acknowledgement of their suffering. Where the perpetrator risks prosecution, this is unlikely to occur, but where an amnesty is coupled with grassroots mechanisms, it is more likely to be possible. The potential for amnesty to contribute to individual reconciliation is, however, clearly constrained by the diversity of needs and responses among victims' groups, and no victims should be pressurised to reconcile or forgive (Daly and Sarkin 2007, p. 45).

[79] For a discussion see Minow (1998, p. 88–89). Daly (2001). See also the view expressed by the *South African Constitutional Court in Azanian Peoples Organization (AZAPO) v the President of the Republic of South Africa* (CCT 17/96) (8) BCLR 1015 (CC) [17].

Amnesty could be argued to contribute to communal reconciliation where it is accompanied by alternative transitional justice mechanisms, such as truth commissions or community-based justice programmes. Such mechanisms could help foster communal reconciliation through the truth that they uncover, particularly by illustrating that all sides suffered during the period of violence. Furthermore, funding for redevelopment or reintegration projects could encourage communities to work together with former combatants who are seeking to return. Communal reconciliation cannot, however, be forced (Daly and Sarkin 2007, p. 186) as to do so would be unrealistic and could cause further harm to individual victims who are trying to regain control of their lives and their place in society.

Finally, amnesty could help to foster national reconciliation[80] where policies of forgiveness contribute to the establishment of a common identity and where truth-recovery mechanisms facilitate the development of a common history. An amnesty could also strengthen transitional power-sharing arrangements by reducing the fears of combatants that they will be punished if they surrender, enabling them to participate in the transitional government. Where an amnesty contributes to the end of violent conflict, it could also help to promote national reconciliation by contributing to stability, which enables economic growth and development, and the improvement of the living conditions of the population. For any amnesty programme to contribute effectively to national reconciliation, it is desirable that it is implemented following widespread consultation.

This chapter began by arguing that traditional understandings of "amnesty" as a tool to cast the crimes of the past into oblivion should be rejected in favour of more flexible conceptions of the term. These should recognize that today states are introducing amnesties that are more nuanced and are accompanied by transitional justice mechanisms, which can work to meet the needs of victims where formal prosecutions are not possible. Although traditional understandings of amnesty may have helped to fulfil "thinner" conceptions of reconciliation by contributing to an end to violent conflicts, this chapter has argued that for a society to move towards "thicker" reconciliation the amnesty must be tailored to suit the specific needs of the transitional state and must incorporate measures to restore (or create) harmonious relationships between previously antagonistic groups. Indeed, amnesty as a policy of forgiveness and compromise can, if introduced in good faith as part of a wider reform package, act as a tool to promote reconciliation.

Acknowledgment The author wishes to thank Prof Kieran McEvoy, Prof Tom Hadden, Prof Kai Ambos, Mark Freeman and Andrew Reiter for their comments and encouragement. This study was commissioned by the German Development Agency and the ideas contained in this study are explored more fully in the author's monograph: *Amnesties, Human Rights and Political Transitions: Bridging the Peace and Justice Divide* (Hart Publishing, Oxford 2008).

[80] The final category of international reconciliation has been excluded here as there are very few international amnesties in modern times. It should be noted, however, that in many conflicts and transitional situations there are strong regional dimensions which should be considered when designing transitional justice programmes. For a detailed consideration of these issues, see Chandra Lekha Sriram, "Conflict Mediation and the ICC: Challenges and Options for Pursuing Peace with Justice at the Regional Level".

List of Literature and Other Materials Used

Adam H, Adam K (2001) The politics of memory in divided societies. In: James WG, van de Vijver L (eds) After the TRC: reflections on truth and reconciliation. Ohio University Press, Athens
AFP (1997) Afghan Taliban chief asks rivals to surrender, offers amnesty. Agence France Presse (Islamabad, 20 May 1997)
AFP (2004) Pakistani Governor offers amnesty to "foreign fighters". Agence France Presse (Peshawar, 1 April 2004)
Aguilar P (2001) Justice, politics and memory in the Spanish transition. In: Barahona De Brito A, González-Enrıquez C, Aguilar P (eds) The politics of memory: transitional justice in democratizing societies. Oxford studies in democratization. Oxford University Press, Oxford
Alley R (2005) Restorative approaches in societies emerging from conflict. Presentation to the VUW Institute of Policy Studies symposium: towards a restorative society, 10–11 October 2005
Ambos K (1999) Impunidad y Derecho Penal Internacional, 2nd edn. Ad Hoc, Buenos Aires
Ambos K (2004) Selected issues regarding the "Core Crimes" in International Criminal Law. In: International Association of Penal Law (AIDP) (ed) International criminal law: Quo Vadis? Proceedings of the international conference held in Siracusa, Italy, 28 November – 3 December 2002, on the Occasion of the 30th Anniversary of ISISC. 19 Nouvelles Etudes Pénales, Toulouse, 2004
Americas Watch (1989) Challenging impunity: the "Ley de Caducidad" and the referendum in Uruguay. Report, 1 March 1989
Asmal K (2000) Truth, reconciliation and justice: the South African experience in perspective. Mod Law Rev 63:1
Baines E (2005) Roco Wat I Acoli – restoring relations in Acholi-land: traditional approaches to reintegration and justice. Liu Institute for Global Issues, Vancouver
Baines EK (2007) The haunting of alice: local approaches to justice and reconciliation in Northern Uganda. Int J Transitional Justice 1(1):91–114
Bassiouni MC (1996b) Searching for peace and achieving justice: the need for accountability. Law Contemp Probs 59:9
BBC (1980) Amnesty for "several hundred" in Eritrea. BBC Summary of World Broadcasts (Addis Ababa, 26 April 1980)
BBC (1989) Benin Political Bureau announces amnesty measure. BBC Summary of World Broadcasts (31 August 1989)
BBC (2001) Armenian court amnesties six defendants in parliament shooting case. BBC Worldwide Monitoring (20 June 2001)
BBC (2006a) "Amnesty" for Uganda rebel chief. BBC News (4 July 2006)
BBC (2006b) Fines amnesty for overdue books. BBC News (30 August 2006)
Bell C (2003) Dealing with the past in Northern Ireland. Fordham Int Law J 26:1095
Bhargava A (2002) Defining political crimes: a case study of the South African Truth and Reconciliation Commission. Columbia Law Rev 102:1304
Boed R (1999) An evaluation of the legality and efficacy of lustration as a tool of transitional justice. Columbia J Transnational Law 37:357
Boraine A (2000) A country unmasked: inside South Africa's Truth and Reconciliation Commission Oxford University Press, Cape Town
Bourdon W (1999) Amnesty In: Gutman R, Rieff D (eds) Crimes of war book. Wiley, Chichester
Bowyer Bell J (1993) The Irish troubles: a generation of violence, 1967–1992. Gill and Macmillan, Dublin
Bull C (2001) Amnesty November 2001. Prepared by Carolyn Bull for Interim Office, Commission for Reception, Truth and Reconciliation in East Timor
Call CT, Stanley W (2001) Protecting the people: public security choices after civil wars. Global Governance 7:151

Cassel D (1996) Lessons from the Americas: guidelines for international response to amnesties for atrocities. Law Contemp Probs 59:197
Cassese A (2003) International criminal law. Oxford University Press, Oxford
Chigara B (2002) Amnesty in international law: the legality under international law of national amnesty laws. Longman, Harlow
Clark P (2008) Recreating tradition: assessing community-based transitional justice in Northern Uganda. In: Allen T, Vlassenroot K (eds) The lord's resistance army: war, peace and reconciliation. James Currey, Oxford (forthcoming)
Cobban H (2007) Amnesty after atrocity? Healing nations after genocide and war crimes. Paradigm, Boulder
Coonan TS (1996) Rescuing history: legal and theological reflections on the task of making former torturers accountable. Fordham Int Law J 20:512
Crocker DA (1999) Reckoning with past wrongs: a normative framework. Ethics Int Aff 13:43
Daly E (2001) Transformative justice: charting a path to reconciliation. Int Legal Persp 12:73
Daly E, Sarkin J (2007) Reconciliation in divided societies: finding common ground. University of Pennsylvania Press, Philadelphia
Deák I, Gross JT, Judt T (2000) The politics of retribution in Europe: World War II and its aftermath. Princeton University Press, Princeton
Dexter T, Ntahombaye P (2005) The role of informal justice systems in fostering the rule of law in post-conflict situations: the case of Burundi. Centre for Humanitarian Dialogue, Geneva
Diamond L (2004) What went wrong in Iraq. Foreign Aff 2004(Sept/Oct)
Dugard J (2005) International law: A South African perspective. Juta, Cape Town
Elster J (2004) Closing the books: transitional justice in historical perspective. Cambridge University Press, Cambridge
Fletcher LE, Weinstein HM (2002) Violence and social repair: rethinking the contribution of justice to reconciliation. Hum Rights Q 24:573
Freeman M (2001) Lessons learned from amnesties for human rights crimes. Transparency Int Newsletter December 2001 3
Frei N (2002) Adenauer's Germany and the Nazi past: the politics of amnesty and integration. Columbia University Press, New York
Gallagher K (2000) No justice, no peace: the legalities and realities of amnesty in Sierra Leone. T Jefferson Law Rev 23:149
Gavron J (2002) Amnesties in the light of developments in international law and the establishment of the International Criminal Court. Int Comp Law Q 51:91
Graybill LS, Lanegran K (2004) Truth, justice, and reconciliation in Africa: issues and cases. Afr Stud Q 8:1
Hadden T (2004) Punishment, amnesty and truth: legal and political approaches. In: Guelke A (ed) Democracy and ethnic conflict: advancing peace in deeply divided societies. Palgrave Macmillan, Basingstoke
Hanlon K (2007) Peace or justice? Now that peace is being negotiated in Uganda, will the ICC still pursue justice? Tulsa J Comp Int Law 14:295
Harlacher T, et al (2006) Traditional ways of coping in Acholi. Caritas, Kampala
Harper E (2005) Delivering justice in the wake of mass violence: new approaches to transitional justice. J Conflict Security Law 10:149
Hayner PB (2001) Unspeakable truths: confronting state terror and atrocity. Routledge, New York
Herz JH (ed) (1982) From dictatorship to democracy: coping with the legacies of authoritarianism and totalitarianism. Contributions in Political Science. Greenwood, Westport
IRIN (2005) Mauritania: Junta declares general amnesty for political prisoners. IRIN (Dakar, 5 September 2005)
Isima J (2004) Cash payments in disarmament, demobilisation and reintegration programmes in Africa. J Security Sector Mgmt 2. http://www.ciaonet.org/olj/jssm/jssm_2_3/jssm_2_3_isj01.pdf. Accessed 10 June 2008
Jamieson R, McEvoy K (2005) State crime by proxy and judicial othering. Br J Criminol 45:504

Jones T, Newburn T (2005) Comparative criminal justice policy-making in the United States and the United Kingdom: the case of private prisons. Br J Criminol 45:58

Justice and Reconciliation Project (2007) The cooling of hearts: community truth-telling in Acholiland. Report, July 2007

Kritz NJ (2004) Dealing with the legacy of past abuses: an overview of the options and their relationship to the promotion of peace. In: Massard MB, Sisson JP (eds) Dealing with the past: critical issues, lessons learned, and challenges for future Swiss policy. Swiss Peace Foundation, Bern

Larsen SU, Hagtvet B (eds) (1998) Modern Europe after fascism. Social Science Monographs. Columbia University Press, Boulder

Le Sage A (2005) Stateless justice in Somalia: formal and informal rule of law initiatives. Centre for Humanitarian Dialogue, Geneva

Llewellyn JJ, Howse R (1999) Institutions for restorative justice: the South African Truth and Reconciliation Commission. U Toronto Law J 49:355

Mallinder L (2007) Can amnesties and international justice be reconciled? Int J Transitional Justice 1:208

Mallinder L (2008) Amnesty, human rights and political transitions: bridging the peace and justice divide. Hart, Oxford

McEvoy K (2008) Truth, transition and reconciliation: dealing with the past in Northern Ireland. Willan, Cullompton

McEvoy K, McConnachie K, Jamieson R (2007) Political imprisonment and the "war on terror". In: Jewkes Y (ed) Handbook on prisons. Willan, Cullompton

Minow M (1998) Between vengeance and forgiveness: facing history after genocide and mass violence. Beacon, Boston

Moore JJ Jr (1991) Problems with forgiveness: granting amnesty under the Arias Plan in Nicaragua and El Salvador. Stan Law Rev 43:733

Murray I (1986) Israeli Shin Bet leader resigns / Avrahom Shalom granted presidential pardon over 1984 hijacker killings. The Times, Jerusalem, 26 June 1986

OHCHR (2007) Making peace our own: victims' perceptions of accountability, reconciliation and transitional justice in Northern Uganda. Report. Office of the High Commissioner for Human Rights, Geneva

Orentlicher DF (2007) "Settling accounts" revisited: reconciling global norms with local agency Int J Transitional Justice 1:10

O'Shea A (2002) Amnesty for crime in international law and practice. Kluwer Law International, Hague

Rubin BR (2003) Transitional justice and human rights in Afghanistan. Int Aff 79:567

Sadat LN (2006) Exile, amnesty and international law. Notre Dame Law Rev 81:955

Sarkin J (2004) Carrots and sticks: The TRC and the South African amnesty process. Intersentia, Antwerp

Sarkin J, Daly E (2004) Too many questions, too few answers: reconciliation in transitional societies. Colum Hum Rights Law Rev 35:661

Schabas WA (2004) Amnesty, the Sierra Leone Truth and Reconciliation Commission and the Special Court for Sierra Leone. U C Davis J Int Law Policy 11:145

Scharf MP (1996) The letter of the law: the scope of the international legal obligation to prosecute human rights crimes. Law Contemp Probs 59:41

Sebba L (1977) The pardoning power – a world survey. J Crim Law Criminol 68:83

Sikkink K, Walling CB (2007) The impact of human rights trials in Latin America. J Peace Res 44:427

Slye RC (2000) Justice and amnesty. In: Villa-Vicencio C, Verwoerd W (eds) Looking back, reaching forward: reflections on the Truth and Reconciliation Commission of South Africa. Zed Books, London

Slye RC (2002) The legitimacy of amnesties under international law and general principles of Anglo-American Law: is a legitimate amnesty possible? Va J Int Law 43:173

Subotic J (2005) Hijacked justice: domestic appropriation of international norms. Paper presented at International Studies Association Annual Conference, Honolulu, Hawaii, 2 March 2005

Theissen G (2005) Supporting justice, co-existence and reconciliation after armed conflict: strategies for dealing with the past. In: Bloomfield D, Fischer M, Schmelzle B (eds) Berghof handbook for conflict transformation. Berghof Research Center for Constructive Conflict Management, Berlin

Trumbull CP (2007) Giving amnesties a second chance. Berkeley J Int Law 25:283

Truth and Reconciliation Commission of Sierra Leone (2004) The Final Report of the Truth and Reconciliation Commission of Sierra Leone, 5 October 2004. http://www.trcsierraleone.org/drwebsite/publish/index.shtml. Accessed 10 June 2008

UNCHR (2005) Updated Set of principles for the protection and promotion of human rights through action to combat impunity, 8 February 2005. UN Doc E/CN.4/2005/102/Add.1 (prepared by D. Orentlicher)

UNGA (2005) Basic principles and guidelines on the right to a remedy and reparation for victims of gross violations of international human rights law and serious violations of international humanitarian law. 16 December 2005. UNGA Res 60/147

UNSC (1999) Seventh report of the Secretary General on the United Nations Observer Mission in Sierra Leone. 30 July 1999. UN Doc S/1999/836

UNSC (2000) Report of the Secretary-General on the role of United Nations peacekeeping in disarmament, demobilization and reintegration. 11 February 2000. UN Doc S/2000/101

UNTAET (2001) Regulation No. 2001/10 on the Establishment of a Commission for Reception, Truth and Reconciliation in East Timor, 2001

US Department of State (1994) Human rights practices 1993: Malawi. 31 January 1994

Van den Wyngaert C (1980) The political offence exception to extradition: the delicate problem of balancing the rights of the individual and the international public order. Kluwer, Hague

Vinjamuri L, Boesenecker A (2007) Accountability and peace agreements: mapping trends from 1980 to 2006. Centre for Humanitarian Dialogue, Geneva

Watson J (2005) A model pacific solution? A study of the deployment of the regional assistance mission to Solomon Islands. Working Paper No. 126 (Land Warfare Studies Centre Working Papers). http://www.defence.gov.au/ARMY/LWSC/docs/WP_126.pdf. Accessed 10 June 2008

Weschler L (1998) A miracle, a universe: settling accounts with torturers. University of Chicago Press, Chicago

Xiaoyi Q (1993) Malawi on process of political transition. Xinhua News Agency (Lusaka, 28 December 1993)

Zaman A (2003) Turkish parliament approves amnesty for Kurdish rebels. Voice of America News (Ankara, 29 July 2003)

Legal Texts

Amnesty Act 2000 (Uganda)

Chittagong Hill Tracts Peace Treaty 1997 (Bangladesh)

Loi portant amnistie, 2003 (Côte d'Ivoire)

Comprehensive Peace Agreement Between the Government of Liberia and the Liberians United for Reconciliation and Democracy (LURD) and the Movement for Democracy in Liberia (MODEL) and Political Parties ('Accra Peace Accord'), 2003 (Liberia)

Decree No. 7338, 1989 (Albania)

Décret N° 62–328 portant amnistie de faits commis dans le cadre des opérations de maintien de l'ordre dirigées contre l'insurrection algérienne, 1962 (France)

Decreto-Ley No 33–82, Diario Oficial No 84, tomo 218, 1982 (Guatemala)

Indo-Sri Lanka Accord, 1987
Law n° 46–729 Loi Portant Amnistie, 1946 (France)
Law on General Amnesty and National Reconciliation, 1990 (Nicaragua)
Lei 11/96, 1996 (Angola)
Ley 35, Diario Official N° 36133 bis, p. 529 'por la cual se decreta una amnistía y se dictan normas tendientes al restablecimiento y preservación de la paz', 1982 (Colombia)
Ley 37 de 1981 por la cual se declara una amnistía conditional, Diario Official No. 35760, 14 May 1981, p. 442 (Colombia)
Loi d'amnistie générale n° 84/91, 1991 (Lebanon)
Ley de Obedencia Debida, No. 23.521 (4 June 1987) (Argentina)
Loi N° 53–681 portant amnistie, 1953 (France)
Décret N° 62–328 du 22 Mar 1962 portant amnistie de faits commis dans le cadre des opérations de maintien de l'ordre dirigées contre l'insurrection algérienne (France)
Loi portant amnistie d'infractions contre la sûreté de l'Etat ou commises en relation avec les événements d'Algérie, 1966 (France)
Loi N° 68–697 portant amnistie, Journal officiel, 1968, at 77521 (France)
Loi N° 74–643 portant amnistie, 1974 (France)
Loi N° 81–736 Loi Portant Amnistie, 1981 (France)
Loi no 82–1021, 1982 relative au règlement de certaines situations résultant de évènements d'Afrique du Nord, de la guerre d'Indochine ou de la seconde guerre mondiale (France)
Loi relative au rétablissement de la Concorde civile, Loi No 98–08, 1999 (Algeria)
Maunikau Accord, 2000 (Fiji)
Peace Agreement between the Government of Sierra Leone and the Revolutionary United Front of Sierra Leone 1999 ('Lomé Accord') (Sierra Leone)
Promotion of National Unity and Reconciliation Act, No 34, 1995 (South Africa)
Simla Agreement on Bilateral Relations between India and Pakistan, 1972
UNTAET, Regulation No. 2001/10 on the Establishment of a Commission for Reception, Truth and Reconciliation in East Timor, 2001 (E. Timor)

Case Law

Inter-American Commission on Human Rights, Garay Hermosilla et al. v Chile, Case 10.843, Report 36/96, OEA/Ser.L/V/II/95 (1996)
Azanian Peoples Organization (AZAPO) v the President of the Republic of South Africa (CCT 17/96) (8) BCLR 1015 (CC)
Barzilai v Government of Israel, ('Shin Bet Affair') Case HCJ 428/86, [1986]

Part II
Peace Process Considerations: Mediation, Reconciliation and Development

Justice Mechanisms and the Question of Legitimacy: The Example of Rwanda's Multi-layered Justice Mechanisms

Barbara Oomen

Abstract Legitimacy, this contribution argues, plays a key role in connecting transitional justice mechanisms to sustainable peace, and strengthening people's perceptions of legitimacy should be of concern to all those involved in these institutions. Here, it is important to take an empirical, people-based approach to legitimacy, with regard for its dynamic quality. This approach should focus on all three dimensions of legitimacy: the input into transitional justice mechanisms, the popular adherence to the demos that sets them up, and their output. In addition, legitimacy requires an explicit deliberation by means of justificatory discourse, and the involvement of all stakeholders. Drawing on the example of Rwanda's multi-layered justice mechanisms this model then draws attention to the processes through which various internal and external actors can seek to (de)legitimate transitional justice institutions, and what this entails for the legitimacy of these mechanisms in general.

1 Introduction

"Peace", as the Secretary-General of the United Nations wrote in 2004, "cannot be achieved unless the population is confident that redress for grievances can be obtained through legitimate structures for the peaceful settlement of disputes and the fair administration of justice"[1]. In a way, his words echoed the sentiment expressed by a prominent Rwandan observer who, eying the remnants of the onslaught in his country a decade earlier, stated that "what we need now is justice and cash, in that order".

B. Oomen
Roosevelt Academy/Utrecht University, Lange Noordstraat 1 4330 CB, Middelburg, The Netherlands
e-mail: B.Oomen@roac.nl

[1] UNSC, The rule of law and transitional justice in conflict and post-conflict societies (3 August 2004) Report of the Secretary-General S/2004/616 3.

K. Ambos et al. (eds.), *Building a Future on Peace and Justice: Studies on Transitional Justice, Peace and Development.*

In the case of Rwanda, that justice came in many forms. Genocide justice is not only dispensed by the International Criminal Tribunal for Rwanda in Arusha, and universal jurisdiction procedures in a host of countries over the world, but also by a National Unity and Reconciliation Commission, the domestic courts, and the neo-traditional *gacaca*. As such, the Rwandan "legal laboratory" forms one of the most poignant examples of the central features of transitional justice in our days: the strong involvement of the international community, the search for alternatives to the classic retributive mechanisms, the tenuous linkage with wider political and socio-economic processes and the ongoing debate on the relationship between justice and reconciliation.

It also, 13 years after the genocide, offers an opportunity to look into that feature deemed crucial by not only the Secretary-General, but frequently under-researched: legitimacy. What is meant by the legitimacy of transitional justice institutions, what have been the dimensions of legitimacy and strategies of legitimation in Rwanda's search for justice and what general lessons can be drawn from this? In answering these questions, this contribution first offers a definition of legitimacy, and argues why the issue should be approached empirically rather than normatively, and subsequently focuses on perceptions instead of assumptions. Such an empirical assessment, as Sect. 3 argues on the basis of the literature, should focus on all three dimensions of legitimacy in these cases: the input in the transitional justice process, both in terms of procedures and principles; the adherence to the demos concerned, whether this is the international community, the nation-state or the locality; and the output. It should also take into account two crucial preconditions for establishing legitimacy: a communicative strategy geared towards deliberation on, and justification of, choices made on all three dimensions, as well as involvement of all stakeholders, not merely a majority, in all three dimensions. A next section applies this model to the Rwandan context and thus points out some of the strengths and weaknesses of all Rwanda's justice mechanisms, and the strategies of (de)legitimation employed by key actors. These lessons, then, form the basis for a number of observations and recommendations concerning legitimacy in a final section.

2 Legitimacy in an Era of Global Governance

2.1 From Assumptions to Perceptions

There are many definitions and understandings of legitimacy, but the one used here will be that "legitimacy is a generalised perception or assumption that the actions of an entity are desirable, proper, or appropriate within some socially constructed system of norms, values, beliefs, and definitions" (Suchman 1995, p. 571, 574). A crucial feature here is that legitimacy is about compliance, and the voluntary acceptance of costly rules: it is about accepting the jurisdiction of the court that sentences your brother to life-long imprisonment, and not doubting the procedures followed, even if the outcome is adverse (Risse 2004). For legal institutions, Gibson and Caldeira

(1995, p. 459, 460; see also Risse, 2004) argue, no attribute is more important than legitimacy as this gives them the "latitude necessary to make decisions contrary to the perceived immediate interests of their constituents". In a famous trilogy Kratochwil distinguished three motivations for rule acceptance: fear of punishment, a cost-benefit calculation and acceptance of the norm as binding, and indicated how the rule concerned could only be considered legitimate in the third instance (cf. Steffek 2003, p. 249, 254).

This bridging of the moral component of rules and institutions and their popular acceptance sets legitimacy apart from related concepts like legality, credibility and accountability. Legality points at the lawfulness of rules and institutions, and how these comply with preset norms, but does not deal with their moral qualities, or popular acceptance. Credibility concerns the capability of eliciting belief, but does not indicate whether this belief is indeed present with the people concerned. Accountability, on the other hand, points at a particular relationship between actors, while legitimacy concerns a quality of institutions like courts and rules (Risse 2004, p. 7).

Legitimacy, in Suchman's definition, concerns a generalised *perception* or *assumption*, and can thus be approached either empirically, through social-scientific research into popular perceptions, or normatively, through the avenue of political philosophy (Follesdal 2004). Over times, a marked shift has taken place from more normative to more empirical approaches to the issue. Of old, legitimacy was bestowed upon the sovereign on the basis of a moral-theological conception rooted in divine cosmology. After the Vienna Congress legitimacy came to be associated with constitutionalism, and was firmly clamped to the notion of the nation-state, again from a more philosophical and normative standpoint (Clark 2005).

In the early nineteenth century, Weber explicitly shifted focus from the normative to the empirical and from assumptions to perceptions, holding that rule is legitimate when those governed believe it to be so (Weber 1978). Here, the litmus test for legitimacy became "not the truth of the philosopher, but the belief of the people" (Schabert 1986, p. 102). Legitimacy, in Weber's rendering, was intimately coupled to authority and domination, that could either be charismatic (the family, religion), traditional or legal-rational (as is the case with the modern state and its bureaucracy) (Weber 1993). Habermas, building on Weber's work, emphasised the dynamic character of legitimacy, and the role of law-making in giving an order binding force (Habermas 1998).

Rules, and courts, thus play a key role in strengthening legal-rational authority and establishing a legitimate order. For, although discussions on legitimacy often concern a political community as a whole, generalised procedural and substantive rules are a key mechanism in guaranteeing the acceptance of outcomes. At the same time, the legitimacy of rules and courts themselves can be looked into, as is the case in this paper. While examples of such research are relatively scarce, they include studies on the popular acceptance of the South African and the Sierra Leone Truth and Reconciliation Commission, the European Court of Justice or the US Supreme Court (Gibson and Gouws 1997, p. 173; Gibson et al. 1998, p. 343, 354, 2003; Kelsall and Sawyer 2007; cf. Carothers 2003).

2.2 Legitimacy and Global Governance

If legitimacy has always been a key concept in political and socio-legal studies, recent changes in the world order have made it even more relevant. The notion of a nation-state as the sole political order with the right to rule, and a monopoly of force, is increasingly confronted with a more multi-faceted reality: global governance has brought hybrids like side-by-side governance (where local and international non-governmental organisations rule together with governments) and web governance (by governments, elites, mass publics, transitional corporations, NGOs, INGOs) (Rosenau 2002, p. 81). In addition, there is a stark rise of decentralised power-holders, whether local governments or chiefs. On the international plane, Fukuyama (2004, p. 97) argues how "in Somalia, Cambodia, Bosnia, Kosovo, East Timor, and now Afghanistan, the 'international community' ceased to be an abstraction and took on a palpable presence as the effective government of the country in question". The ICC, with which state parties voluntarily share their monopoly of force, could well be the best example of how Weber's one-actor model of political society hardly fits today's world anymore.

If the legitimacy of the nation-state is debated and contested by a variety of actors all over the world, this is even more so in Africa. Here, discussions concerning the legitimacy of the state have often circled around "l'état importé", and posed the question as to whether the state institutions – structures of governance and courts alike – are endogenous and can claim some historical continuity, or have been superimposed by the colonial state (Englebert 2000, 2003). In Pham's words: "by and large, the contemporary African state is not endogenous. It supplanted pre-existing political institutions, underlying norms of social and economic behaviour, and customary sources of law and authority" (Pham 2005, p. 31; cf. Oomen 2005a).

Just as a colonial history puts particular challenges to normative theories concerning the legitimacy of the nation-state, so do many post-conflict situations. Whether the case is East-Timor, Afghanistan, Iraq or Columbia, the state itself was often a key actor in the conflict, leaving its institutions not only ruined physically but also severely delegitimised. Courts and rules in general then become mechanisms for re-establishing legitimacy.

2.3 Transitional Justice and Its Empirical Legitimacy

The global era and the post-colonial and post-conflict condition thus all necessitate increased attention for issues of legitimacy, approached in an empirical, people-centered manner. This also applies to the burgeoning field of transitional justice. Transitional justice, as is well-established, concerns both a set of institutions and a debate. The institutions can range from international(ised) tribunals, national courts, truth commissions, vetting procedures to local courts. The debate is about the aims best suited to make the transition from violent upheaval to sustainable peace: reconciliation, truth-telling, retribution, reparations or otherwise (Bell et al., 2004 Humphrey 2002; Roht-Arriaza and Mariezcurrena 2006; Teitel 2000). The debate was long held in terms of dichotomies: Truth vs. Justice; Reconciliation vs. Retribution; National courts vs. International Tribunals. Recent insights, however, have strongly underlined the need for more holistic strategies (Bloomfield et al., 2003). As the Secretary-General put it in his 2004 report on the rule of law and transitional justice:

> Our approach to the justice sector must be comprehensive in its attention to all of its interdependent institutions, sensitive to the needs of key groups and mindful of the need for complementarity between transitional justice mechanisms.[2]

In establishing the merits of these comprehensive, holistic "justice packages" it is crucial to take an empirical, people-centered perspective. To again quote the Secretary-General:

> Our experience in the past decade has demonstrated clearly that the consolidation of peace in the immediate post-conflict period, as well as the maintenance of peace in the long term, cannot be achieved unless the population is confident that redress for grievances can be obtained through legitimate structures for the peaceful settlement of disputes and the fair administration of justice.[3]

Here, both the normative *assumptions* and the empirical *perceptions* of legitimacy are deemed important in working towards peace: the institutions have to be legitimate in moral terms, but the general public – in all its diversity – also has to perceive them as such.

For a long time, empirical research into the legitimacy of transitional justice institutions was hardly carried out. Baxter pondered in 2002 why the decision to put in place a Truth and Reconciliation Commission in South Africa was not based on empirical research (Baxter 2002), while Pouligny (2005, p. 2) notes a similar disregard for "what people believe about themselves, the other, the nature of justice, the requirements of community, and the proper structure of rights and responsibilities that determine, at least in part, post-conflict politics, social action, and communal life". Other authors, like Mokhiber (2000) and Carothers (2003), extend these findings to the whole justice sector.

Recently, however, a number of NGOs and scientists have carried out empirical research on people's perceptions and expectations of transitional justice mechanisms. In a carefully drafted and carried out study, Stover and Weinstein (2004, p. 11, 18) show how "the views and opinions of those most affected must be solicited and given careful consideration", and, on the basis of field research in Rwanda and former Yugoslavia, work towards an "ecological paradigm of social reconstruction". The International Center for Transitional Justice (2004), correspondingly, carried out survey research on people's opinions on transitional justice institutions in countries like Iraq, Uganda and Columbia (Hovil and Lomo, 2005).

However strong the need for such empirical research, a number of cautionary remarks related to the dynamic quality of legitimacy and the value of such research for policy formulation have to be made. The first concerns the lack of knowledge and understanding of transitional justice institutions that many interviewees are likely to

[2] UNSC The rule of law and transitional justice in conflict and post-conflict societies (3 August 2004) Report of the Secretary-General S/2004/616 3.

[3] ibid.

have at the time of research. One of the central lessons in socio-legal studies is that the more people know about courts, the more they tend to appreciate them: "to know courts is to love them, because to know them is to be exposed to a series of legitimizing messages focused on the symbols of justice, judicial objectivity, and impartiality" (Gibson et al. 1998, p. 345). Also, people's institutional preferences are generally not formed by a preset legal culture – like Asian Confucianism – but determined by the range of institutional options available (Friedman 1969, p. 29). People's perceptions of legal institutions can, therefore, increase with the knowledge that people have of them and the degree to which they are deemed to be available.

What is needed, then, is a conceptual model that puts people's perceptions and appreciation of transitional justice structures at its core, and at the same time recognises the dynamic quality that is essential to gaining and maintaining legitimacy. In the following sections such a model will be elaborated, and applied to that "legal laboratory" of a thousand hills.

3 Conceptualising Legitimacy: Input, Demos and Output

Legitimacy, with all its understandings, becomes a bit like the blind men's elephant: the trunk to the one, the tusk to the second and the tail to the third. In order to capture tail and trunk alike, but also the movement of the animal concerned, the model will distinguish three dimensions determining the legitimacy of transitional justice institutions that come close to the threefold distinction of democracy made by Lincoln in his Gettysburg address: government *of* the people, government *by* the people and government *for* the people (Scharpf 1998). Translated, the legitimacy of courts, truth commissions and the other institutions concerned is made up by the procedural and substantive *input* (of the people); the adherence to the wider community that puts the institutions in place, the *demos* (by the people) and the acceptance of the *output* of the institutions, whether in the short term (specific case law) or the long term (reconciliation).

On the basis of the philosophical and the socio-scientific literature, the following can be postulated: First, the legitimacy of transitional justice institutions hinges on all three dimensions: an Truth Commission in which the input is considered legitimate, but that lacks output or was put in place by an entity that people do not adhere to will still suffer a lack of legitimacy. Second, the legitimacy of an institution is not static, but can fluctuate over time. It has to be both assumed (normatively) and perceived (empirically) and *deliberative* democracy, with an explicit justificatory discourse, helps bridge the gaps between the two (Habermas). Whereas the model follows Ignatieff (2003, p. 175) in stating that "the truth, if it is to be believed, must be authored by those who suffered its consequences" and thus puts the people's perspective first, it is equally important to involve all *stakeholders* in these discursive processes. Attempts to enhance the legitimacy of transitional justice procedures should therefore be concerned with the input, the demos and the output, take a discursive approach and involve as many stakeholders as possible. The following sections will discuss the foundations and the importance of each of these prerequisites.

3.1 The Input Dimension

The *input* dimension of legitimacy, as introduced by Scharpf, concerns the procedural and substantive elements that go into designing transitional justice institutions. Input is the classic locus of legitimacy, and the only one to some theorists and practitioners. It points at a faith in the design of institutions, the procedures followed and the underlying values that will ensure acceptance of decisions made by – for instance – courts, even if they have adverse effects for the people concerned.

Procedural fairness is at play when the setting up of institutions follows preset rules, and takes place by authorities who have the right to do so. It points at procedural correctness and a lack of arbitrariness in the way in which institutions are set up: not as a political, behind-closed-doors arrangement in the transition process, guaranteeing (for instance) amnesty to members of the former regime, but through an open procedure. An element can be public participation in the design and the staffing of the institutions. In South Africa, for instance, the job interviews with Truth Commissioners were held on public television, for all the country to follow. In addition, mandates have to be fair, covering all actors involved (including the international community) and all human rights abuses committed (including those committed by the victors).

Input legitimacy is also enhanced through building on values that enjoy broad acceptance among the community (Friedman and Rogelio 2003). Classically, universal human rights are best suited to act as these values through their emphasis on equality and procedural fairness. At the same time, it is important to build on the underlying values in national law, and in traditional and religious cosmology. As a woman in East Timor said about the community reconciliation process "it is because we also involve the traditional leaders, and swear oaths as in our tradition, that forgiveness becomes true" (Scheeringa 2005, p. 48).

3.2 The Demos

The way in which input in transitional justice procedures is valued is closely related to stakeholders' acceptance of the polity that puts in place the institutions concerned. This polity – the "people" in the *by* the people referred to by Lincoln – can be the international community, the nation-state or the locality.[4] Even if, as discussed before, all these polities might consist of a host of actors once unpacked, their mythical identity as coherent communities of belonging continues to exist (Clark 2005; Steffek 2003). While the demos can be conceptualized in legal-rational terms, as the polity given the right to rule by its citizens, its added legitimacy lies in its mythical qualities: that of the imagined community and the fact that this causes the institution concerned to be perceived as "our court" or "our commission".

[4] These are, of course, not all forms of demos thinkable: in the context of transitional justice the church and other non-government organizations might also function as communities of belonging that set up specific transitional justice procedures.

The mythical quality poses particular challenges in each of the three polities concerned, but arguably most poignantly where it concerns the international community (Falk 2004). As Risse states:

> there is no global "demos" available in terms of a world community of citizens in whose name governance could take place. At best, governance beyond the nation-state relies on a rather "thin" layer of collective cosmopolitan identity of "world citizens". … solidarity with the global community is restricted to particular issue-specific publics organised in transnational networks of like-minded people. (Risse 2004, p. 1)

Here, justification of actions and narratives of belonging becomes even more important in order to gain popular legitimacy. That this is not always the case is demonstrated by the relative lack of support for the Yugoslavia tribunal amongst Bosnians, Croats and Serbs, of whom many feel that "The Hague Tribunal is a big mockery" (Corkalo et al. 2004, p. 147; cf. Fletcher and Weinstein 2000, p. 102).

While the nation-state arguably has the strongest credentials to act as a mythical community of belonging to all its citizens, this myth has often been thoroughly shattered during the war and requires rebuilding around common narratives of ancestry, history, the war and the future that often take generations. Whatever national government is involved in setting up transitional justice procedures – democratically elected, interim or a government of national unity – its legitimacy is likely to be challenged by those who feel marginalised. A reinterpretation of the past, a rephrasing of a common identity, a record of what took place and why, is crucial towards re-establishing this legitimacy.

In this context, it is vital that the state is perceived to strive for the common good: that it seeks to dispense socio-economic justice and treats all its citizens fairly in providing goods like employment, schooling and housing (Uvin and Mironko 2003, p. 219). A transitional justice process, however legitimate the input and the output, will not be perceived as legitimate if there are doubts concerning the degree to which the *demos* truly acts in the common interest.

It is precisely because of the tattered and tarnished image of the nation-state as a community of belonging that policy-makers have increasingly focused on the locality as more suitable, legitimate demos within which to initiate transitional justice initiatives. The community programs in East Timor and Sierra Leone can serve as an example. For all the merits in this approach, there are also dangers in romanticizing post-conflict communities: often, these are characterized by a high degree of social tension (Berkeley 2001; Stover and Weinstein 2004). In these uneasy day-to-day arrangements memories of intimate violence and discourses of insiders and outsiders, perpetrators and victims linger right below the surface, and preclude the notion of a communal identity.

In sum, for all these polities to be the legitimate author of transitional justice strategies they themselves have to be rebuilt as well, through narratives of belonging and day-to-day actions that include all stakeholders. These wider processes are of high importance in ascertaining the role of justice in rebuilding peace in general, and in making for successful transitional justice institutions.

3.3 Output

As people are often highly sceptical of the demos that sets up transitional justice institutions, the output of these institutions becomes more and more important. This shift from *input* to *output* legitimacy as a result of global governance has often been noted: how an institution was set up and who did so becomes less important, as long as it gets the work done (Scharpf 1998). "We don't care too much who tries the members of the Pol-Pot regime, as long as they go to jail", as a Cambodian respondent said (De Wijn 2005, p. 56).

In discussing output legitimacy it is important to distinguish between the direct output and the outcome; the divergent aims that transitional justice mechanisms seek to achieve. In terms of output legitimacy is attained through, amongst others, the speediness of procedures, the amount of cases heard, the accessibility (both physical and in terms of language) and – importantly – the selection of cases. A court that has a well-designed mandate but is perceived to try only certain actors in the conflict risks a loss of legitimacy, as in the case of the International Criminal Tribunal for the former Yugoslavia (ICTY), on which a Serb man said: "The Hague is dictated by the Americans. Those that they want to send to The Hague are sent there. And the wrong people are being tried" (Stover and Weinstein 2004, p. 147).

Even more important, be it difficult to research empirically, is public support for the underlying aims of transitional justice procedures: to what extent do people want retribution, reconciliation, truth-telling, reparations to play the role that they do in the given institution? Ideas and expectations in this field might differ strongly. In South Africa, reconciliation was deemed to be the main aim of transitional justice, while empirical research pointed out how most South Africans found retribution to be equally important (Hayner 2002, p. 144; Gibson and Gouws 1997; Wilson 2000, p. 75). Similarly, the scarce attention for reparations in justice procedures in Guatemala, East Timor and Sierra Leone proved to be a great disappointment for many participants (Roht-Arriaza and Mariezcurrena 2006).

3.4 The Importance of Deliberation, and Justificatory Discourse

Assumptions and perceptions of legitimacy can come closer to one another in processes of justification. The issue is subsequently to not only attain legitimate input and output, and to strengthen the legitimacy of the *demos*, but to engage in ongoing processes of legitimation and justificatory discourse. Habermas (1998), for instance, asserts how legitimate law-making stems from the formation of public opinion and will-formation that produces communicative power that in turn influences social institutions. Justification, arguments for the choices made, the input, the right of the *demos* to act on behalf of the stakeholders and the value of the output are key elements in strengthening legitimacy.

One example are the outreach programs of the International Criminal Court (ICC) and other international(ised) courts that seek to explain their mandate and procedures at the level of the locality. In designing such programs, it is important to keep the three dimensions in mind: an international court has the greatest chance of being perceived as legitimate if it involves the people concerned in its set-up, includes values held and procedures respected locally and explicitly communicates its underlying values, justifies the fact that it acts on behalf of a community of belonging, and – in its selection of cases and wider aims – takes people's perceptions into account and communicates its results to them. The way in which the media are involved in broadcasting information on a wide range of transitional justice initiatives in countries like Sierra Leone, East Timor and Rwanda, often at village level, can serve as an example.

3.5 Stakeholders

Legitimacy, like beauty, is in the eyes of the beholder. In processes that bring closure to a period of horrific human rights violations there are often many actors with very divergent interests: the perpetrators and their families, who can put the emphasis on reconciliation and forgiveness; the ex-combatants, whose primary interest might be reintegration into society; the victims, who often have a legitimate desire for revenge and retaliation; the by-standers, who value socio-economic justice; NGOs, which seek to work on a wider culture of accountability and adherence to universal human rights; elites, who might or might not have played a role in the conflict; international donors, with their own agenda's and political interests; the international community at large, which – more often than not – could have played a greater role in preventing the conflict than it did.

In this context, legitimacy theory points at the overriding importance of *consensual* (as opposed to majoritarian) decision-making and involving all stakeholders in strengthening each of the dimensions of legitimacy: in designing the institutions, in the wider community that is the *demos* and also in delivering justice: the output side (Clark 2005; Mokhiber 2000). One example is the involvement of victims in court procedures, an issue underscored by the International Criminal Tribunal for Rwanda (ICTR) and the ICTY, but well catered for within the ICC.

The conceptual model as set out above is summarized in Table 1. It shows how legitimacy can only be enhanced through attention for its three different dimensions, and the importance of justificatory discourse and involvement of stakeholders, in all of these dimensions. In what follows, the model will be applied to the multi-layered justice mechanisms of Rwanda, explaining the sources of legitimacy of each of these mechanisms, what strategies to (de)legitimise the transitional justice process were successful and why.

Table 1 General model of the legitimacy of transitional justice institutions

Dimensions → *Preconditions for legitimacy↓*	*Input*	*Demos*	*Output*
Legitimacy in *general; procedures*	Institution set up in open process, according to preset norms	Whether the international community, the nation-state or the locality: constituted through democratic elections or other procedures that elicit confidence	Procedural fairness: trying all parties in a conflict, speedy, expedient justice, accessible in terms of language and distance
Legitimacy in general: principles	Universal human rights, national law and traditional, religious values	A mythical community of belonging	Outcome: reconciliation, retribution, truth, reparations?
Justificatory discourse	Explicit two-way communication	Narratives of common identity, history and future, combined with socio-economic justice	Explicit discussion on the aims of transitional justice procedures and short-term output
Involvement stakeholders	Open procedures, all stakeholders	Consensual decision-making, attention for minorities	Involvement of victims, bystanders, perpetrators and support of NGOs and international community

4 Rwanda and Its Multi-Layered Justice Mechanisms

Moving, now, from the theoretical plane to the issue of legitimacy in the "legal laboratory" in the country of a thousand hills, it is necessary to first give a very brief sketch of the 1994 genocide and its causes. As is well established, the starting point of the killings was the shooting of the plane that carried Rwanda's president Habiyarimana on April 6. In the hundred days that followed, an estimated 800,000 Tutsi and moderate Hutu were murdered, often by acquaintances or intimates, with machetes and other farming utensils (African Rights 1994; Des Forges 1999; Prunier 1995). One of the poignant features of the Rwandan genocide is the scale of the killings and the widespread involvement in it: recent reports have estimated the number of killers at 750,000, one out of four Rwandan adults at the time (Penal Reform International 2006).

In looking into the causes of the genocide, and with it the potential for justice and sustainable development, a number of issues are important. There is, for one, the legacy of authoritarianism and obedience, dating back to the times of the *mwami*, king. But there is also the colonial legacy of ethnic differentiation, the overpopulation and general economic pressures at play in the early 1990s, the Rwandan Patriotic Front (RPF) invasion of the country in 1990, the role of the extremist government and its use of the media, the role of the international community and, of course, the culture of impunity.

Rwanda is one of the few African countries where "l'état importé" is not an issue, and which still more or less has the borders of the pre-colonial kingdom of the *mwami*, that was highly hierarchically organised and centralised (Mamdani 2002). While the exact nature of the historical relationship between Hutu and Tutsi at the time remains subject to vehement debate amongst historians, a number of issues are established (Lemarchand 1970; Newbury 1989). One is that the Hutu and Tutsi people might have different historical origins, but that they have long shared the same religion, language and territorial space. The differentiation between the groups was mostly socio-economic in nature, distinguishing agriculturalists from pastoralists and allowing for social movement between the two.

It was only during Belgian colonisation after the First World War that these social categories became ethnicised, and that favouring Tutsi in access to employment and education became common practice. This systematic discrimination sowed, or at least nurtured, the seed for the ethnic violence that erupted after independence in 1959 (causing many Tutsi to flee to, amongst others, Uganda), but also in 1962 and 1972 when Rwandan Hutu killed and expelled thousands of Tutsi.

The actual build-up to the genocide took place over a number of years. Even if Rwanda was a success-story in developmental terms, land scarcity had long been a problem and became even more so in the 1990s (Bigagaza et al. 2002). In addition, the plummeting of the worldwide coffee and tea market in this period hit the country hard. The general sense of uncertainty was further heightened by the RPF Tutsi-led invasion from Uganda in October 1990.

The increasingly extremist Hutu government, under internal pressure to carry out the democratisation agreements of the Arusha accords, channelled this general uncertainty into a discourse of exclusion. Via the newspapers and radio stations like Mille Collines Tutsi were presented as *inyenzi*, cockroaches, to be exterminated before they would wipe away the Hutu population. Moderate voices were increasingly silenced, and when the presidential plane crashed on April 6 a long-planned scenario, on the basis of death lists and well-trained militia and involving the majority of the adult population, was carried out (Des Forges 1999; Reyntjens 1995, p. 281).

Later analyses have all pointed at the failure of the international community, both in foretelling the genocide and in stopping it once it unfolded (Barnett 2002; Dallaire 2003; Gourevitch 1999; Power 2003). Uvin (1995, p. 8), in analysing the role of the development community in Rwanda in the 1990s, argued that it "interacted with the processes that underlay the genocide. Aid financed much of the practices of social exclusion, shared many of the humiliating practices, and closed its eyes to the racist currencies in society". Once the genocide started, under the eyes of the world media, the unwillingness of the international community to label it as such and thus to stop it was one of the reasons why the killers could go on for so long, and why the death toll could rise to one tenth of the population (Power 2003).

A final, often-cited partial explanation for the genocide lies in the culture of impunity that had accompanied the cycles of violence since independence. Once the genocide had been stopped by the RPF, which in turn killed tens of thousands of Rwandan Hutu and caused 2 million people to flee, one of the first priorities felt by the new government was that of justice. The international community, which returned to the country en masse after June 1994, enthusiastically supported this ambition through helping to conceptualise, finance and often administer a wide variety of transitional justice mechanisms.

Hence, post-genocide Rwanda came to be characterised by a true proliferation of justice mechanisms, often with very divergent aims and conceptions of the type of justice to be done. Of these mechanisms, the most important are the ICTR, trials in other countries on the basis of universal jurisdiction the national courts, the National Unity and Reconciliation Commission and the neo-traditional local courts, the *gacaca* (Zorbas 2004). All these institutions are characterised by a high degree of foreign involvement, which can be explained in part by the guilty conscience of the international community, and in part by the increased interest in transitional justice in general (Oomen 2005b, p. 887; Sarkin 2001, p. 143).

The ICTR is, of course, most strongly placed in the international sphere, and aims to prosecute persons responsible for committing genocide and for serious violations of humanitarian law in Rwanda in 1994. Another example of primarily retributive justice are the prosecutions of Rwandan nationals in countries like Canada, Switzerland and Belgium under the doctrine of "universal jurisdiction" (Amnesty International 2002). In the same vein Rwanda's domestic courts made retribution in the wake of the genocide into their central objective. Rwanda's Organic Law on Genocide of 1996 established special chambers to try acts of genocide as defined in the Genocide Convention of 1948, those crimes in the Rwandan Code Pénal committed in relation to the genocide, and crimes against humanity. In addition, but with a very different approach to justice in mind, the Rwandan government also installed a National Unity and Reconciliation Commission (NURC) in 1999. While the international community had pressurised for a full-fledged Truth and Reconciliation Commission along the lines of the South African TRC, and the government had toyed with this idea, it ended up with a body with much less far-fetching powers. Finally, there are the *gacaca*, the local courts erected on virtually every one of Rwanda's ten thousand hills, in which community members are supposed to collectively come to terms with the past and try the guilty amongst them. In the following sections we will briefly consider the legitimacy and legitimation of each of these justice institutions.

5 Multi-Layered Justice Mechanisms and Their Legitimacy

Rwanda's manifold justice mechanisms each have their own sources of legitimacy, and strategies of legitimation invoked by the various stakeholders involved. A brief overview of these dimensions and debates in the ICTR, universal jurisdiction procedures, the NURC, national courts and the *gacaca* can not only shed light on people's perceptions of the justice process, and what informs them, but also on the potential of each mechanism to truly contribute to sustainable peace.

Table 2 The ICTR

Dimensions → *Preconditions for legitimacy↓*	*Input*	*Demos*	*Output*
Legitimacy in general: procedures	In line with international human rights and humanitarian law	International community; Rwanda involved in setting up, critical afterwards, will take over after 2008	Slow, bureaucratic, accusation of victor's justice as no RPF crimes have been included
Legitimacy in general: principles	In line with international human rights	International community not democratically elected, "democratic deficit"	Emphasis on retribution, criticised for lack of contribution to reconciliation
Justificatory discourse	Little communication on aims in Rwanda	Rwandan national debate centres on guilt of the international community	Little known on tribunal in Rwanda, limited outreach
Involvement stakeholders	International community, NGOs, Rwandan government	Rwanda antagonistic towards international community, because of its failure to prevent the genocide	Little attention for victims in procedures

5.1 The International Criminal Tribunal for Rwanda

The establishment of the Rwanda tribunal by the Security Council in 1994 was, together with its sister ICTY, a shining example of how Ignatieffs "Age of Implementation" of human rights had finally come about (Table 2). The Tribunal's mandate followed the Genocide Convention of 1948 and the Geneva Conventions of 1949 in including genocide, war crimes and crimes against humanity and its temporal jurisdiction was wide enough to cover both the genocide and the crimes committed by the RPF as it invaded Rwanda from the North (Morris and Scharf 1998; Van den Herik 2005). Procedurally, the emphasis would come to lie on common law, with its more adversarial approach. In terms of stakeholder involvement and communicating its results the tribunal, vested in Tanzania, did not get as much attention as its sister in The Hague, but was still fed and followed by countless NGOs, amongst which organisations like Hirondelle which published good media reports of the proceedings.

This input legitimacy was further heightened by the fact that it was Rwanda itself, at the time a member of the Security Council, that had asked for the Tribunal to be put in place. In spite of this early Rwandan support, however, the *demos* from which the Tribunal derived its legitimacy was strongly that of the international community. Even at the inception, the Rwandan government presented the ICTR as a mechanism by means of which the international community could make up for its historical debt of not having prevented the genocide from taking place, and withdrew its support once prosecutor Del Ponte indicated that she might also issue arrest warrants for members of the RPF government. As of that moment, communication about the ICTR within Rwanda became frosty, with Kigali emphasising mishaps above accomplishments (Reydams 2005, p. 977).

This detachment from the locality can be felt in Rwanda, where 56% of the people interviewed in 2002 claims to be "not well informed" about the Tribunal and where people were generally more negative about the Tribunal than about the national courts and the *gacaca* (Longman et al. 2004, p. 213–215; cf. Uvin and Mironko 2003). It can also be felt in Arusha itself, where the Tribunal is dominated by a polyglot international legal community with a good Italian coffee bar, but surprisingly little Rwandans, both in the staff and in the audience (Cobban 2003; Vokes 2002, p. 1). This, however, might change as the Tribunal moves to Rwanda, to complete its large cases in the *demos* for which it was primarily set up.[5]

While the input legitimacy of the Tribunal was generally laudable, the legitimacy of the demos was problematic, and the real problem that the Tribunal had in establishing legitimacy came with its output. As of May 2008 the Tribunal had only handed out 30 judgment concerning 36 accosed. The Tribunal has been criticised for its bureaucracy and costliness, even though administration became a little more expedient over the years. Whilst the Tribunal managed to set a number of important legal precedents – establishing that rape can constitute the crime of genocide, convicting the former prime minister Kambanda, looking into the role of the media – recent criticism has focused on one glaring omission: the fact that the RPF crimes were not tried, and the possibly political reasons for this. This background caused the Sierra Leone Chief of Prosecutions to argue that "the lack of eagerness on the part of the Prosecutor to initiate investigations about crimes committed by members of the Rwandan Patriotic Front ... challenges the image of independence of the Prosecutor".[6] Here, the accusation of victor's justice lurks close around the corner.

Also, in terms of the output and outcome of the Tribunal, its day-to-day workings have been strongly criticised by victim's organizations, for instance in the adversarial approach in rape testimonies, the disclosure of the identity of certain witnesses, and the fact that perpetrators – in the beginning – would receive HIV/Aids medication whilst their victims would not. The emphasis on retribution is also valued differently: some victims might prefer an even stronger emphasis on retribution, including the death penalty. Academics, on the other hand, have pointed at the failure of the ICTR to make true its ambition of contributing to reconciliation; mostly through its simplistic narrative of the 1994 events (Hurst 2007; Uvin and Mironko 2003).

Universal Jurisdiction Procedures

The Rwandan genocide, perhaps more than any other tragedy in the twentieth century led to a relatively widespread resolve to make true the essence of the 1948 Genocide Convention: that certain crimes are of such gravity that no person or entity that committed them enjoys immunity and their punishment is the responsibility

[5] The first request of transfer of a case to Rwanda took place on the 11th of June 2007, cf. www.ictr.org.

[6] Sierra Leone Chief of Prosecutions Côté, quoted in Reydams (2005).

of the whole international community (cf. Reydams 2003). Following this doctrine of universal jurisdiction, a number of states – including Belgium, Switzerland, Spain, Finland, Canada and the Netherlands – instigated procedures against persons involved in the Rwandan genocide, often after these had applied for asylum in the countries concerned. Belgium, for instance, convicted four Rwandans, amongst whom two Benedictine nuns, to imprisonment for war crimes in the "Butare Four" case.

The main challenge to the legitimacy of these procedures lies in the demos and its perceived interests. The procedures concerned are often followed critically by Rwandan perpetrators, victims and the Diaspora, especially where they concern ex-colonisers or nations with some form of involvement in the 1994 events (Eftekari 2001, p. 1032). The Belgian resolve to try Bernard Ntuyahaga for his suspected role in the killing of ten Belgian paramilitaries on April 7, 1994 is understood, because of the direct interest in the matter. The work of the French anti-terrorism judge Bruguière has, however, met a great deal of Rwandan criticism. In 2006 Bruguière published a research report accusing Rwandan president Kagame of responsibility for the 1994 plane crash, and recommended that Kagame (who enjoys immunity as a head of state) be tried by the ICTR, whilst issuing arrest warrants for nine senior Rwandan officials (Rémy 2004). In response, the authorities in Kigali not only accused France of seeking to destabilise Rwanda, and instigated a civil suit concerning defamation against the French judge, but also stated that "The French are trying to appease their conscience for their role in the genocide and are now trying to find someone else to hold responsible for their acts here".[7]

5.2 The National Unity and Reconciliation Commission

As opposed to these primarily retributive processes in the ICTR and national courts all over the world Rwanda's National Unity and Reconciliation Commission strongly puts the emphasis on reconciliation (NURC 2003). While many donors had initially pushed for a South African-style independent Truth and Reconciliation Commission with the power to establish a historical record and offer amnesties, the government opted for a government body with relatively little powers instead (Vandenginste 1998, p. 30). The NURC was established in 1999, and aims to "serve as a forum for Rwandan people of different categories to exchange on their problems and find solutions in truth, freedom and mutual understanding" (NURC 2002, p. 23), for instance through the organisation of neo-traditional *ingando* seminars and solidarity camps for prisoners about to reintegrate into society.

Thus, even though the NURC is hardly a full-fledged justice institution, it is important to discuss its legitimacy and strategies of legitimation as it plays a central role in rebuilding the Rwandan demos around a particular government-sponsored narrative of history and common identity (Mgbako 2005, p. 201; Mironko 2004,

[7] "Rwanda fury at Kagame trial call" *BBC News* (London, 21 November 2006) <http://news.bbc.co.uk/2/hi/africa/6168280.stm>.

p. 47). In broad lines, this narrative emphasises the common Rwandan past and national identity, and blames the Belgian coloniser in junction with the Hutu extremist government for the events in 1994. It leaves very little room for individual accountability and dangerously charges the whole Hutu ethnic group with responsibility for the genocide, while positing all Tutsi as victims and glossing over the defects of the current government (Penal Reform International 2004a, p. 19; Tiemessen 2004, P. 57). This narrative is backed up by the constitution that prohibits "divisionnisme" and any mention of a Hutu–Tutsi divide. This narrative, which is the way in which the NURC seeks to foster "a spirit of patriotism" amongst Rwandan people is presented at conferences but also at the *ingando*, the neo-traditional solidarity camps that students, politicians, church leaders, prostitutes, ex-soldiers, ex-combatants, genocidaires, *gacaca* judges, and others have to attend. It risks the danger of leaving little room for individual accountability and throwing a blanket of reconciliation over the remaining trauma, anger and feelings of resentment (cf. Pottier et al. 2002).

Donor participation in the NURC is high, as in all Rwanda's justice mechanisms, with a large number of foreign donors financing the proceedings (Oomen 2005b). As such, the main stakeholders here are the government, in conjunction with the international community, which both thus strongly put the emphasis on reconciliation.

5.3 Rwanda's National Courts

Even if the Rwandan national courts have received relatively little attention in the debate over genocide justice in Rwanda, they have played an important role, which has only been strengthened over time (Table 3). Just after the genocide, the Rwandan

Table 3 The national courts

Dimensions → *Preconditions for legitimacy↓*	*Input*	*Demos*	*Output*
Legitimacy in general: procedures	Generally in line with international human rights standards	Started of as highly donor-driven, became more of a Rwandan enterprise over the past decade	Increased strongly, in terms of quality and quantity, over time
Legitimacy in general: principles	Death penalty, not administered after 1998	Judiciary accused of being "Tutsified", not the perception of Rwandans	Emphasis on retribution, criticised for lack of contribution to reconciliation
Justificatory discourse	Little communication		Little communication of results
Involvement stakeholders	International community, NGOs, Rwandan government		

judicial system was completely shattered: only 40 of the eight hundred judges and lawyers practicing in Rwanda were still in the country by July 1994, and the rest had either fled the country or been killed and many courthouses had been destroyed. Rwanda's Organic Law on Genocide of 1996 established special chambers to try acts of genocide as defined in the Genocide Convention of 1948, those crimes in the Rwandan Code Pénal committed in relation to the genocide, and crimes against humanity.[8]

It took a number of years to rebuild the completely destroyed (and previously also relatively weak) Rwandan justice system: the first years after the genocide were characterised by lawyers flown in from abroad explaining the principles of criminal law to judges who more often than not had no primary or secondary education (cf. Reyntjens and Marysse 2002). Over time, however, this changed, and the courts managed to strengthen their output legitimacy by churning out a steady stream of about a thousand genocide cases on a yearly basis. Also, the amount of qualified lawyers and judges had increased dramatically: while it was estimated that only 5% of the Rwandan legal personnel actually had legal training in 1995, this had risen to 95% in 2006.[9]

Generally, Rwanda's national courts have not only been strengthened over the past decade, with new legislation passed, staff trained and courthouses built, but also become more independent over the years. The Rwandan constitution, for instance, holds some safeguards for judicial independence. On the one hand, the independence of the judiciary cannot be separated from the authoritarian climate in post-genocide Rwanda, with, for instance, Supreme Court nominations linked closely to ethnic background (Des Forges and Longman 2004, p. 60; Reyntjens 2004, p. 177, 188). Nevertheless, Longman et al. (2004, p. 215), in conducting research on people's attitudes towards the national courts, not only found that people were generally more positive towards them than towards the ICTR but also that ethnicity did not significantly influence attitudes.

5.4 The Gacaca

What might be the most interesting quest for legitimacy is made in the context of Rwanda's *gacaca*, the neo-traditional courts that are held on each of Rwanda's ten thousand hills (Table 4). In legitimising these institutions, stakeholders refer to traditional authority – in the Weberian sense – as well as to more legal-rational forms of authority. The *gacaca*, which are the courts of first instance in all genocide cases heard in Rwanda had been debated since 1998, and have both a pragmatic and an ideological background. From a practical point of view Rwanda was faced with a backlog of over 120,000 prisoners, living in abject conditions, by 1999, and with the sheer impossibility of trying them within the domestic court system. But there

[8] Loi organique du 30 août 1996 sur l'organisation des poursuites des infractions constitutives du crime de génocide ou de crimes contre l'humanité, commises à partir du 1er octobre 1990, Art. 1.

[9] According to B. Johnston, President of the Rwandan High Court, The Hague, 6 December 2006.

Table 4 The gacaca

Dimensions → *Preconditions for legitimacy↓*	*Input*	*Demos*	*Output*
Legitimacy in general: procedures	Lack of fair trial guarantees, limited mandate Link with traditional procedures	A community-owned or a government (and donor) sponsored project?	High degree of cases heard, concerns about fairness of trials, trying the amount of accused (750,000) problematic
Legitimacy in general: principles	Underlying values combine "traditional" preference for reconciliation with international criminal law		Shifted from retribution to reconciliation over time; mandatory reconciliation could well lead to further polarisation
Justificatory discourse	Good communication strategy before starting	Strongly conceived as community projects and responsibility	Great deal of national and international attention for the *gacaca*
Involvement stakeholders	High	Communities often still highly fragmented	Victims hesitant, perpetrators fear collective incrimination

was also a more ideological reason for opting for the local courts, with the emphasis both on the cultural authenticity and the reconciliatory character of these institutions. After a series of pilots the *gacaca* system finally took off in 2005. Below, we will discuss some of the different dimensions, the justificatory discourse and the involvement of various stakeholders in the *gacaca* (Table 4).

In terms of their input, the *gacaca* have been designed to deal with crimes ranging from genocide to crimes against property.[10] They consist of three levels, the *gacaca* courts of the cell, the *gacaca* courts of the sector and the *gacaca* appeal courts. The local level courts function as courts of first instance, which can classify the crimes committed during the genocide into three categories: the first category comprises masterminding the genocide, rape and killing with exceptional zeal, the second category consists of killing and assault, and the third category covers crimes against property. Whilst the local-level *gacaca* only impose sanctions in the latter category, they make an inventory of all the crimes committed in the community and are responsible for the classification. Community presence has been mandatory as of 2004, and the *gacaca* are presided over by a minimum of nine village judges, the *inyangamugayo* or intègres, who are often illiterate (of Oomen 2006).

In terms of their input legitimacy, the procedural safeguards within the *gacaca* have been criticised from their inception. Organisations like Amnesty International (2002) openly doubted whether the village courts could guarantee basic fair trial standards like an open, independent and competent tribunal, and whether the notion of equality of arms would not be compromised if suspects did not have a right

[10] Organic law No 40/2000 of 26/01/2001 setting up "Gacaca jurisdictions" and organizing prosecutions for offences constituting the crime of genocide or crimes against humanity committed between October 1, 1990 and December 31, 1994.

to defence (Penal Reform International 2003a, b, 2005; Uvin 2003). Also, the fact that confessions can lead to a severely reduced sentence has been criticised. As with the national courts, the fact that the *gacaca* could not try RPF crimes severely comprised their input legitimacy in the eyes of some stakeholders. In terms of procedures the *gacaca* draw loosely on the traditional way of solving disputes "on the lawn", with the community. Also, government discourse emphasised the degree to which reconciliation, as a core value, is in line with African tradition. There are crucial differences, of course, in terms of the subject matter under discussion: genocide instead of land issues and cattle theft (Reyntjens 1990, p. 31).

One of the strongest points in establishing input legitimacy is the involvement of a very high amount of stakeholders in the process. In spite of the human rights concerns, the international community massively supported the process and provides by far the largest part of the funding of the *gacaca* (Oomen 2005a; Uvin 2001). Victims' organisations like Ibuka have also given their hesitant support to the process. In addition, over 200,000 *gacaca* judges were trained and all adult village members are obliged to partake in the process. An extensive communication intervention, drawn up with assistance of John Hopkins University, made that 96% of the Rwandans had heard of the *gacaca* by 2003 (Babalola et al. 2003). The public attitude towards the *gacaca*, as looked into in 2002, was generally positive, with 82% of the people interviewed claiming that they had confidence in the *gacaca* process (Longman et al. 2004; p. 217).

The demos at play here is thus that of the community. While often romanticised, the *gacaca* that have been held since 2005 have also brought some of the tensions that exist at this level to the surface. While participation in the weekly *gacaca* was voluntary in the pilot phase, it was the reticence to participate that caused the government to make it mandatory after 2004 (Penal Reform International 2004a, b). Reasons for this hesitation were both pragmatic and ideological. People often preferred to work on the fields instead of attending the lengthy meetings. But many also feared, and continue to fear, the *gacaca* procedures: the reopening of old wounds, the sense of victor's justice, the accusations of friends and family members (Penal Reform International 2004a, b). Often, the *gacaca* are considered more of a government project than a local initiative, and support for the process could well be linked to support for the national Rwandan demos. The degree to which this wider demos has legitimacy, in the sense of voluntary compliance, is highly debated: while president Kagame received 95% of the votes in the 2003 presidential elections, human rights organisations speak of a "dictatorship under the guise of democracy" (International Crisis Group 2002; cf. Human Rights Watch 2003). The influence of this authoritarian climate on reconciliation could well be tragic: as Tiemessen (2004, p. 58) writes: "the state-imposed approach of command justice has politicised the identity of the participants in Gacaca – perpetrators remain Hutus and victims and survivors remain Tutsis".

If the input legitimacy and the adherence to the demos concerned provide a rather mixed picture that has shifted over time, the same goes for the *gacaca* output. On the one hand, the amount of cases that had been treated by the *gacaca* by 2007 was impressive: nearly 820,000 cases were classified, including that of a Belgian priest and important authorities.[11] At the same time this classification led to the realisation that there are over 750,000 suspects of the *gacaca*, an amount that will take years to try and for which the overloaded Rwandan prisons do not have the space. In addition, NGOs have issued disconcerting reports on intimidation and disappearances of *gacaca* witnesses, and villagers fleeing in order to evade being tried by the *gacaca*.[12] The intended *gacaca* outcome has also undergone a shift, from a pragmatic instrument for the punishment of over a hundred thousand perpetrators to fora in which reconciliation is mandatory, and that might for that reasons not only cause frustration among the victims but also "intensify a retributive sense of justice and a desire for vengeance among the Hutu majority" (Corey and Joireman 2004, p. 73, 74).

6 Conclusions and Recommendations

Legitimacy is the core feature linking transitional justice institutions to sustainable peace. This study has pointed at the importance of an empirical assessment of legitimacy, most particularly in the current constellations of global governance that characterise many transitional justice settings. While studies into people's perceptions, as opposed to normative assumptions, on the legitimacy of truth commissions, international(ised) tribunals, trials and other justice mechanisms are important, they should merely function as a baseline. Legitimacy, as legal sociologists teach us, is a dynamic quality, and people's perceptions of transitional justice institutions fluctuate depending on their knowledge of them, and their availability. In the absence of a credible national procedure, for instance, people might prefer an international tribunal. Or adversely, people might express support for traditional justice institutions if they feel that this is the only option to have some form of justice done. This, then, says less about legal culture than about the range of available options. A first, more general, recommendation to come out of this research is then somewhat paradoxical: it is important to conduct empirical research on what justice mechanisms people deem desirable, proper and appropriate, but to simultaneously realise that such preference can alter strongly over time.

A first dimension of legitimacy to look into is the input. Input legitimacy concerns the degree to which people adhere to the procedures by which transitional justice mechanisms were set up and the principles on which they are based. It is especially at the international level that input legitimacy runs the risk of becoming conflated with legality: as long as the establishment of, for instance, international(ised) tribunals has followed the right rules, and is based on international human rights law, these are deemed to be legitimate.

---

[11] Rwanda National Service of Gacaca Jurisdictions (2006) The achievement in gacaca courts. http://www.inkiko-gacaca.gov.rw/pdf/Achivements%20in%20Gacaca%20Courts.pdf. Accessed 1 October 2007

[12] Cf. Human Rights Watch reports on Rwanda, <http://hrw.org/doc/?t = africa_pub&c = rwanda>, accessed 1 October 2007.

True input legitimacy goes further. Procedurally, for one, transitional justice institutions have to be set up in procedures involving all stakeholders, not merely the majority. At the international level, it is crucial to have the initial support of the country concerned, as was the case in setting up the Rwanda tribunal but also in the state referrals to the ICC by Uganda and the Democratic Republic of Congo. The way in which the situation in Darfur was brought to the attention of the ICC, via the Security Council, risks a lack of local legitimacy through its non-involvement of key Sudanese actors.

The same need for the involvement of all stakeholders, and consensual as opposed to majoritarian decision-making is at play at the national level. Procedures which exclude major stakeholders, whether they are perpetrators, victims or the international community, risk being considered illegitimate by these stakeholders from the beginning. This is why the process of designing transitional justice institutions has to be as open as possible, and to truly incorporate the suggestions offered from all different sides.

In addition, procedurally, the mandate of the institution concerned is of key importance: the role of all actors, including that of the international community, in the conflict has to fall under the jurisdiction of, for instance, the court concerned. East Timor is a case in point, where the fact that the Special Court could not look into Indonesia's central role in the atrocities delegitimised the tribunal in the eyes of many Timorese right from the start.

Concerning the principles on which transitional justice mechanisms are based, examples like Rwanda's gacaca teach us that it is important to not only found institutions on universal human rights, but to also build on, for instance, religious and traditional values where possible. These two sources do not have to be mutually exclusive, and relying on both can substantially strengthen the input legitimacy of a tribunal or truth commission, giving it the quality of "our institution". The fact that South Africa's Truth Commission also departed from the African notion of ubuntu – "people are people through other people", and the reliance on *nahe biti* – a traditional dispute resolution mechanism – in East Timor all served to enhance the legitimacy of these institutions in the eyes of key stakeholders, without substantially derogating human rights guarantees. Meanwhile, such institutions should not lead towards forced reconciliation or lack of redress; as Allen (2005, p. 5) wrote "there is no reason to believe that Africans are more inclined towards reconciliation than other people". In addition, it is important to explicitly communicate and justify the principles and procedures on which the mechanisms are based from the very beginning.

Classically, theorists of legitimacy often stopped at the input dimension. The recent rise of global governance and the resulting fragmentation of politics also call for an explicit focus on the legitimacy of the demos setting up the transitional justice mechanisms and the degree to which this is a mythical community of belonging.

This challenge is most poignant at the international level. The failure of the international community to intervene in the Rwandan genocide, for instance, has led to a severe lack of legitimacy within Rwanda that influences people's perceptions of the ICTR and donor support to other institutions alike. At a more general level, the international community is, these days, only a community of belonging to a particular group of people and – at worst – labelled as pro-Western and imperialist. At the international level, then, justificatory strategies and the involvement of all stakeholders in processes of decision-making becomes more important than ever, as does a principled commitment to socio-economic justice in, for instance, the field of development cooperation.

The most important Rwandan lessons concerning the role of the legitimacy of the demos in determining the legitimacy of transitional justice mechanisms might well lie at the level of the nation-state. The first is how the nation-state is still the most logical community of belonging, and the priority in setting up transitional justice mechanisms should lie at this level, hooking on to processes of nation-building and narratives of belonging and strengthening them. This is important to note at a time in which a great deal of donor attention and resources goes to international institutions, which have budgets that greatly exceed those of the national court systems. An empirical perspective of legitimacy adds extra weight to the doctrine of complementarity and makes a case for putting more resources into strengthening the domestic court systems than it is currently the case. In Rwanda, for instance, the completely ruined national judicial system was rebuilt to a generally acceptable level within a decade.

Of course, this national demos then has to be legitimate in the eyes of all its citizens. This is where the core problem in Rwanda lies. The most crucial flaw in each of Rwanda's justice mechanisms – the NURC, the domestic courts, the gacaca – is that the compliance with state rules is hardly voluntary, the key feature of legitimacy. Even if Rwanda has had multiparty elections in which president Kagame won 95% of the votes, this is read by most analysts as an indication of the fear that rules the country rather than an adherence to government principles. Majoritarian decision-making, as established by theorists, is not enough to establish legitimacy: there needs to be consensus on the shared nature of the national dream.

This also translates into justice mechanisms, where the quality of voluntary compliance is as important as ever. Forced reconciliation, as it takes place in Rwanda, with little or no space for alternative narratives, individual accountability and feelings of anger and grievance can help perpetuate the very narratives that played such a large role in the genocide. True truth-telling requires openness on the whole messy political reality of the past, and holding all those responsible accountable, whether they are members of the government or of the international community. Thus, the hearing of a Belgian priest played an important role in legitimising the *gacaca* in the eyes of some local actors, while the impossibility of looking into RPF-crimes remains a crucial flaw.

The legitimacy of the demos, furthermore, is not only related to the consensual character of decision-making, but lies also in its capacity to achieve socio-economic justice. People interviewed on their preferences, whether in Uganda, Rwanda or East Timor, often list security and access to food, housing and education above justice. Even if the input and output of justice mechanisms are perceived as fair, they will still lack legitimacy if they operate within a context of ongoing discrimination and deprivation.

Finally, and as important as the input, is the output of all transitional justice mechanisms involved. The conceptual model makes a distinction between output and outcome, and argues that both are equally important. Important elements in the output of transitional justice procedures include accessibility in terms of distance and language, the pace of the procedures and their cost-effectiveness. The costliness of the ICTR, for instance, in combination with its slow pace, dampened enthusiasm for the Tribunal amongst internal and external actors alike. The Rwandan domestic courts, on the other hand, made up for their serious initial flaws by a reasonable output.

One of the main concerns and strongest grounds for delegitimisation in terms of output is a perceived bias in prosecutorial policies. The fact that the ICTR has, to date, failed to incriminate members of the RPF, in spite of overwhelming evidence of grave human rights abuses on its side, severely delegitimised the Tribunal in the eyes of the perpetrators but also, for instance, members of the international human rights community. A very pragmatic recommendation here would be to truly put the interests and expectations of the population concerned, in all its diversity, first in drawing up prosecutorial policies.

Looking at output legitimacy through the eyes of those most concerned also shows once again that retribution and reconciliation are not mutually exclusive concerns but should function – in the words of a Timorese activist – "as the two wings of an aeroplane". An exclusive focus on reconciliation is as destructive as the purely retributive approaches of the Nuremberg paradigm. Here, cooperation between institutions geared primarily towards retribution, and others focused on reconciliation becomes very important.

Finally, looking at the case of Rwanda has shown how legitimacy is not a given, but a quality that has to be gained, and explained, on a case by case basis, while physically rebuilding the country and reweaving common narratives of belonging. Nowhere is this more difficult than in those societies that have been torn apart in countless cruelties over, at times, decades. But then again, nowhere is working on the "generalised perception or assumption that the actions of an entity are desirable, proper, or appropriate within some socially constructed system of norms, values, beliefs, and definitions" more important.

References

African Rights (1994) Rwanda: death, despair, defiance. African Rights, London

Allen T (2005) War and justice in northern Uganda: an assessment of the international criminal court's intervention. Crisis States Research Centre. www.crisisstates.com/download/others/AllenICCReport.pdf. Accessed 1 October 2007

Amnesty International (2002) Gacaca: a question of justice. Amnesty International, London

Babalola S, Karambizi J, Sow B, Ruzibuka JB (2003) Evaluation of the gacaca promotional campaign in Rwanda: summary of main findings. ONAPO, Ministry of Justice and JHU/PCS, Kigali

Barnett M (2002) Eyewitness to a genocide: the United Nations and Rwanda. Cornell University Press, Ithaca

Baxter V (2002) Empirical research methodologies of transitional justice mechanism. Stellenbosch, South Africa, 18–20 November 2002. http://shr.aaas.org/transitionaljustice/mtjm/. Accessed 1 October 2007
Bell C, Campbell C, Ni Aolain F (2004) Justice discourses in transition. Social Legal Studies 13:(3):305–328
Berkeley B (2001) The graves are not yet full; race, tribe and power in the heart of Africa. Basic Books, New York
Bigagaza J, Abong C, Mukarubuga C (2002) Land scarcity, distribution and conflict in Rwanda. In Lind J, Sturman K (eds) Scarcity and surfeit. Institute for Security Studies, Pretoria
Bloomfield D, Barnes T, Huyse L (eds) (2003) Reconciliation after violent conflict: a handbook. International Institute for Democracy and Electoral Assistance, Stockholm, 179 pp
Carothers T (2003) Promoting the rule of law abroad: the problem of knowledge, Carnegie Paper No. 34. Carnegie Endowment for International Peace, Washington
Clark I (2005) Legitimacy in international society. Oxford University Press, Oxford
Cobban H (2003) Healing Rwanda. Can international court deliver justice? In: The Boston Review. Boston. http://bostonreview.net/BR28.6/cobban.html. Accessed 1 October 2007
Corey A, Joireman SF (2004) Retributive justice: The gacaca courts in Rwanda. Afr Aff 103: 73–89
Corkalo D et al. (2004) Neighbors again? Intercommunity relations after ethnic cleansing. In: Stover E, Weinstein HM (eds) My neighbor, my enemy: justice and community in the aftermath of mass atrocity. CUP, Cambridge
Dallaire R (2003) Shake hands with the devil. Random House, Toronto
De Wijn M (2005) Global justice and legitimacy in Cambodia: the Khmer Rouge Trials and local concepts of justice. MA Thesis, University of Amsterdam
Des Forges A (1999) Leave none to tell the story: genocide in Rwanda.. Human Rights Watch, New York, 807 pp
Des Forges A, Longman T (2004) Legal responses to genocide in Rwanda. In: Stover E, Weinstein HM (eds) My neighbor, my enemy: justice and community in the aftermath of mass atrocity. CUP, Cambridge
Eftekari S (2001) International criminal justice: Rwanda and French human rights activism. Hum Rights Q 23: 1032–1061
Englebert P (2000) State legitimacy and development in Africa. Lynne Rienner, Boulder
Englebert P (2003) Back to the future? Resurgent indigenous structures and the reconfiguration of power in Africa. In: Vaughan O (ed) Indigenous structures and governance in Africa. Sefer, Ibadan
Gibson JL, Caldeira GA (1995) The legitimacy of transnational legal institutions: compliance, support and the European Court of Justice. Am J Polit Sci 39:459, 460
Gibson JL, Gouws A (1997) Support for the rule of law in the emerging South African democracy. Int Social Sci J 152:173–191
Gibson JL, Caldeira GA, Baird VA (1998) On the legitimacy of national high courts. Am Polit Sci Rev 92:343
Gibson JL, Caldeira GA, Spence LK (2003) Measuring attitudes toward the United States Supreme Court. Am J Polit Sci 47:354
Gourevitch P (1999) We wish to inform you that tomorrow we will be killed with our families: Stories from Rwanda. Picador, New York
Falk R (2004) Legality to legitimacy: the revival of the just war framework. Harvard Int Law Rev 26:40–44
Fletcher L, Weinstein HM (2000) Justice, accountability and social reconstruction: an interview study of Bosnian judges and prosecutors. Berkeley J Int Law 18:102. Human Rights Centre; International Human Rights Law Clinic, Berkeley
Follesdal A (2004) Legitimacy theories of the European Union. In: ARENA Working Papers No. 15/2004. Centre for European Studies, University of Oslo. http://www.arena.uio.no/publications/working-papers2004/papers/04_15.xml. Accessed 1 October 2007
Friedman LM (1969) Legal culture and social development. Law Soc Rev 4:29–44

Friedman LM, Rogelio Perez-Perdomo (eds) (2003) Legal culture in the age of globalization: Latin America and Latin Europe. Stanford University Press, Stanford

Fukuyama F (2004) State-building: governance and world order in the twenty-first century. Cornell University Press, Ithaca

Habermas J (1984) What does a legitimation crisis mean today? Legitimation problems in late capitalism. In: Connolly W (ed) Legitimacy and the state. Basil Blackwell, Oxford, pp 134–155

Habermas J (1998) Between facts and norms: contributions to a discourse theory of law and democracy. MIT, Cambridge

Hayner P (2002) Unspeakable truths: facing the challenge of truth commissions. Routledge, London

Hovil L, Lomo Z (2005) Whose justice? Perceptions of Uganda's Amnesty Act 2000: The potential for conflict resolution and long-term reconciliation. In: Refugee Law Project Working Papers, 32. RLP, Kampala

Human Rights Watch (2003) Preparing for elections: tightening control in the name of unity. Human Rights Watch. http://hrw.org/backgrounder/africa/rwanda0503bck.htm. Accessed 1 October 2007

Humphrey M (2002) The politics of atrocity and reconciliation: from terror to trauma. Routledge, London

Hurst A (2007) Reconciling Rwanda? PhD thesis, Newcastle University

Ignatieff M (2003) Human rights as politics and idolatry. Princeton University Press, Princeton, 216 pp

International Center for Transitional Justice (2004) Iraqi voices: attitudes towards transitional justice and social reconstruction. University of California, Berkeley. http://www.ictj.org/downloads/IraqDesigned.pdf. Accessed 1 October 2007

International Crisis Group (2002) Rwanda at the end of the transition: a necessary political liberalisation.. International Crisis Group, Nairobi/Brussels. Africa Report No. 53. http://www.crisisgroup.org/home/index.cfm?l= 1&id= 1555. Accessed 1 October 2007

Kelsall T, Sawyer E (2007) Truth vs justice. Popular opinions on the truth and reconciliation commission and special court for Sierra Leone. Online J Peace Conflict Resol 7(1)

LeMarchand R (1970) Rwanda and Burundi. Praeger, New York

Longman T et al (2004) Connecting justice to human experience: attitudes towards accountability and reconciliation in Rwanda. In: Stover E, Weinstein HM (eds) My neighbor, my enemy: justice and community in the aftermath of mass atrocity. CUP, Cambridge, pp 213–215

Mamdani M (2002) When victims become killers: colonialism, nativism and the genocide in Rwanda. Princeton University Press, Princeton

Mgbako C (2005) Ingando solidarity camps: reconciliation and political indoctrination in post-genocide Rwanda. Harvard Hum Rights J 18(Spring): 201–220

Mironko C (2004) Igitero: means and motive in the Rwandan genocide. J Genocide Res 6(1):47–60

Mokhiber C (2000) Local perspectives: foreign aid to the justice sector. International Council on Human Rights Policy, Geneva. http://www.ichrp.org/paper_files/104_p_01.pdf

Morris V, Scharf MP (1998) The International Criminal Tribunal for Rwanda. Transnational, Irvington

Newbury C (1989) The cohesion of oppression: clientship and ethnicity in Rwanda, 1860–1960. Columbia University Press, New York

NURC (2002) Report on the evaluation of national unity and reconciliation. National Unity and Reconciliation Commission, Kigali. www.grandslacs.net/doc/2805.pdf. Accessed 1 October 2007

NURC (2003) Opinion survey on participation in gacaca and national reconciliation. National Unity and Reconciliation Commission, Kigali

Oomen B (2005a) Chiefs in South Africa: law, power and culture in the post-apartheid era. James Currey, Oxford. University of KwaZulu-Natal, Pietermaritzburg. Palgrave, New York

Oomen B (2005b) Donor-driven justice and its discontents: the case of Rwanda. Develop Change 36:887–910

Oomen B (2006) Rwanda's gacaca: objectives, merits and their relation to supranational criminal law. In: Haveman R, Olusanya O (eds) Sentencing and sanctioning in supranational criminal law. Intersentia, Oxford, pp 161–184

Penal Reform International (2003a) PRI research report on the gacaca: The guilty plea procedure, cornerstone of the Rwandan justice system. Rep. IV. Penal Reform International, Kigali

Penal Reform International (2003b) Research on the Gacaca. Rep. V. Penal Reform International, Kigali

Penal Reform International (2004a) Research report on gacaca courts: gacaca and reconciliation – Kibuye case study. Penal Reform International, Kigali 19

Penal Reform International (2004b) From camp to hill: the reintegration of released prisioners. In: Research reports on the Gacaca, 110. Penal Reform International, Kigali

Penal Reform International (2005) Gacaca courts and community service. Penal Reform International, Kigali

Penal Reform International (2006) Information-gathering during the national phase. Gacaca Research Report No. 8. Penal Reform International, Kigali. http://www.penalreform.org/monitoring-and-research-report-on-gacaca-information-gathering-during-the-national.html. Accessed 1 October 2007

Pham PJ (2005) Legitimacy, justice and the future of Africa. Hum Rights Hum Welfare 5:31

Pottier J, Lonsdale JL, Peel JDY, Sender J (2002) Re-imagining Rwanda: conflict, survival and disinformation in the late twentieth century. Cambridge University Press, Cambridge, 272 pp

Pouligny B (2005) The forgotten dimensions of 'transitional justice' mechanisms: cultural meanings and imperatives for survivors of violent conflicts. In: Pouligny B (ed) Re-imagining peace. CERI, Calgary. http://www.ceri-sciencespo.com/themes/re-imaginingpeace/va/resources/forgotten_dimensions_pouligny.pdf. Accessed 19 September 2006

Power S (2003) "A problem from Hell": America and the age of genocide. Perennial, New York, 656 pp

Prunier G (1995) The Rwanda Crisis: History of a Genocide. Hurst, London

Rémy J-P (2004) Le président rwandais Paul Kagamé récuse avec virulence l'enquête. Bruguière, Le Monde, Paris

Reydams L (2003) Universal jurisdiction: international and municipal legal perspectives. Oxford University Press, Oxford

Reydams L (2005) The ICTR ten years on: back to the Nuremberg paradigm? J Int Criminal Justice 3: 977–988

Reyntjens F (1990) Le gacaca ou la justice du gazon au Rwanda. Politique Africaine 40:31–41

Reyntjens F (1995) Rwanda. Background to a genocide. Bulletin des Seances Academie Royale des Sciences d'Outre Mer 41(3):281–293

Reyntjens F (2004) Rwanda, ten years on: from genocide to dictatorship. Afr Aff 103:177–210

Reyntjens F, Marysse S (2002) L'afrique Des Grands Lacs, Annuaires 1996–2004. Harmattan, Paris

Risse T (2004) Transnational governance and legitimacy. In: Paper presented at the ECPR, Standing Group on International Relations, The Hague, September 9–12 2004. www.fu-berlin.de/atasp/texte/tn_governance_benz.pdf. Accessed 1 October 2007

Roht-Arriaza N, Mariezcurrena J (2006) Transitional Justice in the twenty-first century. Cambridge University Press, Cambridge

Rosenau JN (2002) Governance in a new global order. In: Held D, McGrew A (eds) Governing globalization: power, authority and global governance. Polity, Cambridge

Sarkin J (2001) The tension between justice and reconciliation in Rwanda: politics, human rights, due process and the role of the gacaca courts in dealing with the genocide. J Afr Law 45:143

Schabert T (1986) Power, legitimacy and truth: reflections on the impossibility to legitimise legitimations of political order. In: Athanasios Moulakis (ed) Legitimacy/Légitimité. Proceedings of the Conference held in Florence, June 3 and 4, 1982. De Gruyter, Berlin

Scharpf FW (1998) Interdependence and democratic legitimation. In: MPIFG Working Papers 98/2. Max Planck Institute for the Study of Societies, Cologne

Scheeringa S (2005) Transitional justice: the local legitimacy of the commission for truth, reception and reconciliation in East Timor. MA Thesis, University of Amsterdam
Steffek J (2003) The legitimation of international governance: a discourse approach. Eur J Int Relat 9(2):249–275
Stover E, Weinstein HM (eds) (2004) My neighbor, my enemy: justice and community in the aftermath of mass atrocity. CUP, Cambridge
Suchman MC (1995) Managing legitimacy: strategic and institutional approaches. Acad Manage Rev 20(3):571–610
Teitel RG (2000) Transitional justice. Oxford University Press, Oxford
Tiemessen AE (2004) After Arusha: gacaca justice in post-genocide Rwanda. Afr Stud Q 8(1):57
Uvin P (1995) Aiding violence: the development enterprise in Rwanda. Kumarian, West Hartford
Uvin P (2001) Difficult choices in the new post-conflict agenda: the international community in Rwanda after the genocide. Third World Q 22(2):177–189
Uvin P (2003) The Gacaca tribunals in Rwanda. In: Bloomfield D, Barnes T, Huyse L (eds) Reconciliation after violent conflict: a handbook. International Institute for Democracy and Electoral Assistance, Stockholm
Uvin P, Mironko C (2003) Western and local approaches to justice in Rwanda. Global Governance 9:219–231
Vandenginste S (1998) A truth and reconciliation approach to the genocide and crimes against humanity in Rwanda. University of Antwerp Institute of Development Policy and Management Working Paper, 30
Van den Herik L (2005) The contribution of the Rwanda tribunal to the development of international criminal law. PhD thesis, Free University, Amsterdam. 337 pp; In: Developments in International Law, vol 53. Brill Academic, Leiden
Vokes R (2002) The Arusha tribunal: whose justice? Anthropol Today 18(5):1–2
Weber M (1978) Economy and society. In: Roth G, Wittich C (eds) Economy and Society. University of California Press, Berkeley
Weber M (1993) What is politics? In: Lemert C (eds) Social theory: the multicultural and classic readings, 672. Westview, Boulder
Wilson R (2000) Reconciliation and revenge in post-apartheid South Africa. Curr Anthropol 41(1):75–98
Zorbas E (2004) Towards justice and reconciliation in Rwanda: taking stock. In: Pambazuka News

Reconciliation and Development

Karen Brounéus

Abstract Reconciliation has become an important part of postconflict peacebuilding rhetoric and practice in recent years. As nearly all conflicts today are intrastate, former enemies, perpetrators and victims, must continue living side by side after the war. Yet, attitudes and behaviors do not change at the moment of a declaration of peace. Since coexistence is necessary, the need for reconciliation is profound.

The aim of this chapter is to give a shared point of departure for discussion on the critical issues of reconciliation and development after war. Reconciliation is defined and seen from a pragmatic and societal perspective. Reconciliation involves finding a way to balance issues such as truth and justice so that the slow changing of behaviors, attitudes and emotions between former enemies can take place. It is the pragmatic work of building relationships and confidence that will hold for the pressures on peace.

In order to structure the analysis, reconciliation is suggested to be examined from three societal levels: top-level, middle-range, and grassroots. An overview is provided of some key concerns regarding reconciliation in relation to justice, security, and politics respectively, and their respective policy implications discussed. Security risks have not previously been included in the theoretical literature on truth telling and reconciliation. However, recent research indicates that if security is not provided, the process of reconciliation may risk to backlash in increased violence or in suppression of truth. Political initiatives for reconciliation through for example legislation are crucial. However, the post-conflict state is often quite weak thus tensions may easily arise between reconciliation needs, development ambitions, and politics. Finally, truth telling being one of the major components in reconciliation processes around the world today, the concerns of truth telling with regard to trauma, reparation, and culture are briefly highlighted.

K. Brounéus
Department of Peace and Conflict Research, Uppsala University, P.O. Box 514, 75120 Uppsala, Sweden
e-mail: Karen.brouneus@pcr.uu.se

K. Ambos et al. (eds.), *Building a Future on Peace and Justice: Studies on Transitional Justice, Peace and Development.*

The chapter concludes that there is no magic formula for reconciliation; each reconciliation process needs to be designed according to the specific context. However, we urgently need empirical research to learn of general trends regarding the promises and pitfalls for processes of reconciliation.

1 Reconciliation and Development in Postconflict Peacebuilding

In recent years there has been increasing discourse concerning reconciliation as a postconflict measure for the prevention of further conflict. After the groundbreaking work of the Truth and Reconciliation Commission in South Africa, reconciliation – through truth commissions, official apologies, memorials, etc. – has become an almost routine element of post-conflict peacebuilding rhetoric and practice. Peru, Sierra Leone, Ghana, Timor Leste, Liberia and Rwanda, to name but a few, have embarked upon processes of reconciliation in the new millennium. Reconciliation has become a high-level concern for national development initiatives as well as for international development assistance in postconflict societies.

One reason for the increased focus on reconciliation may be that nearly all conflicts today are intrastate.[1] After peace settlements, former enemies, perpetrators and victims, must continue living side by side just as before the atrocities were committed. However, attitudes and behaviors do not change from genocidal to collegial at the moment of a declaration of peace. Since coexistence is necessary, the need for reconciliation is profound. How to design and support reconciliation processes is a crucial question for national and international postconflict development initiatives.

Seen from an academic point of view, reconciliation is anything but a conceptualized tool for peacebuilding, or an operationalized term for postconflict analysis. Few empirical studies have been conducted in the field of reconciliation. The gap between theory and practice is vast. Claims made of the relationship between for example truth, justice, peace, and reconciliation are in need of empirical backing (Weinstein and Stover 2004; Mendeloff 2004). Research is needed to define the advantages, risks and obstacles connected with reconciliation efforts in societies emerging from conflict. In order to promote development and "do no harm" (Anderson 1999), we need informed decision-making that can strengthen reconciliation and avoid undermining fragile relations.

This chapter focuses on reconciliation and development after internal conflict and provides an overview of some key concerns in the field and their policy implications. Reconciliation is seen from a pragmatic and societal perspective. The aim is to give a shared point of departure for discussion on the critical issues of reconciliation and development after war.

[1] In 2006, 32 intrastate conflicts were recorded in the Uppsala Conflict Data Program while no interstate conflicts were active (Harbom 2007). During the years 1989–2006, the number of annual intrastate conflicts ranged from 25 to 50 per year, whereas interstate conflicts varied only from zero to two. The Uppsala Conflict Data Program continually and systematically collects worldwide data on armed conflict. Coding rules and definitions can be found at www.ucdp.uu.se.

2 Defining Reconciliation

There are many different views of the meaning of reconciliation. Some definitions hold religious connotations, some are more political, some psychological. In a previous overview of the field (Brounéus 2003), the following definition of reconciliation was proposed which will also be used in this chapter: "Reconciliation is a societal process that involves mutual acknowledgment of past suffering and the changing of destructive attitudes and behavior into constructive relationships toward sustainable peace".

Apart from distilling many definitions into one, the strength of this definition lies in its clear specification of the central components involved in reconciliation: changes in emotion (mutual acknowledgment of suffering), attitude, and behavior.[2] It emphasizes that reconciliation is a *societal* process after armed conflict, that is, reconciliation involves changes within and between former enemy groups regarding themselves and the other. Finally, it is a *process*, not a remote goal to be achieved when war has ended. This definition lies in line with others who see reconciliation as a pragmatic process in which relations are rebuilt to enable coexistence and sustainable peace (Bloomfield 2006; Staub 2006; van der Merwe 1999).

3 On Forgiveness, Accountability and Amnesia

Forgiveness is often spoken of as a condition for reconciliation. However, it might be wise to regard forgiveness and reconciliation as two separate processes; forgiveness being a one-way process, while reconciliation emphasizes mutuality, involving both perpetrator and victim. Our definition of reconciliation does not rule out the possibility of forgiveness; it may occur in a long-term process, but forgiveness is not considered necessary for reconciliation. Moreover, "[f]orgiveness is not... a political task of the state. Forgiveness demands more than statecraft can deliver", as Villa-Vicencio (2006) observes.

Reconciliation is part of the growing literature on transitional justice where the balance between retributive justice and restorative justice for postconflict societies is discussed (more below). Reconciliation does not mean avoiding accountability for the sake of truth, neither does it entail collective amnesia to avoid the risks of truth telling. It means finding a way to balance issues such as truth and justice so that the slow changing of behaviors, attitudes and emotions between former enemies can take place. It is the pragmatic work of building relationships and confidence that will hold for the pressures on peace.

---

[2] The report was commissioned by the Swedish International Development Cooperation Agency (Sida) and can be downloaded at: http://www.pcr.uu.se/publications/other_pub/SIDA2982en_ReconWEB_brouneus.pdf.

4 Top-Down, Middle-Out, Bottom-Up

In order to structure the analysis of reconciliation, it can be examined from three societal levels: top-level, middle-range and grassroots – each with its own actors and methods.[3]

International and national criminal tribunals, important *top-level* methods for reconciliation, play a central role in the reconciliation process for two reasons. First, accountability and punishment of certain crimes are considered in both theory and practice to be important for reconciliation; there is a legal and moral perception that the most severe crimes, such as instigating genocide, must be punished. Second, a functioning legal system is vital for reinstating a sense of order and safety after violence. The importance of training leaders should also be mentioned as they are top-level actors with the potential to promote reconciliation. Their attitudes and behavior concerning issues such as suffering, coexistence and the past will be reflected in the national work for peace and thus have a "top-down" effect on the population's rehabilitation and reconciliation.

Middle-range initiatives for reconciliation are projects that influence emotions, attitudes, and behavior in both top-level decision makers and the grassroots community. They are close to both constituencies, reaching both "middle-up" and "middle-down". Middle-range actors are, for example non-governmental organizations, civil society groups, religious groups, medical and psychosocial staff, and the media. The media has an exceptional role in influencing attitudes and behavior. This has been used to provoke hatred – but increasingly also to promote peace.[4] Another significant middle-range method for reconciliation is the truth commission, which has become a central part of development practice for peacebuilding in the past decades (Hayner 2001). In the best of cases, truth commissions affect top-level politics and engage the population, hopefully promoting reconciliation on both levels. However, risks for retraumatization and security threats as a result of truth telling have been demonstrated in recent empirical research (Brounéus 2008d; Byrne 2004). Identifying the strengths and risks with truth commissions is an area in crucial need of research (Barsalou 2007; Mendeloff 2004).

In all societies there are methods for handling conflict without violence; people who are turned to when there are disagreements to be sorted out or cleansing rituals for healing. Experiencing constructive relationships with former enemies – with the sufferings of the past in mind – the peace of the present might be too precious to waste on further war. By strengthening and empowering local actors for peace, the foundations are laid for national reconciliation. This is the "bottom-up" approach

---

[3] These categories build on John Paul Lederach's classification of approaches to peacebuilding (Lederach 1997).

[4] For example, *Search for Common Ground's* children's television programmes with the aim to reduce negative stereotypes and increase respect in for example Macedonia, for more information see www.sfcg.org; Radio drama programmes on trauma, healing and reconciliation in Rwanda, Burundi and the DRC by Professor Ervin Staub, Dr Laurie Pearlman and the organisation *La Benevolencija*, see www.heal-reconcile-rwanda.org.

to reconciliation and includes meetings between grassroots leaders and their communities with the aim to build collaboration and eventually understanding between former enemy groups.

5 Reconciliation and Justice

The question of how to deal with the atrocities of the past in a country emerging from internal conflict is critical and enormously complex. Should there be tribunals to punish perpetrators? Should amnesty be granted in order to avoid disturbing a fragile peace? Or should a truth commission be established to ensure that the past will be acknowledged and not repeated, and dignity restored in victims and survivors? What does the justice versus stability equation look like and what is best for the process of reconciliation? There is strong consensus that, as Bar-Tal puts it, "justice is indispensable for reconciliation".[5]

Within the literature on reconciliation, there has been much discourse in recent years concerning retributive versus restorative justice. *Retributive justice*, also called criminal, procedural, or legalistic justice, focuses on crime as the violation of law. Crime is a matter between the perpetrator and the state. Punishment is decided upon by the criminal justice system, transferring "the individuals' desire for revenge to the state or official body" (Minow 1998). *Restorative* or *reparative justice*, on the other hand, focuses on crime as a conflict between individuals as well as on the injuries crime inflicts on all parties: the victim, the perpetrator and the society (Zehr 2001). The interest of the justice system is here to reconcile and heal conflictive relationships in order to end the vicious circle of crime, revenge, and recurring crime. This is done for example by official acknowledgment of the past, formalized apologies, and reparations to victims.

Truth commissions are hoped to provide a judicial balance for postconflict societies. However, in one of the most cogent critiques of the field, Mendeloff (2004) argues that the beneficial claims made in the literature of truth-telling and truth-seeking mechanisms on reconciliation and peace have been based on flawed assumptions and on faith rather than on empirical evidence. He argues that there is a necessity to restrain the enthusiasm for these mechanisms in the absence of empirical knowledge and stresses the urgent need of systematic research in the area.

One of the few empirical studies that has tested the link between truth and reconciliation is Gibson's South Africa survey from 2004 (Gibson 2004). The results of the survey showed that among white South Africans, accepting the truth contributed to reconciliation. The same seemed to be true among Asian and Colored South Africans. However, among black South Africans, truth did not lead to reconciliation. Gibson points out that even though this may be a "disappointing finding…truth does not contribute to irreconciliation either" – a fear many had when gruesome testimonies were made (Gibson 2004, p. 215).

[5] Speech held at the "Stockholm International Forum: Truth, Justice, and Reconciliation", April 23–24, 2002. For more on the issue of amnesty, please see Louise Mallinder of this volume.

On the other hand, Meernik (2005) recently tested the impact of the International Criminal Tribunal for the Former Yugoslavia (ICTY) on societal peace in Bosnia. Meernik calls into question the effects of justice when decided and initiated by the international community (as in the case of the ICTY). Contrary to the common assumptions regarding truth-telling, peace, and reconciliation, Meernik finds that arrests or judgments of war criminals in the ICTY were more often than not correlated with increased hostility between ethnic groups. His conclusion is that the ICTY does not have a meaningful effect on societal peace in Bosnia.

These initial empirical results lead to the notion that we must include a risk calculation when discussing the balance of truth, justice and reconciliation. For a process of reconciliation after conflict, one must take into consideration the society's ability to sustain the pressure and tension of exposing difficult truths without collapsing into renewed violence (Nordquist 2002). Finding the balance between truth and justice is not an undemanding venture.

Transforming judicial institutions in order to build a sustainable capacity for handling justice and accountability in the postconflict society itself is crucial. In most cases, the infrastructure has been destroyed and the staff, including the academic elite, is decimated. Rebuilding the infrastructure and supporting education for capacity building is an important area for development with direct links to reconciliation; if the administration of justice is just, a large step toward reconciliation has been taken. Preparing a country to legally engage with war crimes, or to take over cases from an international tribunal as is currently being discussed with regard to the ICTR and Rwanda's national judicial capacity, is an area where development assistance can have a significant impact. By asserting the importance of considering for example ethnic dimensions and the role of a just peace for all, institutions which previously have been associated with authoritarianism and threat may be transformed to playing an important role in relation-building through justice.

6 Reconciliation and Politics

The tensions that may arise between reconciliation needs on the one hand and development ambitions and politics on the other are evident. Postconflict societies are most often in the beginning of a democratization process and the state quite weak. Politics is steered by conditions in office and the support of the population, all the more difficult in the brittle state of postconflict. Large focus on structural and economic development in postconflict nationbuilding is needed for reasons of both well-being and politics; issues of reconciliation may at times be paid lip service to conform to requests from the international community. Thus, reconciliation initiatives may be signals more to the international community than to the population. Factors such as the character and the genuineness of the reconciliation initiative, which may in turn be affected by how the conflict ended, may influence how the reconciliation initiative is perceived by the people, and thus, how it will affect reconciliation (Brounéus 2008a). If the conflict ended in victory for one party or by a negotiated peace agreement will effect to what extent the former enemy must be taken into account in such initiatives.

Nevertheless, symbolic acts by political leaders indicating remorse in order to promote reconciliation have been an increasingly frequent phenomenon over the last years. German Chancellor Willy Brandt was a pioneer, falling to his knees in the Old Jewish Ghetto in Warsaw in 1970, gesturing an apology for Germany's atrocities during World War II. Other examples include the IRA apologizing for having killed civilians in its 30-year anti-British campaign, and the Japanese Prime Minister Koizumi in 2001 expressing remorse for the Korean suffering under Japanese rule during World War II. The UN Secretary General Kofi Annan apologized to Rwanda for the UN's inability to act and prevent the 1994 genocide; former US president Bill Clinton did the same. In February 2008, Australian Prime Minister Kevin Rudd apologized for past mistreatment and suffering caused by successive governments on the indigenous Aboriginal population. Official acknowledgment of, and expression of remorse for, past wrongs has a significant role in today's world politics.

Political initiatives for reconciliation within a country after war can also be made in official statements, either to disclose a perception of what kind of atmosphere the government believes should be present in society between former enemies or to demonstrate that a clear strategy has been decided upon at the political level to promote reconciliation. Political initiatives for reconciliation include initiating judicial measures such as truth commissions, building new political institutions while taking earlier conflictual ethnic divisions into account, and through constitutional restructuring and legislation. Through legislation, behavior is regulated which can be used for reconciliation. For example, by criminalizing ethnic violence and discrimination, behavior must change, and slowly with time, this will also affect attitudes and emotions. Increased awareness among top-level leaders regarding the importance of official self-reflection and acknowledgment of past atrocity committed by the state does seem important for reconciliation. Such concerns would be of importance to development assistance and the international community when considering how to support the work for reconciliation at the highest political level.

7 Reconciliation and Security

In most truth commissions, survivors testify in public. In South Africa, for example, the hearings were broadcasted on the radio and television as an attempt to involve the whole nation in the process of reconciliation. Very rarely (in recent truth commissions), are the proceedings performed behind closed doors or the survivors' identity kept confidential. Many victims and witnesses in the International Criminal Tribunal for the Former Yugoslavia (ICTY) reported feelings of fear and abandonment on their return home after testifying (Stover 2004). Similarly, witnesses in the South African TRC described being stigmatized, abandoned and threatened by their community as a result of participating in the TRC (Backer 2007). Likewise, security for the accused when returning to their home communities has been a major concern for the International Criminal Tribunal for Rwanda (ICTR).[6] However, security risks are not included in the theoretical literature on truth telling and reconciliation.[7]

In Rwanda, where the largest officially driven reconciliation process in the world today is taking place (over 10,000 village tribunals are underway, called the *gacaca*, involving the entire population through mandatory participation) the issue of public testimony is carried to an extreme. Here, the village assembles to hear witnesses and the accused, thus the witness is surrounded by neighbors and family members of the accused.[8] Recent research in Rwanda suggests security should be included into the truth, justice and reconciliation equation.

In this research, insecurity as a result of the truth telling process emerged as one of the most crucial issues at stake (Brounéus 2008d).[9] Interviewed witnesses were threatened before the *gacaca* to deter from giving testimony, during the hearings to quiet them, and after, as punishment. This study suggests a novel understanding of the complexity of reconciliation at the grassroots level and raises questions about the relationship between truth commissions and security. If security is threatened, this may lead to a number of outcomes: physical injury, psychological anxiety and ill-health, an increase of violence in order to silence the truth, acts of revenge from either group, or skewed testimonies leading to a distorted picture of the past which may lay the grounds for renewed conflict.[10] In designing reconciliation processes for a nation, the individual participants must be taken into account. It is at this level, between former enemies, where the cycles of violence risk to be renewed.

---

[6] Statement by Justice Hassan B. Jallow, Prosecutor of the ICTR (Personal communication February 1, 2007).

[7] Luc Huyse importantly points out the significance of a minimum of security for a process of reconciliation as well as of the protection of members of truth commissions (Huyse 2003a,b) as does (van der Merwe 1999), however, this overview has failed to find any discussion in the literature on security risks as an *effect* of the reconciliation process. For a more detailed discussion on this topic, see (Brounéus 2008b).

[8] The crimes of the genocide in Rwanda have been divided into three categories: Category 1 consists of instigators and leaders of the genocide and sexual violence; Category 2: killings and serious attacks that may or may not have caused death; Category 3: offences against property. The accused in Category 1 are tried in the national courts or the ICTR (International Criminal Tribunal for Rwanda). Accused in Categories 2 and 3 are treated in the gacaca (pronounced "gatchatcha") courts in their home communities. Gacaca literally means "grass" in Kinyarwanda, referring to the tradition of assembling outdoors on the grass for the proceedings. The gacaca can be seen as a *functional equivalent* to a truth and reconciliation commission. For more on the multi-layered judicial process in Rwanda, please see Barbara Oomen of this volume.

[9] This research project, "The gacaca and psychological health", was funded by the Swedish International Development Cooperation Agency (Sida) which is gratefully acknowledged.

[10] A recent report from Human Rights Watch, "Killings in Eastern Rwanda" (January 2007), gives worrying information on this subject: two incidents of reprisal killings were reported in November 2006, now against Hutu. In the first incident, after the murder of a genocide survivor, eight Hutu, including five children, were killed in a reprisal attack the same day by a group of genocide survivors. In the second incident, three Hutu men died in alleged extrajudicial executions by the police after the murder of an Inyangamugayo (gacaca judge). These incidents have not been followed up by the police and thus the "culture of impunity", which is much discussed by the government, is at risk of being perpetuated.

8 Truth Telling and Reconciliation

Reconciliation is the pragmatic work of changing behaviors, attitudes and emotions between former enemies. Truth telling is one of the most important components of reconciliation processes around the world. In the following we will briefly highlight three additional concerns for reconciliation with regard to truth telling: trauma, reparation, and culture.[11]

8.1 Truth Telling and Trauma

The underlying assumption in much of the peacebuilding literature, as well as in political rhetoric, is that truth telling is cathartic or healing and thereby will advance reconciliation. However, there is very little empirical knowledge of these processes. As Kotzé (2002) observes: "We still await studies about the psychological impact of truth commissions". DeLaet (2006) states that "scholars and practitioners of transitional justice must give greater attention to individual psychological processes [in truth commissions] if they genuinely believe healing and reconciliation are integral to promoting peace and justice in the long term". Shaw (2005) has argued that if truth commissions are not built on established practices of healing, they risk jeopardizing psychological recovery. Considering that it is "the victims' suffering that is now at the core of how truth commissions operate" (Hamber 2006), it is their experience that requires analysis. In addition, psychological research would suggest a contrasting expectation of truth telling, namely, that there may be risks for retraumatization. Recent findings would support this hypothesis. To investigate the assumption that truth telling is healing, a multistage, stratified cluster random survey of 1,200 Rwandans was conducted in 2006 (Brounéus 2008c). The results of the survey are disconcerting. Witnesses in the gacaca suffered from significantly higher levels of depression and posttraumatic stress disorder than non-witnesses also when controlling for important predictors for psychological ill-health such as gender or trauma exposure. Together with the above mentioned in-depth interviews in Rwanda (Brounéus 2008d), these results challenge the claim that truth telling is healing, suggesting instead that there are risks for the individuals on whom truth-telling processes depend.

Official acknowledgement of past atrocities and injustices is important for working with individual traumatic experience because it validates past experiences and may help restore dignity and self-esteem. However, to speak of traumatic wounds, which often have left feelings of deep humiliation, shame, and guilt, is difficult, painful, and may lead to stigmatization. It is of great importance how the talking and listening is done and that the victim is aware that revealing may not lead to instant healing (Backer 2007; Hamber 2006; Stover 2004).

[11] One key concern that has emerged from current research on reconciliation and truth telling is the importance of studying the experiences of both women and men in these processes. Please see Nahla Valji of this volume for the crucial question of gender and reconciliation.

Truth commissions rely on the survivors' participation, but also on the accused, on witnesses who were affected through their family members, on the truth commission staff. The proceedings affect neighbors and those who were not yet born at the time of the conflict – whether by radio and television broadcast or in the form of attending village tribunals as in Rwanda. With regard to this massive national impact of truth commissions, Gibson's South Africa survey mentioned above raises one interesting question: do truth commissions lead to more reconciliation amongst the people who were not directly affected by the conflict by giving them a deeper understanding of the past even though no effect on reconciliation is seen in victims or those who were directly involved? If this is the case, truth commissions may play a vital role at the national level of reconciliation. However, as there may be significant risks for those involved, the policy implications are straightforward: we must take risk into account when designing reconciliation processes in order to minimize detrimental effects for the people at the focal point. Here, development support can serve a crucial function.

8.2 Truth Telling and Reparations

Peace and security are essential for reconciliation. Studies show that post civil war societies are more likely to experience civil war again than societies with no prior experience of war. Research suggests that improvement in economic well-being together with increased political openness significantly decreases the risk of experiencing war anew (Walter 2002). As war greatly strains the economy, there is a risk for a trap of economic deterioration and repeated conflict that may also spill over in neighboring countries, leading to instability in the region and the risk of expanded conflict (Collier and Sambanis 2002). So, how does economy relate to reconciliation? Firstly, economic development seems essential for peace, and peace in turn is fundamental for reconciliation. Secondly, survivors of atrocity and injustice have often been denied access to large parts of society such as education, jobs, housing, and medical care. In post-conflict societies, the gaps between former perpetrators and survivors are often vast, not least in relation to economic well-being. If these gaps are not addressed, economic inequality will undermine relation-building and provide a basis for further conflict.

For reconciliation in particular, the importance of economic reparations in the work of truth commissions around the world has become unmistakable. Money can never compensate the death of loved ones, but can help a surviving family build a better life as well as serve as "...an official, symbolic apology" (Hayner 2001). In a recent study investigating how victims experienced economic reparations, Byrne (2007) conducted in-depth interviews with Black South African survivors of human rights violations during apartheid. Three major themes emerged from these interviews. First, some survivors attributed a literal meaning to the money they had received ("just money to feed the family"), for others it held a symbolic meaning ("acknowledgment of past suffering"). Second, the survivors described their current suffering and unfulfilled needs despite the economic reparations they had received, for example a lack of access to health care. Third, the survivors spoke of their disappointment with the government after having received reparations: they felt betrayed and that the government no longer recognized them as survivors of apartheid or recognized contributions they had made. Other reports from South Africa indicated that failing to deliver promised financial reparation may lead to decreased support in the reconciliation process and renewed feelings of anger and humiliation in survivors (van der Merwe 2001; Vandeginste 2003).

Policy implications for reconciliation involve the following factors: supporting governments in delivering financial reparations to survivors and family members of those killed or missing for giving testimony in truth commissions. How reparations should be administered should preferably be decided in dialogue with the surviving community, who know their own situation best and who have suggestions if consulted (Byrne 2007). Economic development must also reach those who choose not to take part in a truth commission through projects seeking to reduce the postconflict economic gaps in society, thereby strengthening relation-building.

8.3 Truth Telling and Culture

Culture is the rich and complex blend of beliefs, attitudes, and behavior regarding everything from food to art to politics and religion in a society. Culture shapes how we perceive ourselves and others. Violence, fear and hatred during war result in the modernization of old myths and stereotypes to explain one's own or some other group's behavior – and thereby justify whatever gruesome atrocities are committed. After the war, the societal and cultural fabric is drenched with these beliefs. They can be seen in how history is described, how the language is used, in education, the media, theatre, etc. In order to live in peace, these beliefs must be questioned and transformed. The changing of stereotyped beliefs is a crucial step in the process of reconciliation.

The search for sustainable peace in a society after conflict must begin from its own roots, importing from outside whatever can be of use, but basing the society's transformation on its own unique set of traditions and cultural heritage. The importance of acknowledging the power of cultural heritage and tradition for postconflict relation-building has been discussed in the literature (Assefa 2001; Bloomfield 2003). A well-known example is the South African Truth and Reconciliation Commission's use of the African notion of *ubuntu*. *Ubuntu* entails that humanity is intertwined, a person is a person through other people; we are human because we belong. The misconduct of one person reduces the *ubuntu* of everyone while good deeds increase the *ubuntu* and well-being of all. Thus, reconciliation was part of restoring *ubuntu* in both victims and former perpetrators, for everyone is linked together. In this way, the TRC brought together its mission for national reconciliation, which often used Christian vocabulary, with the traditional African cultural heritage in the attempt to pave the way for reconciliation (Tutu 1999).

The religious and in particular Christian undertones of the term reconciliation for many people should be considered. Reconciliation between God and humanity through Jesus is a fundamental theme in Christianity. The Bible's concept of justice emphasizes interpersonal reconciliation, and focuses on compassion, mercy and forgiveness. In contrast, in the Buddhist tradition for example, compassion rather than forgiveness is stressed. The fundaments of the Buddhist Middle Path are acceptance, tolerance, and above all compassion. In a study from Cambodia, some interviewees suggested that truth commissions are a Christian concept as they are based on "confessing and forgiving" (Lambourne 2002). One interviewee explained that it would not be applicable to Cambodian tradition where, in accordance with Buddhism, people who have committed crimes will always be held responsible for them – there is no God who will ultimately forgive. Another interviewee argued on the same lines but drew the opposite conclusion, saying that it would be easy for Cambodians to forgive because they believe the perpetrators will be punished in the next life.

Awareness of the Christian connotations "reconciliation" may have in Christian versus non-Christian cultures appears important for policy. Similarly, supporting local and culturally grounded initiatives for reconciliation will have the highest legitimacy and sustainability in the long run.

9 Some Concluding Remarks

There is no magic formula for reconciliation. Each reconciliation process needs to be designed according to the specific context: the country, the conflict the country has been through, the culture and traditions it has that can strengthen reconciliation. Hearing the survivors and the community is essential in all initiatives for development and reconciliation.

We urgently need empirical research to better understand general trends regarding promises and pitfalls for reconciliation processes. We need evaluations of reconciliation processes, measurements of attitudes, behavior, and emotions towards the other group before, during, and after the reconciliation initiatives are taken. Carefully designed systematic comparative research is needed, to see what lessons can be learned from detailed case studies and from comparisons between a larger number of cases. Despite the best intentions, there are risks involved and we must learn how to improve reconciliation processes for building peace.

References

Anderson MB (1999) Do no harm: how aid can support peace – or war. Lynne Rienner, Boulder

Assefa H (2001) Coexistence and reconciliation in the Northern Region of Ghana. In: Abu-Nimer M (ed) Reconciliation, justice, and coexistence: theory and practice. Lexington Books, Oxford

Backer D (2007) Victims' responses to truth commissions: evidence from South Africa. In: Ndulo M (ed) Security, reconstruction, and reconciliation: when the wars end. University College London, London

Barsalou J (2007) Managing memory: looking to transitional justice to address trauma. In: Peacebuilding and trauma recovery: integrated strategies in post-war reconstruction. University of Denver, Colorado

Bloomfield D (2003) The context of reconciliation. In: Bloomfield D, Barnes T, Huyse L (eds) Reconciliation after violent conflict: a handbook. International IDEA, Stockholm

Bloomfield D (2006) On good terms: clarifying reconciliation. Berghof Research Center for Constructive Conflict Management, Berlin

Brounéus K (2003) Reconciliation: theory and practice for development cooperation. The Swedish International Development Cooperation Agency, Stockholm

Brounéus K (2008a) Analyzing reconciliation: a structured method for measuring national reconciliation initiatives. Peace Conflict: J Peace Psychol 14(3):291–313

Brounéus K (2008b) Rethinking reconciliation: concepts, methods, and an empirical study of truth telling and psychological health in Rwanda. Department of Peace and Conflict Research, Uppsala University, Uppsala

BrounéusK (2008c) The trauma of truth telling: implications of witnessing in the Rwandan Gacaca courts on PTSD and depression. In: Rethinking reconciliation: concepts, methods, and an empirical study of truth telling and psychological health in Rwanda. Department of Peace and Conflict Research, Uppsala University, Uppsala

Brounéus K (2008d) Truth telling as talking cure? Insecurity and retraumatization in the Rwandan gacaca courts. Security Dialogue 39:(1):55–76

Byrne CC (2004) Benefit or burden: victims' reflections on TRC participation. Peace Conflict: J Peace Psychol 10:(3):237–256

Byrne CC (2007) "The bullets are still lodged in their bodies": South African survivors of human rights violations reflect on government's reparation payouts. In: Peacebuilding and trauma recovery: integrated strategies in post-war reconstruction. University of Denver, Colorado

Collier P, Sambanis N (2002) Understanding civil war – a new agenda. J Conflict Resolution 46:(1):3–12

DeLaet DL (2006) Gender justice: a gendered assessment of truth-telling mechanisms. In: Borer TA (ed) Telling the truths: truth telling and peace building in post conflict societies. University of Notre Dame Press, Notre Dame

Gibson JL (2004) Does truth lead to reconciliation? Testing the causal assumptions of the South African truth and reconciliation process. Am J Polit Sci 48:(2):201–217

Hamber B (2006) "Nunca Mas" and the politics of person: can truth telling prevent the recurrence of violence? In: Borer TA (ed) Telling the truths: truth telling and peace building in post conflict societies. University of Notre Dame Press, Notre Dame

Harbom L (2007) States in armed conflict 2006. Uppsala Conflict Data Program, Department of Peace and Conflict Research, Uppsala University, Uppsala

Hayner PB (2001) Unspeakable truths: confronting state terror and atrocity. Routledge, New York

Huyse L (2003a) The international community. In: D. Bloomfield, T. Barnes, L. Huyse (eds) Reconciliation after violent conflict: a handbook. International IDEA, Stockholm

Huyse L (2003b) The process of reconciliation. In: Bloomfield D, Barnes T, Huyse L (eds) reconciliation after violent conflict: a Handbook. International IDEA, Stockholm

Kotzé D (2002) Reviews: truth commissions and formulas. Int Stud Rev 4(1):166–171

Lambourne W (2002) Domestic politics, international obligations and the pursuit of justice and reconciliation in Cambodia and East Timor. In: 43rd Annual ISA Convention. New Orleans, LA, USA

Lederach JP (1997) Building peace: sustainable reconciliation in divided societies. United States Institute of Peace Press, Washington DC

Meernik J (2005) Justice and peace? How the international criminal tribunal affects societal peace in Bosnia. J Peacc Res 42(3):271–289

Mendeloff D (2004) Truth-seeking, truth-telling, and postconflict peacebuilding: curb the enthusiasm? Int Stud Rev 6(3):355–380

Minow M (1998) Between vengeance and forgiveness: facing history after genocide and mass violence. Beacon, Boston

Nordquist K-Å (2002) Försoningens politik: om rättvisa, etik och konflikt efter inbördeskrig [The politics of reconciliation: on justice, ethics and conflict after civil war]. Uppsala University, Uppsala

Shaw R (2005) Rethinking truth and reconciliation commissions: lessons from Sierra Leone. Special Report. United States Institute of Peace, Washington DC

Staub E (2006) Reconciliation after genocide, mass killing, or intractable conflict: understanding the roots of violence, psychological recovery, and steps toward a general theory. Polit Psychol 27(6):867–894

Stover E (2004) Witnesses and the promise of justice in The Hague. In: Stover E, Weinstein HA (eds) My neighbor, my enemy: justice and community in the aftermath of mass atrocity. Cambridge University Press, Cambridge

Tutu D (1999) No future without forgiveness, 1st edn. Doubleday, New York

van der Merwe H (1999) The truth and reconciliation commission and community reconciliation: an analysis of competing strategies and conceptualizations. Institute for Conflict Analysis and Resolution, George Mason University, Fairfax

van der Merwe H (2001) Reconciliation and justice in South Africa: lessons from the TRC's community interventions. In: Abu-Nimer M (ed) Reconciliation, justice, and coexistence: theory and practice. Lexington Books, Oxford

Vandeginste S (2003) Reparation. In: Bloomfield D, Barnes T, Huyse L (eds) Reconciliation after violent conflict: a handbook. International IDEA, Stockholm

Villa-Vicencio C (2006) The politics of reconciliation. In: Borer TA (ed) Telling the truths: truth telling and peace building in post-conflict societies. University of Notre Dame Press, Notre Dame

Walter BF (2002) Does conflict beget conflict? explaining recurring civil war. University of California, San Diego

Weinstein HM, Stover E (2004) Introduction: conflict, justice and reclamation. In: Stover E, Weinstein HM (eds) My neighbor, my enemy: justice and community in the aftermath of mass atrocity. Cambridge University Press, Cambridge

Zehr H (2001) Restorative justice. In: Reychler L, Paffenholz T (ed) Peacebuilding: a field guide. Lynne Rienner, Boulder

Gender Justice and Reconciliation*

Nahla Valji

Abstract This paper examines how women's experiences of conflict and transition differ from that of men because of inherent gendered power relations and that, as a result, women's experiences of violence and needs for justice have until recent times largely been ignored. It speaks to gender justice as the protection of human rights based on gender equality and explores two such tenets: the acknowledgement of and seeking of justice for women's experiences of sexual violence in conflict situations; and the securing of increased representation of women in policy- and decision-making bodies on post-conflict issues and transitional justice mechanisms. The paper then goes beyond these tenets to discuss the specific needs of women within post-conflict systems that are male-orientated, and examines the assumptions of the transitional justice field from a gendered perspective. An examination of truth commissions is used to highlight the advances that have been made in securing redress for gender-based crimes, as well as the limitations. In particular, the article highlights the need to move beyond a focus on individual incidents of sexual violence in conflict to addressing the context of inequality which facilitate these violations as well as the continuum of violence from conflict to post-conflict which becomes visible through a gendered analysis. The paper concludes by suggesting a range of policy recommendations for gender justice and equality in the transitional justice field.

Although at their most brutal in war, sexual abuses against women often stem from longstanding prejudices, a lack of equality and discrimination that had condoned such violence all along. When perpetrators go unpunished, they are emboldened to strike again, perpetuating and encouraging vicious cycles of attack and reprisal even when a country emerges from conflict. Rendering justice to the victims

---

N. Valji
Centre for the Study of Violence and Reconciliation, Cape Town, South Africa
e-mail: nvalji@csvr.org.za

*This paper was originally published as part of Friedrich Ebert Stiftung's Dialogue on Globalization series, No. 35, November 2007.

K. Ambos et al. (eds.), *Building a Future on Peace and Justice: Studies on Transitional Justice, Peace and Development.*

is, therefore, not only a moral imperative, but also a precondition for reconciliation and peace to take hold.

Statement by Louise Arbor, International Women's Day, 2007

Justice, truth, reconciliation and guarantees of non-repetition for victims in the wake of conflict are just some of the core goals pursued by societies through the employment of transitional justice mechanisms. None of these goals however are attainable in a context of exclusion and inequality – as inequality, an injustice in itself, is also a causal factor of conflict. Violence thrives in societies entrenched in hierarchical structures and relations (Moser and Clark 2001; Schmeidl and Piza-Lopez 2002); and no inequality is more pervasive, both vertically and horizontally across the globe than gender inequality.

It is generally accepted that because of gendered power relations, it is women who pay the disproportionate cost of war.[1] This is not to further entrench the stereotype of women's identities in conflict as that of the "perpetual victim" – powerless and acted upon – but rather to acknowledge that women's experiences of both conflict as well as transition differ because of power relations, and that these experiences and accompanying needs for justice have largely been ignored.[2]

The myriad ways in which gender, power and violence intersect during both conflict and transition can be illustrated by the example of Rwanda. During the genocide, mass rape was utilized as a deliberate strategy of the Interahamwe. Beyond the trauma of the actual violation(s), the ongoing consequences for women have included high levels of HIV infection in a context of limited or no access to medical facilities and the responsibility for children born as a result.[3] When the violence receded, most men had either been killed, fled to nearby countries, or were in prison, leaving a national population that was 70% female. Women assumed the position of head of household; daily managing the impact of their own experiences whilst also shouldering the responsibility to ensure the economic survival of those who remained and the reconstruction of communities and social relations. This situation

[1] "...women and girls suffer predominantly or exclusively from specific types of harm during armed conflict both because they are female [and] while entire communities suffer the consequences of armed conflict, women and girls are particularly affected because of their status in society as well as their sex". UN Beijing Platform For Action, Para 131 in Levine (2004). See also Stern and Nystrand (2006).

[2] Reflecting on the tension between painting women as uniformly "victims" and yet highlighting the real impact of conflict, Rehn and Sirleaf (2002, p. 2) write: "[I] have grappled with the dilemma of describing the atrocities experienced by women in war in a way that will not [only] ascribe to women the characteristics of passivity and helplessness. Women are everything but that. But as with all groups facing discrimination, violence and marginalization, the causes and consequences of their victimization must be addressed. If not, how will preventive measures ever focus on women? How will the resources and means to protect women be put in place? How will the UN system, governments and NGOs be mobilized to support women? [It is important to keep writing about the ways women experience conflict as marginalized because] so far, not enough has been done".

[3] Research conducted by the Rwandan women's organization AVEGA in 1999 (based on a sample of 1,125 women living in the prefectures of Kigali, Butare and Kibundo) found that 74.5% had experienced sexual violence of some form. Two-thirds of these women reported being HIV positive (Bop 2001, p. 33).

was compounded by pre-existing gender norms; including cultural values which ascribed the stigma of sexual violence to the victim, and a legal system which forced women to be dependent upon surviving – and sometimes distant – male relatives as a result of an inability to inherit (Rombouts 2006).

Whatever the context, causes or nature of a conflict, all have in common that they are impacted by, and in turn impact upon, gendered power relations. Periods of conflict and post-conflict reconstruction destabilize gender identities and assumptions – during conflict women often assume positions that would have been unacceptable pre-conflict, either by joining one of the fighting parties, assuming the position of head of a household, or occupying positions in the public sphere or other spaces that were previously the exclusive domain of men (Meintjes et al. 2001b; see also Enloe 2004).

These shifts in roles and identities can provide a double-edged sword, whereby conflict has an enormous and devastating impact on women's lives, but can also open new spaces, and challenges, for transformation. As conflict is brought to an end and peace agreements negotiated, societies are faced with the task of reconstructing not only their physical infrastructure, but social infrastructure – including relationships to each other, and between citizens and the state.

Much has been made in feminist literature of the importance of this post-war moment for transforming unequal power relations and furthering gender justice (see in particular, Meintjes et al. 2001b). However it has also been noted that this moment is fleeting; and few, if any, examples can be pointed to where the gains that were made during this period were successfully consolidated and manifested in sustained gender equality and a transformed society.[4]

In part this inability to harness the potentially transformative moment is a result of the demand during post-conflict situations that "women" and "gender" be placed on the back burner for later as priority is once more placed on other issues (Enloe 2004). Equally detrimental is that peace negotiations often downplay issues of justice in an effort to consolidate a peace which is defined narrowly as a silencing of the guns. Where justice issues *are* addressed, "justice" is similarly narrowly defined and does not encompass transformative justice or challenge fundamentally unjust power relations within society; power relations that are often at the heart of the conflict itself.

It is during this moment of flux that transitional justice mechanisms are negotiated and established, with the express mandate to deal with past violations and contribute towards a blueprint for a new society based on principles of justice and equitable relations; and in doing so, ensure that the atrocities of the past will "never again" occur.

[4] Sondra Hale notes that it does not bode well for the struggle for gender equality that "no liberation or revolutionary war, no matter how progressive its ideology regarding the emancipation of women – from Russia and China to Algeria, Vietnam, Cuba, Nicaragua, El Salvador, Guinea-Bissau, Angola, Mozambique, South Africa and the Palestinian intifada – has empowered women and men to maintain an emancipating atmosphere for women after the military struggle and brief honeymoon are over" (Meintjes et al. 2001b, p. 123).

These objectives of transitional justice mechanisms as well as the space they occupy during the transition pose challenges as well as opportunities for the furthering of gender justice. The following paper begins to explore how transitional justice mechanisms can capitalize on the opportunities presented in order to move beyond the reconstruction of pre-war gender relations and instead encourage fundamental transformation of relations and institutions in order to contribute towards comprehensive social justice.

1 Gender Justice

Gender justice can be defined as "the protection and promotion of civil, political, economic and social rights on the basis of gender equality. It necessitates taking a gender perspective on the rights themselves, as well as the assessment of access and obstacles to the enjoyment of these rights for both women, men, girls and boys and adopting gender-sensitive strategies for protecting and promoting them" (Spees 2004).[5]

Incorporation of gender justice into accountability mechanisms has thus far emphasized two key objectives: acknowledging and seeking justice for women's experiences of sexual violence during conflict; and securing increased representation of women in arenas of policy making and decision making on post-conflict issues as well as in the transitional justice mechanisms themselves. The following sections assess the gains made in both these fields as well as select recommendations going forward. The paper then turns to the need to move beyond increased participation of women and the redress of specific violations to an engendering of the field of transitional justice as a whole in order to progress towards sustainable peace and transformative justice.

2 Addressing Sexual Violation as a War Crime

> *Without accountability for crimes against women, the legal foundations of new governments will be weakened, the credibility of governing institutions will be undermined and women will continue to suffer discrimination. Rehn and Sirleaf (2002, p. 89)*

---

[5] Gender as a concept has little to do with the biological categories of 'men' and 'women'. Rather it is about the social roles ascribed to individuals. Incorporating a gender analysis renders visible underlying power relations in society in order to expose what is valued and what is marginalized; and how these assumptions and hierarchies, if ignored, can fundamentally distort what might otherwise be well intentioned policy prescriptions. Introducing gender into transitional justice should not further entrench an essentialization of women as victims and men as perpetrators, but instead problematize these simplifications. The aim is to highlight gendered social relations, hierarchies and assumptions in order to provide a more complex and comprehensive picture which can then inform transitional justice policy prescriptions which are able to achieve their objectives and are not thwarted by faulty premises. See, Moser and Clark (2001); Giles and Hyndman (2004).

In the realm of international law there has been considerable progress in recent years towards acknowledging and addressing women's experiences of sexual violence during conflict. Where crimes of this nature were once covered in a complicit silence by both sides in a conflict, both law and the interpretation of law has shifted in recent years.

The Rome Statute which established the International Criminal Court recognizes sexual crimes as well as persecution on the grounds of gender. In cases before the International Criminal Tribunal for the Former Yugoslavia (ICTY) and the International Criminal Tribunal for Rwanda (ICTR) rape has been confirmed as both a crime against humanity as well as an act of genocide. Other notable initiatives at an international level include Security Council Resolution 1325 which deals specifically with justice for women's experiences of violence during conflict and the 2004 Report of the Secretary General on *The rule of law and transitional justice in conflict and post-conflict societies* which confirms the need for women to be included in all initiatives which seek redress for past violations as well as assurances that these interventions will not revictimize marginalized and at risk groups, in particular women who have been victims of sexual violence.

Similarly, mechanisms for redress in the domestic sphere have increasingly become gender-sensitive and inclusive. This is particularly visible in the way in which national truth commission processes have built upon the best practices of preceding commissions. The first truth commissions in Latin America were "gender blind" and either did not address sexual violence[6] or omitted from their analysis the context of gender inequality. Subsequent commissions have incorporated women's hearings, dedicated gender units and international technical support as well as a broader and more gendered definition of their mandate and harms covered.

3 Policy Implications

- Whilst there have been important gains in the international legal arena with regards to redressing sexual violence during conflict, these have been tempered by the actual number of convictions secured which have been few and far between. Moreover, despite these early victories, subsequent cases of sexual violence have not received the same levels of attention (Orentlicher 2007, pp. 10–12). Precedent setting cases make an important contribution to curbing impunity and sending a message that these violations will be treated with the condemnation due such atrocities, but these gains have little on the ground impact if they are not consistently applied or given sustained attention.
- Beyond the individual cases, international law is in a unique position to serve as a driving force for the reform of national law and the encouragement of domestic prosecutions of sexual violence. This is important as access to justice for the vast majority of women occurs at this level. With regards to legal reform and

[6] As late as 1993, the El Salvador truth commission failed to report on rape during the conflict as it was not defined as a "politically motivated" act but rather as a private crime.

implementation, the Rome Statute has again been a positive step in this regard. By recognizing gender persecution and requiring state parties to bring their own laws into conformity with the provisions of the Statute, the ICC can influence the adoption of domestic remedies and thus broaden access to justice for women in post-conflict states.[7] Again, real impact will require follow through: As states rarely have the political will to prosecute cases of this nature, progress will entail the prioritization of these crimes at an international level with the backing of a credible threat of referral to the ICC.

- Ensuring access to justice for women post-conflict also entails the rebuilding of national justice systems, legal reform and the implementation of effective policing bodies. International institutions and particularly peacekeeping operations are in a unique position to support the reconstruction of local police and courts and address the vacuum often left by the absence of these institutions in a post-conflict period by taking over the functions whilst working to establish new ones. Violence against women in particular flourishes in a context of general insecurity, impunity and an absence of judicial mechanisms. United Nations Mission in Liberia (UNMIL) has played a positive role in addressing widespread and endemic levels of violence against women in that country as well as working with local police to rebuild and reform to meet these challenges on their own (Action Aid 2007).

4 Gender Balance

Women's participation in all spheres of decision-making and policy formulation is both a form of justice and redress and a necessary element of real democratization. No policy process or institution can be credible which fails to incorporate the participation of a majority of the population; and this holds equally true for forums which determine and implement transitional justice policies. Moreover, marginalization and exclusion are often at the heart of the conflict being addressed, and transitional justice mechanisms are intended to both address these causes as well as contribute to the creation of a new society. Creating mechanisms which incorporate the voices of women and women's experiences begins to address old patterns of exclusion and actively lays down new patterns of engagement for the state. By doing so, it contributes to democratization in valuing equal participation in the public sphere, as well as vertical reconciliation as trust is built between previously marginalized populations and state institutions. Beyond being an important end goal in itself, gender balance in all arenas of policy and implementation is a factor in sound

[7] This assumes a functioning and effective judicial system which is often absent post-conflict and as such, international support for legal reform needs to be a coordinated effort which targets both law reform as well as the reform of institutions to serve all citizens where they previously may have been the preserve of only certain groups.

policy formulation and implementation as it brings to the table an increased range of skills and perspectives.[8]

Despite a recognition of the need for gender balance[9] in all policy processes concerned with dealing with the legacy of past crimes, actual progress towards this objective has been inconsistent. A United Nations Development Fund for Women (UNIFEM) study on Security Council Resolution 1325 (Women, Peace and Security) notes that rarely have women been "consulted about the form, scope and modalities for seeking accountability. Women's stake in these processes has been minimized or denied and, in most cases, crimes against them go unrecorded" (Rehn and Sirleaf 2002).

5 Gender Balance: Policy Implications

- Democratization and social justice necessitate that women be involved at every step of post-conflict reconstruction. Pressure should be brought to bear by international institutions and donor agencies for a minimum number of seats to be reserved for women during peace negotiations and in all forums where decisions are being made regarding justice for past crimes.
- A space at the table does not however guarantee that these voices will be heard. To increase effectiveness and impact, international agencies should work with local civil society, and particularly women's organizations, to build the capacity and expertise necessary to strategically represent the needs of previously marginalized constituencies during these deliberations.
- International agencies must reflect the practice they preach. Many such organizations continue to be dominated by men, particularly in those missions operating in a post-conflict context and particularly at higher levels of responsibility. To date, only 2 of the 27 UN peacekeeping missions in post-conflict countries have been headed by women.
- The full and equal participation of women is a goal in and of itself, it does not however necessarily lead to gendered policy. Equally important is the participation and involvement of gender experts – both men and women – at all stages of peace negotiations, and particularly during the foundational discussions on

[8] The UN for example has found that peace operations with higher levels of gender diversity in their staffing have resulted in increased effectiveness in the overall mission, Schmeidl and Piza-Lopez (2002, p. 19). Some also argue that the inclusion of women into decision making forums leads to the improvement of the status of women in society more generally. This is a contested view and assumes a homogeneity of women's interests which is false. Impact also depends on a range of factors such as the type of political system, institutional reform and the overall importance ascribed to values of democracy and inclusion. But whilst impact on outcomes is a factor, women's inclusion in all spheres and levels of policy is on its own a critical component of a just democratic system.

[9] For an overview of "gender balance" and its coverage in international policy documents see "Women's Initiative for Gender Justice on 'What Is Gender Balance?"' in Nesiah et al. (2006, p. 11).

transitional justice policies. This incorporation of gendered expertise should extend to all planning, implementation and evaluation of programs conducted by external agencies in a post-conflict context.

6 Beyond Inclusion

While recent debate in the field of transitional justice has revealed a growing recognition of gender justice as an indivisible component of the overall post-conflict justice and peace agenda, there are huge challenges which remain to be addressed. As the previous sections demonstrate, gains thus far have been predominantly concerned with increasing women's representation in existing mechanisms and addressing experiences of sexual violence. Both of these objectives are of fundamental importance, but neither can achieve in isolation the transformative justice required for sustainable peace and reconciliation.

New laws, seen in isolation, reduce women's experiences of conflict to only that of sexual crimes. They do little to challenge the fundamental assumptions of transitional justice mechanisms; the ways in which these assumptions are gendered or the extent to which such mechanisms take cognizance of or strive to further gender equality and justice as part of a "justice" agenda. Whilst it is essential to make visible the use of rape as a weapon of war, this alone will not address the system of unequal power relations and the use of violence against women as a means to enforce these unequal relations. Gender justice can only be furthered if there is a focus not just on the crime but its context, motivation, and location within a continuum of violence (Cockburn 2004).

There are two elements necessary to incorporating a gender justice agenda into the transitional justice field. The first requires acknowledging the specific needs of women in a system that has been designed to acknowledge and seek justice for crimes experienced and defined by men, as well as inclusion of women in all processes designed to deliver redress for the past. The second element moves beyond inclusion of women into existing mechanisms and instead seeks to examine the core assumptions of transitional justice from a gendered perspective, opening the field to a reassessment of these assumptions as well as the policies they inform. This second step moves beyond a limited reform agenda to addressing the root causes and consequences of conflict.

6.1 Incorporating a "Gender Lens", Challenging Core Assumptions

At its core, transitional justice is concerned with redress for victims of past violations and guarantees of non-repetition. South Africa, a country often cited as a "model" in the field of transitional justice for its innovative Truth and Reconciliation Commission premised on public victims hearings and conditional amnesty, is also a vivid example of the failings of such a mechanism to contribute substantially to gender justice. Today, it is a country with higher levels of violence against women than many countries currently mired in "political" conflict.[10] And it is by no means unique in this experience. Research across post-conflict societies reveals that violence does not simply cease with the signing of a peace accord, but for various reasons – including pervasive trauma, easy access to guns, militarized identities, normalization of conflict and the devastation of judicial systems – violence carries through and can even intensify during a transition period; playing out in ways which have continuity and a rooting in the causes and consequences of the conflict but which can also take on new forms.[11] As one feminist writer observes, "[W]ars don't simply end. And wars don't end simply" (Enloe 2004, p 193). Ongoing insecurity and violence once again intersect with gendered hierarchies and disproportionately impact on certain sectors of society, those historically in positions of less power such as women, foreigners, children, and the elderly.

High levels of violence, specifically experienced by certain sectors, challenge some of the normative foundations of transitional justice. For example, "non-repetition" has been defined narrowly to cover only violent "political" conflict which takes the same form as that experienced in the past. It has not been defined in a forward-looking manner which repudiates *all* violence, prejudice and discrimination. What can guarantees of non-repetition mean to those who continue to experience violations of their basic rights? The treatment of rape in war as exceptional, as has been the focus of international law to date, renders invisible the relationship between sexual violence in conflict and its ongoing and pervasive existence during and after the transition. These mechanisms may lend themselves to the denunciation of violence against women in a conflict setting, however their "exceptional" focus does little to denounce violence in all forms, and in particular violence against women during peace (DeLaet 2006).

The removal of war time rape from the continuum of violence against women in which it is inherently a part, the setting it aside as exceptional or not rooted in larger power relations, also reinforces a false dichotomy of conflict/post-conflict and detracts from the more fundamental goal of human security. Who defines what constitutes "the conflict"; what does it mean to be a "post-conflict" society when so many women can still ask the question "how do we know we are at peace?" (Farr 2000, pp. 23–31); and of what value is a peace agreement if levels of violence experienced by women continue at conflict levels? As Copelon notes, "to emphasize as unparalleled the horrors of genocidal rape is factually dubious and risks rendering rape invisible once again ... when the ethnic war ceases or is forced back into the bottle, will the crimes against women, the voices of women and their struggles to survive be

[10] Rape Crisis (2006) reports that 147 women are raped daily in South Africa. It is estimated that only one in nine rape victims ever reports the crime and of these cases, only 7% are successfully prosecuted (OneinNine.org.za, 2006). Ross (2006).

[11] For a critical overview of the experiences of violence during transition, its continuities and forms in the South African context, see Harris (2005).

vindicated? Or will condemnation be limited to this seemingly exceptional case?" (cited in DeLaet 2006, p. 162).

Similar to the false dichotomy of conflict/post-conflict is the assumption of a dividing line between political and criminal (or "private") acts. This focus on the political in transitional justice is not informed by the experiences of victims, but rather superimposes a false structure which fails to account for the common impact of violations and insecurity; missing as it does the way in which violence transforms through the transition, the merging of the criminal and the political, and the ways in which violence against women in particular becomes the response to transition, destabilization and the reinforcement of traditional norms. As a submission to the South African TRC highlighted, "A political rape has no different consequences. It has exactly the same reason behind it – a violent act against a woman ... In fact the women [are] being punished as women" (Goldblatt and Meintjes 1996).

As the causes of violence against women, particularly during the post-conflict period, emanate directly from the political sphere – and gendered power relations are very much a political construct – the arena of what TJ mechanisms seek to address needs to be expanded beyond the current privileging of a patriarchal notion of what is "political". Just as feminists have strived over the years to break down the false dichotomy of public/private which entrenches and renders invisible larger structures of oppression, similarly, the false distinctions of conflict/post-conflict and criminal/political implicitly entrenched in transitional justice policies must be equally addressed.

Other key assumptions that require revisiting include the very violations that transitional justice seeks to redress. International law reflects a male experience of conflict (Levine 2004; Nesiah 2005), failing to take into account the specific impact conflict has on women's lives – the consequences of a lack of access to basic services; ongoing insecurity; being forced to take on the roles of missing male family members but in a context of ongoing and systematic discrimination such as laws which prohibit women from inheriting land and property, force them to be married to a husband's relative, prevent them from accessing services from the state without a male intermediary, etc. For women the post-conflict period of rebuilding and restructuring their lives is very much focused on everyday survival needs. In this context, terms such as "justice" and "peace" take on a very different meaning. Women's experiences of injustice during conflict are also a result of existing inequalities and as such are not necessarily the crimes that are codified in international human rights law. For example, given existing patterns of feminization of poverty, the aggravation of poverty when a state chooses to shift its spending from social services to military disproportionately affects women and women-headed households. Moreover, the gendered impact of forced displacement, of deliberate bombing and destruction of social infrastructure which places an increased burden on those assigned a care giving role by society, are all ways in which conflict has a gendered impact; one which is not captured or redressed through the rights which are codified in international law, and as such, the rights which are the concern and focus of transitional justice.[12] A gendered analysis would require rethinking even *what* it is that we are seeking redress for. As noted above, the shift in thinking is beginning to occur as experiences of women are incorporated into the work of existing mechanisms, but this incorporation has been limited and has yet to secure justice for the full range of gendered harms.

A focus on gender can also begin to address some of the central questions regarding perpetrators – providing needed information for the prevention of future violence. For example, why is it that men who have never engaged in rape during peace time willingly engage in such acts during conflict? How does this transformation occur? What is the impetus? Given that rape is a crime of power, there is much theorization regarding the use of rape – against both men and women – as a means to humiliate the enemy, encourage "bonding" amongst male soldiers, "reward" combatants, etc. But until more attention is paid to these questions little can be done to prevent these crimes. What role does militarized masculinity play in the mobilization of combatants? What does this mean when those combatants are returned to civilian life post-conflict? More attention also needs to be paid to the use of rape and sexual violence against male combatants and boys – this too is a result of gender constructions and militarized masculinities.

Reassessing key notions of truth, justice and reconciliation from a gendered perspective will undoubtedly complicate the field of transitional justice by destabilizing core assumptions.[13] But it will also lead to different questions being asked, different information being collected and therefore a fuller picture created which can inform policy that furthers a transformation agenda, rather than policy which reinforces unequal power relations (Enloe 2004). Incorporation of gendered analysis in research will give a more accurate picture when establishing TJ mechanisms as well as contribute to a more complete evaluation of these mechanisms and policies.

Given the limited space available it is not possible to examine each of the core areas of transitional justice and assess how incorporating gender would further the end goals of justice and reconciliation. As such, the following section engages with just one key mechanism – that of truth commissions – and outlines briefly the potential contribution they can make to gender justice, key challenges to date and select policy recommendations before making some further general recommendations for the field.

[12] Peru's truth commission report for example documented that there were "important gender dimensions to the economic causes and consequences of human rights violations, such as the widespread displacement of women and children and a phenomenal rise in female-headed households in many communities affected by violence". World Bank (2006, p. 28).

[13] Nesiah notes the dilemma for feminists in the need to "engage and impact a field that has such momentous consequences for women" without being mainstreamed into the already constituted boundaries of that field. She states, "In sum, we may be charged with the seemingly impossible imperative to subvert the terrain that we want to impact" (Nesiah 2005). See also DeLaet (2006).

7 Truth Commissions

Truth commissions have over the past two decades expanded from their limited institutional origins just a step beyond commissions of inquiry, to bodies that today are expected to deliver a range of social goods not just for victims, but for post-conflict societies as a whole: documenting history, encouraging reconciliation, providing public acknowledgment for victims, social sanction for perpetrators and more. Most recently, truth commission reports have gained import as foundational documents of the new society (World Bank 2006; Nesiah et al. 2006); recording not just past history but providing a blueprint for legislation, policy and practice which address the root causes of the conflict and give impetus to the transition towards democracy and good governance.

As a World Bank report on gender and truth commissions notes, in this role, truth commissions have valuable potential for transforming gender relations post-conflict: "A gender perspective in a truth commission's report can help bring about changes in existing laws and patterns of behavior that have contributed to inequality and discrimination" (World Bank 2006, p. ix). Moreover, "... incorporating gender-sensitive approaches into the work of the truth commission not only aids in making effective reparations, but also helps prevent future conflicts" (World Bank 2006, p. ix). This potential however has not been fully harnessed by truth commissions to date.

Early concerns with gender and truth commissions were very much focused on increasing the number of women commissioners, encouraging the employment of women statement-takers and providing a safe space for women to tell their stories of sexual violence. As noted previously, given the history of silence which shrouds women's experiences of sexual violence and the lack of accountability or justice with which these crimes have been treated, creating spaces to hear, record and acknowledge these crimes is no small contribution. This concern with "adding women" however has not adequately examined the core assumptions of truth commissions and how these assumptions may or may not fit the needs of women, gender justice and individual context.[14]

With regards to the focus on recording sexual violence itself, assumptions regarding truth, public acknowledgement and healing need to be questioned regarding their applicability to the specific nature of sexual violations. Are the assertions of truth as a road to reconciliation, or assumptions regarding the enactment of individual scenarios of confession and forgiveness, equally suitable to the nature and damage of sexual crimes? Are the gendered experiences of trauma adequately recognized and catered for in truth seeking mechanisms?

[14] There has been efforts in the most recent commissions, particularly East Timor, Sierra Leone and Peru, to move beyond the focus on recording sexual violations to including context, complexifying the role of gender relations during and after conflict as well as making key recommendations to further equality during the transition. These successes need to be consolidated and built upon further.

The focus almost exclusively on sexual violence reinforces the view of women as victims and prescribes meaning to the event externally. The focus on the one event severs it from a context of violations and oppression that women endure – as well as casts into the shadows the other roles that women have occupied. The issue of the gendered bias inherent in the selection of violations with which transitional justice concerns itself has been covered above. The truth commission is a forum where this emphasis has played out in a visible manner to silence women's complex identities. Some feminists have noted that because of what is valued by these institutions women are implicitly encouraged to assume a victim identity in order to be "acknowledged". The focus on "the" incident strips it of meaning in a wider context, as well as subverts or fails to acknowledge resilience and the complexity of identities which are not frozen in a single identity of victim-hood (Ross 2006). It has been noted that in this regard there is actually a tension established between justice and healing (Franke 2006).

Some have argued that truth commissions can in fact undermine gains made by women during conflict, recording and naturalizing a gender biased history through its focus on specific types of violations – i.e., individual acts of violence perpetrated against largely "politically active" figures or combatants, both of which categories have been historically defined to exclude women's roles – and marginalizing the spaces occupied and the contribution of women. As one activist notes: "Societies focus in the aftermath on finding the truth about atrocities and on the reconciliation process; this diverts women from looking at the advances they made during war and distracts them from creating new blueprints. Because public reward goes to those who died, women's advances – the survival strategies that kept families alive and communities together – are erased from the historical record" Meintjes et al. (2001a, p. 17).

The focus on the single violation also removes it from its context within a broader framework of oppression and strips it of the power to highlight the structural factors.

In South Africa for example, African women's unlawful detention and the fear and intimidation they felt at the hands of white security officers was informed by a lifetime of oppression, humiliation, and abuse at the hands of a white-minority state and its officials. To unravel a single element of the overall picture and convey the story as a single event, devoid of context, does little to promote healing and acknowledgement; and may in fact do harm. The primary focus that was placed on getting women to speak of their sexual violations denied the range of other abuses women endured and shaped the stories that were heard; until "a diversity of harms [became] a story of sexual violation" (Ross 2003). Whilst legal processes necessarily need to focus on the actual crime, transitional justice mechanisms do not have the same limitations, and in pursuit of redress, these bodies need to acknowledge context and address consequence and pain in a more nuanced way which takes into account where women are, what their experiences are, and how their lives have been impacted by the violation.

8 Policy Implications

- International institutions and donor agencies should financially and technically support a research agenda during the transition. Local civil society should be given the resources necessary to carry out research, document victim's perspectives and needs and learn from the experiences of other countries though horizontal networks. Within this research agenda, specific attention should be given to documenting the cultural and political context, power relations and the specific needs of women prior to the establishment of a truth commission or decisions on their mandate or modes of operation.
- There should be no assumptions about what victims of gender-based violence (GBV) need for healing and justice; this needs to be context-specific. For many victims, the difficulties of discussing one's suffering in the public sphere, particularly in a context where speaking of sexual violence will lead to a revictimization and other consequences for the victim, the assumptions of a truth commission regarding revealing and healing may not "restore dignity" but may in fact compound harm. This has been well recognized by commissions to date and much effort has been expended on securing in camera hearings and ensuring adequate numbers of women statement takers. However the assumption does not hold true for all women in all contexts and the assumption should not be made that women *don't* want to speak out. As Nesiah notes, in East Timor and Sierra Leone many women wanted to speak of their experiences publicly (Nesiah et al. 2006).[15] Moreover, there has not been the same concerted focus on encouraging boys and men who have also been victims of GBV – and suffer the same consequences of shame and silence – to come forward. Gender-based violence is not just about women and its use against male victims is equally about gendered power and may need to be addressed in unique ways.
- There must be adequate support given to those who do want to talk, and mechanisms of acknowledgement and redress constituted for those who cannot come forward. The linking of reparations specifically to the disclosure of the violation needs to be reassessed. Even for those that benefit from disclosure, once off unburdening of stories during a hearing is inadequate for full healing, and truth commissions should partner with and feed into a larger network of psycho-social support where available.[16] Different spaces for therapeutic support should also be considered – i.e., group hearings or the use of local or cultural traditions may

[15] Also note that when a group of NGOs got together in 2000 to publicly convene a People's Tribunal to try the crimes committed against over 200,000 girls and women sexually enslaved by the Japanese Army during WWII – a crime that no local or international court has ever tried – 75 survivors came forward to tell their story. UNIFEM notes that what drove these women "was the wish to tell their story before it was lost to history". http://www.unifem.org/filesconfirmed/149/219_chapter07.pdf.

[16] The therapeutic approach may itself be gendered and inappropriate to some contexts. DeLaet (2006, p. 171) notes that in a cultural context "where talking about one's vulnerabilities and problems is not seen as masculine, therapy may not be an appropriate method for fostering truth-telling by male victims of human rights abuses".

not assist a truth commission to put numbers to the crimes, but they could be a more valuable space for victim-centered healing. Given that this is the first priority for commissions, and that in many countries devastation and poverty limits access to any psycho-social support beyond the commission itself, these options should be considered where appropriate. Where survivors do choose to testify in public, power over the story and exchange needs to be given to the survivor. The act of taking control over one's own story in a historical context of uneven power relations can be a form of redress itself and contribute to a sense of justice; it also allows the commission to model equal gender relations in its own dealings where the survivor is female (see DeLaet 2006).

- Public hearings should be harnessed for their potential value for public education. Special hearings on women that are held publicly should capture the full range of women's experiences not reflect them as passive victims or solely as victims of sexual violence. Truth commissions serve an important function in writing/recording a new and ideally more inclusive history. The narrowing of women's stories in this forum merely perpetuates their ongoing invisibility from history and the marginalization of their roles and contributions; and further entrenches gendered notions of who is remembered and valorized and what the new society values and includes.
- Final reports can play an important role in guiding the transformation of society, however the best and most inclusive report serves little purpose if its recommendations are not implemented. It is here that multilateral and donor agencies can make an impact in holding governments to account in the implementation of recommendations, in particular those that concern gender justice where political will is often at its weakest. Tying loans, allocating dedicated program funding or incentivizing for the implementation of these recommendations can have substantial impact (see World Bank 2006). This is particularly important with those recommendations that could be easily implemented given sufficient political will, and which would have a meaningful impact. For example, in Sierra Leone, the TRC recommended that political parties and government reserve 30% of public office positions for women. However the recommendations of the TRC have yet to be implemented and this measure in particular has met with much resistance. Without external intervention it is unlikely that regulations for positive discrimination and historical redress will be adopted in the near future.

9 Further General Policy Recommendations

- *Reparations as a tool for gender empowerment.* Just as an exclusive focus on a specific violation or incident undermines the ability of truth commission's to contribute to a broader agenda of social justice, so too with reparations does the linking of redress to a single incident similarly weaken the potential contribution to social justice. Reparations programs have enormous potential to empower women, address social and economic inequality linked to gender and contribute to a broad social justice agenda. Using reparations policies can serve as a proactive vehicle to redress past harms which are not limited to "the" violation, but rather serve to redress an overall context of oppression and violations of basic rights and a contribution towards furthering gender equality, empowerment and gender sensitive development.

- *Lesson learning from other fields.* Lessons learned from "engendering" policy and practice in other fields should be assessed for their application and use in the field of transitional justice. For example, reparations policies in the past have failed to take into consideration the gendered hierarchies of individual families and the implications for how resources are provided, who benefits and what impact these programs have. In South Africa, reparations took the form of a once-off payment of approximately US $4,000. Despite the fact that the majority of beneficiaries were African women, the policy failed to take into consideration both power differentials within families as well as the historic lack of access to bank accounts amongst this population. Local victims groups reported that the money was often deposited into male family member's accounts and women were given limited or no control over the resources.[17] In some cases, tensions over how money should be spent in households lent itself to family violence. Valuable lessons could be learned for reparations programs from the field of Gender Budgetary Analysis – that is the study of budgets and policy decisions for their gendered impact in order to inform how state spending can be used to target the causes of feminization of poverty; thereby breaking the cycle of poverty and furthering gender-sensitive development strategies that foster real equality. By only seeing half the picture, policies can in fact do more harm than good as they are unable to answer questions regarding how resources should be distributed or services delivered and what impact it will have on gender-relations or the ability of women to access these resources.
- *Integration and coordination.* An integrated approach is needed between various sectors and international and national bodies/donor agencies engaged in all aspects of transitional justice and reconstruction. For example, an integrated approach would coordinate psycho-social support for victims of sexual violence with health services and skills training to assist in reintegration and socio-economic stability in order to break the cycles of violence and poverty.
- *Use of existing resources.* In planning transitional justice mechanisms, policy makers should draw upon and make use of relevant existing information which would allow them to understand the overall context with regards to gender relations. For example, the *Gender Empowerment Measure* (GEM) used by UNDP measures the relative empowerment of men and women and examines whether "women and men are able to participate in economic and political life and take part in decision-making" (Schmeidl and Piza-Lopez 2002). Such information is vital to creating policy which is applicable to the context. Also, Security Council Resolution 1325 on Women, Peace and Security should be given concerted attention and resources by all governments and should guide all work that is done

[17] Research conducted for the report Makhalemele (2004); see also, Goldblatt (2006).

in a post-conflict setting. Beyond its implementation however, there is a need to revisit the original resolution to ensure that new developments in the field of transitional justice are adequately addressed.

- *Funding of research.* It is vital to have victim informed policies and research that is gender disaggregated and challenges cultural assumptions. For example, it is often stated that prosecution may not be a priority for women, however this is an untested assumption. Whilst the sequencing of social justice issues such as access to health, housing and education may be a first priority, it is difficult to conclude whether this is an "either or" choice unless there is further research. TJ mechanisms must meet the needs of all victims, not only one part of this constituency. This data should similarly be disaggregated for age, location, socio-economic background, etc. Women are not a homogenous category and creating policy that works means knowing who you're creating it for and what the context is.
- *Selective audit of mechanisms to date.* A multi-country audit should be commissioned to review the range of TJ policies and mechanisms to date and examine not just how women's participation can be increased but the relationship between transitional justice and gender justice; what these mechanisms have contributed to gender justice; how they should be restructured; and what additional policies or procedures would strengthen their impact to this end. There is scant research on these questions thus far.
- *Dedicated funding.* There is a need for dedicated funding to ensure that these issues are given adequate attention. For example, the dedicated funding provided by the UN's Office of the High Commissioner for Human Rights (OHCHR) in the case of the Peruvian truth commission and by UNIFEM in the form of technical support and expertise in the case of the Sierra Leone truth commission, ensured that these issues could not be relegated to the margins or constrained by an absence of resources (World Bank 2006).
- *Increased representation of women in all levels of international institutions operating in a post-conflict setting.* Initial evidence from Liberia in the months after the deployment of the UN's first all-women peacekeeping unit showed that not only were they making services more accessible to women who had experienced sexual violence but they were also becoming role models and challenging domestic thinking on the roles and abilities of women.
- *Support for local women's organizations.* Intervention, funding and technical support should be provided to women operating at a grass-roots level to bridge the divide post-conflict and forge reconciliation based on shared needs and concrete projects. This is not to essentialize women as being inherently peaceful, but rather to acknowledge that given the traditional roles and place in society occupied by many women, there is evidence across conflict zones of marginalized women seizing these roles in order to mobilize for change based on concrete projects. Examples such as the Women in Black in Yugoslavia, numerous initiatives by Hutu and Tutsi women to jointly care for children orphaned by the genocide in Rwanda, examples in Burundi, Israel/Palestine and elsewhere all demonstrate a mobilization across the divide based on concrete needs

(Cockburn 2004). Support for these initiatives encourages community-level reconciliation whilst also supporting projects which address basic survival needs post-conflict.

- *The role of local mechanisms*. Local or traditional rituals can play a strong and positive role in community reintegration of victims and combatants as well as for healing and reconciliation as they are likely to resonate with the local population and have buy in. However some of these practices may perpetuate inequality or undermine the rights of women and girls – such as the practice of exchanging a girl of marriageable age as "compensation" for a life taken or a crime committed. National governments and international institutions should aim to audit local practices in a country during the transition phase to look at what practices could contribute to reconciliation and reintegration, draw out the positive principles to be encouraged and address those that undermine justice and equality. Traditions are not static but evolve according to context. Building on the positive elements of these practices can contribute to establishing locally informed mechanisms for justice and healing and can also have a positive impact on society more generally by initiating the reform of practices that are antithetical to gender justice – and leave a legacy of evolved traditions that are more conducive to the rights of all.
- *Sustained and long term funding for a range of initiatives*. Psychosocial support for example requires long term investment and is not a one off event. Dealing with trauma is integral to halting the cycle of violence and implementing sustainable reconciliation, but victims of gender-based violence in particular may not be ready to access psycho-social assistance until there has been some space and time from the actual conflict, and until immediate issues of security are addressed.
- *The need for a holistic and integrated approach*. Security is a precondition to reconciliation and given the pervasive levels of insecurity experienced almost uniformly by women in post-conflict situations, an integrated response is required which includes: rebuilding the justice and policing sector; implementing DDR programs which aim to demilitarize society and minds, not just collect weapons; removal of small arms from circulation; access to opportunities for both former combatants and marginalized populations; addressing of root causes; and rebuilding of social development networks amongst other issues. Donors and international agencies should create forums for coordination and regular feedback which involves and is driven by a national agenda. Also, there will be little impact if TJ mechanisms focus on gender equality within a context characterized by ongoing oppression and discrimination. There needs to be an integrated response with other key role players who are concerned with legal reform including the signing of all relevant human rights instruments, particularly CEDAW; establishment of quotas for all levels and spheres of government; public education to address cultural practices which disadvantage women, etc.

10 Conclusion

Engendering the field of transitional justice will entail a fundamental rethinking of the goals, structures and foundational assumptions upon which the field is built as well as the future incorporation of a gendered perspective in all levels of planning and implementation. Whilst this may destabilize accepted practices in the short term, continuing to sideline this perspective only contributes to an unjust and partial reconciliation premised upon pre-conflict inequitable power relations; laying the foundations for future violence and conflict and subverting the very goals transitional justice mechanisms are intended to secure.

References

Action Aid (2007) UNMIL: International engagement in addressing violence against women. Recommendations for change

Bop C (2001) Women in conflict, their gains and their losses. In: Meintjes S, Turshen M, Pillay A (eds) Aftermath: women in post-conflict transformation. Zed Books, London

Cockburn C (2004) The continuum of violence: a gender perspective on war and peace. In: Giles W, Hyndman J (eds) Sites of violence: gender and conflict zones. University of California Press, Berkeley

DeLaet DL (2006) Gender justice: a gendered assessment of truth-telling mechanisms. In: Tristan Ann Borer (ed) Telling the truths: truth telling and peace building in post-conflict societies. University of Notre Dame, Notre Dame

Enloe C (2004) The curious feminist: searching for women in a new age of empire. University of California, Berkeley

Farr V (2000) How do we know we are at peace? Reflections on the Aftermath conference. Agenda 43:23–31

Franke K (2006) Gendered Subjects of Transitional Justice. Columbia J Gender Law 15(3): 813–828

Giles W, Hyndman J (eds) (2004) Sites of violence: gender and conflict zones. University of California Press, Berkeley

Goldblatt B (2006) Evaluating the gender content of reparations: lessons from South Africa. In: Rubio-Marín R (ed) What happened to the women: gender and reparations for human rights violations. Social Science Research Council, New York

Goldblatt B, Meintjes S (1996) Gender and the Truth and Reconciliation Commission: A submission to the Truth and Reconciliation Commission. Available at http://www.doj.gov.za/trc/submit/gender.htm

Harris B (2005) Between a rock and a hard place: violence, transition and democratization. A consolidated review of the Violence and Transition Project. Violence and Transition Series. Centre for the Study of Violence and Reconciliation, Johannesburg

Levine C (2004) Gender and transitional justice – a case study of East Timor. Canadian Consortium on Human Security

Makhalemele O (2004) Still not talking: Government's exclusive reparations policy and the impact of the 30,000 financial reparations on survivors. Centre for the Study of Violence and Reconciliation, Johannesburg

Meintjes S, Pillay A, Turshen M (2001a) There is no aftermath for women. In: Meintjes S, Turshen M, Pillay A (eds) Aftermath: women in post-conflict transformation. Zed Books, London

Meintjes S, Turshen M, Pillay A (eds) (2001b) Aftermath: women in post-conflict transformation. Zed Books, London
Moser CON, Clark FC (eds) (2001) Victims, perpetrators or actors? Gender, armed conflict and political violence. Zed Books, London
Nesiah V (2005) Feminism and transitional justice: towards a critically reflective practice. Paper presented at conference on women and human rights: conflict, transformation and change, Belfast, Northern Ireland, 19–20 May 2005
Nesiah V et al (2006) Truth commissions and gender: principles, policies, and procedures. International Center for Transitional Justice, New York
Orentlicher DF (2007) 'Settling accounts' revisited: reconciling global norms with local agency. Int J Transitional Justice 1(1):10–22
Rehn E, Sirleaf EJ (2002) Women, war and peace – the independent expert's assessment on the impact of armed conflict on women and women's role in peace-building. UNIFEM, New York
Rombouts H (2006) Women and reparations in Rwanda: a long path to travel. In: Rubio-Marín R (ed) What happened to the women: gender and reparations for human rights violations. Social Science Research Council, New York
Ross F (2003) Bearing witness: women and the truth and reconciliation commission in South Africa. Pluto, London
Ross F (2006) An acknowledged failure: women, voice, violence and the South African truth commission (unpublished paper)
Schmeidl S, Piza-Lopez E (2002) Gender and conflict early warning: a framework for action. International Alert / Swiss Peace Foundation, London/Bern
Spees P (2004) Gender justice and accountability in peace support operations. International Alert, London. Available at http://www.international-alert.org/pdfs/gender_justice_accountability_peace_operations.pdf
Stern M, Nystrand M (2006) Gender and armed conflict. SIDA, Stockholm
World Bank (2006) Gender, Justice, and Truth Commission. June 2006

Linking Mediation and Transitional Justice: The Use of Interest-Based Mediation in Processes of Transition*

Lars Kirchhoff

Abstract The aims of this paper are, on the one hand, to further develop and define the relationship between the challenges of transitional justice and different models of mediation and, on the other hand, to illustrate the anatomy of one particular mediation model. It will be discussed which mediation styles and techniques can be employed in the international arena – and what role mediation can play in dealing with the different areas of transitional justice and in designing the larger framework of transition processes. In addition, the paper will offer recommendations on how to elicit and integrate the specific (and potentially conflicting) interests of both the direct parties and the international community during the design of transition processes.

1 Introduction

The prevalence of the term *mediation* in essays and discussions on *transitional justice* implies a close connection between these two concepts. But precisely how may the relationship between transitional justice[1] and mediation[2] be defined, considering that transitional justice consists of a wide range of processes which serve to promote such generic goals as peace, human rights, the rule of law, and

L. Kirchhoff
Institute for Conflict Management, Center for Peace Mediation, Berlin, European University Viadrina, Große Scharrnstr. 59, 15230 Frankfurt/Oder, Germany
e-mail: Kirchhoff@euv-frankfurt-o.de

*Parts of this work have been published in Lars Kirchhoff, Constructive Interventions (Kluwer Law International, The Hague, 2008).

[1] Transitional justice is understood here as comprising the full range of processes and mechanisms associated with a society's attempt to come to terms with past abuses in order to ensure accountability, serve justice, and achieve reconciliation; see UNSC (2004).

[2] In its broadest sense, mediation is understood as a process carried out by an acceptable intermediary who actively supports the parties in negotiating an agreement.

K. Ambos et al. (eds.), *Building a Future on Peace and Justice: Studies on Transitional Justice, Peace and Development.*

reconciliation, while mediation is often perceived as one particular technique to resolve concrete conflicts?

As correctly observed by David Bloomfield (2005, p. 57), the sophisticated debate on peace and justice implies a whole "series of complex questions which arise when we start to unpack the dense concepts of justice, truth, reconciliation, human rights, and peace in a post-violence context." The fundamental insights that justice is merely one aspect of a many-faceted approach needed to secure enduring peace in a transitional society (Goldstone 1996, p. 485, 486) and that the goals of justice and reconciliation might compete, illustrate an inherent tension that poses a number of abstract moral questions and, at the same time, defines highly practical tasks for all actors involved.

Compromises, resulting from the need to strike the right balance between conflicting interests, are necessary elements of coping with conflict on a societal level in a period of transition. Mediation has a lot to offer in facilitating the tension underlying these bargaining processes because it can help to disentangle the knot of interests and needs in a structured and efficient way. The good news about mediation is that it is internationally recognized as a highly promising instrument to broker peace. Often enough, specific power resources of the mediator render success possible. The bad news is that, in some instances, a mediated peace might be achieved at the cost of compromising justice, often related with another source of power, namely that of the parties, and especially when in the hands of the former perpetrators.

Against that background, one might assume that this paper is about power in mediation, reflecting the status quo on the debate and practice of power-oriented mediation approaches. Instead, this research will focus on a model of mediation which, in my view, is almost naturally connected with transitional justice: that of interest-based, facilitative mediation. In essence, transitional justice is all about conflicting interests. Therefore a mediation model that offers a social space as well as an elaborated communication structure (and distribution of roles) which helps to elicit and creatively reconcile existing interests should be a primary tool in the area of transitional justice.

The aim of this essay is to contribute to – and provide an analytical framework for – the further debate on the precise mandate of a mediator in the context of transitional justice and, accordingly, on the roles and techniques that should be used. Instead of focusing on case studies, the paper will consider rather abstract parameters of mediation and transitional justice. It will demonstrate how the model of interest-based, facilitative mediation, exercised with clear references to international law, can meet the various challenges of transitional justice. The paper explains the process of this particular mediation model (Sect. 2) and suggests areas of operation within the wide field of transitional justice (Sect. 3). By way of illustration, the paper will briefly discuss which categories of interests tend to be involved as well as why and how they need to be prioritised (Sect. 4). Finally, conclusions will be presented as well as a number of policy recommendations on how to realize the full potential of mediation in the field of transitional justice (Sect. 5). A short executive summary will follow (Sect. 6).

2 Mediation Models and Styles: Interest-Based, Facilitative Mediation

2.1 A Word on Mediation

The decision to focus on one particular method – mediation – for the purposes of this investigation has been taken for a number of reasons. The most obvious one is the practical relevance and frequent occurrence of mediation efforts in conflict as well as post-conflict situations during the post-World War II period. More importantly, substantial interdisciplinary research has been conducted in the field of international mediation (for an overview see Bercovitch 2002, p. 4) in order to structure and categorise its parameters – conflict resolution in general and mediation in particular have developed from an "art" to a veritable "science".[3] Finally, and most decisively, the specific nature of the mediation procedure makes it a useful topical focus in the context of transitional justice: when compared to inquiry, arbitration or other processes, mediation represents a genuinely different procedural approach in the resolution of conflicts: Unlike inquiry, its declared goal is the resolution of the conflict; unlike arbitration, it does not include binding elements. In its very essence, mediation maximizes the autonomy, sovereignty, and dignity of the conflict actors involved – aims that are closely connected with those of transitional justice.

2.2 Some More Words on Mediation Models

> [A]s long as analysts remain unaware of the existence of the models and their attendant evaluation criteria, they are likely to focus on different sets of indicators while debating the outcomes of one and the same mediation effort. In this case, the scope for confusion between them is large. This changes when they make explicit their ways of looking. Misunderstandings and confusion will give way to clear-cut differences in perspective and normative debates become more transparent. (Kleiboer 1998, p. 192)

For a scholar in the field of international mediation, it is surprising to note to which degree commentators neglect the existence of different analytical models of mediation and, instead, claim that the observed differences simply follow from the concrete case and, in particular, have their source in the respective personalities of the intermediaries (Kolb and Babbitt 1995, pp. 63–64). This approach of "personalizing" mediation is closely related to the perception of mediation as a secret, personal "art" – a view that is emphatically rejected in this paper. The mere fact that in international affairs most actors never have to reveal what they do (Princen 1992, p. 29) and which particular form of mediation they practice does not refute the existence of different models in the first place. As pointed out by Christine Bell, there might be a certain degree of attractiveness to the current state of uncertainty surrounding the task, role, and mandate of mediators. However, I argue that there will

[3] Menkel-Meadow (2003, p. xxi); stressing that conflict resolution involves both behavioral (art) and cognitive (science) components.

be only limited opportunities for meaningful guidelines or codes of conduct for intermediaries as long as there is no transparency and minimum consensus as to what mediators actually do – and as to where the limits of their flexibility lie. As a starting point, three authors and their respective approaches shall briefly be presented (Kirchhoff 2008).

2.2.1 Touval/Zartman

Touval and Zartman, as further elaborated in a joint empirical study on mediating international crises (Wilkenfeld et al. 2003, p. 279), differentiate between three concepts of mediation: the mediator as *facilitator*, the mediator as *formulator*, and the mediator as *manipulator*. This typology is based on the classification of three mediator strategies which are categorized on an ascending level of involvement (see also Touval and Zartman 2001, p. 435).

Facilitation: In facilitative mediation, the mediator primarily serves as a channel of communication. He focuses on the process, organizes the logistics, collects information, delivers messages between parties if face-to-face communication is not possible, and gathers the parties' concessions to help them create a package deal. The facilitative mediator declines to make substantive contributions to the solution, but ensures constructive dialogue between the disputants.

Formulation: Unlike the facilitative mediator, the mediator as formulator is required to enter into the substance of the conflict. She makes substantive contributions to the resolution process, including the development and proposal of new resolution options. At the same time, the mediator as formulator is not in a position to push the conflict actors to endorse any particular outcome, or even to advocate the outcome favoured by her.

Manipulation: The manipulative mediator has all the powers of the formulator and, in addition, he uses his position and leverage to manipulate the parties into agreement. He assumes the maximum degree of involvement by applying his power, influence and persuasion, eventually becoming a veritable party to the conflict, making use of his capacity to add or subtract benefits to or from the solution (and the parties).

> When the obstacle to agreement is the seemingly paltry size of the outcome, the mediator must persuade the parties of his vision of a solution; he must then take measures to make the solution attractive, enhancing its value by adding benefits to its outcome and presenting it in such a way as to overcome imbalances that may have prevented one of the parties from subscribing to it. The mediator may have to go so far as to improve the absolute attractiveness of the resolution by increasing the unattractiveness of continued conflict. (Touval and Zartman 2001, p. 436)

2.2.2 Marieke Kleiboer

Throughout her excellent study analyzing the various "realities" of mediation in the international context, Marieke Kleiboer (1998, p. 186) differentiates between a number of forms of international mediation, being complementary rather than competing in nature. These include the *power-brokerage model*, the *domination model*, the *political problem-solving model*, and the *transformative model*. For each of the paradigms, Kleiboer generates a theoretical ideal type, adopting each model's jargon and linguistic style.

Power-Brokerage: According to what Kleiboer calls the power-brokerage model, the arena of international politics is characterized as essentially conflictual, with interests clashing as a result of a competition for scarce resources. In this world of actors seeking to safeguard their interests in a rather anarchical environment, the rational pursuit of own interests is the primary justification for all action. With conflict being inherent to the system, the elimination of the underlying causes of conflict is an impossible task. The implications of these general perceptions for mediation are far-reaching: The process of a particular conflict is not analyzed as for its own dynamics, but as a mere reflection of the general power structure of the international system and the actors' positions within it. The crucial resources for a mediator are power and the skills to enforce her strategies and ideas through promised rewards or sanctions.

Domination: According to the domination model, international conflict is endemic to the international system. It has led to institutionalized inequalities and dependencies between central and peripheral forces within and between actors. As no mediator can possibly have the necessary economic or political power required to force structural changes, international mediation is seen as a form of domination, "a practice initiated or supported by powers from the centre to suppress peripheries and protect and maintain the international economic and political status quo" (Kleiboer 1998, p. 188).

Problem-Solving: According to the problem-solving model, international conflict is a contingent result of dynamics in the interplay between actors. This approach is based on a more constructive perception of conflict: Conflict arises when actors experience or perceive incompatibilities between their respective goals and values. This approach to mediation recognises the theoretical possibility of conflict resolution – there is no prima-facie reason why a complete resolution of a conflict should be impossible. The mediator's role can be played by any well-informed, established actor with sufficient knowledge of the personalities and belief systems of the parties.

Transformative: According to the line of thought underlying the transformative (restructuring relationships) model of international mediation, conflict is regarded as a "result of the frustration of basic human needs in institutional arrangements perceived by some groups to be unequal, unjust, or illegitimate" (Kleiboer 1998, p. 188). Conflict is perceived more positively, as an opportunity to transform the political arena so as to increase the satisfaction of all discontent parties and to restructure or even transform the relationships involved.

2.2.3 Conny Peck

Another useful categorization within the field of conflict resolution – and resulting international mediation models – can be gleaned from the work of Conny Peck.

The essential categories she uses are the *power-based approach*, the *rights-based approach*, and the *interest-based approach* (Peck 1996, p. 10).

Power-Based: In the *power-based* approach, the conflict and its resolution process is essentially characterized by the attempt to determine who is most powerful. Power relevant to the conflict resolution can be exercised both by the original actors to a conflict and by those who serve as intermediaries during the process of resolution.

Rights-Based: In the *rights-based* approach, the central feature is the determination of who is entitled to certain rights or who is right according to a specified standard. International law is the standard most commonly used. Rights-based approaches to conflict resolution are not necessarily confined to adjudicative tribunals; instead, the application of rights-based standards can occur in arbitrations, mediations, and negotiations. Illustrating this approach, it is evident that blanket amnesties would not serve as bargaining chips in the hands of intermediaries acting according to this rights-based approach.

Interest-Based: Interest-based approaches to conflict resolution focus on the identification and creative response to the essential interests underlying a given scenario. *Interest-based* approaches attempt to reconcile the existing interests by creating solutions which will bridge the different perceptions and aspirations of the parties in a way satisfactory to all.

2.2.4 Observations

This short portrayal of different models of categorizing mediation suffices to illustrate the wide range of the spectrum. Significant overlaps as to the question of which parameters constitute the basic structure of a mediation model can be observed. One such parameter is the question of *power applied by the mediator*, i.e., the question of how much leverage and control is present during the mediation process. A second parameter is the *depth and direction of the conflict resolution approach*, i.e., the question of the role the underlying causes play and of how the restructuring or transformation of the topics is dealt with. A third parameter concerns the question of which *category and number of participants* are chosen for the mediation process, an aspect closely connected with the mediation model in operation.

What is the relevance for the practical purpose of this paper? Each presented model contains the "seeds for a set of policy recommendations to policymakers and (potential) mediators" (Kleiboer 1998, p. 198). If no clear decision is taken for or against a particular mediation approach, the resulting randomness will undermine the efficiency of the process. One recommendation to potential mediators results from the existence of a "proportionality principle": the bigger the power and control element on either side of those involved in a mediation, the less likely it is that deeper, underlying interests and causes will be addressed during the mediation process. Pressure of any kind hampers, rather than encourages, the articulation of interests, which are the building blocks for holistic solutions. As worthwhile as power in the hands of an intermediary may be, for example, to silence guns, as detrimental this very same power can be when it comes to re-establishing trust and restructuring a society.

Another recommendation concerns the question of whether the mediator should enter into the substance of the conflict. As exemplified especially in the categorization of Touval and Zartman, the difference between the mediator as *facilitator* and the mediator as *formulator/manipulator* is significant, especially with regard to the expectations and the ensuing behaviour of the parties. In a context where the authenticity of the conflict parties' perspectives serves as the main safeguard for the sustainability of an agreement, the mediator should in many cases leave the complete responsibility for the substance of the solution in the hands of the parties (as long as this path is compatible with the legal cornerstones of the international arena).

2.3 Mediation and Transitional Justice

This paper argues that different mediation models – each of which deserves a prominent role in international politics – can deal with the specific challenges within the field of transitional justice to widely varying degrees. What is needed in this context is a mechanism that encourages and supports the process of acknowledgment and healing and, at the same time, proves to be result-oriented. The adequate mediation model must offer a structure that manages to prioritize conflicting interests, including those of the international community, without suppressing the articulation of diverging motivations of actors who might otherwise sabotage the process.

In this specific context, one model of intermediary action can be particularly suited to realize the full potential of mediation. Speaking in the terminology of Conny Peck, the basis of the mediation approach in transition processes should be interest-oriented; essential elements of rights-based approaches should be integrated to define the legal limits of mediated agreements, while power and manipulation elements should be categorically excluded. Therefore, while fully acknowledging the role of other mediation models within the contingency model of international conflict resolution, the next part of this paper will be dedicated to the explanation and application of interest-based, facilitative mediation to the context investigated.

2.4 Model of Interest-Based, Facilitative Mediation

A comprehensive introduction to what a mediator working with this model actually does would include the description of possible phase models,[4] roles, and techniques used by the mediator. This short paper can only provide a definition of the concepts of focus on interests and on the potential of options as well as of facilitative style.

[4] An example for a phase model can be found at Mitchell (1993).

2.4.1 Focus on Interests

The heart of the process of interest-based mediation is dedicated exclusively to eliciting and formulating interests. An "interest" is, in this context, the specific, individual aspiration of an actor that fuels its behaviour in a given situation. The definition of the term interest[5] includes, in addition to legally recognized interests, moral, ideological, economic, religious, regional, political interests, or a combination of these.

Accordingly, a mediation process with a focus on interests investigates the distinction between *what* is sought by a given actor – and what actually motivates what is sought, and focuses on the latter. Investing substantial time and energy to systematically explore the individual interests underlying the positions formulated by the parties is one of the essential distinguishing marks between the mediation model examined in this paper and more power-oriented mediation models. The difficulty and the eminence of the exploration of interests, in an effort to develop empathy for all actors involved, can be illustrated by an interview taken from the *International Herald Tribune*, conducted with chief Israeli and Palestinian negotiators:

> Disengaging Israelis and Arabs from the West bank touched so many deep-seated passions, taboos and paranoia on each side – religious, cultural, historical, psychological – that pragmatism was not enough, said Mr. Savir. (...) Gradually the sparring gave way to understanding. Abu Alaa and his team came to understand that Israel's obsession with security was not just a negotiating tactic, and they learned to appreciate the domestic political pressure on Mr. Rabin. Mr. Savir and the Israelis began to understand the importance to the Arabs of maintaining dignity and to appreciate the humiliation of occupation. 'Everything that was security for us was dignity for them', Mr. Savir said, summarizing many a dispute. (Peck 1996, p. 39)

The mediator has to assure that the interests of all relevant actors are carefully analyzed so that for each of them, a comprehensive profile of interests can be elaborated. The resulting profiles of interests are likely to include, for example, a sophisticated combination of personal or strategic interests (with regard to economic or security issues), governance interests (for example to support norms related to transparency and good governance), and humanitarian interests (including ethical imperatives for action). Later in this paper, a matrix of possible interests in scenarios of transitional justice will be elaborated (see part D).

2.4.2 Focus on the Potential of Options

The multiplicity of interrelated topics to be dealt with in post-conflict societies highlights the significance of value creation and issue linkages during transition processes. The creative stages of a mediation provide a useful procedural space for this task: Once the parties have stated their concrete positions, ascertained information, and identified underlying interests, the mediator supports the process of

[5] As formulated in the *Dictionnaire de la terminologie du droit international* (International Union of Academies 1960, p. 342): Terme désignant ce qui affecte matériellement ou moralement une personne physique ou juridique, l'avantage matériel or morale que présente pour elle une action ou une abstention, le maintien ou le changement d'une situation.

developing options. In doing so, it is vital to explore the full range of possibilities with the direct involvement of the parties who are affected by the proposals. The mediator needs to counteract the tendency of any party to discard valuable options simply because they spontaneously consider them to be ultimately unacceptable. To avoid this, it is best for the parties first to collect multiple options without evaluating them. By deferring judgment on any option to a later stage, the invention of more creative solutions is encouraged. While creativity should be the guiding principle in generating options, caution should be exercised when actually choosing the most suitable ones among them. For the context of transitional justice, the limits of flexibility when choosing options will be examined below (see Sect. 4.3).

2.4.3 Facilitative Style

The facilitative style of mediation implies that the mediator neither uses power techniques nor evaluates the scenario according to her own values and preferences. Facilitation as understood in this paper, however, does not keep the mediator from formulating, along with the parties, resolution options,[6] as long as she does not try to convince the parties of the merits of her own proposals.

2.4.4 Resulting Mediator Roles and Techniques

The spectrum of adequate mediator roles and techniques depends on the respective model of mediation. The following compilation of aspects is specific to the interest-based mediation model.[7]

Process Chairman: Within the interest-based, facilitative mediation model, the mediator has full process control but no outcome control. By exercising process control, the mediator can change the dynamics through reconfiguring the structure of the bargain, he can control the pace and formality of meetings as well as the physical environment in which the process takes place. He establishes the protocol, suggests procedures, controls the timing and structures the agenda.

Communication Facilitator: In his role as facilitator of communication, the mediator identifies issues and gathers information, helps to clarify facts, to provide missing information and thereby to determine whether or not sufficient bargaining space exists.

Formulator of Interests: Given the high relevance of interests in this model of mediation, both eliciting and formulating these interests is one of the most crucial functions of the mediator.[8] Eliciting interests as well as accurately formulat-

---

[6] In order to avoid misunderstandings: facilitative mediation as understood here includes elements from both facilitation and formulation in accordance with the model by Zartman and Touval described above.

[7] For further elaboration on some of these roles, see Hopmann (1996, pp. 230–234).

[8] For the practical aspects of this task, see Eidenmüller 2003, p. 155).

ing those interests under conditions of conflict pressure can be highly sensitive and challenging tasks.

Facilitator of Cognitive Change: The study *Barriers to Conflict Resolution* (Arrow et al. 1995) identifies cognitive barriers as a valuable explanation why negotiations fail so often – even where some of the possible options would obviously serve the disputants' goals. Especially post-violence peace-building means "dealing with a complex area of human activity which by its very nature involves a degree of confused, illogical and contradictory thinking and behaviour" (Bloomfield 2005, p. 59) and therefore underlines the role of the intermediary as facilitator of cognitive change. Above all, it requires a substantial cognitive change for the parties of transition processes to quit the pattern of perceiving one another as enemies (Hopmann 1996, p. 234) and to instead view each other as partners faced with the task to jointly rebuild a society. The interactive nature of mediation provides an excellent framework for dealing with these cognitive barriers.

Agent of Reality: This role is most important in situations where stalemate is caused more by different or wrong perceptions of the same issues or other psychological factors, rather than by conflicts of interests. A mediator can help to dissolve psychological distancing, such as stereotyping, scapegoating, and partisan perceptions, and ensure that all actors have a more rational perception of the threat or value potential of a given scenario. He can also be supportive in separating negotiable from non-negotiable issues, a point which will be further elaborated under Section 5.

Provider of Creativity: Another essential role of the mediator is that of supporting parties in the generation and subsequent selection of options during the process of finding the proper solution. The application of brainstorming methods, the creation of an atmosphere where it is possible to develop ideas without instantaneously committing to them, is a role genuinely attributed to the mediator. It can also be his task to suggest ways of creating more space for bargaining, i.e., through possible issue linkages (Hopmann 1996, p. 231).

2.4.5 Model-Specific Limits of the Mediator's Role

In order to ensure the clear communication of the mediation model under investigation, it is essential to mention which roles and techniques the mediator should actually *not* employ when applying this model.

Integrating Own Interests: The tendency of many international mediators to – explicitly or implicitly – integrate own interests into the process can pose a threat to the mediation success. The fact that the mediator articulates own interests can easily lead to the perception of one or more parties that the mediator is biased and favours one specific solution. Combined with the fact that he might use his process control to emphasize his own interests, he loses his greatest asset – the trust of the parties in his impartiality.

Representing (Absent) Parties: Parties absent from the negotiating table pose another challenge to interest-based, facilitative mediation processes. In the very moment where the mediator starts to speak for one particular actor, absent or present, the clarity of role central to the performance of the mediator's task is endangered.

Rewarding and Sanctioning: Both positive and negative stimuli presented by the mediator – in other words carrots as well as sticks – involve the danger that parties feel manipulated into agreement. Of course, assets in the form of money or economic support will be distributed in many post-conflict processes, but these resources should not be closely connected with the person of the mediator.

3 Areas of Application

Evidently, in transition processes, intermediary action in general and mediation initiatives in particular can have many forms – reaching from short mediated conversations between victims and perpetrators to comprehensive design processes for institutional reforms with the involvement of dozens of actors. With regard to interest-based, facilitative mediation in transition processes, two concrete areas of application are illustrated in the following: that of mediating particular elements of rebuilding a society, and that of designing the overall framework of intervention.

3.1 Mediating Peace and Justice

In an effort to roughly sketch some areas where interest-based, facilitative mediation can make a significant contribution in transition processes, and being fully aware of the discussions surrounding the "catch-all phrase"[9] reconciliation, this expression can nevertheless serve as the adequate umbrella term for the larger process of rebuilding relationships between actors alienated by violence. According to Bloomfield (2005, p. 62), in the context of transitional justice processes, reconciliation has the following ingredients:

- A justice process that punishes past violence and deters future repetition; justice that is built on human rights principles, democratic practice, and international legal norms; and social justice in the distribution of social goods that promises fairness for all in the future.
- A process of acknowledging experiences, uncovering unknown events, giving voice to the previously unheard, and addressing interpretations of history, often referred to as truth-seeking or truth-finding.
- A process of healing, whereby victims repair their lives by coming to terms with their suffering.
- A process of reparation through real and/or symbolic compensation for loss.

[9] Bleeker (2005, p. 162), stressing that due to its religious connotations, it is essential to define a precise, context-specific meaning.

Against that background, also paying tribute to the observation that there exists "increasing consensus around a view which holds that transitional justice has four main pillars: establishing the facts, justice, reparations, and institutional reforms" (Bleeker 2005, p. 161), the possible roles of mediation in processes of transition can be described as follows.

3.1.1 Role of Mediation in the Justice Process

It is an essential task within the field of transitional justice to mediate between the differing and potentially conflicting aspects of a wider concept of justice (Bloomfield 2005, p. 60). This wider concept of justice contains but is not limited to retributive justice (focusing on the offender), restorative justice (focusing on the victim), moral and social justice (focusing on shared concepts of fairness), and distributive justice (focusing on the fair sharing of goods). While the application of some of these facets of justice can be subject to individual bargaining processes, other components are non-negotiable. A mediator can make a substantial contribution to the peace process by disentangling these elements and clarifying which weight or priority should be attributed to the respective elements of justice during the various periods of a transition process.

3.1.2 Role of Mediation in Establishing Facts

Truth-finding cannot be mediated. Therefore, the process of mediation can only be of indirect help during the task of uncovering past events. The eminent task of establishing facts is much better served under the auspices of truth commissions. In addition, the activities of international criminal tribunals must be embedded in the overall strategy of truth-finding. Only as a second step, when it comes to the acknowledgement of experiences and the interpretation of the subjective perception of history, mediation processes can be supportive. The interactive character and the direct contact with the perceptions, underlying interests, and suggested options of the involved parties can significantly facilitate the necessary step of acknowledging the possibility of different perceptions of the same facts and events.

3.1.3 Role of Mediation in Determining Reparations

Additional processes of balancing and interest-based bargaining in which mediators can be highly useful are those concerning questions of reparation. One essential challenge in the practice of providing reparations to victims is that the task of repairing harm cannot be fulfilled in a collective fashion, but, rather, is an individualistic undertaking. The adequate provision of benefits demands a systematic and transparent exploration of the interest structure of the actors on behalf of which reparation measures are taken. Two additional aspects complicate things: First, the "impossibility of compensating victims in proportion to the harm they have suffered",[10] and second, the pressure to award reparations in a systematic fashion which lives up to standards of fairness in the eyes of all actors involved, including those victims that cannot be compensated but nevertheless strive for a measure of recognition. Reconciling these interests is a task that can efficiently be approached through mediation processes. Insights gained in domestic judicial systems in the context of victim-offender-mediation[11] prove that determining the adequate reparation from the range of possible material and symbolic benefits can only be done on a case-by-case basis. As pointed out by de Greiff (2005, p. 54), in order to avoid the impression that reparations constitute the currency with which the state tries to buy the silence of victims, open, deliberative, and participatory processes must be designed. The suggestion is to design these processes, including the coordination of individual reparation measures in the overall reparation program, according to the interest-based approach introduced above.

3.1.4 Role of Mediation in the Process of Healing

Every process of healing is, by definition, highly individual; even the widespread assumption that it takes considerable time until a healing process is accomplished does not necessarily apply to all cases. Unlike formal mechanisms such as trials, an informal mechanism such as mediation depends on the direct contact between the involved actors, often including emotional responses and non-verbal manifestations which can accelerate healing processes significantly. Unlike power-based mediation techniques (which, due to the possible effect of feeling *manipulated into* rather than *autonomously elaborating* an agreement, might even increase the impression of victimization), mediation practiced in the facilitative style allows all participants to uphold their sovereignty and dignity – or even re-establish it through the participation in the autonomous act of decision-making. Mediation itself can, therefore, be a significant building-block in the healing process.

3.1.5 Role of Mediation in Institutional Reforms

Finally, interest-based mediation can support the process of institutional reform. After the loss of confidence in the functioning of authorities and institutions in the aftermath of conflict, mediation techniques can be useful when integrating the potentially conflicting interests of various society actors into one process of institutional design.

---

[10] See de Greiff (2005, p. 51), referring to de Greiff (2006).

[11] For a recent contribution see Umbreit et al. (2005).

3.2 Mediating the Framework of Intervention

In addition, mediation can be used for elaborating the framework of intervention. The fields of coordinating the actors and "designing" the adequate process in cooperation with those primarily affected by its results – instead of this decisive course of action being determined from the outside – bear great promise for the success of the transition.

3.2.1 Coordinating the Actors

The country-specific context has a crucial impact on attempts of designing transitional justice programs. Relevant factors include the regime's and the opposition's level of legitimacy, the strength and shape of civil society, and the presence of international actors. During the configuration of the framework of any transitional justice program, any lack of coherence and effective coordination between external players can threaten the success of the process. As actors may duplicate, if not actually undermine each other's efforts, developing an adequate response in post-conflict situations requires a comprehensive act of coordination between governments, non-governmental organizations, civil society, and international organizations. This task may include the weighing and bargaining of priorities and the allocation of money according to conflicting donors' agendas as well as according to urgent needs of the populations or institutions involved. In addition, given the multiplicity of actors interested in the fate of societies in transition, the number of possible intermediaries and the possibility of multi-channel mediations, the sophisticated coordination between these framework actors and their respective motivations is essential. Mediating between those willing to mediate should be done according to an interest-based rather than power-based model.

3.2.2 Designing the Process

The flexibility of the mediation process makes it possible to actively discuss the suggested "process design" with the participants and adapt the design according to the particular interests elaborated. For example, it should be discussed and negotiated with the parties whether all relevant actors are present, or whether the interests of additional parties might become so relevant that their presence would be necessary. Especially in sensitive situations it might be useful to start the transition process with a small group of participants on the track two level and, as a second step, invite representatives on a more formal level once the agenda has been clarified. Another question that has to be discussed is the definition of what will constitute agreement in the absence of pre-defined decision-making rules. Although the basis is the assumption that all decisions require unanimity, other options should be discussed especially in processes involving a large number of parties. Steps of the process have to be sequenced and specific transitional justice mechanisms have to be coordinated.

4 Eliciting Interests and Defining Priorities

The following section of the paper shall illustrate the actual heart of interest-based mediation processes: the spectrum and diversity of interests that have to be taken into account when mediating the tensions between peace and justice in transitional societies.

4.1 Matrix of Interests

A brief delineation of possible profiles of interests underlying mediation processes shall serve three purposes: stressing that interests can be competitive as well as non-competitive in nature, illustrating how flexible the task of eliciting interests must be approached, and explaining how a focus on interests defines the methodological course of action of the mediator. For the purpose of illustration, being well aware that the dividing line between some of the categories can be blurred, potential interests of the individual victims, the society in transition, the international community, and the former perpetrators are presented.

4.1.1 Interests of the Individual Victims

I would like to start my short investigation into the possible interest structures and profiles of former victims by putting a question mark behind the statement that victims "understandably gain a sense of satisfaction when they see their perpetrators punished in the name of society" (Bloomfield 2005, p. 60). This may, but need not necessarily be true. The interests of individual victims show significant differences; acts that trigger satisfaction in one victim might trigger disgust in another person. The exploration of the past can be an essential part of a healing process for one person but result in further victimization in the case of his neighbour.

It can, however, be safely assumed that the following interests will be among those essential to most victims:

- Recognition as bearers of equal rights
- Solidifying the status of victims not as victims, but rather as citizens
- Reception of some form of reparation (meaning the provision of benefits of whichever nature)
- Receiving respect for the intimate and personal character of dealing with the status as victim, including the deconstruction of expectations to forgive the perpetrators

Interests that may differ significantly (or may be completely absent) include:

- Desiring revenge (for example by seeing the perpetrator punished and excluded from societal relationships)
- Maximizing transparency and knowledge with regard to the own past, e.g., by offering names and precise acts of offenders

- Defining the adequate degree of contact with the perpetrator (on a spectrum between establishing a personal encounter or completely avoiding contact)

4.1.2 Interests of the Society in Transition

Intermediaries in transitional processes must deliver to the populations and societies. Given that each society consists of a significant number of entities and subsections (the interests of which might be divergent or complementary in character), comments on interest profiles of transitional societies are of a particularly speculative nature. In any event, it is decisive to perceive the society in transition as the bearer of its own and specific interests. Again, a set of interests likely to be present in transitional societies can be detected:

- Ensuring some form of collective memory of the events with tools of participatory remembrance (from collections of data to monuments and memorial days)
- Improving community life and rebuilding the social fabric
- Strengthening the political will and increasing local ownership
- Supporting the emergence of a culture of non-violent management of conflicts
- Discouraging future human rights violations
- Establishing new leadership and working military
- Reconstructing trust in institutions
- Establishing structures for a smooth functioning of the society, including the suppression of organized crime and prosecution of criminals
- Supporting domestic reform constituencies

When eliciting the interests of societies in transition, it is particularly relevant to adequately acknowledge the specific political, cultural and social context in order to avoid an attitude of overbearing universalism. If the profile of interests is not carefully analyzed, criticism of transitional justice as a formal, predetermined, almost imperialistic mechanism imposed by the Western world can be more than justified. Examples for these possible, highly individualistic interests include:

- Defining and limiting the role of external players' intervention (for example, confining it to a specific arena)
- Deciding about the degree of commitment to a democratic future
- Defining a new national ethos (which may or may not be in accordance with the general value system of the international community)
- Establishing respect for the nature and structure of the country's legal system, traditions, and institutions

4.1.3 Interests of the International Community

As the norms of sovereignty have changed, the perception of what constitutes an international as opposed to a domestic concern has changed as well (Cronin 2002, p. 147). The international community – abstractly defined as "an ensemble of rules, procedures and mechanisms designed to protect collective interests, based on a perception of commonly shared values" (Tomuschat 2001, p. 88) – has emerged not only as an abstract concept, but as a veritable actor, as an interested third party to international transactions. More concretely, situations exist in which the goals of the international community and the other actors' goals may not be aligned, which illustrates that in transition processes, interests of the international community may be at stake that by far exceed the mere interest in peace as such:

- Shielding the international system from further transaction costs of a conflict
- Preserving and developing the universally accepted basic norms in the areas of human rights
- Clarifying the role of ad-hoc criminal tribunals and the International Criminal Court
- Holding individuals accountable for serious crimes in order to prevent or at least discourage future human rights violations and to further establish the rule of law
- Establishing respect for and trust in the agencies of the international community involved in the process of transitional justice
- Creating precedents for future transition processes with the involvement of the international community
- Respecting, incorporating and applying international standards for fairness, due process and human rights in the administration of justice
- Supporting the emergence of a culture of non-violent management of conflicts
- Preserving the close-knit network between the various international actors involved in the processes of transitional justice
- Identifying the general role of the United Nations in peace operations

4.1.4 Interests of Former Perpetrators

Due to their considerable relevance during peace negotiations, a fourth group should be prominently mentioned, namely that of the former perpetrators. Interests relevant for this group of actors include:

- Restoring the dignity of the perpetrators (Lindenmann 2005, p. 133)
- Receiving attention for the intimate and personal character of dealing with the status as perpetrator and the changed status and reputation in society
- Ensuring the application of just and fair patterns and mechanisms for allocating guilt and punishment

Again, the interest profiles of the perpetrators can differ widely. Some of those more individualistic interests are:

- Determining a suitable degree of transparency and knowledge with regard to the own past (which can mean an interest in systematically exploring one's motives and the fate of the victims of one's actions or in turning the page as fast as possible, leaving the past in complete darkness)

- Defining an adequate degree of contact with the victim(s) (again, on a spectrum between establishing a direct encounter or completely avoiding contact)
- Defining a new status in the society that is compatible with the existing measure of self-esteem as well as with the perceived degree of guilt

4.2 Observations

Three observations shall be made. The first regards the fact that, with the exception of the clear-cut universal interests of the international community, profiles of interests have to be analyzed on a case-by-case basis. This underlines the necessity to employ communication and mediation methods which can elicit interests and support individuals and societal actors in formulating their perspective on past events and current preferences. Secondly, it can be observed that the international community has a whole number of genuine interests when being involved in processes of transitional justice, some of which are not shared by any other actor. To make this point more graspable: the individual citizen cannot be expected to understand or even share the interest in fostering the legal foundation of the international community. And thirdly, it becomes evident that, while some interests are compatible or could easily be combined if some creativity is injected in the negotiating process, others are clearly competitive in nature. Therefore, one of the essential questions is how to prioritise these interests.

4.3 Prioritising Competing Interests

Once the specific profiles of interest (including those of the victims and perpetrators, of the society in transition and of the international community) have been elaborated and matching options been generated, two priorities must be closely observed. First, there must be an overriding focus on the interests of the victims as compared to those of the perpetrators, and second, the most fundamental interests of the international community cannot be subject to any deal-making and negotiation – they have an overriding character with regard to all other interests involved.

4.3.1 Focus on Victims' Interests

It may well be argued that in situations where interests of victims and interests of perpetrators collide, those of the victims should prevail. This principle is likely to find application with regard to questions like access to information as well as to the establishment *vel non* of direct contact between victims and perpetrators.

4.3.2 Overriding Status of International Community's Interests

The following, ambivalent statement by Juan Méndez (2005, p. 17) can be seen as quite telling when it comes to defining the status of (international) law:

> International law and the practice of states and international organizations provide guidelines to policymakers in framing the questions that a peace process must address. This is not to say that mediators cannot use their own discretion in offering incentives at the negotiating table. The law provides a framework, not a straightjacket. Even so, there are ethical and legal limits to the pursuit of peace, beyond which peace may be little more than silencing of the guns, without justice.

Although in many respects, international law provides nothing but a framework, in other respects it has started to provide a straightjacket, and this fact is of one of the most remarkable developments in the international legal arena. The international community has given an absolute quality to some fundamental norms, which cannot be subject to derogation. Despite the fact that the roots of fundamental norms of the international legal system can be traced back to natural law (Verdross 1973, p. 25), explicit, residual categories for fundamental norms only developed after the Second World War (Kleiboer 1998, p. 128). It is essential for the further development of the idea of an international community that this community is capable of enforcing its most fundamental interests and values. As clarified by Christian Tomuschat:

> The litmus test for the fruitfulness of the concept of international community must be whether, impelled by its driving forces, rules, procedures and mechanisms have been established with a view to vindicating and enforcing the common interest recognized by all States. Should nothing of specific legal significance have materialized, we would know that we still find ourselves in the antechamber of politics, waiting for the law to see the light of the day. (Tomuschat 2001, pp. 78–79)

For the context of mediation in transitional scenarios this means that blanket amnesties are simply not an option (Grono and O'Brien 2008, p. 18), and that there is a strict policy against endorsing amnesty in respect to war crimes, genocide, crimes against humanity or gross violations of human rights (UNSC 2004). Mediation in transitional justice processes has to take place in the shadow of – and with close reference to – the fundamental norms of public international law. This normative commitment to core principles has to be beyond doubt in order to ensure transparency and predictability.

5 Recommendations

It has been the declared aim of several initiatives in the field of peace and justice to conceptualize the interplay between the conflict resolution perspective, the justice/human rights perspective and the social, economic and political development perspective. This study illustrates the contribution that one specific field within the large arena of contemporary conflict resolution theory and research can offer – that of international mediation.

Consensus exists with regard to the fact that mediators should not work with templates. In essence, the task of mediators active in transitional justice processes is a twofold one: to help negotiate every single aspect of peace that actually *is* negotiable with all the creativity and methodological skills possible – and to strictly avoid and counteract negotiations about topics that are *not* negotiable. While power on the side of the mediator is not necessary for the fulfilment of the first task (in fact, pressure hampers rather than encourages the articulation of interests), power in the hands of the mediator can be even detrimental to fulfilling the second task. Only if the mediator bases his authority exclusively on the resources of legitimacy, process expertise and access to information (rather than on a system of rewards and coercion), the expectations of the parties will adapt accordingly.

The consequences are that specific models of mediation prove to be more useful than others, and that the selection of intermediaries for transition processes deserves the fullest attention and care of the international community. This short investigation into the linkages and the interplay between mediation (models) and transitional justice arrives at the following conclusions:

I. Clarity in Terms of Models and Roles in Mediation: The discussion on transitional justice would benefit from a more precise perception of the significant differences between mediation models. Some commentators and practitioners still understand mediation as a tool of foreign policy-making that is being used especially by powerful intermediaries to impose their own interests. Many others see it as a sophisticated instrument based on the principles of conflict theory and cognitive psychology, used by non-partisan third parties in order to optimize self-determined processes of conflict resolution and decision-making. The blurring of the lines between these two categories of mediation diminishes its reputation and effectiveness.

II. Focus on Interest-Based Mediation: In many instances, for ending hostilities, power-based mediation approaches are necessary. However, during the later stages of peace-building, and especially when designing transition processes, only sophisticated efforts of eliciting and observing the essential interests of all actors can ensure durable peace. In the context of transitional justice, interest-based, facilitative mediation with direct reference to the fundamental norms of international law proves to be a valid method for dealing with the tension between peace and justice and the multiple facets thereof.

III. Selection of Intermediaries:

> To understand why some parties – governmental or nongovernmental – make better mediators and are able not only to gain entry into a conflict but also to sustain a process of negotiation, we argue that one has to look beyond the kinds of resources and leverage these mediators bring to the table to their status, legitimacy, and broader political relationships with the parties concerned. (Crocker et al. 1999, p. 667)

When choosing the suitable mediator for processes in the context of transitional justice, two aspects should be observed: First, in order to ensure the self-determination of the parties, mediators should have full legitimacy but no significant power resources at their disposal if they want to engage in an authentic process of interest-based mediation. Second, to ensure neutrality and impartiality, the mediator should not have significant own interests in the substantive issues.

IV. Integration of the International Community: The international community needs to participate in mediated processes of transitional justice in a rather specific role. As shown above, there exists a whole number of situations where the international community no longer is an external entity, but a *genuine party*. In these instances, taking the role of the mediator and at the same time adequately representing the genuine interests of the international community would be a contradiction, because it would inevitably lead to role conflicts obstructive to the mediation process. Therefore, where interests of the international community are at stake, it has to be represented at the table – but not in the role of the mediator. Therefore, in these scenarios, the adequate consequence in terms of process design would be that a representative of the international community takes part in the mediation process as an additional party to the proceedings.

V. Fostering International Legal Order in Transition Processes: Justice and human rights topics may be seen by certain parties as flexible issues worth compromising. What is needed is a clear commitment to the overriding status of the fundamental rules of the international community, and clear limits to the temptation to use the exceptional nature of the case at hand as an excuse for acting against those minimum standards. A clear communication that any mediator active in transitional justice processes is bound by the core principles embodied in international law will make his work much more easy, transparent and sustainable. In transitional justice processes, flexibility finds its limits where fundamental legal norms are infringed upon. This rule, along with other moral and ethical principles, must be translated into all relevant guidelines for the practice of mediation in the field of transitional justice:

> Those who presume to intervene in the lives of others, especially in critical situations of conflict, need to consider very consciously the moral and ethical consequences of their actions. (Fisher 2004, p. 26)

In a nutshell, actors and decision-makers in the field of transitional justice should:

- Sharpen their perception of the differences between existing mediation models and focus on interest-based, facilitative approaches
- Ensure that sophisticated analyses and subsequent consideration of the interest profiles of all relevant actors are included in the mediation process and its outcome (including, but not limited to, the victims, the society, the perpetrators, and the international community), because each category of actors is in a position to sabotage the transition process if its interests are ignored
- Solidify the prohibition of amnesties in cases where fundamental norms of the international community have been violated and communicate ever more clearly that the core elements of the international legal order are not at the disposal of the mediator

6 Summary

- In the international arena, a considerable spectrum and diversity of mediation styles can be observed. Each mediation model contains the seeds for a set of recommendations to policymakers and mediators.
- For the context of transitional justice, the model of interest-based, facilitative mediation, exercised in the shadow of and with clear references to public international law, seems to be particularly useful for mediating the tension between peace and justice inherent in transition processes. The specific role of the intermediary can help to disentangle the knot of personal and collective interests involved in a structured and controlled way.
- Areas for the promising application of this mediation model include such diverse fields as the mediation of possible trade-offs between the various aspects of justice, the precise shape and distribution of adequate reparations, the coordination between the various actors willing to support the transition period, and the overall design of the peace-process.
- In addition, non-power-based mediation processes maximize the autonomy, sovereignty, and dignity of the conflict actors involved, aims closely connected with those of transitional justice, and can thereby contribute to the process of healing.
- In the heart of interest-based, facilitative mediation processes, the interests and needs of all relevant actors in post-conflict societies must be carefully analyzed so that for each of them, a comprehensive profile can be elaborated. The character and intensity of the interests of individual victims differ significantly. When eliciting the interests of a specific society in transition, it is particularly relevant to adequately acknowledge the political, cultural and social contexts in order to avoid adopting an overbearing universalism. On the side of the international community, interests may be at stake in transition processes that by far exceed the mere interest in peace as such.
- The rules for prioritizing potentially conflicting interests are straightforward: there must be a priority on the interests of the victims as compared to those of the perpetrators, and the most fundamental interests of the international community have priority over all other interests involved. For the context of mediation in transitional scenarios this means that some topics are simply not negotiable, and that there is a strict policy against endorsing amnesties in respect to war crimes, genocide, crimes against humanity or gross violations of human rights.
- All this should result in an ever more sophisticated selection both of the mediators active in the field of transitional justice and, in particular, of the methodological approaches and techniques they apply.
- Interest-based, facilitative mediation can, of course, not be the one answer to the fundamental questions arising in the context of transitional justice. But it provides a social space to bring together the relevant actors and enable a productive, joint quest for the specific answers relevant in each individual case. In essence, if transitional justice can be perceived as a "tool for shaping a new society" (Bleeker 2005, p. 160), then interest-based mediation can be seen as one essential device to further optimize and sharpen this tool.

References

Arrow KJ, Mnookin RH, Tversky A (eds) (1995) Barriers to conflict resolution. W. W. Norton, New York

Bercovitch J (2002) Introduction: putting mediation in context. In: Bercovitch J (ed) Studies in international mediation: essays in honor of Jeffrey Z. Rubin. Palgrave Macmillan, Basingstoke

Bleeker M (2005) Challenges to the implementation of transitional justice. In: Bleeker M (ed) Dealing with the past and transitional justice: creating conditions for peace, human rights and the rule of law, 24–25 October 2005. Political Affairs Division IV, Swiss Federal Department of Foreign Affairs, Bern

Bloomfield D (2005) Strategies for reconciliation: are justice and peacebuilding complementary or contradictory? In: Bleeker M (ed) Dealing with the Past and transitional justice: creating conditions for peace, human rights and the rule of law, 24–25 October 2005. Political Affairs Division IV, Swiss Federal Department of Foreign Affairs, Bern

Crocker CA, Hampson FO, Aall P (1999) Rising to the challenge of multiparty mediation. In: Crocker CA, Hampson FO, Aall P (eds) Herding cats: multiparty mediation in a complex world. United States Institute of Peace, Washington

Cronin B (2002) Multilateral intervention and the international community. In: Kerren M, Sylvan D (eds) International intervention. Frank Class, London

de Greiff P (2005) Reparations and the role of international cooperation. In: Bleeker M (eds) Dealing with the past and transitional justice: creating conditions for peace, human rights and the rule of law, 24–25 October 2005. Political Affairs Division IV, Swiss Federal Department of Foreign Affairs

de Greiff P (ed) (2006) The handbook of reparations. Oxford University Press, Oxford

Eidenmüller H (2003) Interessen verstehen und gewichten. In: Duve C, Eidenmüller H, Hacke A (eds) Mediation in der Wirtschaft. Otto Schmidt, Köln

Fisher RJ (2004) Methods of third-party intervention. In: Fischer M, Bloomfield D (eds) The Berghof handbook for conflict transformation. Berghof Research Center for Constructive Conflict Management, Berlin. http://www.berghof-handbook.net/articles/fisher_hb.pdf. Accessed 5 June 2008

Goldstone R (1996) Justice as a tool for peace-making: truth commissions and International Criminal Tribunals. NYU J Int Law Policy 28:485, 486

Grono N, O'Brien A (2008) Justice in conflict? The ICC and peace processes. In: Waddell N, Clark P (eds) Courting conflict? Justice, peace and the ICC in Africa. Royal African Society, London. http://www.crisisstates.com/download/others/ICC%20in%20Africa.pdf. Accessed 5 June 2008

Hopmann PT (1996) The negotiation process and resolution of international conflicts. University of South Carolina Press, Columbia

International Union of Academies (1960) Dictionnaire de la terminologie du droit international. Sirey, Paris, 342

Kadelbach S (1992) Zwingendes Völkerrecht. Duncker & Humblot, Berlin

Kirchhoff L (2008) Constructive interventions. Kluwer Law International, The Hague

Kleiboer M (1998) The multiple realities of international mediation. Lynne Rienner, Boulder

Kolb DM, Babbitt E (1995) Mediation practice on the home front: implications for global conflict resolution. In: Vasquez JA, Jaffe S, Johnson JT, Stamato L (eds) Beyond confrontation: learning conflict resolution in the post cold war era. University of Michigan Press, Ann Arbor, pp 63–64

Lindenmann J (2005) Transitional justice and the international criminal court. In: Bleeker M (eds) Dealing with the past and transitional justice: creating conditions for peace, human rights and the rule of law, 24–25 October 2005. Political Affairs Division IV, Swiss Federal Department of Foreign Affairs, Bern

Méndez J (2005) Peace, justice and prevention: dilemmas and false dilemmas. In: Bleeker M (ed) Dealing with the past and transitional justice: creating conditions for peace, human rights and the rule of law, 24–25 October 2005. Political Affairs Division IV, Swiss Federal Department of Foreign Affairs, Bern

Menkel-Meadow C (2003) Dispute processing and conflict resolution: theory, practice and policy. Ashgate, Aldershot

Mitchell C (1993) The process and stages of mediation: two sudanese cases. In: Smock D (ed) Making war and waging peace. United States Institute of Peace, Washington

Peck C (1996) The United Nations as a dispute settlement system. Kluwer Law International, The Hague

Princen T (1992) Intermediaries in international conflict. Princeton University Press, Princeton

Tomuschat C (2001) International law: ensuring the survival of mankind on the eve of a new century. Recueil des Cours de l'Académie de Droit International

Touval S, Zartman W (2001) International mediation in the post-cold war era. In: Crocker CA, Hampson FO, Aall P (eds) Turbulent peace – the challenges of managing international conflict. United States Institute of Peace Press, Washington, DC

UNSC (2004) The rule of law and transitional justice in conflict and post-conflict societies. Report of the Secretary-General, UN Doc S/2004/616

Umbreit MS, Coates R, Vos B (2005) Victim offender mediation: evidence-based practice over three decades. In: Moffit M, Bordone R (eds) The handbook of conflict resolution. Jossey Bass, San Francisco

Verdross A (1973) Die Quellen des universellen Völkerrechts. Rombach, Freiburg

Wilkenfeld J, Young K, Asal V, Quinn D (2003) Mediating international crises. J Conflict Resol 47:279

Part III
Specific Challenges in Pursuing Justice During or after Conflict

Pursuing Justice in Ongoing Conflict: A Discussion of Current Practice

Thomas Unger and Marieke Wierda

Abstract This study seeks to explore current practices in the pursuit of justice within a situation of active hostilities prior to a peace agreement, drawing on recent experiences in Afghanistan, Colombia, the DRC, Sierra Leone and Liberia, Sudan, Uganda, and the former Yugoslavia. In dealing specifically with the complex questions that arise from the exercise of criminal justice during conflict, the paper seeks to identify factors which govern the decisions of prosecutors, in particular regarding the question of the timing of indictments. The paper also lists the potential considerations of various constituencies on the question of delivering justice in the context of ongoing conflict, such as the interests of victims, governments, the Security Council and other UN actors, regional organisations, humanitarian organisations, traditional leaders, and mediators. Finally, the paper highlights the challenge of conducting an investigation in a situation of ongoing conflict and elaborates on steps that can be undertaken to preserve justice options for the future. Throughout the paper, reference is made to the experience of the International Criminal Court which, at the moment, only has active investigations operating in contexts of ongoing conflict, therefore placing it at the heart of this question.

1 Introduction

Prior to the 1990s, it would have been unthinkable to pursue justice claims during an ongoing conflict. Wars are often attended by particularly severe forms of criminality, including the perpetration of war crimes, massive or systematic violations

T. Unger
ICTJ Brussels, Blvd. Bischoffsheim 11, 8th Floor, 1000 Brussels, Belgium
e-mail: TUnger@ictj.org

M. Wierda
International Center for Transitional Justice
e-mail: MWierda@ictj.org

K. Ambos et al. (eds.), *Building a Future on Peace and Justice: Studies on Transitional Justice, Peace and Development.*

of human rights, crimes against humanity, and genocide. Apart from the fact that justice institutions may be inaccessible during active hostilities, many conflicts owe their origins to the fact that justice has not been dispensed fairly or independently. The demand for justice is often postponed to be dealt with (or more likely dismissed) at the negotiating table by those who have committed violations. Those whose rights have been violated often find no place at that table, and their views are frequently not heard. Where justice is implemented, it is usually within a post-conflict context or part of a transition, as was the case in Argentina.

But the past 10 years have seen a dramatic new development in the pursuit of justice in times of ongoing armed conflict, with the emergence of international jurisdictions. The first tribunal to be established in a situation of ongoing conflict was the International Criminal Tribunal for the former Yugoslavia (ICTY). Subsequent international jurisdictions established during conflicts have included the Special Court for Sierra Leone (SCSL) and, particularly, the International Criminal Court (ICC). The ICC has issued arrest warrants in at least three ongoing conflicts, including in Uganda, the Democratic Republic of the Congo (DRC), and the Sudan.[1]

The implications for tensions between peace and justice are obvious. First, there is the question of the legitimacy and accountability of the international prosecutor. What are the experiences to date? How should decisions on tensions be made? What positions have been taken by key stake holders, including victims, and what is their role? What have been the opinions of the UN Security Council and regional organizations? How do these link or clash with those of organizations on the ground, such as humanitarian organizations and traditional and religious leaders? How should states' own efforts to deliver justice, such as the Justice and Peace Law in Colombia, be evaluated, particularly if they seek to meet the "complementarity" threshold of the Rome Statute?

On the other hand, in the absence of an international prosecutor, we need to ask if it is possible to investigate in a situation of ongoing conflict, and what steps might assist in preserving justice options now or in the future. What are the technical dimensions of investigations in situations of ongoing conflict?

This paper sets out to explore current practices in the pursuit of justice within situations of active hostilities before a peace agreement – drawing on recent experiences in Afghanistan, Colombia, the DRC, Sierra Leone and Liberia, Sudan, Uganda, and the former Yugoslavia. The paper deals specifically with the exercise of criminal justice during a conflict, although some of the techniques aimed at preserving future justice options also have obvious utility for other transitional justice mechanisms, such as truth commissions and reparations.[2]

---

[1] This analysis does not deal with the case of Iraq and the work of the Iraqi High Tribunal. The ICTJ has contributed extensively to monitoring the trials of Saddam Hussein and other senior Ba'athists in Iraq, but we consider the circumstances of those trials so unique in terms of problems of security, legitimacy and politicization, that its lessons are also not easily applied elsewhere to date. Neither does the paper deal with the recent establishment of the Special Tribunal for Lebanon which is similarly unique and which may be premature to include in this analysis.

[2] For a thorough account of the legal framework see Kai Ambos, "The legal framework of Transitional Justice", elsewhere in this volume.

2 Considerations Governing the Work of the International Prosecutor

2.1 *Early Examples: The ICTY and the Special Court for Sierra Leone*

International prosecutors usually have a wider scope of investigative and prosecutorial discretion than national systems, depending on limitations on jurisdiction and any other factors reflected in the statutes of their jurisdictions.[3] However, they operate in a complex environment. National courts are closer to affected populations and better equipped to understand the background that led to the commission of crimes. Their legitimacy may be less in doubt, while international jurisdictions may face a constant struggle for legitimacy and comprehension by local populations. The issue of how to communicate with the latter is crucial in a situation of ongoing conflict.

Within these limitations, the early prosecutors of the ICTY have displayed a strict view of their obligation to prosecute. For instance, Richard Goldstone has recently written that when he chose to indict Karadžić and Mladić he believed that the Security Council had mandated him (under Chapter VII of the UN charter) to investigate and prosecute serious violations of humanitarian law in the former Yugoslavia. As a result, he had no option but to indict because the potential indictees were participating in peace talks.[4] As he put it, "our duty was clear" (Bass 2003, p. 7). In dealing with the argument as to whether prolonged conflict could lead to the commission of additional crimes, Goldstone said:

> A peace accepted by society with the willingness and ability to heal, with the willingness and capacity to move itself beyond the abuses of the past, is the only really viable peace. Such is the peace the international community should be seeking to promote. A peace masterminded by and in order to accommodate the concerns of vicious war criminals defiant of all fundamental international law prescriptions or norms is no such effective or enduring peace. (Goldstone 1998, p. 198)

---

[3] There may be limitations on subject matter and temporal or territorial jurisdiction. Furthermore, the current legal framework is limited in its ability to address the humanitarian consequences of conflict, such as mass displacement, death from disease or other humanitarian circumstances in displacement camps, or the violation of social and economic rights. Temporal limitations are usually framed by political decision, and may seem particularly arbitrary. Other limitations may include a reference to "those bearing the greatest responsibility," as was the case in Sierra Leone, or references to "gravity" as essential to case selection, as found in the Rome Statute.

[4] In the period leading up to the issue of the indictment, Goldstone was under close scrutiny, particularly by the UN Secretary General Boutros-Ghali. On various occasions, the Secretary General voiced his disquiet about the decision to indict Karadzic and Mladic while the war was still being fought. He did not, however, attempt to intervene. See Goldstone (2000, p. 103). The media too were initially critical of the fact that only the "small fish" had been indicted and asked specifically for an indictment against Karadzic and Mladic (Goldstone 2000, p. 107).

Likewise, at the press conference to announce the indictment of Slobodan Milošević, Louis Arbour said:

> I do not think that it is appropriate for politicians – before and after the fact – to reflect on whether they think the indictment came at a good time; whether it is helpful to a peace process. This is a legal, judicial process. The appropriate course of action is for politicians to take this indictment into account. It was not for me to take their efforts into account in deciding whether to bring an indictment, and at what particular time. (Coté 2005, p. 9)

Nevertheless, it is clear that prosecutors may have discretion beyond that which they care to admit.[5] Prosecutors live in a political reality and must use their discretion to make certain choices. In doing so, they may choose to consider the views of important stakeholders. What considerations should govern their decisions? To examine this question in more detail, it is instructive to study the exercise of discretion in the timing of indictments.

2.2 Considerations Governing the Timing of Indictments

The debate on timing tends to focus on two interrelated concerns. First, could indictments during conflict hinder justice and prolong conflict and suffering – by precluding otherwise optimal political arrangements for peaceful transition to a more just society in exchange for non-prosecutorial alternatives? Second, could indictments possibly have positive effects? Might they deter political actors from expediency when insistence on prosecution would ultimately prove preferable? Can they deter existing or prospective war criminals engaged in the conflict from future crimes? In other words, could early indictment provide a sort of conflict-specific deterrence that is distinct from the goal of general international deterrence?

History offers little empirical evidence to answer these questions, and existing cases caution against easy generalizations. The experience of the ICTY has given rise to two instances in particular that provoked debate about the timing of charging decisions. These are the indictments of self-styled Bosnian Serb President Radovan Karadžić and General Ratko Mladić in 1995 a few months before the Dayton peace negotiations, and the indictment of Yugoslav President Slobodan Milošević in 1999 during NATO's Operation Allied Force. Although some U.S. and European diplomats worried that the indictments would hinder peace negotiations in Bosnia, as mentioned former ICTY Prosecutor Justice Richard Goldstone has argued that the action was essential to peace because Karadžić and Mladić's subsequent exclusion from the negotiation of the historic Dayton peace accord facilitated the participation of Bosnia's Muslim-led government in those talks (Goldstone 2000, p. 103).

[5] Like his predecessors, David Crane of the Special Court for Sierra Leone also saw his mandate in narrow terms and stated at the time of the indictment of Charles Taylor: "Regarding the timing of our announcement, we reiterate our legal and moral obligations for unsealing the indictment. He has been indicted based on evidence, and [...] my job is to investigate and prosecute." See the press release of June 2003 by Prosecutor David Crane, available on-line at www.sc-sl.org/Press/prosecutor-060503.html (visited May 2007).

Closer examination of these events, however, fails to yield clear answers. Goldstone's account that the indictments themselves resulted in the exclusion of these individuals from diplomatic negotiations is anecdotal and highly contingent. The chief negotiator for the Bosnian Serbs at Dayton was Serbia's Slobodan Milošević, who would later find himself on trial at the ICTY for crimes such as genocide and crimes against humanity – many of which were committed before Dayton. Croatian President Franjo Tudjman negotiated on behalf of both Croatia and the Bosnian Croat leadership, and provided the international community with an essential, if not wholly welcome, ally in opposing Milošević. But he too has been accused of war crimes and his death sparked much speculation on whether a sealed indictment existed in his case.

The underlying assumption rests on a moral distinction: that is, the international community should refuse to negotiate with indicted war criminals while continuing to deal with known criminals who have not faced the formality of indictment. This is certainly not a correct reading of the situation. Many scholars hold the view that the timing of the Karadžić and Mladić indictments had little if any effect on the resolution of the Bosnian conflict. The marginalization of the Bosnian Serbs resulted not from legal formalities, but from political calculation. It is possible that the indictments affected their political calculation.

Some have pointed out that the turning point in Bosnia was the result of US strategy and not the indictments. The US increasingly saw Karadžić and Mladić as useless interlocutors, in contrast to the way they viewed Milošević. There is also no evidence, before or after these indictments, that the most critical actors in the international community saw amnesty for Karadžić or Mladić as an effective or realistic strategy for achieving peace.

The indictment of Milošević, 4 years later and in the middle of NATO's military intervention in Serbia, was the first ever international indictment of a sitting head of state. It provoked similar concerns that the action might inhibit peace negotiations.[6] Although the indictment seemed to have little impact on his behavior during the conflict, Milošević later agreed to a ceasefire that included UN governance of Kosovo backed by NATO troops and contained no promise of amnesty for him. Milošević may have realized that an ICTY indictment had little meaning for his hold on power unless he was first removed by international intervention or domestic effort. It is unlikely that any deterrent threat arising from those prospects would be

[6] Of Milošević, it was said that the evidence against him would have been sufficient to issue an indictment, even before the Dayton peace accord. Lord Owen said in this respect: "When I met Goldstone or the people close to the Tribunal, I did not recommend against indicting Milosevic or the others. Such a recommendation would not have been wise, since I did not have a word to say about whether they must or must not issue an indictment. On the other hand, I explained to them the details of the negotiations, showed the difficulties [we faced]. The conclusion that they could easily draw was that it would not be very wise to indict the heads of state if we wanted to arrive at a negotiated peace between them and with them. I believe that Goldstone and [his successor Louise] Arbour had this pragmatic attitude, this common sense judgment, and thc tribunal only indicted Milosevic when the prosecutor understood that he was no longer an obstacle, politically. Because after Kosovo there were no means to negotiate with Milosevic." Hazan (2000, p. 107).

much amplified by the formal existence of an ICTY indictment. As it turned out, it took both a domestic revolution and extraordinary international pressure to deliver Milošević to The Hague.

As with the Karadžić and Mladić indictments, there is no concrete evidence that the Milošević indictment in and of itself scuttled any realistic effort to trade amnesty for peace. It is also unclear whether it would have deterred international political actors from following that route had it looked otherwise attractive, although it would have probably been difficult. An international indictment may frustrate amnesty deals. This leaves prosecutors with some difficult choices.

Chief Prosecutor David Crane of the Special Court for Sierra Leone faced a similar dilemma when he decided to unveil the sealed indictment of Liberian President Charles Taylor in 2003, while Taylor was attending peace talks in Ghana in August 2003.[7] Although the Special Court for Sierra Leone had already issued the indictment under seal in March 2003, its existence had been the subject of speculation, based on the format of the public indictments in other related cases.[8] When Charles Taylor left Liberia to attend peace talks in Accra, Ghana, in August 2003, Crane publicly announced the indictment against him and the Ghanaian authorities were requested to arrest him. Rather than complying with this request and executing the warrant of arrest, Ghana chose to facilitate Taylor's speedy return to Liberia, prompting considerable criticism of the Special Court Prosecutor's timing. The decision to unseal the indictment at that time was clearly intended to reduce Taylor's ability to negotiate in Accra. However, a further explanation was that the Special Court was intended to have a limited lifespan of 3 years, and the Court was already more than a year into that timeframe when the indictment was unsealed.

But subsequent events also showed the inherently political nature of the exercise. Taylor's unexpected departure from the peace talks risked prolonging the conflict in Liberia, where government forces and the Liberians United for Reconciliation and Democracy (LURD) were engaged in a dangerous deadlock over the center of Liberia's capital, Monrovia (and success at Accra was far from certain). Indeed the conflict continued for another 2 months while the talks continued in Accra. Nevertheless, on August 11, 2003, Taylor was escorted out of Monrovia by three African leaders: Olusegun Obasanjo of Nigeria, Thabo Mbeki of South Africa, and Joaquim Chissano of Mozambique. It was alleged that, in return for relinquishing power, Taylor was promised asylum in Nigeria, arranged by the African Union (AU) and supported by the Economic Community Of West African States (ECOWAS), the UN, the US, and UK governments. The offer of asylum was conditional on Taylor halting his political activities in Liberia and refraining from further interference in Liberian politics.[9]

---

[7] For a thorough account of the peace talks in Accra, Ghana, see Hayner (2007).

[8] Indictees in special court indictments are referred to in capital letters and Charles Taylor was always referred to in capitals in the other indictments. Also, the indictments were numbered, starting with 2.

[9] By asylum we do not mean refugee status in international law.

While some may be of the view that Taylor's departure from the talks prolonged the conflict, it is clear that LURD's attack on Monrovia was preplanned and designed to put pressure on negotiations. Taylor's re-entry into that situation was not necessarily directly related to his indictment, as much would have depended on how long the talks would have lasted in any case.

By all accounts then, it is not possible to claim that the indictment alone forced Taylor out of office, although it probably contributed greatly. For instance, it eroded the potential of his demands to continue in the Presidency. Although international tribunals cannot force political actors to enforce their edicts, the existence of indictments may nevertheless influence public opinion and political thinking in ways that make otherwise appealing amnesty deals, whether formal or de facto, less palatable. Even those willing to promote amnesty in specific contexts must recognize that doing so involves a trade-off. Indictments issued during ongoing conflicts may serve to highlight the nature of this trade-off, encouraging political actors and the publics to which they are accountable to consider more deeply whether moral considerations truly justify forsaking prosecution in particular instances.

In June 2006, Charles Taylor was transferred from the custody of the Special Court for Sierra Leone to the International Criminal Court in The Hague, allegedly at the request of the Governments of Liberia and Sierra Leone, amongst others on the grounds of regional security.[10] His trial is being conducted by a special arrangement which allows the Special Court to use the premises of the ICC. The trial is of great symbolic significance to the region, but his removal to The Hague has to some extent hampered efforts to publicize the trial in Sierra Leone and Liberia.

Most recently, controversy regarding the role of an international arrest warrant in domestic politics has arisen on 26 May 2008, with the arrest of Congolese Vice President Jean-Pierre Bemba in Belgium at the request of the ICC, for crimes committed in the Central African Republic.[11] Bemba was transferred to The Hague and made his initial appearance in Court on 4 July 2008. Proponents of the arrest welcome his transfer to the ICC as in full compliance with its mandate to pursue those bearing the greatest responsibility.[12] Opponents of the arrest warrants feared a violent reaction by supporters in DRC, which to date has not materialized. They also point to the fact that Bemba was likely to be elected opposition leader, and argue that his arrest constitutes an interference with Congolese politics by an international court and a former colonial power, in a move which favors President Kabila. Thus international arrest warrants for senior political leaders will continue to be controversial and their impact remains subject to further study.

[10] See ICTJ press release, "Taylor Trial Should be Moved from Sierra Leone Only as Last Resort", 3 April 2006.

[11] ICC Press Release, "ICC Arrest Jean-Pierre Bemba – massive sexual crimes in Central African Republic will not go unpunished", The Hague, 24 May 2008, ICC-OTP-20080524-PR316_ENG.

[12] ICC OTP on Jean-Pierre Bemba surrender: this is a day for the victims, The Hague, 3 July 2008, ICC-OTP-20080703-PR336-ENG.

2.3 *The International Criminal Court and Ongoing Peace Negotiations*

The ICC is a permanent international criminal institution, which implies that it will usually be active during ongoing conflict. This is borne out in the current caseload of the Court, which deals only with situations of ongoing conflict.

This gives the ICC the difficult role of seeking to prevent ongoing crimes on the one hand, while simultaneously pursuing those who may be committing them. The ICC Statute is more explicit than the statutes of the ICTY or SCSL in recognizing the tensions between peace and justice. For instance, the Prosecutor is given limited discretion to apply to the Pre-Trial Chamber to halt an investigation or prosecution "in the interests of justice" (Art. 53 of the Rome Statute), although the pretrial chamber must make the decision. Also, the Security Council can choose to defer an investigation for a period of 12 months, renewable under Article 16. Finally, admissibility challenges can still be made under Article 19 if a peace process results in a change in the situation whereby a State finds itself in the position to be able genuinely to investigate or prosecute, and embarks on that course.

The ICC has already been confronted with several peace processes of varying promise. In Uganda, there have been two separate peace processes on which the ICC's actions have had the potential to impact: the first was the Betty Bigombe process, which peaked between December 2004 and February 2005. In this case, the ICC announced the opening of its investigation in January 2004. At times, when it looked as if the peace process had a chance of succeeding, the Prosecutor chose to proceed with his investigation. However, he adopted a "low profile" approach, which entailed refraining from public statements and vocal outreach campaigns. Despite this, the ICC's presence was a matter of much controversy and local sentiments could be summed up in the demand: "Peace First, Justice Later." When the Betty Bigombe process faltered in the second half of 2005, arrest warrants against senior LRA leaders were unsealed in October 2005.

In the summer months of 2006, a new peace process began at Juba, mediated by Riek Machar, Vice President of the Government of South Sudan. These talks are known as the "Juba peace talks" and are widely considered one of the best possibilities for achieving peace. The arrest warrants had already been issued, and senior leaders from the Lords Resistance Army (LRA) maintained from an early stage that the ICC arrest warrants are the most important obstacle to the success of the peace talks (International Bar Association 2007). For instance, the senior LRA leaders, for whom arrest warrants existed, have not been in personal attendance in Juba for fear of being arrested. This has led to complications in determining whether the delegation representing the LRA at Juba, many of whose members are noncombatants, is truly representative of the combatants. Throughout the tumultuous Juba process, the delegation was replaced several times, adding to doubts about its representative nature.

In the course of its interaction with the peace processes in Northern Uganda, the ICC OTP has maintained the following: (1) it is possible for the peace process and the arrest warrants to proceed simultaneously, on "parallel tracks" (2) arrest warrants should be viewed not as a stand-alone option, but as part of a comprehensive solution to conflict. In essence, the parallel tracks approach implies that international actors involved in peace negotiations should do as they see fit to promote a peaceful solution, without being hindered or inhibited by the actions of the Prosecutor. Simultaneously, the OTP should promote the enforcement of the arrest warrants without necessarily deferring to the peace process. In order not to detract from the peace process, the OTP chose to proceed mostly in a non-public manner.

It is too early to state conclusively whether the idea of proceeding with criminal proceedings and peace negotiations on parallel tracks can succeed in practice. Many expressed doubts that the arrest warrants would scuttle a final agreement at Juba, and senior LRA leaders repeatedly stressed this in media interviews. The Prosecutor, on the other hand, took the view that pressure to execute arrest warrants have contributed to the decrease of supplies to the LRA in Southern Sudan and their resulting move to Eastern Congo. The OTP has highlighted that this reduced the violence in Northern Uganda. The OTP has also argued that the arrest of the key suspects will contribute to the deterrence of further conflict[13] and that "the arrest warrants have helped speed up peace negotiations and the reduction of violence. Their arrest is essential for peace and justice."[14]

This approach by the ICC Prosecutor leaves us, however, with questions such as: Can peace and justice proceed on parallel tracks, and what does this mean for the pursuit of justice in ongoing conflict? Does such a process send out messages that are too blatantly contradictory? For instance, are States Parties motivated to execute arrest warrants in a climate in which they are anxious to reach an agreement?

Sequencing is often referred to as part of the solution to resolving tensions between peace and justice. For instance, there are some who promote the idea that a peace agreement should be silent on the issue of accountability, and that this can be dealt with in the post-conflict situation. However, this neglects the fact that sequencing is often made impossible by demands from perpetrators for assurances that they will not be tried, for instance through an amnesty. It also ignores the fact that once the ICC has issued arrest warrants, the only possibilities for a temporary or permanent discontinuation of the proceedings are found in Articles 16, 19 and 53 of the Rome Statute. It must be presumed that those negotiating peace agreements, including those who have perpetrated crimes, are politically astute and able to calculate the risks of a "peace first, justice later" approach without such assurances. In this respect, while the Charles Taylor situation is considered a victory for justice in many human rights circles, it is also commonly referred to by the LRA as the scenario that they are keen to avoid.[15]

---

[13] Fifth Session of the Assembly of States Parties, Luis Moreno Ocampo, prosecutor of the International Criminal Court, "Opening Remarks" (23 November 2006).

[14] Interview with Luis Moreno-Ocampo on May 15, 2007, see at www.la-croix.com/article/index.jsp?docId=2303077&rubId=1094# (visited May 2007).

[15] It should be noted that the ICC Prosecutor has not put forward a specific doctrine on deterrence or prevention of crime. This seems prudent, as the link between the prevention of crimes and the existence of the ICC would be very difficult to prove. Moreover, it is well known in national

Amid tensions of peace and justice, in early summer 2007, delegates at Juba faced the question of Agenda Item 3.[16] On 31 May 2007, the delegates held a one-day workshop on the issue, facilitated by Rwot David Arcana II, Paramount Chief of the Acholi. The discussions were long and difficult, they produced several conclusions that paved the way for the Preliminary Agreement on Accountability and Reconciliation. For instance, delegates drew the important conclusion that the traditional justice systems under discussion (including those from Acholi, Lango and Teso) were more appropriately viewed *in parallel* to formal justice, rather than as an alternative to it. Besides agreements about traditional justice, delegates concurred that there should be a *national approach* to accountability and reconciliation and that this would require the government to challenge the jurisdiction of the ICC under the Rome Statute.

These discussions paved the way for an Agreement on Agenda Item 3, signed at Juba on 29 June 2007. Most importantly, the Agreement establishes a general national framework and approach as a foundation for further discussions about specific accountability and reconciliation mechanisms. It states specifically that "formal criminal and civil justice measures shall be applied to any individual who is alleged to have committed serious crimes or human rights violations in the course of the conflict." For non-state actors (in this case LRA personnel not facing ICC warrants), the agreement specifies that an "alternative regime of penalties" will be introduced, and that these shall take into account the gravity of the crimes but also the need for reconciliation. In this respect, the Agreement resembles Colombia's 2005 law on Justice and Peace (see below Sect. 3.2.2).

The Agreement also refers to the need to carry out an "analysis of the conflict" and its root causes as well as the need for reparations for victims and for due process and effective legal representation for the accused. Victim participation in accountability processes and the special needs of women and children also feature in the Agreement. Traditional justice mechanisms are recognised as "a central part of the framework of accountability and reconciliation." Finally, the Agreement requires the government to undertake to "address conscientiously the question of the ICC arrest warrants relating to the leaders of the LRA/M." The government and the LRA agreed to put further issues relating to the mechanisms to a public consultation.

After a period of public consultations described below, the Government and LRA signed an Annexure to the Agreement on 19 Feb. 2008. The Annexure specifies the mechanisms that will be established for transitional justice in Uganda, which include (1) a special division of the High Court will be established to try persons responsible for serious crimes, in particular persons responsible for widespread or systematic attacks against civilians or grave breaches of the Geneva Conventions; (2) a "Commission of inquiry into the past and related events" with functions similar to those of a truth commission; (3) reparations, and (4) "traditional justice will play a central part of the alternative justice and reconciliation framework referred to in

criminal justice systems that it is not the consequences as such, but the likelihood that there will be a consequence, which serves as a deterrent. In other words, the deterrent impact of the Court could be properly measured only if it could count on unwavering support in enforcement.

[16] For a more extensive discussion see Otim and Wierda (2008).

the Agreement." Much speculation remains on what may be envisioned in terms of sentencing, an issue on which the Annexure is conspicuously silent. There are also still question marks about whether all provisions will apply equally to both sides.

International human rights groups have been quite critical of the Annexure. For instance, in a press release of 20 Feb. 2008, Amnesty International stated that "It is not acceptable for the Ugandan government and the LRA to make a deal that circumvents international law," and that Uganda would still need to hand senior LRA leaders over to the ICC. These positions seem to suggest that a challenge by Uganda of complementarity is not possible or unlikely to succeed as the Court has already investigated the crimes itself. However, it is important to remember that Uganda originally referred the situation in relation to the LRA to the Court not because they were unable to *try* the LRA but unable to *arrest* them. If that factual situation should reverse, the terms of the Rome Statute make it possible for Uganda to challenge admissibility without first having to surrender LRA leaders to The Hague. Of course Uganda would have to demonstrate ability and willingness to genuinely investigate and prosecute.

The Agreement and Annexure are potentially of great significance in allowing for peace without ignoring or rejecting the importance of Uganda's international obligations. A national solution and comprehensive approach to justice, if properly implemented, could have far reaching implications for Uganda's future. However, many in Uganda and elsewhere were disappointed when Joseph Kony failed to sign a Final Peace Agreement in April 2008. Also, new violations were committed by the LRA in the Central African Republic and in South Sudan in May and June 2008. Speculation abounds that the continuing validity of the arrest warrants prevented him from signing: however, it is equally or more likely that the national accountability option presented is not attractive to him.

In any case, the impact of the existence of arrest warrants on the negotiations has been quite profound. It has meant that the issue of accountability was put squarely on the table as central to the negotiations from the outset. The standards of the Rome Statute and the requirements of complementarity also gave rise to a discussion of the use of the national justice system, rather than recourse to amnesty or other options. It may be too early to speak of a shift, but it is possible that future negotiations would go through similar discussions based on Rome Statute obligations.

3 Views of the Various Constituencies

The work of any prosecutor must follow the principles that regulate judicial activities, particularly the fundamental principles of the independence and of impartiality of justice, and the correlated concept of the independence of investigatory and prosecutorial organs. Full and unconditional respect for these principles is essential to guarantee the legitimacy and credibility of judicial work, and also to foster its credibility amongst and acceptance by all concerned parties.

At the same time, it is obvious that the views of numerous stakeholders will have an influence on the process. The views and mandates of these stakeholders may compete with those of justice actors and may result in tensions. These are some of the key questions that need to be asked:

1. How should the views of victims be taken into consideration?
2. What are the duties of state parties for cooperation and promoting the Rome Statute in ongoing conflict? What are the factors that may guide an exercise of complementarity in such a situation?
3. What should be the role of the Security Council?
4. What has been the experience with UN peacekeeping missions, and what are some of the tensions in mandate that may arise?
5. What has been the experience with regional actors to date?
6. What are some of the views and concerns expressed by humanitarian organizations?
7. How should the Court interact with traditional and religious leaders, who may promote alternative forms of justice?
8. Do mediators interact with international prosecutors?

3.1 The Interests of Victims

An ethical prosecutorial policy should be informed (but not bound) by the views of victims. Rather than being viewed as simple vessels of evidence or sources of investigative leads to be introduced in the trial at strategic moments, victims should be involved from the outset and be consulted on various decisions. The Rome Statute gives victims a clear position as key stakeholders in the process of justice. This includes initiating prosecutions by communicating information on violations to the prosecutor during the preliminary investigations stage; participating throughout the proceedings, and being able to claim reparations. Victims' interests are also considered when deciding to discontinue a proceeding "in the interests of justice" pursuant to Article 53 of the Rome Statute.

Article 53 states that the Prosecutor can decide to discontinue investigations where, "taking into account the gravity of the crime and the interests of victims, there are nonetheless substantial reasons to believe that an investigation may not serve the interests of justice." The same is true for a prosecution, although additional grounds are given here: "taking into account all the circumstances, including the gravity of the crime, the interests of victims and the age or infirmity of the alleged perpetrator, and his or her role in the alleged crime." Also, in such a case, the Pre-Trial chamber has the power to review the Prosecutor's decision.

In a draft Policy Paper on how to interpret "the interests of justice," the Prosecutor argues that the Rome Statute generally implies that the interests of victims will weigh in favor of prosecution, and decisions to halt ongoing investigations or prosecutions should be taken only in highly exceptional circumstances. The Prosecutor acknowledges, however, that due consideration must be given to the sometimes divergent views of victims, their communities and the broader society. It will be necessary systematically to seek the views of victims and local communities throughout the process.[17] For the Prosecutor, the "interests of victims" includes the victims' interest in seeing justice done, but includes other essential interests such as their security and protection.[18] In doing so, the OTP takes a view that differs from certain human rights organizations, which have argued that the interests of victims referred to in Article 53 is in justice and justice alone.

The Prosecutor has introduced a number of methods to measure the interests of victims. An important one is dialogue and consultation. The OTP has used this method to in a number of situations under investigation to fully explore the "interests of victims."[19] Another methodology – not carried out by the ICC itself but by other organizations – is survey work. Surveys enable the gathering of representative views of certain communities, using scientific methodology such as random sampling. For instance, in the report, *The Forgotten Voices*, the International Center for Transitional Justice and Human Rights Center of the University of Berkeley decided to interview 2,500 respondents in four districts in Northern Uganda on their views of peace and justice (ICTJ 2005a).[20] The report demonstrated that victims' perspectives on these difficult questions are diverse. Although such reports may be instructive, they cannot replace the need for consultation by official actors, including those involved in peace mediation. Uganda has also set an important precedent in this regard by the official consultation of affected communities by the parties to the Juba peace process from September to December 2007.

The difficult question of who speaks on behalf of victims remains. Diversity of views will be common. The absence of organized victim groups may be another complicating factor. Another question relates to the depth of victims' understanding and their ability to make informed choices even when consulted. Studies on ICC outreach activities in the past have shown that victims still have very limited

---

[17] The Office of the Prosecutor, Draft Policy Paper on the Interests of Justice. http://www.icc-cpi.int/otp/otp_docs.html.

[18] Article 68(1) places an obligation on the whole court, including the office of the prosecutor, to take appropriate measures to protect the safety, physical and psychological wellbeing, dignity and privacy of victims and witnesses. Article 54(1) (b) requires the prosecutor to respect the interests and personal circumstances of victims and witnesses in carrying out effective investigations. Investigations are likely often to take place in unsafe or unstable circumstances.

[19] According to the OTP, 25 missions to Uganda were undertaken for the purpose of listening to the concerns of victims and representatives of local communities. Two meetings with leaders from several local communities were also held in The Hague. Also, in the DRC, the OTP conducted multiple missions to Kinshasa and Ituri for the purpose of consulting with civil society groups and victim representatives. The purpose was to understand the concerns of local populations. Since 2003, several seminars have also been organized in The Hague, gathering various organizations and victim representatives. Finally, three missions were conducted in Kinshasa, Bunia and Ituri by multidisciplinary teams to analyze the probable consequences of OTP action for local populations, including victims and witnesses.

[20] A follow up study was conducted by the same organizations and the Payson Center for International Development at Tulane University in 2007 (ICTJ 2007).

knowledge of the court's existence and actions.[21] Conducting meaningful consultation with victims about these issues remains a tremendous challenge.

3.2 *States Parties, Peace and Justice, and the Rome Statute*

3.2.1 State Cooperation

In times of conflict, as in any other time, the principal obligation to investigate and prosecute certain crimes falls squarely on the state. States directly concerned and under a duty to act are those in the territory in which the crimes have been committed, or those whose nationals have either committed or been victims of the crimes. In times of conflict, states have the additional obligation to respect and ensure respect for the norms defined under international humanitarian law.[22] If war crimes are committed, the obligation to prosecute or extradite those responsible extends to all states (*aut dedere aut judicare*).

In addition to prior existing obligations, the Rome Statute formally commits States Parties to "putting an end to impunity for the perpetrators of these crimes and thus to contribute to their prevention."[23] This includes either investigating and prosecuting these crimes themselves, or rendering assistance to the ICC if a state party is unwilling or unable to proceed. The Prosecutor has sometimes referred to this as a "legal revolution."[24] States Parties no longer have the option of foregoing justice options during conflict or conflict resolution. But how is this "legal revolution" manifesting itself?

The reality is that, where it concerns genocide, crimes against humanity and war crimes, states and their structures are often among the main perpetrators, and many of these crimes are pursued as a matter of state policy, as demonstrated in the Balkans over the past few decades.

Nonetheless, state cooperation remains essential for international courts without their own police forces. The operational paradox for the ICC makes this particularly clear: on the one hand, the ICC is expected to intervene in countries that are either

---

[21] See, ICTJ Report, *Sensibilisation à la CPI en RDC: Sortir du "Profil Bas,"* www.ictj.org/images/content/6/3/638.pdf.

[22] The four Geneva Conventions, adopted on August 12, 1949, define the core of what constitute war crimes. They have been universally ratified. They are complemented by relevant national legislations. War crimes are also defined in Article 8 of the Statute of the International Criminal Court.

[23] Preamble of the Rome Statute.

[24] This evolution in international law is complemented by other developments, such as the UN's position that it cannot condone amnesties for genocide, war crimes, and crimes against humanity. For an in-depth analysis on state practice regarding amnesties see, Louise Mallinder, *Exploring the Practice of States in Introducing Amnesties*, elsewhere in this volume.

unable or unwilling to investigate and prosecute those responsible for the worst crimes, while on the other, the ICC has to rely on the support of those very states to carry out its mandate.[25]

The situation in Sudan, described in further detail below, demonstrates this dilemma in stark terms. The Security Council referred the case of Darfur to the ICC on 31 March 2005, as permitted by Art. 13 (b) of the ICC Statute. On 2 May 2007, the Pre-Trial Chamber issued arrest warrants for crimes against humanity and war crime against Ahmed Mohammad Harun, Minister for Humanitarian Affairs and former Minister of the Interior, and Ali Kushayb, a *janjaweed* leader. Sudan's stance has been one of non-cooperation. The Sudanese government admits that crimes were committed on its territory but maintains that it will try such crimes itself, in part through the creation of a Special Court for Darfur. In his report to the Security Council on 5 June 2008, the Prosecutor alluded to the fact that he will soon apply for additional arrest warrants, perhaps for government officials who are senior to Harun. This has caused widespread speculation that the Sudanese government will cease cooperation in the deployment of the hybrid AU/UN peacekeeping force, UNAMID, and that it may expel humanitarian organizations from its territory (Flint and de Waal 2008). Attacks may occur on peacekeepers or humanitarian workers. There are also fears that the arrest warrants will destabilize the fragile Comprehensive Peace Agreement between North and South Sudan concluded in 2005, which call for crucial elections next year.

On occasion, a close relationship with a State Party may also give rise to a perception of bias in an ongoing conflict, especially where a government has referred cases against ongoing rebellions. For instance, in Uganda, the Prosecutor is dependent on the Ugandan army to provide security for his investigations in the North. Moreover, the Prosecutor first appeared with President Museveni to announce the investigation at a press conference in London in January 2004. The fact that there are currently no arrest warrants for members of the Ugandan army (UPDF) has given further rise to a perception of bias.

Confusion has also arisen about the obligations of state parties under Part 9 of the Statute, which deals with international cooperation and judicial assistance. In Uganda, the question arose whether third states can take steps to support peace processes that involve persons who are the subject of arrest warrants before the ICC. When arrest warrants against senior Lord's Resistance Army (LRA) leaders were issued, some took the view that they would no longer be able to support peace processes involving those LRA leaders financially or otherwise, as this would contravene Part 9 of the Rome Statute. With time, this position was abandoned and now several state parties give direct support to the Juba talks. However, there has been some controversy around the nature of assistance to the Juba talks and whether the funds that were made available may have been used by the LRA to rearm. The ICC, in endorsing a parallel tracks approach, implicitly seems to reject the view that states are in contravention of Part 9 of the Statute if they support an ongoing peace

[25] This tension has been particularly clear in the case of Sudan, where the OTP has taken the view that it should try to elicit Sudanese cooperation where possible.

process, but it has also been critical of the lack of monitoring on how funds are used. But how far do state obligations in this respect reach? Do states parties have an active duty to assist a peace process to arrive at a solution that is acceptable under the Rome Statute? Does that situation change if additional crimes under the Statute are committed?

3.2.2 Complementarity: A Study of Colombia

With the advent of the ICC, certain states are confronting the challenge of forging solutions based on peace and justice at the national level as they seek to resolve their own conflicts. There is always pressure to take the threat of prosecutions off the table early in a peace process and combatants at all levels of the political and military hierarchies have a tremendous interest in securing an amnesty, or "to ensure that peace prevails over justice." Nonetheless, if justice actors are unable to act, because the threat of prosecution is constantly trumped by a peace process, its value as a deterrent will be fundamentally compromised.[26]

The Rome Statute states clearly in Article 17 that, under the principle of complementarity, "a case will be inadmissible if it is being investigated or prosecuted by a state which has jurisdiction over it, unless the state is unwilling or unable genuinely to carry out the investigation or prosecution." Under Article 19, challenges to admissibility may be made either before or at the commencement of a trial. Ideally, complementarity should serve not just to deter the ICC from pursuing cases that are already the subject of a genuine national process, but also to initiate cases because of the existence of the ICC. The Rome Statute, in its preamble, expresses a preference for the exercise of criminal jurisdiction.

As mentioned, the Rome Statute requires states to be willing or genuinely able to investigate or prosecute. It is silent on the requirements for punishing those found guilty. This silence on punishment was cleverly identified and used in the context of Colombia. Colombia has suffered a longstanding conflict between leftwing guerilla fighters (FARC and ELN) and rightwing paramilitary groups. President Uribe came to power in 2002 on an election promise to return security and sovereignty to Colombia. He introduced a scheme known as the Justice and Peace Law (JPL).[27] In its current form, this provides for reduced sentences for ex-paramilitaries (the AUC) in exchange of a full (complete and genuine) disclosure of crimes. Previously, the law was suggesting a range of penalties that formed alternatives to incarceration, including temporal disqualification for public duty, prohibition of carrying weapons, prohibition to live in or visit certain places where the crimes were committed or where the victims reside; and restricted geographic movement for instance to agricultural estates.

The original intention of the government was to avoid using politically contentious amnesty language by offering demobilized paramilitary combatants judicial

[26] Transcript, Second Public Hearing of the Office of the Prosecutor, NGOs and Other Experts, The Hague, 2006, 27.

[27] See also Catalina Diaz, *Bid for Justice and Peace*, elsewhere in this volume.

pardons within the context of the criminal justice system. The initial law, which was adopted by Congress in 2005, reflected this intention and was heavily criticized by victim groups, human rights organizations, and the Office of the High Commission for Human Rights (OHCHR), which condemned it as too generous to the AUC and in violation of the rights of victims to an effective remedy under the constitution and international law.

The Constitutional Court ruled on 18 May 2006 that some of the law's main provisions were incompatible with both constitutional and international law. But the court in general terms approved the law as an instrument for overcoming the internal armed conflict, holding that it introduced a new balance between benefits for former combatants and victims' rights to truth, justice and reparations. The court ruling improved the law regarding reparations to victims; and ruled that all benefits of the law are forfeited if ex-paramilitaries do not confess the whole truth as part of the "version libre" that they are required to give.[28] Regarding the provision for reduced sentences, the Court held that prison terms should be no fewer than 5 years and no more than eight. This, it found, does not disproportionately compromise the rights of victims under the Constitution. The Constitutional Court ruling was generally welcomed by international and local civil society.

However, serious questions remain about the implementation of the JPL. The government challenged the ruling and sought to weaken its effect by executive decrees that, it argues, will make the ex-paramilitaries more cooperative. The JPL law has been flooded with cases, not all of which have to do with the commission of serious crimes. In early June 2008, fourteen senior paramilitary leaders subject to the JPL were extradited to the United States for drug-related offences and face potentially high sentences.[29] This development may diminish incentives to participate in the JPL. In addition, no effective measures are yet in place to let victims participate meaningfully in the process, and to protect witnesses and victims who testify against paramilitary leaders under the JPL. Victims too have been dissatisfied that the focus remains on perpetrators and that they have no opportunity to participate directly in the "version libre" given by paramilitaries, and there remain many challenges in regard to their effective representation in the proceedings. Moreover, the Justice and Peace Unit of the prosecutor general's office remains lacking in capacity to investigate the allegations of system crimes alluded to in the testimonies of paramilitaries. Civil society has urged actors in the process to move swiftly if the JPL is to have any significant effect.

The Colombian approach, at least on paper, may offer a potentially important new model to other governments seeking to resolve internal armed conflict, but the question whether the Colombian Justice and Peace Law meets the complementarity threshold under the Rome Statute remains unanswered and it may only be after

[28] Other conditions are cooperation with judicial authorities in the demobilization process and the making of comprehensive reparation to victims, including release of persons, forfeiting of illegally-obtained assets, public apologies and promises of non-repetition, and collaboration in locating remains of disappeared persons.

[29] ICTJ Press Release, "Extradition: Colombia's and the United States' Mistake", May 14, 2008: http://www.ictj.org/en/news/press/release/1677.html.

some of the cases have concluded completely, that it will be possible to make an evaluation. One important incentive for demobilized paramilitaries who have committed serious crimes to opt for prosecution under the JPL is that they believe it will shield them from ICC prosecution in the future, although again threats of extradition to the US may erode this concern.[30] A report by the International Crisis Group stated that: "the Uribe administration has been acutely aware of this possibility and has attempted to draft the JPL in such a way that it could preclude ICC prosecution of crimes against humanity because the perpetrators were sentenced sufficiently by Colombia's judicial system"(International Crisis Group 2006). The maximum prison term contemplated by the JPL is 8 years; if prosecuted under other Colombian criminal statutes law, the paramilitaries could receive maximum sentences of up to 60 years for the kind of crimes of which they are accused. A great deal will depend on whether proceedings in the context of the JPL are conducted independently and impartially with the intention to bring persons to justice, or whether the system will be subject to continued executive interference in its implementation.

3.3 The Security Council's Powers to Defer a Case

The international organization most involved in issues relevant to justice and conflict situations is the United Nations (UN). Within the UN, the prime stakeholder in this respect is the Security Council (or UNSC). In view of its specific mandate to preserve international peace and security and its broad powers under the UN Charter, the Security Council is directly involved in matters pertaining to peace negotiations and peace missions.[31] It also became directly involved in justice issues when it established the ICTY and the International Criminal Tribunal for Rwanda (ICTR), by way of Chapter VII resolutions.[32]

Because the primary task of the Security Council is to maintain international peace and security, it may in certain circumstances decide that peace or peace

[30] The ICC Prosecutor wrote a letter to President Uribe in March 2005, asking for information on what the Colombian government was doing to address crimes that were potentially within the jurisdiction of the ICC.

[31] The term "peace missions" is used loosely in this paper to encompass peacekeeping and peacemaking operations, armed or not, irrespective of their unilateral, bilateral or multilateral character.

[32] In so doing, the council referred to the close link between peace and justice in the preamble of resolution 827 of May 25, 1993, when it indicated that the tribunal would "contribute to ensuring that... such violations ... are halted and effectively redressed." It was hoped that by bringing to justice those accused of massacres and similar egregious violations of international humanitarian law, both belligerents and civilians would be discouraged from committing further atrocities. The ICTY was also "to contribute to the restoration and maintenance of peace," according to the terms of Resolution 827. Similarly, in Resolution 955 of November 8, 1994, creating the ICTR, the Council declared itself: "convinced that in the particular circumstances of Rwanda, the prosecution of persons responsible for serious violations of international humanitarian law would enable this aim to be achieved and would contribute to the process of national reconciliation and to the restoration and maintenance of peace."

negotiations should prevail over justice, at least temporarily. This paramount role of the Security Council is recognized very explicitly in the ICC Statute, which provides in Article 16 that:

> No investigation or prosecution may be commenced or proceeded under this Statute for a period of 12 months after the Security Council, in a resolution adopted under Chapter VII of the Charter of the United Nations, has requested the Court to that effect; that request may be renewed by the Council under the same conditions.[33]

This provision has been criticized by some human rights NGOs as an intrusion on justice and its independence. While this concern is legitimate to a point, depending on the possible future use of such powers by the Security Council, the provision exists primarily in recognition of the implicit hierarchy that governs the UN – particularly the Security Council – and the ICC. The suggestion has been made that a State Party initiating an Article 16 resolution to allow persons to evade ICC jurisdiction is in breach of the object and purpose of the Rome Statute, but since the Statute itself contains this provision, this argument may be difficult to sustain.

However, it remains to be seen if and how Article 16 will be used in practice. The only occasion to date where it has been used is to grant a form of blanket immunity to peacekeepers – an initiative of the United states but certainly not the purpose for which Article 16 was intended.

Recently, some have suggested that an Article 16 deferral may be sought in the case of Uganda. Prominent in raising this as a possibility has been the International Crisis Group, and this option also seems to be supported by several of those involved in observing the talks including the United States.

Article 16 has the advantage of removing the difficult question of peace and justice to another actor and recognizing that this is a political decision, beyond the scope of the law. The 12 month renewable reprieve may enable difficult situations to be resolved by allowing those who wish to escape to a jurisdiction beyond the reach of the Court if they so choose. It may also create "breathing space" for the implementation of a peace agreement. On the other hand, the use of Article 16 in any situation would potentially set a negative precedent for future conflicts in terms of becoming part of the regular demands of fighting factions before signature of any agreement. Furthermore, where the Security Council has had no previous role in passing resolutions related to the conflict, such as in the case of Uganda, the idea of intervening with the sole purpose to allow for the LRA to escape accountability should be questioned. This may be different in the case of Sudan, where the Security Council was involved from the outset, but where an Art. 16 Resolution would require a complete about face in its position.

After all, the Security Council itself has become increasingly seized with accountability issues. In this respect, several members of the Security Council were slow to put their weight behind the talks facilitated by Riek Machar, believing that any process that entertained the idea of providing amnesty to those indicted by the ICC – even one that began a dialogue with the five commanders – would run the risk of contravening the Rome Statute (Security Council Report 2006). Following a

[33] Article 16 of the ICC Statute, entitled *Deferral of investigation or prosecution*.

briefing by former Under-Secretary-General for Humanitarian Affairs Jan Egeland, states remarked that the peace talks must not come at the price of ending impunity – coupling lasting peace with accountability for crimes against humanity.[34] As the talks developed, these same states moderated their positions, and eventually backed a presidential statement welcoming the Cessation of Hostilities Agreement and inviting member states to support efforts to bring an end to the conflict.[35]

In any case, the triggering of complementarity in the case of Uganda should make resort to Art. 16 of the Statute unnecessary. Some suggest that Article 16 could be used to endorse a deal even if it does not meet the complementarity threshold (International Crisis Group 2007). If that is the case, is the Security Council in a position to fundamentally undermine the complementarity framework? Should justice itself not be viewed as a measure for preventing future breaches of peace and security?

3.4 UN Field Operations and Other UN Actors

The relationship between international courts and UN field operations has often been uneasy. Court officials may require the cooperation and support of the UN peacekeeping mission to carry out their judicial work, including investigations or arrests of suspects or accused. On the other hand, a mandate to arrest war criminals is disruptive and may run counter to other objectives of a peacekeeping mission. This tension was demonstrated by the relationship between the ICTY and the successive peace keeping missions in Bosnia-Herzegovina – whether UNPROFOR, IFOR, or SFOR. SFOR and IFOR did not make a single arrest until July 1997 (Scharf 2000, p. 951). NATO's early position was to deny itself any power to execute arrests (Kerr 2004, pp. 154–155; Maogoto 2004, p. 157) and, until mid-1997, literally to follow a restrictive policy of apprehending only those individuals indicted by the ICTY (when it encountered them in the in the course of IFOR/SFOR duties). People spoke of high profile war criminals indicted by the ICTY living freely in their neighborhoods, with NATO patrols deliberately modifying their route so as to avoid them (Maogoto 2004, pp. 156–157). It was only after a combination of political and judicial pressure that NATO was persuaded to shift its policy with respect to the arrest of indicted individuals (Zhou 2006, p. 216).

Furthermore, peacekeeping missions may find the mere presence of a court disruptive to their own mandate. In Sierra Leone, the Special Court originally had a quite ambivalent relationship with UNAMSIL, the UN peacekeeping mission. To begin with, UNAMSIL took the view that the SCSL posed a potential threat to Sierra Leone's fragile peace process and thus offered little technical, logistical, or

[34] Briefing by the Under-Secretary General for Humanitarian Affairs and Emergency Relief Coordinator, Security Council 5,525th Meeting, Sept 15 2006, S/PV.5525. See also Briefing by the Under-Secretary General for Humanitarian Affairs and Emergency Relief Coordinator, Humanitarian situation in the Great Lakes region and the Horn of Africa, Security Council 5,677th Meeting, May 21, 2007, S/PV.5677.

[35] Statement by the President of the Security Council, S/PRST/2006/45, Nov 16, 2006.

administrative support (Perriello and Wierda 2006, p. 30). With time and the express support of the Secretary General for the Special Court, the relationship between UNAMSIL and the Court improved. UNAMSIL peacekeepers have also been vital to facilitating arrests for the Special Court (Perriello and Wierda 2006, p. 34).

While the relationship between the ICC and the UN is generally governed by an overall relationship agreement that stipulates cooperation between the two organizations, the court may also seek to conclude a further Memorandum of Understanding with the field mission in a particular situation or country. In the DRC, MONUC has committed itself to supporting the Congolese government in fulfilling its obligations under the Rome Statute. This arrangement may go some way toward alleviating tensions that may otherwise exist about issues of sovereignty. All in all, what is needed is an integrated approach by the UN system.

In terms of Darfur, when this situation was first referred to the ICC in March 2005, the local peace-keeping mission, UNMIS, expressed some concerns at the outset about how the activities of the ICC might affect its mandate. UNMIS has argued that the ICC investigation gives Sudan a reason to oppose extending a UN peacekeeping mission to Darfur, thereby prolonging the violence and leading to increased casualties. However, it is clear that the causes of the crimes being committed in Darfur are the responsibility of the Sudanese government and rebel factions. Also, as the failures of the African Union Mission in Sudan (AMIS) painfully demonstrated, the presence of a relatively small peacekeepeing force in a large area does not, in itself, prevent atrocities. Resistance to a UN force for Darfur surfaced at least 18 months before the ICC's referral. Nonetheless, a joint African Union and United Nations hybrid operation (UNAMID) was approved by the Security Council in Res. 1769 on 31 July 2007. Current fears are that the Sudanese government will resist the further deployment of UNAMID if further arrest warrants for senior members of the regime are issued.

What should be the balance between the goals of peacekeeping and the pursuit of criminal justice? At ICTY, an unusual situation occurred when a UN mission argued for provisional release of a particular accused for the sake of peace. UNMIK (and privately also several states) intervened with the ICTY Prosecutor to dissuade her from proceeding with the indictment of Prime Minister of Kosovo Ramush Haradinaj. They argued that the need to guarantee the stability of Kosovo should be taken into consideration, and that Haradinaj's indictment could result in political unrest. In fact, his indictment for war crimes and crimes against humanity committed as a commander of the Kosovo Liberation Army between March and September 1998 was issued without resulting in violence, and he voluntarily surrendered to the court. Thereafter, UMMIK again raised the issue of stability, arguing that Haradinaj should be allowed to return to Kosovo on provisional release to await his trial, which was granted by the ICTY.[36] On 3 April 2008, a Trial Chamber of the ICTY acquitted Haradinaj of all the charges against him on grounds that it was not "satisfied beyond reasonable doubt" that he had taken part in a joint criminal

[36] Prosecutor v. Ramush Haradinaj, Idriz Balaj, Lahi Brahimaj, "Decision on Ramush Haradinaj's Motion for Provisional Release", June 6, 2005, case No. IT-04-84-PT, at www.un.org/icty/haradinaj/trialc/decision-e/050606.htm.

enterprise targeting civilians for the purposes of committing war crimes or crimes against humanity. However, the judgment explicitly mentioned the significant difficulties encountered by the Chamber in securing the testimony of a large number of witnesses, and Presiding Judge Orie commented that the Trial Chamber had "gained a strong impression that the trial was being held in an atmosphere where witnesses felt unsafe."[37]

There are other grey areas. For instance, the official view taken by the UN so far seems to be that arrest warrants do not rule out meetings with political leaders (although this may vary within the UN system). UN representatives such as former Head of OCHA Jan Egeland and UN Special Representative Joaquim Chissano have met with senior LRA leaders such as Joseph Kony and Vincent Otti, despite the arrest warrants issued by the ICC. Is this appropriate, or does it contribute to legitimizing alleged war criminals? On the other hand, would preventing those interactions risk the loss of opportunities to encourage indictees to surrender, to release noncombatants or women and children in their ranks, or to remain engaged in a faltering peace process?

3.5 Regional Organizations and Actors

Regional organizations and actors have also started to play an increased role in issues of peace and justice, particularly through the mediation of conflict. A prominent example is the response of regional actors in Africa to the indictment of Charles Taylor by the Special Court for Sierra Leone.

As mentioned, Charles Taylor was President of Liberia when he was indicted. This meant his case had enormous political significance in the region. A Ghanaian Foreign Ministry official denied receiving any documents relating to the arrest warrant. The Special Court said it had not notified Ghana in advance because of the risk that certain officials would have warned Taylor. The Ghanaians briskly refused to comply and gave Taylor a presidential plane to return quickly to Liberia. The Ghanaian government complained that it was blindsided and embarrassed by the "surprise" request to send Taylor to the Court. In an interview in New African Magazine, Ghanaian President John Kufour said he:

> ...Felt betrayed by the international community ... Five African presidents were meeting in Accra to find ways of kickstarting the Liberian peace process, and Mr. Taylor had been invited as president of Liberia. We were not even aware that a warrant had been issued for his arrest. Incidentally, the African leadership had taken the initiative to convince Mr. Taylor to resign and allow all the factions in Liberia to negotiate. It was when the presidents were leaving my office for the Conference Centre where Mr. Taylor was expected

[37] ICTY Press Release, "Haradinaj and Balaj acquitted of all charges, Brahinaj guilty of cruel treatment and torture in Jablanica compound", The Hague, 3 April 2008.

> to make a statement that word came in that a warrant had been issued for his arrest. I really felt betrayed by the international community (and) I informed the United States of the embarrassment that the announcement caused.[38]

African and American officials sponsoring the talks in Accra were angry that their efforts had been thwarted. They complained that the "overzealous" Prosecutor was jeopardizing their peace initiative. The Prosecutor, however, continued to assert that he did as he was mandated; that the parties at the peace talks needed to be aware that they were trying to negotiate with an indicted war criminal whom – in his opinion – could never be trusted, and that Charles Taylor had violated at least 17 prior ceasefires and agreements.

After Charles Taylor had been allowed to seek refuge in Nigeria, political pressure began to mount on Nigeria to hand Taylor over to the Special Court. Due to considerable pressure from the United States at the highest levels, including a threat from President Bush to cancel a planned meet with President Obasanjo, who was in the US at the time, the latter agreed for Taylor to be transferred to Liberia and from there to the Special Court for Sierra Leone in March 2007.

While international justice advocates celebrated Taylor's arrest and surrender to the Special Court, this was privately condemned by many African leaders. The Libyan leader, Mu'ammar Al-Qadhafi expressed the views of many African leaders when he denounced the Taylor arrest, saying, "It means that every head of state could meet a similar fate. This sets a serious precedent" (Grainger and James 2006, p. 16). Many criticized Nigeria for failing to refer the matter to the AU, which had brokered the initial deal. They condemned Nigeria's unilateral decision to hand one of their own to "a white man's court" to be tried in The Hague.[39] Perhaps as a consequence, in the case of former Chadian dictator Hissène Habré, in 2007, the AU requested Senegal, where Habré is under nominal house arrest, to try the former Chadian Dictator. On April 8, 2008, the National Assembly of Senegal voted to amend the constitution to clear the way for Habré to be prosecuted in Senegal.[40]

The question of how regional actors may react, considering particularly their role in conflict mediation, has spurred the ICC to reach out to the African Union, clearly a critical actor in its realm of operations. To date, however, the ICC has not succeeded in concluding a Memorandum of Understanding with the AU. Despite this, many would agree that the role of regional actors in seeking peaceful solutions to conflict ought to be encouraged. At the same time, such actors may be beyond the reach of legal standards drawn up by the United Nations and of institutions such as the ICC. What are the implications for impunity? How should these organizations seek to set their own standards?

[38] Interview with NewAfrican magazine, March 2004, at www.ghanacastle.gov.gh/president/castle_newsp_details.cfm?EmpID=195.

[39] The decision to transfer Taylor to The Hague was not announced until after his transfer to the SCSL in Freetown.

[40] Les députés modifient la Constitution pour juger Hissène Habré, Senegal, 8 avril 2008, AFP: http://www.jeuneafrique.com/pays/senegal/article_depeche.asp?art_cle=AFP45458lesdprbahen0.

3.6 Humanitarian Organizations and Their Considerations

In recent years, with the functioning of international criminal jurisdictions, humanitarian organizations have increasingly sought to consolidate their position on the role of international courts and tribunals. Broadly speaking, the protection-oriented mandate of humanitarian aid is consistent with the underlying principles of international criminal justice. The International Committee on the Red Cross's (ICRC) Note for Humanitarian Organizations on Cooperation with International Tribunals concludes that: "while the primary purpose of most organizations is to provide lifesaving services to populations in need, if those populations are subject to violent attacks many see the value of helping to bring the attackers to justice" (Mackintosh 2004). Many humanitarian organizations support international justice in their central policies. At a recent meeting on transitional justice and humanitarian concerns, participants recognized that past failures in justice have frequently led to humanitarian crises, which in turn can lead to repeated violations of human rights.[41]

Nonetheless, there are real tensions between the mandates of international tribunals and humanitarian organizations in terms of activities on the ground.[42] This has played out dramatically in Uganda. Since the government of Uganda referred the situation concerning the Lord's Resistance Army (LRA) to the ICC in December 2003, humanitarian agencies have voiced strong concern that the court's involvement might have harmful effects on civilian protection and humanitarian access.[43] This is in a context where prior to the Cessation of Hostilities Agreement in 2006, the humanitarian crisis in northern Uganda could hardly be more severe. A health and mortality survey-conducted by the World Health Organization (WHO), government of Uganda Ministry of Health and other international organizations in 2005-found that the internally displaced persons in the northern districts of Gulu, Pader and Kitgum (upwards of 90% of the region's population) are "experiencing a very serious humanitarian emergency."[44]

The commencement of the investigation by the ICC in Uganda gave rise to much concern by humanitarian organizations that had been active in the north for some time, and that had widely lobbied for a peaceful solution to the conflict. Concerns

---

[41] Meeting on Transitional Justice and Humanitarian Concerns, Conference Report, Geneva, May 16–17, 2006.

[42] See Code of Conduct for the International Red Cross and Red Crescent Movement and NGOs in Disaster Relief. International Federation of Red Cross and Red Crescent Societies. 1994.

[43] See CSOPNU (n.d.). CSOPNU is made up of the following organizations: Care; Concerned Parents Association; Development Network of Indigenous Voluntary Associations; Gulu NGO Forum; International Rescue Committee; Norwegian Refugee Council; Oxfam; Pader NGO Forum; Save the Children in Uganda; SODANN; Uganda Child Rights NGO Network.

[44] World Health Organization (2005). The humanitarian situation in the north has reached such high crisis levels over the past 20 years that former UN Under-Secretary General for Humanitarian Affairs, Jan Egeland, famously referred to it as "the biggest forgotten, neglected humanitarian emergency in the world today", War in Northern Uganda World's Worst Forgotten Crisis: UN. Agence France-Presse, Nov 11 2003, Nairobi. A report issued in 2006 by Oxfam International and the Civil Society Organizations for Peace in Northern Uganda finds that approximately 3,500 people die from easily preventable disease each month (CSOPNU 2006).

about the Court commonly voiced by humanitarian organizations the Court included complaints that: "it is biased; it will exacerbate the violence; it will endanger vulnerable groups – notably witnesses and children; it is spoiling the peace process by undermining the Amnesty and the ceasefire; and it ignores and dis-empowers local justice procedures" (Allen 2005, p. 44). Several humanitarian organizations came out with statements urging prudence in moving forward with the investigation. In December 2004, a coalition of international and local humanitarian organizations – named Civil Society Organizations for Peace in Northern Uganda (CSOPNU) – argued that, "removing all possibilities of amnesty means that there is no incentive for the senior command of the LRA to stop fighting. Indeed, it is probable that it will lead to an escalation in violence if the cornered rebels seek to fight to the last" (CSOPNU 2004, p. 111).

While so direct an effect might be difficult to prove in practice, especially in relation to a conflict that has had many ebbs and flows, there was an increase in attacks on humanitarian organizations immediately following the issue of the arrest warrants in October 2005 (IDMC 2006, p. 14). Before that time, humanitarian organizations had generally not been targeted, although attacks on their vehicles had occurred. This caused great alarm and fears that, if targeted violence continued, the mandate of humanitarian organizations to assist victims of violent conflict might conceivably be jeopardized (Perrin 1998, pp. 319–333). However, in retrospect, analysts generally do not believe that these attacks were linked to the arrest warrants.

Due to concern about the potential impact of arrest warrants in northern Uganda, many organizations involved in humanitarian issues in this region originally urged the ICC to adopt a "wait and see" policy, or advocate an approach of "Peace First, Justice Later" (Hovil and Quinn 2005). In a joint press release, the Refugee Law Project and Human Rights Focus stated that: "given the international community's overriding commitment to contributing to peace, the logic of prosecution is untenable. It unreasonably devalues an opportunity to seek to end a destabilizing humanitarian crisis. . . ."[45] This created a dynamic in which support of the current pursuit of justice or the ICC became rather unpopular and was seen as reckless. As a CSOPNU (n.d.) press release from before the Juba talks states: "Our greatest concern is to secure peace for the people of Uganda."

Similar concerns are increasing in the context of Darfur. It is conceivable that actors on the ground suspect international humanitarian organizations of collusion with the Court. This makes them increasingly vulnerable to attack. Moreover, many fear that if the stand-off between the Court and the Government escalates over new arrest warrants, that humanitarian organizations will be further hampered from delivering crucial services to the camps.

The relationship between the ICC and humanitarian organizations is complicated by a further consideration. Apart from concerns about how the ICC may affect an ongoing peace process, humanitarian organizations may also face difficult decisions about whether they should choose to share information with an international court,

[45] "Refugee Law Project and Human Rights Focus, Not a Crime to Talk: Give Peace a Chance in Northern Uganda." Press statement. Kampala, July 24, 2006.

or legitimately fear being called upon as witnesses in trials, when disclosing such information could ultimately impair their access to victims. A humanitarian organization such as the ICRC, involved specifically in conflicts and abiding by the principles of independence, neutrality and impartiality enshrined in its statute, deems it fundamental to remain neutral in all situations. In the light of the specificity of the ICRC mandate, which is recognized under international humanitarian law, the ICTY recognized in *Simić et al* that the ICRC benefits from a privilege and that its former employees cannot be forced to testify. A similar privilege is recognized in Rule 73 of the ICC Rules of Procedure.[46]

3.7 Traditional and Religious Leaders

In Northern Uganda, religious and traditional leaders had already pursued several of their own justice-related initiatives when the ICC became involved. For instance, religious leaders lobbied hard for an Amnesty Act of 2000, which orders that any Ugandan who has engaged in war against the government since 1986 should not be prosecuted for their participation in the rebellion.[47] The main reason why traditional leaders were so strongly supportive of this initiative is because so many of the LRA rank and file combatants had been abducted, and there was a strong push to "welcome our children home."

Another initiative on behalf of traditional leaders is that of Acholi traditional justice. Traditional justice and particularly the ceremony of the Mato Oput has been put forward assertively by local leaders as an alternative to the International Criminal Court. Zachary Lomo (2006), formerly of the Refugee Law Project, has suggested that: "the people of northern Uganda have the right to self-determination, and this implies the primary prerogative of determining how to end the conflict in northern Uganda." The debate about which form of justice is appropriate in this context has become trapped in a broader debate about universalism versus local tradition. Much of the discourse has centered on a resentment at the imposition of "Western" or "retributive" justice on a local population that is more interested, first and foremost, in peace, and then in restorative forms of local justice. This juxtaposition of choosing the route of "forgiveness," or "reconciliation" and "restorative justice" as opposed to "revenge" and "retributive justice" is often touted by politicians, and has been used in contexts as diverse as in the Colombian transition and the recent resolution granting amnesty passed by the Afghan Parliament. However, research indicates that victims usually have diverse views on forms of justice. In northern Uganda, victims were asked: "what would you like to see happen to those LRA leaders who are responsible for violations." Twenty-two percent opted for forgiveness (including reconciliation and reintegration) and 66% for punishment (including trial, imprisonment or death) (ICTJ 2005a, Table 4).

[46] Prosecutor v. Blagoje Simic, Miroslav Tadic, Simo Zaric. Case No. IT-95-9-T. International Criminal Tribunal for the Former Yugoslavia, Oct 17, 2003.

[47] Amnesty Act, 2000.

Furthermore, some of the claims put forward about traditional justice and its legitimacy deserve to be tested. Following 20 years of armed conflict in the North, the Acholi population is almost entirely displaced and the current generation has known nothing but conflict (Uganda Conflict Action Network 2007). Although the traditional leaders, Rwot Moo, was officially recognized in the Ugandan constitution in 1995, displacement had so disrupted hierarchical relationships and people's connections to the elders that those raised in the camps began to lose touch with their cultural legacy (Liu Institute for Global Issues 2005). Also, public trust began to shift from the elders to agents that could provide for their daily needs, including state representatives (LCs) and camp leaders (Liu Institute for Global Issues 2005).[48]

In northern Uganda, traditional structures have been recently revived and are consolidating into a degree of permanence. The Ker Kwaro Acholi was established in 2005, in part as a means to address the ongoing conflict (Liu Institute for Global Issues 2005). The Ker Kwaro Acholi has yet to gain full legitimacy in Acholi. Nonetheless, tradition may be an important coping mechanism in conflict, as suggested in the recent book, *Living with Bad Surroundings*, by anthropologist Finnström (2003), who writes that "cultural life is the lens through which people interpret their surrounding instability, and by which they continuously struggle to build hope for the future." Culture may also serve as a building block for future peace and stability. Finnström (2003) cites the peace accords in the west Nile in 1986 as an example where two warring parties applied local mechanisms to achieve reconciliation. In most situations, religious and traditional leaders are essential to finding long-term solutions to conflict and reweaving the social fabric of a society.

A further interesting and unanticipated consequence of the ICC's engagement in Northern Uganda has been that ICC involvement has assisted in legitimizing local leaders. In northern Uganda, Acholi elders and traditional leaders voiced early concerns that the ICC investigation and subsequent indictment would jeopardize longstanding peace efforts (James Latigo Ojera 2006). In March 2005, a delegation of Acholi religious and traditional leaders traveled to The Hague to meet the Chief Prosecutor of the ICC.[49] These interactions had the effect of casting traditional leaders as the intermediaries between victim populations and the ICC, thus bolstering their legitimacy.

However, it is not yet clear whether traditional mechanisms are suited to playing a role that deals with atrocities committed during the conflict with the LRA.[50]

---

[48] In the July 2005 survey, Forgotten Voices (ICTJ 2005a), a total of 15% of respondents in Gulu and 7% in Kitgum said they felt that their views were best represented by traditional leaders, while 34% and 38%, respectively, named their government representatives. Camp leaders were named by 14% of Gulu respondents and 17% of those in Kitgum.

[49] Statements by ICC Prosecutor and the visiting delegation of Acholi leaders from northern Uganda. International Criminal Court Press Release, The Hague, March 18, 2005.

[50] For instance, in interviews with clan elders and traditional leaders (Rwodi) a report by the Liu Institute for Global Studies finds that the majority felt that processes such as Mato Oput cannot easily be adapted "to play a role in realizing justice in the current circumstances" as "reconciliation cannot be fostered until the conflict ends; and the specific requirements of Mato Oput do not immediately translate to the scope and scale of the present conflict." Additionally, the Acholi traditional justice instruments require full consent of all participants; practically speaking, this would

Moreover, Acholi rituals do not apply to other affected groups in the north such as the Langi or Iteso (or for that matter to affected groups in south Sudan such as the Dinka). In a situation as complex as this, it will be difficult devise a traditional justice mechanism that is acceptable to all who have been affected (Allen 2005).

What is clearer is the fact that traditional justice mechanisms are unlikely to be accepted as meeting the threshold set out in the Rome Statute for a complementarity challenge. During the Juba process, Kony and Otti have suggested they are willing to participate in locally-based justice mechanisms, which has given rise to a lot of speculation as to whether these mechanisms will be included in the final peace agreement (Agence France Presse 2006). The question of local versus global justice remains. How should a global justice institution gain local legitimacy? How should it interact with religious and traditional leaders that may seek to pose their own solutions?

3.8 Mediators

The relationship between peace mediators and international courts will likely remain ambivalent. Mediators may take the view that the existence of international courts complicates their work, and may even fear being called to testify, although the risks of this happening are minimal (ICTJ 2005). On the other hand, there can be little doubt that the existence of the ICC may complicate the work of a mediator, in that it restricts the options that can be offered as part of an agreement.

The ICC Prosecutor and mediators have embarked on dialogues aimed at better understanding each other's mandates. In recent years, there have been a number of conversations between senior mediators and ICC officials, hosted by the Geneva-based Center for Humanitarian Dialogue. Their goal is to help senior mediators to understand the ICC better, and for the ICC to develop its understanding of the concerns and techniques used by senior mediators. Apart from this initiative, there exists little opportunity for direct interaction between the ICC and mediators, particularly in the context of specific negotiations.

It can be argued that the existence of the ICC clarifies the stance of mediators in the sense that the issue of future prosecutions by the ICC is outside of their control. Nonetheless, it remains to be seen how mediators will choose to position themselves vis-à-vis that fact. Some mediators, under UN instructions, are in any case bound not to ratify agreements that allow for amnesties for genocide, war crimes and crimes against humanity. On the other hand, mediators from organizations other than the UN are usually free from such restrictions.

Mediators also often face other challenges and concerns, including the halting of ongoing violence. Work on ongoing violations should begin before and not be

---

mean an admission of guilt on behalf of all parties involved (Liu Institute for Global Issues 2005). See also Thomas Harlacher and Caritas Gulu Archdiocese (2006).

deferred to the negotiating table. Lastly, it is relevant to note that mediators remain at liberty to approach the Security Council if they deem an Article 16 resolution necessary.

4 Preserving Justice Options During Ongoing Conflict

In some situations, justice will have to wait, particularly in areas where there is no jurisdiction for the International Criminal Court, or no inclination by the Security Council to act. This may be the case despite the fact that widespread crimes have occurred. Recent examples where the international community has not shown impetus to take action include situations in which there were massive human rights violations, such as Afghanistan, Liberia, DRC (before 2002), and Iraq (for violations other than those committed by Saddam Hussein). In such situations, there are a number of strategies that can assist to preserve or determine justice options at a later stage. These include consultation of the public on justice options and documentation of past and current abuses. Some situations may also require a rapid response in terms of evidence preservation.

Even if investigations do proceed, different approaches are needed to preserve the investigative effort and narrow the exposure of victims and witness.

4.1 Consultation on Justice Options

The peace versus justice dilemma has played out dramatically in recent years in Afghanistan. First, while many originally thought that peace would arrive for Afghanistan with the fall of the Taliban in December 2001 and the subsequent Bonn Agreement, violence has resurged in the south and conflict between NATO and the Taliban/Al-Qaeda continues. Second, since Bonn the international community invited many Northern Alliance leaders into the government, despite the fact that many are known human rights abusers. The current government's lack of credibility has contributed to further violence in the south. Third, international policy makers have always argued that the warlords should not be tackled as they may destabilize Afghanistan further. Instead, Afghanistan remains inherently unstable and the warlords have consolidated their power, including securing official government positions or posts as Parliamentarians.

In the face of this, the Afghan Independent Human Rights Commission created under the Bonn Agreement took important steps to promote the cause of justice in Afghanistan. In 2004, it carried out a nationwide consultation in very difficult security conditions, interviewing over 6,500 persons on their views on justice. The AIHRC presented its results and recommendations in an important report, A Call for Justice, published in January 2005.[51] The report showed clearly that most people believed that there is an integral link between justice and security: 76% of respondents said that bringing war criminals to justice would increase rather than decrease security.[52]

The report made a strong impact on the government and President Karzai "ordered" its implementation. This led to the formulation of an Action Plan on Peace, Justice and Reconciliation by the government, which was adopted in December 2005. The Action Plan – in itself a very ambitious government commitment to deal with the past – states in its preamble:

> To build sustainable peace and stability, deal with past abuses, reconcile victims, perpetrators and other stakeholders, and to move from a divided past into a shared future is a difficult task in almost any post conflict situation where institutions tend to be weak, there are few resources, unstable security and a war-affected population. In order to transition into a peaceful life and to strengthen national reconciliation in Afghanistan, the past should be dealt with in a bold and just way that avoids revenge. We should explore ways to build co-existence amongst the citizens of this country based on the principles of tolerance, forgiveness and the requirements of a social order premised on law and order.

Nonetheless, warlords remain powerful in Afghanistan. Many are now members of parliament which, on March 10, 2007, passed a resolution for their own amnesty (see also Nader Nadery 2007). This constitutes a setback, and may affect implementation of the Action Plan. At the same time, Afghanistan demonstrates the difference that the power of consultation and a single actor – in this case, the Afghan Independent Human Rights Commission – can make.

4.2 Evidence Gathering and Documentation

Documenting crimes to a sufficient standard is an essential first step in preserving justice options during an ongoing conflict. Nonetheless, it is rare for actors (domestic or international) to engage in the kind of documentation that goes beyond reporting violations to gathering the kinds of evidence useful to a subsequent criminal procedure. In order to understand the strategies and techniques of documenting mass crime in situations of ongoing conflict, it is important to understand some of the intricacies of investigating and prosecuting these crimes. Crimes such as genocide, crimes against humanity and war crimes differ from ordinary crimes in they are generally of such a scale that they require a degree of organization or system to perpetrate. The key challenge in prosecuting system crimes does not normally lie

---

[51] For a copy of the Afghan Independent Human Rights Commission's report "A Call for Justice", see: www.aihrc.org.af/Rep_29_Eng/rep29_1_05call4justice.pdf.

[52] Also, 44.9% of respondents were of the view that war criminals should be tried now; 25.5% said within 2 years; 18.8% said within 2–5 years, and only 8.4% said 5 years or more from now. When the report was presented to President Karzai in Jan 2005, he mandated a three-person expert committee to work on an action plan to implement the recommendation. The action plan was adopted by the Afghan government in December 2005 and launched in early 2007.

in proving that facts occurred, but on the nature of participation and the knowledge and intent of those "behind the scenes" (Seils and Wierda 2005, p. 321).

Investigation techniques for "system crimes," as developed initially at Nuremberg and later by the ad hoc tribunals, differ from those of ordinary crimes (OHCHR 2006, p. 11). In addition to traditional investigation techniques-such as the reconstruction of the crime-scene and forensic analysis – investigation into system crimes requires a detailed analysis of the particular practices and structure of military and paramilitary organizations (OHCHR 2006, p. 12). In order to present an accurate understanding of how these events occurred, it is essential that investigators uncover the nature of political, historical and institutional relationships. An analysis of the local context and dynamics of violence – as well as analyses of documentary evidence – are other important elements in the investigation of system crimes. The testimony of so-called "insiders" can be particularly crucial, but is also very difficult to obtain.

Another important element in investigating system crimes is the recording, recovery and preservation of documentary evidence (Seils and Wierda 2005, p. 321). Such evidence offers several key advantages: it is less susceptible to challenges by the defense and does not face the same challenges to credibility likely in the case of human testimony. Documentary evidence, however, is vulnerable to physical destruction.

A key question in the documenting of crimes relates to the admissibility of evidence in criminal trials. In general, common law systems take a more technical approach to admissibility. Civil law systems tend to be more liberal in their admissibility of evidence, due to the role of the investigative judge, and are guided mainly by the criteria of relevance. International criminal courts have followed a hybrid approach, being relatively flexible in the admission of evidence, and taking into account the difficulties of securing evidence in the case of system crimes (e.g., there may be only a few surviving witnesses and physical evidence may have been destroyed). The general standard is that probative evidence is admissible regardless of its format, unless the rights of the accused are to be deemed prejudiced by admission (Seils and Wierda 2005, p. 323). Hearsay and uncorroborated evidence are admissible in certain circumstances.

Groups active on the ground during an ongoing conflict may contribute to the gathering of documentation and evidence that could assist justice options at a future stage, but will not usually be able to fulfill the same role as an investigative judge or prosecutor if they do not know which procedural rules will apply. However, their efforts in documenting may still be very useful for the following purposes:

- *Identifying, establishing links and maintaining contact with potential witnesses.* The guiding principle when protecting potential witnesses must be to "do no harm" and to ensure their wellbeing, prior, during and after the proceedings (OHCHR 2006, p. 18). Apart from protection measures, sensitivity to the needs of witnesses is of the utmost importance. This can be achieved by effective and regular communication with witnesses and by providing treatment that respects cultural and social particularities. The aim should always be to create a relationship of trust and respect with the witness. Civil society organizations can play a very important role in this respect, particularly in situations where there may be significant displacement – in which case potential witnesses may be difficult to locate in the future.

- *Retrieving and preserving documentary evidence.* NGOs will usually lack capacity to conduct full investigations into systems and may encounter challenges in attempts to gather relevant documentation, for instance from military archives.
- *Taking statements from victims and witnesses.* It may be common for civil society organizations such as human rights or victim groups to seek to take statements from victims in the immediate aftermath of an event. This area should, however, be approached with care, not least because inconsistencies in prior statements may be used to challenge the credibility of a witness at trial.
- *Documenting statements by perpetrators that may reflect their intent.* On occasion, civil society and particularly the media have played an important role in documenting statements by perpetrators that can subsequently be used to prove knowledge and intent. The role of journalists in this regard is very important and, while they may on occasion provide valuable testimony, their mandate in terms of protecting their sources should also be recognized.
- *Conflict mapping.* Conflict mapping is a particular technique, the purpose of which is to be able to make a quantitative analysis that can help identify trends and patterns of abuses. These documents serve in many instances as a lead for further criminal investigations. Some international NGOs such as No Peace without Justice and the Europe and Eurasia Division of the Rule of Law Initiative of the American Bar Association (ABA CEELI), have engaged in conflict mapping or have trained national actors in these techniques in different contexts, including Kosovo, Sierra Leone, and Afghanistan (NPWJ 2004).

4.3 Rapid Response?

Investigations during or in the immediate aftermath of conflict may be considered urgent because evidence may be lost, destroyed or weakened with the passage of time. There may be a risk of intentional contamination or destruction of evidence, particularly by those seeking to distort the course of investigations (Seils and Wierda 2005, p. 322). It is important to put mechanisms in place to ensure the effective protection of evidential sites or documents for future investigations. Protocols may be required to govern the chain of custody and other such considerations (OHCHR 2006, p. 15). Ad hoc international assistance might be sought on issues such as forensics.[53] NGOs like Physicians for Human Rights and volunteer teams of forensic scientists have often been deployed to assist the investigation process, or to safeguard the opportunity for a subsequent prosecution.[54]

---

[53] See discussion in the context of "Justice Rapid Response" initiative, at www.justice rapidresponse.org/.

[54] Their work has been used by the ICTY, and at national trials and truth commissions. For example, the UN/OAS Mission in Haiti brought in a team of Argentine forensic experts in 1997 to investigate

On the other hand, urgency should not be exaggerated. In the absence of specific attempts to destroy evidence or harm witnesses, system crimes such as genocide or crimes against humanity may generate large numbers of witnesses or other forms of evidence that can be retrieved at a later date, when it may be more secure to do so.

In some situations, states may wish to take steps to preserve evidence but may lack the capacity to do so. A current intergovernmental initiative, known as the Justice Rapid Response Initiative (JRRI), seeks to establish an international cooperative mechanism, which could provide a wide range of investigative assistance to states and international institutions on request.[55] Voluntary assistance could be rendered by a state or by a multi-state team at the request of another state or international institution, in order to identify, collect and preserve information that could assist a wide range of justice mechanisms. The specific functions envisaged for such a JRRI include: patterns of violence investigation; conflict mapping; identification of potential witnesses; documentary and physical evidence investigation; forensic mapping; visual image collection; identification and facilitating the preservation of the integrity of massacre and burial sites; and identification of possible focuses for further investigations – in full consideration of the physical and psychosocial safety of those affected by such activities.

The advantage of JRRI is that it could put in place mechanisms that would avoid the need for complex bilateral ad hoc arrangements on the giving of such assistance, or the need to generate a request by the United Nations. JRRI could thus significantly reduce response times by providing assistance that is both impartial and meets international standards.[56] However, there is still confusion about the cope of such a mechanism. For instance, should assistance be given only at the earlier stages of a process or also during the prosecution that may follow? Can that still be said to constitute rapid response? On the other hand, what is the purpose of collecting evidence when there is no mechanism to feed into? While JRRI may provide a useful contribution, it may still be some time before it becomes a functional mechanism.

The Office of the High Commissioner for Human Rights (OHCHR) also has an Emergency Response Unit. Its purpose is to respond to directives of the Security Council and the newly established Human Rights Council to deploy fact finding missions. It is also mandated to conduct ad hoc investigations and commissions of inquiry in areas that have recently experienced grave human rights violations, war crimes, and crimes against humanity (O'Neill 2007, p. 6). The reports of such commissions of inquiry may be admissible in subsequent criminal trials (OHCHR 2006, p. 15). In 2006, the Unit responded to requests to send special investigators to

---

a mass grave and prepare evidence for a trial in the national judiciary where several senior Haitian army officers were accused of murder. Neither the mission's human rights officers nor the Haitian institutions had the necessary equipment or expertise.

[55] See JRR outcome document, New York March 13, 2007, at www.justicerapidresponse.org/public_area.htm.

[56] Seven meetings have taken place to help define and launch the JRR concept: New York (April 2004, December 2004 and 2005, March 2007, November 2007); The Hague (June 2004) and Venice (June 2006). These involved representatives of governments, civil society and international justice institutions. See also Justice Rapid Response Feasibility Study, October 2005, at www.justicerapidresponse.org/public_area.htm.

the Lebanon (twice), Darfur[57] (twice), Guinea, Liberia, Chad, Nepal, the Occupied Palestinian Territories, and Timor-Leste. Of particular significance has been the International Commission of Inquiry on Darfur, which led to Security Council resolution 1593, which referred the situation in Darfur since 1 July 2002 to the Prosecutor of the ICC.[58] The UN established this commission of inquiry – also known as the "Cassese Commission" – in 2004 to investigate reports of crimes committed in Darfur.[59]

4.4 Investigations into Ongoing Conflict: Practices of the ICC

To meet the challenges of investigating in situations of ongoing conflict, the Office of the Prosecutor (OTP) of the ICC developed certain overall strategies and policies aimed at reducing the length and scope of its investigations, thereby minimizing the exposure of victims and potential witnesses.[60] Consistent with the approach adopted by the Special Court for Sierra Leone (SCSL), the ICC adopted a policy of focusing efforts on the most serious crimes and on those who bear the greatest responsibility for these crimes. This enabled it to deal with only a limited number of cases.[61] The approach is sequenced, meaning that one case at a time in a situation will be investigated.[62] Cases are selected according to their gravity.[63] Criteria for establishing that a case is of particular gravity have been developed by the OTP. In assessing the

---

[57] The Commission of Inquiry on Darfur established by SC Resolution 1,564 of September 18, 2004 developed its own working method. The commission made it clear from the outset that it was not a judicial body. The commission discussed the standard of proof that it would apply in its investigations. It decided that it could not comply with the standards normally adopted by criminal courts (proof of facts beyond a reasonable doubt), nor with those used by international prosecutors and judges for the purpose of confirming indictments (that there must be a prima facie case). It concluded that the most appropriate standard was that, "requiring a reliable body of material consistent with other verified circumstances, which tends to show that a person may reasonably be suspected of being involved in the commission of a crime." The commission did not make a final judgment on criminal guilt; rather, it made an assessment of possible suspects and thus tried to pave the way for future investigations, and possible indictments, by a prosecutor.

[58] Security Council Resolution 1,593 (2005), March 31.

[59] Pursuant to Security Council Resolution 1,564, September 18, 2004. The commission was presided over by Professor Antonio Cassese, an authority in international law and human rights law, who also served as the first president of the first UN International Criminal Tribunal for the former Yugoslavia.

[60] Second Public Hearing of the Office of the Prosecutor, NGOs and other Experts, New York, October 18, 2006, 1.

[61] Second Public Hearing of the Office of the Prosecutor, NGOs and other Experts, New York, October 18, 2006, 1. This approach was also developed largely for efficiency reasons.

[62] Second Public Hearing of the Office of the Prosecutor, NGOs and other Experts, New York, October 18, 2006, 1. In the DRC, the OTP started by investigating the case against Thomas Lubanga, who was associated with the ethnic group of the Hemas. The OTP will announce a second case in the near future.

[63] See Article 17(1)(d) of the ICC Statute.

gravity of the act that constitutes a crime, the Prosecutor has indicated that the scale, nature, manner of commission, and impact of the crimes committed will be relevant (OTP 2006, p. 5; see also OTP 2003). The degree of participation in the commission of the crime is mentioned as an important criterion to establish gravity.[64] This limited approach should assist the office in reducing the number of witnesses called to testify, which it considers essential to ensuring the security of those affected.[65] The approach is also tailored to be sensitive to the political realities of limitations on resources.

However, in taking a narrow approach to investigations, the ICC has faced criticism in its investigations in the DRC, notably from NGOs (including local civil society organizations). For instance, in the case against Thomas Lubanga, a leader of one of the major militias in Ituri associated with the Hema ethnic group, NGOs have argued that the charges are too narrow and do not represent the range and nature of the crimes committed during the conflict.[66] Human Rights Watch (HRW) has argued that sequencing in this case may have negative implications for the perception of the Prosecutor's impartiality by the local population. The organization has also said that the absence of warrants against Lendu leaders has led to a strong perception among the Hema community and others that the ICC is carrying out "selective justice" on charges.[67] Others have argued that the charges of enlisting and conscripting children and using them to participate in hostilities are too narrow, and that child recruitment is not generally perceived as a crime in eastern Congo, let alone as the gravest. Finally, there are those who have argued that restricting charges to high-level accused eliminates the possibility of dealing with perpetrators who have a direct link with victims. This gives rise to an impression that justice is not being done in their particular case (Human Rights Watch 2006, p. 13). The recent proceedings in the Lubanga case, resulting in the Trial Chamber ordering a stay of proceedings and the release of Thomas Lubnaga (both decisions by the

[64] The PTC has affirmed that focusing on those in leadership positions is a core component of the gravity threshold in the Rome Statute. PTC I found that the gravity requirement under article 17(1)(d) "is intended to ensure that the court initiates cases only against the most senior leaders suspected of being the most responsible for the crimes within the jurisdiction of the court allegedly committed in any given situation under investigation." Prosecutor v. Thomas Lubanga Dyilo, ICC, Case No. ICC-01/04-01/06, "Decision on the Prosecutor's Application for a Warrant of Arrest", Article 58, February 24, 2006, www.icc-cpi.int/library/cases/ICC-01-04-01-06-8-US-Corr_English.pdf, para. 50.

[65] Second Public Hearing of the Office of the Prosecutor, NGOs, and Other Experts, NY 2006, 1.

[66] Joint letter to the Chief Prosecutor of the International Criminal Court, by Avocats Sans Frontières, Center for Justice and Reconciliation, Coalition Nationale pour la Cour Pénale Internationale – RCD, Fédération Internationale des Ligues des Droits de l'Homme, Human Rights Watch, International Center for Transitional Justice, Redress, Women's Initiatives for Gender Justice, at hrw.org/english/docs/2006/08/01/congo13891_txt.htm.

[67] Second Public Hearing of the Office of the Prosecutor, NGOs, and Other Experts, NY 2006, 6. In the meantime two ICC arrest warrants have been successfully executed against two members of the Hema community, Germain Katanga and Mathieu Nqudjolo Chui.

ICC Trial Chamber I were subject to appeal upon writing), have demonstrated the vulnerability of the case.[68]

The question is therefore whether the OTP's approach to narrow investigations lends itself well to effective deployment in complex conflicts. In Uganda, the focused nature of the investigation has generally been acknowledged to be efficient; but progress on investigations on certain other conflicts, including Sudan, has at times been slow. A sequential approach may also lead to tensions between different fighting factions. Also, a situation-based focus risks ignoring regionalized aspects of the conflicts. On the other hand, narrow and focused investigations have the advantages of allowing the Court to contact fewer witnesses and strictly limit contact and exposure.

4.5 Security and Protection of Victims and Witnesses

Situations of ongoing conflict raise particular challenges to the need to provide protection. Some of the obstacles include problems arising from a total collapse of functional institutions, the absence of programs or legislation to protect victims and lack of state cooperation. Effective measures of protection have been a constant challenge for the ICC and other tribunals, due to the nature of the crimes. Factored in is the lack of ability to rely on organs of the state, which may not function to full capacity during the conflict, or which may be unreliable. The measures for the protection of victims are kept confidential; court officials have recently reported that to date, no-one identified as a potential witness has been harmed.

A critical question in an ongoing conflict is whether protection should encompass only those who will testify, or whether protection should extend more broadly to victim populations that may be affected by the actions of the court. In Dafur, the court solicited several opinions on this issue – including from the UN High Commissioner for Human Rights and from Professor Cassese, who had headed the ICI in Darfur. Professor Cassese argued that the obligation to protect victims under the Rome Statute encompasses both the protection of victims as potential witnesses in trial proceedings and the protection of victims in general.[69] The obligation to protect therefore goes "beyond the scope of trial proceedings and is more humanitarian in nature." Its main aims are to terminate and deter serious offences against victims, "in particular for such vulnerable categories as civilians, women and children."[70]

[68] ICC Press Release, "Trial Chamber imposes a stay on the proceedings of the case against Thomas Lubanga Dyilo", The Hague, 16 June 2008, ICC-CPI-20080616-PR324-ENG; ICC Press Release, "Trial Chamber I ordered the release of Thomas Lubanga Dyilo - Implementation of the decision is pending", The Hague, 2 July 2008, ICC-CPI-20080702-PR334-ENG; "ICC to Hear Arguments Tuesday About the Possible Release of Congo Rebel Leader Lubanga", Voice of America June 24, 2008: http://www.ictj.org/en/news/coverage/article/1780.html.

[69] Observations on Issues Concerning the Protection of Victims and the Preservation of Evidence in the Proceedings on Darfur Pending before the ICC, August 25, 2006, ICC-02/05, 3.

[70] Observations on Issues Concerning the Protection of Victims and the Preservation of Evidence in the Proceedings on Darfur Pending before the ICC, August 25, 2006, ICC-02/05, 3.

He recommended certain measures in this respect to the ICC, including to take steps to establish expeditiously the criminal responsibility of those causing instability and insecurity in the affected area. He recommend to the ICC Chamber to call on the government of Sudan to protect victims, and summon Sudanese officials to report on specific measures implemented to protect witnesses and to hold perpetrators accountable. The ICC should also call on third states and other entities (including NGOs) operating in Darfur to provide full assistance to victims (medical, humanitarian and psychological) of such crimes. Noncompliance with the measures ordered by the chamber should be reported to the Security Council.[71]

The High Commissioner for Human Rights argued in her submission to the Court that it is possible to conduct investigations into serious violations of humanitarian law in situations of ongoing conflict without imposing an unreasonable risk of reprisal on victims and witnesses.[72] Furthermore, she observed that the mere presence of the Prosecutor on the ground could have the potential to lead to increased protection of vulnerable groups. The Prosecutor took a different view. He argued that: "the continuing insecurity in Darfur is prohibitive of effective investigations inside Darfur, particularly in light of the absence of a functioning and sustainable system for the protection of victims and witnesses."[73] As a consequence, investigative efforts by the Prosecutor have so far been conducted outside Darfur.[74] According to the Prosecutor, this has not impeded the Court's ability to gather significant amounts of information and evidence on crimes committed.[75]

In general, the OTP stated that criminal investigations should contribute to the protection of the civilian population in Darfur, in particular by preventing future crimes being perpetrated against the civilian population. But it argued that neither the OTP nor the chamber have the responsibility to enhance security for victims of crimes in Darfur.[76] The responsibility for security of the civilian population in Darfur rests solely with the government of Sudan and, where appropriate, with other

[71] Observations on Issues Concerning the Protection of Victims and the Preservation of Evidence in the Proceedings on Darfur Pending before the ICC, August 25, 2006, ICC-02/05, 3.

[72] Observations of the United Nations High Commissioner for Human Rights invited in Application of Rule 103 of the Rules of Procedure and Evidence, October 10, 2006, ICC-02/05.

[73] Prosecutor's Response to Cassese's Observation on Issues Concerning the Protection of Victims and the Preservation of Evidence in the Proceedings on Darfur Pending before the ICC, September 11, 2006, ICC-02/05. Ibid, 19.

[74] In response to the OHCHR, the Prosecutor observed that the risk for victims and witnesses in the context of a criminal investigation is higher compared to inquiries on Human Rights violations as conducted by the OHCHR, since the former will have more severe consequences for the respective perpetrator.

[75] This was confirmed when the PTC issued arrest warrants against two accused in Darfur. Prosecutor v. Ahmad Muhammad Harun ("Ahmad Harun") and Ali Muhammad AL-ABD-AL-Rahman ("Ali Kushayb"), Decision on the Prosecution Application under Article 58(7) of the Statute, ICC-02/05-01/07.

[76] Prosecutor v. Ahmad Muhammad Harun ("Ahmad Harun") and Ali Muhammad AL-ABD-AL-Rahman ("Ali Kushayb"), Decision on the Prosecution Application under Article 58(7) of the Statute, ICC-02/05-01/07; Prosecutor's Response to Cassese's Observation on Issues Concerning the Protection of Victims and the Preservation of Evidence in the Proceedings on Darfur Pending before the ICC, September 11, 2006, ICC-02/05, 8.

actors such as the UNSC and the AU. The Prosecutor also emphasizes that the mandate to protect victims and witnesses, "can not realistically be viewed as a duty to protect all the victims in Darfur regardless of their lack of connection to the investigation."[77]

It is obvious that the Prosecutor cannot be responsible for the broader consequences of violence or even for attacks on persons that may be presumed to be associated with the court. On the other hand, it is equally clear that the Prosecutor has a responsibility to work in way that will minimize the risk of the Court's activities to broader populations in conflict areas, including victim populations and humanitarian groups. Protection and the monitoring of security are complex imperatives, involving the overlapping responsibilities of numerous actors.

5 Conclusion

This paper has sought to analyze some of the current practices followed when dealing with justice in ongoing conflict. It is not possible to be empirical about experiences to date, in terms of suggesting whether indictments during ongoing conflicts promote or hinder the achievement of peace. However, it is clear that with the advent of international prosecutors, justice will increasingly be pursued before conflicts end. In some instances, such as Uganda and Colombia, the existence of the ICC may be leading to a different approach to justice in ongoing conflict than was the case prior to its establishment.

For these purposes, it is essential to envisage a landscape where a range of actors try to implement their mandates, in order to promote increased understanding of the issues and challenges as viewed by each. Both the mandates of peace negotiators and those of prosecutors are vitally important. This environment concerning justice in ongoing conflict is highly complex and emotive, and polarization in the debate easily occurs and speculation abounds. This should be avoided. Prosecutors should proceed with prudence, whereas negotiators should continue their task with a thorough understanding of new realities. Furthermore, it is necessary to develop and employ techniques that serve to preserve justice options or to conduct careful investigations.

Acknowledgments Our thanks and deep gratitude to Richard Bailey, Cecile Aptel, Abdul Tejan Cole and Caitlin Reiger, all from the Prosecutions Program of the International Center for Transitional Justice, for their valuable contributions to this paper, often stemming from their personal experience with these important questions. The authors are Program Associate and Director at the Prosecutions Program at ICTJ respectively. The views are those of the authors and other contributors listed here, and not those of the organization.

[77] Prosecutor's Response to Cassese's Observation on Issues Concerning the Protection of Victims and the Preservation of Evidence in the Proceedings on Darfur Pending before the ICC, September 11, 2006, ICC-02/05, 30.

References

Agence France Presse (2006) Ugandan rebel leader ready to face justice at home; officials. Agence France Presse – English, December 21, 2006

Allen T (2005) War and justice in Northern Uganda: an assessment of the International Criminal Court's intervention. Crisis states Research Centre, Development Studies Institute, London School of Economics. February 2005 (draft)

Bass GJ (2003) Stay the hand of vengeance: the politics of war crimes tribunals. Princeton University Press, Princeton

CSOPNU (n.d.) Failure to embrace peace a bitter blow for Northern Uganda. Press release. Civil Society Organizations for Peace in Northern Uganda

CSOPNU (2004) Nowhere to hide: humanitarian protection threats in Northern Uganda. December 2004. Civil Society Organizations for Peace in Northern Uganda

CSOPNU (2006) Counting the cost: twenty years of war in Northern Uganda. March 30, 2006. Civil Society Organizations for Peace in Northern Uganda

Coté L (2005) Reflections on the exercise of final discretion in International Criminal Law. JICL 2005:9

Finnström S (2003) Living with bad surroundings: war and existential uncertainty in Acholiland, Northern Uganda. Uppsala University Library, Uppsala

Flint J, de Waal A (2008) Justice off course in Darfur. International Herald Tribune, 28 June 2008

Goldstone RJ (1998) Bringing war criminals to justice during ongoing war. In: Moore J (ed) Hard choices, moral dilemmas in humanitarian interventions. Rowman & Littlefield, Lanham

Goldstone RJ (2000) For humanity: reflections of a war crimes investigator. J Conflict Security Law 5:63–103

Grainger S, James J (2006) Head hunted. Focus on Africa magazine, October–December 2006

Hayner P (2007) Negotiating peace in liberia: preserving the possibility of justice. HD and ICTJ report, 2007. http://www.ictj.org/en/news/pubs/index.html

Hazan P (2000) La Justice à Face a la Guerre, de Nuremberg à La Haye. Stok, Paris

Hovil L, Quinn J (2005) Peace first, justice later: traditional justice in Northern Uganda. Refugee Law Project, Working Paper No. 17, July 2005

Human Rights Watch (2006) The selection of situations and cases for trial before the International Criminal Court. October 2006

ICTJ (2005a) Forgotten voices: a population-based survey on attitudes about peace and justice in Northern Uganda. July 2005. International Center for Transitional Justice and the Human Rights Center, University of Berkeley. www.ictj.org/images/content/1/2/127.pdf

ICTJ (2005b) The ICC and conflict mediation. June 2005. International Center for Transitional Justice. www.ictj.org/images/content/1/1/119.pdf

ICTJ (2007) When the war ends: a population-based survey on attitudes about peace, justice and social reconstruction in Northern Uganda, Dec. 2007. International Center for Transitional Justice, Human Rights Center of the University of Berkeley, and Payson Center for International Development at Tulane University. http://www.ictj.org/images/content/8/8/884.pdf

IDMC (2006) Only peace can restore the confidence of the displaced, 2nd edition. Refugee Law Project and the Internal Displacement Monitoring Centre of the Norwegian Refugee Council

International Bar Association (2007) ICC monitoring and outreach programme, Second Outreach Report, May 2007, 16. www.ibanet.org/images/downloads/ICC/ICC%20Outreach%20report_%20May%202007.pdf

International Crisis Group (2006) Colombia: towards peace and justice? Latin America Report No 16, March 14, 2006

International Crisis Group (2007) Northern Uganda: seizing the opportunity for peace. Africa Report No. 124, April 26, 2007

James Latigo Ojera (2006) The Acholi traditional conflict management. Uganda Living Law J 4(1)

Kerr R (2004) The International Criminal Tribunal for the former Yugoslavia: an exercise in law, politics and diplomacy. Oxford University Press, Oxford

Liu Institute for Global Issues (2005) Roco Wat I Acoli / Restoring relationships in Acholi-land: traditional approaches to justice and reconciliation. September 2005. Liu Institute for Global Issues, Gulu District NGO Forum and Ker Kwaro Acholi

Lomo ZA (2006) Why the International Criminal Court must withdraw indictments against the top LRA leaders: a legal perspective. Refugee Law Project, Makerere University Faculty of Law, August 2006

Mackintosh K (2004) Note for humanitarian organizations on cooperation with international tribunals. International Review of the Red Cross Current Issues and Comments 86(853):131–146

Maogoto JN (2004) War crimes and realpolitik: international justice from Word War I to the 21st century. Lynne Rienner, London

Nader Nadery A (2007) Peace or justice? transitional justice in Afghanistan. Int J Transitional Justice 1(1):173–179

NPWJ (2004) Conflict mapping in Sierra Leone, violations of international humanitarian law from 1991 to 2002. No Peace Without Justice, Freetown

Office of the Prosecutor, International Criminal Court, "Criteria for Selection of Situations and Cases," draft policy paper, June 2006, 5.

Office of the Prosecutor, International Criminal Court, "Paper on some policy issues before the Office of the Prosecutor," September 7, 2003

OHCHR (2006) Rule of law tools for post conflict states, Prosecution Initiatives. www.ohchr.org/english/about/publications/docs/ruleoflaw-Prosecutions_en.pdf

O'Neill WG (2007) Justice rapid response options, draft dated February 22, 2007

Otim M, Wierda M (2008) Justice at Juba: international obligations and local demands in Northern Uganda. In: Waddell N, Clark P (ed) Courting conflict? justice, peace and the ICC in Africa. Royal African Society, London

Perriello T, Wierda M (2006) The special court for Sierra Leone under scrutiny. International Center for Transitional Justice Prosecutions Case Studies Series, p. 30. www.ictj.org/static/Prosecutions/Sierra.study.pdf

Perrin P (1998) The impact of humanitarian aid on conflict development. Int Rev Red Cross 1998(323):319–333

Scharf MP (2000) The tools for enforcing international criminal justice in the new millennium: lessons from the Yugoslav tribunal. De Paul Law Review 2000:951

Security Council Report (2006) Monthly forecast, Uganda, October 2006

Seils P, Wierda M (2005) Evidence. In Dinah L. Shelton (ed) Encyclopedia of genocide and crimes against humanity, vol 1. Macmillan, Detroit

Thomas Harlacher, Caritas Gulu Archdiocese (2006) Traditional ways of coping in Acholi: cultural provisions for reconciliation and healing from war. Kampala

Uganda Conflict Action Network (2007). Conflict background. www.ugandacan.org/history.php. April 20, 2007

World Health Organization (2005) Health and mortality survey among internally displaced persons in Gulu, Kitgum and Pader Districts, Northern Uganda. Government of Uganda Ministry of Health, UNICEF, UNFPA, WFP and the International Rescue Committee. July 2005

Zhou (2006) The enforcement of arrest warrants by international forces. ICJ 4(2):216

Conflict Mediation and the ICC: Challenges and Options for Pursuing Peace with Justice at the Regional Level

Chandra Lekha Sriram

Abstract Whilst accountability and mediation processes are largely state-focused, many conflicts and attendant human rights violations are transboundary and even regionalized. This creates difficulties for traditional political and legal mandates tied largely to territorial states. As a result broader dynamics may be missed and state-focused solutions may end up neither addressing the true underpinnings of conflict or the human rights violations. This dilemma may pose a bigger challenge to mediation and accountability than the straight justice/peace tension, making holistic peace and justice even more elusive. What are the challenges at regional level in contemporary practice? What is the range of options in this context that mediators may put to the parties? Are they the same as the range in domestic processes, such as criminal accountability, truth and reconciliation processes, traditional justice, vetting, limited amnesties, processes with pardons, and if so how might they be modified to suit the context?

1 Introduction

In keeping with the theme of this conference, this paper will focus upon challenges and opportunities for pursuing "holistic" peace and justice simultaneously, with a focus upon options for mediators and others designing both peace and accountability processes. I do not assume or argue that "peace" or "justice" are mutually exclusive, though I recognize the tensions that may emerge in practice. While the paper will not focus upon mediation processes *per se* but rather challenges and options for mediators. While the paper will consider the possibility of accountability processes both through and beyond the International Criminal Court (ICC), it will take special account of the role that the ICC may play. I will argue that the challenge of pursuing

---

C. L. Sriram
University of East London School of Law, Duncan House, Stratford High Street, London E15 2JB, UK
e-mail: c.sriram@uel.ac.uk

K. Ambos et al. (eds.), *Building a Future on Peace and Justice: Studies on Transitional Justice, Peace and Development.*

peace with justice is particularly complex where both conflicts and the patterns of human rights violations have been transboundary or regional. I argue that this is the case because mediators are generally authorized to address country-specific causes of conflict and actors, be they state or non-state, and because the design of accountability mechanisms generally focuses upon crimes committed on the territory of (or against the territory of) a particular nation-state. Where key players are found outside state borders, holistic peace and accountability processes may be difficult to craft or implement.

2 Beyond Peace Vs. Justice: Can Holistic Approaches Be Developed?

The purported tension between peace and justice is well-known, and while it continues to be real and important, should not be our focus here. Rather, I will only outline it very briefly, before turning to specific debates about the issue in relation to the ICC, and to a variety of options and challenges in practice. As is by now elaborated in an ever-expanding literature, demands for accountability are often in tension with goals of conflict resolution (Parlevliet 2002; Lutz et al. 2003; Hannum 2006; Putnam 2002; Bell 2003; Human Rights Watch 2004), never more so than when accused perpetrators continue to hold significant power, whether as state actors or non-state armed groups. In either circumstance, those accused of serious violations may have the capacity to disrupt or terminate peace negotiations, or to stall, undermine, or terminate implementation of peace agreements once they have been reached. The risk is not simply that of reverting to armed conflict, however; peace agreements and processes, and accountability processes, seek to (re)install democracy and the rule of law, and here they may have at least some complementary, if difficult to achieve, aims.[1]

Of course, as is well understood by now, the choice is never merely peace or justice. Rather, what may be and often is agreed in peace processes, or resolved before or after them through bureaucratic processes or informal bargaining, are a range of measures, including, and between, the two extremes on the continuum from widespread prosecution to blanket amnesty. These may include limited prosecution, limited or conditional amnesty, vetting or lustration, reform of the judicial or security sectors, reform of the constitution, reparations, and truth commissions. Decisions about accountability are not made in a vacuum, however: given political realities on the ground, options will be circumscribed.[2] Further, many measures that may appear in direct contradiction to accountability may also be negotiated, in addition to or instead of partial or full amnesty. These may include, *inter alia*, measures to integrate ex-fighters, whether state or non-state, into the security forces, measures to allow

[1] On the challenges of transitional justice generally, and of developing transitional institutions and rebuilding rule of law and security, see Teitel (2000); Roht-Arriaza (1995); Sriram (2004a); and Mani (2002).

[2] Sriram (2004a, chaps. 2 and conclusion) discuss these trade-offs or choices in comparative perspective. On truth commissions, see Hayner (2000); Rotberg and Thompson (2000).

former rebels to participate legally in the political process, and even form political parties. It may also include measures to allow all parties to a conflict (or selected ones) a portion of, or a stake in the governance of, the state's economic resources. Finally it may include measures granting a group or groups a degree of territorial autonomy over a particular region (Sriram 2008a). Given that fighting forces will most likely have been involved in some degree of violations of human rights, any such concessions have consequences not only for accountability generally, but for past and potentially future victims, but these concessions are fairly common, perhaps increasingly so (Hartzell et al. 2001, p. 183; Hoddie and Hartzell 2003; Walter 2002; Sisk 1996; Roeder and Rothchild 2005).

The range of options for mediators is thus wide, and while there can be no single prescription for all negotiated peace processes, a "holistic" process of peace and accountability is likely to contain elements of accountability, but also limits to it, along with other incentives to parties to actually implement any agreement. And in purely "domestic" peace and accountability processes, these compromises will generally be legally and politically permissible. However, internationally-sponsored peace processes may be under greater constraints not to sacrifice accountability, and particularly not to condone full or even partial amnesties, particularly where they function in the shadow of the International Criminal Court (ICC).[3] I turn next to the potential place or impact of the ICC in peace and accountability processes.

3 The ICC in the "Peace-Justice Dilemma"

With the entry into force of the statute of the International Criminal Court in mid-2002, an important new venue emerged for pursuing accountability. Its central features are its permanence and international nature, bringing distinct advantages over some domestic transitional processes and some *ad hoc* processes. The role of the ICC in relation to conflict mediation is well addressed elsewhere, including in this volume, so I will touch on just a few issues here (Seils and Wierda 2006). The ICC can be seen as part of the progressive development of transitional justice, transnational justice, and international criminal accountability since the end of the Second World War, notably advanced by the work of the *ad hoc* International Criminal Tribunals for the former Yugoslavia and Rwanda (see generally Sadat 2002). The ICC might be seen, however, not just as a challenge to impunity, but also as a potential challenge or impediment to peace negotiations and agreements, particularly given the court's wide mandate, the lack of recognition of domestic amnesties before the court, as well as the increasing lack of recognition of amnesties by international courts generally (Seils and Wierda 2006; Meisenberg 2004).[4]

[3] And, of course, foreign courts are not bound to respect amnesties imposed by domestic processes in other states either, as we have seen in a number of cases involving the exercise of universal jurisdiction. See generally Sriram (2005); see also Sadat (2004).

[4] *The Prosecutor v. Morris Kallon and Brima Buzzy Kamara*, Special Court for Sierra Leone, SCSL-2004-15-AR72(E) and SCSL-2004-16-AR72(E), Decision on Challenge to Jurisdiction: Lomé Accord Amnesty (Appeals Chamber, 13 March 2004).

If the Office of the Prosecutor (OtP) chooses to pursue a case, assuming that the court has jurisdiction, the case may proceed, regardless of peace negotiations that may be occurring simultaneously. This has been the case in the context of investigations and indictments of members of the Lord's Resistance Army in Northern Uganda in the context of peace negotiations, discussed later. In such a situation, it might plausibly be the case that the decision to pursue prosecutions could have a negative or positive impact on the peace process. They might, most obviously, serve as a disincentive to negotiations, as accused perpetrators may also be lead negotiators, and may simply terminate negotiations if they fear arrest or prosecution. They may alternatively negotiate amnesties or pardons; while the ICC is not bound to respect them, states in which they might be found might choose to do so. Positive effects might include enabling mediators to more tightly define topics open for discussion, individuals permitted to sit at the table, and to internationalize the process in ways that bring in new incentives. It might also be the case that the specter of prosecutions acts as a partial deterrent.[5] However, it is also arguably the case that the ICC may not loom large in peace negotiations because many cases can be addressed by courts other than the ICC, and because the OtP can defer prosecutions. First, the ICC's jurisdiction is complementary, so it should not address cases unless another relevant court (i.e., a court of the country most affected, but also courts of other countries exercising universal or other bases for jurisdiction) fails to do so. Second, the OtP has at least in the first instance chosen to rely heavily upon state referrals, and these have been forthcoming, up to a point (Bekou and Shah 2006; Sriram 2007a). Finally, the prosecutor may exercise his or her discretion in choosing not to pursue prosecutions "if the interests of justice" would not be served by doing so.[6]

4 Transnational Conflict, Transnational Crimes

Transnational conflict and crimes are evidently complex and interconnected. I will treat transnational or regional conflicts separately here first, however, to illustrate the complex nature of each, but inevitably, just as with "purely domestic" conflicts or crimes, accountability and conflict resolution processes are dynamically linked.

4.1 Transnational or Regional Conflicts

Transnational conflict dynamics and regional conflict formations are not new developments: conflicts and their effects, including refugees, arms flows, fighting groups,

---

[5] These possible positive effects are detailed in Seils and Wierda (2006).

[6] *Rome Statute of the International Criminal Court* (17 July 1998) article 53(1)(c) at http://www.icc-cpi.int/library/about/officialjournal/Rome_Statute_120704-EN.pdf. Seils and Wierda (2006, pp. 10–13).

and further violent conflict, have often spilled across borders with disastrous effects. This dynamic was visible throughout the Cold War period, particularly through conflicts in Africa, and most visibly in West Africa and the Great Lakes region, where transnational fighting and regionalization have marked conflicts, in part because of proxy wars (Väyrynen 1984, p. 337). This phenomenon is of course seen outside Africa as well: Central American conflicts in the 1980s also had a transnational and regional dimension, as do some contemporary conflicts in Central Asia (see generally Sriram and Nielsen 2004). Since the end of the Cold War there has been a visible increase in civil wars that spill across borders, and which often are driven by forces in other countries. Such regionalization and transnationalization means that civil wars are no longer internal, but rather that there may be several purportedly internal conflicts that exist as part of "regional conflict formations".[7] This problem has been most marked in Africa since the end of the Cold War, with governments and armed groups engaged in fighting on neighboring territories for reasons of self-defense, to defeat in particular rebels operating from across borders, or to retaliate against the government of another state or exploit that state's resources (Wallensteen and Sollenberg 1998, p. 621; Lembach 2007). "The role that African governments play in supporting, sometimes even instigating conflicts in neighbouring countries must be candidly acknowledged," noted one report issued by UN Secretary-General Kofi Annan.[8]

However, despite the regional dimension of many contemporary conflicts, nearly all conflict resolution processes either involve only the actors within a given state, or only seek to address conflict dynamics occurring within that state. This is perhaps not surprising given respect for state sovereignty in the international system: peace negotiations will generally only take place between the recognized state authority and those parties that are permitted at the negotiating table (i.e., rebel groups that the state acknowledges) (Sriram and Ross 2007).

This may immediately exclude a variety of actors, making conflict resolution a challenge. For example, non-state armed groups operating transnationally, whether as mercenaries or as forces with specific socio-political claims, may seldom be the subjects of peace agreements. This may be the case with a range of fighters who have taken part in conflicts in West Africa, including Sierra Leone, Liberia, and Côte d'Ivoire. Alternatively, elements of the Lords Resistance Army of Uganda have hidden in the Democratic Republic of Congo and have also recruited members in Southern Sudan. They may thus become what are sometimes referred to as "spoilers": excluded from an agreement, and thus lacking any investment in it, may seek to undermine it, or alternatively may simply foment conflict in another state

[7] On regional conflict formations, see the work of Barnett Rubin at New York University's Center on International Cooperation, at http://www.cic.nyu.edu/archive/conflict/conflict_project1.html.

[8] Report of the Secretary-General, 'The Causes of Conflict and the Promotion of Durable Peace and Sustainable Development in Africa' (1998), UN Doc. S/1998/318; compare UK Department for International Development, 'The Causes of Conflict in Africa: Consultation Document' (2001) at http://www.dfid.gov.uk/pubs/files/conflict-africa.pdf#search=%22dfid%20causes%20of%20conflict%20in%20africa%22.

(on spoilers, see Stedman 1997, p. 5). In either event, a nationally-focused peace agreement may fail to address larger regional sources of conflict.

Alternatively, a nationally-oriented peace agreement that only involves state actors from one territory may overlook the key or even primary promoters of conflict in a territory, which may be other states. The state that is subject to the conflict may not wish to acknowledge the influence of other states, and thus its own vulnerability, or the other states may have no interest in participating in a neighbor's peace process, thereby acknowledging culpability (and potentially risking legal accountability) (see Pugh and Cooper 2004).[9] Or states that have intervened in other states may claim that they have a legitimate security interest in doing so: for example Rwanda justified its intervention in the DRC in part with claims that former Rwandan rebels and genocidaires were hiding in the latter's territory and planning or actually staging attacks in Rwanda. As discussed below, Rwanda was part of peace negotiations for the DRC.

But more frequently, neighboring states are not included in such negotiations. Thus in the case of the conflict in Sierra Leone, while the responsibility of Liberian president Charles Taylor for promoting conflict in the country through his support to Revolutionary United Front rebels is well known, he was not part of the Sierra Leonean negotiations, and indeed would shortly be engaged in negotiations in his own country, receiving a controversial amnesty and exile in Nigeria, albeit a relatively short-lived one. Alternatively, neighboring states might be involved in peace agreements, but only in respect of their activities in that country, rather than the cross-border activities of other actors, such as rebel groups. In such an instance, these states are likely to be drawn back into conflict, or the rebel groups may be left to stir up new conflict. The 1999 Lusaka Accord for the DRC was an attempt to address just such a problem: it involved the governments of the DRC, Angola, Rwanda, Sudan, Namibia, and Zimbabwe, and (eventually) the two major rebel groups. It also included provisions to address the cross-border movement of arms and fighters, and the need to disarm armed groups and militias.[10] Nonetheless, the agreement and the deployment of a UN peacekeeping force, MONUC, failed to stop the fighting.[11] Subsequent agreements between the DRC and Uganda addressed the withdrawal of Ugandan troops from DRC territory and the pacification of areas they had occupied, and between the DRC and Rwanda addressed both the withdrawal of Rwandan troops and dismantling of Rwandan rebel groups operating in DRC

[9] Consider for example the case brought by the Democratic Republic of Congo against its neighbour Uganda for its involvement in the DRC's 1998–2003 conflict: *Case Concerning Armed Activities on the Territory of the Congo* (DRC v. Uganda), General List No. 116 (19 December 2005), in which the ICJ held that Uganda violated principles of non-use of force and non-interference in international relations, violated its obligations under international humanitarian law and international human rights law, and owed the DRC reparations.

[10] *Lusaka Cease-fire Accord* (15 July 1999), at http://www.usip.org/library/pa/drc/drc_07101999_toc.html.

[11] United Nations, 'Democratic Republic of the Congo-MONUC-Background,' at http://www.un.org/Depts/dpko/missions/monuc/background.html.

territory.[12] While the DRC peace processes have proven shaky at best, their inclusive nature, involving a range of armed groups, and neighboring states, might be an important model for future mediation of regionalized conflicts. So too, although these emerged in a different region and time frame, might the Contadora and Esquipulas peace processes in Central America during the 1980s (Sriram 2004b).

4.2 Transnational or Regionalized Crimes

At one level, all human rights abuses occur at the national level, which is to say, they occur within the borders of an existing state. However, it is frequently the case that while they occurred within the territory of one state, they were promoted or even ordered by individuals, whether state or non-state actors, operating in the territory of another state. This may occur in at least two ways. First, human rights abuses may occur in a "simple" transnational sense: an external actor directed it or was complicit in its commission. Second, abuses may occur in a more complex or regionalized sense, in the context of regional conflict formations.

Simple transnational violations of international human rights or humanitarian law may involve the direction by a foreign government of activities that constitute violations: Taylor's support to the RUF with full knowledge of the abuses they were committing, or Uganda's occupation of part of the DRC and concomitant commission of abuses by its army (and failure to prevent other abuses in territory it occupied) are examples of these. So too might the engagement of some multinational corporations in conflict zones, where they knowingly contract with, or otherwise support, abusive government or rebel forces, in order to conduct business, particularly extractive industries. The involvement of Unocal and other oil companies in Burma/Myanmar, of Talisman oil company and now state-run Chinese oil companies in Sudan, are examples of these. Individual state leaders or officials might face criminal accountability, and individual corporations might face civil liability, but this is fairly infrequent, and seldom part of broader accountability processes for the country affected by the conflict and crimes (see Hoffman 2005; Schabas 2005; Sriram 2007b, 2008b).

In conflicts that are regional (often with sustained interventions by the militaries of one or more states into one or more states, or multiple patterns of support to rebels in neighboring states), there may be several sets of actors responsible for human rights violations, and even identifying, much less pursuing, those responsible may be quite difficult. Regional conflicts generate serious abuses of human rights and violations of international humanitarian law both within and across state borders,

[12] Agreement Between the Governments of the Democratic Republic of the Congo and the Republic of Uganda on Withdrawal of Ugandan Troops from the Democratic Republic of the Congo, Cooperation and Normalisation of Relations Between the Two Countries (6 September 2002), at http://www.usip.org/library/pa/drc_uganda/drc_uganda_09062002.html; Peace Agreement Between the Governments of the Republic of Rwanda and the Democratic Republic of the Congo on the Withdrawal of the Rwandan Troops from the Territory of the Democratic Republic of the Congo and the Dismantling of the Ex-FAR and Interahamwe Forces in the Democratic Republic of the Congo (DRC) (July 30 2002), at http://www.usip.org/library/pa/drc_rwanda/drc_rwanda_pa07302002.html.

which means that not only do complex conflict formations have to be resolved, but overlapping and competing claims regarding abuses and accountability will present themselves within and across several countries.[13] However, accountability processes are most frequently focused upon the national state and its actors, which may exempt some culprits from punishment.

4.3 The State-Oriented Nature of Accountability Processes

It may seem strange in the first instance to characterize contemporary accountability processes as state-oriented. After all, anyone with a passing familiarity with recent prosecutions for violations of international human rights or international humanitarian law will be aware that they have taken place at various levels and in various types of fora: domestic, transnational, hybrid, and international.[14] Further, the crimes to be prosecuted are *international* crimes: violations of international humanitarian law and international human rights law. However, there is a critical irony for accountability at any level: while the crimes are ones of international concern, to which any and all states may respond, the state-centric nature of the very international criminal law that shapes prosecutions may mean that key crimes and criminals are not addressed. Thus it may be the case, for example, that a perpetrator of torture or war crimes is prosecuted for those crimes s/he committed in his/her own country, but not those in a neighboring country for which s/he is also responsible, or vice versa. Amnesty at home or exile and amnesty in another country may also mean the perpetrator escapes prosecution. Where there are multiple perpetrators and combatant groups in the same territory, some may be shielded from prosecution while others are not. I first turn briefly to the nature of the crimes of international concern and the state-based nature of international law before taking up the perverse consequences of the combination of these two phenomena.

Thus there is a profound irony at the heart of international criminal justice: international law both condemns certain acts as internationally sanctioned, yet until recently, has delegated responsibility to states, who are frequently the perpetrators of such acts, to respond.[15] The ICC's power to hear cases comes entirely from state consent: cases are referred to it by states, are permissible because states have signed

[13] While traditionally International Humanitarian Law largely sought to address international armed conflicts, common article 3 of the Geneva Conventions as well as Additional Protocol II address situations of non-international armed conflict, and contemporary practice has further diminished the importance of the international-non-international armed conflict distinction. See for example: *Prosecutor v. Tadic* Case No. IT-94-1-AR72, paras 79–85, 95–137 (2 October 1995); but compare on appeal *Prosecutor v. Tadic* Case No. IT-94-1-A, paras 68–171 (Judgment on Appeal from Conviction, 15 July 1999).

[14] This section draws upon Sriram and Ross (2007, p. 45); for a discussion of the various levels of accountability processes, see generally Sriram (2005).

[15] This is the case even though of course IHL, through Additional Protocol II in particular, addresses internal armed conflict, and individuals can be the subjects of international criminal accountability, as, potentially, legal persons such as corporations might be, according to some analysts. See generally Clapham (2006).

and ratified the Court's statute. Even the one mode of referral to the ICC that may occur over the objection of the relevant state, referral by the United Nations Security Council, requires the affirmative votes of states on the Council and that veto-holders do not exercise the veto.[16]

However, while decisions about accountability are still largely limited by state consent, the acts of concern in post-conflict justice – gross violations of human rights and international humanitarian law – are crimes of international concern. This is the case not only because they may frequently occur in situations of international or transnational conflict, but because they are considered to offend our common humanity (Broomhall 2004; Reydams 2004; Sadat 2006, p. 970). For this reason, there are certain *jus cogens* obligations, obligations from which no derogation is permitted: prohibitions on genocide, war crimes, crimes against humanity, torture, and slavery. These obligations are binding upon states whether or not they have signed specific conventions. They are *erga omnes* obligations, binding upon all states in the international system. However, the legal mechanisms that might impose accountability upon individuals or responsibility upon states may not have jurisdiction over such states. Thus the obligation may be universal, but enforcement mechanisms may not be available.[17]

Herein lies the central challenge. Crimes are, thus, on the one hand recognized as of international concern, but often, due to the state-centric nature of international law, legal mechanisms and responses are tailored in such a way as to exclude crimes committed outside a state territory or inside another. Further, attempts at accountability will be contemporaneous with, or dictated by, peace processes that generally seek to develop peace within a single state even where a regional conflict has occurred. In such a context, is truly "holistic peace with justice" really feasible?

5 Challenges of Peace and Justice in a Regional Context

Given the transnational dimensions of conflict and conflict resolution, determinations about justice and amnesty, like determinations about peace agreements, should not be, but often are, treated as single-country affairs. This combination – linked conflict and human rights violations in a context of linked, transnational, or regional conflicts – will make the mediator's task of pursuing peace with accountability especially tricky.

---

[16] Of course such referrals may be rare given that the United States, an adamant opponent of the ICC, holds a veto; it might however be prepared to acquiesce to compromise resolutions such as that crafted in Resolution 1593. UN Security Council Resolution 1593 (2005), UN Doc. S/RES/1593. All five permanent members can insulate themselves and key allies from a Security Council referral.

[17] For example, the International Court of Justice found itself unable to consider a case brought by the Democratic Republic of Congo against Rwanda for activities on Congolese territory because it lacked jurisdiction. The Torture Convention was excluded as a source of jurisdiction because Rwanda was not a party to it. *Case Concerning Armed Activities on the Territory of the Congo (DRC v. Rwanda)* (Jurisdiction and admissibility) General List No. 126 (3 February 2006), at http://www.icj-cij.org/icjwww/idocket/icrw/icrwframe.htm.

This is the case because even if a country-specific deal could be brokered that achieves a satisfactory degree of accountability, while embedding a robust peace agreement, it may have adverse effects upon the pursuit of peace or accountability (or both) in a neighboring country.

The strange case of Charles Taylor may serve to illustrate this point in several ways. First, the Comprehensive Peace Agreement for Liberia, reached in August 2003, terminated the country's armed conflict, and allowed (now) former Liberian president Charles Taylor to go into exile in Nigeria.[18] This may have facilitated the peace agreement in Liberia, but protected him not only from the courts of Liberia, but those of Sierra Leone, where he was also responsible for a wide range of crimes. Further, decisions about accountability made through the Special Court for Sierra Leone have had or could have direct effects upon attempts at either making peace or pursuing accountability in Liberia. The prosecutor of the Special Court unsealed an indictment against Taylor during Liberia's peace negotiations in Ghana, and asked Ghana to execute an arrest warrant. This incident could have derailed negotiations and did cause some diplomatic embarrassment; Ghana allowed Taylor to leave the country untouched. Taylor was subsequently arrested while trying to flee Nigeria, but he is not to be tried in Sierra Leone: instead he was transferred to the Hague, at the request of the new Liberian president and the Court itself, for trial, due to security concerns.[19] However, the trial of Charles Taylor, wherever it is held, will not address crimes committed against his own people and country, thus any accountability process, to the degree that it "works", will have done so for Sierra Leone only. This is not a result that will satisfy all Liberians, who have a truth and reconciliation commission but may never have trials of those who caused that country's devastating wars and attendant crimes (Yoch 2006).

In a different vein, peace negotiations in northern Uganda have raised the possibility of an amnesty for Joseph Kony and other LRA leaders. Such an amnesty has been rejected by the ICC prosecutor, who issued warrants for Kony and four of his commanders in July 2005, and who issued statements objecting to the offers of amnesty while negotiations were ongoing during summer 2006.[20] Nonetheless, while the peace process has not been completed, there have been interim agreements, and the prospect of amnesties and the use of traditional justice processes within Northern Uganda (Grainger 2007; International Crisis Group 2007). But the LRA has posed a threat in the DRC and Southern Sudan as well. The government of Southern Sudan, which has been mediating the talks, has indicated that it is prepared to offer Kony and his colleagues a safe haven in exile. This poses a number of dilemmas for the ICC and for the UN's envoy, former Mozambican President

[18] Comprehensive Peace Agreement Between the Government of Liberia and the Liberians United for Reconciliation and Democracy (LURD) and the Movement for Democracy in Liberia (MODEL) and Political Parties (18th August 2003) at http://www.usip.org/library/pa/liberia/liberia_08182003_cpa.html.

[19] UN Security Council Resolution 1688 (2006), UN Doc. S/RES/1688; Website of the Special Court for Sierra Leone, at http://www.sc-sl.org/Taylor.html.

[20] *The Prosecutor v. Joseph Kony, Vincent Otti, Raska Lukwiya, Okot Odhiambo and Dominic Ongwen* ICC-02/04-01/05, at http://www.icc-cpi.int/cases/UGD/c0105.html; Sriram and Ross (2006).

Joacquim Chissano, in any revived talks. The governments of Uganda and Southern Sudan may be prepared to see the LRA evade responsibility for its crimes in their territories, but this would not take account of the wishes of the government or people of the DRC (Doyle 2006). Further, the government of Southern Sudan may be playing a dangerous game, facilitating negotiations for Northern Uganda, but failing to address the presence and threat posed by LRA members not just from Uganda, but from Sudan as well, even as it undertakes a flawed peace implementation and demobilization process.

The ICC prosecutor too faces a dilemma in considering how actively to pursue the arrest of Kony and other LRA members. The prosecutor of course cannot legally defer to amnesties, but he can use his discretion to delay or halt prosecutions. This might of course have unintended consequences for the other cases on his docket, including crimes committed in Darfur, should the prosecutor appear to be engaged in selective prosecutions. Similarly, the Prosecutor has indicated his intent to monitor the situation in Colombia, where the Ley de Justicia y Paz has provided for amnesty or reduced sentences for ex-paramilitary fighters in exchange for their demobilization, notwithstanding the alleged commission of crimes against humanity and war crimes, including massacres of civilians, and demands for extradition of some of their commanders by the United States.[21]

From the forgoing, it should be evident that pursuing peace and justice in a holistic fashion in a regional process will be a difficult, if not impossible, challenge. That does not however mean that the international community, including scholars and policymakers, can afford to shy away from it. The dilemmas I have presented are more than complex but academic problems: they are ones faced by mediators and to a lesser degree the ICC prosecutor right now. Thus, some attempt to identify options should be made, however preliminary and speculative it may be.

6 Holistic Peace and Justice in a Regional Context?

This part of the paper is necessarily more speculative, as it seeks to identify ways to craft not just peace with justice, which is challenging enough, but to do so in a regional context. In the first instance, we must consider what tools might be available to address the oft-competing demands of peace and justice. We can presume that they will include, at least in part, mechanisms that have been utilized in "purely domestic" processes, already noted above. These include, although they are certainly not limited to: criminal accountability, truth and reconciliation processes, traditional justice, vetting, limited or total amnesties, and accountability processes with pardons. Is it simply a matter of transposing such tools to a regional process, or are some of these better suited than others for regional peace and justice processes, and are there other tools we might consider? Once I have identified the range of possible

[21] Colombia, *Ley de justicia y paz* Law No. 975 (2005) at http://www.fiscalia.gov.co/justiciapaz/Imagenes/Documentos/Esquema_Ley975_Justicia_Paz.pdf; "ICC Probes Colombia on War Crimes," (2005), at http://news.bbc.co.uk/2/hi/americas/4399027.stm.

tools and their modification, I will turn to an obvious issue – even if regional tools could be identified, are such processes really feasible?

6.1 Transposing Tools

First, which of the "tools" might be utilized in a regional/transnational context? I will consider each of the standard tools noted above in turn.

Criminal accountability. In principle, criminal accountability is as appropriate a tool in the context of transnational/regional conflicts or crimes and peace/justice processes as it is in domestic ones, and is subject to the same obvious limitations. The International Criminal Court can hear cases pertaining to all parties to a conflict (or those complicit in abuses) if each is a national of a state party or commits a crime on the territory of a state party (or if the UN Security Council refers the situation). However, it has not yet chosen to do so, notwithstanding the obvious appropriateness of doing so in relation to crimes committed in the DRC, where Rwandan or Ugandan officials, or officials of foreign corporations, might well have committed or been complicit in crimes. Alternatively, a regional court, whether permanent or *ad hoc*, might be developed to hear cases involving regional conflicts and crimes. The United States advocated that an African hybrid tribunal be set up to address crimes in Darfur, albeit as part of its long-standing campaign against the ICC.[22] Obviously, any *ad hoc* regional court or prosecution would require state consent, which might be very difficult to obtain.

Truth and reconciliation processes. In principle, truth and reconciliation processes could be held that addressed conflicts and abuses across borders, or in a regional context. In practice, official truth commissions, mandated by governments, are designed to address crimes in a national context. This does not mean that truth commissions and their reports cannot address regional dynamics: the final report of the Sierra Leonean Truth and Reconciliation Commission (TRC) included an extended discussion of the role of external actors (Sierra Leone Truth and Reconciliation Commission 2004). However, the TRC was not designed to hear evidence from actors outside the country, or about abuses outside the country; similarly the Liberian truth commission will be designed to hear testimony regarding abuses in Liberia, but not elsewhere. Given the linked nature of these and other conflicts in the region, perhaps a regionalized process would be appropriate, but as with prosecutions would necessitate the elusive state consent.

Traditional justice. Traditional justice processes are often also linked to traditional conflict resolution processes, and so in principle might be useful routes to pursue peace with justice. They have been utilized in countries such as Rwanda and East Timor, where the formal judicial sector could not manage the volume of cases (Sarkin 2001, p. 143; Hohe and Nixon 2003). In practice, of course, they have proven problematic for a variety of reasons, including abuse of process, failure to

[22] Remarks of US representative Mrs. Patterson at the meeting of the UN Security Council that approved resolution 1593, referring the situation in Darfur to the ICC, (2005) UN Doc. S/PV.5158.

meet international human rights standards, dominance of certain groups, and exclusion in particular of women from decision-making. This does not mean that such processes should never be used, but that caution should be exercised. Further, the local nature of these processes may render them inappropriate to address conflicts that spill across borders, given that they generally take place at a community or tribal level.

Vetting and lustration. Vetting and/or lustration involve governmental policies regarding exclusion from government service, including in the security sector, and in key professional roles, as doctors, teachers, or lawyers.[23] While it is not inconceivable that vetting arrangements could be discussed transnationally, governments are likely to consider these decisions a sovereign preserve and resist such discussions.

Limited or total amnesties, and accountability processes with pardons. As already discussed, total amnesties are not binding on international or foreign courts, and the United Nations rejects them. Limited or conditional amnesties, or prosecutions with pardons or reduced sentences, may find greater favour. Examples include the so-called exchange of truth for justice in the South African Truth and Reconciliation Commission, which provided for individualized amnesty in exchange for testimony before the Commission, with the threat of prosecutions of those refusing to testify (Berat 1995; Sriram 2004a). Any of these processes, like accountability processes, or TRC processes more generally, could be regionalized, subject to state consent.

6.2 Is Regionalization Possible?

Assuming that some or all of the above tools should be regionalized, and that of course remains to be seen, could they be? I have noted in each instance, with the exception of vetting and traditional justice, that regional approaches might be feasible in principle subject to state consent. But what are the odds that states would consent? That is to say, could a mediator reasonably expect to promote a regional peace with justice process in the context of regional conflict formations, in light of the many competing interests, fears, and agendas of numerous state and non-state actors? The prospects seem slim, but worth considering.

Certainly, in many instances state or rebel leaders who are barely able to reach agreement with each other within state borders will not be able to come to agreements with multiple other states who may also have supported rebel groups, either about terms of cessation of fighting, or appropriate measures for accountability. Reaching agreements will not be easy. However, it might be argued that the peace agreements for the DRC, while focused upon cessation of fighting, withdrawal of foreign troops, and stabilization of areas of DRC territory, may offer something of a model for a regionalized agreement. So too might the commitments, albeit broad, made in the Contadora and Esquipulas processes in Central America.

[23] UNCHR (2006); Smith, (1995); International Center for Transitional Justice resource page on "Vetting," at http://www.ictj.org/en/tj/783.html.

Further, the international security architecture is increasingly attuned to the regional dimension of conflict, and might provide institutional support for holistic regional approaches to peace and justice. The UN system, for example, as developed not just country but also a regional peacebuilding support office, in the Great Lakes region, and there is a Special Representative of the Secretary-General for West Africa.[24] UNDP has active regional centres in Bangkok and Colombo as part of its regional bureau for Asia and the Pacific, as well as centres for southern Africa and Europe.[25] In Africa, regional organizations such as ECOWAS and IGAD have played growing roles in supporting or mediating peace agreements, or even deploying peacekeeping missions. And the African Court on Human and Peoples' Rights, while pan-African, and focused on state obligations rather than individual criminal accountability, might speculatively offer a neutral venue (with different judges and mandate, to be sure) for regionalized cases.[26] During my interviews at the Special Court for Sierra Leone, when the subject of the disposition of the court premises following completion of trials was raised, some suggested it should become a regional court for West Africa. None of these processes, institutions, or developments means that regional holistic processes will be easy, or even feasible, but rather may provide some insights as to where to start. In particular, the Mediation Support Unit, created in response to a recommendation of the UN High Level Panel report, and operating as part of the UN Department of Political Affairs, might promote cooperation with regional organizations.[27]

7 Conclusions

I have argued that a critical obstacle to pursuing peace with justice, or holistic processes, is the regional or transnational dimension of contemporary conflicts and abuses of human rights. This not only renders peace or accountability processes more complex, but potentially prevents holistic processes, because traditionally these have been state-generated or focused. Mediators of conflicts, and prosecutions for crimes, have largely been mandated to address conflicts and crimes located within the territory of a specific state. I have argued that rather than state-oriented processes, what may be needed are regionally-oriented ones. Such an approach

---

[24] 'United Nations Political and Peacebuilding Support missions,' at http://www.stimson.org/fopo/pdf/ppbm.pdf; see also the website of the UN Office for West Africa, at http://www.un.org/unowa/.

[25] See the regional bureau's page at http://www.undp.org/rbap/ResourceCentre2.htm; see the listings of other regional bureaus and "SURFS" at http://www.undp.org/energyandenvironment/regsurf.htm.

[26] I do not mean to imply that the Court could hear the cases, but rather that its seat could be of use for symbolic reasons. The Court, while officially established, is far from functional as yet. For the resolution establishing the Court, see http://www.achpr.org/english/_info/court_en.html (last accessed 29 March 2007).

[27] See UN Department of Political Affairs webpage on peacemaking at http://www.un.org/Depts/dpa/peace.html (Last accessed 13 April 2007); Centre for Conflict Resolution (2006).

will clearly be difficult to promote, given state concerns with sovereignty, and the state-centric nature of international law and politics. However difficult developing regional holistic processes may be, however, it may be equally necessary, in order to develop more sustainable peace.

Acknowledgments This paper draws upon fieldwork carried out by Professor Sriram in Sierra Leone under British Academy grant SG-3725, and in Sudan under Nuffield grant SGS/01159/G and a grant from the Carnegie Trust for the Universities of Scotland.

References

Bekou O, Shah S (2006) Realising the potential of the International Criminal Court: the African experience. Hum Rights Law Rev 6(3):499–544

Bell C (2003) Peace agreements and human rights. OUP, Oxford

Berat L (1995) South Africa: negotiating change? In: Roht-Arriaza N (ed) Impunity and human rights in international law and practice. Oxford University Press, Oxford

Broomhall B (2004) International justice and the International Criminal Court: between sovereignty and the rule of law. OUP, Oxford

Centre for Conflict Resolution (2006) United Nations Mediation Experience in Africa, Workshop report

Clapham A (2006) Human rights obligations of non-state actors. OUP, Oxford

DFID (2001) The causes of conflict in Africa: consultation document. UK Department for International Development. http://www.dfid.gov.uk/pubs/files/ conflict-africa.pdf#search = %22dfid%20causes%20of%20conflict%20in%20africa%22

Doyle M (2006) Africa's mixed amnesty precedents. http://news.bbc.co.uk/1/hi/world/africa/5148226.stm

Grainger S (2007) How to punish Uganda rebels. http://news.bbc.co.uk/1/hi/world/africa/7081560.stm

Hannum H (2006) Human rights and conflict resolution: the role of the Office of the High Commissioner for Human Rights in UN peacemaking and peacebuilding. Human Rights Quarterly 28(1)

Hartzell C, Hoddie M, Rothchild D (2001) Stabilizing the peace after civil war: an investigation of some key variables. Int Organ 55:183–208

Hayner P (2000) Unspeakable truths: confronting state terror and atrocity. Routledge, London

Hoddie M, Hartzell C (2003) Civil war settlements and the implementation of military power-sharing arrangements. Journal of Peace Research 40(3):303–320

Hoffman PL (2005) Corporate accountability under the U.S. Alien Tort Claims Act. In: Ballentine K, Nitzschke H (eds) Profiting from peace: managing the resource dimensions of civil war. Lynne Rienner, Boulder

Hohe T, Nixon R (2003) Reconciling justice: 'traditional' law and state judiciary in East Timor. United States Institute for Peace Final Report

Human Rights Watch (2004) Human rights and armed conflict. http://hrw.org/wr2k4/

International Crisis Group (2007) Northern Uganda peace process: the need to maintain momentum. Africa Briefing No. 46 (14 September 2007). http://www.crisisgroup.org/home/index.cfm?id=5078

Lembach D (2007) Close encounters in the third dimension: the regional effects of state failure. INEF Report 87/2007. Institute for Development and Peace

Lutz E, Babbitt EF, Hannum H (2003) Human rights and conflict resolution from the practitioners' perspectives. Fletcher Forum of World Affairs 27(1). http://fletcher.tufts.edu/chrcr/pdf/Lutz4.pdf

Mani R (2002) Beyond retribution: seeking justice in the shadows of war. Polity, Cambridge

Meisenberg SM (2004) Legality of amnesties in international humanitarian law: the Lomé amnesty decision of the special court for Sierra Leone. Int Rev Red Cross 856

Parlevliet M (2002) Bridging the divide. Exploring the relationship between human rights and conflict management. Track Two (11)1. http://ccrweb.ccr.uct.ac.za/archive/two/11_1/bridging.html

Pugh M, Cooper N (2004) War economies in a regional context: challenges of transformation. Lynne Rienner, Boulder

Putnam T (2002) Human rights and sustainable peace. In: Stedman SJ, Rothchild D, Cousens E (eds) Ending civil wars. The implementation of peace agreements. Lynne Rienner, Boulder

Reydams L (2004) Universal jurisdiction: international and municipal legal perspectives. Oxford University Press, Oxford

Roeder P, Rothchild D (eds) (2005) Sustainable peace: power and democracy after civil wars. Cornell University Press, Ithaca

Roht-Arriaza N (ed.) (1995) Impunity and human rights in international law and practice. Oxford University Press, Oxford

Rotberg RI, Thompson D (eds) (2000) Truth vs. justice: the morality of truth commissions. Princeton University Press, Princeton

Sadat LN (2002) The international criminal court and the transformation of international law: justice for the new millennium. Transnational Publishers, Ardsley

Sadat LN (2004) Universal jurisdiction, national amnesties, and truth commissions: reconciling the irreconcilable. In: Macedo S (ed) Universal jurisdiction: national courts and the prosecution of serious crimes under international law. University of Pennsylvania Press, Philadelphia

Sadat LN (2006) Exile, amnesty, and international law. Notre Dame Law Rev 81:970

Sarkin J (2001) The tension between justice and reconciliation in Rwanda: politics, human rights, due process and the role of the gacaca courts in dealing with the genocide. J Afr Law 45:143

Schabas WA (2005) War economies, economic actors, and international criminal law. In: Ballentine K, Nitzschke H (eds) Profiting from peace: managing the resource dimensions of civil war. Lynne Rienner, Boulder

Seils P, Wierda M (2006) The international criminal court and conflict mediation. International Center for Transitional Justice Background Paper. www.ictj.org

Sierra Leone Truth and Reconciliation Commission (2004) Final Report, vol. 3b. http://trcsierraleone.org/drwebsite/publish/v3b-c2.shtml

Sisk TD (1996) Power sharing and international mediation in ethnic conflicts. US Institute of Peace, Washington DC

Smith KE (1995) Decommunization after the 'velvet revolutions' in East Central Europe. In: Roht-Arriaza (ed) Impunity and human rights in international law and practice. Oxford University Press, Oxford

Sriram CL (2004a) Confronting past human rights violations: justice v. peace in times of transition. Frank Cass, London

Sriram CL (2004b) Dynamics of conflict in Central America. In: Sriram CL, Nielsen Z (eds) (2004) Exploring subregional conflict: opportunities for conflict prevention. Lynne Rienner, Boulder

Sriram CL (2005) Globalizing justice for mass atrocities: a revolution in accountability. Routledge, London

Sriram CL (2007a) The ICC Africa experiment: Darfur, Northern Uganda, and the DRC. Paper prepared for CCR workshop on "Peace versus Justice? Truth and Reconciliation Commissions and War Crimes Tribunals in Africa. Cape Town, 17–18 May 2007

Sriram CL (2007b) China, Human Rights, and the Sudan. 30 January 2007. http://jurist.law.pitt.edu/forumy/2007/01/china-human-rights-and-sudan.php

Sriram CL (2008a) Peace as governance: power-sharing, armed groups, and contemporary peace negotiations. Palgrave, London

Sriram CL (2008b) Achieving accountability for non-state armed groups: use of domestic mechanisms for international crimes. In: Policzer P, Capie D (eds) After leviathan: restraining violence by non-state armed groups. University of Pennsylvania Press, Philadelphia (forthcoming)

Sriram CL, Nielsen Z (eds) (2004) Exploring subregional conflict: opportunities for conflict prevention. Lynne Rienner, Boulder

Sriram CL, Ross A (2006) Catch-22 in Uganda: The LRA, the ICC, and the peace process. http://jurist.law.pitt.edu/forumy/2006/07/catch-22-in-uganda-lra-icc-and-peace.php

Sriram CL, Ross A (2007) Geographies of crime and justice: contemporary transitional justice and the creation of 'zones of impunity'. Int J Transitional Justice 1:45–65

Stedman SJ (1997) Spoiler problems in peace processes. Int Security 22:5–53

Teitel RG (2000) Transitional justice. OUP, New York

UNCHR (2006) Vetting: an operational framework. UN Office of the High Commissioner for Human Rights. http://www.ohchr.org/english/about/publications/docs/ruleoflaw-Vetting_en.pdf

Väyrynen R (1984) Regional conflict formations: an intractable problem of international relations. J Peace Res 21:337–358

Wallensteen P, Sollenberg M (1998) Armed conflict and regional conflict complexes, 1989–97. J Peace Res 35:621–634

Walter BF (2002) Committing to peace: the successful settlement of civil wars. Princeton University Press, Princeton

Yoch JM Jr (2006) Liberia group pushing for national war crimes court. http://jurist.law.pitt.edu/paperchase/2006/04/liberia-group-pushing-for-national-war.php

DDR and Reparations: Establishing Links Between Peace and Justice Instruments

Pablo de Greiff

Abstract Disarmament, demobilization, and reintegration (DDR) programs have traditionally been designed and implemented in total isolation from transitional justice measures, of which reparations for victims is one kind. It is only recently that the approach that considers DDR as essentially a technical issue to be decided exclusively on the basis of military and security concerns with no regard for political or justice considerations has begun to be questioned. The incentives to try to bring the worlds of the peace maker and of the justice and human rights promoter together, however, are manifold. The general aim of this paper is to construct an argument about the advisability of drawing links between DDR and reparations programs, not just because this is better from the standpoint of justice, but because it may help DDR programs as well. The paper first briefly presents the facts of two cases, Rwanda and Guatemala, countries that have moved significantly farther regarding DDR than reparations. It then outlines some of the fundamental challenges faced by DDR and reparations programs, respectively. The next section presents conceptions of transitional justice and of DDR that facilitate seeing why implementing DDR programs but no reparations program is problematic. The argument capitalizes on and reinforces the trust-inducing potential of both DDR and transitional justice measures. If the argument is correct, a successful linkage of these measures will strengthen both DDR and transitional justice programs. Focusing on DDR, one of the main advantages this linkage offers to DDR programs is that it would help them mitigate one of the fundamental criticisms to which they have been subject, namely, that they reward bad behavior. The final section provides some comments on the role of the international community in DDR and reparations programs.

P. de Greiff
International Center for Transitional Justice, 5 Hanover Square, 24th Fl NY NY 10004, USA
e-mail: PdeGreiff@ictj.org

K. Ambos et al. (eds.), *Building a Future on Peace and Justice: Studies on Transitional Justice, Peace and Development.*

1 Introduction

It is obvious that one stands in new territory when the first task that the introduction of a paper has to do is to explain the very choice of topics. What is the point of comparing DDR and reparations programs? After all, aren't these very different programs serving different constituencies, and, most importantly, different ends? Isn't it the case that DDR programs are part of the tool box of peace makers and builders as well as development practitioners, whereas reparations programs can be located (if at all) in that of the justice or human rights practitioner? In actual fact, DDR programs have traditionally been designed and implemented in total isolation from transitional justice measures, of which reparations for victims is one kind. Indeed, it is only recently that the traditional approach that considers DDR as essentially a technical issue to be decided exclusively on the basis of military and security concerns with no regard for political or justice considerations has begun to be questioned. While there are now a few documents that argue for the introduction of justice-related considerations into DDR programming, these are still not just few in number but also tentative in nature.[1]

The incentives to try to bring the worlds of the peace maker and of the justice and human rights promoter together are manifold. In the first place, it should be acknowledged that the international legal domain has changed in the recent past. The two most visible manifestations of this change are, perhaps, the (new) disposition to act in accordance with (an older) prohibition against granting amnesties for war crimes and crimes against humanity, and the not unrelated establishment of the International Criminal Court which will now make the effects of any national amnesty for such crimes internationally moot, at least in theory. Peace making, then, now has to be practiced in a way that accommodates at the very least these broad justice concerns.

Aside from these legal considerations, there has of course been a long discussion within the peace building and even the peace making arenas about the role of justice. The long negative *v.* positive peace debate is at least partly about this.[2] Since I have never taken this debate to be about whether negative peace is the best that can be hoped for, but rather about what we ought to be prepared to pay in order to get it (so that then other more substantive goals can be pursued), this means that there are incentives for thinking about the relationship between peace and justice internal to the sphere of peace itself (just as, of course, justice and human rights promoters have a reason to take peace considerations seriously, for war is one of the conditions least conducive to respect for justice and rights).

Although this is a paper written from the standpoint of someone who works in the field of transitional justice, its general aim is to construct an argument about the advisability of drawing some links – to be specified – between DDR and reparations programs, but not just because this is better from the standpoint of justice;

[1] Perhaps SIDDR (2006) goes farther in this direction than any. See Sect. 3.5. In a more tentative vein, see Meek and Malan (2004, p. vii), which talks about "the need to move towards a new DDR framework that is based on human rights."

[2] See some of the papers in Barash (1999).

the argument is that this may help DDR programs as well. Given this aim, I will of course continue to grant significance from the standpoint of justice to the fact that while in circles where DDR is discussed there is strong support for the idea that each and every ex combatant should be a beneficiary of a DDR program,[3] there is, neither in the national nor in the international domain, a similar commitment to the idea that each and every victim of conflict should be made a beneficiary of a reparations program; I will continue to grant significance, from the standpoint of justice, to the observation that the international community acts consistently with its rhetoric, at least at this level, and thus provides much more support for peace and security issues than for justice issues;[4] and I will consider significant that of the 22 countries with ongoing DDR programs in a recent global study, programs involving 1.25 million beneficiaries and the expenditure of more than US $2 billion (ECP 2007), a few have discussed the possibility of establishing reparations programs, but not one of these countries has implemented one. Ultimately, however, one way of seeing, at least initially, the nature of this paper is by considering that whether it satisfies its own end will be determined not so much by whether it successfully deploys justice considerations in the interest of justice, but whether it does so in the interest of peace.[5]

Now, more specifically, the paper will proceed as follows: it will start with a brief presentation of the facts of two cases, Rwanda and Guatemala, countries that have moved significantly farther regarding DDR than reparations (Sect. 2). Then I will outline some of the fundamental challenges faced by DDR and reparations programs, respectively (Sect. 3). In Sect. 4, I will present conceptions of transitional justice and of DDR that facilitate seeing why implementing DDR programs but no reparations program is problematic. The argument will capitalize on and reinforce the trust-inducing potential of both DDR and transitional justice measures. If the argument is correct, a successful linkage of these measures will strengthen both DDR and transitional justice programs. Focusing on DDR, one of the main advantages this linkage offers to DDR programs is that it would help them mitigate one of the fundamental criticisms to which they have been subject, namely, that they reward bad behavior. In Sect. 5, I will provide some comments on the role of the international community in DDR and reparations programs. My hope is that by

---

[3] See, e.g., the statement by the head of Rwanda's Demobilization and Reintegration Commission (RDRC) which is not atypical: "Our mission is to ensure that *all* ex combatants are socially and economically reintegrated in their communities...." See RDRC (n.d., p. 2).

[4] According to the authors of the paper on international aid prepared as part of the present project, in the 11-year period from 1995 to 2005, of the US $2,686 million in aid given to Rwanda by 15 donors, only $111 million (4.1%) was allocated to transitional justice measures. In the same period Guatemala received $2,143 million, and allocated $140 million (6.5%) to transitional justice measures. For my purposes the figures are even more striking, for in the rubric of transitional justice measures the authors of the international aid paper include support for security sector reform, to which in fact roughly half of the total transitional justice budget in each country was devoted. See Petersen et al. (2007, esp. pp. 2, 4, 10, 11).

[5] I say that this is only an initial description of the nature of the paper for in the last analysis I would like the peace *v.* justice vocabulary to be set aside in favor of a more complex conceptualization of their relationship, to which the paper ultimately seeks to make a small contribution.

showing a potential synergy between a peace and security measure on the one hand and a justice measure on the other, the paper will contribute to the promotion of "a sustainable peace concept that comprises not only peace, but also justice, security, development and institutional reforms."[6]

2 DDR and Reparations in Guatemala and Rwanda

2.1 Guatemala

2.1.1 DDR

There were two different dimensions of the issue of "demobilization" in Guatemala treated in the peace agreements, one involving the demobilization of members of different state and parastatal security forces, and another, the demobilization of the Guatemalan National Revolutionary Unity forces (*Unidad Revolucionaria Nacional Guatemalteca* – URNG). The fact that Guatemala's conflict was close to the paradigm of a "vertical" conflict with a huge asymmetry of forces and also of the responsibility for human rights violations must be kept in mind; by the time the peace agreements were signed on 29 December 1996, the URNG was a small force (around 3,000 members of the URNG were demobilized). By contrast, while the total number of regulars in the different security forces was not tremendously high (from 35,000 to 45,000 troops), if the members of paramilitary organizations (formal and informal) are taken into account, the government had people fighting on its side at several orders of magnitude above the URNG. In terms of abuses, the Historical Clarification Commission (*Comisión de Esclarecimiento Histórico* – CEH), also part of the peace agreements, stated in its 1999 report that the armed forces and paramilitary groups were responsible for 93% of the abuses committed during the more than 30 years of conflict and only 3% were the responsibility of the URNG.

Considering the security sector first, the four fundamental obligations undertaken by the government in the peace accords were the following:

1. The demobilization of the so called civil defense patrols (*patrullas de autodefensa civil* – PAC), whose members were largely indigenous men organized by the military since 1981 and legalized in 1982 as part of the National Security and Development Plan of the military government of Efrain Ríos Montt. The evidence of widespread coercion to serve in the PACs belies their real name, i.e., "Voluntary Civil Defense Committees." The precise total number of members remains unknown, with estimates ranging from almost 400,000 (Stanley and Holiday 2002, p. 35) to 1–1.3 million at the peak of the conflict in 1982–83 (Hauge and Thorsesen 2007, p. 16).[7] The PACs had been formally dissolved

[6] This was one of the stated goals of the conference at Nuremberg.

[7] When the ex-PACs finally received some economic benefits in 2005–2006, the program served 544,620 individuals. See Hauge and Thorsesen (2007, p. 43).

by presidential decree in 1994, before the peace agreements were signed, but it was only in 1996, still before the agreements were formally signed, that their structures were effectively dismantled. In fact, until 2005, this is what the demobilization of the ex-PACs amounted to, for individually, they were not part of any formal program, nor the recipients of any benefits whatsoever.

2. The government committed to disbanding the Mobile Military Police (*Policía Militar Ambulante* – PMA), a force of 2,421 men, some of whom performed police functions and others functioned as a "parastatal security company" which provided guards for banks and other institutions (Stanley and Holiday 2002, p. 35). Some of them were incorporated in the new National Civilian Police, and others, predictably, went into private security firms.
3. The government committed to the redeployment of the army consistent with the redefinition of its functions in accordance with the peace agreements, which called for limiting the army to issues of external, not internal, security. This involved a commitment to reducing the number of military zones and closing down bases that had been established as part of the counterinsurgency campaign.
4. The fundamental commitment to demobilization on the side of government forces had to do with the reduction of the size of the military. The peace agreement stipulated a one-third reduction during 1997, down from a benchmark figure of 45,000 members to 31,000. Shortly after the signing of the accords, however, the army reported that its force level actually stood at 35,000, so it only needed a 4,000 troop reduction, which indeed took place (more systematically among rank and file than among the officer corps) (Stanley and Holiday 2002).

Now, as for the demobilization of the URNG forces, the following are the basic facts: as the peace agreements stipulated, a special commission (*Comisión Especial para la Integración* – CEI) with representation from the government, the URNG, and the UN mission in Guatemala (and with observers from the EU, the OAS, UNDP, and USAID) was established in January 1997 to run the DDR program for former URNG forces. The program that was established shortly thereafter[8] led to the demobilization of 2,928 persons (766 females) (Hauge and Thorsesen 2007, p. 28), and the recovery of 1,824 arms (FGT 2006, pp. 42–43). After a two-month long demobilization process involving the cantonment of forces in eight camps, where they received a variety of services, a two-phase reintegration process started. When the process started in 1997 the CEI had negotiated with the international community a total budget of US $27 million.[9] The following summarizes some of the benefits provided by the programs:

Demobilization: Basic medical services were extended to all ex combatants in camps. They were surveyed and offered legal advice and basic vocational training workshops.

[8] The peace agreements called for a very rapid demobilization process: 60 days after the establishment of the UN verification mission (which the agreements themselves call for) the URNG forces had to be demobilized.

[9] This figure was a disappointment compared to the more than $85 million figure that had been mentioned in December 1996 before the agreements were signed, a figure that enticed reticent members of the URNG. See Hauge and Thorsesen (2007, pp. 23, 28).

Reintegration: Upon leaving camps, those ex combatants who had a place to return to (*los dispersos*) were given grants in the form of four checks: three for Q1,080 (US $142) and one for Q540 ($71). Ostensibly, these were intended to cover vocational training costs (Heard 1999, p. 30). Those who had no place to return to (355 persons) were provided with temporary housing in four hostels (*albergues*) and a small monthly stipend of Q150 ($20). Additionally, three cooperative farms were established to permanently settle 235 ex combatants (Heard 1999, p. 32). Basic technical training was also offered in general business administration, masonry, carpentry, auto mechanics, and other trades (Heard 1999, pp. 37, 44). In order to promote the economic independence of ex combatants the "Productive Incorporation Project" was established. The *dispersos* were eligible for grants of Q10,000 ($1,600) and those in *albergues* of Q15,000 ($2,500). These grants were meant to be start-up money for the creation of new businesses, but early reviews showed that the businesses were not sustainable.[10]

In reality, the DDR program basically offered a variety of technical and vocational courses and minimal levels of short-term economic support. The program did include some projects of high symbolic value, such as the three cooperative farms and the Fundación Guillermo Toriello, a foundation that was supposed to institutionalize the participation of the ex combatants in the design and implementation of the DDR program.

2.1.2 Reparations

Again, in a paper such as this one, there is no point in even attempting a detailed history of the discussions about reparations in Guatemala. And the term "discussions" is used with only some exaggeration, for although there has been some political action, and even the assignment of a relatively speaking not ungenerous budget for this purpose, as we will see, there has been little movement in terms of implementation. The story, from my perspective as well as some experience,[11] is a frustrating one of lack of social coordination and poor institutional design.

The issue of mass reparations in Guatemala can be traced back to the comprehensive peace agreements signed in 1996.[12] Two of the 12 accords, those dealing

[10] These businesses turned out to be mostly failures. As the USAID evaluation (Heard 1999, p. 42) laconically puts it, "many of these people are not mini-entrepreneurs."

[11] The author of this paper advised the *Comisión Nacional de Resarcimiento* during a brief period in 2003–2004, under an agreement with GADRES (*Grupo de Apoyo a las Reparaciones*), whose core members included representatives of the Swiss Government, GTZ, UNDP and a few local NGOs.

[12] Long before the accords were signed judicial cases both in front of Guatemalan courts and in the Inter American system, cases which sought the prosecution of those responsible for human rights violations, and at least those in the Inter American system, reparations for victims, constituted the other important leg on which progress on the general topic of reparations stood in Guatemala. The cases in the Inter American system can have an important motivating effect (meeting between the author and Vice President Stein, Guatemala City, 2004). For an illuminating account of the fate of reparations in Guatemala, see Paz y Paz Bailey (2006).

with human rights and with displacement, include a reference to a "humanitarian duty to redress and/or assist the victims of human rights violations during the internal armed conflict" (as quoted in Paz y Paz Bailey 2006, fn. 65, p. 129). Although not the most categorical (or precise) statement of an obligation to provide reparations to victims, its mere appearance in the peace accords and the extension of the duty to the displaced are both notable. Be that as it may, the CEH report of 1999 gave great impetus to the topic by including quite specific recommendations regarding reparations, some of which have survived the vagaries of the discussions. This included the formation of a body that would be responsible for, among other things, following up on the implementation of the CEH's recommendations. This body, *Instancia Multiinstitucional para la Paz y la Concordia*, was created in 1999 under the auspices of the *Procuradoría de los Derechos Humanos* gathering at least 50 civil society organizations. In August 2002 the *Instancia* presented a draft bill for the creation of the National Reparations Plan (*Plan Nacional de Resarcimiento* – PNR) to President Alfonso Portillo. The draft incorporated most of the specifics recommended by the CEH, including its definitions of victims and of beneficiaries, and its typology of the benefits that the PNR was to distribute. After intense further consultations, a modified bill, containing the outlines of the PNR and its ruling executive commission (*Comisión Nacional de Resarcimiento* – CNR) was presented to the President in November 2002. After it became clear that the legislature was not going to pass the law, the President approved the measure via decree (Governmental Agreement) in May 2003.[13]

The 2003 Governmental Agreement created the ruling executive commission (CNR) and gave it wide latitude to design the PNR within a broad framework. The ten members of the commission included a president (who acted as the representative of the President of the Republic and whose vote was tie-breaking), four representatives of ministries and other government institutions, two representatives of victims' organizations, a representative of Mayan organizations, a representative of women's organizations, and a representative of human rights organizations.[14] Independent of whether this structure was promoted with good or bad intentions, in a context in which there were deep cleavages (of various kinds including class, training, familiarity with the instruments and ways of governance, politics, etc.) between the government and civil society representatives, and worse, in which civil society was itself very badly fragmented, the CNR, perhaps predictably, stalemated completely for more than a year after its creation, notwithstanding the fact that the government had in fact assigned a budget to it which under Guatemala's budget rules had to be executed or it would be "lost." The PNR under the CNR's tutelage was given Q300 million (US $37.5 million) a year for each of its 11 years of projected existence.

In 2005 the government decided to modify the Agreement. The CNR was restructured, placing the members of civil society (same in number and same distribution

[13] Governmental Agreement 258–2003.

[14] Governmental Agreement 258–2003, art. 4.

among the different groups as in the former one) in a consultative council.[15] The new decree adopted the definitional work carried out in the documents produced by the former commission, and provided that the following categories of violations would be subject to reparations:

(a) Forced disappearance
(b) Extrajudicial executions
(c) Physical and psychological torture
(d) Forced displacement
(e) Forced recruitment of minors
(f) Sexual violence and rape
(g) Child abuse
(h) Massacres
(i) Other violations as considered by the CNR[16]

Similarly, it adopted from the same sources the definition of the broad categories of benefits that would be provided by the PNR:

(a) Measures tending towards the restoration of the dignity of victims
(b) Cultural restoration
(c) Psychosocial reparations and rehabilitation
(d) Property restitution
(e) Economic compensation[17]

Finally, and still following the lead of the PNR, and therefore of the recommendations made by the CEH, it urged the prioritization of the reparation of victims, taking into account, in the case of individuals, the gravity of the violations and the socioeconomic conditions and conditions of vulnerability of victims, paying special attention to widows, orphans, the handicapped, the elderly, and children. In the case of collectivities, the decree stipulated that in addition to the general criteria above, the program would pay special attention to victims' groups and indigenous groups that were particularly affected by human rights violations.[18]

It goes without saying that even if one could count on more functional institutions, better relations between state and non-state actors, and a less fragmented civil society, a country like Guatemala would have found it difficult to implement this plan. Reportedly, implementation has begun, at a very slow pace, and not regarding

[15] Governmental Agreement 619–2005, arts. 3 and 4.

[16] Governmental Agreement 619–2005, art. 1.

[17] Governmental Agreement 619–2005, art. 1.

[18] Governmental Agreement 619–2005, art. 1. The decree is silent on the other crucial definition that reparations programs must make, namely, that of beneficiaries. But in the *Manual de Calificación de Víctimas* that the CNR had succeeded in producing in 2005 the beneficiaries in the cases of deceased or disappeared victims were the direct family including the father, mother, spouse or common-law partner, and the children, all of whom would share the granted compensation. One more issue concerning the definition of beneficiaries: the *Manual* does not distinguish between civilian and combatant victims; human rights offenders as well as those in lists of ex-PACs are excluded from receiving benefits (Art. 28).

the five types of benefits but only economic compensation and exhumations (which is an important but narrow component of the broader category of measures tending towards the dignification of victims).[19] Beneficiaries of victims of death in massacres, extrajudicial execution, and forced disappearance are receiving around US $8,000 (shared amongst family members). Victims of torture and sexual violations are receiving up to $7,000.[20] It remains to be seen whether any of the other measures will be implemented, and in fact whether all the victims of these types of violations will indeed receive economic compensation.

2.2 Rwanda

2.2.1 DDR

DDR in Rwanda has taken place in two phases, 1997–2001, and 2002 to the present, and has involved dealing with five shifting and sometimes overlapping forces (listed chronologically in terms of their participation in events in Rwanda, not in the order in which they were processed by the DDR program): (1) the FAR (*Forces Armées Rwandaises*), the former Rwandan army, part of the Hutu regime responsible for the genocide of the Tutsi minority which took place in the period between April and July 1994; (2) the RPF (Rwandan Patriotic Front), the Tutsi dominated rebel army which routed the FAR in July 1994, leading to an exodus of a million Hutus including members of the Hutu regime and large numbers of FAR who participated in the genocide; (3) the RPA/RDF (Rwanda Patriotic Army later renamed the Rwandan Defense Forces), the post-genocide Rwandan military; (4) the Hutu rebels whose leadership included a large number of *genocidaires* that continued fighting the RPA/RDF especially in Northwestern Rwanda from 1997 until 1999, when most of them retreated to the Democratic Republic of Congo (DRC) (these forces launched their last, and unsuccessful, major attack in 2001); (5) the "armed groups" (AGs), the Hutu rebels that have stayed behind in the DRC (see Waldorf 2007).[21]

2.2.2 The DDR Program (RDRP)

In terms of numbers, the basic facts are the following: Rwanda has demobilized and reintegrated more than 58,000 ex combatants of all forces in the period 1995 to December 2006. The present army has been reduced from its size at the time of the genocide in 1994, 40,000–50,000 to between 25,000 and 27,000, and it includes

---

[19] Psychosocial support, particularly around exhumations, has long been provided not by the PNR, but by NGOs.

[20] Communication from Martín Arévalo, Executive Director of the CNR (30 May 2007).

[21] The last two groups were treated as part of the category of ex-AG.

both RPF and RPA members.[22] This reduction in numbers has been accompanied by a reduction in defense expenditure, which has dropped from 3.16% of GDP in 2001, to 2.1% in 2006 (see MDRP 2006, p. 7). About 1% of those who have been demobilized are women, for whom the Rwanda Demobilization and Reintegration Program (RDRP) has created special programs and who receive special treatment (more on this below). In this period, a total of 2,943 children have been demobilized through the RDRP (about 5% of the total number of ex combatants) through specially targeted programs as well. The budget of the program as a whole has been US $53.7 million, of which the government of Rwanda has contributed $2.7 million, and the remainder, that is, the bulk of the budget, comes from international sources.[23]

The RDRP has functioned in two different stages. In stage I, 18,692 members of the RPA – of whom 2,364 were children – were demobilized (although the RPA designation is misleading, for at the time 15,000 ex-FAR had already been reintegrated into the RPA ranks). International donors, wary of Rwanda's participation in the conflict in the DRC, provided only US $8.4 million for DDR, which meant that the program gave almost no reintegration assistance, and in particular, none to the 15,000 ex-FAR at the time (Waldorf 2007, p. 6).

After the RDRP became a part of the Multi-Country Demobilization and Reintegration Program (MDRP) – the regional demobilization and reintegration initiative for seven countries in the Great Lakes region – which among other things, made resources from the Multi-Donor Trust Fund (MDTF) available for the program, phase II began in 2000. The following can only sketch the benefits that the program now provides at each stage of the process:

Demobilization: Ex-RDF are quickly channeled into the programs described below. Ex-AG, repatriated from the DRC, are taken to a demobilization center, where children and adults are separated, as are males and females. This is where the formal registration process takes place, at the end of which (and after formal renunciation of the combatant's status) an RDRP demobilization card is issued. A socio-economic profile of beneficiaries is drawn, and they are medically screened (with voluntary HIV/AIDS testing available). Beneficiaries stay at the center for a two-month long "pre-discharge orientation program," which includes instruction on Rwandan history, human rights, the legal and administrative framework of the country (including women's legal rights), as well as more practical instruction on project management, entrepreneurship, and access to credit. Additionally, this is where they are given information about the RDRP's benefits (RDRC n.d., p. 3).

Reinsertion: After an official demobilization ceremony, all ex combatants receive an identification card and a "Basic Needs Kit" (BNK) of 50,000 RwF (US $91). Ex-RDF and ex-FAR, both considered former government soldiers, and therefore civil

[22] The Arusha Accords stipulated a 50–50 split in the officer corps, and a 60–40 split (RPA/RDF) in other ranks. These proportions have not been kept, however. See Waldorf (2007, pp. 2–3).

[23] The World Bank has provided US $28.7 million (a $10.8 million grant, and a $17.9 million credit); the Multi-Donor Trust Fund (MDTF) managed by the World Bank as part of the Multi-Country Demobilization and Reintegration Program (MDRP) gave a $14.4 million grant; and then there is bilateral financing from DFID for $8.8 million and from the German government for $2.7 million. See RDRC (n.d., p. 2).

servants, also receive a "Recognition of Service Allowance" (RSA), which varies according to rank from 150,000 to 500,000 RwF ($273–$909).[24]

Reintegration: The reintegration stage is the weak point of most DDR programs. Whether this is the case with Rwanda's RDRP is an open question, but judging by the amounts of support distributed (particularly relative to the reinsertion support, which is meant to help ex combatants with *immediate* needs), it seems that Rwanda is no exception. Stage II of the program stipulates that ex-AG and ex-RDF have six months after demobilization to submit to Community Development Committees project proposals meant to allow them to invest in an income-generating activity. In addition to basic business advice and information about opportunities in their areas of settlement, the program makes them eligible to receive "reintegration grants" of 100,000 RwF (US $182). The program also encourages beneficiaries to pool resources. A total of 23,960 reintegration grants have been given by the program.[25]

The program makes available one more source of economic support to ex combatants in stages I or II who have exhausted all their previous benefits and who remain vulnerable. These are grants through the "Vulnerable Support Window" (VSW) which offers anywhere from 100,000 to 500,000 RwF ($182–$909) depending on the level of vulnerability. A total of 27,351 Vulnerable Support Grants have been given (MDRP 2006, p. 3).

Recognizing that reintegration is not an economic matter alone, the program provides educational and vocational support, although the numbers here are not particularly high, and part of this support comes through the VSW grants, not in addition to them: in 2005, for example, the total number of ex combatants supported in formal education was 1,024, and 1,027 were receiving training in different trades (RDRC n.d., p. 4). Plans were under way to increase the availability of vocational training to 3,584 ex combatants in the first round of a new vocational training program (MDRP 2006, p. 4).

Finally, the program makes available a variety of services to ex combatants who are chronically ill or physically disabled, including medical support to 4,018 of them (MDRP 2007, p. 5).

In terms of non-individual benefits, the RDRP is starting to provide capacity development and technical advice to associations and cooperatives with significant ex combatant membership, is exploring options to provide psycho-social support, and has initiated an active information and sensitization strategy to provide information about the program and to improve the perception of ex combatants (MDRP 2007, pp. 5–9).

As was said before, the RDRP has made an effort to deal with female and children ex combatants through specially targeted programs, including special quarters for women in demobilization centers and separate facilities for children. Female ex combatants are eligible for all the benefits available to their male counterparts,

---

[24] This allowance is paid into the beneficiaries' bank account in two installments, the first one a month after settlement in the community of return, the second two months after. All the ex-FAR who demobilized (12,969 out of original estimates of 15,000), who had been underserved in Phase I, received the RSA by December 2005 through Phase II.

[25] This last figure is for the period running up to 30 September 2006. See MDRP (2006, p. 3).

but since they are considered particularly vulnerable, they automatically qualify for the Vulnerable Support Grants. Children do not receive cash through reintegration grants but they receive customized reintegration assistance, including educational support.

The following tables summarize some of these results (RDRC n.d., p. 5):

Demobilization (Stage I & II)

	Stage I (1997-2001)	Stage II (Dec. 2001 - Dec. 2006)			
		Target	Demobilized	Totals (I-II)	
Ex-RPA, adults	16,328	-	-	16,328	
Ex-RPA, children	2,364	-	-	2,364	
Ex-RDF, adults	-	20,000	20,039	20,039	100%
Ex-AG, adults	-	14,400	5,526	5,526*	38%
Ex-AG, children	-	1,600	597	597*	37%
Ex-FAR, adults	-	13,000	12,969	12,969	100%
Totals	18,692	51,000	39,131	57,823	

*Challenge: Despite all the accords and the Rome Declaration (San Egidio, 31 March 2005) of the leadership of the FDLR to abandon its armed struggle, disarm its forces and return to Rwanda, an estimated 8,000-10,000 combatants are still active in the eastern DRC.

Reinsertion and Reintegration Assistance (Stage II)

BASIC NEEDS KIT				*REINTEGRATION GRANT*			
	Demobilized	Distributed			Demobilized	Distributed	
Ex-RDF	20,039	20,039	100%	Ex-RDF	20,039	18,805	94%
Ex-AG	5,526	5,526	100%	Ex-AG	5,526	5,526	100%
Totals	25,565	25,565		Totals	25,565	24,060	

RECOGNITION OF SERVICE ALLOWANCE (RSA)			
	Demobilized	Distributed	
Ex-RDF	20,039	20,039	100%
Ex-FAR	12,969	12,969	100%
Totals	33,008	33,008	

SPECIAL ASSISTANCE TO CHILD-XCs		
Support	Provided	
Reunification (back home)	597	Of the 597 child-XCs demobilized (see demobilization table), all received assistance for reunification with their families. After demobilization, child-XCs received reintegration assistance in the form of vocational training, formal education or income-generating activities.
Transit Care (foster family)	58	
Formal Education	84	
Vocation Training (skills training)	148	
Income-generating Activities	103	
Totals	990	

2.2.3 Reparations

Regardless of whatever may be thought about the adequacy of the DDR efforts, there is no question that compared to them, reparations initiatives come off looking significantly worse. Even taking into account the effect of differences in reporting between the two programs – a function, among other things, of the fact that since there has been little to no involvement on the part of international organizations in the reparations efforts, there is much less reporting and therefore much less information readily available – it is clear that the relationship between DDR and justice measures in Rwanda has followed a well-established pattern in international experience: security related measures are implemented long before justice measures, and they typically receive more attention, in every respect, than justice initiatives.

It goes without saying that this disparity has nothing to do with the urgency in the needs of the constituencies of each set of measures. While attending to the needs of 58,000 ex combatants was obviously an urgent matter, not the least because of the security risks that neglecting them may have posed, the situation faced by their victims was not less dire. As a study for the Danish Ministry of Foreign Affairs described it:

> The genocide had profound demographic impacts [sic] in addition to the loss of 12% of Rwanda's population. Currently about one-third of Rwandan households are headed by women and 20% of households by widows. The genocide created about 220,000 orphans of whom some became, and remain, heads of households (...). Within the broadly defined group of 'survivors' that probably numbers around 400,000 the term 'neediest survivors' is generally used to describe those who have been rendered vulnerable as a result of violence directed at them and/or the killing of either their partners, their parents or their families during the 1994 genocide. A 1998 survey by FARG estimated the 'neediest survivors' to number 282,000 of which 48,000 were widows, 147,000 were orphans (fatherless), 10,000 orphans (motherless) and 64,000 orphans (both parents). The needs of these different groups varied considerably. A particular problem for the widows has been that many were raped and infected with HIV/AIDS during the genocide (Borton and Eriksson 2005, p. 32, footnotes omitted).

Given the peculiar use of the term "survivor," to which we will return, and which lowers the numbers of people in this description who would, under any notion of rights, not to speak of humanitarian concern or basic decency, be seen as deserving recipients of reparations, the truth is that to date, there is no comprehensive reparations program for victims in Rwanda.[26]

This does not mean that the issue of reparations has been entirely absent from Rwanda; the "Organic Law" adopted in 1996 to address the legacies of the genocide already mentions the creation of a fund to compensate the victims of those found guilty by the special chambers within Rwanda's existing courts that the law itself created.[27] Two subsequent draft laws were discussed in 2001 and 2002, respectively. The drafts would create a *Fonds d'Indemnisation*, a compensation fund, as well as the criteria and procedures so that victims could access reparations benefits, to cover all victims, rather than only those of perpetrators who stood trial. These drafts were eventually set aside. This is not the place to attempt a full review of these drafts (see

---

[26] Considering that the overwhelming majority of victims were Tutsi and that the post genocide regime is led by Tutsis makes this even harder to understand. Surely, the reasons to explain this lack of action are complex, but according to one analyst, this "underscores the political marginalization of the Francophone Tutsi survivors, who have an uneasy relationship with the mostly Anglophone, Ugandan-born Tutsi who lead the RPF." Waldorf (2007, p. 13).

[27] Loi Organique du 30 août 1996 sur l'organisation des poursuites des infractions constitutes du crime de genocide ou de crimes contre l'humanité, commises à partir du 1er octobre 1990 jusqu'au 31 décembre 1994, Journal Officiel, no. 17, 01/09/1996.

Rombouts 2006, esp. pp. 199–203, 217–220), but the direction in which the second draft moved – not to speak of the fact that neither draft was adopted – reveals huge disparities in the strength of the commitment to attend to the needs of ex combatants vs. the needs of their victims.

The 2001 draft would have provided benefits to the direct and/or indirect victims of genocide and crimes against humanity – that is, to those survivors who suffered harms directly, as well as to the family members of those who did not survive. It recognized three types of harm that call for compensation: material loss, loss of life, and permanent incapacity, and it would have provided benefits according to the harm suffered.[28] The draft, written with insurance compensation schemes in mind, for example, determined the amount of compensation for incapacity as a function of the age of a victim, the degree of incapacity, and for family members, the degree of kinship. The law both required and articulated the basis on which to perform the complicated gradations that it called for. Thus, it recognized a highly differentiated scale of incapacity (from 1% to 5%, from 5% to 10% and so on), three age groups (below 18, between 18 and 55, above 55, roughly corresponding to three stages of professional activity – and therefore of income potential), and varied the compensation according to degrees of kinship (Rombouts 2006).

Perhaps because it came to be understood that even when faced with a universe of potential beneficiaries significantly smaller than Rwanda's, such a scheme was overly complicated (leaving aside the discretion it gives to doctors in the determination of degrees of incapacity, the negative gender impact of the overall approach, among other problems), and less than a year after the draft was floated, the Ministry of Justice proposed a new one. The 2002 draft goes to the opposite end of the spectrum by proposing a flat compensation (12 million RwF, US $21,818) to all beneficiaries regardless of the harm they suffered. The law defines beneficiaries in terms of three categories, namely, first, the "survivors," "the *rescapés* (those persecuted because of their ethnicity or because of their opposition to the genocide); second, the children, legal partners, brothers and sisters and parents of those killed because of their ethnicity or opposition to the genocide; and, finally, those Rwandans living in Rwanda who were not in the country during the genocide but whose children, legal partners, brothers and sisters or parents were killed for the mentioned reasons" (Rombouts 2006, p. 219).

Alas, this draft was not adopted either, so it is not worth elaborating on the advantages and the (many) disadvantages of the approach it took. What is noteworthy about it is that it responds to what I will argue is one of the fundamental challenges faced by reparations initiatives, namely, how to define "victims," and particularly, "beneficiaries," by offering restrictive definitions. This approach is one shared by the only program established by the Rwandan government that provides support for (some) victims of the genocide – although, strictly speaking, this is not a reparations program – and therefore the issue is best discussed in that context.

---

[28] This definition of victims and of the harms that require compensation obviously leaves out important categories of violations that affect women, in particular, including forced pregnancy. See Rombouts (2006, p. 217).

In 1998 the government established a fund for the benefit of victims of genocide – the *Fonds d'Assistance aux Rescapés du Génocide* (FARG), meant to provide support in micro finances, health, education, and housing to a sector of the victim population. Detailed information about its activities is difficult to come by, but on all accounts this has been a problematic exercise: early on it was recognized that the repayment rates for the micro credits were very low, and thus this part of the program never acquired the importance it could have had (see Rombouts 2006, pp. 224–25); housing support has been minimal in terms of numbers compared to demand (3,000 houses constructed in response to a demand from more than 80,000 women and 53,000 men among its target population who declared that they were without shelter), and the housing offered has reportedly also been substandard in terms of quality, durability, and location (see Rombouts 2006, pp. 222–23). In terms of health care support, FARG reached agreements with health care centers so that they would provide card-holders with medical services for all kinds of illnesses, not just those related to the genocide (except trauma counseling, which was supposed to be provided through a specialized program that was never launched). It is known that 68,000 cards were issued, but no data is available about the types of services actually rendered. There is information, however, about some of the centers turning down FARG patients for the latter's failure to disburse payments (see Rombouts 2006, pp. 224, 229). The educational support part of the program is the one that survives. It basically consists of tuition assistance for children in schools and in some cases, in universities. The fact that the program does not include vocational and educational support for adults is a major shortcoming (see Rombouts 2006, pp. 223–24).

Leaving aside persistent allegations of impropriety in the handling of this program (for a recent example, see Munyaneza 2006), there are two points worth elaborating. First, the FARG is not really a reparations program. There are many important differences between victims' assistance programs and reparations programs, but two are fundamental: whereas reparations programs must involve the recognition of responsibility, victims' assistance programs need not involve such recognition, but may provide benefits solely to assuage the dire circumstances in which victims may find themselves. Furthermore, the type of recognition that is a fundamental aim of reparations programs is two-fold: reparations involve recognizing victims not just in their status *as victims*, but crucially, as *rights bearers*.[29] So, while victims' assistance programs may adopt a needs-based perspective, reparations programs must be rights-centered. That is, the conceptual scaffolding around which reparations programs are constructed must be the notion of rights, and this helps to articulate its primary definitions, including the definitions of "victims" and "beneficiaries." FARG, by contrast, is structured not around the notions of rights. The program uses need as a criterion of access to its benefits,[30] and, most importantly, it is not open to all of those whose rights were violated during the period of

[29] For an account of justice in reparations that places recognition at the core of such programs, see de Greiff (2006a). I will return to this topic below.

[30] In contrast to a social welfare program which can of course be structured around the notion of need, a reparations program may use need as a criterion for the prioritization of the distribution of its benefits, but not as a criterion for accessing those benefits in the first place.

violence, strictly speaking, but only to its "survivors" (*rescapés*).[31] Survivors, according to the law, is a much narrower category consisting of those who "escaped the genocide or the massacres committed between 1 October 1990 and 31 December 1994." Since the intentional element of genocide and massacres is emphasized elsewhere in the law, this means that there are whole categories of people, including all those whose rights were violated by the RPF, who are excluded from the program by definitional fiat.[32] So, even if all the considerations against taking FARG as a reparations program could be overcome, one would have to say that it addresses the crucial challenge of defining its beneficiaries in a way that ends up underserving even those beneficiaries to whom the program opens access to its benefits for it does little to entrench the perception of them – as well as their self-perception – as the bearers of rights, even if it does something (in this case not much) to assuage their needs.

This pattern of a huge disparity in the commitment to DDR and reparations is not a peculiarity of the situation in Rwanda. Indeed, the pattern is so well established in international experience that it is close to the norm.

3 The Main Challenges Faced by DDR and by Reparations Programs

Establishing DDR and reparations programs is an immense undertaking in any context, let alone precisely in the situations in which they most need to be established, namely, post-conflict or post-authoritarian societies, which are marked by profound political divisions, weak, ineffective, or mistrusted institutions, and usually, deep scarcity as well. The challenges are of various sorts, ranging the gamut from the design to the implementation stages. Within the domains of design and implementation, of course, multiple factors that generate difficulties are usually at play, and these also cover a broad spectrum that includes lack of expertise, poor funding, weak political commitment, and severe coordination problems amongst the many actors that are (or ought to be) involved at each step of the way if these programs are going to be set up and achieve their goals.

That both reparations and DDR initiatives have been marred by implementation problems there can be no doubt. In this paper, however, I will not focus on these, for, in principle, implementation problems are avoidable. Nor will I concentrate on the sort of problems that need to be resolved if reparations or DDR programs are going to be designed – let alone implemented – in the first place, problems that may be, for short, grouped under the labels of economic feasibility and "political will." I will assume that these latter types of problem have been solved and that indeed, there is interest in establishing the programs in question, and that a modicum of financing

[31] For a discussion of this concept, see Rombouts (2006, pp. 214–16).

[32] To complicate matters even further, to the opacity of the notion of *rescapé* is added the fact that the status is not certified by an impartial body, but by neighbors, victims' organizations, or local authorities or institutions.

has been secured.[33] Hence, I will concentrate instead on design challenges, at least in part because these apply across the board, independently of contextual considerations, and are, in this sense, more revealing.[34]

3.1 Some Challenges Faced by Reparations Programs

3.1.1 How to Define Victims and Beneficiaries

It makes sense to think about reparations, at least ideally, as a three-term relationship in which links are established between the members of a set defined as "victims" (at least for the purposes of the program), and the members of a set defined as "beneficiaries." In this relationship, the links take the form, precisely, of the benefits distributed by the program. The ideal behind a reparations program, then, is to make sure that at least every victim is a beneficiary, i.e., that he or she receives something from the program.[35] If this helps to clarify, at least abstractly, how reparations are supposed to work, it also clarifies one of the fundamental challenges faced by reparations programs, namely, how to define "victims" and "beneficiaries," and how to craft an effective package of benefits.

The real challenge these days concerning the notion of victim, given developments in international law, is not so much with a choice of a general definition,[36]

[33] It goes without saying that gathering the resources and mustering the will are extremely challenging (and, incidentally, interrelated problems). For a thoughtful analysis of financing reparations programs (including the political dimensions of the issue) see Segovia (2006).

[34] As will become obvious, some of the challenges are shared. I derive no special significance from this fact; these are some of the challenges inherent to the design of distributive procedures. My argument about the importance of establishing links between DDR and reparations programs therefore does not rest on the observation that these programs face some common challenges.

[35] This is nothing more than a heuristic; on the one hand, the ideal is indeed more demanding than this suggests, for reparations programs usually provide benefits to a set of people larger than the set of victims (think about unharmed family members who nevertheless, rightly, receive benefits from the program). On the other, however, programs usually fail to provide benefits to all victims (think not just of the many victims of violations of the type of rights that are frequently violated in situations of conflict or authoritarianism but that have never been triggers of reparations through a program, but also of the many people who are victims of the very violations that the program is supposed to provide benefits for, who nevertheless never receive any). To use the vocabulary that the author developed for OHCHR (2008), the former is a problem of lack of "comprehensiveness" in the reparations program, the latter of "incompleteness."

[36] For instance, the Basic Principles and Guidelines on the Right to a Remedy and Reparation for Victims of Gross Violations of International Human Rights Law and Serious Violations of International Humanitarian Law offers a general definition of "victims" which is likely to be adopted by most reparations programs in the near future:

> Victims are persons who individually or collectively suffered harm, including physical or mental injury, emotional suffering, economic loss or substantial impairment of their fundamental rights, through acts or omissions that constitute gross violations of international human rights law, or serious violations of international humanitarian law. Where appropriate, and in accordance with domestic law, the term "victim" also includes the immediate

but with a fundamental question that all reparations programs face, namely, how to select the rights whose violation will trigger access to benefits. In order for a reparations program to satisfy the ideal of at least making sure that every victim is a beneficiary, it would have to extend benefits to the victims of the same broad range of violations that may have taken place during the conflict or repression.[37] Now, no program has achieved this type of total comprehensiveness. Most programs have actually provided reparations for a rather limited and traditional list of rights, concentrating heavily on the more fundamental civil and political rights, leaving the violations of other rights largely unrepaired.

While particularly under conditions of scarcity it makes sense to concentrate on what are perceived to be the worst forms of abuse, it remains true that no program to date has worried about articulating the principles why it chooses to provide benefits for the violations of some rights and not others. One of the predictable consequences of this omission is that violations that affect mainly or predominantly marginalized groups have rarely led to reparations benefits. This has had a nefarious effect on the way that women, for example, have been dealt with by reparations programs.[38] The mere demand that those in charge of designing reparations programs articulate the grounds on which they choose the catalogue of violations that the programs will provide benefits for will have a salutary effect.

Rather than offering a solution to this challenge, I am here interested in highlighting this as one of the crucial challenges that reparations programs always face. In situations of limited resources, choosing a very extensive list of rights will inevitably lead to the dilution of the benefits. On the other hand, choosing a very narrow list will leave out of consideration entire categories of deserving victims, which means not just that important claims to justice will be left unaddressed by the program – making it less effective than it could be – but also, since people tend to persist in their struggles for justice, that the issue of reparations will remain as a contested one in the political agenda.

3.1.2 How to Define the Benefits to Be Distributed by the Program

The term "reparations" in international law is a broad notion closely related to the concept of "legal remedy," and therefore includes measures of restitution, compensation, rehabilitation, satisfaction, and guarantees of non-repetition.[39] No reparation program to date has assumed the responsibility for undertaking measures of all

family or dependants of the direct victim and persons who have suffered harm in intervening to assist victims in distress or to prevent victimization. A person shall be considered a victim regardless of whether the perpetrator of the violation is identified, apprehended, prosecuted, or convicted and regardless of the familial relationship between the perpetrator and the victim. A/RES/60/147, 21 March 2006, p. 5.

[37] If it did that, the program would be "comprehensive" in the technical sense defined in OHCHR (2008).

[38] On this topic, see Rubio Marín (2006) especially the Introduction.

[39] For an account of justice in reparations that places recognition at the core of such programs, see de Greiff (2006a). I will return to this topic below.

these kinds. For purposes of simplicity, in the domain of the design of reparations programs more narrowly conceived, the measures that programs typically distribute can be organized around two fundamental distinctions, one between material and symbolic reparations, and the other between the individual and the collective distribution of either kind. Material and symbolic reparations can take different forms. Material reparations may assume the form of compensation, that is, of payments either in cash or negotiable instruments, or of service packages, which may in turn include provisions for education, health, housing, etc. Symbolic reparations may include, for instance, official apologies, the change of names of public spaces, the establishment of days of commemoration, the creation of museums and parks dedicated to the memory of victims, rehabilitation measures such as restoring the good name of victims, etc. These symbolic measures would fall under the category of "satisfaction" used in the *Basic Principles*.

The combination of different kinds of benefits is what the term "complexity" seeks to capture. A reparations program is more complex if it distributes benefits of more distinct types, and in more distinct ways, than its alternatives.

There are at least two fundamental reasons for crafting "complex" reparations programs combining measures of different kinds. The first has to do with the maximization of resources; programs that combine a variety of types of benefits ranging from the material to the symbolic, and each distributed both individually and collectively, may cover a larger portion of the universe of victims than programs that concentrate on the distribution of material benefits alone, and thus make the program more complete. Since victims of different categories of violations need not receive exactly the same kinds of benefits, having a broader variety of benefits makes this task feasible. Just as important, this broader variety of benefits allows for a better response to the fact that a particular violation can generate harms of different types, and having a range of reparatory measures makes it more likely that these harms can, to some degree, be redressed.

Reparations programs, then, can range from the very simple, that is, from programs that behave as mere compensation procedures, distributing money alone, to the highly complex, distributing monetary compensation but also health care, educational and housing support, etc., in addition to both individual and collective symbolic measures. In general, since there are certain things that money cannot buy (and there are certain things for which there is no money), complexity brings with it the possibility of providing benefits to a larger number of victims[40] and of targeting benefits flexibly so as to respond to a variety of victims' needs. All other things being equal, then, "complexity" is a desirable characteristic in a reparations program. Of course, in most cases not all things remain equal. There are some costs to increased complexity that may make it undesirable beyond a certain threshold.

Now, it is unlikely that complexity, in the sense of the distribution of a variety of types of benefits, will be effective on its own. The types of benefits, ideally, must reinforce one another, making a coherent whole, giving the program "internal coherence" (see, e.g., OHCHR 2008, Sect. IV.6). Thus, a packet of mutually reinforcing

[40] And, particularly in the case of collective symbolic measures such as public apologies and sites of memory, to non-victims as well.

benefits is more likely to satisfy victims than a random assortment of goods. Deliberate planning about the interrelationships between the different types of benefits is called for.

3.1.3 How to Define the Goals of the Program

In the case of isolated civil cases of reparations before courts, the fundamental aim of the proceedings is quite clear: the objective is to make each victim whole, that is, to the extent possible, to return him or her to the status quo ante, to the situation the person was in before his or her rights were violated. This is done, to the extent possible, by providing compensation in proportion to the harm suffered, that is, technically, by satisfying the criterion of *restitutio in integrum*. This is an unimpeachable criterion for the individual case, for its main motivation is, on the side of the victim, to neutralize as far as possible the consequences of the violation suffered, and on the side of the violator, to prevent him or her from enjoying the benefits of crime.

The problem, however, is that there is no massive reparations program that has even approached the satisfaction of this criterion. Typically, victims receive by way of compensation a fraction of what any calculation of the harms endured by the violation of the rights which are normally the triggers of benefits through reparations programs (e.g., disappearance, extrajudicial execution, illegal detention, in general severe violations of the right to freedom and against bodily harm) would suggest they should receive.

This generates at least two challenges. The first is that given that the judicial criterion of compensation in proportion to harm is both perfectly familiar from its application both in national and in regional courts as well as intuitively attractive, victims' expectations are set around this notion. How to manage these expectations by reparations bodies that in all likelihood cannot meet this criterion of justice is a serious challenge. The second, related problem is how to define the aim(s) of the program in the face of the impossibility of satisfying the criterion of justice around which the point of reparations, in general, has traditionally been conceived. If reparations programs cannot make victims whole, what are they trying to do? Are they the same thing as victims' assistance programs? Is the frequent move on the part of governments faced by reparations claims, namely, to argue that since reparations are too expensive they will rather either do development, or do reparations by means of development programs, a legitimate one? To these questions we must certainly return. To anticipate, however, the mediate aims of a reparations program, arguably, are to provide recognition to victims and to foster a minimal sense of civic trust. These aims, which reparations programs can be thought to share with other transitional justice measures, partly explain why it is important for programs to be not merely internally coherent in the sense explained above, namely, that they provide a variety of benefits that reinforce one another, but also *externally* coherent, that is, that they bear significant relationships with other justice initiatives such as truth-telling, prosecutions, or institutional reform.

3.2 Some Challenges Faced by DDR Programs

3.2.1 How to Define the Beneficiaries

Despite the fact that on the face of it the question of who the beneficiaries of a DDR program should be seems to have a ready answer, namely, "ex combatants," it is clear that this does not begin to settle the question, for even in the case of conventional conflicts with well organized armies the boundary between combatants and non-combatants is porous (IDDRS 2006, Sect 5.1, p. 8). This is even more so in the case of non conventional conflicts whose forces are characterized by a great deal of circulation between civilian and conflict related activities of different kinds. Furthermore, however stable (or not) combat functions and positions may be, there is always a large contingent of people in support positions of different types without which combatants could not play their roles, and it is not clear that these should be left out of DDR programming. Even if a security-oriented conception of DDR is adopted (about which more will be said), in contexts in which arms are easily available, leaving out of DDR programs large groups of people who have played important support positions, and moreover, who likely circulated between combat and non-combat roles does not serve security interests very effectively.

The challenge of defining who is eligible for benefits is multidimensional and the fact that it is pervasive and unavoidable does not mean that ready answers have been found. How "beneficiaries" are defined has an impact on the way that procedures for accessing the benefits are designed, and it has a very significant impact on women and children. To illustrate, a good number of the earlier programs made benefits conditional on turning in weapons, in effect defining beneficiaries as those who bear arms. One can of course see why this was at some point considered an attractive alternative: being an incentive for disarming, it was thought to kill two birds with one stone. However, the simplicity of this approach failed to take into account not just that particularly among insurgent forces there are typically more combatants than arms, but that this would by definition exclude from benefits the bulk of women and children in support roles who had no arms to turn in.[41] Variations to

[41] The following chart clearly shows that only exceptionally is there a close to one-to-one relationship between demobilized ex combatants and recovered arms. So, if returning arms is chosen as a criterion of accessing the program, lots of ex combatants will be left out. Source: ECP (2007, p. 30).

Table 12. Weapons handed in per demobilised combatant in selected countries

Country	People demobilised	Weapons handed in	Weapons/person	Years
Afghanistan	62.000	48.819	0,78	2003-2006
Angola	97.115	33.000	0,34	2002-2006
Burundi	21.769	26.295	1,2	2004-2006
Colombia	31.761	18.051	0,57	2004-2006
Côte d'Ivoire (1)	981	110	0,11	2006
Indonesia (Aceh)	3.000	840	0,28	2005
Liberia	101.405	28.364	0,28	2005
Rep. Congo	17.400	11.776	0,68	2000-2006
TOTAL group	**335.521**	**167.525**	**0,49**	
El Salvador (FMLN)	11.000	10.200	0,93	1992
Guatemala (URNG)	3.000	1.824	0,61	1997

this approach, such as the one tried in Sierra Leone, which required not turning in a weapon but demonstrating the ability to assemble and disassemble one, were rapidly met by the sudden availability in the streets of instruction on how to do that (see Ginifer 2003). An entirely different approach, namely, to allow commanders of the forces to be demobilized to define the beneficiaries of the DDR programs by providing lists of names has also encountered difficulties: particularly in the early stages of the process, when confidence levels are low, this is a procedure that lends itself to easy manipulation, and which has frequently led to massive over reporting – not surprisingly, however, not of women and children, who are not well served by this procedure either.[42]

In summary, then, all DDR programs face a challenge not just in defining the beneficiaries (as well as in establishing verification procedures) in a way that avoids both the exclusions that predictably come about as the result of narrow definitions and demanding procedures, as well as the over inclusiveness (with the consequent increase of costs and the potential resentment and friction) that come from loose definitions and lax procedures. Since two notoriously vulnerable groups, i.e., women and children, stand to lose more than others from mistakes, it is imperative to exercise utmost care in establishing these definitions and the attendant verification procedures.

3.2.2 How to Define a Sensible Packet of Benefits

We are used to speaking about DDR programs as if each one of them were a single program. In reality, of course, each DDR program is a complex set of (ideally integrated) initiatives, each one of them serving its own ends: thus, for example, reinsertion measures have specific ends which are distinct from the ends of reintegration programs. This alone explains part of the difficulties that characterize the effort to put together a sensible packet of benefits. Since the ends of both reinsertion and reintegration can be conceived differently, this only increases the complications.[43]

---

[42] The IDDRS has come down in favor of tests to determine an individual's membership of an armed force or group, but adds that "All those who are found to be members of an armed force or group, whether they were involved in active combat or in support roles (such as cooks, porters, messengers, administrators, sex slaves and "war wives") shall be considered part of the armed force or group and therefore shall be included in the DDR programme." (IDDRS 2006, 2.30, Sect. 5.1, p. 2).

[43] See, for example, the definitions of reinsertion and reintegration in IDDRS:

> Reinsertion is the assistance offered to ex-combatants during demobilization but prior to the longer-term process of reintegration. Reinsertion is a form of transitional assistance to help cover the basic needs of ex-combatants and their families and can include transitional safety allowances, food, clothes, shelter, medical services, short-term education, training, employment and tools. While reintegration is a long-term, continuous social and economic process of development, reinsertion is short-term material and/or financial assistance to meet immediate needs, and can last up to 1 year. Reintegration is the process by which ex-combatants acquire civilian status and gain sustainable employment and income. Reintegration is essentially a social and economic process with an open time-frame, primarily taking place in communities at the local level. It is part of the general development of a country and a national responsibility, and often necessitates long-term external assistance. IDDRS (2006, 2.10, p. 5).

Even if there is consensus about what the proper way of understanding these goals might be, there is no single way of pursuing or achieving them. Even the relatively modest goal of reinsertion can be served in many ways. Regarding the more ambitious goal of social reintegration this is even more so. Considering that these are decisions that are made under conditions of scarcity, in contexts in which markets for both labor and goods are partially functioning at best, in which civil society has been disarticulated under the pressure of authoritarianism or conflict, targeting a universe of beneficiaries who in many cases have no skills other than those of waging war and little formal education, and that these decisions are often made by people – including donors – with little familiarity with the local context, it is not surprising that there are so many stories of poorly conceived benefit packages, in particular skills training courses. Benefits drawn with the participation of recipients and on the basis of labor market analyses increase the likelihood that beneficiaries will not only be recipients but that they will actually benefit from the goods and services provided by the program.[44]

3.2.3 How to Define the Goals of the Program

Once again, it may be surprising that programs that were traditionally conceived in narrow, technical terms have ended up encountering difficulties defining their goals. Why this has come about, however, is easier to understand by keeping in mind one inherent and one extrinsic feature of DDR programs; "reintegration," one of the dimensions (and goals) of these programs is a broad notion, whose satisfaction potentially makes reference to and calls for myriad, sustained and long term interventions in a variety of areas. As if this internal factor did not provide a sufficient incentive for the proliferation of aims to be pursued by DDR programs, the fact that in the early stages of a post conflict process DDR programming is frequently the only source of access to international funds has turned these programs into the means to attain the various goals pursued by the myriad projects that get their funding via DDR programs, including in some cases both services and infrastructure (SIDDR 2006, p. 10).

Thus, all DDR programs face a challenge in defining the goals that can be legitimately pursued through initiatives of this sort. As usual, there are pitfalls to be avoided both on the side of conceptual parsimony as well as profligacy; among other problems, a very narrow understanding of DDR may strengthen the tendency to think about it as an exclusively technical issue to be addressed solely in military or security related terms, ignoring thereby the crucially important *political* dimensions of DDR and weakening the incentive for consultation and participation – which will

[44] How to institutionalize the participation of civil society and other stake holders in both reparations and DDR programs is another critical challenge. For reparations programs, see OHCHR (2008, Sect. 4.1). For DDR programs, see IDDRS (2006, 2.30 and 3.30, esp.).

undermine the sense of ownership over the programs, making them in turn more difficult to implement and less sustainable. On the other hand, conceptual profligacy in the definition of the goals of DDR can easily generate expectations – and not just on the part of beneficiaries – which are impossible to satisfy, weakening also the sustainability of the programs.[45] Assigning DDR programs the responsibility to, say, make a significant contribution to economic development and then criticizing the program for failing to achieve this goal is an example of how conceptual profligacy with the goals of DDR programs may discredit them in general.

But the challenge of defining and articulating clearly the goals of DDR programs is important for reasons that go well beyond narrow matters of implementation. It is through the definition of the goals of the program that an answer can begin to be articulated to what is the fundamental challenge that all DDR programs face, namely, the charge that these are programs that reward bad behavior. Particularly in contexts of deep economic scarcity and weak or uneven state presence, the establishment of programs to benefit ex combatants has almost without exception led others to conclude that apparently, the only way to get the attention of the state is to bear and use arms. This is a challenge that these programs cannot afford not to meet, and therefore I will return to this issue below.

4 Conceptualizing DDR and Reparations

I have argued that one of the main challenges that both DDR and reparations programs face is to define the goals that can legitimately be sought through them. In this section, after offering an account of a holistic transitional justice policy and adopting an account of DDR, I argue that a proper conceptualization of these goals helps to explain why it makes sense to think about establishing links between the two types of programs. I will also defend the view that establishing these links helps DDR fend off the objection that these programs reward "belligerents." The section begins with a brief account of a holistic conception of transitional justice and of a comparatively narrow, security oriented conception of DDR. It then tries to show how even this narrow understanding creates a sufficiently rich conceptual overlap to warrant thinking about the relationship between reparations and DDR. Finally, it will show how establishing these links helps DDR programs meet one of the frequent objections raised against them.

4.1 Transitional Justice

I think of reparations as one element of a holistic conception of transitional justice that includes as some of its other elements criminal prosecutions, truth-telling, and

[45] This is true not just of the expectations generated amongst the population as a whole, but even among the groups specifically targeted to receive benefits through the program. See, for example, FGT (2003).

institutional reform. While this list need not be thought to exhaust the elements of a comprehensive transitional justice policy, what is important if this is going to be part of a holistic conception is that the list be more than a random assortment of measures – in other words, that the close relationship among its different elements be articulated. I will do so by means of two arguments.[46]

The first argument focuses on the relations of complementarity that in practice the measures arguably have. I will illustrate the point by reference to reparations measures; the general argument is that reparations in the absence of other transitional justice measures are more likely to be seen by victims as "compensatory" measures that lack the proper connections to justice, connections without which compensation can hardly be seen as *reparations*. A society that responds to norm-breaking exclusively by compensating the victims for the costs that the norm-breaching may have caused them is one which fails to understand that there are dimensions of corrective justice that go beyond the obligation to try to restore victims to their economic status quo ante. A good illustration of this unsatisfactorily narrow approach is that of the Japanese reaction to the euphemistically called "comfort women," the majority of whom have not accepted the benefits offered through a Japanese foundation established to compensate them, for the benefits not only come from private funds, but are unaccompanied by an explicit recognition of fault from the Japanese government (see, e.g., Yoshimi 2002; Stetz and Bonnies 2001). Similarly, and in the opposite direction, a society that responded to crime without redressing victims at all would fail to understand that when violations occur it is not just norms that are broken but lives as well.

Thus, to be more concrete, reparations in the absence of truth-telling can be seen by beneficiaries as the attempt, on the part of the state, to buy the silence or acquiescence of victims and their families, turning the benefits into "blood money." But the relation holds in the opposite direction as well: truth-telling in the absence of reparations can be seen by victims as an empty gesture, as cheap talk. The same bidirectional relationship links criminal justice and reparations: from the standpoint of victims, especially once a possible moment of satisfaction derived from the punishment of perpetrators has passed, the punishment of a few perpetrators without any effective effort to positively redress victims could be easily seen by victims as a form of more or less inconsequential revanchism. But reparations without criminal justice can easily be seen by victims as something akin to the payments of a crime insurance scheme, which does not necessarily involve the assumption of responsibility on the part of anyone, including the state. The same tight and bidirectional relationship may be observed between reparations and institutional reform, since a democratic reform that is not accompanied by any attempt to dignify citizens who were victimized can hardly be legitimate. By the same token, reparative benefits in the absence of reforms that diminish the probability of the repetition of violence are nothing more than payments whose utility, and again, legitimacy, are questionable.

The second argument to explain the holistic dimension of a comprehensive transitional justice policy acknowledges that each of the measures that forms a part of

[46] See de Greiff (2006a) for an elaboration of these arguments.

such a policy – criminal prosecutions, truth-telling, reparations, and institutional reform (of which vetting is one modality[47]) – has its own specific goals, but points out that they share two mediate goals;[48] it can be argued that the different elements of a comprehensive transitional justice policy are meant to provide recognition to victims and to foster civic trust. Very briefly, the various transitional measures can be interpreted as efforts to institutionalize the recognition of individuals as rights bearers. Criminal justice can be interpreted as an attempt to re-establish the equality of rights between the criminal and his or her victim, after the criminal severed that relationship with an act that suggested his superiority over the victim. Truth-telling provides recognition in ways that are perfectly familiar, and that are still probably best articulated by the old difference proposed by Thomas Nagel between knowledge and acknowledgment, when he argued that although truth commissions rarely disclose facts that were previously unknown, they still make an indispensable contribution in acknowledging these facts.[49] The acknowledgment is important precisely because it constitutes a form of recognizing the significance and value of persons – again, as individuals, as citizens, and as victims. Reparations are the material form of the recognition *owed* to fellow citizens whose fundamental rights have been violated, manifesting that the state has taken to heart the interests of those whose rights went previously unrecognized.[50] Finally, institutional reform is guided by the ideal of guaranteeing the conditions under which citizens can relate to one another and to the authorities as equals.

The other aim that, arguably, the different elements of transitional justice share is the promotion of trust among citizens and amongst them and their institutions.[51] The sense of trust at issue here is not the thick form of trust characteristic of relations between intimates, but rather, a thin disposition between strangers that can be characterized initially as a non-hostile disposition that contrasts not just with its direct opposite, but with one that puts a premium on surveillance and the threat of sanctions.

At the most general level, the point can be put in the following terms: law both presupposes and catalyzes trust among individuals and trust between them and their institutions. It can help generate trust between citizens by stabilizing expectations and thus diminishing the risks of trusting others. Similarly, law helps generate trust in institutions (including the institutions of law themselves) among other ways, by accumulating a record of reliably solving conflicts. But the accomplishment of these

---

[47] I am following Alexander Mayer-Rieckh in thinking about vetting as a form of institutional reform, without rehearsing his argument. See Mayer-Rieckh (2007).

[48] They also share two long term goals, namely, democratization and reconciliation, but I cannot address these here.

[49] Thomas Nagel argues that there is "a difference between knowledge and *ac*knowledgment. It is what happens and can only happen to knowledge when it becomes officially sanctioned, when it is made part of the public cognitive scene." Quoted in Weschler (1989).

[50] For a full elaboration of this argument, see de Greiff (2006a).

[51] I have worked out in detail the relationship between reparations and civic trust in de Greiff (2006a), between truth-telling and civic trust in de Greiff (2005), between vetting and civic trust in de Greiff (2007a), and between reconciliation and civic trust in de Greiff (2007b).

goals naturally presupposes the effectiveness of the law, and in a world of less than generalized spontaneous compliance, this means that law, although rational, must also be coercive. And this coercive character at the limit entails criminal punishment.

Truth-telling can foster civic trust in different ways. Among those who were directly affected by the violence – whose trust is obviously particularly difficult to recover – there are two groups, distinguished by their attitudes, for whom organized truth-telling might facilitate the possibilities of trusting their fellow citizens again or anew. First, there are those who are fearful that the past might repeat itself, whose confidence was shattered by experiences of violence and abuse. Their specific fear might be that the political identity of (some) citizens has been shaped around values that made the abuses possible. So, members of minority groups in different contexts fear that majorities have internalized values, dispositions, and attitudes that might lead to violence again. How can trust be fostered among citizens some of whom suspect that others still carry dispositions that either due to their outright wickedness or to their weakness made terror possible and is likely to make it possible again?

Truth-telling, remembering the past in public ways, can be regarded, precisely, as the beginning of the effort to satisfy the requirements of civic trust; we give those who worry about our political identity as well as those who worry about whether they can rely on people who may still be the carriers of dubious dispositions and attitudes reasons to participate in a common political project if we are willing to reflect upon the constitution of our identity and the character of our dispositions. An institutionalized effort to confront the past might be seen by those who were formerly on the receiving end of violence as a good faith effort to come clean, to understand long term patterns of socialization, and in this sense, to initiate a new political project.

Second, we need to worry also about those whose concern is not so much that the past might repeat itself, but rather, that independently of what might happen in the future, we have a debt towards those who perished. They want to receive recognition for their suffering, not necessarily because they fear the recurrence of violence, but because of what they already endured. Here again truth-telling is important, and not merely for pedagogical reasons. Social trust on all sides might increase if there is a willingness to remember those who perished not only as a form of "gratitude" for what they did for us – even if that was only to afford us yet another occasion to learn what human beings are capable of – but as an expression of sheer loss. Remembering the suffering of others, then, is important independently of the knowledge that the suffering ought not to happen again. Trust might be fostered if we know not only that those whom we trust will quickly learn from their offences, but, more important still, if we know that they have a keen perception of the consequences of their transgressions.

Reparations foster civic trust by signaling for victims the seriousness of the state and of their fellow citizens in their efforts to reestablish relations of equality and respect. In the absence of reparations, victims will always have reasons to suspect that even if the other transitional mechanisms are applied with some degree of sincerity, the "new" democratic society is one that is being constructed on their shoulders, ignoring their justified claims. By contrast, if even under conditions of scarcity funds are allocated for former victims, a strong message is sent to them and others about their (perhaps new) inclusion in the political community. Former victims of abuse are given a material manifestation of the fact that they are now living among a group of fellow citizens and under institutions that aspire to be trustworthy. Reparations, in summary, can be seen as a method to achieve one of the aims of a just state, namely inclusiveness, in the sense that all citizens are equal participants in a common political project.

Finally, most post transitional institutional reform is motivated not just by the aims of increasing the efficiency of state institutions – understanding efficiency simply in terms of quantifiable output – but by the richer goals of re-legitimizing the state, and of preventing the recurrence of violence. The achievement of these goals provides reasons to individuals for trusting one another and their institutions.

These two arguments, one centering on the relationships of complementarity between the different transitional justice measures, and the other focusing on the goals that the different measures arguably share, are part of the explanation of the holistic character of a transitional justice policy. My interest here, however, is not simply explanatory or conceptual, but practical. These arguments also provide a motivation to make sure that each of the measures is implemented in an "externally coherent" manner, that is, in a way that reinforces, precisely, the relationship between each of the measures and other initiatives that seek to provide recognition, and, for purposes of this paper, most relevantly, civic trust.

4.2 DDR

The recently completed Integrated DDR Standards (IDDRS) represents, perhaps, the most sophisticated understanding of DDR. One of the reasons that make it so sophisticated is that it certainly makes an effort to go well beyond the (excessively) narrow focus on disarmament and demobilization which has characterized if not the thinking, at least the practice of DDR for so long. As the document puts it, "Integrated DDR places great emphasis on the long-term humanitarian and developmental impact of sustainable reintegration processes and the effects these have in consolidating long-lasting peace and security" (IDDRS 2006, 2.10, p. 1). While this is certainly a measure of great progress, the text is sufficiently ambiguous as to allow for different readings of what it really intends to say about the relationship between DDR and development. To claim that IDDRS places emphasis on the developmental impact of reintegration is not the same thing as saying that development is one of the goals, let alone the responsibilities it attributes to DDR programs. To illustrate the ambiguity again, the text argues that DDR is "a process that helps to promote both security and development." However, the same sentence argues that DDR "is just one of several post-conflict recovery strategies" and that "it must work together with other comprehensive peace-building strategies including socio-economic recovery programmes… " (IDDRS 2006, 2.20, p. 1). What DDR's contribution to (and responsibility for) development might be, exactly, the text does not make explicit. On a charitable reading of the text, one may argue that the contribution that it assigns to DDR is to promote the economic development not of society, generally, but of the program's own beneficiaries. This is plausible but (a) it would be slightly odd to talk about development in such a circumscribed manner[52] and (b) it may clash with its injunctions against "turning [ex combatants] into a privileged group within the community" and its explicit statement that DDR programs seek only to fulfill their "essential needs," which is not a big developmental aim (IDDRS 2006, 4.30, p. 3). It is in these more careful contexts where IDDRS trims its sails and returns to what may be a less ambitious but nevertheless more defensible position which recognizes that "DDR is carried out primarily to improve security" (IDDRS 2006, 4.30, p. 6), more boldly, that it is precisely because returning ex combatants are potential "spoilers" of peace that we provide them benefits through DDR programs even though other war affected groups may be larger (IDDRS 2006, 4.30, p. 3),[53] and where it shifts the main responsibility for developmental tasks to the other, broader "post-conflict recovery strategies" (insisting, nevertheless, on the importance of coordinating these various programs).

Now, this is not the place to engage in a detailed exegesis of IDDRS, for that is not my point. In this paper I will explicitly adopt a narrower understanding of the goals of DDR (at least narrower than the widest but still plausible reading of IDDRS). That is, I will adopt an interpretation of the goals of DDR programs that is more focused on the security enhancement aim of DDR. I will do so not only because I think that this is more realistic (and avoiding defeated expectations in a post-conflict setting in which institutions have both a low level of credibility and a low capacity to deliver is crucial, in my opinion), but also because I do not want my argument to turn on nothing more than definitional fiat; obviously, the possibility of finding interesting overlaps between transitional justice measures in general and reparations in particular, on the one hand, and DDR programs, on the other, increases if one adopts an expansive understanding of DDR. But that would be uninteresting. I would rather take the hardest case, because if it can be shown that even a narrower understanding of DDR is one that relates in interesting and significant ways with transitional justice measures, then that will be even more so for the broader conceptions of DDR.

I will therefore concentrate here on a conception according to which, as the Stockholm Initiative on DDR (SIDDR) (2006, p. 14) is not shy to recognize, "the primary aim of DDR is to contribute to a secure and stable environment in which the overall peace process and transition can be sustained." This understanding of the basic goal of DDR programs is not indifferent at all to further, developmental aims, but it explicitly takes DDR processes to be, at best, *enabling conditions* (see SIDDR 2006, p. 23) rather than direct *causal contributions* to development. The way the SIDDR *Final Report* puts it dovetails with IDDRS when the latter is at its most

52 Particularly given the insistence on the importance of making sure that DDR benefits not just ex combatants but also communities. E.g., IDDRS (2006, 2.30, p. 6).

53 Of course size is not the relevant consideration, *desert* is. But these are waters in which IDDRS chooses not to wade.

cautious; the point is not to go back to a conception of DDR that concentrates exclusively on disarmament and demobilization, but to argue that the more ambitious dimensions of reintegration should be carried out by means of *coordination with other programs* rather than being the responsibility and parts of the DDR program:

> The SIDDR, on the one hand, sets the boundaries of DDR programmes based on the goals of security and stability – and therefore does not encourage thinking that these programmes alone can achieve either a rapid or comprehensive transformation of societal structures. On the other hand, to the extent that the SIDDR promotes the idea that DDR programmes ought to be designed and implemented as part of a comprehensive peace-building framework, it provides an incentive to think about the many ways in which DDR programmes need to be linked with other interventions if they are to support the long-term goals of a larger peace process (SIDDR 2006, p. 19).

So, now, why does this conceptual work matter? In a nutshell, this is the argument: it is significant that both DDR and transitional justice measures can be seen to be measures intended to promote trust. I have already sketched the ways in which transitional justice measures can be thought to have as one of their fundamental goals the promotion of civic trust, and in particular, the trust in institutions. The point is that even a narrow understanding of DDR programs attributes to them a confidence building role. The aim of disarming and demobilizing is both to demonstrate and to cultivate confidence in the prospects of peace, and a minimal sense of trust in one's partners in the process.

Of course, it could be argued that the objects of trust at issue for DDR and for transitional justice measures are not the same: DDR, it could be said, can reasonably be thought to foster trust initially in *partners* in a peace process, whereas transitional justice measures aspire to making a contribution to the trustworthiness of institutions, largely by reaffirming the importance of foundational *norms and values*. While the objection is generally valid, it must also be kept in mind that a norm-based account of trust suggests that trusting individuals is a function of certain convictions of the norms and values on which these individuals act; in other words, partners in peace processes trust one another only to the extent that they have reliable convictions that the other parties will have as one of their reasons for acting certain norms and values.[54]

Now, how does finding this functional and conceptual overlap between DDR programs and transitional justice measures help, concretely? Returning to one of the topics in the introduction to this paper, my interest here, at least at first, is to deploy justice-related arguments in the interest of security. The general point is the following: if the primary goal of DDR programs is to enhance security by avoiding the marginalization of potential spoilers of the peace process, then the goal is better achieved by means of processes that contribute to the reintegration of the ex combatants. And the rub is that justice enhancing measures may facilitate this process. Although it is difficult to generalize conclusively on the basis of a single case and a relatively small sample of participants in that case, evidence seems to support the case I am making here. A recent study of the DDR program in Sierra Leone suggests that the single most important factor in the reintegration of ex combatants is

[54] For the norm-based account of trust on which this argument relies, see de Greiff (2007b).

the reputation of the unit to which the ex combatants belonged: those who belonged to the units that allegedly perpetrated the greatest abuses have had a harder time reintegrating. This is true regardless of whether the individuals in question participated in the DDR programs or not (Weinstein and Humphreys 2005). The argument that I have offered here provides an explanation for these results: to the extent that successful reintegration is not simply a matter of the ex combatants' disposition, but also of the attitudes and reactions of the receiving communities, DDR programs that are completely devoid of any justice component will have no effect on the reintegration process. By contrast, DDR programs (in association with other initiatives) that provide to receiving communities, for example, some certainty that those whom they are expected to readmit are not the worst offenders, or that make a contribution to the clarification of the abuses through, say, creative ways of making information available for truth-telling purposes,[55] or that include safeguards against "recycling" human rights abusers by making them part of new or reformed security forces, may contribute to the reintegration of ex combatants.[56]

Before closing this section, however, I would like to consider how this general argument plays itself out with respect to reparations, for as I have said, one of the frequent charges that are brought against DDR programs is that while these programs distribute benefits to ex combatants, victims, by contrast, receive nothing. In virtually all countries where DDR programs have ever been established, the charge has come up. In Sierra Leone, for example, a victim put the point as follows: "those who have ruined us are being given the chance to become better persons financially, academically and skills-wise" (cited by Ginifer 2003, p. 46). In Rwanda, the Chairman of the RDRC acknowledged that this disparity in the treatment of ex combatants versus victims upsets some survivors who feel "you recompense killers but you forget the victims" (see Waldorf 2007, p. 26). The basic point is the same: resistance on the part of receiving communities, particularly victims, may diminish if they are given reasons to think that they will also be attended to. DDR programs have taken this presumption on board, and hence IDDRS, for example, emphasizes the importance of "balancing equity with security," of making sure that "reintegration support for ex-combatants is not... regarded as special treatment for ex-combatants, but rather as an investment in security for the *population as a whole*" (IDDRS 2006, 4.30, p. 6, emphasis added) and ultimately, by arguing that "*all war-affected populations*... should be given equal access to reintegration opportunities" (IDDRS 2006, 4.30, p. 6, emphasis added). But this is not enough; victims call for measures that not only improve their security to the extent that everyone's security improves, or for measures that benefit them alongside everyone else. After all, while it is true that

---

[55] This need not be thought of in terms of sharing information that may compromise individuals, and therefore increase the resistance on the part of ex combatants to participate in DDR programs to begin with, but might consist exclusively of information about the more "structural" dimensions of the parties to the conflict.

[56] Notice the modality. They *may*. Whether they do in fact is an empirical issue that depends upon many factors including highly contextual considerations, among which a sense of whether returning ex combatants are "our boys (and girls)" or not is an important one. The strength of the tendency to forgive "our boys" for what they have done to *others* should not be underestimated.

under conflict or authoritarianism everyone suffers, the suffering of victims is special and calls for special recognition. Providing benefits to ex combatants without attending to the claims of victims not only leaves victims at a comparative disadvantage, but gives rise to new grievances, which may exacerbate their resistance against returning ex combatants. By contrast, guaranteeing that the claims of victims will be addressed may diminish such resistance. This is the argument for establishing links between DDR and reparations programs.

Now, how, exactly are those links to be drawn? The point is *not* that DDR and reparations programs should be folded into one, for despite the fact that both programs overlap around the notion of trust, it is still the case that their immediate goals differ. The urgent security needs that motivate DDR programs guide the design of such programs by considerations having to do, at least initially, with estimates of what is sufficient to avert the risks posed by potential spoilers. The considerations that should guide the design of reparations programs are, by contrast, related to an understanding of what justice requires in situations of massive human rights violations. Although this is not an argument against making some of the benefits distributed through DDR programs available to victims and to the community at large, the element of recognition that is part and parcel of reparations, and that makes them different from mere compensatory schemes, will typically require targeting victims for special treatment. This is part of what it means to give them recognition, and part of the reason that transitional institutions can give them to motivate their trust. So, rather than dissolving reparations programs into DDR programs, this is an argument for some type of coordination between them, for a particularly broad type of "external coherence" between programs that have heretofore never been thought of in relation to one another. Ultimately, because it is not just that these programs serve different constituencies and pursue different immediate aims, but also because they typically move in accordance with very different calendars, one way of putting the point is that what needs to be coordinated is not so much the programs, but the commitments; although time after time victims have shown themselves reasonable enough to understand the importance of security and are willing to countenance the provision of benefits to those who may thwart a peace process, they need reasons to think that this does not amount to surrendering their claims to justice. Were they to be given assurances that this will not happen, these justice-based reasons may facilitate the achievement of security aims.

5 Recommendations

What recommendations follow from the preceding argument and from an analysis of the data collected for this project about the distribution of aid between security and justice concerns (see Petersen et al. 2007)? What should be made of the readiness of the international community to put resources and expertise behind DDR programs, which contrasts with its reluctance to commit itself similarly to reparations programs, and what are some sensible reactions to this tendency? Again, at a broad level of generality, these are jarring disparities. However, one should not rush to judgment; even from the standpoint of justice there are considerations that ought to be kept firmly in mind:

- While the argument of the paper has moved in the direction of establishing the relevance for peace of justice considerations, we do well to remember the relevance of peace for justice. Justice measures stand a better chance of being implemented after the peace is secured. This assumes, of course, that in the process of attaining peace justice is not permanently compromised through, e.g., the granting of blanket amnesties. Hence the importance of DDR programmers improving their familiarity with the requirements of justice, so at the very least they can display a "do no harm" attitude and maintain the possibility of justice measures being implemented down the line.
- Since reparations measures are not mere compensatory schemes, it therefore matters *who* covers their costs. This is one more reason not to take the disparity in aid to DDR versus aid to reparations as evidence that international aid is being distributed unfairly.[57] Having said this however, it is not that the international community is flooding with resources other transitional justice measures less sensitive to considerations about who covers their costs than reparations. There is, indeed, a disparity in the level of commitment of the international community to security over justice-related programs. So, what can the international community do about this besides increasing its overall level of support for justice initiatives? Concerning reparations specifically, it can, without violating the constraints imposed by the notion that responsibility for human rights abuses entails the responsibility to pay for their reparation (see de Greiff 2006b):
  - Provide technical assistance in the design and implementation of reparations programs.
  - Support local groups involved in reparations discussions.[58]
  - Given the involvement of some international actors in the area of justice, the international community can play an important role in pressuring governments not to leave behind the more victim-centered justice initiatives, thus making a contribution to the coherence of a comprehensive transitional justice policy.
  - Pressure multilateral institutions to foster conditions under which post-conflict economies can afford to pay due attention to the victims of conflict.
  - Rethink, at least in those cases in which international actors have played an important role in a conflict, its reluctance to provide direct material support to reparations efforts.

[57] Indeed, Guatemala has received international aid for reparations. But notice that this has been for exhumation initiatives and not for the more traditional direct benefits usually associated with reparations programs. See Petersen et al. (2007), and accompanying charts.

[58] This is important not just because recognition requires participation. Beyond this, there is an additional important consideration: in the end, whether a reparations plan is implemented or not depends heavily on a political struggle in which the participation of local groups is absolutely imperative.

Acknowledgments This paper was commissioned by the Working Group on Development and Peace (FriEnt), which published it in November 2007 under the title "Contributing to Peace and Justice. Establishing Links between DDR and Reparations." My gratitude to Natascha Zupan and Sylvia Servaes, who gave comments on earlier drafts. Roger Duthie and Paige Arthur at the ICTJ also provided useful commentary. This paper does not necessarily represent the ICTJ's position.

References

Barash D (ed) (1999) Approaches to peace. Oxford University Press, Oxford

Borton J, Eriksson J (2005) Lessons from Rwanda – lessons for today. Ministry of Foreign Affairs, Copenhagen

de Greiff P (2005) Truth-telling and the rule of law. In: Borer TA (ed) Telling the truths. University of Notre Dame Press, South Bend

de Greiff P (2006a) Justice and reparations. In: de Greiff P (ed) The handbook of reparations. Oxford University Press, Oxford

de Greiff P (2006b) Reparations and international cooperation. In: Dealing with the past and transitional justice: Creating conditions for peace, human rights, and the rule of law. Swiss Ministry of Foreign Affairs, Berne

de Greiff P (2007a) Vetting and transitional justice. In: Mayer-Rieckh A, de Greiff P (eds) Justice as prevention: Vetting public employees in transitional societies. Social Science Research Council, New York

de Greiff P (2007b) The role of apologies in national reconciliation processes: On making trustworthy institutions trusted. In: Gibney M et al. The age of apology. Facing up to the past. University of Pennsylvania Press, Philadelphia

ECP (2007) Analysis of the disarmament, demobilisation and reintegration programs existing in the world during 2006 (Barcelona, March 2007). Escola de Cultura de Pau, Bellaterra

FGT (2003) Lecciones de la incorporación a 7 años del acuerdo. Fundación Guillermo Toriello, Guatemala. http://www.c.net.gt/fgtoriello/infgral/lecciones_aprendidas.html

FGT (2006) La incorporación de la guerrilla Guatemalteca a la legalidad. Fundación Guillermo Toriello, Guatemala

Ginifer J (2003) Reintegration of ex-combatants. In: Meek S et al. (eds) Sierra Leone: Building the road to recovery. Institute for Security Studies, Pretoria

Hauge W, Thorsesen B (2007) El destino de los ex combatientes en Guatemala. Magna Terra, Guatemala

Heard J (1999) Guatemala: Demobilization and incorporation program. Evaluation prepared for USAID. January 1999

IDDRS (2006) Integrated Disarmament, Demobilization and Reintegration Standards. UN DDR Resource Center

Mayer-Rieckh A (2007) On preventing abuse. In: Mayer-Rieckh A, de Greiff P (eds) Justice as prevention: Vetting public employees in transitional societies. Social Science Research Council, New York

Meek S, Malan M (eds) (2004) Identifying lessons from DDR experiences in Africa. Pretoria, South Africa

MDRP (2006) Rwanda country report, Oct. 4–6, 2006, circulated at the MDRP Partners Meeting, Paris, 20 November 2006. MDRP Joint Partner Mission

MDRP (2007) Rwanda demobilization and reintegration program. World Bank / MDRP Secretariat Implementation Support Mission, Aide-mémoire

Munyaneza J (2006) Ministers discuss FARG, order audit. The New Times, 19 June 2006. http://www.rwandagateway.org/article.php3?id_article = 2010&var_recherche = FARG

OHCHR (2008) Rule-of-law tools for post-conflict states: Reparations Programmes United Nations, Geneva

Paz y Paz Bailey C (2006) Guatemala: Gender and reparations for human rights violations. In: Rubio Marín R (ed) What happened to the women? Gender and reparations for human rights violations. Social Science Research Council, New York

Petersen S, Samset I, Wang V (2007) Aid to transitional justice in Rwanda and Guatemala 1995–2005. Working Group on Development and Peace, Bonn

RDRC (n.d.) Demobilization and reintegration. Rwanda's Demobilization and Reintegration Commission. http://www.mdrp.org/rwanda.htm

Rombouts H (2006) Women and reparations in Rwanda: A long path to travel. In: Rubio Marín R (ed) What happened to the women? Gender and reparations for human rights violations. Social Science Research Council, New York

Rubio Marín R (ed) (2006) What happened to the women? Gender and reparations for human rights violations. Social Science Research Council, New York

SIDDR (2006) Final report of the Stockholm Initiative on DDR. Ministry for Foreign Affairs, Sweden

Segovia A (2006) Financing programs of reparation: Reflections from international experience. In: de Greiff P (ed) The handbook of reparations. Oxford University Press, Oxford

Stanley W, Holiday D (2002) Broad participation, diffuse responsibility: Peace implementation in Guatemala. In: Steadman SJ et al (eds) Ending civil wars: The implementation of peace agreements. Lynne Rienner, Boulder

Stetz M, Oh B (eds) (2001) Legacies of the comfort women during World War II. ME Sharpe, New York

Waldorf L (2007) Transitional justice and DDR in post genocide Rwanda. Paper produced for ICTJ's research project on DDR and Transitional Justice. International Center for Transitional Justice, New York

Weinstein J, Humphreys M (2005) Disentangling the determinants of successful demobilization and reintegration. Center for Global Development, Working Paper 69, September 2005

Weschler L (1989) Afterword. In: State crimes: Punishment or pardon. Aspen Institute Report, Washington DC

Yoshimi Y (2002) Comfort women: Sexual slavery in the Japanese military during World War II. Columbia University Press, New York

Transitional Justice in Bosnia and Herzegovina: Coherence and Complementarity of EU Institutions and Civil Society*

Iavor Rangelov and Marika Theros

Abstract This study interrogates the engagement of the European Union in the process of transitional justice in Bosnia and Herzegovina. It first reviews developments in the various mechanisms of transitional justice and related efforts of civil society, highlighting common challenges such as the nature of the violence in 1992–1995, the design of the peace negotiated at Dayton, and the shortcomings of reconstruction agendas in the period of transition. The analysis then turns to EU involvement in transitional justice in Bosnia, focusing particularly on coherence between the "peace-building" and "enlargement" approaches and complementarity with civil society. The study concludes that the strategy of disengagement with issues and civil society actors related to war crimes and justice, pursued by the Union, has served to compromise Europe's own objectives of peace-building and progress towards accession. A way forward is suggested for EU policy in Bosnia and Herzegovina, emphasizing the benefits of adopting a justice-sensitive approach to peace-building and European integration, as well as the need to broaden EU engagement with civil society to incorporate victims associations and social movements alongside the NGO sector.

1 Introduction

Transitional justice is the process by which societies emerging from armed conflict or oppressive rule deal with the legacy of mass atrocity and past human rights abuse. The mechanisms of transitional justice are directly related to the goals of conflict

I. Rangelov
Centre for the Study of Global Governance, London School of Economics and Political Science, Houghton Street, London WC1A 2AE UK, e-mail: i.p.rangelov@lse.ac.uk

*A previous version of this paper was published in Iavor Rangelov and Marika Theros, "Maintaining the Process in Bosnia and Herzegovina: Coherence and Complementarity of EU Institutions and Civil Society in the Field of Transitional Justice", (FriEnt, Bonn 2007).

K. Ambos et al. (eds.), *Building a Future on Peace and Justice: Studies on Transitional Justice, Peace and Development.*

transformation and democratic transition: ending the culture of illegality and rebuilding the rule of law by establishing accountability for perpetrators and justice for victims of mass atrocity; marking a clear break with past abuse and recognizing historical injustice by articulating truth-telling narratives in the transition; and deterring future conflict and promoting peace through reconciliation and restorative efforts.

The central mechanisms of post-conflict transitional justice are criminal prosecutions, truth commissions, vetting, and reparations. Criminal prosecutions can be conducted by international courts and tribunals, national courts, and mixed or hybrid tribunals that combine elements of national and international law, jurisdiction, and staffing. Truth commissions vary in their mandate and methodology from more narrow fact-finding inquiries conducting analysis of evidence and documentation, to broader truth and reconciliation initiatives that incorporate victims and perpetrators through a process of public hearings. Vetting takes an individualized approach to assessing the integrity of persons in order to determine their suitability for employment in the public and particularly the security sector, while lustration disqualifies groups of individuals from holding public office on the basis of their membership or employment in certain organizations. Finally, reparations can be provided to victims of human rights abuse either within state-sponsored reparation programs, or by courts and other judicial bodies on an individual basis. Other forms of redress and modalities of transitional justice include restitution, apology, memorialisation, and education.

This study begins with an overview of transitional justice efforts in BiH and elaborates the role and activities of civil society organizations within that context. It then discusses the involvement of the European Union in transitional justice in BiH, with added emphasis on issues of coherence and complementarity with civil society. Finally, the study closes with conclusions and recommendations to address identified gaps and opportunities.

2 Transitional Justice in Bosnia and Herzegovina

Bosnia and Herzegovina (BiH) presents a post-conflict case study that spans the entire range of transitional justice mechanisms, pursued with varying degrees of success at the international, state, Entity and local levels since conflict ended in 1995. It illustrates well the central dilemma of transitional justice after armed conflict and mass atrocity: high demand for justice within society coupled with little state resources and capabilities to be employed for addressing that demand. The war in BiH was marked by a high level of violence, most of which was directed against civilians and took the form of "ethnic cleansing" through large-scale killings, torture, rape, expulsions, and extensive property destruction (Kaldor 1999, pp. 31–68). While broad segments of society have experienced different forms of victimization and may now demand justice and redress, the conflict effectively destroyed state structures and 13 years later BiH remains a weak state with scarce institutional and material resources.

Ethnicity, coupled with nationalism, presents an additional challenge since it was central to the commission of crimes in the conflict and has served to politicize the calls and efforts for justice during the transition. The Dayton Peace Agreement for BiH has also contributed to the continued politicization of ethnicity that undermines the process of transitional justice, by entrenching a constitutional structure based on Bosniak, Croat and Serb "constituent nations" and effectively mediating political power and participation through ethnic identity. In this context, most developments in transitional justice in BiH have come as a result of pressure exerted by the international community, most notably the Office of the High Representative (OHR), often by enforcing a compromise on the ethnic elites in charge in the Federation and Republika Srpska, without broad public consultations or engagement with victims and other civil society groups.

2.1 Criminal Prosecutions

The bulk of the jurisprudence of the International Criminal Tribunal for the Former Yugoslavia (ICTY) in The Hague has dealt with war crimes, crimes against humanity and genocide committed on the territory of BiH. Despite attempts to strengthen outreach and pursue ethnic balance in the trials, the ICTY remains disconnected from its local constituencies, perceptions of its work are largely modified by ethnic identity, and practices such as plea bargains are criticized by victims groups (Biro et al. 2004, pp. 183–205). In recent years, intensified international pressure and EU accession conditionality have helped improve the cooperation of Bosnian authorities with the Tribunal. Republika Srpska, however, has been more problematic in comparison with the Federation, and until recently, the overall record of BiH failed to satisfy EU demands, acting as a roadblock for accession negotiations.

As part of the Exit Strategy of the ICTY, scheduled to complete all proceedings by 2010, a special War Crimes Chamber (WCC) at the State Court of BiH was established in 2004 with international assistance, operating with national and international staff. The Chamber was created to deal with cases transferred from the Hague Tribunal pursuant to Rule 11*bis* of the ICTY Statute, as well as with the most sensitive cases initiated in Bosnia. This means that the vast majority of war crimes cases will be left to the local courts, which so far have failed to address the scale of atrocity – Republika Srpska has conducted only a handful of trials, while the Federation has performed slightly better. The local courts are currently disabled by two sets of factors when compared with the WCC. First, they are much more vulnerable to political pressure and ethnic bias in the administration of justice. Second, they lack the staff and equipment that international assistance has secured for the WCC. Local courts would not be able to handle adequately 90% of the war crimes caseload, as is currently intended, without addressing both of these weaknesses (HRW 2004).

2.2 Truth Telling

An official national Truth and Reconciliation Commission (TRC) in Bosnia has failed to materialize despite repeated attempts to establish one. International actors, namely the United States Institute of Peace (USIP), have taken the lead in consecutive efforts that reflected largely the international agenda rather than local ownership of truth-telling processes in Bosnia. The ICTY opposed the initial attempt to create a TRC fearing it would overlap with its mandate and interfere in the prosecution of war crimes. Subsequently, the ICTY did endorse an effort in 2001, which, however, did not attract the necessary political backing and nothing concrete emerged. The more recent USIP-led initiative in 2005 once again failed to garner local legitimacy in the planning process and suffered the same fate. Among other shortcomings, the Working Group, coordinated by USIP and tasked with writing the draft law,[1] did not consult broad segments of civil society and one of its members was forced to resign after victims groups shed light on his wartime activities. Similarly, the government-led Sarajevo Truth Commission (2006), with a mandate confined to investigating the wartime suffering of the population in Sarajevo (mostly Serbs), has created little interest and debate in the public domain once it was established (BIRN 2007; HLC 2006). The Srebrenica Commission in Republika Srpska (2004) remains the only successful local fact-finding body in BiH, its reports produced with High Representative Paddy Ashdown pressuring and sacking uncooperative officials.

Where government efforts have faltered, civil society in Bosnia has taken the lead in confronting the past and engaging the public in truth-telling. Initiatives have ranged from documentation efforts on war crimes and missing persons, to artistic, cinematic, and literary projects, to inter-communal dialogue and public forums. Civil society organizations, victims groups, academics, and media groups are seeking to foster truth-telling processes and stimulate public debate on war crimes and justice issues. Three key NGOs from BiH, Serbia, and Croatia have come together to propose the creation of a regional victims commission, which would examine the atrocities committed in the conflicts, and are seeking broad involvement of civil society, including victims groups, in the consultation process.[2]

2.3 Vetting

Comprehensive vetting efforts in BiH in the judicial and security sectors, executed as part of the institutional reform process, have produced mixed results. The Dayton Peace Agreement provides that no person indicted by the ICTY can hold public office; that civilian law enforcement agencies must operate in accordance with internationally recognized standards; and, requires the prosecution or dismissal of police

[1] Draft Law on the Truth and Reconciliation Commission in BiH (on file with the authors).

[2] For civil society initiatives at the regional level, see Rangelov (2006a, pp. 121–130).

officers and public servants responsible for serious violations of minority rights.[3] In addition, the OHR is empowered by the Dayton Peace Agreement to remove civil servants from public office for reasons ranging from their wartime record to obstructing the implementation of the peace process.

While generally regarded as successful, vetting processes for the security services in BiH have lacked transparency and clear criteria. Both NATO's screening of high ranking officers in the Bosnian army (2004) and the UN review of 24,000 police officers (2002) have led to accusations of procedural shortcomings and united public opinion across the constituent communities against the decertification decisions (Zupan 2006, pp. 332–333). Vetted police officers filed complaints with the Human Rights Commission and, in February 2007, Bosnia's Human Rights Ministry established a commission to review the nearly 800 police dismissals. Although the UN refuses to disavow the vetting process, a Commission Delegation official in Sarajevo stated that EU representatives are currently involved in meetings at the UN Secretariat in New York to discuss a resolution of this issue.[4]

Apart from these procedural shortcomings, the vetting process itself was incomplete. Media reports regularly surface indicating that police officers and public officials implicated in war crimes continue to serve. The findings of the Srebrenica Report corroborate these reports. Moreover, the UN did not institutionalize formal screening procedures for police recruitment and new recruits are not subject to a review of their wartime activities (Freeman 2004, pp. 13–14).

Vetting within the judiciary in BiH has proven more successful after several bungled attempts in the early post-Dayton period. In 2001, the High Representative established an internationally-appointed Independent Judicial Commission to oversee the review and re-appointment of all judges and prosecutors undertaken by the three permanent High Judicial and Prosecutorial Councils (HJPC), created by the HR in 2002. Although the initial background checks into the applicants alleged wartime activities were limited, a process of reviewing, appointing, and disciplining judges has now been institutionalized.

2.4 Reparations and Restitution

Reparations in BiH have failed to attract significant public debate or international attention and a comprehensive state-sponsored reparations program has not been considered so far. Instead, individual and collective compensation claims have been brought before the Human Rights Chamber, which in 2004 became the Human Rights Commission of the Constitutional Court. In its best-known case on Srebrenica, the Chamber ordered Republika Srpska to investigate the atrocities, make a single payment of KM 2 million (approx. EUR 1 million) and four additional

[3] General Framework Agreement for Peace in Bosnia and Herzegovina (initiated at Dayton, Ohio 21 November 1995 and signed in Paris 14 December 1995) (Dayton Peace Agreement) Annex 4, art 9 and art 3.

[4] Interview, EC Delegation, Sarajevo (Telephone, 19 April 2007).

payments of KM 500,000 over 4 years to the Foundation of Srebrenica-Potocari (Zupan 2006, pp. 331–332). While the Commission is making progress to finish all pending cases, the Court continues to receive scores of new applications, and problems persist in securing compliance with past decisions.

In 1993 Bosnia instituted proceedings against then Yugoslavia for alleged violations of the Genocide Convention before the International Court of Justice (ICJ), but in February 2007 the Court ruled that Serbia cannot be held responsible for planning and perpetrating genocide and did not award the requested billions in wartime damages.[5] Federation authorities immediately denounced the ICJ decision with chagrin while victims organized street protests. Finally, significant restitution and rebuilding of property has been accomplished through legislation and the post-war reconstruction effort.

3 Civil Society and Transitional Justice in BiH

3.1 The Character of Civil Society in BiH

The literature on civil society in BiH underscores three interrelated factors that affect the nature of civil society work on the ground. These are the nature of the armed conflict in 1992–1995, the constitutional structure put in place by the Dayton Peace Agreement, and the approach adopted by the international community in assisting civil society development during the transition.

The war in Bosnia and Herzegovina has been interpreted not only as an ethnic conflict but also as a war against civil society. The violence was directed not simply against the civilian population but against civility itself: the values of tolerance, dialogue, and individual autonomy. Intellectuals and advocates of multicultural values and peace were often the first casualties of the war. Young people and the educated middle classes fled the conflict in large numbers, leaving a vacuum for developing alternatives to extremist nationalist forces that eventually prevailed. While civil society requires a framework of order, security, and law in order to operate, the war in BiH entrenched a climate of fear, disorder, and insecurity leading to the effective collapse of the state. In the early 1990s, a broad anti-war movement in Bosnia challenged the nationalist rhetoric and violence, often linking up with similarly minded movements in other parts of Yugoslavia. Since ethnicity provided the basis for assaulting civilians, the space for challenging and crossing divides diminished and the majority of people sought refuge into their respective sectarian identities and communities (Kaldor 1998, p. 205).

The peace process in BiH has not been able to reverse the logic of conflict. The Dayton Peace Agreement rewarded the nationalist extremists by establishing

[5] *Case Concerning the Application of the Convention on the Prevention and Punishment of the Crime of Genocide (Bosnia and Herzegovina v Serbia and Montenegro)* (Judgment) General List No 91 [2007] ICJ.

a system of power-sharing built on ethnic membership in the "constituent nations": Bosniak, Croat, and Serb. The constitutional structure of Bosnia reflects the ethnic principle by splitting the country into two Entities, Republika Srpska and the Bosniak–Croat Federation, and the autonomous Brcko District. Political participation in post-Dayton Bosnia is mediated through ethnicity, obstructing the emergence of a shared political and civic space for debate and negotiation. Civil society has slowly returned but as a weak and fragmented force, reflecting the legacy of conflict and the design of the peace. Few civil society organizations operate on a state-wide basis. The majority of NGOs, victims associations, and veterans groups conduct their activities either at the local or Entity level. Ethno-religious divides are reflected not only in their scope and activities but also in their failure to cooperate and establish links with organizations from other communities.[6]

The process of civil society development in BiH reflects the top-down approach of the international community and donor agendas rather than authentic bottom-up initiatives and priorities. Much of civil society assistance has been channelled to NGOs providing service delivery, effectively taking on functions of the state. Most beneficiaries of donor funding are professionalized NGOs in urban centres, some of which have even been created in response to available funding schemes. By contrast, civic associations and interest groups have been largely ignored both as interlocutors and beneficiaries of international donors (Zivanovic 2006, p. 37). This has diminished the space for autonomous civil society actors, necessary to build an accountable and responsive state. Such organizations have been marginalized because they are seen as politicized and often have not been able to professionalize. Victims associations illustrate this point. On the one hand, they are usually perceived as too political and exclusivist. On the other hand, these are often rural associations that lack the skills to draft complicated proposals and cannot fit their concerns within donor priorities.

3.2 *Civil Society, War Crimes and Justice*

Civil society in Bosnia remains weak, divided, and largely donor-driven. Civil society work on issues of war crimes and justice exhibits these characteristics as well. Transitional justice activities discussed in this section include documentation, support for criminal prosecutions, truth-seeking initiatives, reparations and advocacy of victims groups, peace-building and reconciliation, memorials, public education, and debate.

Documentation of war crimes and missing persons has been an ongoing activity in BiH since the very beginning of the war. The Research and Documentation Centre (RDC) in Sarajevo has developed, over the year, a comprehensive database on victims and atrocities within the project "Population Losses 1992–1995". Within the project, in 2007 the organization produced a report on population losses in BiH.

[6] Our research on civil society draws on a data set of 22 interviews with civil society groups in Bosnia and Herzegovina. For the complete list, please see the Appendix.

The RDC has also taken the lead on monitoring war crimes trials in BiH as part of a regional initiative with partner organizations from Serbia and Croatia.[7] Documentation has also been done at the local level. For example, the Mostar-based Center for Peace and Interethnic Relationships has created an archive on the Mostar region.

Civil society has been both active and largely ignored in the process of establishing a truth and reconciliation commission (TRC) for BiH. The Citizens Association for Truth and Reconciliation was established by Jakob Finci in order to lobby for the creation of a TRC. It successfully liaised with the ICTY and secured their support for a truth-telling body. But the draft law that resulted from this effort failed to attract political backing. The second TRC initiative involved the United States Institute of Peace (USIP) taking the lead in partnership with the local NGO Dayton Project, created to facilitate the process. This initiative coordinated a working group composed of the eight leading political parties to draft legislation. It provoked an outcry among civil society and the public since both were excluded from the process of consultation and negotiation (Jelacic and Ahmetasevic 2006).

While this process has been frozen, the RDC has initiated a regional consultation exercise on a TRC with the Humanitarian Law Center (HLC) in Belgrade and Dokumenta, Zagreb. This network is organizing public debates in Sarajevo, Zagreb, and Belgrade with broad civil society participation, discussing the various aspects of a possible regional victims commission for the former Yugoslavia. The Srebrenica Commission and the Sarajevo Truth Commission have not provided for any participation of civil society either through consultations or public hearings (Rangelov 2006a).

With respect to reparations, civil society groups have been making use of the available legal mechanisms for redress. Avenues they have explored include the Human Rights Chamber (now the Human Rights Commission at the BiH Constitutional Court) as well as civil suits for compensation in foreign courts. Examples include the 49 cases of victims from Srebrenica submitted to the Human Rights Chamber by the Association "Women of Srebrenica", seeking information on their missing relatives as well as compensation. Women victims of sexual violence have brought reparation cases in American courts under the Alien Tort Claims Act and the Torture Victim Prevention Act.[8] Relatives of the Srebrenica victims have filed a lawsuit for compensation in the Netherlands against the Dutch government and the UN for failure to prevent the Srebrenica massacre.

Associations of the families of missing persons started organizing in 1996–1997 and expanded across Bosnia in 1998. They mobilized in response to the indifference of the political class to their problems and concerns. These groups are primarily based in rural areas, most harshly hit during the war. In the beginning, they used controversial methods to protest and focus public attention on their demands, such as blocking roads and public building entrances, and were widely seen as radical and highly politicized. With the support of the International Commission for Missing Persons, the various missing persons victims associations have connected to engage

[7] Interview with Mirsad Tokaca, Executive Director, Research and Documentation Centre Sarajevo (Telephone, 10 April 2007).

[8] *Kadic v Karadzic* 74 F.3d 377 (2d Cir. 1996).

in joint actions. In RS, they initially worked within an umbrella organization that included war veterans, civilian victims, the war disabled, and other groups. In order to better represent their demands related to missing persons, they have become more autonomous over time.

On the Federation side, most Bosniak and Croat associations have engaged in cooperation, except for the area of Central Bosnia where the nature of the conflict makes such cooperation more difficult. The Srebrenica victims have remained largely outside of this network and operate independently.[9] The collaboration of the associations coming from the different sides succeeded in pushing through the Law on the Missing, which was adopted in 2004 with substantial input from these groups. The envisioned Trust Fund for compensating the family members of the missing remains inoperative due to lack of funds – there were expectations that any war damages awarded to BiH by the ICJ might be channelled into the Fund, and the recent decision unsurprisingly sparked protests across the Federation.

The relative success of mobilizing associations of families of missing persons has become an example for other victims associations to follow. Former prisoners of war (POWs) have more recently come together at the Entity level and cooperation between Croat and Bosniak former POWs has developed over time. They have established some contacts with similar associations in Republika Srpska, but so far have kept these conversations private, away from the public. A common priority for this emerging network is to secure compensation for ex-POWs.

War veterans associations have also become more active locally and at the Entity level. For example, the War Veterans Associations 90–95 in Tuzla have created a "Self-Help" project to respond to marginalization and high rates of suicide in their ranks. The training and education combined with individual and group therapy is in high demand and now the Tuzla Associations want to replicate and share their experience with other war veterans groups. It remains difficult for war veterans who fought on different sides to establish links among themselves. Other victims groups worth mentioning for their recent activities are women victims of sexual violence during the war. These associations of the sexually harassed emerged within the space created by the widely publicized Foca case at the ICTY and the release of films like "Grbavica" ("Esra's Secret").

Civil society has been a key agent of public debate around issues of war crimes and justice in BiH with individual intellectuals, journalists, and civil society activists often taking the lead on these sensitive subjects. Documentaries, films, and art projects have provided alternative avenues for stimulating public debate on dealing with the past. For example, XY Films was established specifically to produce documentaries and television programs on the crimes committed during the war.[10] The demand for producing narratives of the war has become another way of facing mass atrocity, such as Emir Suljagic's internationally acclaimed *Postcards from the Grave* (Suljagic 2005).

---

[9] Interview with Alma Masic, Regional Coordinator for SEE Programs, Royal Danish Embassy (Sarajevo, 23 April 2007).

[10] See website for XY films www.xyfilms.com.

Organizations such as the Association of the Alumni of the Center for Interdisciplinary and Post-graduate Studies for Sarajevo have contributed to academic research and debate. At the grassroots level, the Nansen Dialogue Network organizes public debates within the framework of the Dialogue for Democracy Project. In addition to publishing books and producing films on dealing with the past, the Center for Nonviolent Action has organized public forums with war veterans in towns throughout BiH. Finally, NGOs such as the Helsinki Committee for Human Rights in RS and the RDC in Sarajevo have strong media presence and actively participate in public debate on a range of transitional justice issues.[11]

Civil society in Bosnia has also mobilized around honouring the victims of the war and erecting memorials to capture the suffering of the different communities during the conflict. Each year, thousands gather in Srebrenica-Potocari to commemorate the victims of the massacre at a memorial established after the Human Rights Chamber's ruling in the Srebrenica case. Other memorials have also been erected to commemorate victims on each side of the conflict. However, this process has been ethnically focused and divisive, causing resentment and competition between communities. For instance, a monument was quickly set up in Kravica for Bosnian Serb victims of 1992–1993 in response to the Potocari memorial. A similar pattern occurred in Prijedor. In spite of the large number of Bosniaks killed there, only memorials for Serb civilians and soldiers existed until Bosniak victims mobilized to build one at Omarska camp. Years after the end of the war, inclusive commemorations of the victims in Bosnia are yet to emerge (Aucoin and Babbitt 2006, pp. 156–157).

Much civil society effort has focused on peace-building and reconciliation. Activities for rebuilding interethnic trust and tolerance represent the core work of the International Multi-religious and Intercultural Center, while the Youth Initiative for Human Rights works specifically to build trust between young people through seminars and exchanges. TERCA (Training, Education, Research, Consulting, Action) defines its projects as peace-building through dealing with the past. The Center for Building Peace – Sanski Most runs peace camps, conducts workshops for "former enemies", and implements conflict transformation programs for young people. While education, particularly on recent history, has been recognized as necessary in the peace-building and reconciliation effort, civil society has not been able to overcome the ethno-religious divides entrenched in the school system. The Nansen Dialogue Network is currently working with high schools to address the problem of "Two Schools under One Roof", whereby the student body is ethnically segregated within the same school buildings.[12]

International assistance to civil society has been much more forthcoming in areas such as legal aid and the socio-economic aspects of refugee return and reintegration, i.e., activities related to service delivery. Donors have mostly avoided support-

[11] The data on civil society activities draws on our interviews. Our research on civil society draws on a data set of 22 interviews with civil society groups in Bosnia and Herzegovina. For the complete list, please see the Appendix.

[12] Our research on civil society draws on a data set of 22 interviews with civil society groups in Bosnia and Herzegovina. For the complete list, please see the Appendix.

ing civil society work on sensitive and politicized issues of transitional justice.[13] Furthermore, it is in the nature of transitional justice to focus on advocacy and the broader political process rather than the measurable outcomes and deliverables preferred by the donor community. Where civil society projects on transitional justice have received funding, the beneficiaries have usually been professionalized human rights NGOs, perceived to be neutral and objective and able to draft complicated proposals and reports. The dense network of victims associations representing the interests of missing persons, former prisoners of war, and women, as well as war veterans groups, have been excluded from both the political dialogue facilitated by the international community in BiH and the assistance priorities of donors.[14]

4 EU Involvement in Transitional Justice in BiH

4.1 Policy Framework

EU policy with respect to BiH reflects a two-pronged strategy combining active engagement on the ground and monitoring of the country's performance against benchmarks and conditions. The first approach stems from the armed conflict that took place on the territory of BiH in 1992–1995 and the goals of post-conflict stabilisation and the consolidation of peace. The European Security Strategy adopted in 2004 stipulates that the long term objective of the EU is a stable, viable, peaceful and multiethnic BiH.[15] The Council of the EU has deployed significant resources in the country to address a situation which may deteriorate and harm the Union's objectives in the context of the Common Foreign and Security Policy (CFSP) and the European Security and Defence Policy (ESDP). The European Union Special Representative (EUSR) in BiH is also the High Representative in BiH, tasked to coordinate the implementation of the Dayton Peace Agreement and subsequent Peace Implementation Council (PIC) conclusions and declarations. In the framework of CFSP/ESDP, the Union maintains a peace-keeping force and a police mission in BiH. The EUFOR/Althea operation, with 2,250 troops, and the European Union Police Mission (EUPM) both operate in line with the general objectives of the Dayton Agreement.

The second approach of the EU with respect to BiH resembles the standard "stick and carrot" strategy employed for all countries aspiring to join the Union, spearheaded by the Commission and its DG Enlargement. In this context, the progress of candidate countries is continuously monitored against sets of criteria and conditions,

[13] But note that the Charles Stewart Mott Foundation is funding the Court Support Network for victims to come forward and give feedback on prosecutions. Interview with Walter Viers, Program Officer, Charles Stewart Mott Foundation (London, 30 March 2007).

[14] Interview with Bogdan Ivanisevic, International Center for Transitional Justice (Belgrade, 26 March 2007).

[15] Council of the EU "A Secure Europe in a Better world: European Security Strategy" (European Council, Brussels, 12 December 2003).

and supported with EU assistance to match accession priorities. The Thessaloniki European Council in 2003 introduced the European Partnerships as a means to integrate the Western Balkans into the Union, within the framework of the Stabilization and Association Process (SAP) which would govern relations with these countries until accession. While the first European Partnership with BiH dates back to June 2004, the country has only recently met the conditions necessary to secure a Stabilization and Association Agreement (SAA).

EU accession conditionality for the countries of the Western Balkans comprises two sets of criteria. First, the Copenhagen European Council of 1993 defined political, economic and institutional criteria for all candidate countries, elaborating the political criteria to include stability of institutions guaranteeing democracy, the rule of law, human rights and the protection of minorities.[16] Second, there are conditions set specifically for the SAP for South East Europe, which include, *inter alia*, full cooperation with the ICTY, respect for human and minority rights, the creation of real opportunities for refugees and internally displaced persons to return, and a visible commitment to regional cooperation. Each European Partnership incorporates the core SAP conditions and elaborates further priorities specific to the respective applicant country. Community assistance under the SAP to the Western Balkan countries is conditioned on further progress in satisfying the Copenhagen criteria as well as progress in meeting the specific priorities of the European Partnership. The Commission makes assessment of progress and reports regularly to the Council of the EU and the European Parliament through annual country progress reports.

EU conditionality in the SAP for Bosnia has been dominated by one aspect of transitional justice – the criminal prosecutions taking place at the ICTY, while at the same time it has ignored domestic transitional justice mechanisms. Cooperation with the ICTY has been consistently emphasized as a central priority of the European Partnership, and together with police reform and public broadcasting, it remained the central obstacle to concluding an SAA with the Union until the spring of 2008. In January 2006 the Council reiterated as a key priority of the European Partnership that BiH must fully cooperate with the Tribunal in apprehending all ICTY indictees at large.[17] The BiH 2006 Progress Report of the Commission concluded that while the Federation's cooperation with the ICTY was satisfactory, the RS efforts remained insufficient.

Recently the RS authorities have handed over to The Hague parts of its wartime archives and have made efforts to undermine the support networks of indictees. A turning point was the arrest in May 2007 of Zdravko Tolimir, a high-level suspect indicted in relation to atrocities in Srebrenica and Zepa. This improved record of cooperation was reflected in the recent EU decision to proceed with an SAA for BiH. Despite its firm commitment to international justice, however, the EU has shown little interest in domestic mechanisms for dealing with the legacy of war crimes. Apart from identifying the need to staff and finance the State Court of BiH, which includes Section I for War Crimes, transitional justice issues are not mentioned among the

[16] Presidency Conclusions, Copenhagen European Council, 21–22 June 1993.

[17] Council Decision (EC) 2006/55 on the principles, priorities, and conditions contained in the European Partnership with BiH and repealing decision 2004/515/EC, [2006] OJ L35.

European Partnership priorities and are largely excluded from Commission assessments of the Copenhagen criteria and Community assistance schemes.[18]

4.2 Instruments

4.2.1 The European Union Special Representative in BiH

The European Union Special Representative in BiH, appointed by the Council, is responsible for the overall political coordination of all EU actors on the ground. He acts also as High Representative of the international community, mandated to promote continued progress in the implementation of the Dayton Peace Agreement, in accordance with the OHR's Mission Implementation Plan, and to support the policy objectives of the EU in support of the accession process.[19] The EUSR directs the European Union Police Mission (EUPM), provides guidance to the EUFOR Commander, and offers EU advice and facilitation in the political process. As High Representative, he can exercise the so-called Bonn Powers to intervene in all aspects of Bosnian political life and can remove officials from office, quash judicial decisions, and enact legislation necessary to advance the peace process.

Since the Dayton Peace Agreement did not set out a comprehensive vision for justice, transitional justice efforts undertaken by the OHR have been ad hoc and incomplete, primarily focused on prosecutions and vetting. The OHR created the War Crimes Chamber and a corresponding special department for war crimes within the Prosecutor's Office. He has supported the ICTY by freezing bank accounts and assets of indicted war criminals. In addition, consecutive High Representatives, using the Bonn Powers, have dismissed a total of 185 public officials, barring them from holding public office until further notice, and have established a process to review the appointment of judges and prosecutors (ICG 2007, p. 4–6).

EUSR/HR, Dr. Christian Schwarz-Shilling, who took office in early 2006, pursued a different strategy. He declared that he would refrain from using the Bonn Powers, unless a serious threat to peace and stability emerged, so that BiH authorities could assume ownership of and full responsibility for the reform process. He envisioned 2007 as the year of change in BiH, with a transition from an OHR-led reform process to an EU presence that emphasizes reform without international community imposition. In 2006, the HR did not impose any major reforms required for European integration and enacted far fewer executive decisions than his predecessor.

Until Schwarz-Shilling, each previous HR augmented the use of the Bonn Powers, achieving significant breakthroughs, especially in weakening the support networks for war crimes suspects (ICG 2007, p. 4–6). Despite his reluctance to

[18] Commission (EC), "Bosnia and Herzegovina 2006 Progress Report" (Commission staff Working Document) COM (2006) 649 fina (08 November 2006).

[19] Council Joint Action (EC) 2006/49/CFSP on appointing the European Special Representative in BiH (30 January 2006).

interfere, Schwarz-Shilling has made use of his Bonn Powers to overturn previous OHR vetting decisions removing and barring individuals from public life. Schwarz-Shilling rehabilitated 18 officials and put forth two decisions in 2006, effectively allowing formerly barred officials to assume positions in public institutions and to serve in political parties, regardless of the reason for dismissal.

The decision to shut down the OHR by June 2007 was revised at the Peace Implementation Council meeting held at the end of February 2007. The PIC prolonged the OHR mandate, with its Bonn Powers, for another year until June 2008. The EU stated that it will strengthen its engagement with BiH in line with the expected OHR closure through a revised and reinforced EUSR mandate and appointed Dr. Miroslav Lajcak to the post in June 2007. His ongoing term in office has been marked by intensified effort to facilitate international and domestic actors in order to allow Bosnia to fulfil the accession conditions set by the Union. This has not involved an increase in the use of the Bonn powers but rather pro-active mediation and coordination on the ground.

4.2.2 European Union Police Mission

In January 2003, the EU deployed its first ESDP mission, the European Union Police Mission (EUPM) in BiH, which replaced the UN-led International Police Task Force (IPTF). Under the direction of the EUSR, the EUPM's aim is to establish a sustainable, professional, and multiethnic police service, operating in accordance with the best European and international standards. Its mandate is to strengthen Bosnia's police forces through monitoring, mentoring, and inspecting activities, emphasizing local ownership of the reform process and local police capacity for fighting organized crime. It concentrates on providing technical assistance in order to improve the police services' organizational capacity and to facilitate policing on complex forms of crimes, such as organized crime, trafficking, and money laundering.

The mandate of the EUPM was extended in November 2007 to assist local authorities in fighting organised crime and strengthening the criminal justice system, with special emphasis on police–prosecutor relations. The EUPM works with the State Investigation and Protection Agency (SIPA) to build its operational effectiveness in fighting organized crime, including the dismantling of support networks for war criminals, and assists in the development of the State Border Service and the Ministry of Security. In addition, it monitors the police force throughout the entire investigation process to ensure it meets appropriate standards.

By concentrating primarily on technical issues and working with a weak mandate, which lacks executive powers, the EUPM has encountered significant difficulties in establishing a professional and independent police force. The lack of effective investigation of war crimes has been a principal obstacle to rebuilding the rule of law in BiH. Police, especially in the RS, often serve the narrow interests of nationalist politicians and arrests of indictees have often resulted from political pressure (ICG 2002, p. 2). Despite the declared success of the IPTF vetting process, police officials with questionable wartime backgrounds remain a problem, confirmed by the RS Government Srebrenica Report, which lists hundreds of individuals taking part in the massacre as active duty officers. Unlike the IPTF, the EUPM has not been mandated to decertify obstructionist police officers or those implicated in war crimes and it has abstained from making such requests to the EUSR/HR.[20]

4.2.3 European Union Force/Althea

In December 2004 the EU launched its military operation in BiH, EUFOR/Althea, in order to strengthen the EU presence and replace the NATO-led SFOR.[21] Operating under an UN Chapter VII mandate, EUFOR's mission is to maintain a stable and safe environment for the implementation of the military and civilian aspects of Dayton through deterrence and reassurance. NATO retains a small headquarters presence in Sarajevo to provide advice on defense reforms and to support EUFOR efforts to apprehend indicted war crimes suspects, under the so-called "Berlin Plus" arrangements.

EUFOR's primary task is to support the ICTY and relevant authorities, including the detention of persons indicted for war crimes, and to combat organized crime through the Integrated Police Unit, its military police force. The IPU enables it to conduct anti-organized crime operations without informing local police. To date, EUFOR has conducted several operations aimed at collecting illegal weapons, disrupting organized criminal activity, pursuing war crimes fugitives and attacking their support networks. EUFOR has worked closely with Bosnian law enforcement agencies on combating organized crime, including conducting joint anti-crime operations and arrests. It cooperates with NATO and SIPA in hunting down and arresting war criminals.

Based on a positive evaluation of the security situation in BiH, the EU decided to implement a transition of EUFOR/Althea in late February 2007. The EU reduced the size of EUFOR to 2,250 troops at the end of June 2007. However, it will maintain a reserve force for rapid deployment in case the security situation deteriorates. The reduced force retains the same robust peace-enforcement mandate under Chapter VII and will continue to provide support to the ICTY while noting that responsibility for cooperation rests with BiH authorities.

4.2.4 The Reform Process Monitoring

The main operational instrument for political and technical dialogue between the EU and BiH is the Reform Process Monitoring (RPM), which is the successor to the Consultative Task Force. It is the primary mechanism established for the European Partnership in the Stabilisation and Association Process. Each year, approximately two to three plenary RPM meetings are held, bringing together representatives from

[20] Interview, Rule of Law Section, EC Delegation BiH (Telephone, 19 April 2007).

[21] Council Joint Action (EC) on the EU military operation in BiH 2004/570/CFSP (12 July 2004).

the BiH government and the EC, to assess the progress made in implementing reforms.[22] A total of seven plenary meetings have been held so far. In addition, sectoral RPM meetings are organized every few months to discuss technical aspects of reform implementation. Officials in Brussels have stated that the impact of this dialogue has been limited.[23] While the RPM meetings have focused on full cooperation with the ICTY, they have *de facto* ignored domestic transitional justice mechanisms, both as priorities of the European Partnership and as a subject of monitoring by the Commission. As Bosnia moves from stabilization and association to the next level of negotiations, an opportunity arises to broaden the scope of EU conditionality and set new priorities to address the shortcomings from the previous period.

4.3 Assistance

EU financial assistance to Bosnia has been declining since 2001 with only €332 million being earmarked for the 2007–2010 period. The EU has distributed aid through the Community Assistance for Reconstruction, Development and Stabilization (CARDS) program in 2000–2006 and continues to fund civil society through the European Instrument for Democracy and Human Rights (EIDHR). On 1 January 2007, the EU introduced the Instrument for Pre-Accession to replace CARDS as the financial instrument of the SAP.[24] The IPA has distributed a total of €62 million in 2007 and funding will increase annually to reach €110 million by 2010.

The CARDS funding has been allocated to match primarily the institution-building and economic development priorities of the European Partnership.[25] CARDS assistance for "Democratic Stabilization" has focused on return and reintegration of refugees and internally displaced persons, media reform, and civil society, but has ignored the right to justice and reparation for past human rights abuse and the subject of missing persons. Under "Good Governance and Institution Building", support was given for general public administration reform and capacity building (customs and taxation; public finance; health sector; local government) and justice and home affairs (combating corruption, financial and organized crime; border management and police; technical assistance to the national judiciary; restructuring ministries of justice). While CARDS co-funded the establishment of the War Crimes Chamber of the State Court of BiH, support was not provided for training war crimes police

[22] Interview, DG Enlargement, European Commission (Brussels, 28 March 2007).

[23] Interview, DG Enlargement, European Commission (Brussels, 28 March 2007).

[24] Council Regulation (EC) 1085/2006 establishing an Instrument for Pre-Accession (IPA) [2006] OJ L210.

[25] Council Regulation (EC) 2666/2000 on assistance for Albania, Bosnia and Herzegovina, Croatia, the Federal Republic of Yugoslavia and the Former Yugoslav Republic of Macedonia, repealing Regulation (EC) No. 1628/96 and amending Regulations (EEC) no. 3906/89 and (EEC) No. 1360/90 and Decisions 97/256/EC and 1999/311/EC (CARDS), [2000] OJ L306.

investigators, prosecutors or judges, establishing witness protection and relocation programs, or funding fact-finding bodies across the region. Similarly absent was assistance in relevant police reform to deal with war crimes and ethnically-motivated crimes.

The IPA primarily focuses on transition assistance, institution building, and regional and cross-border cooperation. The main areas of intervention in support of the Copenhagen political criteria include public administration reform; constitutional reform; assistance to minorities and returnees; and support to civil society and the media. The IPA will continue to fund the War Crimes Chamber and will support cooperation between police, prosecution, courts, and the penitentiary system. Assistance will be provided to strengthen regional cooperation in criminal matters between the countries of the former Yugoslavia but only at the State Court of BiH. Support to local courts will not include specific assistance for the prosecution of war crimes at the local level. Assistance for a witness protection and relocation program remains missing.

The second priority for IPA assistance is the development of the NGO sector in Bosnia. For 2007, the IPA allocated 1.5 million to strengthen cooperation across civil society and to further its involvement in the reform processes. An emphasis is placed on building civil society capacity to act as a watchdog and partner of the government. To that end, the IPA designates funding in support for a State-level Economic and Social Council as a framework of civil society dialogue with the government. While assistance is earmarked for work with vulnerable groups (children, the elderly, the disabled, and minorities), no provision is made for support of the associations of war crimes victims.

The EIDHR funds civil society organizations, through macro- and micro-projects that promote the rule of law, respect for human rights, protection of minorities, and political pluralism.[26] Past and ongoing assistance includes civil society initiatives for fighting torture and impunity with a special emphasis on international criminal courts; the promotion of children's and women's rights; education reform; strengthening democratisation and good governance; and combating discrimination against minorities. It should be stated that the failure to spell out the general programmatic areas to include explicitly transitional justice, has effectively banned access of NGO war crimes work in Bosnia to EIDHR funding. Moreover, war crimes and justice are not currently envisioned as possible priorities for future funding.[27]

---

[26] Council Regulation (EC) 976/1999 laying down the requirements for the implementation of Community operations, other than those of development cooperation, which, within the framework of Community cooperation policy, contribute to the general objective of developing and consolidating democracy and the rule of law and to that of respecting human rights and fundamental freedoms in third countries (EIDHR), [1999] OJ L120.

[27] Statement by official at Democratic Stabilisation and Social Development Section, EC Delegation, BiH (Personal email correspondence, 25 April 2007).

5 EU Coherence and Complementarity with Civil Society

5.1 Policy Coherence

Bosnia and Herzegovina presents a challenge for the European Union because the legacy of conflict remains an obstacle to the consolidation of peace. At the same time, the country aspires to join the European Union and has entered into a standard process of negotiations involving EU conditionality and monitoring. The ambiguity of Bosnia's status as a post-conflict zone and a "normal" country on track to accession is reflected in the two approaches that the Union has developed to tackle the challenge: peace-building within the ESDP and EU integration. The Council of the EU has deployed significant resources to prevent the situation on the ground from deteriorating and presenting regional threats to peace and security, including the EUSR, EUFOR, and EUPM. Alongside the peace-building effort, the European Commission has incorporated Bosnia in the Stabilisation and Association process through European Partnerships, elaborating key priorities and reforms as preconditions for the eventual accession of the country to the EU. Interviews at the Commission confirm that the relationship between the two approaches has not been conceptualized at the EU level and the incentives that come with integration have not been clearly linked to the objectives of peace-building.[28]

So far, these two approaches are integrated in an EU policy framework that establishes the role of ESDP missions in support of the overall objective of BiH's integration through the SAP. As peace implementation by the international community phases out and less resources and powers are used to that objective, the accession framework is intended to absorb the residual conflict-related issues on the ground. But the standard "stick and carrot" approach used for integrating other Eastern European countries might on its own prove inadequate to achieve both consolidation of peace and accession to the EU. Without taking into account and addressing directly the legacy of war, the potential for instability remains, which would undermine both the achievements in peace implementation and the process of EU integration.

Conflict transformation in BiH has not been completed to the point where it is irreversible. The recent speculations of RS Prime Minister Dodik suggesting the possibility to hold a referendum for the Entity's secession have reignited divisive rhetoric in public debate on the very viability and integrity of the state. The difficulties in agreeing on constitutional reform demonstrate the reluctance of the ethnically-divided political class to achieve compromise on their own and to prioritize state-building over narrow political interests. War crimes issues that have been largely ignored by the international community continue to undermine the political process and to reinforce existing grievances at the level of communities and individuals in society. For example, the RS representatives at the State Parliament effectively blocked its operation for a month in 2006 over delays in setting up the Sarajevo Truth Commission (ICG 2007, pp. 4–6). The shortcomings of vetting of

[28] Interview, DG Enlargement, European Commission (Brussels, 28 March 2007).

the police services remain a persistent source of popular resentment in BiH, since the process is seen as both incomplete and unfair. More recently, the ICJ judgment exculpating Serbia for genocide reinforced divides as Serbs in the RS celebrated while Bosniaks in the Federation protested and mourned.

These conflict-related issues cannot be easily ignored by the EU if it takes its peace and integration objectives in BiH seriously. Instead of sidelining them in the political dialogue with Bosnian authorities and the assistance framework, a better approach might involve rethinking how such issues should be integrated coherently in its overall strategy. In order for the EU to effectively facilitate the resolution of the remaining problems stemming from war and mass atrocity, while it prepares BiH for membership, the accession framework must be adapted to take into account these potential sources of conflict and instability. The SAP did not articulate a coherent strategy for the consolidation of peace and integration in EU structures, and it remains to be seen how the Union will tackle this problem in the next stage of negotiations. The challenge is not a matter of better coordination between the Council and the Commission. Rather, a coherent strategy would involve first, deepening the ESDP engagement with conflict-related issues and second, incorporating specific priorities that will address such issues in the negotiations of the *acquis communautaire.*

War crimes remain one of the outstanding conflict-related issues with high potential to galvanize tensions between communities, to obstruct the political process, and to undermine the legitimacy and stability of transition. Transitional justice offers a security strategy and an institutionalized framework for processing the legacy of war crimes. On the one hand, it opens up space for negotiating conflicting and often competing narratives of injustice across communities and at the individual level. The opportunity for articulating grievances and claims for justice in a public policy debate commits people to the democratic political process and the rule of law, minimizing incentives for seeking extra-judicial and extra-political forms of redress. On the other hand, transitional justice can provide a rule-based methodology for disabling those elements within society that might have a stake in the culture of illegality and state weakness linked to the conflict.

In order to advance its goals in BiH, the ESDP framework should take a justice-sensitive approach to security and peace-building. Council officials have confirmed that war crimes issues were discussed at the Ministerial level only with respect to the ICTY.[29] So far, the ESDP missions on the ground have not been mandated to reflect the role of justice mechanisms in enhancing security and peace-building on the ground. Key tasks of the EU-led force are to provide support to the ICTY and relevant authorities, including the arrests of persons indicted for war crimes, and to provide the security environment in which the police can act against networks of organised crime. However, the overall security environment is compromised by the significant number of war criminals at large, not only the remaining few ICTY indictees. Similarly, EUFOR efforts to facilitate local authorities in combating organized crime depend on explicitly tackling the links between wartime networks and organized crime.

[29] Interview, Council of the EU (Telephone, 11 April 2007).

The mandate of the EUPM to build a professional police service, through mentoring, monitoring, and inspecting, effectively ignored the key contentious issue of vetting.[30] The vetting implemented by IPTF was incomplete in purging war criminals from the structures; unfair in conducting recertification; and failed to institutionalize a review process for recruitment. It is difficult to see how the EUPM can achieve its goals given the persistent obstacles inherited from the flawed process of vetting. A coherent ESDP approach would entail facilitating the EUPM in completing its mandate by reopening the issue of vetting in the Dayton framework. Given that the EUSR is tasked with the overall coordination of the peace implementation process, the responsibility for implementing a coherent justice-sensitive approach across ESDP missions should be centralized under his authority, within a framework adopted by the Council.

Since the negotiations of the *acquis communautaire* will provide the overall framework for the EU in BiH over the next period, deepening the ESDP component must take place within this framework to address outstanding conflict-related issues in the country. The European Partnerships and the Reform Process Monitoring were potentially useful instruments for absorbing the disruptive war crimes and justice issues within the political process and the rule-of-law structures. However, they were never used to that effect. The Council put a premium on cooperation with the ICTY as a key priority for the European Partnership with BiH, while neglecting domestic transitional justice mechanisms. The Commission interpretation of the Copenhagen political criteria placed full cooperation with The Hague and domestic war crimes trials in the section assessing progress on regional issues and international obligations, rather than in its judicial system reporting. The Commission assessment of administrative reform ignored the problems related to vetting in evaluating police reform. Apart from the Human Rights Commission, mechanisms for dealing with war crimes and justice for mass atrocity were not part of the assessment of national institutions guaranteeing democracy, rule of law, and human rights.[31]

By leaving aside these highly politicized and sensitive demands of transition, the EU has failed to engage Bosnian authorities and the broader public in a political dialogue that could help find policy solutions to address the legacy of conflict. Furthermore, since domestic transitional justice did not feature in the SAP and Copenhagen conditionality, it was also largely excluded from EU assistance that matched reform priorities. The EU has missed valuable opportunities to trigger political dialogue, public debate, and the emergence of institutional capacity for dealing with the divisive aspects of the past. Brussels officials have openly stated that the EU takes a future-oriented approach to BiH and an overemphasis on war crimes is a stumbling block for rebuilding the country. However, this analysis ignores both the potential of past injustice to jeopardize the entire project of state-building, and the forward-looking contribution of transitional justice to the consolidation of peace and EU integration of BiH. To operationalize a coherent framework that addresses war crimes and justice in Bosnia, these issues must be incorporated at the level of

[30] Council Joint Action (EC) on the EUPM in BiH 2005/824/CFSP (2005).

[31] Commission (EC), "Bosnia and Herzegovina 2006 Progress Report" (Commission staff Working Document) COM (2006) 649 fina (08 November 2006).

the Copenhagen conditionality and the negotiation of the *acquis*, and by providing matching assistance through the Instrument for Pre-Accession and the European Instrument for Democracy and Human Rights.

5.2 Operational Aspects of Coherence and Coordination

Given the complexity of EU engagement in BiH, alongside multiple international actors, coordination to ensure coherence has been a continuous challenge. Arrangements are in place for external coherence between Brussels and Sarajevo and for internal coherence between the different EU missions within BiH. Decision-making authority on CFSP/ESDP is concentrated at the level of the Council, the Political and Security Committee (PSC), and the Council Working Groups, while the Commission and Parliament oversee relevant financial arrangements. The Council, through its Secretary General, must ensure coherence between the various ESDP instruments while the Commission is responsible for developing its assistance programs along the lines of Council priorities. While coherence at this level remains a challenge, the Secretary General is tasked to guaranteeing that funding matches policy. The PSC coordinates and provides strategic direction to ESDP missions. The Commission provides regular progress reports to the Council and Parliament, incorporating contributions from its Delegation, the government of BiH, the Member States, European Parliament reports, and information from various international and non-governmental organizations.

Internal coherence and overall political coordination in Bosnia is the responsibility of the EUSR. In this role, the EUSR convenes weekly meetings with EU Heads of Mission, monthly EC assistance coordination meetings, and chairs monthly operational meetings with EUFOR, EUPM, Commission Delegation, EUMM, and the EU Presidency.[32] The EUSR directs the EUPM while providing only political guidance to the EUFOR Commander. In the case of disagreement between EUFOR and the EUSR, both report to their separate chains of command to seek clarification. In the fight against organized crime, tensions existed between the EUPM, instructed to delegate to local police authorities, and EUFOR, which was instructed to bypass them. Coordination improved after EUPM's mandate was strengthened and revised to allow it to take the lead in coordinating operations to counter organized crime.[33]

Since the EUSR is the High Representative, he also must coordinate with other international actors operating in BiH. The permanent members of the Steering Board of the PIC (Canada, France, Germany, Italy, Japan, Russian, UK, US, the Presidency of the EU, the Commission, and the Organization of the Islamic Conference, represented by Turkey) meet once a week in Sarajevo to provide the OHR with political guidance and coordination. A Board of Principles was established as the main coordinating body in 2002, meeting once per week to ensure coherence and prevent

[32] Interview, DG Enlargement, European Commission (Brussels, 28 March 2007).

[33] Interview, Rule of Law Section, EC Delegation BiH (Telephone, 19 April 2007).

overlap in activities. The Board of Principals brings together the OHR, EUFOR, NATO, OSCE, UNHCR, EUPM, the European Commission, IMF, and the World Bank. Another level of coordination involves formal and informal donor meetings, specifically to support the State Court of BiH, which have been managed by the International Registry quite successfully.

International organizations active in the field of transitional justice issues include the OSCE, the International Commission for Missing Persons (ICMP), the ICRC, USIP, UNDP, and other development agencies. Within its Dayton mandate to monitor the human rights situation in BiH, the OSCE currently monitors domestic war crimes trials, including those transferred from the ICTY pursuant to Rule 11*bis*, and provides technical assistance in the process of trying war crimes cases. It also coordinates the effort for education reform. The ICMP and the ICRC have overall responsibility for the remaining missing persons, exhumations of mass graves, and support civil society efforts for dealing with the past. USIP has facilitated the initiatives for establishing an official truth-telling mechanism. The UNDP has conducted a survey of transitional justice in BiH in an attempt to develop a comprehensive approach to the process. Currently, it provides support to the War Crimes Chamber of the State Court, some assistance to local courts, and is planning to broaden their work in this field. Individual Member States have also committed resources to the War Crimes Chamber and to NGOs working in the field.

While there are multiple international actors involved in different aspects of transitional justice work in Bosnia, there is lack of coordination among them, limiting the impact of their work. Our interviews suggest that no international agency is prepared to take the lead on the highly sensitive and politicized problems of war crimes and justice. Furthermore, the EU is perceived within this group as largely disengaged and reluctant to take the issues on board.[34] Given that all international actors are committed to working within the framework established by the EU in the accession process, the European Union is best positioned to coordinate these efforts. The logical steps to ensure coherence among international organizations in the field of transitional justice include commissioning an assessment or mapping study to clarify the activities of all relevant actors and proposing a coordination structure. Within his mandate to coordinate all ESDP and Community activities in BiH, the EUSR is the most relevant body to implement these tasks.

One policy area with clear lack of coherence and coordination between international actors is the domestic prosecution of war crimes in BiH. The EU and Member States have largely focused their efforts on establishing and making operational the War Crimes Chamber of the State Court of BiH. Yet this War Crimes Chamber will be able to prosecute no more than 10% of the war crimes case load likely to come before Bosnian courts in the next period. The vast number of criminal prosecutions will have to take place at the poorly equipped, understaffed, and under-funded 16 local courts that have already begun to hear cases (UNDP 2005). Without a coordination effort between the EU and the other agencies committed to supporting local war crimes trials, the discrepancy between a well-established and well-funded

[34] Interview, Rule of Law Section, UNDP Sarajevo (Telephone, 12 April 2007).

War Crimes Chamber and weak local courts with limited capacity, is likely to persist. It should be noted that the EU's overall goal of seeing war crimes processed through domestic courts, as the ICTY is phasing out its operations, would be better served if it engages more closely with other actors that can channel their resources towards the 16 local courts that the EU currently does not support. For example, recent UNDP assessments identify their commitment to take the lead in that respect. Rather than calling for an across-the-board increase in EU funding and engagement with specific transitional justice mechanisms, this case suggests that the more pressing need is for the EU to map and pool existing international resources in a coherent framework.

However, improving the operational coordination of European missions, on its own, will have a limited impact on transitional justice processes in BiH. As already noted, the EU lacks a coherent policy framework matched with adequate assistance for addressing transitional justice as part of the conflict-related obstacles to peace-building and EU integration of Bosnia. Without deepening and fine-tuning EU engagement in war crimes and justice, the multiple EU agents on the ground can achieve little, regardless of efforts to improve coordination. However, given that the Union intends to strengthen its engagement over the next period, if it adopts a justice-sensitive approach within its policy and instruments, this would have to be matched with structural adjustments on the ground. Currently, transitional justice efforts involve the infrastructure for security and rule of law provided by the EU and the relevant local stakeholders. In this sense, transitional justice emerges at the intersection of security structures, rule of law activities, conditionality and dialogue, as well as the provision of technical and financial assistance, all of which depend on the interaction between the EU and BiH.

One avenue for facilitating the necessary interaction between different stakeholders involved in the process is provided by the emerging methodology of interface units. This methodology is particularly relevant for a context that involves multiple actors and multilateral coordination needs. This study proposes the creation of a War Crimes Interface Unit within the office of the EUSR. The Unit should provide permanent infrastructure and staff for coordination of justice-related activities of the EU missions (EUSR, EUFOR, EUPM, the Commission Delegation) and key local agencies and ministries dealing with justice, security and policing. Directed by the EUSR, the Interface Unit should perform coordination functions with view to ensure the necessary support and interaction between all active members. Specific functions can include, *inter alia,* coordinating the effort for cooperation with the ICTY within the accession process; coordinating support for the War Crimes Chamber and the sixteen local courts working on war crimes; and, coordinating issues of regional cooperation in criminal matters.

The Interface Unit additionally would provide a forum where local stakeholders and EU representatives can bring up problems and identify pragmatic solutions to day-to-day challenges, within a framework of dialogue. The sensitive issues of transitional justice have so far been dealt with by the international community, either through direct action, sidelining local counterparts, or by using the instruments of political pressure. The Unit would provide an opportunity to engage in a technical discussion that can operationalize policy and help generate ideas and strategies that can be taken up to relevant decision-makers on both sides.

Since the appointment of Lajcak, the EUSR has taken the lead to improve coordination between international actors and local authorities on the issue of cooperation with the ICTY. There has been a marked shift in integrating the ESDP and enlargement strategies on the ground even though so far, this trend has been reflected only on ICTY conditionality. The EUSR has emphasized his two-pronged strategy of pressure and assistance in his recent report to the UN Secretary General:

> I continue to place a high priority on cooperation with the ICTY. Since my last report, international forces and domestic law enforcement agencies have applied continuous pressure on and scrutiny over persons and networks suspected of supporting ICTY fugitives. My office cooperates with and supports the activities conducted by ICTY, NATO, EUFOR, the RS police, the BiH Intelligence and Security Agency (OSA), and others involved in efforts to bring the four remaining fugitives to justice. This has resulted in greatly improved coordination and unity of effort, as well as more efficient use of our limited resources. (OHR 2008)

The success of Bosnia in securing a Stabilization and Association Agreement with the European Union came after the EUSR strengthened his role in coordinating the effort to meet ICTY conditionality. Furthermore, the other major obstacle in the negotiations with the EU, police reform, has been resolved to a satisfactory level only after similarly active intervention on the part of the EUSR. Lajcak's role in exerting pressure on Bosnia's political class and facilitating their dialogue has led to the adoption of key legislation necessary for police reform in the spring of 2008. These two examples illustrate the potential of a shift in the EU's strategy in Bosnia and suggest the way forward with respect to other aspects of transitional justice. By integrating coherently the peace-building and enlargement efforts, the EU can tackle the residual conflict-related issues even more effectively at the next stage of the accession process. As Bosnia begins negotiations of the *acquis,* the Union's leverage to incorporate transitional justice beyond the ICTY increases. In particular, the benchmarks for opening negotiations on Chapter 23, Judiciary and Fundamental Rights, provide a convenient framework to elaborate conditionality with respect to domestic prosecution of war crimes, truth-telling, vetting, and reparations.

5.3 A Regional Approach to Transitional Justice in the Western Balkans

The war in Bosnia was not a traditional civil war and was *de facto* a regional conflict. The cross-border and inter-ethnic nature of the war requires a regional approach to dealing with the legacy of mass atrocity. In BiH and across former Yugoslavia, domestic war crimes trials are conducted in a situation in which perpetrators, victims, witnesses, and evidence are often located across state borders. This requires regional cooperation in criminal matters, which is currently regulated by bilateral agreements but is obstructed by political, technical, and financial problems (Rangelov 2006a). Cooperation at the investigation and prosecution stages must be enabled through training and resource allocation to fit current agreements. Furthermore, without regional witness relocation and exchange programs, the witness protection legislation that Bosnia and the other ex-Yugoslav countries have adopted, remains inoperative. Both the War Crimes Chamber in Sarajevo and local courts depend on witnesses and evidence that can be obtained only in a regional framework.

Since the SAP was established for all Western Balkan countries, a coherent approach to transitional justice at the next stage of negotiations can emerge only within a regional framework. Adopting a justice-sensitive approach to EU accession in Bosnia must be replicated in Serbia and Croatia, which would provide incentives for the governments in the region and help prevent the politicization of the issue in each context. If transitional justice is a priority in BiH, it must be a priority in the other countries implicated in the conflict as well, in order for the Union to be seen as fair-handed. A regional approach is necessary to ensure the effectiveness and coherence of overall EU policy, as well as the strengthening of regional cooperation in criminal matters. Our interviews at the EC Delegation in Sarajevo demonstrate that local staff is aware of this need. The Delegation has been coordinating a project that brought the regional war crimes prosecutors together to discuss the matter.[35] The project has exposed the need for more support and pressure at the political level. Moreover, it has clarified the current lack of coherence – cases on Srebrenica, for example, have been opened in different countries without coordination at any level.

5.4 Complementarity with Civil Society

The European Union has engaged in a political dialogue in Bosnia that has sidelined civil society as an interlocutor and partner in the transition. The SAP framework and the Reform Process Monitoring did not provide for mechanisms to engage non-state actors. Furthermore, the European Partnership priorities did not even mention civil society, which meant that the third sector was effectively excluded from the agenda of EU negotiations with BiH authorities. The literature on post-conflict reconstruction has long emphasized that civil society is a key factor for the political and economic development of weak states. Given that Bosnia remains a weak state, the Union has ignored the potential role of civil society in state-building to the detriment of its own policy goals and efforts. The potential of civil society for development is significant, both with respect to building responsive and transparent state structures and as a partner in the reconstruction effort.

Recently, EU policy for engaging with and supporting civil society organizations in BiH has been reconsidered and is moving in a positive direction. The background for policy change was provided in the Thessaloniki Agenda for the Western Balkans, stipulating that consolidation of peace, stability, and democratic development cannot be achieved without thorough involvement of local stakeholders. Thessaloniki further established that strengthening the capacity of civil society in partner countries

[35] Interview with Isabel Royo Pla, Task Manager for Judiciary and Justice Issues, EC Delegation BiH (Telephone 3 April 2007).

should be given a priority and the financial means should be made available for non-state actors when drawing up programmes of financial support.

As a result, civil society was consulted for the first time in the planning for the current IPA assistance programming for 2007–2009.[36] In 2005, the Commission carried out a Mapping Exercise for civil society, shared the results with BiH authorities, and used it as the basis for the development of its 2007 project "Capacity-Building of Civil Society to take part in Policy Dialogue".[37] The purpose of the project is to strengthen civil society both as partner and as a watchdog of the government in the reform process. The project also aims to develop better communication and cooperation among non-state actors, as well as between Entities and the constituent peoples, in this way facilitating greater understanding between citizens of BiH. As already mentioned, the EU has committed resources for the development of a State-level Economic and Social Committee. Once established, this body will initiate an institutionalized policy dialogue between civil society and the government.

This intensified involvement of the European Union with the third sector does not include engagement and consultation with civil society actors working on issues of transitional justice. Indeed, our extensive interviews with key NGOs and victims groups suggest that the European institutions in Bosnia have pursued a deliberate strategy of avoiding engagement with transitional justice issues and actors. For example, Mirsad Tokaca, head of one of the strongest and most vocal outfits, the Research and Documentation Centre in Sarajevo, stated that the EU ignores those groups in civil society that work on war crimes.[38] Key organizations for dealing with the past such as Helsinki Committee for Human Rights in Republika Srpska, Center for Nonviolent Action, Youth Initiative for Human Rights, and the Association of the Families and Missing Persons in Zvornik, among others, have never been contacted by EU representatives for consultations or discussion of war crimes and justice issues.[39] Where links exist, they are often based on personal contacts rather than coherent policy.

Not surprisingly, EU assistance for civil society work on war crimes issues also reflects this general strategy for disengagement. The distribution of funds from the EIDHR incorporates only civil society projects providing services to war victims, for example, support for therapy and rehabilitation of torture victims, carried out by the NGO Citizen Association "Vive Zene" in Tuzla. Activities such as monitoring war crimes trials, truth-telling, or advocacy on behalf of war victims are not supported. In this sense, one cannot speak of any effort on the part of the Union to complement civil society activities on transitional justice in BiH. The lack of complementarity is not simply a result of how EU missions operate. Rather, it stems

[36] Statement by official at Democratic Stabilisation and Social Development Section, EC Delegation, BiH (Personal email correspondence, 25 April 2007).

[37] Directorate for European Integration / Division for EU Assistance Coordination, BiH "Project Synopsis: Capacity Building of Civil Society to take part in Policy Dialogue" working document (November 2006) (on file with the authors).

[38] Interview with Mirsad Tokaca, Executive Director, Research and Documentation Centre Sarajevo (Telephone, 10 April 2007).

[39] Our research on civil society draws on a data set of 22 interviews with civil society groups in Bosnia and Herzegovina. For the complete list, please see the Appendix.

from the reluctance of Council and Commission policy to seek any engagement on these issues with the civil society actors pursuing them.

EU officials in Brussels and Sarajevo explain that war crimes and justice are not covered by EIDHR and the IPA because there is no consensus on this subject in BiH itself.[40] Furthermore, as the situation on the ground has deteriorated in the last year, they don't foresee future assistance anytime soon. They state that the only opportunity to pay more attention to mass atrocity would come if Bosnian authorities agree amongst themselves to prioritize the problems in this field. However, this approach contradicts the notion that civil society is an autonomous sphere, separate from the state and reflecting interests and priorities that are often ignored by state institutions. When civil society is expected to perform watchdog functions, again the assumption is that the officials should not be the only ones to determine what is best for the citizens and should be responsive to demands coming from the bottom-up.

By disengaging the broad segments of Bosnian society that have a stake in transitional justice, the European Union has failed to identify an alternative source of legitimacy in the political process. Groups of victims of torture and sexual violence, prisoners of war, associations of the families of the missing, and war veterans comprise the part of civil society with the highest demand for justice and the one that can provide legitimacy to efforts to address mass atrocity. These groups can be a powerful partner of the international community in the peace-building effort especially since they often feel neglected and betrayed by the ethnic elites and political classes. Rather than abstaining from war crimes and justice for fear of destabilization, the EU would be better served if it recognized the potential of bringing in and empowering civil society that is currently marginalized on all sides of the ethnic divides. Indeed, it is precisely the most victimized groups in Bosnian society that have been seeking inter-ethnic cooperation as a result of their common experiences during the war and their shared struggle for justice and redress during the transition. Together with NGOs that already work across communities, these victims groups constitute a powerful resource that can generate the legitimacy necessary to transcend ethnic divides in the state-building project.

This study suggests that a meaningful engagement of the European Union with civil society groups active in transitional justice would involve not only complementing their current efforts but also helping them reclaim their voice and agency in the political process. This would require rethinking the meaning and role of civil society as seen from Brussels, to adopt a broader concept that includes more loosely organized victims groups and social movements as well as the professionalized NGO sector.

In order to operationalize such a concept, the Commission can conduct a mapping study in Bosnia that incorporates this broader set of actors and civil society forces. The EU should then establish a mechanism for dialogue on transitional justice between civil society and EU representatives. This presents an opportunity for the EU to justify a future engagement in war crimes issues since civil society can lend legitimacy to bringing demands for justice into the political process. The dia-

[40] Statement by official at Democratic Stabilisation and Social Development Section, EC Delegation, BiH (Personal email correspondence, 25 April 2007).

logue can also generate policy solutions through a participatory process, emphasizing local ownership on this most sensitive subject. Such a process of engagement has the potential to provide the EU and civil society with counterarguments to the divisive ethnic rhetoric of the political elites, stressing shared demands and problems of victims across communities. As a last step, based on its mapping exercise and the dialogue with civil society, the EU will be prepared to devise an adequate strategy for financial assistance to support civil society action in transitional justice.

6 Concluding Remarks

The major obstacle to the consolidation of peace in Bosnia and Herzegovina is the failure to adequately address the legacy of armed conflict and mass atrocity from 1992–1995. The Dayton Peace Agreement successfully ended the war but at the same time, established constitutional structures that further entrenched ethnic divides. Rather than seeking to confront and deal with conflict-related issues in the transition, the Dayton framework and the engagement of the international community have ignored the potential of transitional justice to contribute to peace-building and stabilisation. The limited developments in transitional justice in BiH have come as a result of pressure exerted by the Office of the High Representative (OHR) on the political class, without broad public consultations or engagement with victims and other civil society groups.

Civil society in Bosnia is weak, divided, and largely donor-driven. It reflects the nature of the ethnic conflict, the Dayton constitutional structure, and the top-down approach of the international community in providing assistance. Civil society activism on issues of war crimes and justice rarely crosses the ethnic divide and attracts donor funding for service delivery rather than more politicized forms of advocacy and engagement.

EU policy towards Bosnia and Herzegovina reflects a two-pronged strategy: peace-building within the European Security and Defence Policy and the standard "stick and carrot" strategy for integration into the EU. However, the relationship between the two approaches has not been conceptualized at the EU level and the incentives that come with integration have not been clearly linked to the objectives of peace-building. Apart from international war crimes trials, transitional justice has been largely ignored by Brussels since the EU takes a future-oriented approach that sees war crimes as a conflict-generating issue. However, without taking into account and addressing directly the legacy of war, the potential for instability remains, which would undermine both the achievements in peace implementation and the process of accession to the Union. Our main recommendation is to rethink the EU's overall policy approach to Bosnia, by integrating transitional justice directly within both the peace-building and the accession effort.

The Union has overlooked the potential of transitional justice as a security strategy that can provide an institutionalized framework for processing the legacy of war crimes. The process of transitional justice opens up space for negotiating conflicting narratives of injustice. In this way, it commits people to the democratic political process and the rule of law, minimizing incentives for seeking extra-judicial and extra-political forms of redress. Moreover, it provides a rule-based methodology to sideline individuals who propel the culture of illegality, state weakness, and ethnic polarization. In this context, the challenge for the EU is not merely to enhance the coherence between the ESDP and the accession framework in their current form. Rather, the EU should deepen ESDP engagement with war crimes and justice issues and incorporate specific priorities on these issues into the accession process.

Our analysis suggests that the ESDP framework for Bosnia should take a justice-sensitive approach to security and peace-building. In order to incorporate war crimes and justice within ESDP missions, the EU will have to adjust and refocus their mandates. This would entail enhancing the European Union military force (EUFOR) to support local security agencies in apprehending war criminals, whether indicted by international or national courts. Another key recommendation is to reopen the issue of vetting in order to deal with the problem of war criminals active in the police services.

Given the regional nature of the conflict in Bosnia, another main conclusion of this study concerns the need for a regional approach by the European Union to transitional justice that focuses on the Western Balkans as a whole. Across the region, war crimes trials involve evidence, witnesses, and suspects located outside of the affected country. The current framework for regional cooperation would need to be strengthened with political will and technical support in order to operationalize any bilateral agreements.

While the EU has begun to work more closely with the third sector, it has not involved or consulted with civil society actors active in the field of transitional justice. As a consequence of this strategy of disengagement, one cannot speak of any effort on the part of the Union to complement civil society activities on these highly politicized and sensitive problems. A rethink of the EU's approach to non-state actors should involve broadening the very concept of civil society to involve victims groups, alongside the NGO community. Only then can the EU proceed to establish mechanisms for dialogue and appropriate schemes for assistance.

Appendix: Civil Society Organizations Surveyed

Name of organization/person	Date	Communication
Nansen Dialogue Center, Sarajevo, Ljulijeta Goranci Brkic	3 April 2007	Email
Human Rights Center, University of Sarajevo, Sasha Madacki	3 April 2007	Email
Association of the Alumni of the Centre for Interdisciplinary Post Graduate Studies (ACIPS), Ivan Barbalic	3 April 2007	Email

Nansen Dialogue Center, Mostar, Elvir Djuliman	3 April 2007	Email
TERCA (Training, Education, Research, Consulting, Action), Sarajevo, Goran Bubalo	4 April 2007	Email
Bureau for Human Rights, Tuzla	10 April 2007	Telephone
Helsinki Committee for Human Rights in BiH, Sarajevo, Zivica Abadzic	10 April 2007	Telephone
Youth Organization ODISEJ, Bratunac, Cedomir Glavas	11 April 2007	Telephone
Helsinki Committee for Human Rights in RS, Bijeljina, Aleksandra Letic	12 April 2007	Telephone
Nansen Dialogue Centre, Banja Luka	13 April 2007	Email
IMIC: International Multi-religious and Intercultural Centre, Sarajevo	16 April 2007	Email
Center for Nonviolent Action, Sarajevo	17 April 2007	Telephone
Center for Building Peace – Sanski Most, Vahidin Omanovic	17 April 2007	Telephone
Citizen's Association "Viva Zene", Mima Dahic	17 April 2007	Email
Citizen Association "Truth and Reconciliation", Jakob Finci	17 April 2007	Email
Research and Documentation Centre, Sarajevo	17 April 2007	Email
Youth Initiative for Human Rights, Sarajevo, Dejana Grbic	18 April 2007	Email
Association of the Families of Prisoners and Missing Persons in the Zvornik Municipality, Tuzla	20 April 2007	Telephone
Association of War Veterans 1992–1995, Tuzla, Alija Mouratovic	20 April 2007	Telephone
Association of Camp Prisoner "Omer Filipovic", Kljuc, Mehmet Begic	25 April 2007	Telephone
Youth Cultural Centre "Abrasevic", Mostar, Hussein Orucevic	26 April 2007	Telephone
Youth Centre Gornji Vakuf-Uskoplje, Gornji Vakuf-Uskoplje,	27 April 2007	Email

References

Aucoin L, Babbitt E (2006) Transitional justice: assessment survey conditions in the former Yugoslavia. UNDP, Belgrade

BIRN (2007) No progress for Sarajevo truth commission. Justice Report, 23 February 2007. Balkan Investigative Reporting Network

Biro M, Ajdukovic D, Corkalo D (2004) Attitudes toward justice and social reconstruction in Bosnia and Herzegovina and Croatia. In: Stover E, Weinstein H (eds) My neighbor, my enemy: justice and community in the aftermath of mass atrocity. Cambridge University Press, Cambridge

Freeman M (2004) Bosnia and Herzegovina: selected developments in transitional justice. International Center for Transitional Justice, New York

HLC (2005) Strategy for transitional justice in the Former Yugoslavia. Humanitarian Law Center, Belgrade

HLC (2006) Transitional justice in the post-Yugoslav countries: report for 2006. Humanitarian Law Center, Belgrade. www.hlc-rdc.org

HRW (2004) Justice at risk: war crimes trials in Croatia, Bosnia and Herzegovina, and Serbia and Montenegro. HRW Report 16, 7(D). Human Rights Watch, New York

Huyse L (1995) Justice after transition: on the choices successor elites make in dealing with the past. Law Social Inquiry 20:51

ICG (2002) Policing the police in Bosnia: a further reform agenda. Balkans Report No. 130. International Crisis Group, Sarajevo/Brussels

ICG (2007) Ensuring Bosnia's future: a new international engagement strategy. Europe Report No. 180. International Crisis Group, Sarajevo/Brussels

Jelacic N, Ahmetasevic N (2006) Truth commission divides Bosnia. Balkan Insight, 31 March 2006. www.iwpr.net

Kaldor M (1998) Transnational civil society. In: Bianchini S, Schopflin G (eds) State building in the Balkans: dilemmas on the eve of the 21st Century. Longo Editore, Ravenna

Kaldor M (1999) New and old wars: organized violence in a global era. Polity Press, Cambridge

Koulouri C (ed) (2001) Teaching the history of Southeastern Europe. CDRSEE, Thessaloniki

Koulouri C (ed) (2002) Clio in the Balkans: the politics of history education. CDRSEE, Thessaloniki

OHR (2008) Thirty-third report of the High Representative for implementation of the peace agreement on Bosnia and Herzegovina to the Secretary-General of the United Nations, 1 October 2007 – 31 March 2008. Office of the High Representative and EU Special Representative. www.ohr.int

Rangelov I (2006a) EU war crimes policy in the western Balkans. In: Denisa Kostovicova, Vesna Bojicic Dzelilovic (eds) Austrian presidency of the EU: regional approaches to the Balkans. Renner Institute, Vienna

Rangelov I (2006b) EU conditionality and transitional justice in the former Yugoslavia. Croatian Yearbook Eur Law Policy 2:365

Suljagic E (2005) Postcards from the Grave. Saqi Books, London

UNDP (2005) Transitional justice in Bosnia and Herzegovina: situation analysis and strategic options. Mission report. United Nations Development Program, Sarajevo

Zivanovic M (2006) Civil society in Bosnia and Herzegovina: lost in transition. In: Benedek W (ed) Civil society and good governance in society in transition. Belgrade Center for Human Rights, Belgrade

Zupan N (2006) Facing the past and transitional justice in countries of the former Yugoslavia. In: Fischer M (ed) Peacebuilding and civil society in Bosnia-Herzegovina: ten years after Dayton. Lit, Munster

Documents

Council of the EU (05.12.2000) Council Regulation No. 2666/2000 on assistance for Albania, Bosnia and Herzegovina, Croatia, the Federal Republic of Yugoslavia and the Former Yugoslav Republic of Macedonia, repealing Regulation (EC) No 1628/96 and amending Regulations

(EEC) No 3906/89 and (EEC) No 1360/90 and Decisions 97/256/EC and 1999/311/EC, 2000/2666.EC (CARDS)
Council of the EU (29.04.1999) Council Regulation No 976/1999 laying down the requirements for the implementation of Community operations, other than those of development cooperation, which, within the framework of Community cooperation policy, contribute to the general objective of developing and consolidating democracy and the rule of law and to that of respecting human rights and fundamental freedoms in third countries, 1999/976/EC (EIDHR)
Council of the EU (12.12.2003) *A Secure Europe in a Better World: European Security Strategy*
Council of the EU (14.06.2004) *Council Decision on the principles, priorities, and conditions contained in the European Partnership with BiH*, OJ L 221/10 22.06.2004
Council of the EU (14/06/2004) *Council Decision on the principles, priorities, and conditions contained in the European Partnership with BiH*, 2004/515/EC
Council of the EU (12.07.2004) *Council Joint Action on the EU Military Operation in BiH*, 2004/570/CFSP
Council of the EU (24.11.2005) *Council Joint Action on the EUMP in BiH*, 2005/824/CFSP
Council of the EU (30.01.2006) Council *Joint Action appointing the European Special Representative in BiH*, 2006/49/CFSP
Council of the EU (30.01.2006) *Council Decision on the principles, priorities, and conditions contained in the European Partnership with BiH and repealing Decision* 2004/515/EC, 2006/55/EC
Council of the EU (10.03.2006) *Council Common Position renewing measures in support of the effective implementation of the mandate of the ICTY*, 2006/204/CFSP
Council of the EU (20.12.2006) Regulation of the European Parliament and the Council on establishing a financial instrument for the promotion of democracy and human rights worldwide. 2006/1889/EC (EIDHR)
Council of the EU (25.07.2006) Council Joint Action amending the mandate of the EUSR in BiH, 2006/523/CFSP (2)
Council of the EU (07.02.2007) Council Joint Action amending and extending the mandate of the EUSR in BiH, 2007/87/CFSP
Council of the EU (17.07.2006) Council Regulation No. 1085/2006 establishing an Instrument for Pre-Accession Assistance (IPA) OJ L 210 of 31.07.2006
Directorate for European Integration / Division for EU Assistance Coordination, BiH (2006) "Project Synopsis: Capacity Building of Civil Society to take part in policy dialogue"
Directorate for European Integration / Bosnia and Herzegovina Council of Ministers (2006) "EU Integration Strategy for Bosnia and Herzegovina – April 2006"
Draft Law on the Truth and Reconciliation Commission in BiH (on file with the authors)
European Commission (26.05.1999) Commission Communication to the Council and the European Parliament on the SAP for countries of South-Easter Europe. COM (1999) 235
European Commission (03.04.2002) Report from the Commission – The Stabilisation and Association process for South East Europe First Annual Report, COM (2002) 163
European Commission (26.03.2003) Report from the Commission – The Stabilisation and Association process for South East Europe – Second Annual Report, COM (2003) 139
European Commission (30.03.2004) Report from the Commission – The Stabilisation and Association process for South East Europe – Third Annual Report, COM (2004) 202
European Commission (08.11.2006) Communication from the Commission to the European Parliament and the Council – Enlargement Strategy and Main Challenges 2006–2007, COM (2006) 649
European Commission (08.11.2006) Bosnia and Herzegovina 2006 Progress Report, Commission Staff Working Document. COM (2006) 649
European Commission (24.05.2006) A Concept for European Community Support for Security Sector Reform, Communication from the Commission to the Council and the European Parliament, COM (2006) 253
European Commission (27.01.2006) The Western Balkans on the road to the EU: Consolidating stability and raising prosperity, COM (2006) 27
General Framework Agreement for Peace in Bosnia and Herzegovina (Dayton Peace Agreement) (14.12.1995). http://www.ohr.int

Law on Protection of Witnesses under Threat and Vulnerable Witnesses. (Consolidated Version) Official Gazette of BiH, 3/03, 21/03, 61/04, 55/05
Law on Court of Bosnia and Herzegovina, adopted 3rd July 2002. Official Gazette of BiH No. 15/02
Parliamentary Assembly of BiH. Law on Missing Persons, adopted on 21st October 2004
RS Government/RS Prime Minister Dragan Mikerevic (2004), Conclusions of the RS Government regarding the Srebrenica Commission Final Report
OHR (23.05.2002) Decision of the High Representative Enacting the Law on the High Judicial Council of BiH, Official Gazette of BiH, 15/02
OHR (05.07.2004) Decision establishing the Police Restructuring Commission

Abbreviations

BiH	Bosnia and Herzegovina
CARDS	Community Assistance for Reconstruction, Development and Stabilization
CFSP	Common Foreign and Security Policy
EC	European Commission
EU	European Union
EIDHR	European Instrument for Democracy and Human Rights
ESDP	European Security and Defence Policy
EUFOR	European Union Force
EUMM	European Union Monitoring Mission
EUPM	European Union Police Mission
EUSR	European Union Special Representative
HJPC	High Judicial and Prosecutorial Councils
HLC	Humanitarian Law Center in Serbia
ICJ	International Court of Justice
ICMP	International Commission for Missing Persons
ICRC	International Committee for the Red Cross
IPA	Instrument for Pre-Accession
IPTF	International Police Task Force
NATO	North Atlantic Treaty Organization
NGO	Non-governmental Organization
OHR	Office of the High Representative
OSCE	Organization for Security and Cooperation in Europe
POWs	Prisoners of War
RDC	Research and Documentation Center in Sarajevo
RPM	Reform Process Monitoring
RS	Republika Srpska
SAA	Stabilization and Association Agreement
SAP	Stabilization and Association Process
TRC	Truth and Reconciliation Commission
USIP	United States Institute of Peace
WCC	War Crimes Chamber (Section 1) of the State Court of BiH

Part IV
Case Studies on Resolving Tensions between Peace and Justice

Transitional Justice for Burundi: A Long and Winding Road

Stef Vandeginste

Abstract This paper constitutes a summary attempt at reconstructing Burundi's approach to dealing with the past. First, a brief presentation is made of the kind of legacy of violence Burundi is facing. Next, I will summarize how in the immediate aftermath of the various cycles of violence, justice was rendered (or, more adequately, not rendered). Thirdly, a presentation will be made of what, at least at the level of public discourse – both at the national and at the international level – constituted the stated transitional justice policy for Burundi. Fourthly, the paper will show how essentially political parameters have determined the practice of transitional justice during and after the period of transition. In Sect. 6, the current state of affairs will be summarized. Section 7 briefly refers to the traditional Bashingantahe mechanism. Finally, some tentative conclusions will be formulated.

1 Introduction

In September 1996, Neil Kritz[1] started off his presentation to the conference "Creating an Agenda for Peace in Burundi" (USIP, Washington) with the following opening sentence: "Some observers would suggest that the best way to achieve reconciliation in a situation such as that present in Burundi is to leave the past in the past". Somewhat further on, he stated his own opinion on the Burundi peace negotiations process and the importance it should award to transitional justice: "If the goal, however, is something more than a tenuous, temporary pause in the violence,

S. Vandeginste
Institute of Development Policy and Management, University of Antwerp, Prinsstraat 13, 2000 Antwerp, Belgium,
e-mail: Stef.vandeginste@ua.ac.be

[1] In 1995, Neil Kritz edited the seminal work *Transitional Justice. How Emerging Democracies Reckon with Former Regimes* (Kritz 1995a), three volumes that launched the term "transitional justice" on the international scene.

K. Ambos et al. (eds.), *Building a Future on Peace and Justice: Studies on Transitional Justice, Peace and Development.*

dealing in a clear and determined manner with past atrocities is essential". And he concluded with the following recommendation for immediate implementation: "the parties should agree in principle that the subject of justice and impunity will be part of the agenda for negotiations" (Kritz 1995b).

More than a decade later, we can conclude that Kritz' recommendation has been put into practice. Important attention was paid to transitional justice during Burundi's peace negotiations process and the successive cease-fire agreements (concluded in 2000, 2003 and 2006) do pay attention to how justice should be rendered for a legacy of several decades of gross and systematic human rights violations. At the same time, however, we are also forced to conclude that, in reality, Burundi has gone through a process of political transition[2] without meaningfully dealing with its own past. Negotiations between the United Nations (UN) and the Government of Burundi (GOB) – which was put in place following democratic parliamentary elections in 2005 – about the establishment of a Special Tribunal (ST) and a Truth and Reconciliation Commission (TRC) are dragging on, facing several fundamental difficulties.

Overall, Burundi is a fascinating case in which both at the national and at the international level, the use of formal retributive justice mechanisms was strongly favoured by the large majority of political and other players, but where, in practice, there has so far been a complete failure to establish any kind of mechanism to deal with truth, accountability, reparation and/or reconciliation. The objective of reaching a negotiated settlement for the armed conflict and for more than a decade of political instability has constantly outweighed the transitional justice agenda. For mainly political reasons, no traditional dispute settlement mechanism has been used either. Compared to the past fourteen years, and despite a short flare-up of hostilities in April–May 2008, Burundi is now significantly more peaceful.[3] Despite repeated institutional stalemates (see, in more detail, Vandeginste 2008), it is also politically more stable. The truth about the past has not been told, hardly anyone had been held accountable for the crimes that were committed and victims are left without any reparation for the injury suffered. Should much more be done in order to end the long-standing culture of impunity in Burundi and in order to ensure long-term political stability? Or would any serious attempt to deal with the past inevitably mean that short-term stability is under threat and that a new cycle of violence might start? Is this the right time or is it simply too early to engage in a true transitional justice exercise for Burundi? The current position of the Burundian government comes close to the position suggested in Kritz' opening sentence of 1996 referred to above: reconciliation and forgiveness should be the top priorities, criminal justice should

[2] When using the term "political transition" here, we essentially refer to the process through which one political regime is replaced by another political regime (with, in the case of Burundi, important constitutional and institutional reforms and a significant change of the top political leadership). It is too early to tell to what extent the Burundian transition also fully meets the classical definition of "political transition" under the transition paradigm, i.e., of a transition from an authoritarian regime to a democratic system of governance. See, i.a., Carothers (2002, p. 6); O'Donnell and Schmitter (1986). Some observers have expressed concern at what they consider to be an increasingly authoritarian drift, see International Crisis Group (2006).

[3] "Peace" should here be understood as "negative peace", the absence of armed conflict of other political violence.

be no more than an auxiliary instrument to "motivate" those otherwise unwilling to firmly commit themselves to the reconciliation process.

2 Brief Historical Overview: The Nature of Burundi's Legacy of Violence

After its accession to independence (1 July 1962), Burundi has been the scene of different cycles of gross and systematic human rights violations that have decisively shaped its post-colonial identity. Although four decades of violence can certainly not be reduced to specific "incidents", there were five outbursts that were marked by remarkably intense and large-scale crimes (in 1965, 1972, 1988, 1991 and 1993 and beyond). In the report of the UN assessment mission on the establishment of an international judicial commission of inquiry for Burundi,[4] it is suggested that the future transitional justice mechanisms concentrate particularly on these five sets of events.[5]

(1) In October 1965, following important power struggles within the leading political party (Uprona) and increasingly ethnico-political tensions, a coup attempt was staged by Hutu military officers. The coup was suppressed and over one hundred Hutu military and political leaders were either physically eliminated or politically sidelined. In turn, in Muramvya province (the region most strongly associated with Hutu opposition leaders), Tutsi families were attacked, their houses set fire to and many Tutsi were killed. By means of retaliation, an estimated five thousand Hutu civilians were killed at the hands of Tutsi military and associated armed groups. In 1966, a one-party system was installed and the monarchy was overthrown through a military coup led by Minister of Defence Michel Micombero (member of a Tutsi Hima clan from Rutovu, in southern Bururi province), who became the first president of Burundi. Political power was increasingly concentrated in the hands of southern Tutsi Hima.

(2) In April 1972, a Hutu led insurgency and violent uprising was launched in the southern part of the country, with some groups of insurgents crossing the border from Zaïre and Tanzania. Government posts and military installations were at-

[4] Hereinafter referred to as the "Kalomoh report", named after the Assistant Secretary-General for Political Affairs in lead of the mission. As we will explain below, the mission was dispatched at the request of the UN Security Council (UN Doc. S/2004/72 of 26 January 2004) to consider to advisability and feasibility of establishing an international judicial commission of inquiry, as provided for in the Arusha Peace and Reconciliation Agreement of August 2000. The Kalomoh report (UN Doc. S/2005/158 of 11 March 2005) forms the basis for the ongoing negotiations between the UN and the Burundian Government on the establishment of a Truth and Reconciliation Commission and a Special Tribunal for Burundi.

[5] The term "events" (or "événements") is the euphemistic and neutral term that Burundians themselves use to describe the horrendous crimes that were committed. Alternatively, each of thc five events described above, is sometimes also referred to as "the crisis" (e.g., "la crise de 1993"), also in order to avoid having to use more contentious terms as "the 1993 genocide".

tacked and thousands of Tutsi were killed. In return, from mid-May onwards, in what appeared to be a well-orchestrated campaign of so-called "pacification", all educated and wealthy Hutu and their families were targeted. The Hutu "elite" that was targeted included teachers, priests, civil servants, skilled workers, medical personnel, agronomists, school children, etcetera. Estimates of the number of casualties of what is sometimes called a "selective genocide"[6] range from 100,000 to 300,000 Hutu. Some 200,000 Burundians went into exile (see, in more detail, Manirakiza 1992; Minority Rights Group 1974; Chrétien and Dupaquier 2007).

(3) One year after Major Pierre Buyoya (also a Tutsi Hima from Rutovu) came to power, Marangara and Ntega, two districts in the northern provinces of Ngozi and Kirundo, were the scene of an outburst of ethnic and political violence in 1988. A Hutu uprising, during which hundreds of Tutsi were killed, their houses burned and destroyed, was violently suppressed by the army, in a manner which, according to Amnesty International (1988), was aimed at repression rather than at merely restoring order. The estimated number of casualties ranged from some 5,000 to 20,000. In response to these events, President Buyoya engaged in a process of political liberalization.

(4) This process of political liberalization went too far for some (notably on Tutsi side) and too slow for others (notably on Hutu side). While a new Constitution – reintroducing multipartyism – was under preparation, a new Hutu uprising in November 1991 was followed by a severe repression of Hutu civilians suspected of sympathizing with the clandestine Palipehutu[7] movement. Lemarchand (1994, p. 154) estimated that hundreds of Tutsi civilians were killed, while the estimated number of Hutu casualties ranged from 551 (official government figure) to nearly 3,000 (Erler and Reyntjens 1992).

(5) Democratic presidential and parliamentary elections were held in June 1993. They resulted in the victory of the predominantly Hutu party Frodebu. Melchior Ndadaye became the first Hutu president of Burundi. In October 1993, Ndadaye and most of the political leadership (including the speaker and deputy speaker of the National Assembly) were killed during a coup attempt by a group of Tutsi military.[8] In an immediate reaction to the coup staged in Bujumbura, violent attacks were launched against Tutsi (or even Hutu supporters of the Uprona party), either as a spontaneous reaction by Hutu or as the result of a systematic operation – sometimes qualified as genocide[9] – organized and supported by local

[6] See United Nations, Commission on Human Rights, Sub-Commission on Prevention of Discrimination and Protection of Minorities, *Revised and updated report on the question of the prevention and punishment of the crime of genocide. Prepared by Mr. B. Whitacker*, E/CN.4/Sub.2/1985/6, 2 July 1985.

[7] *Parti pour la libération du peuple hutu.*

[8] Although the coup attempt was aborted, in particular because of the international reaction, a process of destabilisation of the institutions was irreversibly set in motion and, in July 1996, the "creeping coup" (the term was used by Reyntjens 2000, p. 14) was "officialised" by the return to power of Major Pierre Buyoya.

[9] United Nations, Security Council, *Letter dated 25 July 1996 from the Secretary-General addressed to the President of the Security Council*, S/1996/682, 22 August 1996, § 483.

authorities (many of whom were Frodebu members). This was the start of years of civil war between the army and a Hutu rebellion (primarily the CNDD-FDD[10] and the Palipehutu-FNL[11]). A peace negotiations process started in June 1998, with former Tanzanian president Julius Nyerere as mediator. After his death in October 1999, he was replaced by former South African president Nelson Mandela. As we will deal with in further detail below, the Arusha Peace and Reconciliation Agreement for Burundi was signed on 28 August 2000,[12] between the government, the national assembly and two coalitions of a total of seventeen political parties (one predominantly Hutu, the other predominantly Tutsi). The Arusha Agreement did not bring an end to the civil war. It took until 16 November 2003 before a Global Ceasefire Agreement was concluded between the transitional government and the main rebellion, the CNDD-FDD. General elections were held in 2005, resulting in a victory of the former rebel movement and the election of its chairman Pierre Nkurunziza as the new president of Burundi. On 7 September 2006, a Comprehensive Ceasefire Agreement was signed with the last remaining rebel movement, the Palipehutu-FNL.[13]

This short historical account can be concluded with the following observations on the main characteristics of the Burundian legacy of large-scale past abuses, in particular insofar as these are relevant from a transitional justice perspective.

(a) The degree of victimization is enormous. Even if only for merely logistical and quantitative reasons, telling the truth, establishing responsibilities, dealing with reparations, etcetera, is an enormous challenge.
(b) The subsequent cycles of violence together span a lengthy period of time. Since, furthermore, they are closely related to one another, isolating and disregarding some of them would be artificial. This obviously has important repercussions on the temporal mandate of any transitional justice mechanism.
(c) Each cycle of violence shows elements of repetition and reciprocity. Despite many possibly important differences between and within each of the abovementioned sets of events (for instance as far as the degree of intention and orchestration is concerned), part of the violence of each cycle repeats or is done in retaliation (or fear of repetition) of violence carried out during a previous cycle or during the new cycle.
(d) From the immediate post-colonial violence to the recently ended civil war, the past violence shares the common characteristic of being primarily political in nature. It is about control of governance functions and access to resources. Essentially political violence is based on a combination of shifting ethnic, regional and clan alliances or cleavages.

---

[10] *Conseil National pour la Défense de la Démocratie – Forces pour la Défense de la Démocratie.*

[11] *Forces Nationales de Libération.*

[12] Text available on the USIP website: http://www.usip.org/library/pa/burundi/pa_burundi_0828 2000_toc.html.

[13] One year and a half later, the implementation of this ceasefire agreement remained highly problematic. See, i.a., International Crisis Group (2007).

(e) The context in which the legacy of large-scale past abuses was committed was one of, partly, one-party authoritarian rule and, partly, (failed) democratisation evaporating into civil war.
(f) The political transition that came to an end with the 2005 elections started off through an internal reform process but was decisively shaped through compromise and negotiated settlement.
(g) From the 1993 events onwards, there was an increasingly active involvement and intervention by the international community, through different actors, including the United Nations, the Organization of African Unity, the European Union and the Regional Peace Initiative for Burundi.
(h) Written Burundian sources provide us with sometimes radically different accounts of what happened. Very factual data are presented differently, using different terminology, providing different interpretations, referring to different contextual explanatory factors, and this very often occurs along ethnic lines. This in itself is indicative of both the importance and the difficulty of truth telling.

3 Responses in the Aftermath of the Events

Current negotiations between the UN and the GOB are about a transitional justice policy and the establishment of transitional justice mechanisms (a TRC and a ST) that would – ideally – deal with the entire post-independence period. One of the stated objectives is to put an end to the cycle of impunity. This raises the question how, in the weeks, months and years after the above-mentioned events, issues of truth, accountability, reparation and reconciliation were dealt with. It is impossible to describe this in much detail here, but, generally, the following types of aftermath-responses can be distinguished. Sometimes, several of them were combined. All of them were designed and implemented at the national level, without any significant international involvement. This radically changed from the aftermath of the 1993 events onwards.

(1) In some instances, the state of emergency was declared and the government established military tribunals to replace all civil courts, including to prosecute civilians through summary trials. This was the case, for instance, in the days after 19 October 1965, when a coup attempt was staged by a group of Hutu military.[14]
(2) On several occasions, amnesty legislation was adopted in order (not) to deal with the past. In some cases, the amnesty was collective but nevertheless one-sided, benefiting only those perpetrators that were friendly to the regime in power. In other cases, under the stated objective of national reconciliation, the amnesty

[14] Arrêté royal N° 001/792 du 20 octobre 1965 instaurant le régime militaire et d'exception dans toutes les provinces du Royaume, *Bulletin Officiel du Burundi (B.O.B.)* 12 (1965) 845; Arrêté-loi N° 001/795 du 21 octobre 1965 modifiant l'arrêté-loi N° 001/791 du 20 octobre 1965 déterminant les règles applicables au régime militaire et d'exception, *B.O.B.* 12 (1965) 841.

legislation was more or less balanced and benefited members from different ethnic and political groups. In most cases, amnesty was limited to so-called political offences, although these were defined very broadly. In all cases, the amnesty legislation prevented the truth from being told. Reference can be made here to amnesty laws of 1 September 1962,[15] 27 November 1967,[16] 30 August 1990[17] and 9 September 1993.[18]

(3) On various occasions, grossly unfair trials were instrumentalized to eliminate (politically but sometimes also physically) political opponents, such as the trials against Tutsi Banyaruguru, opponents of the Tutsi Hima, for an alleged conspiracy in 1971. Thousands of Hutu suspects were arrested – very often on an arbitrary basis – and spent years in pre-trial detention – almost systematically in violation of the Code of Criminal Procedure – for their alleged involvement in the 1993 massacres. What constituted a systematic and repressive abuse of criminal procedure for the suspects and their relatives, was – at the same time – by others experienced and denounced as a failure to render justice to victims and their families.

(4) Very often, gross and systematic human rights violations were followed by *de facto* impunity, in particular as far as those responsible at the top political level or in the military hierarchy were concerned. This was the case after the events of 1965 and 1988, both as far as Hutu as well as Tutsi casualties were concerned. The massacres of Hutu in 1972 probably constitute the most striking example of this long-standing culture of impunity.

(5) At the institutional level, there has been a quasi-permanent control of the government on the judicial branch. Taking into account the constitutional context of the time, this was not even all that surprising. Under the constitutions of 1974 and 1981, the judicial branch was put under the control of the Uprona party. It was not until 1992 (at the same time as when multi-partyism was introduced) that the independence of the judicial branch was laid down in the Constitution. The interference by the executive branch became furthermore apparent in the activities of the commissions that were put in place to deal with land disputes and property restitution issues for returnees.

International concern for the lack of truth, accountability and reparation in Burundi was largely absent during nearly three decades. In particular after the 1993 events, the attention of the international community for Burundi gradually increased. Its top priority, however, was to negotiate an end to the violent conflict, through power-sharing arrangements.[19] Transitional justice, and in particular the

---

[15] Arrêté royal N° 1/80 du 1er septembre 1962 portant actes de clémence à l'occasion de l'indépendance du pays du Burundi, *B.O.B.* 8 (1962) 195.

[16] Décret-Loi N° 1/119 du 27 novembre 1967 portant actes de clémence en faveur de détenus et auteurs de certaines infractions, *B.O.B.* (1968) 51.

[17] Décret-Loi N° 1/034/90 du 30 août 1990 portant mesure d'amnistie en faveur de prévenus ou condamnés de certaines infractions, *B.O.B.* (1990) 287.

[18] Loi du 9 septembre 1993 portant amnistie, *B.O.B.* (1993) 543.

[19] Three days after the coup of 21 October 1993, UN Secretary-General Boutros-Ghali sent his Special Envoy on a good offices mission to promote the return of the country to constitutional rule.

establishment of mechanisms to prepare for the criminal prosecution of politicians, top government army officials and rebel leaders for their involvement in the large-scale violence, was time and again delayed in order not to undermine ongoing efforts to negotiate short-term stability. Several missions were sent by the UN, all of which issued reports, most of which were made public with considerably delay and none of which ever received any further follow-up.[20] The Government Convention of 10 September 1994, which was signed by most of Burundi's political parties and which essentially rendered the 1992 Constitution and the outcome of the 1993 elections meaningless, had explicitly called for the establishment of an international judicial commission by the UN to investigate the 1993 events.[21] Against the background of a radicalisation of (armed/rebel) forces at both Hutu and Tutsi side, this clause was never put into practice. This embryonic transitional justice process in response to the 1993 events was decisively aborted when a new coup in July 1996 formalised the "creeping coup" that had been taking place since October 1993 and brought back Pierre Buyoya to power.

4 Burundi's Stated Transitional Justice Policy

Burundi did never officially decide to forget the past. There was no publicly stated discourse in favour of forgetting and no formally declared "pact of silence" that was openly advocated as the most viable strategy to ensure a peaceful and stable future of unity and reconciliation. On the contrary, on various occasions, starting with the above-cited Government Convention of September 1994 and culminating in the Arusha Peace and Reconciliation Agreement of August 2000, the use of (national and international) formal retributive mechanisms was strongly favoured and agreed upon, by most – if not all – political parties, by the successive transitional governments and by the international mediators. Nevertheless, in practice, there has been a complete failure to establish any kind of truth, accountability and/or reparation mechanism. Before summarizing Burundi's stated transitional justice policy and contrasting it with its transitional justice practice (in Sect. 5), we will, by way

After the mission of the Special Envoy, the UN SG appointed a Special Representative for Burundi, Mr. Ould Abdallah who took up his duties on 25 November 1993.

[20] Reference is made here to the following reports: United Nations, Security Council, *Report of the Preparatory Fact-finding mission to Burundi to the Secretary-General*, S/1995/157, 24 February 1995 (also known as the Ake-Huslid report); United Nations, Security Council, *Letter dated 7 September 1994 from the members of the Security Council mission to Burundi addressed to the President of the Security Council*, S/1994/1039, 9 September 1994; United Nations, Security Council, *Report of the Security Council mission to Burundi on 10 and 11 February 1995*, S/1995/163, 28 February 1995; United Nations, Security Council, *Report of the Special Envoy appointed to examine the feasibility of establishing either a commission on the truth or a judicial fact-finding commission in Burundi*, S/1995/631, 28 July 1995 (also known as the Nikken report); United Nations, Security Council, *Letter dated 25 July 1996 from the Secretary-General addressed to the President of the Security Council*, S/1996/682, 22 August 1996.

[21] The text of the Government Convention was reproduced in Guichaoua (1995, pp. 588–598).

of an introduction, briefly refer to Jelena Subotic' analysis of why states adopt certain policies and models of transitional justice. This may help in understanding and explaining the gap between Burundi's stated policy (or public discourse) and actual practice.

4.1 Introductory Note: Why was a Transitional Justice Policy Adopted?

In her paper "Hijacked Justice: Domestic Appropriation of International Norms", Subotic argued that:

> the motivation of states to adopt international models of transitional justice has changed over time. The transitional justice norm – that posits that war crimes and massive human rights abuses must be dealt with in a proper legal setting and not through "victors' justice" or impunity – was institutionalized in large part as the result of a strong domestic demand for transitional justice in countries like Argentina and South Africa. However, as this norm began to diffuse through the international system, states began to adopt international justice but now for very different reasons – to achieve international legitimacy, to get rid of domestic political opponents, to appease international coercion, or out of uncertainty. (Subotic 2005, p. 2)

Without analyzing this aspect in much further detail here, it is clear that Burundi's stated transitional justice policy was not the result of a strong domestic demand. This is not so much due to the fact that there was no such demand – it would require further anthropological research to verify this – but because, assuming that the demand were there, the channels through which society at large might participate in the policy debate about transitional justice were largely absent. Burundi's stated transitional justice policy – laid down in peace agreements and partially incorporated in national law – was largely based on the other factors mentioned by Subotic: (a) comparative experiences of other countries and the international trend to incorporate human rights and transitional justice concerns into peace agreements in order to legitimize negotiated settlements, (b) the growing activism and lobbying by international[22] groups (including non-governmental human rights organisations) to end Burundi's tradition of impunity, (c) political calculations by negotiating parties and also by mediators. Some further explanation is needed to explain this third element.

For the international mediators, the particular transitional justice arrangement that was laid down in the peace agreements and their various protocols had at least one major advantage. It enabled them to postpone the "thorny" issue of accountability (and punishment) for human rights abuses. From this particular perspective, a transitional justice approach was designed that could, at the same time, give international legitimacy to the negotiated peace settlement and be used as delaying tactics in order not to jeopardize the negotiated settlement.

[22] It should be noted that these concerns were also voiced at the national level through a (relatively small) group of Bujumbura-based civil society organisations.

For the negotiating parties, transitional justice was among the instruments used in order to maintain, attain or reinforce political power. Two examples may illustrate this.

(i) During the negotiations process, the predominantly Tutsi parties urged that transitional justice mechanisms be put in place before elections were held. This would have at least two favourable effects. First, elections would be delayed, at a time when the predominantly Tutsi parties did not have much reason to hope for an electoral victory.[23] Secondly, it could reasonably be expected that a number of Hutu politicians, in particular those who had joined the armed rebel movements, were to fear for criminal prosecution and, as a result, the end of their political career.
(ii) For the leaders of the armed rebellion, the transitional justice arrangement needed to be designed in such a way as to temporarily protect them against possible prosecution for war crimes (or other crimes of international law). Furthermore, they had every reason to belief that, after the elections, the political context would drastically change[24] and that they would have much more control on the (possible) implementation of the stated transitional justice policy. The latter scenario indeed materialized. We will elaborate this in more detail below.

4.2 What Transitional Justice Policy was Adopted?

The Burundian peace process has left a "complex documentary trail",[25] composed of pre-negotiation agreements, substantive agreements and implementation agreements between various (political and/or armed) parties to the conflict. Several of them contain provisions that deal with transitional justice.

Table 1 implicitly refers to some of the politically relevant aspects of the successive peace agreements.

First of all, while, in legal terms, the Burundian government is a signatory to all of the three agreements and its constitutive parts, the dominant political actors within the government are fundamentally different for each of the three. At the time of signing of the Arusha Agreement, the government was politically dominated by the Buyoya regime installed following the July 1996 coup d'Etat, with, however, important modifications brought about by the internal partnership for peace. At the

[23] In 1993, the elections had resulted in an overwhelming victory of the predominantly Hutu party Frodebu.

[24] This was true despite the important consociational power-sharing arrangements that were laid down in the Arusha Agreement, in the transitional Constitution of 28 October 2001 and in the post-transition Constitution of 18 March 2005. See in more detail Vandeginste (2006).

[25] The Burundian peace process nicely meets the description by Christine Bell who noted that "Most peace processes leave a complex documentary trail, as different issues are dealt with at different stages, as political actors come and go, as agreements are accepted and rejected, and as agreements themselves shape a conflict, and its central issues mutate accordingly" (Bell 2000, p. 20).

Table 1

Signatories	Date of signature	Title
1. The Government (of President P. Buyoya) 2. The National Assembly 3. A total of 17 political parties	28/08/2000 Arusha	*Arusha Peace and Reconciliation Agreement for Burundi*, made up of: – Protocol I. Nature of the Burundi conflict, problems of genocide and exclusion and their solutions – Protocol II. Democracy and Good Governance – Protocol III. Peace and Security for All – Protocol IV. Reconstruction and Development – Protocol V. Guarantees on Implementation of the Agreement
1. The Transitional Government (of President D. Ndayizeye) 2. The CNDD-FDD (of P. Nkurunziza)	16/11/2003 Dar Es Salaam	*Global Ceasefire Agreement* (GCA), including as integral parts:
	02/02/2002	– The Ceasefire Agreement
	27/01/2003	– The Pretoria Protocol
	08/10/2003	– The Pretoria Protocol on political, defence and security power-sharing
	02/11/2003	– The Pretoria Protocol on outstanding issues
	02/11/2003	– The Forces Technical Agreement
1. The Government (of President P. Nkurunziza) 2. Palipehutu-FNL (of A. Rwasa)	07/09/2006 Dar Es Salaam	*Comprehensive Ceasefire Agreement* (CCA), including as an integral part:
	18/06/2006	– The Dar Es Salaam Agreement of Principles towards Lasting Peace, Security and Stability

time of signing of the GCA, the Burundian state was represented by a transitional government, led by President Domitien Ndayizeye (Hutu, Frodebu). At the time of signing of the CCA, the Burundian government was dominated by the former rebel movement CNDD-FDD. In particular from the side of predominantly Tutsi political parties, this has been the subject of major criticism. The CCA constitutes, in their view, an agreement among allied anti-Tutsi rebel movements, namely the CNDD-FDD and Palipehutu-FNL.

Secondly, closely related to the above, the chronological order of the three agreements is not a coincidence. The transitional government concluding the GCA was put into place as a result of the Arusha Agreement. In turn, the CCA was signed as a result of negotiations conducted by a government that emerged from the elections that were held after the signing of the GCA.

As a result, the political willingness to implement the transitional justice provisions under the Arusha Agreement is not necessarily the same for those who negotiated and signed the GCA and the CCA. Particularly because of the new post-electoral political context, this has indeed turned out to be a relevant issue in practice, despite the fact that the GCA explicitly refers to the Arusha Agreement as being part of one overall agreement.

We will, in our analysis, refer to the peace agreements[26] and to subsequent legal and institutional reforms that were adopted to implement the agreed transitional justice approach.

4.2.1 Accountability Legislation and Mechanisms

The Arusha Agreement considered combating the impunity of crimes as one of the solutions for the Burundian conflict. It was agreed in Prot. I, Chap. II, that legislation needed to be enacted to counter genocide, war crimes and other crimes against humanity, as well as other human rights violations (art. 6, para. 9).[27] More specifically, the Agreement stipulated that the transitional government request the establishment by the UN Security Council of an international judicial commission of inquiry on genocide, war crimes and crimes against humanity. This commission would be responsible for (a) investigating and establishing the facts relating to the period from independence to the date of signature of the Agreement; (b) classifying them; (c) determining those responsible. Furthermore, the Arusha Agreement stipulated that the government would request the establishment of an international criminal tribunal by the UN Security Council to try and punish those responsible "should the findings of the report point to the existence of acts of genocide, war crimes and other crimes against humanity". On 24 July 2002, nearly two years after

[26] As far as their legal status is concerned, it should be noted that these peace agreements have been adopted as law by the National Assembly and therefore constitute a legal source of Burundi's transitional justice.

[27] As agreed, national legislation was adopted to integrate the crimes of genocide, crimes against humanity and war crimes in Burundi's national criminal law (*Loi* N° *1/004 du 8 mai 2003 portant répression du crime de génocide, des crimes contre l'humanité et des crimes de guerre, B.O.B.*, 5 (1 May 2003) 136). With explicit reference to the Statute of the International Criminal Court – which Burundi ratified on 21 September 2004 – and other international human rights conventions, the law of 8 May 2003 defines the above-mentioned crimes as criminal offences under Burundian criminal law (art. 2–4).The law also defines the criminal sentences applicable to those found responsible (art. 8–18). The law of 8 May 2003 is, however, because of its final provisions, not an instrument to deal with past violations but solely creates the possibility to prosecute crimes of international law committed after its promulgation. In its final provision, the law of 8 May 2003 integrates the Arusha Agreement insofar as it relates to crimes of genocide, crimes against humanity and war crimes committed prior to the promulgation of the law: "*l'enquête et la qualification des actes de génocide, des crimes de guerre et des autres crimes contre l'humanité commis au Burundi depuis le 1 juillet 1962 jusqu'à la promulgation de la présente loi, seront confiés à la Commission d'Enquête Judiciaire Internationale*" (art. 33, para. 1). Should the report of the Commission conclude that crimes of international law were committed during that period, the government will call upon the UN to establish an international criminal tribunal for Burundi (art. 33, para. 2).

the signature of the Arusha Agreement and some nine months after the establishment of a transitional government, interim President Buyoya addressed a letter to the UN Secretary-General, requesting the establishment of an international judicial commission of inquiry for Burundi.[28] Nearly one year later, during a mission of the UN Security Council to Central Africa, in June 2003, the request was discussed with the Burundian government. The report[29] of that mission noted that "the Government asked the mission to respond positively to the request of the transitional Government for the establishment of an international judicial commission of inquiry, as provided for in the Arusha Agreement, to help Burundi put an end to impunity" (para. 39). The mission recommended that urgent attention be paid to putting an end to impunity in Burundi and that the Security Council "assist Burundi in this regard and that it consider carefully the Government's request for the establishment of the international judicial commission of inquiry as provided for in the Arusha Agreement" (para. 44). It was not until 23 January 2004 that the UN Security Council, in response to the letter by President Buyoya, approved the terms of reference of a mission to be sent to Burundi.[30] These terms of reference were not those of the international judicial commission of inquiry requested by the Burundian government, but of an assessment mission by the UN Secretariat, of which the objective was "to consider the advisability and feasibility of establishing an international judicial commission of inquiry for Burundi, as requested by the President of Burundi" (para. 1). Among the subjects mentioned for consideration by the assessment mission was the division of competencies between the requested international judicial commission of inquiry and the national truth and reconciliation commission provided for under the Arusha Peace Agreement. The timing and the delay in dealing with President Buyoya's request were clearly no coincidence. The Security Council decision came one month after South African Vice-President Jacob Zuma, the main facilitator of the Regional Peace Initiative on Burundi, declared to the members of the Council that "We can now say without fear of contradiction that the Burundi peace process has entered a decisive and irreversible stage".[31] The timing was fully in line with the UN's earlier strategy on Burundi, of prioritizing (at least in chronological terms) peace and political stability over the transitional justice process.[32] We will deal in more detail with the report of the UN assessment mission below.

---

[28] The Transitional Constitution of 28 October 2001 reaffirmed these provisions of the Arusha Agreement (art. 228). Neither the GCA nor the CCA altered or supplemented any of the provisions of the Arusha Agreement relating to this specific issue.

[29] United Nations, Security Council, *Report of the Security Council mission to Central Africa, 7 to 16 June 2003*, S/2003/653, 17 June 2003.

[30] United Nations, Security Council, *Letter dated 26 January 2004 from the President of the Security Council addressed to the Secretary-General*, S/2004/72, 26 January 2004.

[31] United Nations, Security Council, *Report of the meeting of 4 December 2003*, S/PV.4876, 3.

[32] According to the former Minister of Human Rights Eugène Nindorera, "*A mon avis, je pense que l'ONU n'est pas du tout pressé. Je doute même de sa volonté de mettre en place une CEJI et surtout un Tribunal pénal international pour le Burundi. Comme une enquête sérieuse devra nécessairement mettre en cause les signataires des compromis négociés durement avec son concours, l'ONU peut ne pas vouloir prendre le risque de déstabiliser un équilibre et une situation déjà bien fragiles*" (Nindorera 2003, p. 13).

4.2.2 A Truth and Reconciliation Commission

Prot. I, Chap. II of the Arusha Agreement provided for the establishment of a National Truth and Reconciliation Commission (TRC) (art. 8), with three main functions: (a) investigation, (b) arbitration and reconciliation, and (c) clarification of history. First, the Commission was charged with bringing to light and establishing the truth regarding the serious acts of violence committed during the cyclical conflicts committed between 1 July 1962 and 28 August 2000. The Commission was also requested to classify the crimes and establish the responsibilities, as well as the identity of the perpetrators and the victims. This provision endowed the Commission with an important component of accountability and raises the issue of how the Commission would be able to interact with judicial investigative bodies, an issue that would continue to complicate the negotiations on Burundi's transitional justice process for years to come. It was furthermore specified that the Commission would not have the powers to classify acts of genocide, crimes against humanity and war crimes (art. 8, para. 1, (a) in fine). The latter provision has an obvious impact on the Commission's truth telling potential: how to tell the truth about events without using the appropriate terms? Second, in order to promote reconciliation, it was stipulated that the Commission shall, upon completion of its investigations, (a) adopt or propose to the competent institutions those measures that are likely to promote reconciliation and forgiveness, (b) order indemnification or restoration of disputed property, or (c) propose any political, social or other measures it deems appropriate. This provision left some ambiguity as to the powers of the Commission to merely recommend or to actually decide on measures in a wide range of areas, including those related to reparation. One of the latter measures the Commission might possibly find appropriate was explicitly mentioned in the Agreement: "the transitional National Assembly may pass a law or laws providing a framework for granting an amnesty consistent with international law for such political crimes as it or the National Truth and Reconciliation Commission may find appropriate" (art. 8, para. 1 (b) in fine). This provision, as well, turned out to be one among the thorny issues for the negotiations process on Burundi's transitional justice. Finally, the Commission was to be given the responsibility to clarify the entire history of Burundi, "going back as far as possible in order to inform Burundians about their past", with the overall purpose "to rewrite Burundi's history so that all Burundians can interpret it in the same way" (art. 8, para. 1 (c)). In December 2004, a law on the establishment of a national TRC was promulgated.[33] In general, the TRC was endowed with the mandate and the powers agreed upon in the Arusha Agreement. In article 2, it was reaffirmed that the TRC did not have the powers to legally qualify offences as being acts of genocide, crimes against humanity or war crimes. Article 3 provided for the TRC to be operational during a period of two years, with the possibility of extending its mandate for one year or more. On the possibility to propose an amnesty law in order to promote reconciliation, the law reaffirmed the principle laid down

---

[33] *Loi* N° *1/018 du 27 décembre 2004 portant missions, composition, organisation et fonctionnement de la Commission Nationale pour la Vérité et la Réconciliation*, *B.O.B.*, N°12bis/2004, 1 December 2004, 924.

in the Arusha Agreement: "*La Commission peut déterminer les crimes politiques pour lesquels une loi d'amnistie pourrait être votée*" (art. 4, para. 1). However, it was specifically mentioned in a second paragraph that genocide, crimes against humanity and war crimes could not be amnestied: "*Les crimes de génocide, les crimes contre l'humanité et les crimes de guerre ne sont past amnistiables*" (art. 4, para. 2). The law of 27 December 2004 was never implemented and a TRC was never put in place. The CCA of 7 September 2006 stipulated that the TRC needed to be given a new name: "the Commission of Truth, Forgiveness and Reconciliation" ("*Commission Vérité, Pardon et Réconciliation*"). Although the CCA failed to elaborate on the specific implications of this newly named Commission, it is clear that the general objective had changed. Its mission was defined as bringing to light the facts and establish the responsibilities of the various actors ("*dégager les responsabilités des uns et des autres*"), in order to promote forgiveness and reconciliation among Burundians. Terminology under the Arusha Agreement, including "crimes" and "perpetrators", was no longer mentioned, which, at the very least, was indicative of a different vision on the role of the commission.

4.2.3 The Kalomoh Proposal

The report of the UN assessment mission (which is commonly referred to as the Kalomoh report) was submitted to the Security Council on 11 March 2005.[34] The Kalomoh report noted that the delineation between the mandate and the powers of the national TRC and the IJCI as envisaged by the Arusha Agreement was blurred. As a result, there was a serious risk of overlapping jurisdictions, contradictory findings and a waste of resources. This led the assessment mission to the recommendation that a combination of both mechanisms was preferable, through the creation of a single truth commission of mixed (national/international) composition (para. 31). The mandate of the TC would, in accordance with the Arusha Agreement, consist of (a) establishing the facts and determine the causes and nature of the conflict in Burundi, (b) classify the crimes committed since independence and identify those responsible for crimes of genocide, crimes against humanity and war crimes committed during the various cycles of conflict. The TC would be composed of two units. The research unit would be responsible for establishing the causes and facts of the conflict and the nature of the crimes committed during the various cycles of violence. The investigative unit would be responsible for investigating the crimes and identifying those responsible. It was added that "while the investigation conducted by the truth commission would not be a criminal or judicial investigation, investigators would conduct their information-gathering activities in full respect of the rights of witnesses and due process of law" (para. 56, c). In addition to a national TC of mixed composition, the Kalomoh report also recommended the establishment of a judicial accountability mechanism in the form of a Special Chamber within the

[34] United Nations, Security Council, *Letter dated 11 March 2005 from the Secretary-General addressed to the President of the Security Council*, S/2005/158, 11 March 2005.

court system of Burundi, composed of national and foreign judges. The report found inspiration in the model of the War Crimes Chamber which, at that time, was in the process of being established in the State Court of Bosnia and Herzegovina. It was proposed that the Special Chamber (SC) have jurisdiction to prosecute those bearing the greatest responsibility for the crime of genocide, crimes against humanity and war crimes. Its temporal mandate would be limited to specific phases of the conflict and would include, as a minimum, the events between 1972 and 1993 (para. 61). The report also warned that a follow-up on the side of the UN was essential: "It is the view of the mission that the United Nations can no longer engage in establishing commissions of inquiry and disregard their recommendations without seriously undermining the credibility of the organisation in promoting justice and the rule of law" (para. 72). It was therefore recommended that the Security Council mandate the Secretary-General to engage in negotiations with the government on the practical implementation of the proposal to establish both mechanisms. On 20 June 2005, the UN Security Council unanimously adopted resolution 1606. Three pre-ambular paragraphs indicated the approach which inspired the SC. First, the SC expressed the view that, in order to consolidate peace and reconciliation in Burundi, it was necessary (a) to establish the truth, (b) to investigate the crimes, (c) to identify and bring to justice those bearing the greatest responsibility for crimes of genocide, crimes against humanity and war crimes committed in Burundi since independence, (d) to bring an end to the culture of impunity, in Burundi and in the region of the Great Lakes of Africa as a whole. Furthermore, the SC emphasized that appropriate international assistance was needed to help the Burundian people end impunity, promote reconciliation and establish a society and government under a rule of law. Finally, the SC acknowledged the crucial importance of reconciliation for peace and national unity in Burundi and shared the view that a future truth commission should contribute to it. On that basis, the SC requested the Secretary-General "to initiate negotiations with the government and consultations with all Burundian parties concerned on how to implement his recommendations, and to report to the Council by 30 September 2005 on details of implementation, including costs, structures and time frame" (operative paragraph 1) and decided to remain seized of the matter (operative paragraph 2).

Two rounds of negotiations between the Government of Burundi and the UN have so far taken place, in March 2006 and in March 2007. At the time of writing, the negotiations process is suspended while national consultations on the establishment of transitional justice mechanisms are being prepared. Tough initially planned for early 2008, the launching of these consultations has been delayed, mainly as a result of fundamental disagreements between the UN and the Government. We will return to the difficulties met during the negotiations process in Sect. 6 when presenting the current state of affairs. First, in Sect. 5, we will confront the stated transitional justice policy (including the agreement to establish the above-mentioned mechanisms) with actual transitional justice practice.

5 Burundi's Transitional Justice Practice

Between August 2000 and today, none of the above-mentioned agreements and proposals has been implemented in practice. Other provisions, however, have determined Burundi's actual transitional justice practice.

5.1 Temporary Immunity

In its Prot. II (Democracy and Good Governance), Chap. II (Transitional Arrangements), the Arusha Agreement contained a provision stating that the national assembly – as one of the signatories of the Agreement – agreed to enact, within four weeks following its signature, "such legislation as is necessary for the granting of temporary immunity against prosecution for politically motivated crimes committed prior to the signature of the Agreement" (art. 22, para. 22, (c)).[35] While recognizing the need to fight impunity (both during the period of transition and after the end of the transition), it was at the same time felt that a temporary shelter against criminal prosecution needed to be inserted, which was done through the provision on the granting of a so-called provisional or temporary immunity. Several reasons may help to explain why this was done. First, the Arusha Agreement did not put an end to the civil war nor to the peace negotiations process. It was clear that additional negotiations would be necessary, both on the implementation of Arusha Agreement and on several issues that were left unresolved, as well as with those rebel movements that had not signed the Agreement. Secondly, several political leaders had left the country and lived in exile. As a condition for their return, they requested a guarantee that they would not be prosecuted by what they considered to be a one-sided and arbitrarily operating judicial system. In order to implement this part of the Arusha Agreement, the law of 21 November 2003[36] defined immunity as the suspension of criminal prosecution: beneficiaries could not be arrested, indicted or prosecuted ("*arrêté, inculpé ou poursuivi*") during the period of the immunity (art. 1 and 3).

Article 2 of GCA Pretoria Protocol on Outstanding Matters of November 2003 stipulated that:

> 2.1. The parties agreed that all leaders and combatants of the CNDD-FDD shall receive temporary immunity; 2.2. They agreed that this shall also apply to the security forces of

[35] Art. 22, para. 22 (c) left considerable ambiguity, as the Arusha Agreement did not specify what should be understood as "politically motivated crimes". Neither did it define the scope of the immunity, nor its "temporary" (or, according to the French version, "provisional") character. These issues were left to the legislator to determine.

[36] *Loi* N° *1/022 du 21 novembre 2003 portant immunité provisoire de poursuites judiciaires en faveur des leaders politiques rentrant de l'exil*, *B.O.B.*, N° 11/2003, 1 November 2003, 780. The adoption of the law on 27 August 2003 by the National Assembly had given rise to a major controversy. A group of 28 members of parliament, calling themselves "a coalition of MP's against genocide" boycotted the vote. Other opposition members considered the law to be part of a political deal between Uprona and Frodebu to grant themselves "*a kind of auto-amnesty*" (IRIN 2003).

> the Government of Burundi; 2.3. They agreed to establish a Joint Commission, which shall study individual cases of civilians currently serving sentence to determine that they should be granted temporary immunity.

There are some remarkable developments when comparing the notion of provisional immunity under the Arusha Agreement and under the GCA. Firstly, there is no longer any restriction *ratione materiae* to "politically motivated crimes". Secondly, there is an explicit reference to the scope *ratione personae*: the temporary immunity would benefit all leaders and combatants of the CNDD-FDD as well as members of Burundi's security forces. Thirdly, the immunity would also benefit to civilians already serving sentence, when a Joint Commission considered them to be eligible. The latter provision adds to the already ambiguous nature of the immunity. While, normally, immunity (both personal and functional immunity of individuals as well as state immunity) constitutes a safeguard against criminal prosecution, and, more generally, immunity from jurisdiction, the intention of the signatories of the GCA was clearly to extend immunity also to people already serving sentences as a result of a completed criminal trial. The text of the GCA remained unclear on how exactly this should be understood. In order to clarify and implement the latter provision of the GCA, a decree was adopted on 23 March 2004.[37] The decree established a commission, charged with identifying CNDD-FDD combatants, their "collaborators" as well as members of the security forces in detention and eligible for a provisional immunity in accordance with the GCA (art. 1). The notion of collaborators was defined in article 2 and covered a broad range of persons, including: people who supplied weapons or other equipment, people who fed combatants, people who transported combatants, ammunition or equipment, people who incited the population to join the rebel movement, people who provided information, etcetera. Members of the security forces were further defined as being "in particular" those army soldiers fighting rebel fighters, members of the police force who supported the army as well as members of the "gardiens de la paix" militia (art. 3). The decree also explicitly stated that combatants and military guilty of acts of genocide or crimes against humanity were excluded from the provisional immunity (art. 6). However important as a statement of principle, in practice, article 6 was meaningless, since no detainee in Burundi's prisons had ever been convicted for genocide or crimes against humanity. Only people suspected of or convicted for offences committed after 24 November 1994 (the date of creation of the CNDD-FDD) were eligible for immunity (art. 5). This meant that those detained for their (suspected) involvement in the massacres of 1993 were not concerned by the decree. Many persons, including those who under the terms of the decree did not fall within the scope of application, put all their hope in the work of the commission, rather than in the justice system. By the end of 2004, some 539 people had been released on the basis of this decree and of the work of the commission established the same day (quoted in UNDP 2005, p. 90).

[37] *Décret* N° *100/023 du 23 mars 2004 portant modalités d'application de l'immunité provisoire prévue par l'Accord Global de Cessez-le-feu du 16 novembre 2003.*

The difficulty with applying the notion of immunity to people who have already been found guilty of a criminal offence was further exacerbated by the introduction and legal treatment of another notion, that of political prisoners. This culminated, in early 2006, in the release (on the basis of a provisional immunity) of approximately 3,300 political prisoners, primarily those suspected of or convicted for involvement in the 1993 massacres.

5.2 The Release of "Political Prisoners"

The replacement of the late Tanzanian president Julius Nyerere by former South African president Nelson Mandela gave rise to an increasingly central role of the issue of political prisoners[38] during the negotiations process between January and August 2000. International Crisis Group convincingly demonstrated how diametrically opposed positions on the prisoners' issue nearly jeopardized the whole peace process (International Crisis Group 2000, pp. 40–58). On the one hand, there was CNDD-FDD leader Jean-Bosco Ndayikengurukiye who considered many (if not most) of Burundi's prisoners to be "people who voted for democracy". Their release was a pre-condition for his movement to participate in the negotiations. On the other hand, the government stated that Burundi's prisoners and pre-trial detainees were people found guilty or suspected by Burundi's justice system of having committed serious crimes, including homicide, rape, theft, arson, etcetera (in other words, they were "common law criminals", "criminels de droit commun").[39]

In Chap. II of Protocol II of the Arusha Agreement, it was agreed that:

> the Transitional Government shall within 30 days of the commencement of the transition establish a commission under the chairmanship of a judge to investigate, as a matter of urgency, and to make recommendations on: (i) the conditions in jail, the treatment of prisoners and the training and conditions of service of warders, (ii) the release of prisoners awaiting trial in respect of whom there has been an undue delay in the prosecution of their cases, (iii) the existence of and release of any political prisoners (art. 15, para. 20).

One month after its establishment by law on 30 October 2001, the transitional government created the commission, which would soon become known among prisoners and the general public as "the political prisoners' commission" (much to the dissatisfaction of several of its members, who insisted that the very existence of political prisoners remained to be determined by the commission itself).[40] The

[38] When using the term "political prisoners" throughout this section, we merely rely on the terminology used in the various sources mentioned, without agreeing or disagreeing with the qualification of the persons involved as political prisoners.

[39] As of March 2000, Burundi's prison population totalled 9,173 persons, including 6,717 pre-trial detainees and 2,456 convicts. The official capacity of the prison system was limited to 3,650 people. The very large majority of detainees were Hutu, suspected of or convicted for their involvement in the 1993 massacres of Tutsi and/or their support to the armed rebel movements.

[40] Author's interviews conducted in September 2004.

government appointed eight members[41] and "took notice" of the members proposed by the UN. The commission was chaired by a French judge, Philippe Chemithe. The commission report noted, first of all, that not only in the Burundian context, the definition of a political prisoner or a political crime was far from unequivocal. It also found that the issue of political prisoners was particularly divisive in Burundian society, already characterized by important other ethnic and socio-political cleavages. Furthermore the commission noted that there was an important degree of confusion and assimilation between the concepts of political prisoner on the one hand, and, on the other, impunity, absence of guilt, infringement of victims' rights, oblivion, pardon, amnesty, etcetera.[42] The Commission failed to find a consensus on how to define political prisoners in the specific Burundian context and to formulate clear recommendations. The government decided to make use, within the limits of the law, of provisions allowing for a provisional release of pre-trial detainees ("*mise en liberté provisoire*") and a conditional release of convicts ("*libération conditionnelle*"). In all, by the end of 2004, around 3,200 persons had been released, including those benefiting from provisional immunity.

In the GCA of November 2003, the term "political prisoners" was not explicitly used. However, the agreement laid down in the Pretoria Protocol on Outstanding Matters, "to establish a Joint Commission, which shall study individual cases of civilians currently serving sentence to determine that they should be granted temporary immunity" (art. 2, para. 3) is obviously quite directly linked connected to the issue of political prisoners. Indeed, shortly after the Nkurunziza government was sworn in (in August 2005, after the parliamentary elections), a new commission was established through presidential decree on 7 November 2005, in charge of identifying political prisoners in all of Burundi's prisons. A presidential decree of 3 January 2006 decided that all those identified by the commission would benefit from a provisional immunity. Three ministerial orders by Minister of Justice Niragira gave further effect to this decree, as a result of which around 3,300 persons (nearly all of them Hutu) were released. The Minister motivated the measure by referring to the necessity of a national reconciliation and underscored that the release was in all cases provisional, since all released persons would need to be heard by the Special Chamber or the TRC that would be set up as a result of the negotiations between the Government and the UN (Ndikumana 2006). On 9 March 2006,

[41] *Décret* N° *100/028 du 30 novembre 2001 portant nomination des membres burundais de la Commission indépendante chargée d'étudier les questions relatives aux prisonniers conformément au paragraphe 20 de l'article 15 du protocole II de l'Accord d'Arusha pour la paix et la réconciliation au Burundi*, *B.O.B.*, N° 11ter/2001, 1 November 2001, 1609. It is worth noting that one of the members of the Commission was Ms. Clotilde Niragira, at that time a lawyer and member of the bar, who later became Minister of Justice in the Nkurunziza government after the 2005 elections and who, as of early 2006, decided on the release of some 3,300 prisoners through ministerial order.

[42] Commission indépendante chargée d'étudier les questions relatives aux prisonniers, *Rapport de mission*, (Bujumbura, 14 February 2002) 36.

three civil society groups introduced a procedure before the Constitutional Court requesting the annulment of the two ministerial orders on the basis of a violation of article 48 of the Constitution and of the International Covenant on Civil and Political Rights (OAG, FORSC, Ligue Iteka 2006). According to OAG, FORSC and Ligue Iteka, the ministerial orders constitute an "amnesty in disguise" for grave violations of human rights, which is contrary to national and international law. In accordance with article 230, para. 2 of the Constitution, the request was declared inadmissible by the Constitutional Court.[43]

6 Current State of Affairs

The above analysis of Burundi's long and winding road towards transitional justice shows a remarkable discrepancy between stated policy and actual practice. Notwithstanding the principled stance against impunity that was reaffirmed time and time again, Burundi has been remarkably creative in circumventing – at least temporarily – the amnesty prohibition for crimes of international law by combining three instruments: (a) the reference to a yet to be established international judicial body as the sole institution with jurisdiction to investigate and prosecute acts of genocide, crimes against humanity and war crimes; (b) the use of temporary immunity legislation; and (c) the broad interpretation of the notion of political prisoners, in combination with the use of temporary immunity. In the meantime, in the public discourse of the new Burundian government, the need to promote reconciliation as the basis for sustainable peace and stability – even the term "forgiveness" is being used here and there – has gradually taken priority over the need to fight impunity as far as the crimes of the past are concerned.[44] In the current government's vision of how to deal with the past, the "reconciliation procedure" before the TRC is placed centrally. We will now further explain this position while briefly summarizing the current state of affairs of the negotiations process between the UN and the Government.

In October 2005, a Governmental Delegation was established, in charge of negotiating the establishment of a TRC and a Special Tribunal[45] for Burundi. A first session of negotiations between the Governmental Delegation and a UN Delegation

---

[43] Individual persons and legal persons, such as the three associations, can only challenge the constitutionality of laws, not of presidential or ministerial decrees (art. 230, para. 2, of the Constitution).

[44] See, i.a., the letter by Minister of Foreign Affairs Antoinette Batumubwira to the UN Assistant Secretary-General for Legal Affairs, Nicolas Michel (Bujumbura, 15 June 2006).

[45] During the negotiations process, the model of a Special Tribunal – similar to the one established for Sierra Leone – has gradually replaced the model of a Special Chamber that was initially proposed in the Kalomoh report. The proposed mixed composition (of foreign nationals and Burundian nationals) was maintained.

was held in March 2006.[46] No agreement was reached. A second round[47] of negotiations was held in March 2007.[48] Again, talks ended unsuccessfully. In addition to several technical modalities that remain to be agreed upon, two major hurdles remain to be taken on Burundi's long and winding road to transitional justice: the issue of amnesty legislation (1) and the relationship between the TRC and the Special Tribunal (2). In order to buy time and find a solution, it was agreed to launch national consultations on the transitional justice process (3).

(1) The Memorandum of the Governmental Delegation stipulated that, amongst other things, the TRC should be mandated to "determine those cases for which an amnesty law might be enacted" (para. 27, (h)). Compared to the law of 27 December 2004, this provision was far less restrictive.[49] Indeed, the Memorandum did not explicitly rule out amnesty for international crimes, nor did it restrict the possibly proposed amnesty legislation to political crimes. This vision is furthermore confirmed by the provision laid down in paragraph 65: "*Aucun acte, aucun fait établi par la Commission n'est d'avance exclu du processus de réconciliation*". During the first session of the negotiations, the UN Delegation confirmed the position of the UN – referring to its long-standing practice in a variety of countries – stating that amnesty needed to be unequivocally ruled out for genocide, crimes against humanity and war crimes in the legal documents on the establishment of the transitional justice mechanisms. While not explicitly differentiating between collective amnesty measures and possible individualized and conditional amnesty measures (possibly tailored after the South African model), the UN Delegation excluded "any kind of amnesty"

[46] This was done, i.a., on the basis of a memorandum that spelled out the Burundian government's proposal. Two versions were prepared of the memorandum. We will here refer to the latest version. See République du Burundi, *Mémorandum de la délégation burundaise chargée de négocier avec les Nations Unies la mise en place d'une Commission de la Vérité et de la Réconciliation et d'un Tribunal Spécial au Burundi* (Bujumbura, 26 March 2006).

[47] In his report to the fourth session of the UN Human Rights Council, the Independent Expert on the situation of human rights in Burundi noted that a second round was initially planned for the end of 2006 (United Nations, Human Rights Council, *Interim report of the independent expert on the situation of human rights in Burundi, Akich Okola*, A/HRC/4/5, 26 February 2007, §16). The two main contentious issues he identified in his report were "the principles of non-immunity or amnesty for genocide, war crimes and crimes against humanity as well as the neutrality and independence of these bodies".

[48] For this second round, a draft General Framework Agreement was prepared by the UN Delegation: *Accord-cadre général entre l'Organisation des Nations Unies et la République du Burundi relatif à la création d'une Commission Vérité et Réconciliation et d'un Tribunal Spécial au Burundi* (20 February 2007).

[49] Article 4, para. 2 of the law ruled out amnesty legislation for acts of genocide, crimes against humanity and war crimes.

("*toute forme d'amnistie*"[50]).[51] In a letter by the Minister of Foreign Affairs to the UN Assistant Secretary-General of Legal Affairs, the government's position was reaffirmed, namely that the TRC – composed of national and international members – should have the discretionary power to decide in which cases and under which conditions an amnesty could be granted. This in turn demonstrates the importance of the composition of the TRC and the procedure to appoint its members. In the case of a TRC composed of a majority of Burundian nationals,[52] appointed by the President, the issue of amnesty indirectly remains under the control of the government. During the second session of negotiations, the amnesty issue remained highly contentious. Towards the end of the session, a breakthrough seemed to have been reached. This was reflected in the first version of the draft Joint Press Communiqué of Friday 9 March 2007 which read:

> Sur la question de l'amnistie, conformément à la politique et à la pratique des Nations Unies solidement établies, et tel que reflété dans le loi burundaise, le Gouvernement et les Nations Unies réaffirment que le crime de génocide, les crimes contre l'humanité et les crimes de guerre ne sont pas amnistiables. Le principe de non-amnistie pour ces trois crimes s'applique, même devant le Tribunal Spécial. (para. 4)

Some hours before releasing the Joint Communiqué, the Governmental Delegation presented a new version, from which the final sentence – which explicitly stated that amnesty was ruled out as a matter of principle also before the Special Tribunal – was taken out. The remaining part of the paragraph merely confirmed the general principle and did not signal that any progress had been reached during the session on this issue. The refusal by the UN Delegation to sign the second version of the draft Joint Communiqué was partly inspired by the new paragraph 4, though another contentious issue had been subject to even more far reaching last minute modifications by the Governmental Delegation, namely the relationship between the TRC and the Special Tribunal and the independence of the prosecutor of the Special Tribunal.

---

[50] *Compte-rendu thématique des discussions et des négociations entre la Délégation burundaise chargée de négocier avec les Nations Unies la mise en place d'une Commission pour la Vérité et la Réconciliation et d'un Tribunal Spécial au Burundi et la Délégation des Nations Unies, réunies du 27 au 31 mars 2006 à Bujumbura*, attached to the letter of 19 May 2006 by the Assistant Secretary-General Nicolas Michel to Minister of Foreign Affairs Batumubwira, 4.

[51] It is worth referring to a paragraph that was added to the Thematic Report as some kind of footnote, but which possibly revealed dissenting opinions within the Burundian government. The paragraph noted that towards the end of the first session of the negotiations, the First Vice-President of the Republic, Martin Nduwimana, talked to the members of the UN Delegation about the amnesty issue and stated that the Government of Burundi did not recognize amnesty legislation awarded for the crime of genocide, crimes against humanity and war crimes (para. 18). It should be recalled that both Nduwimana as well as his principal advisor – who was at the same time president of the Governmental Delegation – are Tutsi, members of Uprona.

[52] In the initial version of the Memorandum of the Governmental delegation, it had been proposed that the TRC be made up of five members: three Burundian nationals and two foreign nationals. At the explicit request of the government (see the *Communiqué du Gouvernement sur le Conseil des Ministres du 2 février 2006*), this was changed in the second version of the Memorandum. It is now proposed that the TRC be composed of seven members: four Burundian nationals and three foreign nationals. Even if the Burundian membership is – as can be expected – ethnically balanced, this does not necessarily guarantee their operational independence vis-à-vis the government.

(2) The Memorandum of the Governmental Delegation left some room for interpretation[53] as to whether the Prosecutor of the ST would only investigate cases that were deferred to the ST by the TRC, or whether the Prosecutor would also be able to investigate cases *proprio motu*, for instance in cases where the reconciliation had been successfully completed but where the Prosecutor nevertheless considered prosecution to be necessary and in the interest of justice, or in cases that had not been brought to the attention of the TRC. During and after the first session of the negotiations, the UN Delegation had clearly insisted on the independence of the ST and its prosecutor (who, it was agreed, would be a foreign national).[54] Both as a matter of principle and in light of a long-standing practice, the prosecutor of the ST must, in the view of the UN Delegation, be independent, vis-à-vis the UN, the Burundian government or any other government, as well as vis-à-vis any other transitional justice mechanism. The UN Delegation stressed the need for the Prosecutor to be able to exercise his powers to investigate and prosecute at his own discretion. During the second session of the negotiations, this part of the draft GFA turned out to be the most contentious issue of the discussions. A comparison between the two versions of the draft Joint Press Communiqué clearly reveals the continuing divergence of opinions between the two delegations on this issue. The first version, of 9 March 2007, read as follows:

> Elles ont en outré convenu que les deux mécanismes d'établissement des responsabilités seront indépendants. Ils exerceront leurs responsabilités dans un esprit de complémentarité et dans le respect de leur mandat, statut juridique, prérogatives et compétences respectifs.
>
> Les Délégations ont conclu que le Procureur agira en toute indépendance dans l'instruction des dossiers et l'exercice des poursuites contre les auteurs du crime de génocide, des crimes contre l'humanité et des crimes de guerre. Elles ont convenu par ailleurs de

---

[53] According to the memorandum, cases would be referred by the TRC to the Special Tribunal in those cases where the reconciliation procedure was unsuccessful. This was further specified as follows: (a) in case a suspect refuses to appear before the Commission, (b) in case the person does not confess his responsibility for acts confirmed by the Commission, (c) in case the person refuses to participate in the reconciliation procedure, (d) in case the person refuses to implement the reconciliation measures decreed by the Commission (para. 71). It remained however unclear from the document whether these were the only situations in which prosecution before the Special Tribunal would be possible. Several other observers also regretted the ambiguity in the Memorandum. See, i.a., Nindorera (2006, p. 19).

[54] In the note submitted to the UN Delegation on the occasion of the first session, Iteka, FORSC and OAG had expressed doubts about the Government's readiness to accept a truly independent judicial mechanism: "*Au moment où les Nations Unies et le Gouvernement du Burundi étaient déjà en concertation pour mettre en place les mécanismes de justice transitionnelle, les mesures d'élargissement massif des prisonniers qualifiés de politiques se comprennent difficilement. Egalement, de nouvelles nominations des magistrats à tous les niveaux ont été opérés montrant une volonté du gouvernement de maintenir un contrôle serré sur le système judiciaire. L'adoption de la loi organisant le Conseil supérieur de la magistrature et la nomination de ce dernier, avec une prépondérance de personnes nommées par l'exécutif n'augurent d'aucune volonté gouvernementale de favoriser la mise en place d'un système judiciaire réellement indépendant de l'exécutif*" (OAG, FORSC, Ligue Iteka 2006, para. 4).

> poursuivre leurs discussions sur l'indépendance du Procureur par rapport aux travaux de la Commission Vérité et Réconciliation.

Drafted at the initiative of the Governmental Delegation, the second version, as of 10 March 2007, amended the latter paragraph as follows:

> Les deux Délégations ont convenu par ailleurs de poursuivre leurs discussions sur les rapports entre la commission vérité et réconciliation et le Tribunal Spécial.

While the first version explicitly confirmed the independence of the prosecutor yet indicated that further negotiations were needed on how exactly this independence would relate to the operations of the TRC, the second version reiterated the *status quo*, namely that the issue of the mutual independence of the two bodies vis-à-vis each other remained subject to further negotiations.

In May 2007, the CNDD-FDD, the government's leading party, published a memorandum in which it expressed its position on the TRC and the ST. The main novelty was likely to render further negotiations with the UN even more difficult. According to the CNDD-FDD proposal, the very establishment of the ST should be made dependent on the conclusions and recommendations of the TRC.[55]

The question whether or not the government is ready to accept the independence of the prosecutor of the Special Tribunal touches upon the very fundamentals of the Burundian transitional justice issue and even of Burundi's political transition itself. As long as the executive branch is reluctant to accept that the judicial branch (be it at the national level or at the level of a Special Tribunal) exercises its judicial powers in full independence, it seems reasonable to conclude that the political transition has simply not come to an end. Separation of powers, independence of the judiciary and rule of law are fundamentals of any successful political transition.[56] From that perspective, the way in which "recent" human rights violations – i.e., those violations which are not part of the country's legacy of the past but were committed under the incumbent regime – are dealt with is extremely revealing and, unfortunately, not very promising.

(3) A third stumbling block was – seemingly – overcome during the March 2007 round of negotiations. The UN delegation strongly insisted on the organization of a broad and inclusive consultation process, in order to ensure a greater transparency and ownership of the transitional justice process by the Burundian people. An agreement was found with the Governmental Delegation that a national consultation process was to be held countrywide and at all levels of society. In early November 2007, a Framework Agreement was signed between the UN and the Government, establishing a Steering Committee to prepare the

---

[55] "*Le parti CNDD-FDD estime que c'est sur base des conclusions de la Commission Vérité et Réconciliation qu'on décidera ou non de l'opportunité de mettre sur pieds un Tribunal Pénal Spécial*" (CNDD-FDD, *Mémorandum du parti CNDD-FDD sur la Commission Vérité et Réconciliation et le Tribunal Spécial pour le Burundi* (Bujumbura 2007), 8.

[56] Here, I am using the term in its classical meaning under the transition paradigm (see footnote 2).

national consultations process.[57] The Steering Committee is composed of six members, with two representatives from the government, the UN and civil society. From the very start, fundamental disagreements remained about the very purpose of the consultations. For the government, the conclusions drawn from the consultation process should logically determine Burundi's transitional justice policy, even if, for instance, this amounted to amnesty being granted for war crimes. This option is unacceptable for the UN and has even been ruled out in the Framework Agreement.[58] Funding for the national consultations process has been requested from the UN Peace-Building Fund. In May 2008, the UN Secretary-General reported highly critically about the lack of substantive progress, for which it blamed both the government as well as (internal divisions within) the civil society component of the Steering Committee.[59] At the time of writing (in May 2008), it remains highly unsure when the consultations will effectively start and, if so, what approach will be adopted and how the outcome will affect the actual transitional justice policy and mechanisms.

7 Burundi's Traditional Dispute Settlement Mechanism: The Bashingantahe

During the ongoing negotiations process about Burundi's transitional justice process, reference has sometimes been made to the possible use of the traditional dispute settlement mechanism (the Bashingantahe) as a transitional justice mechanism.[60] "Regarded as the embodiment of universal values and personal integrity, the 'wise men' who made up the institution played many roles in the communities they were chosen but the most important was the peaceful resolution of conflicts" (Dexter and Ntahombaye 2005, p. 6). There is little doubt that the use of modernized, formalized and institutionalised gacaca tribunals in Rwanda to prosecute genocide suspects and the donor money this has generated, may have offered inspiration to some people in neighbouring Burundi. While the Arusha Agreement referred in very general terms to the need to promote and revalorize the spirit of Ubushingantahe, the peace agreements do not provide for a specific role for the Bashingantahe in dealing with the past. Within the framework of this paper – and in the absence of further field re-

[57] *Accord cadre entre le Gouvernement de la République du Burundi et l'Organisation des Nations Unies portant création et définition du mandate du Comité de pilotage tripartite en charge des Consultations nationales sur la Justice de transition au Burundi*, Bujumbura, 2 November 2007.

[58] "*Le Comité ne soulèvera pas de questions en cours de négociation entre le Gouvernement du Burundi et les Nations Unies, notamment la relation entre la Commission Vérité et Réconciliation et le Tribunal Spécial, ni l'opportunité de l'une ou l'utilité de l'autre mécanisme, ainsi que des questions qui pourraient être en porte-à-faux avec le droit international*" (art. 10).

[59] United Nations, Security Council, *Third report of the Secretary-General on the United Nations Integrated Office in Burundi*, S/2008/330, 15 May 2008, paras. 71, 72 and 96.

[60] See, i.a., Conseil National des Bashingantahe, *Mise sur pied de la Commission 'Vérité et Réconciliation' et du Tribunal Spécial au Burundi. Propositions du Conseil National des Bashingantahe/Sages traditionnels* (Bujumbura 2006).

search – we will limit ourselves to formulating two remarks on the potential role that Bashingantahe could possibly play in telling the truth, establishing accountability, offering reparation and promoting reconciliation.[61]

First, it is very clear that the Bashingantahe-tradition has strongly suffered from the political context in which it was and is operating. In summary, we may state that as much as the Bashingantahe were increasingly instrumentalised under the one party-regime by the Uprona party, they are now politically sidelined and disliked by the regime dominated by the CNDD-FDD. In addition, the traditional authority of the Bashingantahe may well, at the local level, be increasingly contested by the community level authorities that were elected during the local elections in September 2005. The current political context is therefore certainly not conducive to introducing this alternative approach in the current debate.

Secondly, although there is quite some literature (see, i.a., Ntahombaye et al. 1999; Manirakiza 2002, pp. 39–58) about the role Bashingantahe traditionally (and ideally) played in settling disputes at community level, little anthropological research appears to have been done about the role they have actually been able to play in the aftermath of, e.g., the 1972 or the 1993 massacres. Where they a vehicle of truth telling, did they provide a forum to rebuild civic trust, did they mediate between victims and perpetrators as far as restitution or other forms of reparation was concerned, were they instrumental in reintegrating former child soldiers in the local community, et cetera? Or was the tradition itself among the victims of the armed conflict? Any discussion about the possible formal recognition[62] of the Bashingantahe as a transitional justice mechanism should be based on a careful evaluation of the role they have "spontaneously" played in dealing with the past (as there is no reason why tradition would "wait" for an agreement between the government and the UN to be signed before rendering justice – assuming that it still has the potential of doing so).

8 Tentative Conclusions about an Uncertain Destination[63]

The Burundi case raises fundamental issues about how to deal with the past. Some of our tentative conclusions are situated at an empirical level. Other findings are related to strategy and policy. Finally, questions also arise about the need to normatively intervene and how to do so. Rather than formulating definitive answers, this concluding section will primarily highlight some of the problems and issues that stem from the Burundi case-study.

---

[61] For an excellent analysis of the concept, its strengths and weaknesses, see Naniwe-Kaburahe (2008, pp. 149–179).

[62] In addition, this obviously raises the question – as with any other kind of traditional justice mechanism – how much interference by external actors the Bashingantahe tradition can afford without being fundamentally altered.

[63] The title is a wink to O'Donnell and Schmitter (1986).

Burundi's transitional justice practice was decisively determined by political parameters. Its stated transitional justice policy was the result of a lengthy negotiations process between various parties. The gap between stated policy and actual practice was also primarily due to the political context. There was no winner or loser to the military conflict. Political power was, over the past fourteen years, spread over a large group of political and military players. The international community (successfully) tried to reach a compromise that would, in the first place, ensure political stability and peace. Transitional justice was not a priority concern. Compared to the situation in neighbouring Rwanda, the situation in Burundi was fundamentally different. After the Rwandan 1994 genocide, there was a clear winner and a new political regime dominated by the former rebellion that had won the war. In such a setting, it was much more "easy" for the international community to establish an international criminal tribunal to prosecute those responsible. (Note however that, before the ICTR, only "losers" – in the political and military meaning of the term – have so far been brought to justice, see, i.a., Cruvellier 2006; and Reydams 2005, pp. 977–988.) Today, Burundi is more stable and peaceful than ever before during the past fourteen years. Was "not dealing with the past" an acceptable price to pay? Was it a necessary price to pay? Is it a price Burundi should continue to pay today and also tomorrow?

People on all sides have suffered losses, in many ways (lives, relatives, friends, limbs, houses, trust in their neighbours, earnings, hope, et cetera). Do we know what people want in terms of "justice" and has it really mattered so far? The issue of popular consultation about people's expectations and views on transitional justice has come up only very recently in the debate about Burundi's transitional justice mechanisms. Ownership and participation by victims, survivors, returnees, internally displaced people and the population in general has been almost non-existent in the discussions so far. If peoples' expectations and views do matter indeed – could we possibly conclude otherwise? – how then do we design a process that allows people to voice their concerns, in a country where there is no track record at all of people having a say in political decision making at the macro-level? And should we also accept the outcome of such a (supposedly genuine, inclusive and representative) consultative process, even if it turns out to be the case that, for now, a large majority favours peace, stability and a return to normalcy instead of establishing accountability mechanisms, prosecuting and punishing?

What measures can be taken during (possibly lengthy) periods of transition? If truth is ever to be told, harm ever to be repaired, perpetrators ever to be held responsible, which kind of interim measures need to be taken in order to safeguard essential information? And how should trials or reparation processes (e.g., related to restitution of land) that are organised by the outgoing regime or during the period of transition but which are considered to be grossly unfair by local and international observers be integrated in the transitional justice process?

The growth of international human rights norms and the increasing number of human rights bodies that deal with monitoring and/or enforcement of these norms, have an obvious impact on the possibilities for States and societies to design their own transitional justice approach. For instance, the use of blanket amnesty legislation is no longer acceptable as a way to deal with crimes of international law. However, the Burundi case-study demonstrates how creative decision-makers can find ways to – at least temporarily – circumvent or hijack the international amnesty prohibition, even while incorporating the international norms in national legislation. What constitutes an appropriate response to this finding? Should norms be elaborated much further, so as to restrict national escape lanes? Is there a need for more and stronger international bodies to enforce international norms (but then how should these relate to international mediators who may need temporary escape lanes as part of their peace negotiations agenda)? Or should international law during periods of political transition tolerate a certain degree of hijacking of international norms?

The Burundi case finally raises a fundamental question about the very essence of transitional justice. How much truth, accountability, reparation and reconciliation can one reasonably expect in situations where the political transition has not yet come to an end? In its early days, the very notion of transitional justice was defined on the basis of the experience of "emerging democratic societies", undergoing a political transformation from authoritarian to more liberal rule (see, i.a., Kritz 1995a,b; and Teitel 2000). When transplanting this transitional justice experience to states that undergo a different kind of transition, or societies that struggle with a particular stage in their transition, new difficulties inevitably arise, some of which may be temporarily insurmountable.

References

Amnesty International (1988) Burundi: killings of children by government troops. London

Bell C (2000) Peace agreements and human rights. Oxford University Press, Oxford

Carothers T (2002) The end of the transition paradigm. J Democracy 13 (1):6

Chrétien J-P, Dupaquier J-F (2007) Burundi 1972 – Au bord des génocides. Karthala, Paris

Cruvellier T (2006) Le tribunal des vaincus. Calmann-Lévy, Paris

Dexter T, Ntahombaye P (2005) The role of informal justice systems in fostering the rule of law in post-conflict situations. The case of Burundi. Centre for Humanitarian Dialogue, Geneva

Erler B, Reyntjens F (1992) Les événements de novembre-décembre 1991 au Burundi: rapport d'une mission d'enquête. NCOS, Brussels

Guichaoua A (ed) (1995) Les crises politiques au Burundi et au Rwanda (1993–1994). Analyses, faits et documents. Karthala, Paris

International Crisis Group (2000) Unblocking Burundi's peace process: political parties, political prisoners and freedom of the press. Brussels, June 2000

International Crisis Group (2006) Burundi. Democracy and peace at risk. Brussels

International Crisis Group (2007) Burundi: Conclure la paix avec les FNL. Brussels

IRIN (2003) Approval of temporary immunity law sparks heated debate. Nairobi, 3 September 2003

OAG, FORSC, Ligue Iteka (2006) Communiqué de Presse. Bujumbura, 9 March 2006. Observatoire de l'Action Gouvernementale (OAG), FORSC (Forum pour le Renforcement de la Société Civile) and Ligue Iteka

Kritz N (ed) (1995a) Transitional justice. How emerging democracies reckon with former regimes, vols. 3. USIP, Washington DC

Kritz N (1995b) The problem of impunity and judicial reform in Burundi. Washington

Lemarchand R (1994) Burundi. Ethnocide as discourse and practice. Cambridge University Press, Cambridge

Manirakiza M (1992) Burundi: de la révolution au régionalisme 1966–1976. Le Mat de Misaine, Bruxelles

Manirakiza Z (2002) Modes traditionnels de règlement des conflits: l'Institution des Bashingantahe. Au Cœur de l'Afrique 2002:39–58

Minority Rights Group (1974) Génocide sélectif au Burundi. London

Naniwe-Kaburahe A (2008) The institution of Bashingantahe in Burundi. In: Huyse L and Salter M (eds) Traditional justice and reconciliation after violent conflict. Learning from African experiences. International IDEA, Stockholm

Ndikumana E (2006) Burundi: la libération de détenus pourrait raviver les tensions ethniques. AFP, 15 January 2006

Nindorera E (2003) L'agencement et l'applicabilité des différentes lois en matière de lutte contre l'impunité au Burundi. Bujumbura, Octobre 2003

Nindorera E (2006) Pas de réconciliation véritable sans justice. Bujumbura, 30 March 2006

Ntahombaye P, Ntabona A et al (eds) (1999) L'institution des Bashingantahe au Burundi. Etude pluridisciplinaire. Bujumbura

O'Donnell G, Schmitter P (1986) Transition from authoritarian rule: tentative conclusions about uncertain democracies. Johns Hopkins University Press, Baltimore

Reydams L (2005) The ICTR ten years on. Back to the Nuremberg paradigm? J Int Criminal Justice 3:977–988

Reyntjens F (2000) Burundi: prospects for peace. Minority Rights Group, London

Subotic J (2005) Hijacked justice: domestic appropriation of international norms. Human Rights and Human Welfare Working Paper Series, University of Wisconsin. http://www.du.edu/gsis/hrhw/working/2005/28-subotic-2005.pdf

Teitel R (2000) Transitional Justice. Oxford University Press, Oxford

UNDP (2005) Rapport national sur le développement humain. Bujumbura

Vandeginste S (2006) Théorie consociative et partage du pouvoir au Burundi. Discussion Paper, Institute of Development Policy and Management, University of Antwerp. http://www.ua.ac.be/main.aspx?c=.IOBE&n=38974

Vandeginste S (2008) Burundi: entre le modèle consociatif et sa mise en oeuvre. In: Marysse S et al (eds) L'Afrique des Grands Lacs. Annuaire 2007–2008. L'Harmattan, Paris, 55–75

Justice and Reconciliation in the Aftermath of the Civil War in Gorongosa, Mozambique Central*

Victor Igreja

Abstract In the aftermath of the protracted Mozambican civil war (1976–1992), the national political authorities opted for an unconditional amnesty law for wartime crimes. Neither the cadres from the Frelimo-led government, nor the Renamo leadership offered public explanations as to why no politico-legal initiatives were to be forthcoming in the post-civil war period to actively address issues of accountability for the wartime crimes. The representatives of Christian religious groups and the members of the international community, who played a key role in brokering the Mozambican peace agreement, also remained silenced vis-à-vis issues of accountability in post-civil war period. War survivors were simply advised to forget what had happened, to forgive and to reconcile with one another. The only reference to justice was the emphasis placed on "you shall not take revenge upon your fellow man." Robert Cover had insightfully observed that in a society "each group must accommodate in its own normative world the objective reality of the other. There may or may not be synchronization or convergence in their respective understandings about the normative boundary and what it implies" (quoted in Minow et al. 1995, p. 125).

Following this perspective of multiple normative sources and boundaries, in a society, the Mozambican state officials failed to consider the implications that their enacted unconditional amnesty law would have in the communities that had been severely affected by the civil war violence. In some of these communities, the normative world or ethics of reciprocity demands accountability over serious past wrongs. In the former war zones of the Gorongosa district, one of the features of the ethics of reciprocity is that *micero ai vundi*, i.e., a conflict does not get rotten unless

V. Igreja
Post-Doctoral Fellow at the Australian Centre for Peace and Conflict Studies,
The University of Queensland, Brisbane, Australia,
e-mail: vigreja@yahoo.com

*This paper is based on a more comprehensive chapter Restorative justice and the role of magamba spirits in post-civil war Gorongosa, Central Mozambique written by V. Igreja and B. Dias-Lambranca and published in the book, *Traditional Justice and Reconciliation after Violent Conflict: Learning from African Experiences* (International, IDEA, Stockholm, 2008).

K. Ambos et al. (eds.), *Building a Future on Peace and Justice: Studies on Transitional Justice, Peace and Development.*

when there is an active resolution by the legitimate institutions. Based on the rule that implies the rejection of silence as a mechanism to cease a conflict, this paper analyses the enactment of the local ethics of reciprocity through the intervention of a civil-war-related spirit named *gamba* (*magamba* in plural) in the former epicentres of the civil war in Gorongosa district, in the centre of Mozambique.

1 Introduction

This paper addresses the ways in which the survivors of the protracted civil war in Gorongosa managed to create justice to peacefully deal with the legacies of an extremely violent past.[1] The focus is on *gamba* spirits and the manner in which these spirits break the post-war conspiracies of silence regarding a violent past, joust for truth and justice, and foster peace and reconciliation. In their struggle for truth and justice in post-war Mozambique, *gamba* spirits form part of the local ethics of reciprocity that indicates that *micero ai vundi*, i.e., a conflict does not get rotten; it does not fade away simply because people stop thinking or talking about it. Instead, there is a need of a participatory conflict resolution by the legitimate institutions. In this context, *gamba* spirits powerfully bespeak the necessity of actively engaging with the horrors of civil war in order to achieve a durable conflict resolution and subsequent social stability (Igreja et al. 2008). In a broader context and from a cross-cultural perspective, *gamba* spirits suggest the need to recognize the availability worldwide of diverse strategies to peacefully deal with the legacies of civil war violence.

Processes of conflict resolution for serious past abuses and crimes through the intervention of spiritual forces have been observed in various societies. For instance, anthropological studies in Southwest China describe the transformation of collective ancestral spirits into wild ghosts as a way of coming to terms with the legacies of the violent Cultural Revolution (Mueggler 2001). Similarly, in Sri Lanka, the increasing popular experiences of ghost manifestations are related to the war and the failure of the official mechanisms of justice (Perera 2001). Judy Rosenthal (2002, p. 316) demonstrates how certain forms of Vodu religious practices through spirit possession in southern Ghana and Togo are "vehicles of cultural resistance to the abuses of state power." These studies provide some indications of ethics of reciprocity in different communities, in which the manifestations of spirits can be seen as part of "struggles to enunciate calls for justice and to articulate longings for reconciliation" (Mueggler 2001, p. 9). In fact, these spiritual phenomenon are a contemporary example of what Douglas Fry (2006) calls the "the human potential for peace." From this perspective, one issue to consider is that there are multiple ways of thinking about truth, justice, peace and reconciliation in post-conflict countries.

[1] This paper was written based on a decade (1997–2007) of continuous field research in the centre of Mozambique. An early version of this paper was presented at the conference "Building a Future on Peace and Justice," Nuremberg June 2007.

This paper is organised in three sections. Following a brief introduction, this section also describes some aspects of the context of the civil war violence in Gorongosa and some of the features of the transition from civil war to peace and reconciliation. Section 2 describes the emergence of the *gamba* spirits in the Gorongosa district and presents some mechanisms by which these war-related spirits break the prevailing conspiracies of silence over a past of civil war violence. This section also presents how *gamba* deal with issues of truth, justice and reconciliation. In Gorongosa, reconciliation is a multidimensional phenomenon and *gamba* spirits demonstrate the multiplicity of reconciliation processes and achievements. Section 3 gives the main conclusions suggests the necessity of taking seriously the variety of socio-cultural and non-state approaches to deal with the complexities of transitional justice issues in post-conflict societies.

1.1 The Mozambican Civil War and its Consequences

The protracted Mozambican civil war (1976–1992) was ruthless. Although the war was spread all over the country, rural areas were the most affected in terms of war destruction and human suffering. The war was fought between the Frelimo-led governmental troops and the former rebel movement Renamo. Around the mid 1980s, the Zimbabwean army joined the war by supporting the Felimo-led government. The civil strife was a low-intensity war, i.e., the parties in conflict largely struggled for control over populations. This fight for control over civilians gave rise to divisions between areas controlled militarily by governmental troops, and other areas controlled by Renamo. The people continuously shifted between one area and another, or even moved around "no man's land" in search of better security conditions.

Not only did the war destroy the country's socio-economic infrastructure, it also created deep divisions and hatred between family and community members. People living within the war zones were compelled to spy on one another, with hints of murder contributing to the erosion and depletion of the trust and relationships of socio-economic reciprocity that had bonded communities together historically. Young virgin daughters were abducted to military bases for sexual violation and forced marriage. Young boys were forcibly recruited and compelled to murder their own relatives and burn their own villages. Mutilation of male and female body organs was carried out on some occasions. Forced labour and forced displacement were also common practices. Thousands of civilians were killed, although the numbers of the dead are not known for certain. Some observers of the Mozambican civil war estimate a figure of 100,000 civilian deaths; others place the figure at one million (Hanlon 1991); still others suggest that "A more realistic guess would be that some 50,000 victims lost their lives directly as a result of rebel military action throughout the entire war" (Thomashausen 2001, p. 98). Regarding the forced population displacement, it is estimated that at least four million people fled into the urban centres, becoming internally displaced; others sought refuge in neighbouring countries. The extreme events of the civil war brought profound divisions and mistrust among many community members in Mozambique. These divisions and enmities still prevail in this post-war era in different social and political contexts of the Mozambican society (Igreja 2008, forthcoming).

1.2 The Transition from Civil War to Peace and Reconciliation

The civil war did not terminate in a military victory of one side over the other. In order to attempt to end the civil war, the Frelimo party promulgated two amnesty laws: The Laws no. 14/87[2] and 15/87[3] of December 19 (Trindade 2003, p. 114). However, these legal initiatives failed to achieve their aim. At the end of the 1980s it became clear that the Frelimo slogan of "when we are at war, the first priority is war," meaning that "it is necessary to make war in order to end the war," was disastrous propaganda. It was not possible for either side to reach a military solution to the conflict. Initiatives to end the conflict through peace talks came from Christian religious groups. Eventually in 1990 peace negotiations began between the Frelimo-led government and the Renamo rebels. After two years of mediated and direct negotiations in Rome, Italy, the Mozambican government and Renamo reached a peace agreement on October 4, 1992 and publicly swore never to return to the violence of war as a mechanism for resolving disputes. This sworn peace, which was witnessed nationally and internationally, marked the cessation of the protracted cycle of extreme violent hostilities.

The signing of the Mozambican General Peace Agreement (AGP) was an important reconciliation event (Long and Brecke 2003). An incremental step was given after the reconciliation event when the Mozambican General Peace Agreement was attributed legal status through the law no. 13/92 promulgated by the then Frelimo-led Popular Assembly. This political accord completely neglected the fact that the civil war hostilities had extensively breached conventional rules dealing with victims of war (Geneva law), and the rules governing the conduct of hostilities (The Hague law) (Tomuschat 2003, p. 14). That is, no measures in the post-war period were developed to hold accountable those individuals who had been responsible for the most egregious acts of violence. The peace agreement was founded upon what Stanley Cohen (2001) has termed *cultures of denial*, in which political authorities "encourage turning a collective blind eye, leaving horrors either unexamined or normalized as being part of the rhythms of everyday life" (p. 101). Such neglect by the Mozambican political authorities in assuming their responsibilities over past abuse and war crimes was believed by many political authorities, non-governmental

[2] Article 1st, no. 1, states that, "amnesties for the crimes against the Security of the People and of the Popular State, foreseen in the Law no. 2/79 of March 1, committed by Mozambican citizens that, by any way, have combated or promoted violence against the People or the Mozambican state, within or outside of the national territory, as long as they voluntary give up themselves."

[3] Preamble. It concedes pardon for the punishment to the actors of crimes against the security of the State that by their behaviour, "have revealed the purpose to reintegrate in peace in the society and to redeem through socially useful work."

officials and intellectual elites to be the most effective mechanism for achieving a resolution for the Mozambican civil war (Hayner 2001).

Insisting upon the need to address the violence and crimes of the past does not imply that the serious difficulties in achieving justice and peace in transitional periods should be ignored. The issue is that "consolidating democracies have a wide range of options with regard to justice and accountability: they can pursue selective prosecutions, purges and even commissions of enquiry that lay bare the legacy of the past" (Sriram 2004, p. 2; Teitel 2000).

Instead, the culture of denial was nationally formalised in Mozambique when the Frelimo-led single party parliament enacted the law no. 15/92 that granted generalised and unconditional amnesties for crimes committed between 1979 and 1992 in Mozambique. The law no. 15/92 states that it, "Amnesties the crimes committed against the security of the people and of the popular State, foreseen in the law no. 2/79, of March 1 and in the law no. 1/83, of March 13, the crimes against the security of the state, foreseen in the law no. 19/91, of August 16, and the military crimes foreseen in the law no. 17/87, of December 21, and still those whose criminal procedures were not yet established by July 1 of 1988."[4]

From the top to the bottom of the political hierarchy there was no explanation as to why no politico-legal initiatives were to be provided. War survivors, having been given no advice or support other than to forget past events and to avoid the extraction of revenge, went back to their villages of origin in order to start new lives by building houses in which to live and cultivating the land for subsistence farming.

One compelling reality of the post-war settlement, however, was that these former war-zone villages were not to be inhabited solely by individuals and families who shared a collective memory as victims of war violence. The ex-soldiers from the two former belligerent armies (the Frelimo-led government army and Renamo) and their associates, who had committed the most pervasive abuses and war crimes, did not forfeit the right to live in these villages. On the contrary, they went back, quite unconcernedly, to live in those same villages.[5] In general, there were few reports of former soldiers swaggering and strutting about in the villages, but their very presence was a continuous reminder of wartime crimes and abuse. Under those conditions of military crimes and abuse and post-war political abandonment, the following questions are raised that require careful examination: how can war survivors live in peace when their perpetrators roam freely in the same villages? What kind of truth, justice and reconciliation is it possible to attain amid cultures of denial and impunity? To what extent has the emergence of the *gamba* spirits contributed to the healing of divisions caused by the civil war, by responding to the needs of truth, justice and reconciliation in Gorongosa?

[4] Boletim da República, I SÉRIE – Número 42. Quarta Feira, 14 de Outubro de 1992. Suplemento.

[5] From the government side they were mostly *secretarios*, *chefes do quarteirão* (chiefs of neighbourhoods), and militia. From the Renamo side they were *mujibas* (vigilantes and collectors of food for the troops), *blocos* (vigilantes), and some local traditional chiefs that remained under their control.

2 Gamba Spirits: Breaking the Conspiracies of Silence

Gamba spirits emerged in a social world that already had a long history and tradition of conceptualising human beings as *homines aperti*, i.e., "the image of a multitude of people, each of them relatively open, interdependent processes" (Elias 1970, p. 121). The idea of *homines aperti* suggests a way of being in and experiencing the world. In Gorongosa, the model of human beings suggests an openness of the men and women who are capable of establishing relations of interdependence not only with other human beings but also with supernatural forces that inhabit the same social world. *Homines aperti* establish continuous interactions with spirits to the extent that spirits not only inhabit the landscape of the region, but they also have the capacity to dwell within the *homines aperti*.

Spirits and healers occupy different positions and perform a variety of complex roles. These positions and roles change over time according to the general metamorphosis through which the society experience. The spirits perform various roles: there are spirits and healers who historically safeguarded the moral and ethical values, social stability and identity of the community; there are spirits and healers who perform healing, in the strict sense of the word; and there are yet other spirits and healers who perform both functions simultaneously.

Gamba is the name of a spirit, an affliction, and also a healer that specialises in *gamba* afflictions (Igreja 2003; Marlin 2001). In general, *gamba* are spirits of male soldiers who died during the civil war. Their bodies were not properly buried, and people living within the war zones and in extreme conditions are referred to as having defiled the corpses of these fallen soldiers to make medicines to protect themselves against the violence of war. Within this context *gamba* spirits return to the world of the living to fight for justice and the focal point of their avenging force is women. *Gamba* spirits also attack men, but less frequently than women.

Women and men who fall prey to *gamba* strikes are those whose relatives were allegedly involved in the use of protective medicines illicitly made from the corpses of the fallen soldiers (known or unknown, but not soldiers related to them), or were allegedly involved in the murder of the soldiers themselves. With the passage of time, the initial configuration associating *gamba* spirits with dead soldiers has evolved to the extent that currently any male who was killed during the civil war is able to return to the world of the living to claim justice.

In order to understand the impact of violence and the local setting of social experience there is a need to analyse "how that local world mediates between broader political forces and the responses of individuals" (Kleinman 1997, p. 183). In this regard, there is clear evidence that the cultures of silence over a grisly past promoted by the Mozambican political elites in the post-war period were also initially incorporated into the everyday life of war survivors in the centre of Mozambique. That is, when the war was over, many war survivors in Gorongosa wished to forget the horrors that they had lived through and to progress with their lives. For instance, in the first five years of peace (1992–1997), *gamba* spirits were generally a silent phenomenon. During my initial observations in April 1997, I came across only very few young men who were considered to be working as healers using the *gamba* spirits.

These observations were confined to remote villages located in the central Gorongosa Mountains. The few *gamba* healers roaming around in 1997 would carry their working instrument (a bayonet) with them at all times, in a scabbard tied to their waist. These bayonets are said to come from the *Kalashnikovs* that stabbed and killed many people during the civil war. The *gamba* healers travelled around with these bayonets as an indication of the presence of a *gamba* healer and of the spirit's puissance.

By 1999 or thereabouts, the unbearable experiences of the war could apparently no longer be relived and processed in silence. *Gamba* spirits broke through the prevailing conspiracies of silence and there was a sharp increase in the number of people possessed by this spirit, particularly young women. A striking aspect of *gamba* is that it manifests itself mainly through spirit possession of the body of its victim. *Gamba* spirits can randomly possess anybody who has a personal or family history of extreme suffering, abuse, abandonment, and death related to the civil war. The manifestation of a *gamba* spirit is always very noisy, bodily enacted and very talkative. Everybody in a village knows who is a host and whom a *gamba* spirit has affected. When someone become possessed by *gamba* spirits, this is a denunciation of the prevailing divisions caused by the civil war within the families and indicates the need to deal openly with the turbulent past.

2.1 Gamba Spirits and Practices of Truth and Justice

The emergence of the *gamba* spirits forced war survivors to change their initial strategy of oblivion regarding their violent past. This capacity to change is referred to here as *cultures of engagement*, which generally means sustainable social practices that are crucial in keeping peace, social stability and generating prosperity at a local level. Specifically, *cultures of engagement* consist of the willingness of war survivors to actively create new resources and access and utilize available endogenous resources to repair their devastated social world by way of reconciling formerly estranged people, and healing the extreme wounds of war. Cultures of engagement for reconciliation and healing are enacted in a way that cannot shun the past of violence. In this regard, after a relatively short period of silence and attempts at oblivion, many people began to be seriously afflicted, and the origins of these afflictions were rooted in the past of violence, i.e., *gamba* spirits.

Possession by *gamba* spirits causes severe afflictions to their hosts and agnates. One particular affliction is the blockage of the reproductive functions (Igreja et al. 2006). Afflictions by these spirits are an indication of violent experiences, involving war-related shameful or amoral acts, which are being concealed. This experience must be publicly disclosed, acknowledged and repaired. In this way, *gamba* spirits also present a potential source for a peaceful resolution of the histories of abuse, denial and concealment that prevail in Gorongosa (Igreja 2003).

Gamba spirits do not disclose "the truth" since in the context of protracted civil war "the truth" does not exist. *Gamba* spirits are concerned with the multiplicities of truths about the past. That is to say, *gamba* spirits create a safe public space in which an afflicted person, her family and the community at large can deal with their past without fear of igniting new cycles of violence and bloodshed.

In post-war Gorongosa, the process of creating collective truths and their usage takes place largely during the public sessions aimed at dealing with *gamba* spirit possession. When someone is afflicted this means that a family member of the afflicted person has done something terrible against someone during the civil war. It is the person who was wronged that returns in the form of a *gamba* spirit to disclose the narrative of the violent events; and these events are extremely serious (Igreja and Dias-Lambranca 2008).

In order to discover the accusation and establish the facts, the *gamba* healer places the afflicted person at the centre of the ceremony. The *gamba* healer re-creates the scenario of war by acting out the actions of the soldiers during the civil war. People participating in the ceremony follow the *gamba* healer by singing songs whose messages evoke war events: abuse, suffering and death. The songs also evoke ideas about the need to voice what happened so that the alleged wrongdoer and the participants in general can acknowledge the truths about the past, and at a later stage, the wrongdoer specifically can repair the havoc.

The scenario of war created by the *gamba* healer and the community in general gives confidence to the afflicting *gamba* spirit to manifest itself to the public via the body of the host. When the spirit assumes full control of the host's body, this implies that the conscience of the host is fully replaced by the personality of the *gamba* spirit. This means that the host cannot be held accountable for anything that happens during this ceremony. When the *gamba* spirit is ready to make the indictments against the alleged perpetrator, these usually refer to the following acts: "killing of one or more people," "eating human body parts," or "stealing the goods of dead people." The indictment of "eating human body parts" is a way of accusing the individuals and society as a whole for their inaction vis-à-vis the need to appropriately take care of the corpses that proliferated in the pathways of Gorongosa former war-zones.

The indictments are rarely free of dispute. The deliberations, which are mediated by a *gamba* healer, are very agitated and can take hours, since initially the indicted person refuses to comply with the accusation. Since the *gamba* healer is also a survivor of extreme experiences and knows very well the politics of denial, he or she mediates the deliberations between the *gamba* spirit and the indicted person, using as a starting point the principle that "*não há fumo sem fogo*" (there is no smoke without fire). In order to lead the people to see the fire that produced the smoke, the *gamba* spirit has to work very hard. Besides making the indictment, the role of the *gamba* spirit is to provide more unknown clues that may increase the indisputability of the accusation. When this level of evidence production is reached the inductee must assume his or her responsibilities in the case.

The formal acceptance of the accusation by the accused is a very reconciliatory act. It is his or her acceptance that will allow the justice, i.e., the transformation processes to be initiated. Justice consists in the transformation of the *gamba* spirit from the status of an alien and wounded spirit to that of an acknowledged spirit.

It also consists of the transformation of the possessed from the status of afflicted patient to the status of being free from the *gamba* spirit. This transformation allows the patient to start the recovery process, as their status changes from that of a perpetrator to that of someone who assumes his or her responsibilities by publicly acknowledging his or her weaknesses at the time of the civil war. The person ceases to live under the shadow of being a perpetrator, whose behaviour always raises motives for suspicion. He or she gains the status of a "cleansed" person.

2.2 Reconciliation after Everyday and Mass Violent Conflict

In Mozambique, the ordinary meaning of reconciliation encompasses both a process and a state. The Gorongosa word for reconciliation is derived from the word *ku batizana* (or *patizana*), which means reconnection. Specifically it is a ceremony that married people undergo after one spouse breaks the sex taboo by being involved in extra-marital sexual intercourse. The consequence of breaking this taboo is that the married couple cannot have sex, as otherwise one of them, or even their children, can become seriously ill. In order to be able to restart their sexual life as a married couple there is a need for *ku batizana*, i.e., for them both to be reconciled. The healer prepares the roots and leaves of different trees to use in the preparation of a bath for the taboo breaker. While taking a bath in private, he or she must narrate the events and make a promise never to repeat the act. The healer also prepares a meal using, among other ingredients, an egg, which culminates in the estranged couple eating together. The state of reconciliation means that the couple is cleansed or free to re-establish their sexual relations without the risk of contamination by disease.

Reconciliation after the civil war does not follow the procedure of *ku batizana*. It is *gamba* spirits that create the possibility of post-war reconciliation to take place. However, post-war reconciliation through *gamba* spirits and *ku batizana* pursue the same goals, in that the state of reconciliation consists in the reconnection of formerly estranged people. *Gamba* spirits not only address issues of truth and justice, they also deal with the reconciliation of people divided by violent conflict.

The magnitude of violence during the civil war has no precedent in the history of the Gorongosa people and of the Mozambicans more generally. The violence disrupted all spheres of human existence and the official post-war settlement challenged war survivors to experience reconciliation in the most basic and fundamental way. That is, perpetrators, victims, bystanders, cowards, traitors, wartime prostitutes and thieves, victims who went on to become perpetrators, perpetrators who went on to become victims, etc., all went on to live at the exact place where they had experienced violence. The processes of reconciliation, therefore, that can effectively address these post-civil war complexities must be comprehensive. *Gamba* seems to be the answer since there are no socio-cultural processes in Gorongosa that more closely deal with a past of violence than that which is initiated by the *gamba* spirits.

The actions ignited by *gamba* spirits deals with three levels of reconciliation that form part of the *homines aperti*: Reconciliation between people; reconciliation between people and the spirits of the dead; and reconciliation between the spirits of the dead themselves.

2.2.1 Reconciliation between People in the Aftermath of the Civil War

Gamba spirits pave the way for reconciliation to take place among war survivors. The presence of these war-related spirits force war survivors to move out of their scattered quarantines of silence. They have to come together to address the divisions caused by the protracted civil war. When someone is afflicted by *gamba* spirits, this is not an individual problem: the family members of the patient must also take part in the healing ceremonies. However, most of the time family members are still bitterly divided because of the events that took place during the civil war and have not yet been reunited since the war came to an end. These divisions within families impair, in the first instance, the possibility of the afflicted person receiving an intervention since no comprehensive intervention can be developed without the presence of family members. Since *gamba* spirits return to disclose war-related shameful events that took place within families, their presence is one of the key factors without which reconciliation cannot begin.

In this regard, the eruption of the *gamba* spirit compels divided families to join together in order to help a relative who is severely afflicted. Community members, particularly neighbours of the *gamba* healer in charge of the case, also participate of their own free will to help in the peaceful resolution of war-related ill-health. Bystanders also take part in the rituals by witnessing "other" people's problems. I place "other" in inverted commas because according to the model of *homines aperti* and the fact that almost everyone in Gorongosa has an experience of the civil war, the appearance of *gamba* spirits must indeed be everyone's concern. Perhaps it is for this reason that neighbours choose to go to the *gamba* healer's house as soon as they know that there is a patient (even one unknown to them) suffering under *a gamba* spirit. This manifested willingness to cooperate in the solution of problems affecting unknown persons afflicted by *gamba* spirits indicates the collective dimension of the *gamba* phenomenon.

2.2.2 Reconciliation between People and Spirits

The world of the living cannot be separated from that of the spirits. Both form part of the same social world. As a result of the extreme abuse and mass killings that took place in the civil war, relations between the living and the spirits of the dead were severely disrupted. The landscape and the social environment were also affected: *phfumbe rawa nhakufa*, i.e., the *dust of the dead* polluted society as a whole. This expression suggests the existence of many corpses from the war that were not properly buried; sacred zones such as cemeteries that were violated during the war with no attempts made in the post-war era to re-establish them; men and women continuing to disrespect the dead by engaging extramarital sexual intercourse either in the forests or in ad-hoc cemeteries; in general, people hardly ever worshipping their ancestral spirits in the privacy of their homesteads. Above all, the *dust of the dead* is an indicator of the existence of large numbers of individuals in communities who have a prowess in conflict and killing. For all these reasons, *gamba* spirits seriously afflict the living, forcing them to know and be continuously and publicly confronted with the images of what war does. In this respect, gamba spirits resemble a kind of collective remembering in which "our bodies, which in commemorations stylistically re-enact an image of the past, keep the past also in an entirely effective form in their continuing ability to perform certain skilled actions" (Connerton 1989, p. 72).

Since the living initially resist the need to assume their individual and collective responsibilities, *gamba* spirits block the most important physiological and social process, i.e., reproduction. *Gamba* impairs society from regenerating. It is at this moment that the living realise that they must reconcile peacefully with the spirits of the dead. Therefore, war survivors gather together in the house of a *gamba* healer, perform for the *gamba* spirit and the *gamba* spirit manifests itself to the public, which is ready to listen. After deliberation, the family concerned asks the *gamba* spirit for forgiveness (*ku lekerera*). They then look for the goods that the *gamba* spirit considers necessary to be given to him to repair the havoc. When this reparation has been completed, the living requests the *gamba* spirit to go home in peace and to leave the afflicted person in peace. The departure of the *gamba* spirit allows in principle procreation to take its normal course, and normal life to resume.

2.2.3 Reconciliation between the Spirits Themselves

In general *gamba* are alien spirits. The initial configuration connected *gamba* spirits to the male soldiers who died in combat in Gorongosa. With the passage of time, *gamba* spirits came to be associated with the unjustified death of any men during the civil war. Although war survivors can recognise some of the soldiers or civilians who return as *gamba* spirits, these spirits are alien because historically Gorongosa was dominated by the existence of ancestral spirits known as *madzoca* spirits. *Madzoca* spirits only possess people who have a history of healing within their lineage.

Gamba spirits changed the prevailing logic of the *madzoca* spirits, as *gamba* randomly possess anybody, as long as the person (or his/her family) has a history of extreme suffering, abuse and death as a result of the war. However, more important than possessing people *gamba* spirits needed to be accepted: to create an institution in society. That is, the transformation of *gamba* spirits into *gamba* healers was only possible because *gamba* spirits made a reconciliatory pact with the ancestral spirits. Under these conditions, the *gamba* spirits established themselves as a valid healing institution in Gorongosa and elsewhere in central Mozambique. A pertinent example of this reconciliation can be illustrated through the fact that the *madzoca* healers initially showed some resistance to the emergence of the *gamba* spirits and healers. Over time, this has changed and various *madzoca* healers have incorporated certain aspects of the *gamba* healing institution into their healing practice. *Gamba* healers have done the same. It is interesting to observe how *madzoca* healers have adopted some of the *gamba* healing techniques, particularly by eliciting their patients' past of war violence, instead of their common ancestral past.

3 Concluding Remarks

In the aftermath of the civil war in Mozambique, the state officials enacted an unconditional amnesty law to avoid dealing with the legacies of the violent past. This legal norm did not accommodate the objective reality of the various communities that had been seriously wronged by both the governmental and opposition troops. One of the rules in Gorongosa is that a wrong cannot cease unless the legitimate institutions deal with it. The state amnesty law that order impunity and silence over the abuses and crimes of the past diverged from the local ethics of reciprocity that orders accountability for serious past wrongs as a precondition for social peace and productive collective action. In this context, the practices of *gamba* spirits to unveil past truths and attain justice and reconciliation have to be analysed in the context of a community that has deep historical and cultural roots in terms of interactions between the living and the spirits of the dead victims.

Gamba spirits appeared in a society that believes that silence is not an effective solution to certain forms of violent conflict since "a conflict does not get rotten." A conflict needs to be actively addressed in order to foster social peace in the society. Although the goals of the *gamba* spirits intersect at certain points with the goals of secular institutions of justice, they differ greatly in scope. Secular institutions of justice are primarily concerned with establishing individual culpability and the modalities of punishment. G*amba* spirits also identify individual culprits, but it is as much about the collective as it is about the individual. For this reason, an intervention by *gamba* spirits cannot take place if the relatives of the host are not present. They must be there in order to participate in the deliberations, and as the person singled out for wrongdoing assumes his or her responsibilities. It is the justice achieved by the spirit that allows the living to move on in their lives. In this context, the secular institutions of justice are clearly limited in the goals that they pursue. As demonstrated above, the *gamba* spirits deal with all the various issues of truth, justice and reconciliation at once. Furthermore, reconciliation is comprehensive since the spirits create conditions for reconciliation between the living people, between the living and the spirits and among the spirits themselves. As Douglas Fry suggests "an anthropological perspective demonstrates that humans are capable of devising and employing a great diversity of conflict prevention and management techniques" (2006, p. 260). That is, state sponsored retributive justice or truth commissions in periods of transition should be seen as one of many mechanisms available to deal with crimes of the past, since there are indeed other ways of thinking about truth and justice. In order to understand the meaningfulness of this diversity of mechanisms to deal with legacies of violent pasts in post-conflict societies, there is a need to develop critical approaches to state power and state action. In this regard,

Carol Greenhouse (2002, p. 6) suggests that "the state is not the endpoint of some evolution of political forms but only one modality of concentrating and representing human agency that always entails alternative, even rival, forms." Gamba spirits and healers represent an alternative form of power to deal with the legacies of modern warfare involving state and rebel armed groups.

Despite the accomplishments of the *gamba* spirits, one lesson that it is important to spell out is that the justice enacted by the *gamba* spirits does not replace national and international formal processes of justice. The reconciliation between ancestral and *gamba* spirits reiterates the political dimension of the *gamba* spirits. These spirits were born out of an extreme armed conflict among factions that were fighting to retain political control and legitimacy (Frelimo), accessing political recognition (Renamo), and paying a political debt and accessing trans-frontier resources (Zimbabwean army). The male soldiers from these three armies are capable of returning as a *gamba* spirit and bear witness to the mass-scale of war violence that ravaged Mozambique over two decades. However, the emergence of *gamba* spirits should not be used as an excuse by political authorities to avoid assuming one of their post-war responsibilities, which is to engage in national processes of truth-seeking, justice and reconciliation.

Although the goals of the *gamba* spirits are comprehensive, they deal principally with transitional processes within families and communities. The individuals directly responsible for the war destruction and crimes nowadays belong to the official institutions of the Mozambican state. These individuals do not physically participate in the *gamba* sessions to be held accountable for their past actions. Usually only their names are referred to. Yet the naming of these figures during the *gamba* sessions are permanent indictments for and reminders of their participation in the orchestration of extreme violent acts against civilians during the civil war.

Under these circumstances it is appropriate to consider complementing sociocultural processes performed by the *gamba* spirits (and similar processes around the globe) with national and international formal processes of transitional justice. The tendency to endorse the idea of complementarity between various types of transitional justice approaches that are applicable in contexts of mass-scale violence, has been gaining momentum since the creation of the *gacaca* justice system in the aftermath of the 1994 Rwandan genocide and the recent demonstration of *mato oput* (bitter root or juice) ceremonies among the Acholi people in northern Uganda. In post-genocide Rwanda the political authorities re-recreated *gacaca*, which is a community mechanism of conflict resolution, in order to "make it applicable to the prosecution of those accused of having committed crimes during the genocide" (Molennar 2005, p. 3). Although the *gacaca* system has been widely criticized for its weaknesses in conforming to due legal procedures, it demonstrates the prospect of various types of legal orders, including grassroots justice approaches, in addressing mass-scale and collective crimes in an African country. In relation to attempts to resolve the conflict in northern Uganda, the elders are said to mediate in the *mato oput* ceremony, in which the wrongdoer must admit responsibility, ask for forgiveness and agree to pay compensation. Both parties drink the blood of a sacrificed sheep mixed with *mato oput*, and the ceremony ends with *gomo tong* (bending spears) to represent reconciliation (Allen 2006, pp. 132–3). *Mato oput* is another example of how people living in contexts of extreme violent conflicts can develop their own ways of achieving resolution. Although during *mato oput* ceremonies nobody is prosecuted, as in the case of *gacaca*, the fact that the wrongdoer is called upon to admit his or her responsibility signals the presence of ideas and practices of accountability in these systems.

The consideration of the idea that there are different ways of thinking and enacting justice should lead us to think that in certain societies ravaged by civil wars, transitional justice by way of formal retribution (national and international) or state sponsored truth commissions are alternatives to the potential embodied and enacted by socio-cultural processes such as that of the *gamba* spirits. If we endorse this proposition and consider it as a serious challenge, then it is appropriate to develop mechanisms for achieving dialogue and cooperation between various forms of post-war truth finding, justice and reconciliation, instead of relying uniquely on state and formal approaches to deal with legacies of civil strife.

Acknowledgments The author wishes to thank NIAS, Africa Study Center (ASC, Leiden), LUMC and CNWS of the University of Leiden.

References

Allen T (2006) Trial justice: the international criminal court and lord's resistance army. Zed Books, London

Cohen S (2001) States of denial: knowing about atrocities and suffering. Polity, Cambridge

Connerton P (1989) How societies remember. Cambridge University Press, Cambridge

Elias N (1970) What is sociology? Columbia University Press, New York

Fry D (2006) The human potential for peace: an anthropological challenge to assumptions about war and violence. Oxford University Press, Oxford

Greenhouse C (2002) Introduction: altered states, altered lives. Ethnography in unstable places: everyday lives in contexts of dramatic political change. Duke University Press, Durham, pp 1–34

Hanlon J (1991) Who calls the shots? Indiana University Press, Bloomington

Hayner P (2001) Unspeakable truths: confronting state terror and atrocity. Routledge, New York

Igreja V (2003) Why are there many drums playing until dawn? Exploring the role of gamba spirits and healers in the post-war recovery period in Gorongosa, Central Mozambique. Transcult Psychiatry 40:459–487

Igreja V (2008) Igreja V (2008) Memories as weapons: the politics of peace and silence in post-civil war Mozambique. J South Afr Stud 34(3): 539–556

Igreja V, Dias-Lambranca B (2008) Restorative justice and the role of magamba spirits in post-civil war Gorongosa, Central Mozambique. In: Huyse L, Salter M (eds) Traditional justice and reconciliation after violent conflict: learning from African experiences. International IDEA, Stockholm, pp 61–83

Igreja V, Kleijn W, Richters A (2006) Women's posttraumatic suffering after the war in Mozambique. J Nerv Ment Dis 194:502–509

Igreja V, Dias-Lambranca B, Richters A (2008) *Gamba* spirits, gender relations and healing in post-civil war Gorongosa, Mozambique. J R Anthropol Inst 14:350–371

Kleinman A (1997) Writing at the margin: discourse between anthropology and medicine. University of California Press, Berkeley

Long W, Brecke P (2003) War and reconciliation: Reason and emotion in conflict resolution. MIT, Cambridge

Marlin R (2001) Possessing the past: legacies of violence and reproductive illness in central Mozambique. Ph.D. thesis, New Brunswick, NJ

Minow M, Ryan M, Sarat A (1995) Narrative, violence and the law: the essays of Robert Cover. The University of Michigan Press, Ann Arbor

Molenaar A (2005) Gacaca: grassroots justice after genocide. African Studies Centre, Leiden

Perera S (2001) Spirit possessions and avenging ghosts. In: Das V, Kleinman A, Lock M, Ramphele M, Reynolds P (eds) Remaking a world: violence, social suffering, and recovery. University of California Press, Berkeley, pp 157–200

Rosenthal J (2002) Trance against the state. In: Greenhouse CJ, Mertz E, Warren KB (eds) Ethnography in unstable places: everyday lives in contexts of dramatic political change. Duke University Press, Durham, pp 316–351

Sriram C (2004) Confronting past human rights violations: justice vs peace in times of transition. Frank Cass, London

Teitel R (2000) Transitional justice. New York, NY: Oxford University Press

Thomashausen A (2001) Mozambique: a case study. In: Conference on Politics of Identity and Exclusion in Africa. University of Pretoria, Pretoria www.kas.de/db_files/dokumente/7_dokument_dok_pdf_5094_2.pdf

Tomuschat C (2003) Human rights: between idealism and realism. Oxford University Press, Oxford

Trindade J (2003) Rupturas e continuidades nos processos politicos e juridicos. In: Conflito e transformação social: Uma paisagem das justiças em Moçambique. Edições Afrontamento, Porto, pp 97–125

Foreign Aid to Transitional Justice: The Cases of Rwanda and Guatemala, 1995–2005*

Stina Petersen, Ingrid Samset, and Vibeke Wang

Abstract Although transitional justice (TJ) has been an area of significant donor engagement for more than a decade, little is known about the scope, trends, and experiences of that engagement. This study examines patterns and priorities of the aid that was given from 1995 through 2005 in support of transitional justice in Rwanda and Guatemala. It is based on statistical data from 15 donors and on interviews with 20 donor officials. The size of the TJ aid to the two countries in this period was modest, only accounting for about 5% of total development aid. While security sector reform received the bulk of the TJ assistance, the distribution of the remaining assistance was diverse. In Rwanda it targeted retributive justice processes including criminal courts and *gacaca*, while in Guatemala it focused on restorative justice institutions such as truth commissions and reparations. In Rwanda most of the TJ aid went directly to the government, and donor priorities by and large reflected government priorities. In Guatemala donor loyalties first and foremost lay with the peace accords, and donor commitment to certain TJ mechanisms was often not matched by a similar commitment on the part of the government. While Guatemala received more TJ support immediately after the end of the conflict, in Rwanda aid levels rose most prominently in the last half of the post-genocide period. While identifying trends such as these is a vital first step to fill the knowledge gap, further research is required to understand how transitional justice aid works across cases, over time and for different actors.

I. Samset
Chr. Michelsen Institute (CMI), Bergen, Norway,
e-mail: Ingrid.samset@cmi.no

*The chapter is a revised version of Samset et al. (2007). For inputs to the revision process the authors wish to thank Rachel Sieder, Siri Gloppen, as well as participants at occasions where drafts were presented: (1) the meeting held on 11 September 2007 of the Rights, Democracy and Development Research Group at Chr. Michelsen Institute (CMI) in Bergen, Norway; (2) the meeting "Donor Strategies for Transitional Justice: Taking Stock and Moving Forward" held on 15–16 October 2007 in London, convened by the UK Department for International Development and the International Center for Transitional Justice; and (3) the workshop "Transitional Justice and the Role of Donors" held on 7 November 2007 as part of the Annual Conference of the Norwegian Association for Development Research at CMI.

K. Ambos et al. (eds.), *Building a Future on Peace and Justice: Studies on Transitional Justice, Peace and Development.*

1 Introduction

Rwanda and Guatemala, two countries far apart and with many differences, both came out of devastating armed conflicts in the mid-1990s. In the aftermath, each sought to address what had happened and to seek some form of justice. For this purpose they drew not only on their own resources, but also received considerable economic assistance from foreign countries and international organisations.

This chapter examines aid given to the two countries' transitional justice (TJ) efforts from 1995 through 2005. Much has been written about Rwanda's and Guatemala's conflicts and their peacebuilding processes,[1] and some more specifically about the development aid they received to rebuild their societies.[2] Yet the aid to the area of transitional justice has not yet been systematically assessed, despite the substantial donor involvement in this field in the two countries.

A comparison between Rwanda and Guatemala is instructive for several reasons. Both countries have received transitional justice assistance at least since the mid-1990s, which makes it possible to map and compare trends in aid allocation over a relatively long period of time. The numerous differences between the cases also shaped divergent courses of action and varying outcomes that we can learn from. Rwanda was poorer and aid's share of overall income was higher there than in Guatemala. The Rwandan conflict was shorter and more intensive than the Guatemalan one, and in Rwanda, the post-war regime was representative of the victims of the previous conflict and pursued a retributive justice approach. Guatemala, by contrast, did not see any substantial reversal of power roles, and somewhat reluctantly pursued a restorative justice approach.

To map and assess the TJ aid in these two cases, we collected data from donors that supported this field in the two countries in the 11-year period under review. 20 donor officials were interviewed by telephone, and statistical data were collected from 15 donor agencies on the size and targets of the transitional justice aid.[3] Our data shed light on the magnitude, origins, distribution, and sequencing of the TJ assistance, and the motivations, priorities and strategies of the involved donors.

2 Theoretical and Empirical Context

2.1 *Aid to Transitional Justice: The Knowledge Gap*

Economic assistance to countries coming out of armed conflict has become a key policy issue after the end of the Cold War. As state sovereignty has been

[1] On Rwanda, see, e.g., Barnett (2002); Hintjens (1999, p. 241); Jones (2001); Mamdani (2001); and Straus (2006). On Guatemala, see, e.g., Booth et al. (2006); Jonas (1991, 2000); Schirmer (1998); and Torres-Rivas and Peralta (1998).

[2] On Rwanda, see, e.g., Hayman (2006); Kimonyo et al. (2004); Uvin (2001, p. 177). On Guatemala, see, e.g., Azpuru et al. (2004); Paris (2004); Sørbø et al. (2002).

[3] The statistical data are on file with the authors and are available upon request. The list of informants is given in Samset et al. (2007).

fundamentally questioned and "peacebuilding" has climbed up on the policy agenda, post-war reconstruction is no longer seen as a matter a country should deal with all on its own. The emerging set of presumed pro-peace policy prescriptions includes not only peacekeeping, economic recovery, and statebuilding but also transitional justice. Transitional justice is assumed to help provide the truth about past violence, reparations for victims, accountability for perpetrators, reconciliation – and through all of this deterrence, "rule of law", and less violence. Mechanisms such as prosecutions, truth-telling, and reparations are thus considered critical in so-called post-conflict situations. In parallel with this normative development, dozens of countries that have gone through civil war, genocide, or authoritarian rule have in the last few decades started taking up the task of dealing with their troublesome histories. Due both to a changing normative framework and to new opportunities and demands for intervention, many of the world's more affluent countries and international organisations have therefore started funding such transitional justice measures.

They have done so, however, in spite of a virtual absence of knowledge about how and how well this type of aid works. To start with, since no cross-donor database on TJ aid yet exists, estimates of the total amounts of aid that have gone into this field are hard to come by. Our knowledge is also scarce on the origins, intermediaries, and targets of TJ aid across cases; the variations in these aid flows over time; perceptions of this aid among different groups in recipient countries; motivations and strategies among donors; and not least on the impact of the TJ aid. Other open questions include how the external support element shapes a country's internal process to deal with its own past, and what the driving forces and consequences of aid to this complex field have been.[4]

This scarcity of academic knowledge on most aspects of TJ aid can be seen as a paradox, given the enormous growth of the literature on transitional justice over the last couple of decades. This research has looked at normative foundations of transitional justice (see, e.g., Kritz 1995; Leebaw 2008, p. 95; Minow 1998; Teitel 2000) and on how mechanisms of transitional justice have worked, with a focus either on mechanisms within single countries (see, e.g., Chapman and van der Merwe 2008; Shaw 2007, p. 183; Waldorf 2006, p. 1), on one mechanism across countries (see, e.g., Hayner 2001; Huyse and Salter 2008), or, more recently and rarely, on different mechanisms across cases.[5] Yet exploring how TJ works is certainly different than understanding how aid to this field works. While aid to TJ might earlier have been seen as a too new or patchy a phenomenon to explore systematically, today such aid has been provided for more than a decade in many regions of the world. There is hence a rich pool of cases and a relatively long time period to examine. More knowledge about TJ aid would enhance chances that the considerable aid amounts be well invested, and that recipient countries get better off as a result. It would also help

[4] The need to improve our understanding of how TJ aid works is also highlighted in the report from a 2007 international meeting about donor strategies within the TJ arena. See ICTJ and DFID (2008).

[5] For a statistical study see Lie et al. (2007). For a literature review see Thoms et al. (2008). For a study of interaction effects between and combined effects of different mechanisms, see Schabas and Darcy (2004).

us understand the normative rise of transitional justice as an international political phenomenon.

There is hence a knowledge gap that needs to be filled, and this chapter takes one step in that direction – by mapping and analysing TJ aid in two cases, Rwanda and Guatemala, from 1995 through 2005. Before we introduce the cases though, let us outline what we mean by aid to transitional justice in this study.

2.2 Classifying Aid to Transitional Justice

We define transitional justice aid in this chapter as foreign economic assistance provided to support mechanisms of transitional justice, as defined, in recipient countries. We hence classify the aid in accordance with the mechanisms targeted by it. In the cases of Rwanda and Guatemala, five such mechanisms were relevant to assess:

- Criminal courts
- Truth commissions
- Mechanisms for traditional justice
- The security sector
- Reparations[6]

Criminal courts comprise, in this chapter, international and domestic attempts to prosecute persons who allegedly perpetrated war crimes, crimes against humanity or genocide during the previous conflict. The category also includes governmental human rights bodies with an investigative or prosecution mandate. The formal courts system – i.e., the courts that do not deal primarily with serious crimes from the past conflict – is not included in this category, but instead in the security sector (see below).

Truth commissions is defined as "institutions outside of the judicial apparatus, established... to uncover evidence about abuses committed under a previous regime or during a civil war" (Gloppen 2005, p. 27). This category covers both the set-up and operation of such commissions as well as the dissemination of their findings.

Traditional justice mechanisms include so-called traditional forms of restorative or retributive justice that can be found beyond the formal justice system.

The security sector involves the police, judiciary, penal institutions and the armed forces. The category includes security sector reform (SSR), which aims at building or strengthening security sector institutions. We also classify programmes of demobilisation, disarmament and reintegration of ex-combatants (DDR) as SSR.[7]

[6] The transitional justice mechanism of vetting or lustration was not relevant to include since no official vetting processes occurred in either of the two cases.

[7] The decision to include SSR as a transitional justice mechanism was made by the commissioner of the study on which this chapter is based (see initial asterisk note), following discussions with the authors. While SSR often is not considered part of transitional justice, judicial and justice sector reform commonly are. The logic for including SSR is that the judiciary is part of the justice sector, and the justice sector is part of the security sector – hence judicial and justice sector reform

Reparations involve the symbolic and material rehabilitation of the victims of the past conflict. The category includes a wide range of efforts aimed at rehabilitation, such as financial compensation, exhumations of mass graves, mental health programmes and the building of memorials, museums and monuments.

2.3 Rwanda and Guatemala from 1995 through 2005

The 11 years from 1995 through 2005 was a time of transition from past periods of massive armed violence in both Rwanda and Guatemala. Rwanda went through a civil war from 1990 to 1993 and genocide in 1994, while Guatemala put an end to a 36-year long civil war in 1996 which had involved acts of genocide against indigenous groups. Table 1 provides key facts about the two countries and their conflicts.[8]

While the transition from the mid-1990s onward involved gradual moves towards electoral democracy in both countries, it was triggered by the end of large-scale violent conflicts. Rwanda's conflict had been relatively short and highly intensive; Guatemala's long and of lower intensity. The way the wars ended impacted on the nature of the post-war regimes and their transitional justice policies. In Guatemala, both the civil war and the negotiated transition were characterised by a strong imbalance of forces between a militarily weak guerrilla movement and a strong army.[9] This hampered any substantial efforts to redistribute power in the post-war period. In Rwanda, by contrast, it was the party representing the victims of the conflict that gained power at the transition, overthrowing the previous regime that had been instrumental in carrying out the genocide. Partly as a result of these differences, the post-conflict regime in Rwanda vigorously pursued a retributive justice approach,

---

are part of, and sometimes inseparable from security sector reform. By excluding SSR from the analysis, we would hence have missed much of the aid that targeted the TJ mechanism of judicial and justice sector reform. Granted, by including SSR we do adopt a broad definition of transitional justice which includes not only "backward-looking" mechanisms such as criminal courts, truth commissions and reparations, but also "forward-looking" ones such as judicial reform. This is not necessarily problematic however, since it is clear that SSR aims to fill important functions of transitional justice such as accountability, deterrence, and the rule of law. A more problematic aspect of including SSR is that the term comprises reform of the police, military, and intelligence sectors, and reform of these institutions is not commonly seen as a TJ mechanism. A more ideal solution might therefore have been to include judicial and/or justice sector reform only. The reason why we did not was largely practical: that in donors' statistics, especially from the early years, aid to judicial reform or the justice sector was often included in the SSR category. While including SSR in the study implied stretching the transitional justice concept, leaving it out thus implied a risk of excluding a key part of transitional justice from examination. SSR was therefore included.

[8] The table draws on the following sources: CEH/Historical Clarification Commission (1999); Davenport and Stam (2008, p. 24); EIU (2006, 2007); HRW and FIDH (1999); Lacina and Gleditsch (2005, p. 145); Reyntjens (2004, p. 177); and Wickham-Crowley (1992).

[9] Guatemala's post-war Historical Clarification Commission (CEH) concluded that the agents of the state, mainly the armed forces, were responsible for 93% of the acts of violence that were committed during the civil war while the guerilla was only responsible for 3% (CEH 1999, n 128).

Table 1 Conflict and post-conflict Rwanda and Guatemala: key facts

	Rwanda	Guatemala
Type of conflict[a]	Civil war and genocide	Civil war with acts of genocide
Period of conflict[a]	1990–1993 and 1994	1960–1996
Peaks of violence	1994	1966–1967 and 1981–1983
Number of persons killed during conflict[a]	Civil war: approx. 5,000	At least 200,000
	Genocide: between 500,000 and 1.1m	
Population (2006 estimate)	Approx. 9.2m	Approx. 13m
Size of country	$26,338\,km^2$	$108,889\,km^2$
GDP/capita	272 USD (2006 estimate)	2,535 USD (2005 estimate)
Post-conflict elections to date	2003, 2008	1999, 2003, 2007

[a]We refer to the armed conflicts that occurred immediately prior to the 11-year period analysed

while the one in Guatemala opted for a restorative justice approach which it pursued more reluctantly.

A range of donors supported Rwanda's and Guatemala's efforts to rebuild their war-torn countries from the mid-1990s onwards. They include:

Multilateral donors:

- The European Commission (EC)
- The United Nations Development Programme (UNDP)
- The World Bank (WB)

Bilateral donors:

- Belgium (Belgian MFA and DGDC)
- Canada (CIDA)
- Denmark (Danida)
- Finland (Finnish MFA)
- France (French MFA)
- Germany (BMZ and GTZ)
- The Netherlands (Dutch MFA)
- Norway (Norwegian MFA and Norad)
- Spain (Spanish MFA and AECI)
- Sweden (Sida)
- The United Kingdom (FCO and DFID)
- The United States of America (USAID)

Not all these donors supported transitional justice, but all contributed development aid. To put the TJ assistance in perspective, we assessed the magnitude of the development aid to Rwanda and Guatemala during the period in question. We analysed data on net disbursements of Official Development Assistance (ODA) from 13 of the 15 donors listed above, excluding the UNDP and the World Bank from which data was not readily accessible.[10] We found that Rwanda received approximately 25% more development aid than did Guatemala from the 13 donors in question. From 1995 to 2005 the donors contributed ODA worth approximately 2.7bn USD to Rwanda, while Guatemala received 2.1bn USD. On average per year, Rwanda thus received 244m USD and Guatemala 195m USD in development assistance. Figure 1 shows the distribution per year of the development assistance.

As the figure shows, aid was sequenced rather differently in the two countries. Aid to Rwanda peaked in the initial and final part of the post-conflict period, while aid to Guatemala rose relatively steadily over the 11 years. Rwanda's pattern is a U curve, while Guatemala's is more akin to an upward straight line.

Both countries saw an overall increase in aid in the post-conflict phase however, receiving more in 2005 than they did in 1995. Yet the increase was greater in

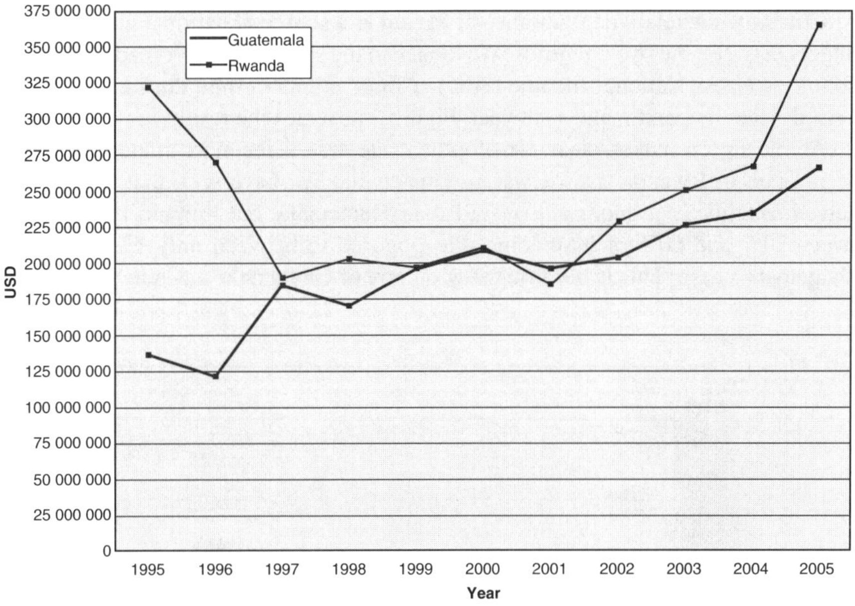

Fig. 1 Development aid to Rwanda and Guatemala, 1995–2005 (in USD)

[10] We used ODA data from the Organisation for Economic Cooperation and Development (OECD), presented in OECD's annual statistical reports (see OECD 2001, 2002, 2006, 2007). Unless otherwise specified, data presented in the following draw on the reports published in respectively 2001 (for the period 1995–1999), 2002 (1996–2000), 2006 (2000–2004) and 2007 (2001–2005). OECD defines official development assistance (ODA) as follows: "those flows to developing countries and multilateral institutions provided by official agencies, including state and local governments, or by their executive agencies, each transaction of which meets the following test: (a) it is administered with the promotion of the economic development and welfare of developing countries as its main objective; and (b) it is concessional in character ... and conveys a grant element of at least 25% per cent". OECD (2006, p. 309).

Guatemala's than in Rwanda's case. Guatemala saw aid rising from around 125m annually in 1995 and 1996, when the peace accords were being negotiated and signed, to 266m in 2005 – more than double. Even if we start from Guatemala's first "real" post-conflict year, 1997, the increase is substantial – from 185m in 1997 to 266m in 2005. In Rwanda, aid dropped from the first to the third post-conflict year and only started picking up again in 2001, the seventh year post-genocide. In line with the U-shaped pattern, total aid grew less in Rwanda than in Guatemala. In 1995 ODA to Rwanda was worth 325m USD, and in 2005 it exceeded this amount for the first time in the whole period – yet with an increase of only some 10%, reaching 365m USD.

Rwanda also saw greater variation in donor contributions. ODA to Rwanda varied between approximately 185m USD in 1997 and 2001 and 365m in 2005, which represents a doubling of the aid over a 4-year period. In Guatemala the amount varied between 122m USD in 1996 and 266m in 2005, which was also more than double but a smaller increase in absolute terms (144m USD) and one that spanned a longer period.

Crucially, the relative importance of the aid as a source of national income varied hugely between the two countries. We looked at the share that ODA made up of each country's Gross National Income (GNI) at three points in time during the 11-year period – the first, sixth, and 11th year. Figure 2 provides the results.

As the figure makes clear, development aid was a far more important source of revenue in Rwanda than it was in Guatemala. We have seen that Rwanda received roughly 25% more aid overall than Guatemala, but this aid made up between 20% and 60% of its income – as opposed to between only 1% and 2% in Guatemala's case. This is because the economy of Guatemala was much larger than

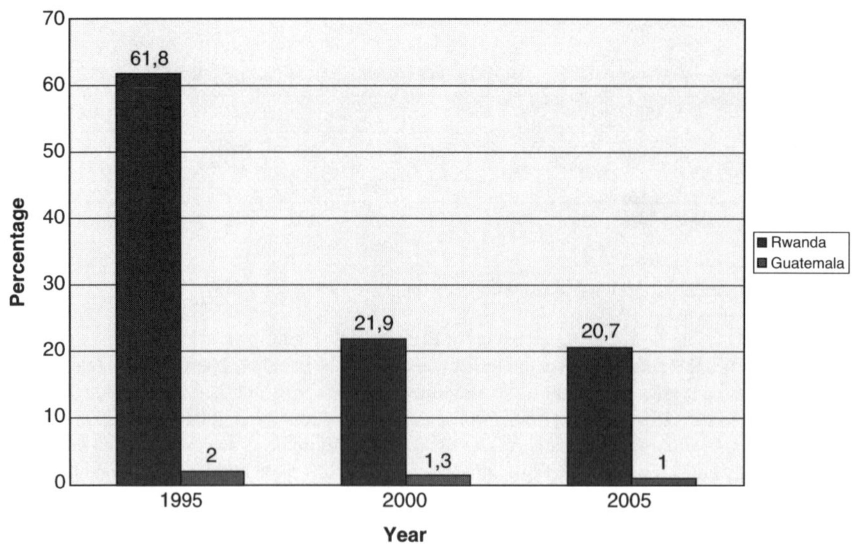

Fig. 2 Development aid's share of gross national income in Rwanda and Guatemala in 1995, 2000 and 2005 (in percent)

that of Rwanda, as revealed in Table 1 – which also showed that Guatemala had roughly a ten times higher GDP per capita. Both countries depended most on aid in the beginning of the post-conflict period, but the divergence remained vast also many years into the peace.

3 Patterns of Aid to Transitional Justice in Post-Conflict Rwanda and Guatemala

In the following we present our analysis of the statistical data we collected from donor agencies on TJ aid flows to post-conflict Rwanda and Guatemala. We outline how much the TJ aid made up of overall development aid; the relative contributions of the different donors involved; what mechanisms the support was channelled into; and finally how the assistance was sequenced over time.

3.1 Transitional Justice Aid Vs. Development Aid

While Rwanda received the most development aid in the period studied, Guatemala received a higher amount of aid to the field of transitional justice. Over the 11 years, Rwanda received 111m USD in support to the TJ mechanisms we assess, and Guatemala 140m USD – approximately 35% more. On average per year, Rwanda received 10.1m USD and Guatemala 12.7m USD in TJ assistance. Figure 3 gives an idea of how this level of TJ aid compared to overall development assistance, and also of how the two types of aid varied over time.

As the figure shows, Guatemala received more aid to TJ than did Rwanda most of the time; that is in the 7 middle years of the 11-year period. It also reveals that TJ aid increased over time in both countries, starting from a low level in 1995–1996 to reach peaks in the last half of the period.

Figure 3 also demonstrates the small share of TJ assistance compared to overall ODA. In effect, during the 11 years only around 5% of the development aid went to transitional justice in the two countries. Rwanda's 111m USD made up 4.1% of total ODA, and Guatemala's 140m USD constituted 6.5%. Figure 4 shows how the relative share of TJ aid to ODA varied over time.

In both countries aid to transitional justice grew considerably, from making up less than 1% of ODA in 1995–1996 to reach peaks of, respectively, 13% in Guatemala in 2002 and 9% in Rwanda in 2004. For Rwanda's part, two phases can be distinguished with regard to the relative importance of the TJ assistance. In the initial 6 years post-conflict, less than 2.6% of ODA went to the transitional justice field, while in the last 5 years the share was 7.3% on average.[11] Guatemala saw more of an inverted U curve, with four periods:

[11] The low level of aid in the first half of the period may partly derive from data bias, as data on transitional justice assistance to Rwanda was more difficult to access for the first half than for the second half of the period.

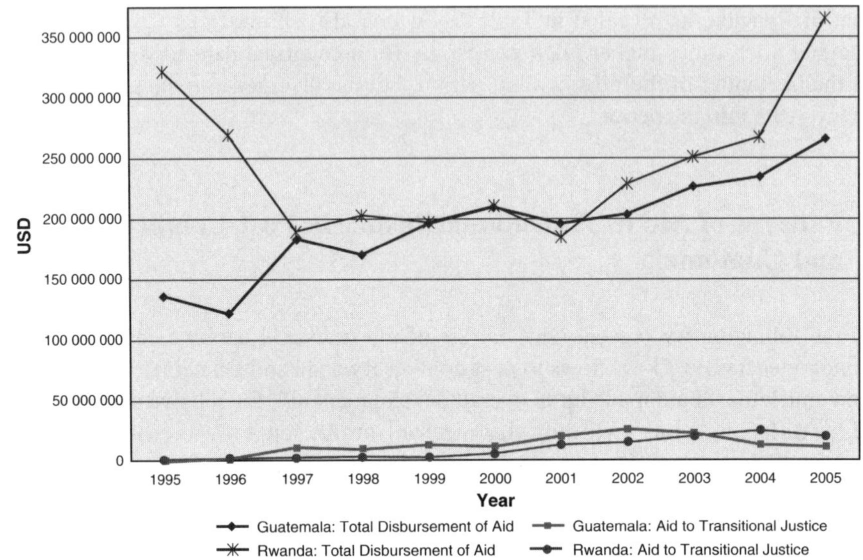

Fig. 3 Aid to transitional justice versus development in Rwanda and Guatemala, 1995–2005 (in USD)

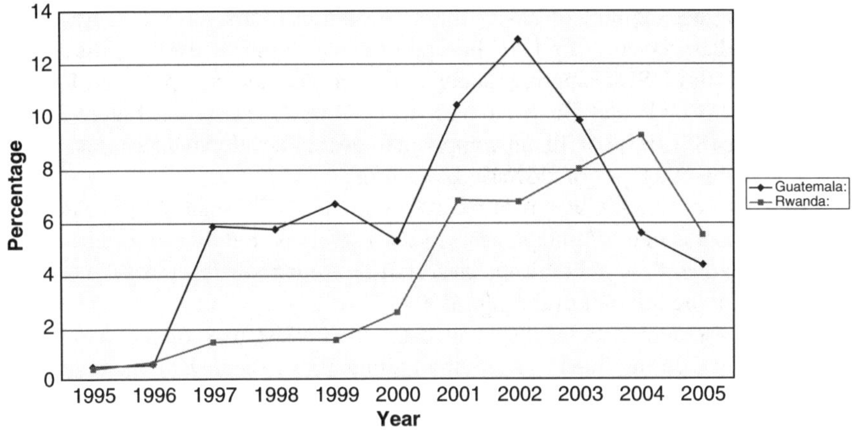

Fig. 4 Share of development aid allocated to transitional justice in Rwanda and Guatemala, 1995–2005 (in percent)

- A first low in 1995–1996, before the final peace accords had been signed
- A medium level during the first four post-war years, when TJ aid made up 5–7% of ODA
- A peak from year 5–7 post-conflict, when it constituted 10–13%
- A return to the medium level of 4–6% of TJ aid out of overall ODA in the eight and ninth post-war year

3.2 The Donors

Not all the donors of development aid were involved in supporting transitional justice. Moreover, we were not able to obtain sufficient data from all relevant donors. Beyond the three multilaterals (the UNDP, World Bank and the EC), we thus assess data from seven to eight bilateral donors in relation to each recipient country. These are:

In Rwanda's case:

- Belgium (Belgian MFA and DGDC)
- Canada (CIDA)
- France (French MFA)
- Germany (BMZ and GTZ)
- The Netherlands (Dutch MFA)
- Norway (Norwegian MFA and Norad)
- The UK (FCO and DFID)
- The USA (USAID)

In Guatemala's case:

- Denmark (Danida)
- Germany (BMZ and GTZ)
- Norway (Norwegian MFA and Norad)
- The Netherlands (Dutch MFA)
- Sweden (Sida)
- The UK (FCO and DFID)
- The USA (USAID)

Compared to our initial list of twelve bilateral donors of development aid, two donors – Finland and Spain – no longer figure, while five donors – Belgium, Canada, Denmark, France, and Sweden – only figure for one of the two countries. The remaining five – Germany, the Netherlands, Norway, the UK and the US – are the only ones for which we analyse transitional justice aid data in relation to both recipient countries. Taking into account the three multilateral donors too, we examine transitional justice aid from eleven donors to Rwanda and ten donors to Guatemala.

How big a share of the total aid to transitional justice did each of the donors contribute? Figure 5 provides the data on this for Rwanda; depicting the relative contribution of each of the eleven donors to the total of 111m USD that Rwanda received for this purpose during the period under review.

As the figure shows, the Netherlands contributed the most transitional justice aid and the UK the least among the eleven donors in this field in Rwanda. While the European Commission was the second biggest donor, only 34% of the funds went through the three multilateral organisations taken together. The UNDP played only a minor funding role. The Netherlands, Belgium and the US together contributed considerably more than the three multilaterals.

Figure 5 therefore also illustrates a general pattern: that in the Rwandan case, the bilateral donors dominated the field of transitional justice and chose to establish direct partnerships with the Rwandan government. In Guatemala by contrast, 59% of the transitional justice aid went through multilateral donors, mainly the UNDP. Figure 6 illustrates that dominance of the multilateral agencies in Guatemala's case.

43% of the aid to transitional justice in Guatemala went through the UNDP, which reflects the fact that many bilateral donors worked through the UNDP instead

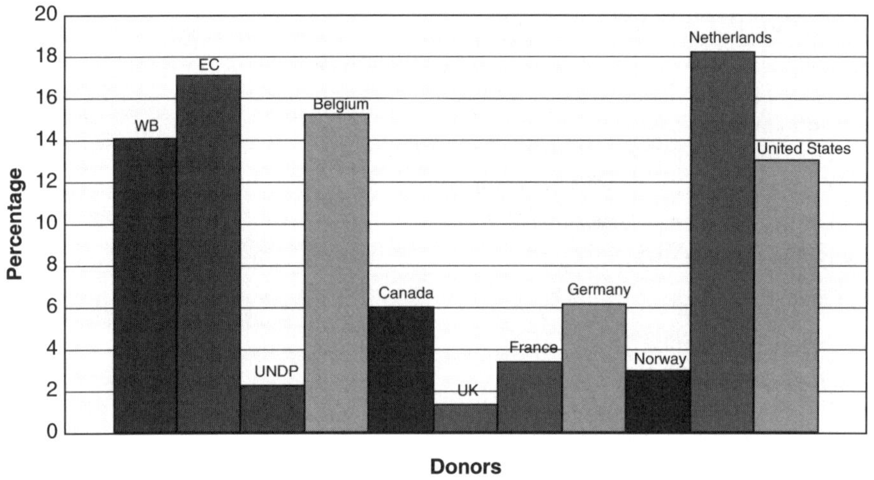

Fig. 5 Share of aid to transitional justice in Rwanda contributed by each donor, 1995–2005 (in percent)

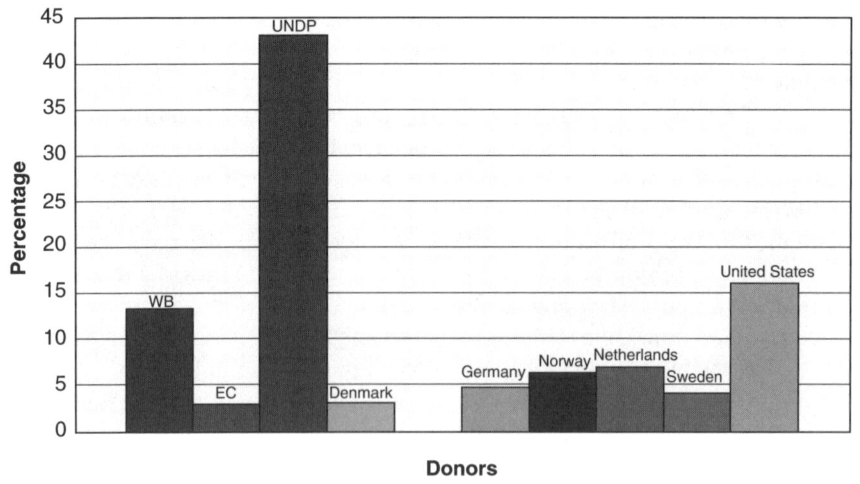

Fig. 6 Share of aid to transitional justice in Guatemala contributed by each donor, 1995–2005 (in percent)

of cooperating directly with the Guatemalan authorities. While the direct bilateral contributions hence were less significant in Guatemala's case than in Rwanda's, the most important bilateral donor was the United States, which contributed some 16% of the aid. The six other bilateral donors gave less than half of that each.

Of the bilateral donors, the Netherlands and the United States hence emerge as the most important contributors to transitional justice in both Rwanda and Guatemala during the period in question. Germany and Norway were also present in both countries, but with smaller inputs.

3.3 Distribution Across Mechanisms

As noted earlier we adopt a fairly broad approach to transitional justice in this chapter; including not only the "classic" institutions of truth commissions, criminal courts and reparations, that are essentially backward-looking; but also "traditional" justice mechanisms and security sector reform, the latter a more forward-looking instrument.

Interestingly, *security sector reform*, which is not always regarded as part of the transitional justice field in the academic literature, was by far the most supported mechanism in both countries. As Figs. 7 and 8 show, SSR aid made up more than half of the aid to TJ in Rwanda and Guatemala; in the latter case almost three quarters.

As for *criminal courts*, a far higher share of the aid went to this mechanism in Rwanda than in Guatemala: roughly 20% in the former and only 3% in the latter case. Institutions in this category include the Human Rights Ombudsman and

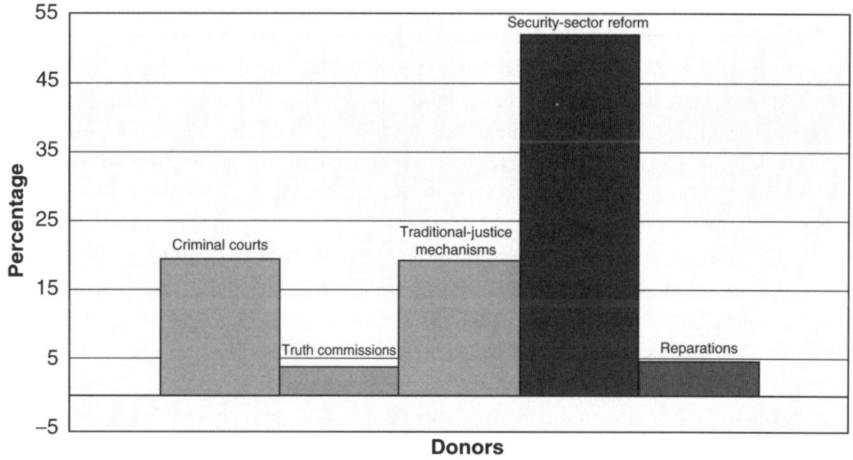

Fig. 7 Distribution across mechanisms of transitional justice aid to Rwanda, 1995–2005 (in percent)

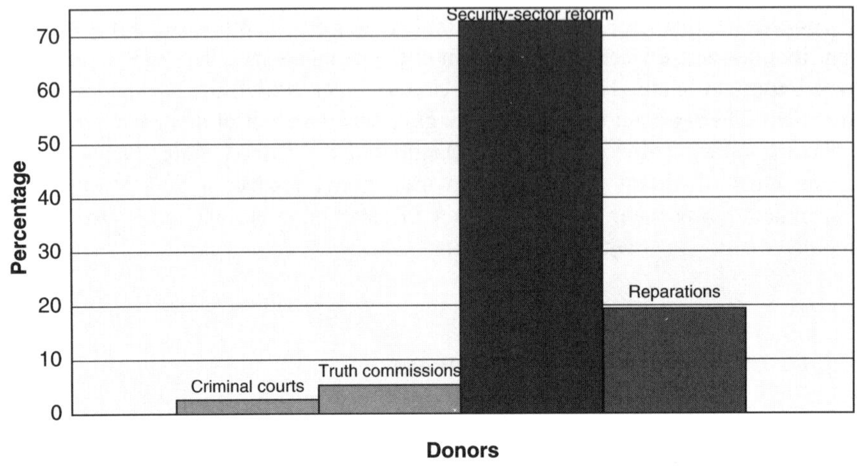

Fig. 8 Distribution across mechanisms of transitional justice aid to Guatemala, 1995–2005 (in percent)

the Women's Ombudsman in Guatemala and in Rwanda the National Commission for Human Rights (CNDH) and the International Criminal Tribunal for Rwanda (ICTR). While our data cover bilateral and multilateral contributions to the ICTR, this tribunal was also supported through the UN system, so criminal courts support in Rwanda's case is therefore likely to have been somewhat higher than what our data suggest. The low level of aid to criminal courts in Guatemala relates to the fact that alleged perpetrators of war-time crimes were not brought to trial internally in the country in the period under study. Civil society groups sought to use Spanish courts and the Inter-American Court of Human Rights for this purpose, yet aid to those attempts is not covered by our data.

Truth commissions received a relatively similar share of the transitional justice aid in both countries – around 5% only. In Guatemala more aid was given to truth commissions than to criminal courts, while in Rwanda the reverse was true. The institutions supported in Guatemala were the Historical Clarification Commission (CEH) and the Recovery of Historical Memory Commission (REHMI), and in Rwanda the National Unity and Reconciliation Commission (NURC). The NURC, however, does not entirely fit our definition of a truth commission (given in Sect. 2.2), since it was established not in order to document what happened during a past period of conflict and to disseminate such information, but rather to promote reconciliation and national unity through educational and more forward-looking activities. While the NURC thus shares the aim of reconciliation with other truth commissions, its chief means towards that end has been different and it might rather be called a hybrid TJ mechanism. We still opt to identify the NURC as a truth commission in this chapter, chiefly for purposes of comparative analysis. Including it enables us to assess how the institution that was most similar to a truth commission in Rwanda was supported, both as compared to other TJ mechanisms in the country and as compared to the truth commission category in Guatemala's case.

As regards *"traditional" justice mechanisms*, Figs. 7 and 8 reveal that only in Rwanda was this category supported, with roughly 20% of the transitional justice aid – about the same share as what went to criminal courts. The only institution in this category is *gacaca*.[12] Yet the location of *gacaca* in the "traditional" mechanism category can also be questioned. In her contribution to this volume, Oomen acknowledges this by identifying *gacaca* as a "neo-traditional" measure, but merely including the term "traditional" might mislead. As Schabas (2005, p. 895) asserts, "although [*gacaca*] defers symbolically to traditional models, it is really nothing more than a very decentralized system of justice administered by non-professionals at the local level". Waldorf (2006, p. 52) elaborates, pointing out that "the new gacaca system is an official state institution intimately linked to the state apparatus of prosecutions and incarceration, and applying codified, rather than 'customary,' law". The mechanism might therefore have been put in the criminal court category. Even though it is "traditional" only in the sense of having been inspired by a conflict resolution mechanism from Rwanda's past, we categorise *gacaca* as a "traditional" measure and not as a criminal court since this enables us to assess its separate importance relative to other mechanisms.

Reparations, finally, is the only category apart from SSR which got a higher share of the TJ funding in Guatemala than in Rwanda: almost 20% in the former and roughly 5% in the latter. In Rwanda, reparations support went to no major institution or programme of financial compensation to victims, but instead to mental health programmes and the building of museums, monuments and memorials. In Guatemala too, reparations funds went to mental health programmes, but also to mass grave exhumations and to efforts to facilitate the set-up and functioning of the National Reparations Program (PNR). By the end of the 11-year period studied here however, hardly any Guatemalan war victims had yet received any financial compensation.[13] And as opposed to Rwanda, reparations aid in Guatemala did not seem to have involved any building of museums and monuments in remembrance of the conflict in the period under study.

To sum up, security sector reform was a key target of TJ aid in both countries. Support to transitional justice went to a wider range of mechanisms in Rwanda than in Guatemala, including local and international courts, yet in Guatemala more was allocated to reparations. Across the two cases, truth commissions received only a fraction of the TJ assistance.

[12] Guatemala too had programmes that might be identified as "traditional" justice, but we classify these within the security sector since they primarily focused on the formal justice system.

[13] Naveda and Hurtado (2007) report that in April 2003, the reparations programme was assigned an annual fund of 300m quetzales (worth approximately 40m USD with a 2007 exchange rate), but by September 2006 only 623 of the 10,000 solicitors had received compensation.

3.4 Sequencing

To find out how the aid to transitional justice in post-conflict Rwanda and Guatemala was distributed over time, we will now take a closer look at the aggregate figures, and then disaggregate the data between the five different mechanisms.

3.4.1 Aggregate Trends

As noted in Sect. 3.1, our data suggest that Rwanda and Guatemala received 111m and 140m USD respectively in TJ aid during the studied period. When comparing this to statistics on development aid, we saw that the aid to transitional justice increased over time in each country, from an initial low point to peaks in the last half of the period (Fig. 3). Figure 9 zooms in on this distribution of the TJ aid across the 11 years we analysed.

The pattern in absolute figures is similar to that of the relative figures, detected in Fig. 4 where trends on TJ aid as a share of ODA were presented. We identified, in Rwanda's case, two sequences during the 11-year period, and in Guatemala's case four. As Fig. 9 shows, these sequences recur in the patterns of the absolute figures of TJ aid. In Rwanda, aid to transitional justice was significantly less during the first six years than during the last five of the period. In Guatemala, by contrast, the aid followed an inverted U pattern, with a medium level during the first four post-war years, a peak during year 5, 6 and 7, and a drop to the medium level again in year eight and nine after the peace deal. In Rwanda, aid during the first sequence grew from 1.4m to roughly 5m USD, while during the last it ranged between approximately 13m and 25m USD per year. In post-war Guatemala, by contrast, TJ aid

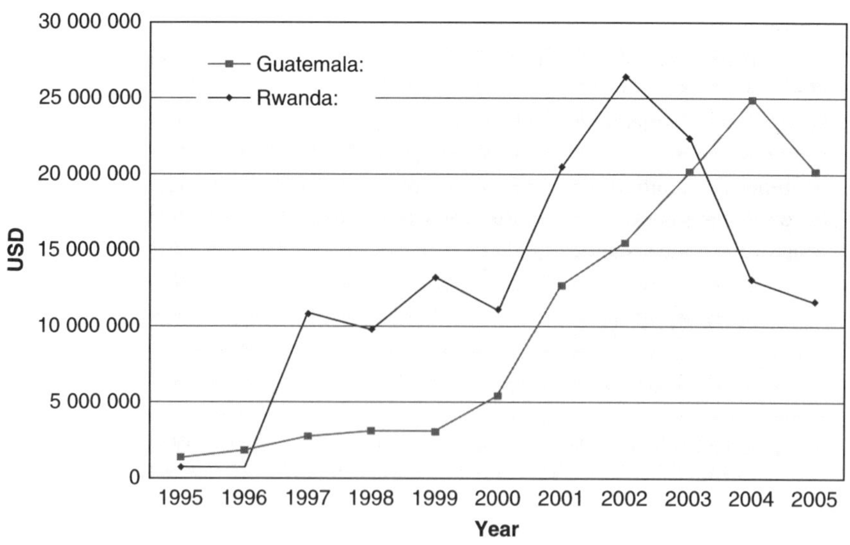

Fig. 9 Sequencing of aid to transitional justice in Rwanda and Guatemala, 1995–2005 (in USD)

ranged between 10m and 14m USD in the first and last phase, while it in the middle phase peaked at between 20m and 26m USD annually.

Donors hence started engaging much earlier in post-conflict justice in Guatemala than in Rwanda. It is striking that while Guatemala received more than 10m USD annually for transitional justice during the first four post-war years (and even more after that) Rwanda got less than 5m USD annually during the first six post-conflict years for the same purpose. Only in the seventh year did Rwanda reach a level similar to that of post-war Guatemala. Even with regard to the last part of the period, on which we have the best data, Rwanda remained below Guatemala's level up to and including 2003. Only 10 years after the genocide did Rwanda get more aid for transitional justice than did Guatemala, which was then in its eighth post-war year. The bulk of the 111m USD that Rwanda received – 93.2m USD – was disbursed between 2001 and 2005.

To understand these patterns, the historical time factor is relevant to take into account. During the last five years of the period, from 2001 onwards, aid to transitional justice reached considerably higher levels than it did during the 1990s, in both countries. This is likely to relate to factors beyond the contexts of Rwanda and Guatemala, such as the increased focus on security in the post-9/11 world. This aspect also helps explain the SSR dominance in the foreign assistance to TJ. The increased inflow of aid during the last half of the period may also relate to the fact that by the early 2000s, experience from aid to a range of post-conflict countries led to a growing consensus that processes to deal with the past are needed to build peace. The time factor may also have contributed to bias in our data however, since transitional justice and security sector reform only consolidated as policy categories in the last part of the examined period. This complicated our collection of data on this issue for the 1990s, since much of the quantitative data for those years were not categorised in transitional justice terms. The skewed pattern we have found, with more aid in the end than the beginning of the period, may therefore be slightly exaggerated.

3.4.2 Trends at the Level of Mechanisms

Figures 10 and 11 show how the distribution of the aid to different TJ mechanisms shifted over time, throughout the 11 years in question.

Criminal courts. Support to this mechanism was sequenced very differently in the two cases. In Rwanda the timing largely paralleled the overall sequencing of TJ assistance. Criminal courts received very little aid during the first five post-genocide years, only around one million per year. In the second half of the period however, this category got between two and six million annually, while in the 11th year aid dropped to reach the level of the 1990s again. In Guatemala by contrast, aid to criminal courts was far smaller, never exceeding one million per year during the first nine post-war years. It was also sequenced in the opposite manner, with a little more aid in the beginning and the end of the period than in the middle years, when hardly any foreign assistance targeted the criminal courts.

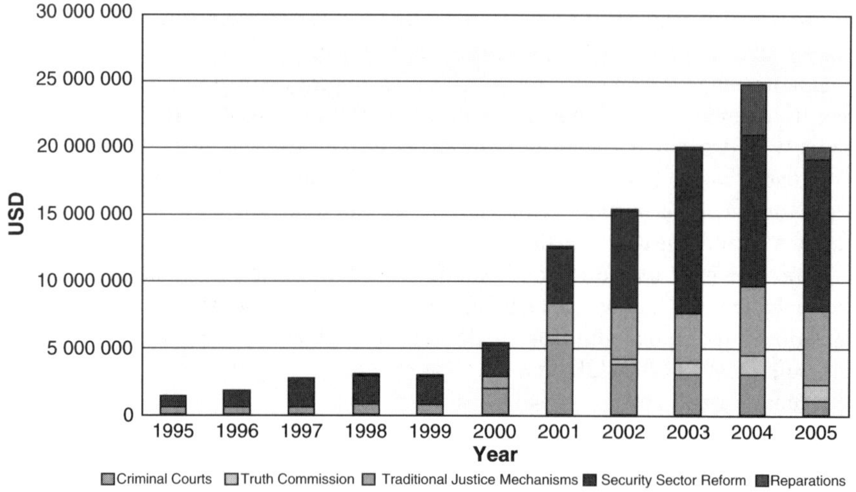

Fig. 10 Sequencing of aid to transitional justice mechanisms in Rwanda, 1995–2005 (in USD)

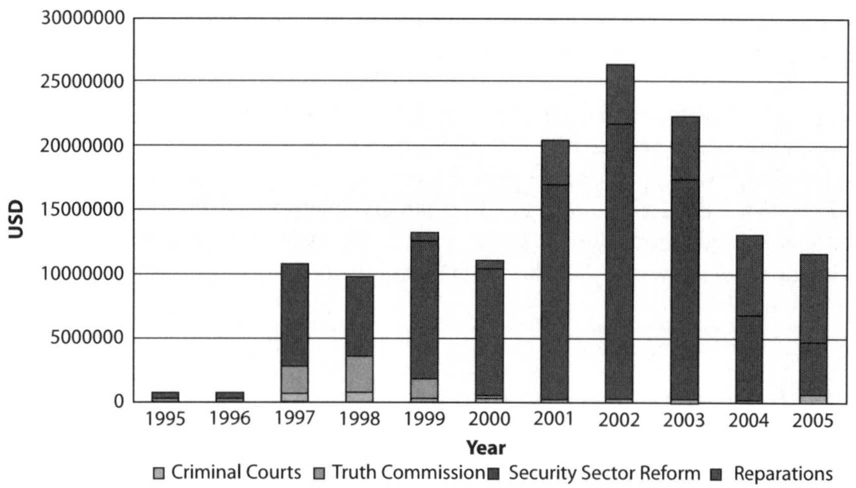

Fig. 11 Sequencing of aid to transitional justice mechanisms in Guatemala, 1995–2005 (in USD)

Truth commissions. Aid to this category was also sequenced differently. Rwanda's most truth commission-like institution, the NURC, was supported only in the last half of the period, while Guatemala's truth commissions were backed only in the first half. In Guatemala the two commissions were operational only in the second half of the 1990s and issued their final reports in 1998 and 1999. Hence, aid flows were largest from 1997 through 1999, when the commissions received 2–3m USD annually. In Rwanda by contrast, the supported commission was established in 1998 and became operational in 1999 (Ingelaere 2006; Kimonyo et al. 2004). Aid to this commission remained minor in 2001 and 2002, and only in 2003 through 2005, half a decade after it was set up, did donors start investing more in it with aid averaging roughly one million USD per year.

"Traditional" justice mechanisms. As noted earlier, aid was channelled into this category only in Rwanda, to the *gacaca* institution. By the time the first *gacaca* legislation was passed in the Rwandan parliament in 2001, donors had already started supporting the process. From a modest start in 2000, when roughly one million USD was given to *gacaca*, aid flows grew in ensuing years, reaching roughly five million USD in 2005 when *gacaca* was launched. Already by 2002 *gacaca* received roughly the same amount of external aid as did criminal courts in Rwanda, and from 2003 onwards more aid was given to the former than the latter.[14] From 2003 onwards *gacaca* was the second-most supported mechanism, surpassed only by security sector reform.

The security sector. During most of the 11 years we examined, security sector reform was the category that received the largest share of TJ aid in both countries. In Rwanda it received roughly half the aid or more in eight of the 11 years (all except 2000, 2001 and 2004). In post-war Guatemala, only in one year (2005) was less than half of the external support channelled into SSR. In absolute figures, SSR aid trends follow the overall trends. In Rwanda, less than three million USD per year went to SSR during the first 6 years, as opposed to between approximately four and twelve million USD per year from 2001 through 2005. In Guatemala, some four to ten million USD annually went to SSR in the first and last phase of the post-war period, but from 2001 through 2003 far more, some 16–21m USD each year. It is illustrative that in some years, aid to security sector reform passed the 10-million mark in Rwanda and the 20-million mark in Guatemala, while other mechanisms hardly went beyond the 5-million mark any given year. SSR clearly dominated the field.

Reparations. Reparations tend to become an issue only some time after the end of an armed conflict, when it becomes clear – often as a result of other mechanisms, such as courts and truth commissions – who among the victims might be eligible for financial compensation. It also tends to take some time before more pressing needs of reconstruction and development are minimally satisfied for space to be opened for memorials, museums, exhumations of mass graves and mental health programmes.

In both Rwanda and Guatemala, aid to reparations followed this pattern of coming in late, towards the end of the first post-conflict decade. But it came later and was far less in Rwanda's case. In Guatemala assistance to this field first emerged in 1999, the third post-war year and at the time when the truth commission reports had just come out. In Rwanda by contrast, only 10 years after the genocide – in 2004 – did reparations aid first emerge, followed by a smaller contribution the year after, which is the last year covered by our data. We hence know little about the extent to which

[14] As noted in Sect. 3.3 though, some of the aid to criminal courts, notably the support to the ICTR, was not covered by our data since it came from other donors than those examined here, such as other UN agencies. Some of our donor informants argued that the *gacaca* received too little support in comparison with, e.g., the ICTR.

reparations aid was sustained over time in Rwanda. The data on Guatemala, by contrast, suggest a strong "staying power" of donors within this field. Reparations assistance was not only given at the time when the truth commissions published their recommendations that victims should be compensated. It also continued for many years after the two reports were published. From 2001 through 2005 reparations aid vacillated between two and five million USD per year in Guatemala, while in Rwanda only some five million USD was provided in total for this purpose. In the former case, most of the aid to reparations was channelled through multilateral channels, as we will further discuss in the next section.

4 Donor Priorities

What shaped the patterns of TJ aid to Rwanda and Guatemala? What underpinned the donors' decisions on mechanisms to support, timing, and magnitude of the aid? In the following we provide answers to these questions based on our interview data.[15]

All the donor officials we interviewed stated that both international obligations, such as international humanitarian law and peace agreements, and the priorities of the recipient country's government and of former parties to the conflict, impacted on their funding decisions. So did shifts in the post-conflict contexts. In spite of these similarities, a striking difference in the donors' approach was that in Rwanda, donors tended to respond to the agenda of the government, while in Guatemala they rather supported the UN-brokered peace accords and, with some exceptions, did not want to get involved in any direct partnership with the Guatemalan authorities.

4.1 Priorities in Relation to Rwanda

The failure by the international community to prevent, let alone stop Rwanda's 1994 genocide triggered a certain guilt complex which is useful to keep in mind when analysing the post-1994 priorities of donor agencies. Our interviewees tended to express some humility with regard to their work and a wish to support the Rwandan government to enable it to set the terms for the country's development. When asked about the background for their support to transitional justice in Rwanda, aid officers emphasised the moral and political imperative their governments felt to enable this post-genocide Central African state to have a well-functioning justice sector. Several expressed a wish to contribute their experiences and resources to make that happen. As one officer put it:

[15] The interviews, which were conducted by telephone by the authors, were based on an agreement with informants that their names would not be identified in direct association with quotes. In the following informants are therefore identified not by name but by institutional affiliation.

> The basis of funding was bilateral agreements and Rwandan politics. The main objective of the Rwandan government was to stabilise the country and improve the governmental work, also the institutions of justice. It is their wish that we are engaged in the field.[16]

The donors were inclined to allocate their money in line with the political interests of the Government of Rwanda. The *gacaca* institution is a clear example of such a nationally driven initiative, which upon the government's request received considerable support from some donors in spite of their lack of experience with such a decentralised justice mechanism. Another field officer thus commented: "... it was also due to priorities of the Rwandan government. *Gacaca* was the Rwandans' choice, although in the preliminary phases *gacaca* was an unknown project to the donors and therefore everyone was sceptical to get involved".[17]

Donors' preference for giving direct aid to the Rwandan authorities was hence justified with reference to the need to strengthen governmental institutions. The nature of the post-war regime, which was more representative of the political interests of the victims than of the perpetrators of the previous conflict, must also be taken into account when assessing the donor approach. The commitment of the Rwandan regime to carry through a coherent transitional justice policy created conditions that were conducive to direct support to the authorities. Yet the donors' choice of partners, as well as the volume and nature of the aid, also responded to the changing situation on the ground. Several representatives remarked that the early years from 1995 to 1998 was a time of emergency in Rwanda. Funding therefore went to humanitarian efforts, while aid to transitional justice was postponed. This helps explain the two-stage pattern of aid to TJ that we have detected. But in the latter part of the period, with the emergency left behind and elections being held, aid to transitional justice picked up, and more of it was channelled directly to the government. The cooperation also shifted to larger-scale and longer-term programmes and became more focused on institution-building. A field officer commented:

> We looked at the capacity – can they implement it? Do they have enough budgets? Hence, our aid was channelled from NGOs to governmental institutions ... Between 2001 and 2003 permanent institutions were still not in place. Therefore, we supported international NGOs in the beginning.[18]

Among the TJ mechanisms, donors in Rwanda clearly prioritised security sector reform, more specifically the building of institutions within that sector. This donor priority was shaped both by the Rwandan government, which encouraged the donors to allocate funds to SSR-related activities, and also by global policy trends in the studied period, when "good governance" and institution-building emerged as key priorities within the broader human rights and democracy discourse. When justifying their SSR funding, donor officials generally referred to overall policy goals such as the imperative to create an independent justice sector within a democratic society.

[16] Interview with representative of the German BMZ.

[17] Interview with representative of the Belgian MFA.

[18] Interview with representative of the Dutch MFA.

In sum, in Rwanda donors allocated their resources according to national priorities as far as possible. Although there were still human rights concerns in Rwanda, the donors tended to be satisfied with the immediate results of their support to the Rwandan government, which managed to achieve increasing capacity in the justice sector.

4.2 Priorities in Relation to Guatemala

A key determinant of donor priorities in Guatemala was the peace accords. While justice sector aspects were covered by altogether five partial peace agreements (Sieder 2003, p. 137, 142), the partial accord entitled "Agreement on the Strengthening of Civilian Power and on the Role of the Armed Forces in a Democratic Society" (AFPC) (MINUGUA 1996) was particularly influential in guiding the allocation of aid to the security sector – which got about three quarters of the transitional justice aid. Why were donors so interested in supporting SSR?

The loyalty of donors to the peace deal framework is part of the explanation. Given the focus in the peace accords on SSR measures as a means to bringing lasting peace, donors became strongly involved in supporting this area. The justice system received substantially more funding than other sections of the accord. The first post-war government followed up on this by establishing the Commission for the Strengthening of the Justice System (CFJ) as well as the Judicial Branch Modernisation Unit. The latter entity had the mandate of coordinating the implementation of the justice reforms (MINUGUA 1996, para 15; 1997, para 41). Both initiatives were supported by funding from multilateral banks and donors (MINUGUA 1998, para 72). But the keen support of SSR also had less positive sides. Our data suggest that there was heavy concentration of aid for the judiciary. Important measures in the AFPC such as the creation of the security advisory bodies and law enforcement units, including the national civilian police, were to some extent neglected. Interviews also suggest that the donors had a long-term funding strategy for SSR, in line with the peace accords. In the immediate aftermath of the civil war, they launched programmes aimed at institution-building, particularly in the justice sector, and this gradually expanded until 2003. But in 2004 and 2005, SSR funding dropped significantly – a result, according to several donor representatives, of the withdrawal of MINUGUA, the UN Verification Mission that had been responsible for a major multi-donor trust fund in the area of SSR.

Aid from Sweden, Norway, Denmark and the Netherlands was particularly coloured by the wish to carry through the 1996 peace accords. The Nordic and Dutch agencies only got engaged in aid to Guatemala after the signing of the peace deal, in view of helping to implement it. A former field officer commented that Norway felt a particular responsibility towards the implementation of the partial peace agreement called the truth commission agreement, signed in Oslo in 1994, since they had been much engaged in the process leading up to its signing.[19] Also, Norwegian authorities wanted to maintain the political position of the warring parties in the post-war regime.[20]

The donors hence tended to care less about the priorities of the successive post-war governments than they did about the guidelines of the peace agreements. Informants related this to an assertion that the Guatemalan authorities did not make substantial efforts to coordinate donor activities. Most donors decided to allocate their aid in UN multi-donor trust funds instead. As one field officer pointed out, this tended to create a state within the state, as MINUGUA took over many state functions. Consequently, some governmental institutions were undermined and did not build up sufficient capacity.[21]

4.3 Comparative Perspectives

Compared with Guatemala, the donor agencies supporting transitional justice in Rwanda seem to have better managed to transfer capacity to governmental institutions in line with the priorities of the national authorities. Though human rights concerns prevailed in post-1994 Rwanda, the apparent state-building effect of the aid is food for thought when compared to post-war Guatemala, where the government was not a key target of TJ aid. A decade after the civil war's end and in spite of the heavy investments in transitional justice over that period, Guatemala found itself in a deep state and security crisis. The justice sector and law enforcement agencies still functioned poorly and violence continued on a scale that made Guatemala one of Latin America's most violent countries.

The donors' reliance on the framework of the peace accords, their embrace of the multilateral framework and reluctance to support the central government in Guatemala must be understood in light of the prolonged transition from war to peace. The negotiated transition was dominated by the political elite of the former regime, which represented the side of the war that had inflicted most of the war-time violence. Conversely, the donors' wish to cooperate with the national government in Rwanda reflects the international community's shock vis-à-vis the 1994 genocide and its shame at having failed to stop or prevent it. The rebel movement that overthrew the genocidal regime and came to power in Kigali, in spite of certain democratic and human rights deficits, got considerable moral and material support. The legitimacy of the two post-conflict governments thus strongly diverged in the eyes of the outside world, as did the respective governments' own willingness to tackle transitional justice issues – considerable in Rwanda, more hesitant in Guatemala – and the way in which they chose to do it. In Rwanda the new regime seems to have had a greater political interest in prosecutions than in truth-telling and reparations,

19 Interview with former representative of the Norwegian MFA in Guatemala.

20 Interview with representative of the Norwegian MFA in Guatemala.

21 Interview with representative of the Danish MFA.

which helps explain the largely retributive approach it opted for. In Guatemala prosecutions proved politically difficult, whereas truth-telling was more feasible. This led in time to an expressed need and demand for reparations and follow-up legal proceedings for which it was far harder to find political support due to the similarities between the in-conflict and the post-conflict regime.

Donor priorities were thus in both cases largely shaped by the balance of power within the post-conflict countries. However, and although it is hard to substantiate this further on the basis of our data, there is reason to suggest that the influence went both ways: that donor choices also helped consolidating emerging patterns of state strength and weakness. An interesting question for further research would be the extent to which and possibly how transitional justice aid, statebuilding and state failure are causally connected in post-conflict contexts like Rwanda, Guatemala and beyond.

5 Conclusions

This chapter has assessed the aid that was given in support of transitional justice processes in Rwanda and Guatemala from 1995 through 2005, identifying its origins, targets, sequencing, and size, and exploring donor priorities. We now sum up main findings and discuss implications for research and policy.

5.1 Main Findings

Transitional justice assistance made up only around 5% of the development aid in the two countries during the period reviewed. Guatemala received more aid to this field than did Rwanda, while Rwanda got more development aid overall. Key bilateral transitional justice donors were the Netherlands, USA, Germany and Norway. In Guatemala most of the TJ aid was channelled through multilateral organisations, while in Rwanda the national government was the chief recipient. More than half of the TJ assistance went to reform of the security sector, in Guatemala almost three quarters. In Rwanda roughly 20% of the TJ support went to criminal courts, and an equal share to the *gacaca* process. In Guatemala, more aid went to reparations efforts and some also to the truth commissions, while criminal courts only received a tiny share of the donors' support. The assistance was also very differently sequenced. In Rwanda transitional justice received little aid during the first six post-genocide years, but far more during the ensuing five. In Guatemala the sequencing pattern assumed an inverted U shape, with considerable amounts allocated during the first four post-war years, more in year five to seven, and smaller but still substantial volumes in the final years studied.

Rwanda was a far more aid-dependent country than was Guatemala. In relation to Rwanda the international community was influenced by a certain guilt complex after the 1994 genocide which it had failed to prevent or stop. While foreign governments surely were committed to backing Guatemala's peace too, they did so by supporting the framework of the peace agreement rather than the central government. In Rwanda, by contrast, donor commitment translated into strong support of the post-conflict government, especially after the early emergency phase. While donor justifications for aiding transitional justice in the two countries were largely similar – the rule of law, human rights and good governance – they chose different strategies for realising these aims. The approaches were associated with divergent outcomes. In Rwanda, where the transitional justice aid targeted the government, the state was strengthened. In Guatemala, where the aid largely evaded the government, the state remained weak.

5.2 Implications for Policy and Research

To understand how aid to transitional justice works, an essential first step is to map the patterns of this aid over time. We need to grasp how large TJ aid has been, what it has gone to, who have been involved and why they got involved. This study has explored these questions in the context of two cases which have received much attention in aid and in TJ debates in recent years. The study's main contribution is to be found in the new facts documented about these two cases. It does not tell the whole story, however. First, our data was limited to donor statistics and interviews; we have not examined the perspectives and experiences of the governments and citizen groups in the recipient countries. Second, we have not studied the impact of the aid. Looking at the impact would shed light on a number of questions that can be asked on the basis of our analysis. One such question is, how did it matter for the countries in question how much aid they got for their TJ processes; how much different mechanisms were backed; how the aid was sequenced; and what priorities the donors had? A study of the impact of the aid will enable us to link the findings on aid size, sequencing, actors and targets to the aid's effects and outcomes, and on that basis formulate lessons for aid policy.

Are the findings pertaining to TJ aid in Rwanda and Guatemala from 1995 through 2005 relevant for other post-conflict cases? Helping recipient countries reach certain goals is the rationale of TJ aid, so knowing more about the impact of the aid in the two cases will also be a crucial next step also to formulate lessons for other countries. The role of TJ aid as compared to other factors in shaping the outcome of the TJ mechanisms will be important to understand in possible future research on Rwanda and Guatemala. Indeed, this is a necessary step before we can draw conclusions on how TJ aid best should be designed in other, more or less similar cases.

While this chapter has contributed to filling the knowledge gap by delineating patterns of TJ aid in a time period when such aid was on the rise worldwide, and in two showcases for such aid; we therefore conclude on a note of caution on drawing policy lessons on the basis of still limited evidence. Further research is indeed required to understand how aid to transitional justice works across cases, over time and for different actors. The mapping of patterns and priorities provided in this chapter helps refine the research questions for this endeavour. For instance, if transitional justice support is found to make up only 5% of aid also in other post-conflict cases, how likely is it that it will help contribute to reaching the lofty aims of truth, restitution, accountability and reconciliation? And if more than half of the TJ aid goes to the forward-looking activity of security sector reform, to what extent does the external support enable the recipient countries to look back and deal with their past? Other emerging questions include; to what extent does the influence of TJ aid depend on the overall level of income and the aid-dependency of the recipient economies? How do the cultures and value systems of the largely Northern donors impact on the TJ outcomes in recipient countries across the globe? Finally, how do the choices TJ donors make impact on the legitimacy and strength of the recipient countries' government and of their civil societies? These are questions this study has shed light on in the contexts of Rwanda and Guatemala, yet that certainly requires closer scrutiny if we are to understand the complex phenomenon of transitional justice aid more fully.

Division of responsibilities. Stina Petersen was responsible for data collection, statistical analysis, preliminary analysis of the qualitative data, initial drafting, and feedback on later versions of the study. Ingrid Samset was responsible for theoretical framework and analysis, introduction and conclusion, and presentations at various workshops. Vibeke Wang contributed to the data collection and gave feedback on successive drafts. Petersen and Samset were jointly in charge of the final revision process.

References

Azpuru D et al (2004) Democracy assistance to post-conflict Guatemala: finding a balance between details and determinants. Democratic Transition in Post-Conflict Societies Project Working Paper 30. Netherlands Institute of International Relations Clingendael, The Hague

Barnett MN (2002) Eyewitness to a genocide: The United Nations and Rwanda. Cornell University Press, Ithaca

Booth JA, Wade CJ, Walker TW (2006) Understanding Central America: global forces, rebellion and change. Westview Press, Boulder

CEH/Historical Clarification Commission (1999) Guatemala: the memory of silence. United Nations Office for Project Services, Guatemala City

Chapman AR, van der Merwe H (eds) (2008) Truth and reconciliation in South Africa: did the TRC deliver? University of Pennsylvania Press, Philadelphia

Davenport C, Stam A (2008) Rwandan political violence in space and time. Contentious Politics workshop, Columbia University, 24 March 2008. http://www.iserp.columbia.edu/workshops/downloads/davenport1.pdf. Accessed 10 July 2008

EIU (2006) Country profile 2006: Guatemala. Economist Intelligence Unit, London

EIU (2007) Country Profile 2007: Rwanda. Economist Intelligence Unit, London

Gloppen S (2005) Roads to reconciliation: a conceptual framework. In: Skaar E, Gloppen S, Suhrke A (eds) Roads to reconciliation. Lexington Books, Lanham

Hayman R (2006) The complexity of aid: government strategies, donor agendas and the coordination of development assistance in Rwanda 1994–2004. PhD Dissertation, Centre of African Studies, University of Edinburgh

Hayner PB (2001) Unspeakable truths: confronting state terror and atrocity. Routledge, New York

Hintjens HM (1999) Explaining the 1994 Genocide in Rwanda. J Mod Afr Stud 37(2):241

HRW and FIDH (1999) Leave none to tell the story: Genocide in Rwanda. Human Rights Watch and International Federation of Human Rights / Fédération internationale des ligues des droits de l'homme, New York

Huyse L, Salter M (eds) (2008) Traditional justice and reconciliation after violent conflict: learning from African experiences. International IDEA, Stockholm

ICTJ and DFID (2008) Donor strategies for transitional justice: taking stock and moving forward (Report). http://www.ictj.org/static/PolicymakerNetworks/080407_IPP_DonorStrategies.pdf. Accessed 10 July 2008

Ingelaere B (2006) Changing lenses and contextualizing the Rwandan (post-)genocide. In: Reyntjens F, Marysse S (eds) L'Afrique des Grands Lacs: Dix ans de transitions conflictuelles. L'Harmattan, Paris

Jonas S (1991) The battle for Guatemala: rebels, death squads, and U.S. power. Westview, Boulder

Jonas S (2000) Of centaurs and doves: Guatemala's peace process. Westview, Boulder

Jones BD (2001) Peacemaking in Rwanda: the dynamics of failure. Lynne Rienner, Boulder

Kimonyo J-P, Twagiramingu N, Kayumba C (2004) Supporting the post-genocide transition in Rwanda: the role of the international community (Report). Netherlands Institute of International Relations Clingendael, The Hague

Kritz NJ (ed) (1995) Transitional justice: how emerging democracies reckon with former regimes. United States Institute of Peace, Washington

Lacina BA, Gleditsch NP (2005) Monitoring trends in global combat: a new dataset on battle deaths. Eur J Popul 21(2–3):145

Leebaw BA (2008) The irreconcilable goals of transitional justice. Hum Rights Q 30(1):95

Lie TG, Binningsbø HM, Gates S (2007) Post-conflict justice and sustainable peace. Post-Conflict Transitions Working Paper no 5, World Bank Policy Research Paper 4191, April 2007. http://www-wds.worldbank.org/external/default/WDSContentServer/IW3P/IB/2007/04/09/000016406_20070409111614/Rendered/PDF/wps4191.pdf. Accessed 10 October 2007

Mamdani M (2001) When victims become killers: colonialism, nativism, and the genocide in Rwanda. Fountain, Kampala

Minow M (1998) Between vengeance and forgiveness: facing history after genocide and mass violence. Beacon, Boston

MINUGUA (1996) Agreement on the strengthening of civilian power and on the role of the armed forces in a democratic society. United Nations, Guatemala City

MINUGUA (1997) First report on the verification of compliance with the peace agreements signed by the Government of Guatemala and the URNG. United Nations, New York

MINUGUA (1998) Third report on the verification of compliance with the peace agreements signed by the Government of Guatemala and the URNG. United Nations, New York

Naveda E, Hurtado P (2007) El programa nacional de resarcimiento mejora su labor. elPeriódico, Guatemala City, 8 April 2007. http://www.elperiodico.com.gt/es/20070404/actualidad/38393/. Accessed 10 October 2007

OECD (2001) Geographical distribution of financial flows to aid recipients: disbursements, commitments, country indicators, 1995–1999. OECD, Paris

OECD (2002) Geographical distribution of financial flows to aid recipients: disbursements, commitments, country indicators, 1996–2000. OECD, Paris

OECD (2006) Geographical distribution of financial flows to aid recipients: disbursements, commitments, country indicators, 2000–2004. OECD, Paris

OECD (2007) Geographical distribution of financial flows to aid recipients: disbursements, commitments, country indicators, 2001–2005. OECD, Paris

Paris R (2004) At war's end: building peace after civil conflict. Cambridge University Press, Cambridge

Petersen S (2007) Peacebuilding and democratic consolidation in post-war Guatemala: a comparative assessment of the impact of civil–military reforms in the peace accords. MA thesis, University of Bergen

Reyntjens F (2004) Rwanda, ten years on: from genocide to dictatorship. African Affairs 103(411):177–210

Samset I, Petersen S, Wang V (2007) Maintaining the process? Aid to transitional justice in Rwanda and Guatemala, 1995–2005 (Report). Working Group on Development and Peace / Fri-Ent, Bonn

Schabas WA (2005) Genocide trials and gacaca courts. J Int Crim Justice 3:879

Schabas WA, Darcy S (eds) (2004) Truth commissions and courts: the tension between criminal justice and the search for truth. Kluwer, Dordrecht

Schirmer J (1998) The Guatemalan military project: a violence called democracy. University of Pennsylvania Press, Philadelphia

Shaw R (2007) Memory frictions: localizing the Truth and Reconciliation Commission in Sierra Leone. Int J Transitional Justice 1(2):183

Sieder R (2003) Renegotiating "law and order": judicial reform and citizen responses in post-war Guatemala. Democratization 10(4):137

Straus S (2006) The order of genocide: race, power, and war in Rwanda. Cornell University Press, Ithaca

Sørbø GM, Skaar E, Stokke H (2002) A review of Ireland aid's human rights and democratisation scheme (Report). CMI Report R 2002:20

Teitel RG (2000) Transitional justice. Oxford University Press, Oxford

Torres-Rivas E, Peralta GA (1998) Desde Autoritarismo a la Paz. Faculdad Latinoamericana de Ciencias Sociales, Guatemala City

Thoms ONT, Ron J, Paris R (2008) The effects of transitional justice mechanisms: a summary of empirical research findings and implications for analysts and practitioners. CIPS Working Paper. http://www.humansecuritygateway.info/documents/CIPS_Transitional_Justice_April2008.pdf. Accessed 10 July 2008

Uvin P (2001) Difficult choices in the new post-conflict agenda: the international community in Rwanda after the genocide. Third World Q 22(2):177

Waldorf L (2006) Mass justice for mass atrocity: rethinking local justice as transitional justice. Temple Law Rev 79(1):1–87

Wickham-Crowley TP (1992) Guerrillas and revolution in Latin America: a comparative study of insurgents and regimes since 1956. Princeton University Press, Princeton

Abbreviations

AECI	Spanish Agency of International Cooperation
AFPC	Agreement on the Strengthening of Civilian Power and on the Role of the Armed Forces in a Democratic Society (Guatemala)
BMZ	Federal Ministry for Economic Cooperation and Development (Germany)
CEH	Historical Clarification Commission (Guatemala)
CFJ	Commission for the Strengthening of the Justice System (Guatemala)
CIDA	Canadian International Development Agency
CNDH	National Human Rights Commission (Rwanda)
Danida	Danish International Development Agency
DDR	Demobilisation, Disarmament and Reintegration
DFID	Department for International Development (UK)
DGDC	Directorate-General for Development Cooperation (Belgium)
EC	European Commission
FCO	Foreign and Commonwealth Office (UK)
GNI	Gross National Income
GTZ	German Technical Cooperation
ICTR	International Criminal Tribunal for Rwanda
MFA	Ministry of Foreign Affairs
MINUGUA	United Nations' Verification Mission in Guatemala
NGO	Non-Governmental Organisation
Norad	Norwegian Agency for Development Cooperation
NURC	National Unity and Reconciliation Commission (Rwanda)
ODA	Official Development Assistance
OECD	Organisation for Economic Cooperation and Development
PNR	National Reparations Programme (Guatemala)
REHMI	Recovery of Historic Memory (Guatemala)
Sida	Swedish International Development Cooperation Agency
SSR	Security sector reform
UN	United Nations
UNDP	United Nations Development Programme
URNG	Guatemalan National Revolutionary Unity
USAID	US Agency for International Development
WB	World Bank

Colombia's Bid for Justice and Peace

Catalina Díaz

Abstract This study aims to offer a critical account on how transitional justice discourses have framed the legal arrangement for the paramilitary demobilization process in Colombia. It seeks to explore not only the official accommodation of concepts of retributive and restorative justice, used to construct an acceptable offer for the paramilitary leadership, but civil society contestation over the meaning, requirements, and ownership of transitional justice processes more generally. In this respect the paper provides a background on the conflict in Colombia, highlights the views of the various constituencies in the process and gives an in-depth analysis of the Justice and Peace law, which has been the subject of a broad debate, both domestically and internationally.

1 Introduction

The extent to which Colombia is undergoing a political transition – and the nature and characteristics of that transition – is a matter of debate among international, national, and local commentators. Nowhere is this more apparent than in the demobilization process of the counter-insurgent paramilitary coalition United Self-defense Forces of Colombia (*Autodefensas Unidas de Colombia*, AUC). This process, operating under the auspices of the controversial "Peace and Justice" Law discussed throughout this study, is presented by the national government, certain political elites, and the paramilitary leadership as a peace process, requiring new and explicitly "restorative" understandings of justice.[1]

C. Díaz
Reparations ICTJ, Colombia Bogotá, Colombia,
e-mail: cdiaz@ictj.org

[1] Ministry of Interior and Justice, "Exposición de Motivos al proyecto de ley estatutaria número 85 de 2003-Senado", 436 Gaceta del Congreso (27 August 2003) at 3 (explaining that the reintegration of armed groups is provided in order to enable them to effectively contribute to national peace).

K. Ambos et al. (eds.), *Building a Future on Peace and Justice: Studies on Transitional Justice, Peace and Development.*

Yet, the positions of what might be termed actors from below – meaning peasant, indigenous, African-Colombian, and urban peripheral organized groups; community-based organizations and their networks; grassroots initiatives; victims' organizations; local nongovernmental organizations (NGOs); and trade-unions – differ markedly. Many such groupings claim that the process of demobilizing paramilitaries is not dissolving *de facto* authoritarian regimes that have been consolidated through paramilitary terror but, on the contrary, might be legitimizing them.

It has become apparent that law and the legal process – particularly criminal law and criminal processes – are to play a leading role in the ways in which transition is constructed in Colombia. The "Peace and Justice" Law constitutes the official vehicle for institutionalized transition. To date, the official "transition" has not resulted in other evidence of radical political transformation, such as a constituent assembly, institutional reform *ad hoc* commissions (police, military, executive, human rights, women issues and land-tenure, among others), or new local and regional governance structures.

This article aims to offer a critical account of how transitional justice discourse has helped frame the legal arrangement for the paramilitary demobilization process in Colombia. It seeks to explore not only the official accommodation of concepts of retributive and restorative justice – used to construct an acceptable offer for the paramilitary leadership – but civil society contestation over the meaning, requirements, and ownership of transitional justice processes more generally.

Section 2 describes the official understanding of the Colombian transition and the basis upon which the national government, political elites and the paramilitary leadership justify the adoption of transitional justice measures. The chapter argues that the official use of the transitional justice rhetoric corresponds to a *thin* understanding of transition. The chapter also outlines why the projected transition is contested, focusing in particular on the perceptions and experiences of the transition by "actors from below". Section 3 discusses the drafting process of the "Justice and Peace" law. The chapter focuses on the use of language relating to truth, justice and the right to reparation and its potential to contest formulas advanced at the official level. Sections 3.4 and 3.5 of the chapter discuss the latest developments of the peace and justice arrangement in Colombia.

2 The Colombian Armed Conflict and the Paramilitary Demobilization Process

2.1 Background to the Conflict

Conservative estimates are that Colombia's internal armed conflict has now lasted between 40 and 56 years. Traditionally, the conflict is viewed by local elites, sectors of the population, and some international actors in far too basic terms. It is often depicted by these constituencies as a war against left-wing guerrillas who have been trying (unsuccessfully) to take national power, but who have achieved control over some of the least accessible parts of the country. Similarly one-dimensional explanations – often encouraged by the U.S. government in particular – have framed the Colombian conflict as a war against drugs and drug-trafficking. More recently, it has also been described as part of the global "War on Terror".

However, as the United Nations Development Program's National Human Development Report for Colombia for 2003 (UNDP INDH 2003) demonstrates, such explanations are simplistic and inadequate. The UNDP INDH 2003 report observes that, "Colombia's war is particularly complex", portraying it as an "eight-faced monster", which can be attributed to three specific circumstances (see UNDP 2003, [5]): First, the multiplicity of actors involved – guerrillas with diverse forms of Marxist allegiances, paramilitary groups with different origins, drug lords as well as smaller and medium-sized traffickers, and an array of different state actors; second, a variety of geographical, historical, cultural, and ethnic settings in which the war is being waged (see UNDP 2003, [5]); and third, the complications caused by the exceptionally long duration of the various confrontations.

The three main illegal armed groups are the *Fuerzas Armadas Revolucionarias de Colombia-Ejército del Pueblo* (FARC-EP),[2] the *Ejército de Liberación Nacional* (ELN),[3] and the former *Autodefensas Unidas de Colombia* (AUC),[4] a coalition of previously existing self-defense/anti-subversive armed groups, which was formed in 1997. As the UNDP INDH 2003 report concludes, each armed group is to varying degrees and simultaneously a political project, a military apparatus, an actor in social conflicts, a rent seeker, a way of life, and a territorial power.

The armed conflict finds its roots in the last partisan armed confrontation between the Liberal and Conservative political parties. Generally known as *La Violencia*, this conflict lasted from 1946 to 1965 and comprised a bureaucratic and ideological dispute to gain control of the state.[5] An estimated 180,000 persons died in a country of 13 million inhabitants. The Liberal modernization enterprise, which involved creating a welfare state, a secular state, trade unions and agrarian reform, met fierce opposition from the Conservative party, along with resistance from within the moderate wing of the Liberal party. The assassination of the leader of the radical populist wing of the Liberal party in 1948 produced an explosion of violence in the capital and in other cities, which did not overthrow the Conservative government but did unleash peasant violence involving Liberal guerrillas and Conservative death-squads. The political violence was fuelled by the social violence and a mixture of party loyalties and agrarian conflicts served to escalate the conflict and remove it from the large cities. While the social struggles took a violent course, the parties' leaders distanced themselves from "their troops".

The political negotiation between the two traditional parties led to a 1957 pact establishing a power-sharing agreement, the "National Front". However, this new arrangement was not enough to extinguish the armed struggle in the countryside.

---

[2] In English the Revolutionary Armed Forces of Colombia – People's Army.

[3] In English the National Liberation Army.

[4] In English the United Self-Defense Forces of Colombia.

[5] In this discussion about the genesis of the conflict, I closely follow UNDP (2003, Chap. 1).

Although the majority of Conservative militias and Liberal guerrillas were demobilized, certain factions of peasant guerrillas linked to the Colombian Communist Party (PCC, created in 1930) persisted as peasant self-defense groups. As the UNDP National Human Development Report 2003 states, "It was in the peasant periphery that the armed struggle was going to be reinvented as a vehicle for the socialist revolution" (UNDP 2003). The FARC were born out of a marriage between liberal peasant guerrillas and the PCC, which did not find space in the center of the political system and was declared illegal in 1954. In 1964, the peasant guerrillas, who were still more defensive than offensive, were converted into a revolutionary army. In 1982, the FARC declared itself to be a Popular Army, "at the service of the socialist revolution"; as put by the UNDP National Human Development Report 2003: "a project for conquering the center of political power, while nonetheless acting from the periphery" (UNDP 2003). As will be discussed below – while it is a political project with its own codes for war conduct – the FARC systematically commits humanitarian law violations and war crimes as part of its policies.[6]

The older anti-subversive/paramilitary groups emerged throughout the 1980s and early 1990s, initially as legal self-defense groups under the auspices of the official military forces, to defend the persons and properties of landowners, wealthy ranchers and merchants from the action of the Marxist guerrillas.[7] In the late 1980s, the self-defense groups had already turned into powerful private armies, controlling large regions of the country by force and terror. Although the legal framework that authorized their creation and their sponsorship by the official military forces was declared unconstitutional in 1989,[8] the Colombian government has never adopted significant measures to combat the self-defense groups or to dismantle their economic and political networks.[9]

The origins of the self-defense/paramilitary groups are also linked to the expansion and protection of drug-trafficking businesses in the country. It is public knowledge that certain paramilitary commanders were major leaders of drug-trafficking cartels and that a significant portion of paramilitary funding comes from the armed front's participation in the various links of the drug-trafficking business chain.[10]

---

[6] For a meticulous contemporary history of FARC's political projects see Dudley (2008).

[7] For comprehensive and detailed accounts of the origins and expansion of the different paramilitary groups, see UNDP (2003); Romero (2003); and Human Rights Watch (2003a). A recent, useful summary in English of existing literature is provided in International Crisis Group (2007).

[8] República de Colombia, Corte Suprema de Justicia, Sentencia del 25 de Mayo de 1989 (Supreme Court of Justice, Judgment of May 25 1989). Various executive decrees authorized civilians to bear combat weapons as well as the military forces to support communal committees buying weaponry and organizing defense strategies. For an interesting and detailed account of the legal history of the provisions authorizing the creation of self-defense groups in Colombia, see Inter-American Court of Human Rights, *Case of the 19 Merchants v. Colombia* (Series C No. 109, 5 July 2004) section 84. http://www.corteidh.or.cr/docs/casos/articulos/seriec_109_ing.pdf, accessed 12 July 2007.

[9] OHCHR (2004) highlights ongoing violations by these groups in spite of the unilateral cease-fire declared by the AUC in December 2002 and "its political commitment to demobilization and cease-fire".

[10] For a detailed account of the relationship between paramilitary groups and narco-trafficking see Cubides (2005).

In fact, in May 2008, 15 paramilitary commanders were extradited to the United States of America for illegal drug trafficking related charges, including money laundering. I will come back to this matter in Sect. 3.4 below.

The paramilitary federation did not confront the state and its armed forces. On the contrary, it defended the status quo. In many cases, the paramilitary fronts conducted joint operations with official military battalions, or counted on open or implicit cooperation of military, police, and intelligence forces.[11] Indeed, the Inter-American Court of Human Rights recently addressed allegations of collusion between paramilitary fronts and state security forces. In five cases, the Court declared the state of Colombia responsible for human rights violations involving paramilitary and state actors.[12]

During the last two decades, the paramilitary groups systematically targeted civilians, accusing them of being supporters of the left-wing guerrillas. Different fronts of the AUC were involved in large-scale massacres involving extreme cruelty;[13] forced disappearances;[14] systematic assassinations of trade unionists, community leaders, and left-wing politicians; forced displacement; sexual violence;[15] and forced recruitment (see, e.g., Human Rights Watch 2003b). According to leading Colombian human rights NGOs, the paramilitary groups have assassinated more

---

[11] See OHCHR (2006); United States of America Department of State "Country Reports on Human Rights Practices-Colombia" (8 March 2006); Human Rights Watch (1996, 2000, 2001).

[12] Inter-American Court of Human Rights, *Case of 19 Merchants v. Colombia* (Series C No. 109, 5 July 2004); *Case of the "Mapiripán Massacre" v. Colombia* (Series C No. 134, 15 September 2005); *Case of the Pueblo Bello Massacre v. Colombia* (Series C, No. 140, 31 January 2006); *Case of the Ituango Massacres v. Colombia,* (Series C No. 148, 1 July 2006).

[13] The "Chengue" massacre constitutes one salient example. Human Rights Watch reported, "On January 17, 2001, an estimated fifty paramilitaries pulled dozens of residents from their homes in the village of Chengue, Sucre. They assembled them into two groups above the main square and across from the rudimentary health center, the *Washington Post* later reported. Then, one by one, they killed the men by crushing their heads with heavy stones and a sledgehammer. When it was over, twenty-four men lay dead in pools of blood. Two more were found later in shallow graves. As the troops left, they set fire to the village. Among the reported dead was a sixteen-year-old boy, whose head was severed from his body". Human Rights Watch (2003a).

[14] The UN High Commissioner for Human Rights reported in 2003, "As compared to 2002, it is a source of concern to note the increase in complaints received by the office in Colombia in relation to forced disappearances, mainly perpetrated by paramilitary groups, in which responsibility is also attributed to the security forces. These complaints involve geographical areas where the security forces were widely present and in control and where tolerance and complicity of public servants with respect to paramilitary activities was reported. Additionally, the investigations aimed at finding the authors and determining their responsibility did not produce results". OHCHR (2004).

[15] See, e.g., Amnesty International (2004). Among many cases, Amnesty International reports the rape, torture and killing of the 16-year-old daughter of a leader of the National Association of Peasant, Black and Indigenous Women of Colombia (*Asociación Nacional de Mujeres Campesinas, Negras e Indígenas de Colombia,* ANMUCIC) in March 2001 as she traveled to Valledupar, department of Cesar. According to the testimony of the mother, the girl was dragged from a bus and taken away: "I don't know who found the body. She had been buried as an unknown person. The AUC had paid for the urn. That's what they do. The indigenous people who lived near the dwell had heard her cries. They told me that she was saying 'Don't kill me, I haven't done anything to you' and that she was calling out for me. The paramilitaries shouted out to her 'What damned mother? If it wasn't for her, we wouldn't be doing this.' They cut off her breasts" [20].

than 30,000 civilians over 20 years and have forced the internal displacement of approximately one million of persons.[16] The paramilitary groups also systematically and forcefully dispossessed peasants, as well as small and medium-size owners of their land.[17] Moreover, as discussed in Sect. 2.3 of this study, the paramilitary groups subjected entire regions of the country to a terrorist regime, infiltrating local and regional democratic processes and public administrations.

The paramilitary groups have been able to commit most of their alleged crimes with almost absolute impunity (see, e.g., Amnesty International 2004; OHCHR 2002, paras. 243–254). In many cases, a formal investigation has not even been undertaken and in many others investigations have remained at a preliminary stage for years, without any identification of those presumably responsible. However, some paramilitary commanders and mid-ranking cadres have been charged or sentenced *in absentia* for some particularly notorious massacres and killings committed in the mid-1990s.[18] Some of the paramilitary commanders have also been sentenced for drug-trafficking activities in Colombian and U.S. courts.

The left-wing guerrillas have also systematically targeted civilians, accusing them of collaborating with official security forces and paramilitary groups. The FARC is responsible for selective killings and massacres; kidnappings and cruel, inhumane and degrading treatment of hostages; sexual violence against civilians and female combatants, including rape, sexual slavery, forced unions, forced sterilization and forced abortion; forced recruitment (see, e.g., Human Rights Watch 2003b); forced displacement; and violence with indiscriminate damage, including the usage of landmines. The FARC has systematically persecuted local and regional democratic elected authorities (governors, majors, members of city councils and province assemblies) and civil servants of local and regional administrations for representing the state. Significant numbers of local and regional officials and civil servants have been assassinated, threatened and forcibly displaced.

Indigenous peoples living in territories under the FARC control have also been targeted by the guerrillas for declaring themselves autonomous and neutral with

---

[16] See, e.g., Colombian Commission of Jurists, "Colombia: en contravía de las recomendaciones internacionales sobre derechos humanos – Balance de la política de seguridad democrática y la situación de derechos humanos y derecho humanitario. Agosto de 2002 a agosto de 2004" (Comisión Colombiana de Juristas, Bogotá, 2004); and Uprimny and Lasso (2004).

[17] Comisión Colombiana de Juristas, *Despojo* (Bogotá, 2007).

[18] See, e.g., the criminal record of paramilitary commander Salvatore Mancuso described by Human Rights Watch: "In April 2003, a judge in Antioquia sentenced Mancuso to forty years in prison for arranging the 1997 El Aro (Antioquia) massacre of at least fifteen people. That same year, the Attorney General's office issued an arrest warrant for Mancuso in relation to his involvement in the 1996 murders of two brothers and another man near San Antonio El Palmito, Sucre. According to the investigation, ten paramilitaries under his command selected the three men using a list of names, then executed them on the spot. In a similar case, government prosecutors also issued an arrest warrant for Mancuso in relation to the massacre of twelve people in villages near Morroa, Sucre, in December of 1996. In total, the Attorney General's office has issued eight arrest warrants for Mancuso related to massacres and selective killings. In December 2001 press interview, Mancuso implied that paramilitaries had abducted and killed Embera-Katio indigenous leader Kimi Domicó in Tierralta, Córdoba. Mancuso is a signatory to the Santafé de Ralito agreement". Human Rights Watch (2003a).

regard to all parties in the conflict (Tattay 1999). Taking hostages for economic purposes has also become an open policy of both the FARC and ELN. According to the leading NGO working with victims of kidnapping and their families, more than 3,000 persons remain kidnapped at the hands of the guerrillas and more than a 1,000 died in captivity between 1996 and 2006 (Fundación País Libre 2006).

The FARC has also entered the drug-trafficking business. Several commanders and mid-ranking cadres are facing prosecution by Colombian and U.S. authorities for drug-related crimes. Two high-ranking combatants have been extradited to the United States by the Colombian government and are standing trial in U.S. courts.

2.2 A "Thin" Transition

After the failure of a 4-year peace process with the FARC-EP Marxist guerrillas, the governor of the province of Antioquia, Alvaro Uribe Velez, won the presidential election in 2002 – largely on the promise that the state would recover territorial control of Colombia and ensure its security. Through his "Democratic Security Policy", Uribe sought to strengthen the military forces, and to promote collaboration among the civilian population as a means to "win the war against terrorism". As a component of the Democratic Security Policy, the peace policy offers socioeconomic and legal benefits to combatants who agree to turn in their weapons and reintegrate into civilian life.

At the height of their "career", having accumulated immense military, economic, social, and political power, several paramilitary commanders accepted the government's offer to engage in a demobilization process (Rangel 2005). Two main reasons have been advanced by analysts to explain why the paramilitary leadership decided to enter into a demobilization process, in spite of the fact that they had not been militarily or politically diminished, but rather precisely when their power was at its height. These were:

- The expectation of favorable legal and political conditions for demobilization, secured by significant national and international support to the President
- The expectation that the government would secure the territories "liberated" from the Marxist threat by the paramilitary fronts

However, with time, these expectations would prove unrealistic.

In July 2003, government representatives and AUC paramilitary leaders signed the Santa Fe de Ralito Accord.[19] The Exploratory Peace Commission, officially established in 2002, as well as three Catholic Church bishops played an important role in the initial stages of the peace talks and the negotiation. The members of the Commission were five prominent Colombian personalities, appointed by the national government. One of them was a former guerrilla combatant demobilized in the early 1990s, who was now in charge of the government's human rights program.

[19] Acuerdo de Santa Fe de Ralito, http://www.altocomisionadoparalapaz.gov.co/acuerdos/acuerdos_t/jul_15_03.htm, accessed 12 July 2008.

Though the Exploratory Peace Commission was soon dissolved, the intervention of the Catholic Church was nonetheless crucial for overcoming several obstacles to peace. In the opening of the one-page Accord, both parties cited "national peace" as their overall objective. Both agreed this goal should be achieved "through the strengthening of democratic governance and the re-establishment of the monopoly of force in the hands of the State".[20] The AUC declared that "its main contribution to the nation in this historical moment is to advance in its reincorporation into civilian life and [to] contribut[e] to the strengthening of the rule of law".[21]

Under the Accord, the paramilitary leadership agreed to demobilize its troops gradually, by 31 December 2005, and the government on its part committed itself to reintegrating the demobilized combatants into civilian life. In point 7 of the Accord, the AUC expressed that it shared the purpose of the government, that is, to liberate the country of drug-trafficking and that the organization supported the official policy against it.

The Santa Fé de Ralito Accord does not address issues related to the legal arrangements needed in order to respond to criminal proceedings already begun against the paramilitary leadership for serious crimes. Media and research centers' reports, as well as various public letters and statements by paramilitary commanders, have shown evidence that the government managed to persuade the paramilitary leadership to accept a legal framework to be debated in Congress. A strong argument was presented by official negotiators for the need for an ironclad instrument that will prevent eventual interventions by the International Criminal Court (ICC) and third-country parties exercising universal jurisdiction.

According to official sources, between November 2003 and August 2006, 31,671 paramilitary combatants were demobilized in 38 public ceremonies throughout the country.[22] Out of the total number of demobilized combatants, 86% were men and 14% women. Furthermore, 19% of these were children.[23] In addition, between August 2002 and September 2007, 9,800 guerrillas voluntarily deserted their organizations, risking retaliation, to avail themselves of the demobilization program.[24]

It is significant to note that the paramilitary demobilization process does not constitute a comprehensive peace process involving other armed actors. Peace negotiations between the FARC and the government are not foreseeable in the near future. As mentioned above, the pillar of the government's policy – responsible for much

[20] Acuerdo de Santa Fe de Ralito, http://www.altocomisionadoparalapaz.gov.co/acuerdos/acuerdos_t/jul_15_03.htm.

[21] Acuerdo de Santa Fe de Ralito, http://www.altocomisionadoparalapaz.gov.co/acuerdos/acuerdos_t/jul_15_03.htm.

[22] República de Colombia, Alto Comisionado para la Paz "Proceso de Paz con las Autodefensas: Informe Ejecutivo" (Bogotá, December 2006), http://www.altocomisionadoparalapaz.gov.co/libro/Libro.pdf, accessed 12 July 2008 [8].

[23] República de Colombia, Alto Comisionado para la Paz "Desmovilizaciones colectivas de las autodefensas: estado de la reintegración" (on file with author) at 2.

[24] República de Colombia, Ministerio de Defensa, "Logros de la Política de Consolidación de la Seguridad Democrática" (Bogotá, September 2007), http://www.mindefensa.gov.co/descargas/Sobre_eLMinisterio/Planeacion/ResultadosOperacionales/Resultados%20Operacionales%20Ene%20-%20Sep%202007.pdf, accessed 12 July 2008.

of its popularity – is its Democratic Security strategy, which includes an ambitious military plan, supported by the U.S., to defeat the FARC in its strongholds of the southern jungles of the country.

Despite certain positive messages included by the President in his inaugural speech before Congress – stating that the Democratic Security strategy does not exclude exploring avenues for a negotiated end to the violence[25] – the official position on what would be required for a political negotiation is still very far from that of the FARC. First, while the government sees an unconditional cessation of hostilities as a preliminary step in the process, the FARC views any kind of peace talks as conditional upon the demilitarization of a large territory in the south of the country, in order to guarantee the security of guerrilla negotiators. Second, while the government publicly states that a peace negotiation would primarily concern economic and legal conditions for demobilization and reintegration of combatants, the FARC demands that substantive national economic and social policy issues be included on the negotiating agenda. In an open letter in October 2006, the guerrilla movement listed the topics that it would expect to be discussed at the negotiating table. These included *inter alia* the free-trade agreement with the U.S.; agrarian reform, including property restitution to peasant victims of the conflict; counter-narcotics policy; extradition treaty; Colombia's energy policy; economic compensation to victims of the conflict by the government; and the formation of a constituent assembly.[26] Even though Uribe's government has expressly referred to the possibility of a constituent assembly at the conclusion of a peace process, it has also stated that it will not subordinate the national agenda to holding negotiations with the guerrillas.

Military and political developments in 2008 could be evidencing a turning point in the war dynamics: the Democratic Security policy could be proving its success in defeating the FARC.[27] In March 2008 two key members of FARC's Secretariat – its maximum political and military authority – fell in bold military operations. Raul Reyes, the second man in command after FARC's historic leader fell in a bombardment to his camp in Ecuador and the youngest member of the Secretariat was killed by the chief of his personal guard, who had entered into negotiations with military intelligence, and who was after granted demobilization benefits.[28] Female commander alias Karina, the woman holding the highest rank within FARC, demobilized in May 2008 also persuaded by military intelligence. She is currently part of moving television demobilization campaigns. FARC's founding member and legendary leader, Manuel Marulanda Vélez, died in the jungle at the age of 79 from a heart attack.

But probably the most significant military success was the spectacular rescue operation of 17 hostages – including Ingrid Betancourt, the three American contractors

---

[25] República de Colombia, Alto Comisionado para la Paz, "Declaración del Presidente electo" (May 26 2002), http://www.altocomisionadoparalapaz.gov.co/pre_paz/05_26_2002.htm, accessed 12 July 2008.

[26] FARC-EP, Secretariado del Estado Mayor Central, (October 1 2006), http://www.farcep.org/?node=2,2324,1, accessed October 2007.

[27] "El Fin de las FARC", *Revista Semana* No. 1350 (March 15 2008).

[28] "Así cayó 'Ríos", *Revista Cambio* (March 12 2008).

and 15 police and military officers – in early July 2008, the majority of whom had been in FARC's hands for almost 10 years. Military intelligence personnel penetrated the insurgent units and conducted a fake humanitarian mission in which the hostages were supposed to be transferred from the southern jungles to the camp of the new maximum guerrilla leader. The hostages were rescued in two civilian helicopters, without entering into any military confrontation.

Previous separate national and international efforts aimed at negotiating a humanitarian agreement for the liberation of hostages and a reciprocal release of the FARC combatants currently serving prison sentences, never materialized. However, under decisive initiative by Venezuelan President Hugo Chávez and, apparently, with Fidel Castro's intervention, six hostages – five former Congress men and women and Ingrid Betancourt's Vice-president Clara Rojas – were unilaterally released between January and March 2008. Chavez called the international community to exclude the FARC from the terrorists' lists and to grant them belligerence status. Latin-American as well as European countries expressly opposed the proposal.

In December, 2005, the less powerful ELN entered into a series of formal exploratory dialogues with government representatives in Cuba. During the sixth round, in April 2007, the government accepted ELN's proposal for a "transitory and experimental" cease-fire, but insisted on adequate verification and assembling of the troops.[29] The ELN had rejected previous calls for assembling its troops, arguing that this would constitute political and military suicide. It remains to be seen if the cease-fire will materialize. At the core of the debate is a fundamental – and somewhat predictable – contradiction around the structure and priorities of the basic terms of the Accord. The government demands a cessation of hostilities, assembling and demobilization as the first step in the process. The ELN insists on inclusion of certain humanitarian, social, and political issues on the agenda, along with the cessation of hostilities (see, for example, Luis Eduardo Celis 2007).

In terms of the paramilitary demobilization, the success of the process is far from assured. Official governmental and inter-governmental sources have reported the persistence of different modalities of illegal armed structures involved in various forms of criminality, coercion and political control in several regions of the country. The National Reparations and Reconciliation Commission presided by a delegate of the Vice-president of the Republic, the monitoring mission of the Secretary-General of the Organization of American States and the UN High Commissioner for Human Rights have evidenced the mutation of paramilitary groups into new armed structures and the emergence of new paramilitary groupings.[30] There is also official

---

[29] República de Colombia, Alto Comisionado para la Paz, "Proceso de Diálogo Gobierno Nacional-ELN, Informe Ejecutivo-Marzo 29 de 2007" and "Entrevista del Alto Comisionado para la paz, Luis Carlos Restrepo a la FM de RCN" (April 18 2007), http://www.altocomisionadoparalapaz.gov.co/noticias/2007/abril/abr_18_07.htm, accessed 12 July 2008.

[30] For example, The UN High Commissioner for Human Rights reported in March 2007 the presence of a new paramilitary organization in Nariño called "Peasant Self-Defense Forces–New Generation". According to the UNHCHR, the paramilitary organization is very well armed, militarily organized, with clear command structures and the capacity to exert territorial control. The

information about paramilitary factions that did not participate in the demobilization process and are occupying territories formerly controlled by the blocs and fronts from which they come.

The Organization of American States' Mission to Support the Peace Process in Colombia (MAPP/OEA) expressly recognizes that positive developments have, in general, occurred in the demobilization process. The Mission has reported that blocs and fronts have been broken up and that the majority of ex-combatants have returned to their regions. However, MAPP/OEA's February and August 2006, February, July and October 2007 and June 2008 reports also allude to the fact that three forms of illegal armed activity involving ex-combatants remain. First, the ex-combatants are regrouping in criminal gangs that exercise control over certain communities and pursue illegal economic activities. Second, factions of demobilized fronts remain active. Third, the reports point to the appearance of new armed actors and/or the strengthening of pre-existing ones in areas left by demobilized fronts (OAS 2006a). These newly transformed armed groups count on significant participation and leadership of former mid-ranking paramilitary combatants. Their main activities are linked to drug trafficking and their *modus operandi* is highly similar to that of the paramilitary groups that formerly operated in the same areas (OAS 2006a).

The first comprehensive report on demobilization, disarmament and reintegration by the National Reparations and Reconciliation Commission (CNRR 2007a), agrees with the characterization of the three phenomena of illegal armed action in which demobilized (remobilized) paramilitaries are taking part. CNRR offers a refined typology: dissidents, rearmed and emerging groups. Dissidents include groups that belonged to the AUC and never entered the negotiation process as well as those who did enter the process but finally refuse to demobilize and factions of demobilized blocs and fronts that remain active (CNRR 2007a, p. 38). The category of rearmed comprehends those demobilized combatants who are re-joining previously existing or newly organized criminal structures (CNRR 2007a). Emerging groups refer to already exiting groups at the time of the demobilization process with little visibility, as well as to newly constituted groups (CNRR 2007a). The official report documents the existence of 34 new illegal armed groups with 3,955 members approximately, including demobilized combatants (high and mid-ranking cadres and rank and file troops) and newly recruited personnel (CNRR 2007a, p. 48).

While, according to CNRR's analysis, it is yet not clear the extent to which the new illegal armed structures participate of a counter-insurgent project, there is enough evidence of their implementation of social and political control strategies towards civil population in various regions of the country. Such strategies are similar to those displayed by the old paramilitary federation.

The MAPP/OEA concluded in its August 2006 report that the success and sustainability of the peace process will depend on the attention paid to communities affected by violence, official recovery of the territories controlled by illegal groups, and the effective reintegration of demobilized ex-combatants (CNRR 2007a). In June 2008 the MAPP/OEA confirmed that in the post-demobilization phase communities

organization is allegedly responsible for two massacres. Human Rights Council (2007). See also International Crisis Group (2007).

are the "fundamental subject of the peace process": the protection of the population and reconstructing the social fabric of those communities affected by paramilitary violence should be top priorities of the State policy (OAS 2008).

2.3 The Transition as Experienced from Below

The political and economic agendas of community and civil society actors received little consideration in the political negotiation. As a result, issues that were crucial for these actors – including restitution, redistribution of land, and reducing paramilitary interference in local community development and governance bodies – have not been addressed by institutionalized transitional mechanisms. This omission has been referred to specifically by the National Movement of Victims of State Crime (*Movimiento Nacional de Víctimas de Crímenes de Estado,* MOVICE),[31] a broad coalition of more than two hundred associations of victims and social organizations which have been specifically targeted by paramilitary groups and state actors. The MOVICE has argued that a "genuine" transitional justice arrangement should include the following:

> recognition of victims of State crime and the participation of the State in the creation of the paramilitary project; a holistic approach to reparations including not only financial compensation but the reconstruction of political projects and collective organizational structures; the return of property and territories, and environmental damage to African-Colombian and Indigenous communities; adequate punishment for the architects of such activities and for those who benefited from paramilitary violence; and the return of property illegally acquired by the paramilitaries, their friends and families. (MOVICE 2006)

National human rights NGOs and their networks, social organizations, and national victims' organizations have claimed specifically that the paramilitary demobilization does not reflect a peace process and that it is not oriented toward dismantling the paramilitary project, but rather to legitimating it. For example, MOVICE questions whether Colombia is experiencing a transition at all and therefore contests the application of the transitional justice framework being articulated, particularly in regard to the Justice and Peace Law (see MOVICE 2006). It claims that, "in order for transitional justice to exist, a transition is needed" defining transition as, "a political transformation requiring that those who brandished weapons decisively contribute to peace, democracy, and reconciliation" (MOVICE 2006). MOVICE's view aligns with that of many other community and civil society organizations claiming that Colombia is in fact witnessing the consolidation of *de facto* authoritarianism exercised by the paramilitary leaders and their organizations. As a human rights leader from Barrancabermeja, one of the cities in the country most affected by paramilitary violence puts it, the paramilitary groups have established "para-institutional

[31] The MOVICE symbolizes the extermination campaign conducted by paramilitary groups in conjunction with official military, police, and intelligence units particularly against left-wing political forces, trade-unions, grassroots, cooperatives and other communal associations. The MOVICE has become the widest victim's network in the country.

governance systems" in the territories under their control, replacing the authority of the state with *de facto* regimes (Meza 2006, pp. 139–157). The paramilitary demobilization thus risks institutionalizing those *de facto* regimes into *de jure* regimes (Hincapié 2006, pp. 93–111).

In studying the transformation of paramilitary dominance structures in Colombia, researcher Michael Reed (2008) explains how the paramilitary demobilization process allowed for paramilitary control over communities through "legalized and formalized structures". Building on effective control gained by tactics of terror, transformed paramilitary units are occupying social and political spheres in the villages, exercising their power through legal mechanisms (Reed 2008).

Similarly, in interviews conducted by American anthropologist, Kimberley Theidon, the great majority of ex-combatants in paramilitary areas were very skeptical about the collective demobilization process. With few exceptions, the ex-combatants refer to the process as a "sham" and a "mockery". For example, a former paramilitary combatant commented that, "the negotiations are not changing anything. They are just transforming the illegal into the legal" (Theidon and Betancourt 2006). Similar concerns have been expressed by the Women and Armed Conflict Working Group,[32] a national research and coordination initiative comprised of more than 20 women's groups, community and grassroots organizations, and human rights NGOs. It discusses the demobilization process and the consolidation of paramilitary power in the Magdalena river valley in its annual report for June 2004 through June 2005,[33] stating that the paramilitary project there has developed – as in many other regions of the country – in three consecutive phases: incursion, consolidation, and legitimization (Mesa de Mujer y Conflicto Armado 2005). The report implies that the legitimization phase is perfectly compatible with the demobilization process. As a woman who attended one of the meetings convened by the paramilitary front controlling her town, subsequently reported: "[T]hey [the paramilitaries] say '[d]emobilization does not mean the end of the organization, but precisely the legitimization of our struggle" (Mesa de Mujer y Conflicto Armado 2005). The report goes on to observe the following:

> In the legitimization phase, the paramilitaries penetrate local economies and local power structures supporting the expansion of capitalism and the liberal-conservative, two-party system. In this phase paramilitary resources are generated by legally bought businesses. Paramilitaries create foundations and cooperatives in order to promote productive projects; they participate in community-based initiatives, particularly in poor areas; and they try to control political and electoral processes at the regional and national levels. As the paramilitaries strengthen their control and neutralize their opponents, some human rights violations decrease, but they maintain the control over the lives of the inhabitants of the communities. (Mesa de Mujer y Conflicto Armado 2005)

For instance, the paramilitaries of the *Bloque Central Bolivar* (BCB) created a "social department" within their organization. The social department is a group in charge of organizing communities around the paramilitary project. The department

[32] http://www.mujeryconflictoarmado.org/.

[33] A vast strategic region of the country which was during three decades under the control of the ELN guerrillas and was during the last decade taken over by the paramilitaries.

leads various initiatives, such as the creation of groups for developing economically productive projects and the promotion of certain candidates running for local and regional public positions. As evidenced by Reed's extensive field research, BCB ex-combatants later established the NGO *Buscando Caminos Buenos* (the name could be translated as *In the search for a good path*), dedicated to the same activities as the old BCB "social department".

A report produced by the *Asociación Nacional de Mujeres Campesinas e Indígenas de Colombia* (ANMUCIC)[34] confirms the implementation of the paramilitary legitimization strategy (Mesa de Mujer y Conflicto Armado 2005). The Association reports the story of the "appropriation" of the communities' organizations and civil society spheres by the paramilitary groups. Organized ex-combatants seek legitimization through positions in the municipal councils, the villages' major offices, and administrative contracting proceedings. Reed has also documented paramilitary control over key community aspects of everyday life, including communal security, public transportation, and regulation of certain economic activities in lower classes suburbs.

Following Ruti Teitel's (2005, p. 839) transitional justice genealogy, the Colombian experience exemplifies how contemporary transitional justice could be progressively abandoning goals of real political transformation, and rather serves as a tool of "conflict resolution". As Teitel (2005) puts it, "the contemporary period (of transitional justice) reflects a chastened commitment to deep political change". Discussing the role of the International Criminal Tribunal for the former Yugoslavia (ICTY) and the Iraqi Special Tribunal, Teitel (2005) affirms that, "Because of the political context of the current trials and their aim of justice-seeking amidst conditions of conflict, the onerous burden of creating a visible normative shift depends upon transitional justice". In the author's words, "vivid construction of transition should be achieved by drawing a clear line distinguishing the past from the present". Can contemporary trials, she asks, constitute that line separating the past from the present? The question is of significant relevance for the Colombian case.

In the Colombian experience, law is playing a crucial role in the construction of the transition. In the absence of other sites of institutional political transformation, the Justice and Peace Law could be bearing the "onerous burden" of drawing a clear line between the past and the present. To date, the Colombian "transition" has not opened other institutional sites of political transformation, such as a constituent assembly, institutional reform *ad hoc* commissions – dealing with police, military, executive, human rights, women issues, land-tenure – or new local or regional governance structures.

In Colombia the official rhetoric has reduced the complex and open-ended concept of political transition to a flawed process of paramilitary disarmament and engagement with a governmental reintegration program. Although formally linking "national peace" with the "strengthening of democratic governance", the paramilitary "peace process" has arguably not been about the widening, deepening, or strengthening of democracy in the country. Political and security institutions remain

[34] In English, the National Association of Indigenous and Peasant Women of Colombia.

largely unchanged and there is little evidence of a genuinely transformative process of legislative or social reform. It remains uncertain whether the criminal justice arena upon which all attention to date has been focused has the potential to itself become a catalyst for such a broader process of transformation.

3 Transitional Justice as "Bottom Up" Resistance: The Potential of the Truth, Justice and Rights to Reparations Discourse[35]

The national government claims that as the paramilitary demobilization process presents a "peace process", the establishment of peace as a key priority necessitates exceptional measures, namely the suspension of ordinary criminal justice.[36] For its part, the paramilitary leadership affirms that the reintegration of ex-combatants would respect "universal principles of truth, justice, and reparations... generously reconciled with ideals of peace, equity, development, and reconciliation".[37]

In July 2005, the Colombian Congress approved Law 975/2005 (hereinafter law 975/2005, Law 975 or Peace and Justice Law), establishing a special criminal justice procedure directed at ex-combatants facing criminal charges or sentences issued *in absentia* for gross human rights violations. Ex-combatants who have been sentenced, charged, or are under investigation for "political crimes" such as rebellion, sedition, and rioting, as well as other related crimes, such as illegal carrying of weapons and ID falsification are eligible for judicial pardon or amnesty benefits depending on the phase of the criminal process. The Colombian Constitutional Court ruled in a previous occasion that crimes such as execution *hors de combat*, kidnapping, and forced disappearance can never been understood as "political".[38]

The great majority of ex-combatants benefit from amnesty provisions, according to Law 782/2002 and Executive Decree 128/2003.[39] In fact, the government first estimated that the new law was expected to deal with no more than 400 ex-combatants.

---

[35] My reflections on the counter-hegemonic use of the rights discourse draw on de Sousa Santos and Rodríguez-Garavito (2005).

[36] República de Colombia, Ministry of Interior and Justice, "Exposición de Motivos al proyecto de ley estatutaria número 85 de 2003-Senado", 436 Gaceta del Congreso (27 August 2003) at 3.

[37] República de Colombia, Alto Comisionado para la Paz, "Proceso de Paz con las Autodefensas-Informe Ejecutivo" (Bogotá, December 2006), http://www.altocomisionadoparalapaz.gov.co/libro/Libro.pdf, accessed 12 July 2008 [123].

[38] República de Colombia, Corte Constitucional, Sentencias C-695/2002 and C-578/2002.

[39] Law 782/2002 and decree 128/2003 enable prosecutors and judges to grant amnesties (in the form of cessation of investigation or prosecution at every stage of the criminal process) and judicial pardons to ex-combatants that have been certified as such by an official "Committee for Weapon Decommissioning" (Comité para la Dejación de Armas, CODA). Ex-combatants are not required to contribute to the clarification of serious crimes that they might have witnessed or heard of – not to say about the crimes that they might have committed themselves but had been never investigated. Neither, are they required to provide any information about the fate of the disappeared or the hostages that their armed front might have taken. For a discussion on the compatibility of law 782 key provisions with international criminal law standards see Ambos (2008, p. 164 et seq.).

Later, it turned out that more than 2,000 expressed their consent to benefit from the provisions of Law 975/2005.[40]

Widely referred to as the "Peace and Justice" Law, Law 975 was adopted after a 2-year public debate in which the national government, the donor community, inter-governmental agencies, local political elites and various civil society actors debated the merits of comparative transitional justice experiences, and their applicability in the Colombian context. Particular attention was given to the applicability and content of the rights to truth, justice, and reparations.

Interpretations about eventual interventions by the ICC or third countries by virtue of the doctrine of universal jurisdiction also played a certain role in the public debate. The government and other actors, including the paramilitary leadership, were fully aware of the fact that the ICC might exercise its jurisdiction over crimes against humanity in the Colombian context, if the country was not able to do justice to victims of those crimes.

While it may be said that the government, paramilitaries, and other elites have adapted the language and discourse of transitional justice for their own political ends, it would be wrong to give the impression that they have done so without challenge.[41] Indeed, community and civil society organizations have themselves increasingly deployed legal and "transitional" terminology in pursuit of their objectives on at least two levels. First, they have actively engaged in the public debate on the legal framework for the demobilization and reintegration process and the drafting of the Justice and Peace Law. Colombian actors from below, backed by international human rights NGOs, inter-governmental agencies and certain European governmental cooperation agencies, have contested the official discourse of transitional justice as intending to evade retributive justice through the manipulation of the right to truth, justice and reparation. Second, grassroots actors are increasingly employing the language on the right to truth, justice and reparation within workshops, research projects, publications, and a variety of campaigns themselves.

For example, victims' support groups and local reconciliation committees in East Antioquia have elaborated on the specifics that the ideals of truth, justice

---

40 As reported by the High Commissioner for Peace in the official speech commemorating the second anniversary of the expedition of law 975/2005, his office persuaded more than a thousand of demobilized paramilitaries to sign to the list of ex-combatants willing to enter the Peace and Justice criminal proceedings, even though not having criminal records. According to the High Commissioner for Peace, the rationale behind the strategy was the need for bringing to justice ex-combatants and cases that were not under the radar of the criminal justice system, in order to demonstrate the virtues of the Peace and Justice Law, based on the voluntary contribution to justice. República de Colombia, Alto Comisionado para la Paz, "Balance de un proceso", (Speech at the Symposium: "Dos años Ley de Justicia y Paz", Bogotá, Universidad Santo Tomas, 25 July 2007), http://www.altocomisionadoparala-paz.gov.co/noticias/2007/julio/documentos/Documento%20de% 20Apoyo.pdf, accessed 12 July 2008.

41 For a very interesting discussion about manipulative and democratic uses of the transitional justice discourse in Colombia see Uprimny and Saffon (2008). An English version of the piece is available in Bergsmo and Kalmanovitz (2007).

and reparations should entail.[42] Similarly, the African-Colombian Conference is conducting a field research project with grassroots initiatives and organized communities to collectively formulate a proposal on truth, justice and reparations for African-Colombian communities (Cuesta 2006). A leading development and human rights NGO in Barrancabermeja published a book describing the paramilitary siege of the city and the contribution of truth, justice and reparations processes in its recovery (Corporación Nación 2006). Finally, the MOVICE offers its affiliates a diploma that includes a truth, justice and reparations module. The practical and legal manifestations of transitional justice discourses in Colombia have become the terrain upon which these very differing meanings are contested throughout society.

3.1 Background to the Justice and Peace Law: The Alternative Penal Draft Legislation

Supported by international actors, local civil society and community organizations played a significant role in the public debate on the drafting process of the Justice and Peace Law. NGOs and social organizations used international legal materials to lobby the Colombian government and influential foreign actors. They made inputs to the various Congressional debates and managed to significantly influence national and international public opinion. This activity was key to securing substantive modifications to early versions of the Justice and Peace Law, in favor of victims' rights.

The first version of the Justice and Peace Law was called the "Alternative Penal draft legislation" and was conceived by the legal team of the Office of the Colombian High Commissioner for Peace on the direct instructions of the President of the Republic.[43] The President's aim was to avoid using politically contentious language on the question of amnesty, by offering demobilized combatants judicial pardons within the context of the criminal justice system. The alternative penal draft legislation was crafted using certain language drawn from the theory and practice of restorative justice but without a clear understanding among officials of the meaning, requirements and applicability of that framework, particularly in a context within which massive human rights violations had been committed. The Minister of Interior and Justice explained that in order to overcome the war, bold alternatives to criminal justice were necessary in order to harmonize Justice and Peace and, as

[42] Conciudadanía, Asociación Regional de Mujeres del Oriente Antioqueño, Programa por la Paz de la Compañía de Jesús, "Primer Encuentro Regional de 'Víctimas a ciudadanas-os': para que otras voces se escuchen y el dolor sea propuesta" (November 2005). On file with author.

[43] Interview with Roberto Mora, at the time Human Rights expert lawyer at the Office of the High Commissioner for Peace, Presidencia de la República de Colombia (Bogotá, 22 May 2006.) The Colombian President happened to be studying at Oxford University when the Good Friday Agreement was signed in Northern Ireland. He personally instructed the High Commissioner for Peace to create a legal mechanism inspired by the early release provisions of that Accord. For a discussion on the provisions of those mechanism see McEvoy (1999, pp. 145–181).

such, these alternatives had to go beyond the notion of justice as punishment. Justice, it was argued, should be understood as a means of fostering co-existence.[44] Even though at that stage the phrase transitional justice was not explicitly used, the law did make some references to the right to truth and reparations for victims.

Under the Alternative Penal draft legislation, the president of the Republic was empowered – when "the interest of national peace is at stake" – to use his discretion to request judges to suspend the execution of prison sentences, if the person sentenced agreed to abide by the following conditions:

- To cease any further commission of crimes
- To contribute to victims reparation, the end of the conflict and peace
- Not to leave the country without previous judicial authorization
- To inform authorities of any change of residence
- To appear before the judicial authority who supervises the execution of the alternative punishment, when required to do so[45]

Those ex-combatants from illegal armed groups that have declared a cessation of hostilities and are actively involved in a peace process, as well as individual deserters, are eligible for suspensions of sentences.[46] This benefit was supposed to cover those crimes for which the ex-combatant was sentenced under ordinary or abbreviated (plea bargaining and confession) proceedings.[47] After a probation period of between 1 and 5 years, in which the demobilized combatant was supposed to comply with the obligations mentioned, the judge would then declare the prison sentence expunged.[48]

Article 11 of the draft legislation provided that in addition, the judge should impose an "alternative sanction" to the prison sentence from a list also contained in the draft legislation, including:

- Disqualification from public duty for a maximum of 10 years
- Disqualification from participating in elections for a maximum of 10 years
- Prohibition from carrying weapons for a maximum of 10 years
- Prohibition from living in or visiting certain places where the crimes were committed or where the victims reside, for a maximum of 20 years
- Prohibition of approaching or communicating with victims

[44] República de Colombia, Ministry of Interior and Justice, "Exposición de Motivos al proyecto de ley estatutaria número 85 de 2003-Senado", 436 Gaceta del Congreso (27 August 2003) [5].

[45] República de Colombia, "Proyecto de Ley Estatutaria No. 85 de 2003", 436 *Gaceta del Congreso* (27 August 2003) Article 2.

[46] República de Colombia, "Proyecto de Ley Estatutaria No. 85 de 2003", 436 *Gaceta del Congreso* (27 August 2003) Article 2.

[47] República de Colombia, "Proyecto de Ley Estatutaria No. 85 de 2003", 436 *Gaceta del Congreso* (27 August 2003) Article 2.

[48] República de Colombia, "Proyecto de Ley Estatutaria No. 85 de 2003", 436 *Gaceta del Congreso* (27 August 2003) Article 5.

- "Geographical restriction of freedom" for a maximum of 10 years, meaning being obliged to reside within certain regions of the country and not to leave it without judicial authorization[49]

From the text, it was not clear, however, whether the various alternative sanctions were cumulative or exclusionary. This was apparently a matter of judicial discretion.

The judge was also vested with the discretion to impose certain reparatory obligations or "acts" to "contribute to the overcoming of the conflict" or to "achieving peace":

- Victims reparation, according to ordinary law
- Community service favoring victims' recovery
- Collaboration with institutions devoted to victims' recovery
- The hand-over of property to the state (through the Reparations Trust Fund) or to institutions devoted to victims' services
- Public expressions of repentance
- Effectively contributing to the clarification of what occurred during the armed conflict
- The provision of information effectively contributing to the dismantling of illegal armed groups[50]

According to Article 6, the imposition of one or several of the measures listed, did not exclude economic compensation. However, as defined in Article 1, "when victim compensation is not possible", measures directed toward the affected community or the society as a whole, should suffice. Thus, the reparations "definitions" in Article 1 made clear that the measures listed to achieve reparation, the termination of conflict, or peace listed in Article 6 were not cumulative, but alternative.

The Alternative Penal draft legislation did not provide genuine mechanisms for reparations to victims. The draft legislation did not make the suspension of the prison sentence conditional upon the effective realization of reparations. Nor did it contemplate the creation of a properly resourced administrative reparations program. Both the Colombian and the international human rights community strongly criticized the initiative, with local human rights NGOs and other civil society actors mobilized against the draft legislation. In conjunction with European and U.S. based human rights networks, the Colombian human rights community launched lobbying campaigns targeted at donor governments and intergovernmental organizations to put pressure on the Colombian government to substantially modify the Alternative Penal draft legislation. Organized indigenous, African-Colombian and peasant communities, trade unions and women rights groups subscribed to NGOs lobby documents and press releases and also incorporated the critique of the Alternative Penal draft legislation into their own agendas and advocacy strategies.

---

[49] República de Colombia, "Proyecto de Ley Estatutaria No. 85 de 2003", 436 *Gaceta del Congreso* (27 August 2003) Article 11.

[50] República de Colombia, "Proyecto de Ley Estatutaria No. 85 de 2003", 436 *Gaceta del Congreso* (27 August 2003) Article 6.

The critique of the draft legislation was framed in terms of the rights to truth, justice and reparation and the violation of international law contained therein.[51] The rights rhetoric was successfully used to oppose official arguments that manipulated transitional justice standards with the avowed intention of overcoming the war. The international community also made clear that its political and financial support for the demobilization process was conditional upon the adoption of a "legal framework" compatible with international truth, justice and reparations standards (International Crisis Group 2006, [14, 15]). The UN High Commissioner for Human Rights, the European Union and the donor community all expressed their concerns about the marginalization of victims' rights within the demobilization process (International Crisis Group 2006).

3.2 Civil Society Effecting Change: The Justice and Peace Law

Due in great part to international pressure, the government was forced to revise the Alternative Penal draft legislation and to discuss modifications to it with certain groups in Parliament who had both criticized the initiative and indeed had drafted an alternative text. A version of the new draft which later became known as the "Peace and Justice Law" was approved in Congress in July 2005 and signed by the president of the Republic.

The Peace and Justice Law maintained the same structure, organizing principles, and procedural mechanisms as the Alternative Penal draft legislation. However, it incorporated key new elements, including a new section establishing the general rights of victims to truth, justice, and reparations (based on international principles), as well as new provisions dealing with specific reparations for victims. According to the Peace and Justice Law, ongoing investigations, prosecutions, and trials against demobilized paramilitaries involving serious crimes will continue. Moreover, the alternative forms of punishment – such as alternatives to a prison sentence – were removed and replaced with a reduced prison sentence of between 5 and 8 years.[52] The Justice and Peace Law did not, however, condition the benefit on a full disclosure of the facts of the crimes. Neither did the law establish any special non-judicial truth-telling mechanism. Rather, it assigned the task of producing a report about "the causes of the emergence and development of the illegal armed groups", to a National Reparations and Reconciliation Commission (CNRR).[53] The CNRR was

[51] See for example the series of press releases and advocacy documents by the Comisión Colombiana de Juristas (Colombian Commission of Jurists), http://www.coljuristas.org/inicio.htm, accessed 12 July 2008.

[52] Ley 975 de 2005, Article 29. However, according to Law 975/2005, the government has the power to determine the facilities where the prison sentences should be served. Based on this provision, the paramilitary leadership claimed that prison sentences can be served on private ranches or "peace villages". Consejo Editorial Ex Comandantes AUC, "Situación actual de las autodefensas: de la crisis a las propuestas" (10 September 2006). For a criminal justice analysis of Law 975 sentence reduction provisions see Ambos (2008, p. 164 et seq.).

[53] Ley 975 de 2005, Article 51.2.

also put in charge of the preparation of a national plan for collective reparations and the formulation of criteria directed to the Justice and Peace magistrates to be considered for the reparations orders, which the tribunals have to include in their final decisions.

In spite of its recognition that ex-combatants who have been declared responsible for serious crimes have a "general duty to repair", Law 975/2005 did not make sentence reduction conditional upon an effective contribution to the reparation of victims, regardless of the considerable financial wealth of paramilitary commanders and mid-ranking cadres. Rather, the law only exhorted ex-combatants participating in the special criminal Justice and Peace process to return illegally acquired assets to the state. Law 975/2005 also failed to establish a clear obligation on the part of the state to provide individual economic compensation.

3.3 Constitutional Court Challenge

As a consequence of these weaknesses in the law, several local human rights NGOs, actively supported by grassroots and community-based organizations, challenged the Justice and Peace Law before the Constitutional Court. In May, 2006, the Court decided to uphold the law, but struck down several of its provisions and declared that the validity of others was conditional upon certain constitutional interpretations. The Constitutional Court admitted that Law 975 was approved as an instrument to assist in resolving the internal armed conflict, and as such, its various mechanisms – that restrict the rights of victims – should be considered in light of the constitutional principle and right to peace.[54]

The Court examined the institution of alternative punishment (*Alternatividad*; in practice reduced prison sentences), strictly balancing the constitutional interest in peace with the rights of victims to truth, justice, and reparations.[55] The Court found the concept of alternative punishment in accordance with the Constitution and ruled that it did not entail a disproportionate compromise of the constitutional principle of justice. It found this considering that the Justice and Peace magistrates will impose an ordinary sentence, according to the rules of the Criminal Code, which will still be enforced if the person sentenced fails to comply by the conditions on which the benefit of sentence reduction is based. However, the Court found that conditioning the alternative punishment on a general collaboration with justice, as required in Article 3, was not specific enough to guarantee the right of victims to truth, justice, reparations, and non-repetition.[56] Consequently, the Court declared the constitutionality of Article 3 conditional upon the interpretation that "collaboration with justice"

---

[54] Corte Constitucional de Colombia, Sentencia No. C-370/2006, Section 5. For an analysis of the proportionality test applied by the Constitutional Court see Ambos (2008, p. 75 et seq.; also in this volume).

[55] Corte Constitucional de Colombia, Sentencia No. C-370/2006, Sections 6.2.2, 6.2.1.3 and 6.2.1.4.

[56] Corte Constitucional de Colombia, Sentencia No. C-370/2006, Section 6.2.1.5.

should be directed to guaranteeing the rights of victims to truth, justice, reparation, and non-repetition.

The Constitutional Court also declared that the criminal procedure established by Law 975/2005 does not "effectively promote full disclosure of the truth". The Constitutional Court clearly stated that the granting of the substantive benefits of sentence-reduction without requiring full (complete and genuine) disclosure of the facts of all the crimes in which the ex-combatant may have participated constitutes a violation of the right to truth.[57] Following its own constitutional jurisprudence[58] and the consolidated jurisprudence of the Inter-American Court of Human Rights, the Constitutional Court declared that the right to truth forms part of the Bill of Rights incorporated into the Colombian Constitution.

According to the Court, the special criminal procedure established through Law 975/2005 did not attribute any real consequences to the deliberate obfuscation of grave breaches by the ex-combatant; neither did it encourage full disclosure of the truth about such crimes.[59] The Constitutional Court highlighted the fact that the procedure created by the law did not punish false or incomplete versions of events, and that the sentence reduction is unaffected despite subsequent evidence suggesting that the complete truth was not revealed. Consequently, the Court struck down the relevant provisions which permitted sentence reduction where crimes were not fully acknowledged in the first instance.

The Constitutional Court stated that ex-combatants who benefit from the provisions of Law 975/2005 should contribute to the financial compensation of victims from their personal estates, including property that they have legally acquired. Accordingly, the Court struck down several sections of Law 975/2005 which required ex-combatants to return illegally acquired assets only "when possible". The Court affirmed that the state is not authorized to exempt those responsible for gross crimes from civil responsibility.[60] The Court explained that under Colombian and international law, economic compensation is an element of the right to reparations of victims and a condition to promote the fight against impunity.[61] Moreover, all the members of a certain demobilized illegal armed front, bloc, or structure should respond collectively to the harm caused by the criminal action of individual ex-combatants.[62]

The national and international human rights communities generally applauded this decision by the Constitutional Court. The paramilitary leadership responded by depicting the decision as a "mortal blow to peace" (Salazar 2006). Indeed, some expressed their specific concerns about the reparations aspects of the decision, as apparently they had expected to keep significant portions of their fortunes.

The key question that remains is whether or not these technical criminal justice processes contained in the Peace and Justice Law have the potential to transform

[57] Corte Constitucional de Colombia, Sentencia No. C-370/2006, Section 6.2.2.1.7.5.

[58] Corte Constitucional de Colombia, Sentencias No. C-228/2002 and No. C-578/2006.

[59] Corte Constitucional de Colombia, Sentencia No. C-370/2006, Section 6.2.2.1.7.15.

[60] Corte Constitucional de Colombia, Sentencia No. C-370/2006, Section 6.2.4.1.11.

[61] Corte Constitucional de Colombia, Sentencia No. C-370/2006, Section 6.2.4.1.12.

[62] Corte Constitucional de Colombia, Sentencia No. C-370/2006, Section 6.2.4.4.7.

entrenched power structures. It is not yet clear whether prosecutions, trials, and reparations under this law together have the capacity to break up the hegemonic influence that paramilitary structures have exercised in significant elements of Colombian public life at the national level. In addition, on the ground, according to many who live and work in the communities in which they operate, paramilitary violence has particularly targeted structures that enable governance and participation in community life. At leadership and middle level structures of local governance, researchers and activists report systemic infiltration and attempts to control such bodies, in effect maintaining paramilitary hegemony through political and lawful means. Can criminal processes against the paramilitary leadership and some mid-ranking cadres under the Justice and Peace Law really impact upon such control strategies in local communities?

Finally, in Colombia the paramilitary "project" of dominance has involved local and regional land-owners, rich merchants, businessmen, and politicians. Their activities would not have been possible without such political, financial, and logistical support. The narrow focus of the Justice and Peace Law upon demobilized paramilitaries in effect obscures that broader architecture of support and complicity among some of the country's most powerful actors.

3.4 The Peace and Justice Criminal Proceedings in Practice

In September 2006, the Ministry of Interior and Justice submitted to the Office of the Prosecutor General the list of ex-combatants who had expressed their will[63] to enter the Justice and Peace criminal proceedings.[64] Up to 2,935 demobilized paramilitary combatants – commanders, mid-ranking cadres and rank and file troops – declared their intention to make use of the Justice and Peace Law during the demobilization phase (CNRR 2007b, [68]). A percentage of these paramilitaries had been sentenced *in absentia,* charged or were under investigation for serious crimes, including assassinations, massacres, forced disappearances and, in a very few cases, forced displacement.

The Peace and Justice Unit of the Prosecutor General's Office (PJU) started to call the ex-combatants on the list, to hear them in proceedings known as *versión libre* (literally, "free versions"), where they are required to confess their participation in the crimes committed as members of the corresponding paramilitary front or bloc. As stated above, the Constitutional Court declared the constitutionality of the provision regulating the so-called "free version" under the condition that the confession given is "complete and thorough".

[63] On the strategy displayed by the Office of the High Commissioner for Peace to get the ex-combatants' consent see n 40.

[64] República de Colombia, Alto Comisionado para la Paz, "Lista de Postulados ley 975 de 2005", http://www.altocomisionadoparalapaz.gov.co/noticias/2007/junio/documentos/postuladosa28deJUNIO2007.pdf, accessed 12 July 2008.

From December 2006 to July 2007, 32 ex-combatants were heard in the first phase[65] of these free version hearings (CNRR 2007b, [69]). According to the Reparations and Reconciliation Commission (CNRR), until March 2008, approximately 127 ex-combatants have been heard in free version hearings, proceedings that are still developing (not finalized);[66] only in one case an indictment has been produced.[67] According to official PJU statistics, 8,634 victims have participated in the hearings; a total number of 125,368 victims have been registered by the PJU.[68]

Several top commanders and mid-ranking cadres have told their stories about the origins, territorial control, and operating protocols of their respective blocs or fronts. The ex-combatants have also admitted their participation in horrendous crimes which were under investigation – in some cases, they have even expanded on unknown details of the crimes – and several of them have confessed other crimes which were not on official records. For example, the former commander of the bloc controlling Cúcuta (the capital city of an eastern province of the country) accepted his responsibility in the assassination of more than 2,000 persons.[69]

The commanders have also given information about their linkages with official military, police and intelligence forces and with local, regional, and national politicians. A former commander, alias "HH", stated, for example, that forced disappearance was a policy of the paramilitary organization, explicitly recommended by official military forces; the ex-combatant explained that when the military

[65] Trough Resolution No. 3938, December 2006, the Prosecutor General regulated the "free version" hearing dividing it into two rounds or sessions. The first session is supposed to address the general aspects of the participation of the ex-combatant in paramilitary activity – his or her role in the armed group, the period of time in which the person belonged to the group and the operation protocols of the group. At the end of the session, the ex-combatant should succinctly list the crimes which he will confess – the confession of specific crimes is the object of the second "free version" session. The prosecutor should organize the participation of victims in the second "free version" session, according to the order of the crimes that the ex-combatant referred to for confession. In practice, however, the PJU prosecutors have found it difficult to follow the sequence designed by the Prosecutor General. Having made tremendous personal and economic efforts to attend the "free version" first sessions, the victims have expressed their anger and deception when listening to extensive justification discourses by the ex-combatants without referring to the specific crimes. On the other hand, some ex-combatants have not respected the proposed order, mixing stories about their political convictions and the origins of the bloc or front with specific "military operations". The prosecutors have adapted the Resolution's instructions in order to address practical problems and to accommodate the various interests at stake.

[66] National Reparations and Reconciliation Commission statistics referred to by Senator Armando Benedetti in a special hearing in Congress. Edición Judicial, "Ex 'paras' no cumplen con la ley: Benedetti", *Diario El Tiempo*, (Bogotá, 16 April 2008).

[67] For a detailed account of the indictment and the appellate proceedings see Comisión Colombiana de Juristas, *Colombia: El espejismo de la justicia y la paz. Balance sobre la aplicación de la ley 975 de 2005*, (Bogotá, Comisión Colombiana de Juristas, March 2008).

[68] National Reparations and Reconciliation Commission statistics referred to by Senator Armando Benedetti in a special hearing in Congress. Edición Judicial, "Ex 'paras' no cumplen con la ley: Benedetti", *Diario El Tiempo*, (Bogotá, 16 April 2008).

[69] Edición Judicial, "Los crímenes de 'Don Antonio'", *Revista Semana* (Bogotá, No. 1303, April 21/2007), http://www.semana.com/wf_InfoArticulo.aspx?IdArt=102300, accessed 12 July 2008.

commanders first noted the public impact of the serial killings, they suggested to "disappear" the corpses in mass graves.[70]

Human rights organizations litigating cases before the PJU and victims' organizations who are participating in the proceedings have questioned the way in which the prosecutors have conducted these sessions. It is noteworthy, however, that prosecutors have interpreted the law and general instructions by the Prosecutor General in different ways, in various cases favoring victims' interests and demands.

First, NGOs and victims see the PJU's approach to guaranteeing the right of victims to access to justice, to participate in the "free versions", and to know the truth as very restrictive. Particularly in a few of the first cases, representatives of victims were denied access to the "free versions" because those victims were not on the PG's database.[71] This type of restrictive interpretations should be corrected according to a general instruction issued by the Prosecutor General that clarifies the standard of proof for demonstrating that someone is a victim.[72] In general terms, neither victims nor their representatives are allowed to enter the room where the ex-combatant is heard, but are permitted to watch the "free versions" through close-circuit television in an annex within the same building. However, a few prosecutors have allowed victims who expressly requested it, to enter the main room and face the perpetrator. Victims' lawyers have so far not been able to cross-examine ex-combatants and they have been only allowed to pass their questions in writing to the prosecutors. Prosecutors have seldom incorporated the questions posed by victims into their investigation strategies; in the majority of the cases the questions are successively read in a mere formalistic way.

Beyond the technical aspects of the proceedings, there is certain frustration among the great majority of victims who had expected that ex-combatants participating in Justice and Peace proceedings would tell them what happened to their loved ones. The great majority of the victims have not found any response to this quest in the paramilitaries' depositions: the ex-combatants have used the first *versión libre* sessions for justificatory narratives about the emergence and development of their respective blocs or fronts. During his first *version libre,* a paramilitary top commander, Salvatore Mancuso, even presented a video showing a village destroyed by the FARC guerillas as visual support for his justificatory discourse.[73] In several cases, the ex-combatants have referred to assassinations and disappearances as "military operations" against guerrillas, and have repeatedly referred to the victims as military targets. These statements were given as victims were watching the *version libre* without an effective opportunity to contradict the ex-combatants or to give their versions of the facts. In most cases, ex-combatants have not shown

---

[70] Comisión Colombiana de Juristas, *Colombia: El espejismo de la justicia y la paz. Balance sobre la aplicación de la ley 975 de 2005*, (Bogotá, Comisión Colombiana de Juristas, March 2008) [147].

[71] Comisión Colombiana de Juristas, "Audiencias de recepción de la versión libre: informe preliminar" (Bogotá, 2007). On file with author.

[72] Fiscalía General de la Nación, Resolución No. 03998 de 2006.

[73] Comisión Colombiana de Juristas, "Audiencias de recepción de la versión libre: informe preliminar" (Bogotá, 2007). On file with author.

any remorse or repentance for their acts. For example, a former commander, when asked about the fate of the victim's disappeared family members, confessed without shame to having thrown the bodies into a river.

The dissatisfaction of victims with the process also has to do with the fact that they have not had the opportunity to tell their stories and be heard by state officials as well as the wider public. So far, the perpetrators have been the main characters of the story. While ex-combatants receive official economic and legal support, victims remain in very precarious economic situations and are not receiving proper governmental attention. There are no specific psychosocial programs for victims and no financial support is granted for travel and accommodation expenses resulting from their participation in the Justice and Peace proceedings. This lack of official support aggravates victims' frustration around the Justice and Peace criminal proceedings.

Human rights NGOs have claimed that the *version libre* should be made public through mass media. Thus, they argue, the right of victims and society as a whole to know the truth could be guaranteed. The national government, the Prosecutor General, and certain sectors of the public endorsed the claim at first. However, additional considerations have since been made about the implications for the integrity of the investigation, the security of victims and witnesses, and about the kind of narrative that the public would receive. A leading human rights NGO litigating cases before the PJU lodged a constitutional action asking for live broadcasting of *versión libre* sessions on television, radio and the internet. The competent chamber of the Constitutional Court decided against, arguing that the criminal investigation is subjected to a secrecy principle.[74]

One of the most critical issues for the Peace and Justice criminal proceedings was the extradition in May 2008 to the United States of America of 14 top paramilitary commanders for illegal drug trafficking related charges; the ex-combatants were taking part of Peace and Justice proceedings and several of them had been already sentenced by ordinary courts for gross human rights violations. The President of the Republic argued that the commanders were committing crimes from prison and infringing their commitments under the Peace and Justice Law. The Government also explained that US authorities accepted to have official representatives in the trials and to cede any assets recovered from the paramilitary commanders to the reparations trust fund in Colombia.[75] But, as Human Rights Watch pointed out, the decision to extradite the paramilitary commanders came only after some had actually started to cooperate, and others announced plans to do so, by beginning to talk about their links with Colombian military and government officials.[76] There is certain suspicion in Colombia that the National Government decided to extradite the paramilitaries to the United States to prevent them from naming more names.

---

[74] Corte Constitucional de Colombia, T-049/2008 (24 January 2008).

[75] President of the Republic of Colombia, "President Alvaro Uribe of Colombia speaks on the occasion of the delivery in extradition of persons subjected to the Law of Justice and Peace" (Bogotá, 13 May 2008), http://www.cancilleria.gov.co/wps/portal/!ut/p/.cmd/cs/.ce/7_0_A/.s/7_0_1PI/_th/J_0_CI/_s.7_0_A/7_0_1PI/_s.7_0_A/7_0_1PI, accessed 12 July 2008.

[76] Human Rights Watch, Letter to Attorney General Mukasey, (Washington D.C., 16 May 2008), http://hrw.org/english/docs/2008/05/16/colomb18870.htm, accessed 12 July 2008.

The Colombia Office of the UN High Commissioner for Human Rights (UN-HCHR), the Inter-American Commission on Human Rights and several Colombian and US based human rights NGOs criticized the extraditions. The Inter-American Commission on Human Rights noted that:

> This extradition affects the Colombian State's obligation to guarantee victims' rights to truth, justice, and reparations for the crimes committed by the paramilitary groups. The extradition impedes the investigation and prosecution of such grave crimes through the avenues established by the Justice and Peace Law in Colombia and through the Colombian justice system's regular criminal procedures. It also closes the door to the possibility that victims can participate directly in the search for truth about crimes committed during the conflict, and limits access to reparations for damages that were caused. This action also interferes with efforts to determine links between agents of the State and these paramilitary leaders.[77]

Furthermore, the Peace and Justice Law does provide for adequate punishment to those ex-combatants who were in principle eligible for the special proceeding, but violate the commitments under the Law. At any time during the process the demobilized who is rejoining criminal activity could be excluded from the Peace and Justice special proceeding and sent to the ordinary prosecutorial and/or judicial authorities. What the Colombian Government did not explained was why to privilege prosecution for illegal drug-trafficking related charges in the US and not prosecution for war crimes and crimes against humanity in Colombia. The Peace and Justice proceedings involving the extradited paramilitaries might well continue – as the Government has explained – but the absence of those implicated will extremely complicate the processes.

For its part, the National Reparations and Reconciliation Commission (CNRR) is facing significant challenges. After adopting basic elements for a participatory construction of its "road map" and its "strategic definitions" in August 2006, the CNRR is yet to play a more active role in the Colombian Peace and Justice arrangement. It is composed of direct representatives of the executive[78] and a variety of civil society sectors; this arrangement complicates the internal consensus necessary to fulfill its obligations. At a national level, The CNRR has not played a particularly active role in the guaranteeing of victims' access to justice; certainly, more could have been done in terms of inter-institutional coordination and dissemination of information. By virtue of its monitoring role, CNRR presented in August and September 2007 two comprehensive reports: the first one evaluating the various processes aiming at restoring victims' rights to truth, justice and reparations (CNRR 2007b) and the second examining the demobilization process from a DDR perspective and analyzing the various forms of criminal activity involving paramilitary combatants (CNRR 2007a). Despite the excellent analytical contribution made by both expert

---

[77] Inter-American Commission on Human Rights, "IACHR expresses concern about extradition of Colombian paramilitaries" (Washington D.C., 14 May 2008) Press Release No. 21.

[78] The vice-president of the Republic acts as CNRR's president, the director of the official humanitarian assistance agency (Acción Social) as its technical secretary and the delegates of two ministers as commissioners.

teams, CNRR has not shown enough political leadership to put their main conclusions and recommendations in the public agenda. It seems to be certain disconnect between the technical level and the political muscle of the Commission.

Certain CNRR's regional offices are well-known exceptions, however. They have shown significant leadership with regard to other regional and local authorities and have organized massive information and orientation sessions for victims. A separate and special mention should also go to the "Historical Memory Working Group", an academically independent body constituted by CNRR to produce the report on the causes for the emergence and development of the illegal armed groups. The members of the group are respected and well-known academics from diverse fields – including anthropology, history, psychology, economics and law – who have extensive experience in studying the internal armed conflict and its effects from various perspectives. The working group is increasingly gaining legitimacy among a wide spectrum of civil society organizations, including the human rights community and victims sectors.

It is obviously too soon to adequately asses the Justice and Peace criminal proceedings and their impact, given that they are in their very initial stages. The challenges are becoming evident, however:

- The extent to which the PJU will be able to build systematic crimes cases
- The extent to which justificatory narratives will dominate and how victims' stories will come to the fore
- Whether the PJU will be able to prosecute the more than 2,000 ex-combatants who are presumably involved in serious crimes
- Whether victims will find satisfaction in Peace and Justice criminal proceedings

3.5 Beyond the Justice and Peace Law: Congress, Supreme Court and Media Activism

Opposition parties, the Criminal Chamber of the Supreme Court of Justice and the leading newspapers and political weekly magazines have decisively contributed to coin a new word in the Colombian lexicon: para-politics. It refers to the joint venture of paramilitary groups and national, regional and local politicians for the economic, social and political control of multiple territories of the country.[79] The association of paramilitaries and Colombian political leaders had been documented by human rights NGOs for several years, but it is only now that it has become part of public debate.

With the discovery of a lap-top belonging to a paramilitary commander from the Northern Bloc with detailed information on the operation and finances of the group, the office of the Prosecutor General started investigations against several

[79] For an excellent account of the alliance between paramilitary groups and politicians, see a special report by Corporación Nuevo Arco Iris, *Paramilitares y Políticos,* in Revista Arcanos, Bogotá, March 2007.

Congressmen, governors, majors, and members of regional and local assemblies and councils for their links with paramilitary groups. The investigations resulted in the unprecedented detention of 50 politicians, who have been indicted for "association for delinquency", financing of paramilitary groups and a few of them for kidnapping and homicide.

Among the detained, there are 15 Congressmen from various political coalitions aligned with the president of the Republic. A significant piece of evidence against the politicians is their signatures in an accord – known as the San José de Ralito Pact – between the paramilitary leadership and several senators, members of the Chamber of Representatives, governors and majors with the purpose of "re-founding the nation". The accord was signed in July 2001. In March 2002, after the Congressional election, paramilitary commander Salvatore Mancuso publicly expressed that the paramilitary federation AUC had gained control over 35% of the Congress. At that time, the public opinion was surprised by the statement, but with recent discoveries its full meaning is becoming increasingly clear.

The para-politics prosecutions by the Supreme Court of Justice are unveiling one of the pillars of the paramilitary project: its association with local, regional, and national political enterprises. This is opening a new – and highly unexpected – site for truth-telling and political debate about the nature, territorial coverage, and modus operandi of the paramilitary federation.

4 Conclusion

The Colombian context vividly illustrates that contemporary transitional justice should not simply be viewed as synonymous with political transition from oppressive regimes to democratic ones or with negotiated ends of armed conflict. Rather, contemporary transitional justice can form part of a partial, messy, and uneven process of state-sponsored transformation, directed at one element of the conflict. Colombia is certainly not experiencing a transition in the sense of negotiating the end of its 40-year internal armed conflict with the guerrilla groups and FARC in particular. Neither is the country going through a process of radical political transformation with new institutional sites for deepening or widening democracy.

What the national government and the paramilitary leadership present as the *transition,* is perceived and experienced in a completely different way by players from below. While the former present the paramilitary demobilization process as a "peace process" that is enabling the State to recover control over the territory of the country, many of those on the ground in various regions of the country are experiencing the demobilization as paramilitary "legitimization" processes – ex-combatants becoming organized in participating in community governance structures and local economic, political and administrative life. At one level this is often precisely the goal of demobilization processes – to ensure that ex-combatants are given the opportunity to retake their role in civic and political life. However, such a perspective pre-supposes a change in mindset and strategies amongst the ex-combatants themselves. Despite the rhetoric and powerful symbolism of the televised demobilization ceremonies, many in Colombian civil society are deeply skeptical as to whether paramilitaries have in reality abandoned their oppressive techniques for the exercise of power in the local communities where they are strong.

Despite the contested nature and meaning of the Colombian *transition,* transitional justice discourse has become a key instrument – both for actors from above and actors from below – to advance their causes. At a political level, the Colombian experience suggests that transitional justice discourses may be used as a strategy of resistance by certain sectors of civil society and communities affected by violence. In particular, the deployment of the truth, justice, and reparations rights discourses has proven to be a powerful tool for such "players from below" in their struggle against impunity. Building alliances with international human rights networks and deploying these discourses, such actors have successfully shaped the terms of the debate at the national level. They provided an antidote to official formulas which advocated the sacrificing of the interests of victims' and communities in the name of a "new concept of justice" which was used to justify the accommodation with the paramilitaries. Transitional justice rights face gave such actors a language and framework to challenge a state sponsored attempt to use transitional justice as a cover for a much more base political accommodation.

The implementation of the Justice and Peace Law, however, is creating new challenges for the materialization of the rights to truth, justice, and reparations. A first series of issues has to do with material obstacles in the access to justice; a second with legal interpretations of the participation of victims and their representatives in the "free version" proceedings; and a third, with imbalances between the uncovering of truths related to paramilitary collusion and the lack of truth about the fate of those subjected to forced disappearance and the reasons for having committed atrocious crimes. Though it is too soon to adequately assess the Justice and Peace criminal proceedings, it is clear that the issues raised thus far will require careful monitoring in the near future.

Given the role that law – and particularly criminal law – has been assigned in the ways transition is constructed in Colombia, close attention should be paid as to how Justice and Peace criminal proceedings are transforming and/or reinforcing entrenched power structures. A key question is whether and if how criminal proceedings will impact paramilitary control over governance and democratic participation at the local level. Another crucial question is the extent to which criminal proceedings will contribute to breaking up hegemonic narratives about the paramilitary enterprise, its ends and means.

Acknowledgments This piece is based on my article "Challenging Impunity From Below: The Contested Ownership of Transitional Justice in Colombia" in McEvoy and McGregor (2008). I would like to thank Marieke Wierda, Javier Ciurlizza, Pedro Díaz and Michael Reed for their insightful comments to earlier versions of the study.

References

Ambos K (2008) El proceso de paz en Colombia, a la luz del derecho penal internacional. In: Ambos K, El marco jurídico de la justicia de transición. Editorial Temis, Bogotá

Amnesty International (2004) Scarred bodies, hidden crimes: sexual violence against women in the armed conflict, 2004. http://web.amnesty.org/library/pdf/AMR230402004ENGLISH/$File/AMR2304004.pdf. Accessed 12 July 2008

Bergsmo M, Kalmanovitz P (eds) (2007) Law in peace negotiations. International Peace Research Institute in Oslo (PRIO), FICJC Publication Series 2

CNRR (2007a) Disidentes, rearmados y emergentes: Bandas criminales o tercera generación paramilitar? Bogotá, August 2007. Comisión Nacional de Reparación y Reconciliación. http://www.cnrr.org.co/new/interior_otros/informeDDR.pdf. Accessed 12 July 2008

CNRR (2007b) Informe al Congreso-Proceso de Reparación a las víctimas: balance actual y perspectivas futuras. Comisión Nacional de Reparación y Reconciliación, Bogotá, August 2007. http://www.cnrr.org.co/new/interior_otros/informe_congreso2007.pdf. Accessed 12 July 2008

Corporación Nación (2006) Agendas Civilistas de Verdad, Justicia y Reparación en Barrancabermeja. Corporación Nación, Barrancabermeja

Cubides F (2005) Narcotráfico y paramilitarismo: matrimonio indissoluble? In: Rangel A (ed) El Poder Paramilitar. Fundación Seguridad y Democracia y Editorial Planeta, Bogotá

Cuesta E (2006) Construcción Colectiva de una Propuesta Marco para el Ejercicio de los Derechos a la Verdad, Justicia y Reparación desde las Comunidades Afrocolombianas. In: Instituto Popular de Capacitación, Píldoras para la Memoria. Instituto Popular de Capacitación de la Corporación de Promoción Popular, Medellín

de Sousa Santos B, Rodríguez-Garavito CA (2005) Law, politics and the subaltern in counter-hegemonic globalisation. In: de Sousa Santos B, Rodríguez-Garavito CA (eds) Law and globalisation from below: towards a cosmopolitan legality. Cambridge University Press, Cambridge

Dudley S (2008) Walking ghosts. Murder and guerrilla politics in Colombia. Routledge, New York

Fundación País Libre (2006) Estadísticas secuestro a 2006. Bogotá. http://www.paislibre.org/images/PDF/secuestroestadisticasgenerales%202006%20org.pdf. Accessed 12 July 2008.

Hincapié SM (2006) Propuestas de políticas públicas para la verdad, la justicia y la reparación. In: Instituto Popular de Capacitación de la Corporación de Promoción Popular, Píldoras para la Memoria 2006:93–111

Human Rights Council (2007) Informe de la Alta Comisionada de las Naciones Unidas para los Derechos Humanos sobre la situación de los derechos humanos en Colombia. A/HRC/4/48, 5 March 2007

Human Rights Watch (1996) Colombia's killer networks: the military–paramilitary partnership and the United States. 1 November 1996

Human Rights Watch (2000) The ties that bind: Colombia and military–paramilitary links. 1 February 2000

Human Rights Watch (2001) The 'sixth division': military–paramilitary ties and U.S. policy in Colombia. September 2001

Human Rights Watch (2003a) Colombia's checkbook impunity: a human rights watch briefing paper. 22 September 2003. http://hrw.org/backgrounder/americas/checkbook-impunity.htm. Accessed 12 July 2008

Human Rights Watch (2003b) You'll learn not to cry: child combatants in Colombia. September 2003. http://www.hrw.org/reports/2003/colombia0903/. Accessed 12 July 2008

International Crisis Group (2006) Uribe's re-election: can the EU help Colombia develop a more balanced peace strategy? Crisis Group Latin America Report, No. 17, 8 June 2006. http://www.crisisgroup.org/home/index.cfm?id=4166&l=1. Accessed 12 July 2008

International Crisis Group (2007) Colombia's new armed groups. Latin America Report No. 20, May 10 2007

Luis Eduardo Celis (2007) En las conversaciones en Curso en La Habana entre gobierno y ELN, hay que ser moderadamente optimistas. Revista Semana, Bogotá, 18April 2007. http://www.semana.com/wf_InfoArticulo.aspx?idArt=102245. Accessed 12 July 2008

McEvoy K (1999) The agreement, prisoner release and the political character of the conflict. Fordham Int Law J 26(1):145–181

McEvoy K, McGregor L (eds) (2008) Transitional justice from below. Grassroots activism and the struggle for change. Hart, Oxford

Mesa de Mujer y Conflicto Armado (2005) Quinto Informe sobre violencia socio política contra mujeres, jóvenes y niños en Colombia. November 2005. http://www.mujeryconflictoarmado.org/pdfs/mca_5to_informe_2005.pdf. Accessed 12 July 2008

Meza JC (2006) Situación de los Derechos Humanos y propuestas para la incidencia en políticas públicas en verdad, justicia y reparación frente a la paz en Barrancabermeja. In: Instituto Popular de Capacitación de la Corporación de Promoción Popular. Píldoras para la Memoria 2006:139–157

MOVICE (2006) Carta a Guillermo Hoyos y a los demás organizadores del seminario 'Verdad y reparación desde la perspectiva de las víctimas'. 8 May 2006. Movimiento Nacional de Víctimas de Crímenes de Estado. http://www.movimientodevictimas.org/node/76. Accessed 12 July 2008

OAS (2006a) Sixth quarterly report of the secretary general to the permanent council on the mission to support the peace process in Colombia (MAPP-OEA). OEA/Ser.G CP/doc.4148/06, 16 February 2006. Organization of American States, Permanent Council

OAS (2006b) Seventh quarterly report of the secretary general to the permanent council on the mission to support the peace process in Colombia (MAPP-OEA). OEA/Ser.G CP/doc.4148/06, 30 August 2006. Organization of American States, Permanent Council

OAS (2008) Decimoprimer informe trimestral del Secretario al Concejo Permanente sobre la Misión de Apoyo Al Proceso de Paz en Colombia (MAPP-OEA). 25 June 2008. http://www.mapp-oea.org/documentos/informes/Decimoprimer_Informe-_Espanol.pdf. Accessed 12 July 2008

OHCHR (2002) Report of the United Nations High Commissioner for Human Rights on the human rights situation in Colombia. E/CN4/2002/17. Office of the High Commissioner for Human Rights

OHCHR (2004) Report of the United Nations High Commissioner for Human Rights on the human rights situation in Colombia. E/CN.4/2004/13. 10 March 2004. Office of the High Commissioner for Human Rights. http://www.hchr.org.co/documentoseinformes/informes/altocomisionado/Informe2003_eng.doc. Accessed 12 July 2008

OHCHR (2006) Report of the United Nations High Commissioner for Human Rights on the situation of human rights in Colombia. E/CN.4/2006/9. 16 May 2006. Office of the High Commissioner for Human Rights

Rangel A (2005) Prólogo: A dónde van los paramilitares? In: Rangel A (ed) El Poder Paramilitar. Fundación Seguridad y Democracia y Editorial Planeta, Bogotá

Reed M (2008) Elementos Analíticos sobre la Reestructuración paramilitar en Colombia (forthcoming)

Romero M (2003) Paramilitares y Autodefensas – 1982–2003. Instituto de Estudios Políticos y Relaciones Internacionales, Universidad Nacional de Colombia and Editorial Planeta, Bogotá

Salazar H (2006) Colombia: proceso de paz en duda. BBC Mundo.com, 19 May 2006. http://news.bbc.co.uk/hi/spanish/latin_america/newsid_4999000/4999218.stm. Accessed 12 July 2008

Tattay P (1999) Farc y población indígena: una muestra de relación con la población civil. In: Corporación Observatorio para la Paz, "Las verdaderas intenciones de las Farc". Bogotá

Teitel R (2005) Law and politics of contemporary transitional justice. Cornell Int Law J 38(837):838–862

Theidon K, Betancourt PA (2006) Transiciones Conflictivas: Combatientes Desmovilizados en Colombia. Revista Análisis Político 58

UNDP (2003) Solutions to escape the conflict's impasse: national human development report for Colombia 2003. http://indh.pnud.org.co/pagina.plx?pg=ENdescargaInforme2003&mlat=11)#=EN. Accessed 12 July 2008

Uprimny R, Lasso LM (2004) Verdad, Reparación y Justicia para Colombia: algunas reflexiones y recomendaciones. In: Conflicto y Seguridad Democrática en Colombia. La Fundación Social, La Friedrich Ebert Stiftung en Colombia -Fescol y La Embajada de Alemania en Colombia, Bogotá

Uprimny R, Saffon MP (2008) Usos y abusos de la justicia transicional en Colombia. Anuario de Derechos Humanos 2008, pp 165–195. http://www.cdh.uchile.cl/anuario04/6-Perspectivas_regionales/Rodrigo_Uprimny_Maria%20Paula_Safon.pdf. Accessed 12 July 2008

The Timing and the Scope of Reparation, Truth and Justice Measures: A Comparison of the Spanish, Argentinian and Chilean Cases

Paloma Aguilar

Abstract This paper will present and discuss the scope and the timing of policies directed towards the victims of political violence (both of the civil war and of the dictatorship) in Spain from a comparative perspective. First of all, the paper introduces the main rules on material reparations approved in Spain since Franco's death. Then, it compares the measures of reparation, truth and justice adopted in Spain, Chile and Argentina. This analysis will not be a strictly legal one. Rather, it will focus on the interplay among factors such as social impetus, the time elapsed, the existence of a proactive judiciary, and the type of violence committed by the dictatorship, on the one hand, and the proportions of various kinds of reparation, truth and justice policies, on the other. While differences in the former variables strongly influence the scope and timing of the policies adopted, it is also argued that, if the past is ignored, it will continue to irrupt in a country's life.

1 Introduction

This paper will not discuss in detail the serious and prolonged acts of injustice inflicted by the Francoist regime, both upon those who participated in or sympathised with the faction that was defeated in the Spanish Civil War (1936–1939), and upon all those who did not subject themselves to the regime's dictates (1939–1975).

Throughout the struggle, there were tens of thousands of deaths on both sides due to both legal and extralegal executions. However, the political violence also continued during the immediate post-war years. It is estimated that 50,000 people were executed by military tribunals and summary indictments, without even the most minimal legal safeguards, through the application of unjust and discriminatory legislation, thus causing more victims than the Nazi regime in Germany or the fascist regime in Italy during peacetime (Cazorla 2002). The number of people placed into

P. Aguilar
Universidad Nacional de Educación a Distancia, Madrid, Spain,
e-mail: paguilar@ceacs.march.es; paguilar@poli.uned.es

K. Ambos et al. (eds.), *Building a Future on Peace and Justice: Studies on Transitional Justice, Peace and Development.*

Francoist concentration camps amounted to 300,000 (Rodrigo 2005), similar to the number of those forced to seek asylum after the Spanish Civil War (Alted 2005).

During the almost 40 years that Franco remained in power, he opposed the return of tens of thousands of people to the jobs from which they had been removed as a consequence of the struggle. Franco also refused to grant pensions or any kind of compensation to those mutilated in the war, be they civilians or military personnel, or to the widows and orphans of combatants from the defeated faction. The property of members of other parties or trade unions and of civilians was confiscated simply because they had defended or sympathised with the legal order that was in place prior to the civil war. This was the Second Republic, which the dictatorship had ousted with their weapons. In the meantime, those who had fought or sympathised with the winners enjoyed considerable spoil, such as jobs (particularly in the public sector, benefiting from the already mentioned purges); pensions; compensation payments; sanitary and health care; the right to exhume relatives from mass graves and to give them a proper burial; constant and highly visible signs of symbolic and moral acknowledgement, among others.

Certainly, unjust trials and extralegal executions were also carried out among the ranks of the defeated party throughout the struggle. Yet, regardless of the number of deaths caused by each of the two parties and the specific nature of their respective acts of repression,[1] the fact is that with regard to the acts of violence inflicted during post-war dictatorship, only the heirs of the Francoist party can be held responsible.

In the transitional period from dictatorship to democracy (1975–1982), traumatic memories of the civil war and the obsessive desire to avoid its repetition caused not only the main political actors, but also Spanish society at large to look toward the future, leaving aside the thorniest aspects of the past. There was a firm conviction that this was the only peaceful path toward democracy. Certainly, the correlation of political forces that prevailed in these years, clearly in favour of the reformists of the dictatorship, would have made it extremely difficult to indict those responsible for the main violations of human rights. But even so, it is quite striking that there was not a single political actor of importance or a single social organisation with a minimum of support that called for any kind of sanction against the perpetrators.[2]

[1] According to more detailed studies, the Francoist party was responsible for more deaths than the Republican side. Also, the acts of violence carried out by the former were more systematic and tended to be supported by the authorities (Juliá et al. 1999). There is evidence that the Republican authorities tried much earlier and more directly to stop uncontrolled acts of violence during the first months of the war and even approved measures that considered personal revenge and acts of retaliation a crime. Finally, according to a publication on the administration of justice during the war, the Republican party seemed to be more concerned than the Francoists with maintaining procedures and guarantees (Cancio 2006).

[2] Although Skaar (1999) does not include the case of Spain in her article, she attaches great importance to the strength of public demands when explaining the existence of truth and justice policies in democratization processes. As a second factor, she considers the strength of the outgoing regime to oppose such demands. According to her projections, a combination of a weak public demand and a strong outgoing regime results in no truth nor justice policies (as in Spain); the opposite combination results in both truth commission and trials (as in Argentina); and, finally, an equilibrium situation between public demand and outgoing regime usually conducts to truth commission but no trials (as it happened in Chile in the beginning of its transition).

The maximum that was proposed then, both in the political as well as in the social sphere, was to free political prisoners and to compensate with material measures those who had lost the war and their relatives. It is also true that many international bodies that are today actively committed to combating impunity did not exist in 1975 or hardly had the capacity at that time to exert pressure in a transition to democracy.[3]

The Spanish transition was characterised, among other things, by the fact that the most important rules of the new democratic game were adopted by consensus between those who reformed Francoism and the main political forces of the democratic opposition. Tacitly, they agreed on "gag rules",[4] which amounted to excluding the dictatorial and bellicose past from the public debate and shielding the past against trials, by means of a norm called "*Ley de Amnistía de 1977*" (Law of Amnesty 1977). These moves, together with the provision of material reparations for the defeated faction, would later become known as "the national reconciliation policy". This policy could not have been made earlier, given that Francoism had long marginalized and repressed the losers of the civil war and their ideological heirs. One of the main points of agreement that laid the foundations for Spanish democracy was the principle of "never again". In contrast to such principles in other countries, this does not refer to the dictatorship or its crimes, but instead to the civil war for whose atrocities the guilt was, more or less, generally shared between the two adversaries.

2 Policies of Material Reparation in Spain[5]

Following Franco's death (20 November 1975), in the face of the acts of repression committed under the dictatorship and the lack of reparations for such acts, there was an urgent need to address a number of issues, with a view to ensuring equal rights for the winners and losers. This translated into a stormy legislative process. On many occasions, norms had to be revised or broadened shortly after their approval to ensure that certain groups who, in accordance with the spirit of the law, needed to be covered by specific measures, had been left out. The casuistry was very extensive and extremely complex.

As a start, just 5 days after Franco's death, some limited measures of pardon were approved, such as a pardon on 25 November 1975 on the occasion of the coronation of King Juan Carlos I, which called for "*concordia*" (harmony) while also paying "tribute to the memory of the eminent figure of Generalissimo Franco, architect of the progressive development leading to the peace that Spain had been

[3] For the progressive introduction of principles of international criminal law in Spanish penal legislation, see Gil (2003) in Ambos and Malarino (eds), and Gil (2006).

[4] A "gag rule", according to Holmes (1988, p. 19), is a form of "strategic self-censorship" that is used to "avoid destructive conflict" when facing highly controversial and divisive issues.

[5] For an account of this legislation from the viewpoint of international law, see Chinchón (2007a). This author has also written a book on transitional justice measures in Spain and Latin America (Chinchón 2007b).

enjoying during the past decades". As a result of this pardon, almost 9,000 prisoners would be released. The pardon only allowed for the release of 773 political prisoners (approximately half of the existent), causing the mobilisation of multiple and very diverse sectors of society in an attempt to obtain the release of the rest. The demand of the amnesty was one of the most important events in the country's transition, with a great potential to mobilise the populace.

In July 1976, the first government of the monarchy approved a Royal Amnesty Decree which covered crimes related to politically motivated acts "as long as these (acts) had not endangered or harmed the lives or integrity of persons". This clause was interpreted in such a restrictive sense by the judges – the vast majority of whom were very conservative, if not directly pro-francoist – that in 1977 it was necessary to add both a general amnesty law and specific acts of pardon to overcome the legal obstacles.

The amnesty of 15 October 1977 was the first law approved by the freshly inaugurated democratic parliament that came out of the elections of 15 June of the same year (Aguilar 1997, 2002). It was a groundbreaking law, applying to crimes of political nature and to persons sentenced for conscientious objection of military service. It restored active rights – reintegration into the workforce, except for military posts – and passive rights for those who had been sentenced for political reasons, and cleared their criminal records. As its most progressive element, the law also covered crimes involving bloodshed, committed prior to 15 December 1976 (date when the Law for Political Reform was passed), and between this day and 15 June 1977, as long as the crime could be linked to an intention to "re-establish public liberties" or to demand devolution. This latter clause proved useful because it allowed for prisoners from the terrorist organisation ETA to be freed,[6] which was one of the law's main objectives.[7]

But in its second article, the law also contained two paragraphs that practically passed unnoticed, both in the parliamentary debate and in most of the media commentaries prompted by its approval. These provisions granted a blanket amnesty for "crimes and misconducts that may have been committed by the authorities, officials and public security forces on the occasion and as a result of the investigation and prosecution of acts covered by this law", as well as "crimes committed by officials and guardians of public order against the people exercising their rights". These aspects effectively converted the Amnesty Law into a "Full Stop Law": in exchange for the liberation of political prisoners who had committed violent crimes (it should be remembered that ETA, GRAPO and other minor terrorist organisations of the extreme left had committed 95 murders between the 1960s and the time the amnesty

---

[6] In the early days of November 1977, 118 prisoners were released. The following month, the last Basque prisoner, convicted for crimes of a political nature, was released.

[7] Paradoxically, this amnesty did not help to stop killings by ETA. In fact, its most violent phase began 2 years later. This can be explained in the following terms: On the one hand, the amnesty did not allow for the release of prisoners involved in violent crimes if these had been committed after the first democratic elections (15 June 1977). On the other hand, the most radical part of the terrorist organization considered that they should not stop the killings given that their main aim was to fight the Spanish state, irrespectively of its democratic or authoritarian nature. The amnesty law did not prevent further coup attempts either, an issue that will be dealt with below.

was approved),[8] the Francoist regime was granted impunity, as its perpetrators could no longer be taken to court.

In the parliamentary debate on this law, both the Centre Democratic Union (*Unión de Centro Democrático*, UCD), which lead a minority government, and the left and nationalist formations (Catalan and Basque), invoked the need to overcome the past and to leave aside the hatred derived from the Civil War and the dictatorship, in order to achieve, as a common endeavour, the peaceful establishment and consolidation of democracy. This law, supported by all but the main right-wing party (then the AP – *Alianza Popular*, now the PP – *Partido Popular*), was widely welcomed both by members of parliament and the citizenry. Before its adoption, large and often dramatic rallies had call for its approval. However, at that time, none of the political or social actors had publicly defended the two provisions granting impunity for the dictatorship, and precisely these provisions constitute the main obstacle faced by the democracy in its quest to subject the Francoist past to a legal scrutiny.

Stephen Holmes has defended the convenience of adopting "gag rules" on particularly divisive and polemic issues, especially during such sensitive and uncertain periods as transitions to democracy, and cites the laws of amnesty as especially illustrative of his argument. According to him, "[b]y closing the books on the past, keeping retribution for former crimes off the political agenda, the organizers of a new democracy can secure the compliance of strategically located elites – cooperation may be indispensable for a successful transition from dictatorship to self-government". However, Holmes himself acknowledges the provisional nature of "gag rules". A legislative body – such as the Spanish Congress – may well decide to adopt them, "but it could not gag the public or the press". He also indicates that "gag rules" tend to be "one-sided" and "are seldom neutral; they implicitly support one policy and undermine alternatives" (Holmes 1988, p. 27, 43, 59).

This is precisely what happened in the Spanish case: the ideological heirs of the dictatorship ended up benefiting much more from the "pact of silence" than those who had directly suffered retaliation during the dictatorship. As it had been said above, both parties to the civil war had committed intolerable abuses. But under the dictatorship, some of these abuses were punished and others not, along a clear political divide between losers and winners, or victims and henchmen. As a consequence, the veil of silence that was spread over history benefited mainly those who had held political responsibilities under Franco or had sympathized with his dictatorship.

Subsequent to the Amnesty Law, the adoption of a host of complementary legislation made the point that important issues had been left unattended. First, the Royal Decree Law of 6 March 1978 granted retirement pensions to members of the military and of the Republican Public Order Forces, or to their heirs, if they had been on active duty even before 18 July 1936. Second, in May 1978, the request to amnesty for officials of the *Generalitat de Catalunya* (the Catalan government) was dealt with favourably. Third, in December 1978 a Royal Decree-Law was approved, granting amnesties to purged justice officials. Fourth, a law adopted in September

[8] This figure was taken from the database on political violence during the transition compiled by Ignacio Sánchez-Cuenca and myself.

1979 provided pensions, medical care and social assistance to the widows and relatives of those who had died in the war or as a consequence of war-inflicted wounds or "as a consequence of political or trade-unionist activities", when death "had not resulted from the execution of a sentence or from violence emanating from that person". Fifth, in June 1984, years spent in prison for reasons covered by the Amnesty Law were recognized as credits to Social Security. Sixth, in October 1984 a qualitative leap was made in terms of the rhetoric used, in that "services rendered" for the Army or the (Republican) Forces of Public Order, as well as pensions and other benefits were acknowledged, even when the respective person had joined the forces only after the beginning of the civil war. The preamble of the law reads: "Now that, with the approval of the Constitution of 1978, we are fortunate to have overcome the emotional motives that had prevented us 1 year before, in October 1977, that is, with the Law of Amnesty, from finding a full solution to the problem, it is now essential to adjust the laws to the precepts of our basic law". It is rather revealing that the preamble acknowledges that limitations existed during the transition in terms of doing justice to certain categories of persons.

Seventh, it was not until December 1986 – the date when condemned members of the military regained their active rights – that the most important vacuum left by the Amnesty Law was filled. This vacuum had, for instance, prevented the reincorporation into the army of persons who had belonged to the Democratic Military Union (*Unión Militar Democrática*, UMD).[9] In fact, in the preamble of the 1986 law, it is acknowledged that the amnesty had "unfairly treated those who, in spite of falling within its field of application, held the rank of professional military serviceman or civil servant (...). The principle of non-discrimination, firmly embedded in Article 14 of the Constitution, as well as the principle of equality of all Spaniards before the law, makes it imperative to redress these differences". It is noteworthy that it took legislators 9 years after the approval of the Amnesty Law and 8 years after the adoption of the Constitution, to enact such a measure. This illustrates the degree of influence that the military enjoyed at that time to oppose policies that could affect its internal organisation.

In the meanwhile, some other, easily overlooked groups remained excluded from the amnesty: persons convicted of homosexuality, adultery, cohabitation or the use of contraceptives, which were at the time considered crimes.

The first Spanish rules on reparation were completely silent about the suffering of those who had fought for a legitimate regime or for the reestablishment of democracy. Instead, at almost every occasion there was a mention of the desire to overcome the consequences of the war and the inequalities that it had generated, as well as of the need to offer protection to certain categories of persons and to integrate them as citizens with full rights. Almost invariably, it was said that these inequalities were due to "politically motivated acts". As we have seen, there had been only one case

[9] A clandestine organisation that emerged in 1974 amidst the Francoist armed forces with the aim of helping spread democratic ideas there. Some UMD members who belonged to the military were judged, sent to prison and expelled from the army. The latter specifically refused to reincorporate them, although, under the protection of the amnesty law of 1977, the rest of the population could be reintegrated if they had lost their job for political reasons.

where the law further elaborated on this formula: the preamble of the Amnesty Law of 1977 refers to the motives of "reestablishment of public liberties" and "demand of autonomy". During the first years of the democracy, there was a desire to acknowledge that the losing side had been treated unfairly, and to grant them the same rights as those on the winning side. This was not about acknowledging their motives or recognising the justness of their cause; the word "reconciliation" amounted to "granting the same level of rights", which no one was against, especially if reference was made to the Civil War. And it was equally important not to blame, and not even to mention, neither the dictatorship nor the people who had caused these injustices.

This is precisely what has changed today. In recent years, reparation measures have attempted to pay moral tribute to the victims, by acknowledging the justness of their cause and their contribution to the reestablishment of liberties. Recent reparation measures also refer more explicitly to the circumstances and persons responsible for the discriminations that needed to be redressed through legislative measures ever since the beginning of the transition. Undeniably, there was a clear difference in tone.

The above mentioned law of 8 June 1984, crediting prison years to the eligibility for social security, was the first to mention the "fight for freedom". However, in the 1990 and 1991 laws, which for the first time granted compensation payments for prison terms endured during Franco's regime for at least 3 years, there is no mention of the justness of the cause or the unfairness of people losing their freedom. Surprisingly enough, the first declaration in this respect is one concerning the International Brigadiers. The Royal Decree of 9 January 1996, granting the brigadiers Spanish nationality, states "it is a matter of justice to acknowledge the efforts to promote freedom and democracy, carried out by the volunteers from the International Brigades", and mentions "the gratitude of the Nation" towards them. Later, in the 1998 law which reinstated goods confiscated from the political parties, there is for the first time a criticism, albeit indirect, of some of the actions carried out during the dictatorship: the law talks of "redressing legal situations that had been illegitimately affected by decisions adopted under the umbrella of unjust laws". This law portrays itself as an act of "historical justice" and says that the assets of the political parties had been "snatched". None of these formulations appeared in the law on the devolution of trade union assets, which had been passed 10 years before.

A huge qualitative leap in the wording of the norms on reparation took place in the eighth legislative period (2004–2008), in which the socialist party (*Partido Socialista Obrero Español*, PSOE) has led a minority government.[10] The Royal Decree of 2004, creating the "Interministerial Commission to study the situation of the victims of the Civil War and of Francoism", speaks of the need to examine the situation of the "victims" – referred to for the first time in these terms – who "suffered repressive acts as a consequence of their democratic commitment". The Decree proposes measures of "acknowledgement" and "moral satisfaction". The change in tone is

[10] I would like to remind the reader that my analysis deals only with norms and, therefore, excludes other parliamentary initiatives, such as motions. This question has already been discussed in other studies (Aguilar 2006).

significant; we are now discussing "suffering", "acknowledgement" and "moral satisfaction" and the measures are furthermore referred to as a "sign of the awareness of Spanish society and its wish to compensate, at least in part, for the shortages experienced by a group of citizens who saw their personal and professional prospects curtailed as a consequence of the military takeover against the legally constituted government, that gave rise to the Civil War from 1936 to 1939". This is the first explicit acknowledgement of the "historic debt that Spain owes these citizens", the first reference to the legitimacy of the Republic and, finally, the first time that those who had risen up against the Republic were declared responsible for the civil war.

In 2005, in a law that restituted to the *Generalitat de Catalunya* documents seized during the civil war and created a Documentation Centre on Historical Memory, the expression "historical memory" was used for the first time in legislation – the Law declaring 2006 the Year of Historical Memory was not sanctioned until July 2006 – and the "injustice" and "illegitimacy" of the Francoist legislation was mentioned once again.

The first government headed by José Luis Rodríguez Zapatero also offered financial and health measures for the "Spanish war children".[11] Furthermore, subsidies directed to associations that carry out activities related to reparations for the victims of war and Francoism have been approved for the first time. Never before had the importance of the endeavours of associations working for the "dignity of the victims" been recognised. Now, their activities are considered worthy of "praise and public respect".

In July 2006, the above mentioned Interministerial Commission produced the first draft of the Law "by which rights are recognized and extended, and measures are taken on behalf on those who suffered persecution or violent acts during the civil war and the dictatorship". After a heated debate, this crucial initiative was finally passed in the Parliament at the end of 2007 (hereafter: Law on Reparations)[12].

3 Reparation, Truth and Justice in Spain, Chile and Argentina

After giving an account of the evolution of the relevant Spanish legislation – from securing equal rights for the two sides in the Civil War, an issue which was presented as a simple question of equality before the law, to the recognition of the illegitimacy and injustice of Francoism, the moral rehabilitation of the victims and the praise for their motives to fight – I will now proceed with comparative reflections on the cases of Argentina, Chile and Spain. I will not discuss in great detail the – often considerable – impact that legislation and jurisprudence in the field of criminal law

[11] The "Spanish war children" are children of Republicans, who were evacuated before the Francoist troops advanced. The countries that welcomed them in large numbers were France, Belgium, Mexico, Great Britain and the former USSR. It is estimated that, during the war alone, around 30,000 children were evacuated. It took many years before some of them could get back to Spain and meet their relatives. Many stayed in their country of refuge.

[12] At the time of writing this article, the government had not approved.

have had on the transitions in Argentina and Chile, but will simply refer to the ample literature on these issues.[13]

The processes of change undergone by these three countries were the subject of various types of constraints.[14] The kind of repressive violence exercised by the dictatorships in Argentina and Chile was very different from that of the Spanish dictatorship. The length of the dictatorships was very different, as was the nearness of the worst crimes at the time the transition took place. Finally, judges and human rights associations played very different roles. However, in the middle of the transition process to democracy, decisions had to be made in all three countries about the legacy of human rights violations inherited from the previous regime (see Barahona de Brito et al. 2001). We will consider below the corresponding reparation, truth and justice policies.[15]

3.1 Symbolic Reparation

3.1.1 Monuments and Commemorative Places[16]

From the beginning in Argentina, "initiatives of symbolic character that put an emphasis on acknowledging the past or on paying tribute to the victims were promoted in different parts of the country" (Tappatá de Valdez 2005, p. 104). Nowadays there are many important commemorative sites such as the *Parque de la Memoria* on the Bank of the *Río de la Plata*. Many of the victims were thrown into this river, lending this monument a very special symbolic value. In Buenos Aires, some of the buildings where people were arrested and tortured have been declared "historic sites". Since 1998, the city of Rosario is housing the *Museo de la Memoria*, which is dedicated to the roots of the authoritarian State and its effects on civil populations, as well as to paying tribute to the detained and disappeared. Finally, President Nestor Kirchner created the National Archive for Historical Memory to house documents related to human rights violations, including documents produced by the Truth Commission (*Comisión de la Verdad*) and by the investigations that followed the end of the regime. Furthermore, the former Navy Sub-Officers Mechanics School (ESMA), one of the juntas' main centres of detention, torture and assassination, was converted, on 30 September 2007, into a museum dedicated to the memory of the victims.

---

[13] For a general account on some Latin American countries see Arnold et al. (2006); for a criminal law perspective see Ambos et al. (2008). For the transition in Argentina from a criminal law perspective see Sancinetti and Ferrante (1999); for an analysis of the "impunity" laws see Ambos (1999).

[14] A comparison between the policies of memory in Chile and Spain can be found in Aguilar and Hite (2004).

[15] A detailed description of the policies of material reparation in Argentina and Chile can be found in Guembe (2006) and Lira (2006), respectively.

[16] For a recent synthesis of public memorialization in the Southern Cone, see Jelin (2007).

In 1991, the Chilean government accepted a joint initiative by the Association of Relatives of Disappeared Detainees (*Agrupación de Familiares de Detenidos Desaparecidos*) and the Association of Relatives of Persons Executed for Political Reasons (*Agrupación de Familiares de Ejecutados Políticos*) to build a memorial and a mausoleum consecrated to the memory of, and to give a dignified burial to the victims of the dictatorship; both sites are located in Santiago de Chile's general cemetery. During the first year of Patricio Aylwin's presidency, Allende's body was transferred from its private tomb, and funeral rites took place in the Cathedral.[17] The monument to Salvador Allende (2000) and the museum, *Museo de la Solidaridad Salvador Allende* (rededicated in 1991), also deserve a mention here.

Several symbolic acts also took place under the presidency of Ricardo Lagos. The National Stadium, a former centre of illegal detention, torture and assassination, was declared a national monument in 2003, displaying a permanent exhibition about the events that took place at that location. Another stadium, formerly known as the *Estadio Chile*, now bears the name *Estadio Víctor Jara*.[18] There are also several other monuments whose purpose is to pay tribute to the victims and to prevent the more turbulent aspects of the past from vanishing from popular memory. Among them is *Villa Grimaldi*, an old clandestine detention and torture centre. Michelle Bachelet was the first president to visit these premises. She was also the first to visit the head office of the Association of Relatives of Disappeared Detainees.

In Spain, during the first democratic government (1977–1979), the Senate approved a motion proposing the transfer of the mortal remains of the three heads of state who died in exile: Alfonso XIII, King of Spain until the establishment of the Second Republic in 1931, and two former presidents of the Republic, Niceto Alcalá-Zamora and Manuel Azaña. However, Alfonso XIII was not transferred to the Escorial until 1980. Alcalá-Zamora, whose grandchild had unsuccessfully applied to have his remains transferred from Argentina with the honours befitting a head of state, was eventually transferred by private arrangement in 1977. The remains of Azaña, the last president of the Republic, still lie in the small French cemetery of Montauban. Marshal Pétain forbade him from being honoured as head of state at this burial and prevented his body from being wrapped in the Republican flag. While it appears that Azaña had expressly stipulated that he did not wish to be removed from his burial place, I have found no evidence that either the current head of state nor any Spanish prime minister has ever visited the cemetery to pay official tribute to the man who was the president of a legally constituted regime, and who was illegally and forcibly deposed. For Azaña, in contrast to Allende, there is no statue to honour him in the capital city, nor any museum named after him.[19]

---

[17] "[Allende's] coffin was carried by the funeral entourage and buried once again, this time at the General Cemetery, where other democratic presidents of the country are also laid to rest" (Wilde 1999, p. 483).

[18] Víctor Jara (1932–1973) was a famous Chilean songwriter and theatre director who was imprisoned in that stadium and assassinated on 16 September 1973 in the course of the repression that followed Pinochet's coup d'état.

[19] In his birthplace (Alcalá de Henares) one statue has been erected and a roundabout bears his name.

In Spain, with the exception of the *Valle de los Caídos* (the Valley of the Fallen), which of course does not pay tribute to the dead of both sides, there is no other monument to the victims of war that has similar status and public symbolism as do those of the Chilean and Argentinian people. The only monument aspiring to appeal to the whole nation is located in the *Plaza de la Lealtad* in Madrid. It is very inconspicuous and lacks the strong symbolism of the *Estadio Nacional* or the ESMA. After all, it is a monument from the 19th century, recycled in 1985 on the occasion of the tenth anniversary of the crowning of the King, which pays tribute to all those fallen "for Spain" in Spanish history. The only change that was made for its reinauguration was the addition of a votive flame. On the other hand, the fact that the *Valle de los Caídos* has been left almost intact after the dictatorship is in itself very significant since it is a legacy of that era. Also, in contrast to the other two countries, nowhere in Spain is there a national monument that commemorates the victims of the Francoist dictatorship.

Considering the omnipresence of Francoist iconography that existed in Spain on Franco's death, efforts to eliminate monuments and symbols of the previous government have been particularly slow. The statue of the dictator in Madrid was not pulled down until March 2005, and this was done against the PP's will. A similar statue was retained in the military academy in Zaragoza until August 2006, and the equestrian statues in Santander and Melilla are still standing today. In several provincial capitals and in numerous towns, an array of streets, plaques and monuments bear Franco's name, still paying tribute to the dictator and his regime. Many churches and cathedrals continue to display a list of those "fallen for God and Spain", thus paying an excessive tribute to the winning side.

The Law on Reparations addresses these issues by proposing that all symbols praising the civil war and the dictatorship must be removed from all public buildings, unless there are insurmountable artistic or architectonic obstacles to do so. Regarding private institutions partially subsidized by the State (specifically the Catholic church), the government will be able, by virtue of the law, to withdraw these subsidies if the law is not abided.

Regarding the *Valle de los Caídos*, the above-mentioned symbols should be eliminated. Bus this will be extremely difficult to accomplish, as these symbols are everywhere and some of them affect crucial parts of the building;[20] also, the tombs of Franco and José Antonio Primo de Rivera[21] will remain in the most important part of the Basilica, in spite of the opposition by leftist parties and victims associations). On the other hand, some sort of symbolic re-dedication of the monument is to be expected, as the Law says that the authority responsible for the administration of the monument is supposed to devote it to the memory of all those fallen in the war as well as to the victims of the dictatorship. But even so, it is far from clear whether the victims of Francoism will recognize themselves in this symbolically loaded and hitherto unpopular monument; additionally, the fact that it is, overall, a religious monument, will limit its representativeness for many of the victims. It

[20] The new law also contemplates one crucial exception: if the symbols are of artistic-religious character, these will not be removed.

[21] Founder of the Spanish fascist party (*Falange Española*) and himself a victim of the civil war.

is hard to believe that the Spanish democracy, after more than 30 years, has been unable to build a new and unambiguous monument to these victims.

It took 30 years after Franco's death for a head of the Spanish government, Rodríguez Zapatero, to visit the Mauthausen concentration camp to pay tribute to the Spaniards who had been imprisoned there. This took place in 2005 on the occasion of the 60th anniversary of their liberation. One might ask why in 1995, at the 50th anniversary, the government – also socialist – did not see it fit to make such a gesture, given that 8,000 Spaniards – of whom 6,000 lost their lives – had been imprisoned at Mauthausen. It should be noted, however, that this same head of government (Rodríguez Zapatero) met with the "Spanish war children" in Moscow twice, and that their situation improved under his government.

In Santiago de Chile, a public avenue is still called *Avenida 11 de Septiembre,* named after the date of the coup by Pinochet. Proposals were made in the early 1990s to change the name. The meaning of this date has evolved over time, from one of victory to one of tragedy. Only in August 1998 did the Chilean government manage to win a vote in Congress to discontinue the status of 11 September as a national holiday.[22] In this sense, the Chilean people have taken much longer than the Spanish to rid themselves of a national holiday related to their dictatorship, since both 18 July (the date of the coup against the Second Republic in Spain) and 20 November (the anniversary of both Antonio Primo de Rivera's and Francisco Franco's deaths) lost their status as official holidays a few years after Franco's death (Aguilar and Humlebaek 2002). Since 2007, the Day of the Disappeared Detainee (August 30th) is publicly commemorated in Chile. No official day in Spain commemorates the victims of the civil war or the victims of Francoism.

In Argentina, it seems that few symbols from the dictatorship remain, except for a few street names in small cities or plaques in memory of those "fallen in the fight against subversion" in a small number of barracks. In 2002, a National Remembrance Day for Truth and Justice (*Día Nacional de la Memoria por la Verdad y la Justicia*) has been declared to commemorate the victims of that period (March 24, the day of the 1976 military coup d'état).[23]

3.1.2 Clarification of the Truth

As regards official efforts aimed at clarifying violations of rights, in contrast to the developments in Spain, truth commissions were created in the early days of political change both in Chile and Argentina. They gathered the testimonies of the victims and publicly acknowledged the crimes of the dictatorships.

In Argentina, the National Commission on the Disappearance of Persons (*Comisión Nacional para la Desaparición de Personas*, CONADEP) was created at the behest of President Raul Alfonsín. In 1984 a report titled "Nunca Más" (*Never Again*) appeared. It documents the lives of 8,963 people who "disappeared" (by

[22] See the recent publication by Joignant (2007) about the celebrations and battles around this date in Chile.

[23] Since 2005, as a result of Kirchner's initiative, this is a non-working day.

1999, however, more than 3,000 new cases had been documented and some human rights organisations speak of a total of around 30,000 cases). It acknowledged the existence of more than 340 secret detention centres and listed the names of 1,351 people, including medical doctors, judges, journalists, bishops and priests, who cooperated with the repression.[24] Official investigations of the circumstances behind the disappearances have continued after this report was released by the Human Rights Sub-Secretariat, a department of the Ministry of the Interior (Barahona de Brito 2001, p. 121).

In Chile, the creation of the National Commission for Truth and Reconciliation was also decreed by the President, Patricio Aylwin, and the "Rettig Report", named after the lawyer who presided over it, was published in 1991. In contrast to Argentina, the Chilean press did not publish the names of the perpetrators. The most concerted action Chile has recently taken on this issue was to create the National Commission on Prison and Torture Policy (*Comisión Nacional sobre la Prisión y Tortura*), which has gathered the testimonies of 28,000 people who were tortured. In an emotional speech, President Lagos informed the country of the findings of this report, published in November 2004. It revealed that torture was not carried out by just a few individuals in isolated cases, but that it was an institutionalised and systematic state policy (94% of the detainees confirmed that they had been tortured). Due to the commission's findings, lifelong pension payments have been adopted for the victims, as well as favourable conditions for access to health care, education and housing.

3.1.3 Condemnation of the Past

In September 1999 a Commission of the Spanish parliament approved a motion to "commemorate the 60th anniversary of the exile" with the votes of the majority of the opposition – from the left to the nationalist parties (Catalan and Basque) – and with the abstention of the PP which was then leading a minority government. The opposition took advantage of the motion to introduce some language to "condemn the military uprising against the legitimate, constitutional regime". A similar move was attempted again in December 2000, when the opposition presented another motion to "condemn the military uprising of 18 July 1936". However, at that time, the PP was enjoying a comfortable parliamentary majority and the motion was rejected in February of the following year.

Among the references that the Spanish Congress has made to the past, one has attracted more attention than all others. On 20 November 2002, the Constitutional Commission debated seven motions concerning the acknowledgement of the victims of the Civil War and Francoism. Some of these motions also asked for a condemnation of the dictatorship. Eventually, the single motion that was unanimously adopted agreed to "extend moral acknowledgment to every man and woman who was a victim of the Spanish Civil War, as well as to those who suffered later under the Fran-

[24] The Argentinian Commission did not officially publish the names of the oppressors, but a list of their names was leaked to the press and published to coincide with the publication of the report.

coist dictatorship". The text also included an expression of generic disapproval of totalitarian regimes, but did not explicitly mention Francoism. The Law on Reparations refers to this motion, as well as to a 2006 report by the European Council condemning Francoism and denouncing its serious violations of human rights. It is very revealing that, more than 30 years after Franco's death, the Spanish parliament needs to turn to an international organisation in search of a quote condemning the dictatorship. After the approval of the Law on Reparations, with the opposition of the PP, this party has not explicitly condemned yet nor the military coup of 1936 or the dictatorship that followed.

In Argentina, several laws contain an explicit rejection of the dictatorship. Also, Kirchner apologized in May 2007, in the name of the State, to the victims of dictatorship. He did so in a public act of commemoration of the victims of the massacre that took place in the town Margarita Belén. In Chile, on 4 March 1991, President Aylwin presented in public the results of the report by the National Commission for Truth and Reconciliation. He asked in the name of the nation for "forgiveness from the relatives of the victims", solemnly requesting "the armed forces, security forces, and everyone who participated actively in the excesses committed, that they make gestures to acknowledge the pain that they have caused, and that they help to alleviate it". In addition, Aylwin promoted the approval of measures of moral and material reparation for the victims. In Spain, neither a head of state nor a prime minister has ever asked the victims of the war or the Francoist regime for forgiveness on behalf of the Spanish state.

3.1.4 Admittance of the Truth

Moral reparation can also take the form of revelation of the truth and contrition. In 1995, Argentina witnessed some well-known cases of repentance by torturers and assassins. The head of the army, Lieutenant General Martín Balza, and the head of the Navy, Admiral Enrique Molina, both expressed criticism of the violations of human rights that took place during the dictatorship. The former asked for forgiveness from the relatives of the oppressed for the deeds carried out by the military. In a document published on 25 April 1995, the Army High Command admitted that the armed forces had participated in torture and assassination. "The document had an important domino effect on the Army, the Navy and the Catholic Church, in spite of the degree of clarity with which they had already admitted in their own public documents the role their members had played in both carrying out acts of terror and collaborating with the state on such acts during the dictatorship" (Acuña 2006, p. 207). That same year, Naval Captain Adolfo Scilingo admitted that between 1,500 and 2,000 prisoners had been thrown into the sea in the so-called "death flights".

Around the year 2000, Chilean military officials started admitting to some of the crimes committed under the dictatorship, not the least under the impression of some jurisprudence – also in the cases brought against Pinochet – that qualified disappearances as ongoing cases of kidnapping and therefore not subject to the terms of the Chilean amnesty law. In the first of a series of reports, military officials admitted to throwing the bodies of prisoners into the sea, even going so far as to name some of the victims in a desperate attempt to redeem themselves. Although it soon came to light that the report contained many untruths, it was the first time that officials from the Chilean military had publicly admitted to having committed such acts. A more accurate record of human rights violations committed by the military was only established in November 2004, in the form of a 1,300 page report produced by the National Commission on Political Prisonership and Torture (*Comisión Nacional sobre Prisión Política y Tortura*), which President Lagos had established in 2003. In the wake of the publication of this report, the Supreme Commander of the Chilean Army, General Juan Emilio Cheyre, recognized the "unjustifiable" institutional responsibility of the armed forces for the human rights violations. One of the lessons that can be learned from the Argentinian and Chilean cases is that, without a certain degree of social and political pressure on the perpetrators (produced, among other means, by the publication of the reports by the truth commissions), they would never have admitted to having taken part in the crimes in question.

In Spain, a long time has now passed since the war and its immediate aftermath, which is when the worst atrocities were committed. There have been, however, no cases of public repentance for the crimes perpetrated during the struggle or for the brutal retaliation by Francoists in the post-war period, in which judges and military officials actively participated. Moreover, in contrast to the Argentinian Church, the Spanish Church has not apologised for its connivance with the winning side, nor for the complicit silence that it had kept, with a few exceptions, under the dictatorship. The Argentinian Church publicly asked for forgiveness for the "culpable silence and effective participation (...) in the abuse of liberties, in torture and denunciation", while the Chilean Church never lend its support to the dictatorship in the first place, but instead tried to protect and help the victims and their relatives. In painful contrast, the Spanish Church, which had characterized the Civil War as a "crusade", so far has missed every opportunity to ask for forgiveness. Only once, at the Joint Assembly of Bishops and Priests in 1971, did it come close to doing so, but the proposal did not obtain the necessary majority. It is hard to believe that more than 30 years after Franco's death, the Spanish Church has failed to relaunch an initiative that it had nearly approved towards the end of the dictatorship.

3.1.5 Locating and Exhuming Victims

Another issue related to the moral reparation of the victims and the restitution of the truth, already mentioned before, concerns mass graves and people who "disappeared" as a result of dictatorships. In sharp contrast to what happened to the civil war victims of the Francoist side, in democratic Spain the initiative to locate, exhume and identify remains has been predominantly private. The first subsidies to the associations responsible for this task were not granted, as already stated, until September 2006, although most of the graves date back to 1936.[25] The number of organisations dedicated to paying tribute to the victims increased between 2003 and 2005 from 30 to almost 170, enabling us to speak of a real" explosion of associations" (Gálvez 2006, p. 34). This does not mean organisations of this kind did not exist before,[26] but they did not have the social prestige and impact that some organisations enjoy today, in particular the Association for the Recovery of Historical Memory (*Asociación para la Recuperación de la Memoria Histórica*, ARMH).[27] Generational change, along with developments in international criminal law and the change in the correlation of political forces, have all helped to give fresh impetus to these demands. Impunity and injustice towards the victims certainly seem to be tolerated much less readily than they were in the past. But public support to such private endeavours is still far from sufficient. For example, there has been, to date, no official request for the assistance of those who might help, through information that they possess, to locate the whereabouts of several thousand executed republicans whose remains are still resting in unmarked mass graves, so that their relatives can at long last proceed with the exhumation, identification and burial of their dead. After the Law on Reparations, and against the association's will, the initiative to exhume the common graves of the civil war will continue to be private[28]. However, the Spanish state has now compromised to elaborate a national map of the graves, accessible to all citizens, and to approve a common forensic protocol that will have to be followed by all associations.

In Chile, the state is responsible for locating and exhuming bodies, a task that is carried out by forensic experts and the legal medical service, under the direction of a judge. In Argentina, a human rights body, the Argentinian Team of Forensic Medicine, is responsible for the exhumation and identification of remains. This body, although independent, works in conjunction with the judiciary, helping to provide evidence for relevant cases.

In order to complement the work of CONADEP, the Argentinian government created the Human Rights Sub-Secretariat, which has since become a full secretariat and currently reports to the Ministry of Justice and Human Rights. Among its functions, it must "hold custody of, and systematise the archive consisting of the files that resulted from the denouncements that CONADEP has received", and

[25] Although the exact figure has not been established, it is known that several thousand people from the Republican side were buried in mass graves as a result of extralegal executions that were carried out by the Francoist side, mainly during the first months of the civil war.

[26] For example, as early as January 1976 there were reports of the first attempts to create associations of former political prisoners (*ABC*, 9 January 1976, p. 8).

[27] In 2002, ARMH seized the UN Working Group on Forced Disappearances with several cases of disappearances. In the cases of two republicans presumably shot after 1945 (and therefore falling under the purview of the UN), the Working Group requested the Spanish Government to investigate those disappearances.

[28] This is very likely to change, since in October 2008 Judge Baltasar Garzón has ordered the unearthing of several mass graves of that period.

supervise "compliance with international norms on human rights to which Argentina is a signatory". Within this secretariat, the government created in 1992 the National Commission for the Right to Identity (*Comisión Nacional por el Derecho a la Identidad*), with the aim of identifying more than 600 children who had been kidnapped (Tappatá de Valdez 2005, p. 100). The commission has a database of genetic data, and its work has been "fundamental to tracing disappeared children" (Barahona de Brito 2001, p. 138). No comparable body exists in Spain, although an unknown number of children were kidnapped when their mothers, of the vanquished side, were put in prison (Vinyes et al. 2002).

3.2 Material Reparations to the Victims

In Argentina four pieces of fundamental legislation were approved between 1991 and 1995 to "provide economic assistance to all political detainees during the dictatorship, as well as to the parents and children of the disappeared" (Barahona de Brito 2001, p. 138). In addition, "workers dismissed on political grounds" were indemnified (Tappatá de Valdez 2005, p. 101).

We have already mentioned that a measure providing for economic reparations to the victims of torture was recently approved in Chile, but in fact a law of reparation has been in place for the relatives of the disappeared since 1992. That same year, the National Corporation for Reparation and Reconciliation was created, which "establishes legally the 'inalienable right' of relatives to find disappeared family members (...). The reparations included a monthly wage (...) for each family affected by disappearance or death (...) and diverse health and education benefits, as well as an exemption from military service for the victims and their relatives". In addition there was "an Office of Repatriation to facilitate the return of exiled persons,[29] and a law for the '*exonerados*'[30] which granted provisional benefits to 58,000 public sector employees dismissed between 1973 and 1990" (Barahona de Brito 2001, pp. 131–2). Economic reparations for children born to mothers in captivity and for all detainees in secret detention centres were also considered (Acuña 2006, p. 215).

As already mentioned at the beginning of this paper, various norms were approved in Spain that aimed at the material reparation of the victims of war and their relatives, as well as those whose suffering in prison was politically motivated. Additionally, the Law on Reparations has incorporated some victim's groups that were not covered by the previous legislation. However, in addition to the vacuum that still exists, and which will be dealt with later in this paper, no measures aimed at facilitating the return of tens of thousands of people in exile or rules that offer reparation to the victims of torture were ever approved.

[29] From which 52,557 people have benefited (Lira 2006, p. 73).

[30] Persons removed or purged from their jobs.

3.3 *Justice, Amnesties and Pardons*

3.3.1 Amnesties and Justice for Perpetrators

In Argentina, as regards measures of justice and pardon, the military enacted an amnesty in April 1983 – that is, before power was handed over – which tried to cover both acts of "subversion" as well as the excesses of the "repression". The new democratic government revoked this law in December of the same year. President Alfonsín adopted measures to simultaneously take to trial several military leaders of the Junta and the seven top guerrilla leaders. The country became the "first and only country in Latin America that, in the middle of a democratisation process, took to trial the nine military junta leaders for the murder and disappearance of citizens in their country during the dictatorship from 1976 to 1983" (Hite 2005). After a trial that was televised, albeit without a soundtrack of the protagonists, five of the defendants were sentenced and four were cleared of all charges. Judicial proceedings against human rights violators continued, creating a certain amount of anxiety among the military rank and file – to the extent that a group known as "*carapintadas*" ("painted faces") organised some revolts. The laws known as Full Stop and Due Obedience, which date back to December 1986 and June 1987 respectively, were approved in an effort to put an end to the military revolts and to stabilise democracy. Later, in October 1989 and January 1991, Carlos Menem was responsible for a series of pardons benefiting those towards whom the laws had been directed in the first place.

The proof that "gag rules" are not irrevocable, in spite of their potentially fundamental role in processes of political change, came in June 2005 when the Argentinian Supreme Court revoked the Full Stop and Due Obedience laws on grounds of unconstitutionality. From the beginning of his mandate, President Kirchner showed determination regarding reparations for the victims. On the occasion of the 30th anniversary of the military coup, the Argentinian president "abolished the decree that prevented the extradition of military servicemen" who had been accused of human rights violations (Tappatá de Valdez 2005, p. 109). Also, he urged judges to revoke the pardons that had been approved by Carlos Menem; in July 2007, the Supreme Court decided indeed (in one case, that will in all likelihood serve as a precedent for all other cases) to declare the unconstitutionality of the pardon, considering that crimes against humanity cannot be amnestied.

The crimes of stealing children from detained women and pregnant women who disappeared were never covered by any of the laws already mentioned or by the pardons granted by Menem. This explains why, during the 1990s, the Argentinian justice system continued to take action against some of the leading members of the dictatorship. Throughout these years, "associations of human rights activists, journalists and judges concentrated on the crimes excluded by the Law of Due Obedience (...) in an effort to obtain new trials" (Hite 2005).

On the other hand, the so-called "Truth Trials" have been taking place from 1999 onwards, mainly in the tribunal of La Plata. Their final aim "was not to establish the criminal responsibility of those involved and thus they did not contemplate the possibility of a sentence" (Tappatá de Valdez 2005, p. 97). Instead, these trials constituted a novel and original measure through which "the right to truth and to mourn"[31] is put to work in an effective form. As a result of pressures from human rights organisations, the Argentinian government acknowledged this right and even created a truth commission in 1996.

In Chile, the 1978 Law of Amnesty (which, in contrast to Spain, was approved by the dictatorship) was applied rigorously until Pinochet's arrest in London. This fortuitous event forced Chileans to review some of the agreements on which their process of political change was based. From then on, judges began to reinterpret the law and many considered that the cases of the disappeared constituted "ongoing crimes", a fact that allowed them to re-open cases prior to 1978. In Chile, as in Spain, the Law of Amnesty is still valid, although in Chile, and not in Spain, parliamentary debates have been held over this issue. (In addition, some declarations by President Bachelet indicate that it could be abolished soon.)

In any case, from a very early date and in spite of the Amnesty Law, some judges in Chile opted to conduct investigations into cases of forced disappearances or torture all the way to their end, although they were then obliged to grant amnesty to the accused. In this way, they helped to clarify the facts without violating the law.

Nothing similar to this has happened in Spain. The Amnesty Law, promulgated in 1977 and in force ever since, has been used as an excuse for not launching investigations into violations of human rights committed during the war or under the dictatorship. The Law on Reparations does not contemplate trials for persons responsible of human rights violations. The provisions of the 1977 amnesty law remain intact. In contrast to what has happened in other cases, almost no Spanish judge has invoked national or international norms for the purpose of bypassing the limits of the Amnesty Law.[32]

In Spain – in contrast to the other two countries – military leaders did not see the need to approve a self-amnesty prior to the change of regime. This is probably due to three factors. Firstly, as has already been pointed out, the transition in Spain took place in a context that was less sensitive to the emerging international climate of rejecting impunity. This explains why the officials of the dictatorship were less apprehensive. Secondly, it illustrates the confidence of an important part of the political elite, which had its origins in the Francoist dictatorship, in its ability to control the process of change. Finally, it must also be pointed out that the power of the Francoist dictatorship, in contrast to the Chilean and Argentinian ones, did not lie with the military – notwithstanding the fact that both during and in the post-war, the Francoist army had played a direct role in the repression of thousands of people linked to the Republican side through military tribunals.

---

[31] See Principles 1–4 of the Set of Principles for the Protection and Promotion of Human Rights through Action to Combat Impunity, prepared by Louis Joinet, member of the UN Commission on Human Right's Sub-Commission on Prevention of Discrimination and Protection of Minorities. UN Doc. E/CN.4/Sub.2/1997/20/Rev.1 of 2 October 1997.

[32] For minor exceptions, see Gil (2009) and Aguilar (2008).

3.3.2 Amnesties for Political Prisoners and Repeal of Sentences for Victims of Illegitimate Trials

All three countries covered by this study have eventually approved amnesties for the political prisoners of the dictatorship, albeit implemented at very different times. In Chile, it took more than 4 years to set 400 political prisoners free. We have seen that in Spain, however, amnesty measures were approved from the beginning, and the October 1977 amnesty law was approved less than 2 years after Franco's death. Something very similar happened in Argentina, where the liberation of political prisoners was the first measure adopted by President Raúl Alfonsín. Both in Chile and in Spain, the military deeply opposed the liberation of prisoners who had committed violent crimes against persons.

Regarding unjust sentences imposed by Francoist tribunals, the Spanish Supreme Court has for a long time denied every attempt to review such sentences. In fact, until recently, only some judges and jurists have argued in favour of a revision, and even the annulment, of the military trials during Francoism, including court martial trials. The official repeal of the effects of these judgments – a solution that Joan Queralt, a penal law professor, finds more appropriate than the annulment of the judgments – should follow, according to him, the model of the German federal law of 1/9/1998.[33] The Law on Reparations formally declares, for the first time, the "illegitimacy" of tribunals that had operated both during the civil war and the dictatorial period in disregard of due process rules, and of the sentences imposed for ideological, political or religious reasons. The legal effects of this declaration are still to be seen. Amnesty International (2007) deplores that the declaration of illegitimacy does not grant affected persons an explicit recourse to seek the annulment or repeal of a sentence. However, José Antonio Martín Pallín, a former judge of the Supreme Court, has argued that individual recourses would be possible and that illegitimate sentences could even be voided *ex officio*.[34] Finally, the former prosecutor of the Anti-Corruption Office, Carlos Jiménez Villarejo – who has been advising the parliamentary left in its negotiations with the government – has asked the judiciary "to be brave" when applying the Law on Reparations and even "to initiate itself judicial processes in order to cancel Francoist sentences"[35] (more on this topic in Aguilar 2008).

3.3.3 Memory and the Call for Retribution

As pointed out before, there were extrajudicial executions, forced disappearances and torture not only during the war, but also in the post-war period, and trials were

[33] "Desmemoria histórica", *El País*, 5/1/2007, p. 26, www.derechos.org/nizkor/espana/doc/queralt.html. The German federal law is the "Gesetz zur Aufhebung nationalsozialistischer Unrechtsurteile in der Strafrechtspflege (NS-AufhG)".

[34] *Público*, 20/10/2007, p. 11, www.publico.es/espana/008330/joseantoniomartinpallin/leydelamemoriahistorica.

[35] *Siglo XXI*, 18/10/2007, www.diariosigloxxi.com/texto/mostrar/?ts=20071018200525.

carried out without due process guarantees throughout the entire regime. But, in distinction to what happened in Chile and Argentina, the Francoist repression was much less clandestine and much more covered by the regime's legislation than in the other two cases. In Chile and Argentina, the repression was basically "clandestine and illegal, even according to the laws of the dictatorships" (Barahona de Brito 2001, p. 119). In fact, surprisingly enough, although the death penalty had been re-established in Argentina, it was never practised during the dictatorship. Under Pinochet's dictatorship, the death penalty was only applied in four cases, for reasons that had nothing to do with politics. In contrast, although it is not known exactly how many death sentences were carried out for political reasons by the dictatorship in Spain, they are believed to amount to 50,000, without taking into account those that took place during the Civil War.[36]

Although Jon Elster falls short of proposing a general theory about transitional justice, he observes the following pattern: "When the pre-democratic regime has been of short duration, memories of wrongdoing and suffering tend to be vivid and (other things being equal) emotions correspondingly strong. If it has been of long duration, the intensity of emotion and of the demands for retribution will depend (other things being equal) on when the worst atrocities took place". (Elster 2004, p. 75).

For one, the fact that the worst crimes of the Argentinian and Chilean dictatorship were more recent and more clandestine made them much more awkward to address, and at the same time more difficult to ignore. In Argentina, even though some policymaking regarding the past began with great determination, circumstances forced the official reparation process into an impasse. But this standstill was not supported by certain sectors of society who never stopped, both in Chile and in Argentina, mobilising against impunity and in favour of justice and memory. Also, some judges did not support the impasse. This explains the subsequent progress that justice has brought about in both countries.

Also, the fact that repression in Argentina and Chile was fundamentally clandestine explains why demands for truth and justice were raised with much more insistence than in Spain, where the trials that led to tens of thousands of executions during the first years of the dictatorship were regular proceedings. Nevertheless, it is surprising that, despite the time that has elapsed, no inventory has been taken of the executions that have happened in Spain; this explains why we still do not know their exact number. A truth commission would have helped to clarify these matters. The point is not, as has been said erroneously on occasion, that the State should write the "official history" of the country, but that the State should put its abundant economic and human resources at the service of investigating the main violations of human rights that took place in the country as a whole. We also still have a lot to learn about the extrajudicial killings that were perpetrated in Spain by the winning side during the war and the first phase of Francoism given that, although they were not committed as systematically as in the other two countries examined, they did take place.

[36] In Spain the death sentence was abolished for common crimes in 1978 and for all types of crimes in 1995 (although Article 15 of the Constitution still makes reference to it). In Chile and in Argentina it was abolished for common crimes only in 2001 and 1984 respectively.

There is a great deal of data and it will take historians decades to compile them and to overcome some major difficulties, such as the huge amount of data, their distribution all over the nation, and the difficulty of access (especially during the birth of democracy). Hence the enormous practical utility of truth commissions: within a brief period of time, they can give access to information that is extremely difficult to compile, but indispensable to drawing up a coherent and trustworthy account of a violent past. Furthermore, these institutions also have symbolic or moral utility: not only do they give voice to the victims who wish to present their testimony, which usually has a restorative effect in itself, but they also allow for wide-spread publicity of the worst episodes of rights violations, documentation of the practices of dictatorships, and the unmasking of the lies of the dictatorships regarding their own crimes. And they perform all these functions with the prestige and credibility that such commissions and their members generally enjoy.

4 Conclusions

If we compare the reparation, truth and justice measures that have been taken in these three countries, it can be generally said that Argentina and Chile have gone further in terms of public clarification of the truth (commissions to this end have been created in both cases). They have both succeeded in bringing to trial and imprisoning some of those responsible for the worst violations of human rights, even when the laws valid at the time supposedly prevented it (the Amnesty Law in Chile and the Full Stop Law in Argentina). These laws were bypassed more efficiently than in Spain, thanks to the pressure exerted by society, to the attitude of some judges and to a resolute political will. These countries have also carried out more convincing and visible symbolic reparations of the victims than Spain. However, in Chile, the institutional reforms took longer and were more incomplete than in the other two countries. In Spain, the absence of deep-rooted reforms in several key institutions, such as the police and the judiciary, explains the virtual absence of these institutions as a driving force in the process of transition and the high numbers of fatalities due to state repression throughout the transitional period (1975–1982), as well as the impunity with which the extreme right acted during this time. There are abundant examples of connivance between the extreme right, the judges and the state security forces.

As far as material reparations are concerned, the main group of victims in each of the three countries has been awarded pensions or indemnisation payments, but in the Spanish case the process has taken longer and there are some vacuums yet to be filled. To outline the main vacuums in terms of material and moral reparations: there are those who died for political reasons, but not during the Civil War or as a consequence of it (for example, persons who died through civil guard or police brutality, something that occurred throughout the entire dictatorship, in particular its first decade). If the victims are not directly connected to the Civil War or its immediate consequences, and if victimization took place before 1968, their relatives do not receive a pension. Also, in contrast to other cases, persons who suffered torture have not been paid any kind of pension, nor have those in exile received any help to assist them in their return. Regarding the exiled, the Law on Reparations does not foresee any financial support, though it offers them the possibility of reclaiming the Spanish nationality. According to government estimates, this could affect one million people.

One would think that the great political and economic stability that Spain has enjoyed in the past 20 years – greater in any case than that of Chile and Argentina – would have allowed it to undertake bolder reparation policies. But the truth is that in Spain the social impetus has been very weak, especially if compared with that in the other two countries. Although things have begun to change very recently in Spain, groups there do not have the mobilisation capacity of many human rights organisations, past and present, in Chile and Argentina. Furthermore, as stated previously, judges have not played the same role in Spain as in the two other countries. So far, the Spanish Supreme Court has rejected all applications, but one, for a review of the thousand of trials that took place during Francoism. Spanish judges have not interpreted the laws in a flexible way, nor have they resorted to international law to find ways to prosecute those crimes for which amnesties are considered to be illicit, such as torture, extrajudicial executions and forced disappearances, according to conventions and treaties that Spain has signed.[37] Also, according to Chinchón (2007a), the Spanish legislation does not have a genuine reparatory character, as most of it does not recognize the existence of human rights violations nor the victim condition of the beneficiaries. In addition to resorting to international criminal law, many Argentinian and Chilean judges have worked very closely with human rights organisations to try to find loopholes in their national legislation with the aim of promoting some judicial causes. Nothing similar seems to have happened in Spain.

Another particularity of the Spanish case was the fact that the Spanish Amnesty Law preceded all attempted coups by military leaders, while the Due Obedience and Full Stop laws in Argentina were sanctioned precisely to end such uprisings. Whereas in Argentina these laws were useful in calming military leaders, in Spain the amnesty did not succeed in making military leaders abandon their intentions to oust the democratic rule of law. It has already been explained that this was not the fundamental purpose of the law, but it is nevertheless noteworthy that the impunity that it consecrated did not have the effect of defusing military leaders and the extreme right. The outcome was the opposite: 4 years after the Amnesty Law, there was a serious coup attempt (preceded and followed by other frustrated ones) and the extreme right notoriously increased their levels of political violence, leading to the death of at least 52 people between 1978 and 1982.[38]

It is surprising that in Spain during the last two decades talk about mass graves, the disappeared, kidnapped children and imprescriptible crimes that should have been the target of judicial prosecution, often sounded as if it was referring to foreign, distant cases. The efficacy of Francoism to hide some of its crimes, the length of

[37] For different perspectives on this topic, see Aguilar (2008), Chinchón (2007a), and Gil (2009).

[38] From the database on the political violence of the transitional period compiled by Ignacio Sánchez-Cuenca and myself.

time which has passed since the most repressive phase of the regime and the general wish, not just of politicians but also of the majority of citizens, not to delve into such a tragic past, explains the surprise caused by the recent increase in exhumations and by some of the most recent revelations about forced adoptions.

It seems that in the Spanish case the problem for moving further was – and still is to some extent – a society still not ready to promote measures as bold as those taken in the other two countries. If this is true of the whole society, then it is even more true (according to my analysis of a 2005 survey by the Centre of Sociological Research/Centro de Investigaciones Sociológicas on this issue) of the inhabitants in the rural areas, where the resistance to digging up the past is strong, and, curiously enough, of the generation who played a key role in the process of political change, that is, those born between 1941 and 1950. One has the impression that this age group attributes a large part of the success of the transitional period precisely to the fact that the past was left out of the political debate. Perhaps this helps to explain why this age group is less inclined to promote additional reparation policies, irrespective of a high level of education, and even of ideology (Aguilar 2008).

I would like to conclude with a reflection on the vicissitudes of the debate on memory and oblivion.[39] The transitional period in Spain may only be understood as a combination of the obsessive persistence of memory together with the equally obsessive wish to ignore it and to avoid its recurrence. The voices criticising the "pact of silence" of the transitional period tend to blame the political elites, when, in fact, the decision to leave the past behind was favoured by the vast majority of the Spanish people. But underlying this criticism is also the realization that there are vacuums with regard to material and symbolic reparations for the victims of both the Republican side and of the dictatorship.

The impunity that the perpetrators of human rights violations enjoyed during the dictatorship was also extended to the transitional period. This was not only a matter of the already-cited police connivance with the violence of the extreme right, but also of the government's own brutality in repressing demonstrations led by groups opposed to the dictatorship. The number of fatalities that resulted from police repression in the transitional period (1975–1982) amounts to a minimum of 140.[40] None of the relatives of the dead has been economically or morally compensated to date. Thanks to the Law on Reparations, the victims of political violence will be compensated, but only if the events took place between January 1968 and October 1977.

Gag rules exist precisely because there is no agreement over the past. What has been agreed, at least in the Spanish case, was to leave the past aside. There are times when, in order not to expose irreconcilable interpretations of the past, it is agreed to forge some rather general consensus of the kind that we find in Spain: "we were all guilty for the atrocities committed during the Civil War" without entering into a debate over who mobilised against a legally constituted regime, thus unleashing the Civil War, who committed more crimes, or what type of violence was used by

[39] More on this issue in Aguilar (2006).

[40] According to a database on political violence during the transition prepared by Ignacio Sánchez-Cuenca and myself.

either side. After Franco's death, no one called for a revision of the past, not only because the correlation of forces was averse to this task, but also because the majority in society was afraid of reviving wartime enmities. There were priorities that were considered more important at that time, although this argument has repeatedly been used by governments, in general, to avoid implementing transitional justice measures. Once time has gone by, when democracy has been consolidated, there is usually an invocation of the "opportunity cost": it is not worth investing so much effort and the subsequent political wear and tear in accomplishing these kinds of measures when the same effort could be directed toward policies considered more significant for the correct functioning of democracy. The problem in the Spanish case is that during the transitional period everyone thought that it was too early to adopt certain measures of transitional justice, while today many think that it is too late to do so, which explains certain resistance to the Law on Reparations even within the socialist ranks.

The paradox is that, if it is true that times of political change are extremely unstable and uncertain, they also seem ideal times at which to elicit genuine agreements on delicate issues. Consensus is usually easier precisely because of the fear of breakdown and the violence that results from the characteristic instability of such periods. When democracy is stable and the unique spirit that, on occasions, accompanies transitions, has turned into a matter of the past, it is not so easy for the political forces to rediscover the impetus needed to come together around certain reparation measures, avoiding the temptation to turn the past into a weapon. Once fear of confrontation and breakdown has dissipated, the incentives to reach genuine consensus leaving aside electoral calculus are weakened.

However, this probable lack of consensus does not mean that it is impossible to advance towards truth and justice once democracy has been stabilized, as both the Argentinian and Chilean cases have demonstrated, or, at least, to improve material and symbolic reparations, as the Spanish case has recently shown. Sikkink and Walling (2007) have recently argued, for many other cases, that it is not true that transitional justice measures are to remain forever. They have also reached a crucial conclusion, of high relevance for this book: human rights trials have not exacerbated conflict, nor destabilized democracies, nor increased human rights violations, as some authors have previously claimed.

Acknowledgments I would like to thank Katie Hite, Alfredo Joignant, Patricia Valdez and Valeria Barbuto for their useful comments on matters relating to Chile and Argentina. I am also indebted to Christian Much for his careful and detailed supervision of this text, and to Javier Chinchón for his advice on some juridical aspects of the paper. A different version of this text has been published in Spanish: Aguilar P (2008) Políticas de la memoria y memorias de la política. Alianza Editorial, Madrid.

References

Acuña CH (2006) Transitional justice in Argentina and Chile. In: Elster J (ed) Retribution and reparation in the transition to democracy. Cambridge University Press, New York, pp 206–238

Aguilar P (1997) Collective memory of the Spanish Civil War: The case of the political amnesty in the Spanish transition to democracy. Democratization 4(4):88–109

Aguilar P (2002) Memory and amnesia. The role of the Spanish Civil War in the transition to democracy. Berghahn Books, Oxford

Aguilar P (2006) Presencia y ausencia de la guerra civil y del franquismo en la democracia española. Reflexiones en torno a la articulación y ruptura del 'pacto de silencio'. In: Aróstegui J, Godicheau F (eds) Guerra Civil. Mito y memoria. Marcial Pons, Madrid, pp 245–293

Aguilar P (2007) Los debates sobre la memoria histórica. Claves de Razón Práctica 172:64–68

Aguilar P (2008) Las políticas de la memoria y las memorias de la política. Alianza Editorial, Madrid

Aguilar P, Hite K (2004) Historical memory and authoritarian legacies in processes of political change: Spain and Chile in comparative perspective. In: Cesarini P, Hite K (eds) Authoritarian legacies and good democracies. University of Notre Dame Press, Indiana, pp 191–231

Aguilar P, Humlebaek C (2002) Collective memory and national identity in the Spanish democracy. History and Memory 14:121–164

Alted A (2005) La voz de los vencidos. El exilio republicano de 1939. Aguilar, Madrid

Ambos K (1999) Impunidad y derecho penal internacional, 2nd edn. Ad Hoc, Buenos Aires

Ambos K, Malarino E, Elsner G (cords) (2008) Jurisprudencia Latinoamericana sobre derecho penal internacional. Konrad Adenauer Stiftung, Montevideo

Amnesty International (2007) La Ley sobre víctimas de la guerra civil y el franquismo aunque mejora, no salda la deuda pendiente, 18/10/2007 (Press Office of the Spanish Section) www.es.amnesty.org/noticias/noticias/articulo/la-ley-sobre-victimas-de-la-guerra-civil-y-el-franquismo-aunque-mejora-no-salda-la-deuda-pendiente

Arnold J et al (eds) (2006) Estado de derecho y delincuencia de estado en América Latina: una visión comparativa. Universidad Nacional Autónoma de México, México

Barahona de Brito A (2001) Truth, justice, memory, and democratization in the southern cone. In: Barahona de Brito A, González Enríquez C, Aguilar P (eds) The politics of memory. Transitional justice in democratizing societies. Oxford University Press, Oxford, pp 119–160

Barahona de Brito A, González Enríquez C, Aguilar P (eds) (2001) The politics of memory. Transitional justice in democratizing societies. Oxford University Press, Oxford

Cancio R (2006) Guerra civil y tribunales: de los jurados populares a la justicia franquista. Universidad de Extremadura, Cáceres

Cazorla A (2002) Sobre el primer Franquismo y la extensión de su apoyo popular. Historia y Política 8:303–319

Chinchón J (2007a) El viaje a ninguna parte: Memoria, leyes, historia y olvido sobre la guerra civil y el pasado autoritario en España. Revista del Instituto Interamericano de Derechos Humanos 47:119–233

Chinchón J (2007b) Derecho internacional y transiciones a la democracia y la paz. Hacia un modelo para el castigo de los crímenes pasados a través de la experiencia iberoamericana. Ediciones Parthenon, Sevilla

Elster J (2004) Closing the books. Transitional justice in historical perspective. Cambridge University Press, Cambridge

Gálvez S (2006) El proceso de recuperación de la 'memoria histórica' en España: una aproximación a los movimientos sociales por la memoria. International Journal of Iberian Studies 19(1):25–51

Gil A (2003) España. In: Ambos K, Malarino E (eds) Persecución penal nacional de crímenes internacionales en América Latina y España. Konrad Adenauer Stiftung, Instituto Max Planck de Derecho Penal Extranjero e Internacional, Montevideo

Gil A (2006) Jurisdicción de los tribunales españoles sobre genocidio, crímenes contra la humanidad y crímenes de guerra. Revista Española de Derecho Militar (87):55–88

Gil A (2009) La Justicia transicional en España. De la amnistía a la memoria histórica. Atelier, Barcelona (in press)

Guembe MJ (2006) Economic reparations for human rights violations: The Argentinian experience. In: Greiff P (ed) The handbook of reparations. Oxford University Press, Oxford, pp 21–54

Hite K (2005) The politics of memory, the languages of human rights (unpublished manuscript)

Holmes S (1988) Gag rules or the politics of omission. In: Elster J, Slagstad R (eds) Constitutionalism and democracy. Maison des Sciences, New York, pp 195–240

Jelin E (2007) Public memorialization in perspective: Truth, justice and memory of past repression in the southern cone of South America. The International Journal of Transitional Justice 1:138–156

Joignant A (2007) Un día distinto. Editorial Universitaria, Santiago de Chile

Juliá S et al (1999) Víctimas de la guerra civil. Temas de Hoy, Madrid

Lira E (2006) The reparations policy for human rights violations in Chile. In: Pablo de Greiff (ed) The handbook of reparations. Oxford University Press, Oxford, pp 55–101

Rodrigo J (2005) Cautivos. Campos de concentración en la España franquista, 1936–1947. Crítica, Barcelona

Sancinetti M, Ferrante M (1999) El derecho penal en la protección de los derechos humanos: la protección de los derechos humanos mediante el derecho penal en las transiciones democráticas. Hammurabi, Buenos Aires

Sikkink K, Walling CB (2007) The impact of human rights trials in Latin America. Journal of Peace Research 44(4):427–445

Skaar E (1999) Truth commissions, trials – or noting? Policy options in democratic transitions. Third World Quarterly 20(6):1109–1128

Tappatá de Valdez P (2005) El pasado, un tema central del presente. La búsqueda de verdad y justicia como construcción de una lógica democrática. In: Pacheco Oreamuno G, Acevedo Narea L, Galli G (eds) Verdad, justicia y reparación. Desafíos para la democracia y la convivencia social. IDEA/IIDH, San José

Vinyes R et al (2002) Los niños perdidos del franquismo. Plaza & Janés, Barcelona

Wilde A (1999) Irruptions of memory: Expressive politics in Chile's transition to democracy. Journal of Latin American Studies 31(2):473–500

Conclusions

Report on the Major Findings of the Conference

By Ambassador of Jordan to the USA

HRH Prince Zeid Ra'ad Zeid Al-Hussein
(abridged version)

(...) Two days ago, during the opening ceremony in the Nuremberg Tribunal, Ms Sonia Picado, the Personal Envoy of Costa Rican President Oscar Arias, and Mr Frank-Walter Steinmeier, the German Foreign Minister, both mentioned that this conference was likely to accumulate an unprecedented wealth of information on the peace-and-justice dilemma. Their expectation was correct. We are indeed blessed, even overwhelmed, with an incredible amount of information, opinions and advice. Let me try to attempt some brief and certainly incomplete conclusions:

1. The first point that comes to mind is the most obvious one – sort of the leitmotiv of the conference: justice and peace need not be contradictory forces. Whilst we must acknowledge that the dilemmas are real, a negotiated agreement must build the foundation for both peace and justice. This point was underpinned by generally accepted references to the concepts of sustainable peace, sustainable development and human security. The logical consequence of the complementarity of peace and justice is that the choice is not between some accountability and none, but rather how to build sustainable solutions.
2. The second point is a very basic and commonly accepted one: peace must be understood as "sustainable peace". The silence of the arms, the end of violence and terror, the ability to meet basic needs, public security – these are the expectations of people who have been traumatized by armed conflict and all sorts of brutalities, and therefore these are immensely important categories. But we must not confuse a signature on an agreement, the end of violence and public security with the notion of "sustainable peace".
3. A third point concerns mediation processes. Here, it became clear that mediation happens at many different levels and involves many different actors. It is not just power bargaining between diplomats and the men with guns. At this top level, mediators indeed bear a responsibility to contribute creatively and flexibly to the immediate ending of violence and hostilities with the simultaneous expectation – which is usually part of their own "work ethic" – to promote sustainable

HRH Prince Zeid Ra'ad Zeid Al-Hussein

K. Ambos et al. (eds.), *Building a Future on Peace and Justice: Studies on Transitional Justice, Peace and Development.*

solutions. This requires engagement with a broader constituency of civil society, in particular women and traditionally excluded groups, to keep the parties from entering agreements that are, in all likelihood, doomed to failure. The commitment of mediators to the core principles of the international legal order has to be beyond doubt – there is simply no room for blanket amnesties where the core crimes are concerned – and mediators should promote knowledge among the parties about the normative framework so that the parties can make informed choices. However, there should be a clear understanding of the division of labour where the mediator and the prosecutor have distinct roles to play. There was also broad agreement that mediators needed flexibility and that a degree of ambiguity could provide the necessary scope to address the reality of conflict situations which invariably centre on competing visions of the past. It was also clear that mediation will continue at many points in society after a formal settlement, often going hand in hand with reconciliation.

4. The fourth point is about the notion of justice. As the development of the field of transitional justice has shown, "justice" needs to be – and in fact is – understood in a broad sense. Transitional justice may comprise criminal justice, truth-telling, reparations and institutional reform. The aims should include building trustworthy institutions and addressing marginalization, especially on grounds of gender. Legitimacy is a cornerstone of justice, and means and priorities must be locally defined. All these ideas are now generally accepted, but the challenge is in combining the ingredients of justice in ways that are sensitive to the context of a particular national or regional situation.
5. Here, as a fifth point, I wish to highlight the fight against impunity, culminating in the Rome Statute of the ICC, now ratified by 104 States. This worldwide movement has changed the parameters for the pursuit of peace. There is an emerging norm in international law that amnesties cannot be conceded for war crimes, crimes against humanity or genocide. In any case, the Court will not be bound by amnesties if it has jurisdiction. In addition, there is an emergence of practice at the international level of concentrating on those bearing the greatest responsibility for such crimes. A central feature of the Rome Statute is the principle of complementarity, whereby States have the primary duty to investigate or prosecute those responsible. The precise way in which States implement this duty may vary, but while incentives may be used within the context of criminal prosecutions, amnesty for such crimes is no longer available.
6. Sixthly, in this regard it has sometimes been noted that the pursuit of justice and reconciliation seem to be in tension. However, the workshops have been helpful in demonstrating that the desire for both accountability and reconciliation is common to all continents. Expectations may differ according to social, political and religious context, and views may not be uniform. The "hunger" for justice may vary over time and may grow once worries about survival diminish. But there is broad understanding that accountability and reconciliation can, and in fact do, co-exist.
7. A seventh point is about social, political and economic development. There was general agreement that to deliver on socio-economic justice, transitional justice

mechanisms and development efforts should complement each other. In particular, security sector reforms, disarmament and demobilization and the restoration of a State sector that is able to uphold a public order based on human rights and the rule of law are all valid development goals which should not be pursued in isolation. Efforts at intelligent timing of the various steps, and at pacing and upholding international commitments, remain a big challenge.

8. An eighth, more specific point on development: several people argued convincingly that development aspects go beyond the resource and managerial dimension which I addressed in my previous point. Conflict is too often centred on issues of lack of equitable access to social goods. Therefore the mediator should be attentive to future developmental needs in order that the root causes of conflict are addressed from the outset. This is essential in generating a "peace dividend" (in other words: a sentiment of trust in the superiority of the post-conflict order), which is crucial to reconciliation. It is therefore necessary that the United Nations – notably the Secretariat, the Security Council and the Peacebuilding Commission – work on the integration of developmental and justice perspectives into their peace-building strategies.
9. Finally, in conclusion, please allow me a simple yet obvious point. The peace-and-justice dilemma is at its worst when people expect simple solutions to highly complex situations. This conference was not intended to produce blueprints for the resolution of all tensions between the pursuits of peace and justice. But the conference has reminded us that although the pursuit of peace and justice occasionally results in a moral dilemma, those deciding do not act in a moral or normative vacuum. There can be no doubt about the genuine difficulties involved, and the need for compromise within the parameters already described. But by comparing experiences from many places, and by listening to the varied expertise, the conference has demonstrated that while there is no *one* perfect solution, there is a spectrum of available options and creative approaches can be found.

You must have heard most of these points before, but maybe you have never heard them in conjunction, all in a single, multidisciplinary conference, and underpinned empirically on such a broad scale. I hope that this will be remembered as the legacy of this conference. I also hope that the legacy will not just be an oral one, but that it will be recorded in such a way as to have a more lasting impact – for the benefit of mediators, Governments, international and regional organizations.

Nuremberg Declaration Peace and Justice

United Nations A/62/885

General Assembly

Distr.: General
19 June 2008

Original: English

Sixty-second session
Agenda items 34 and 86

Comprehensive review of the whole question of peacekeeping operations in all their aspects

The rule of law at the national and international levels

Letter dated 13 June 2008 from the Permanent Representatives of Finland, Germany and Jordan to the United Nations addressed to the Secretary-General

In a joint letter dated 3 December 2007 (A/62/580), issued on 12 December 2007, we informed you of the outcome of the International Conference entitled "Building a Future on Peace and Justice", organized by the Hashemite Kingdom of Jordan, Finland and the Federal Republic of Germany, in Nuremberg, Germany, from 25 to 27 June 2007. In that letter, we mentioned that the Conference had aimed at producing concrete recommendations on how to deal with possible tensions between peace and justice. We also announced that, to that end, the Conference organizers would draft a political document to be called the Nuremberg Declaration on Peace and Justice.

It gives us great pleasure to transmit herewith the Nuremberg Declaration on Peace and Justice (see annex). It was elaborated by a group of international experts designated by the Conference organizers and working under the auspices of Óscar Arias, President of Costa Rica. We have approved the text upon consultations with interested practitioners and civil society organizations.

The Declaration contains definitions, principles and recommendations on issues of peace, justice and impunity, and making peace and dealing with the past, as well as promoting development. Although it is not a legal document, it aspires to "guide those involved at the local, national and international levels in all phases of conflict transformation, including mediation, post-conflict peacebuilding, development, and the promotion of transitional justice and the rule of law" and thus to influence the future practice of making and building "just and lasting peace". It is therefore our sincerest hope that this document may also be useful to the United Nations and its States Members.

08-39294 (E) 250608

Nuremberg Declaration on Peace and Justice

K. Ambos et al. (eds.), *Building a Future on Peace and Justice: Studies on Transitional Justice, Peace and Development.*

We would therefore be grateful if you could circulate the present letter together with its annex as a document of the General Assembly, under agenda items 34 and 86.

(*Signed*) Kirsti **Lintonen**
Permanent Representative of Finland

(*Signed*) Thomas **Matussek**
Permanent Representative of the Federal Republic of Germany

(*Signed*) Mohammed F. **Al-Allaf**
Permanent Representative of the Hashemite Kingdom of Jordan

Annex to the letter dated 13 June 2008 from the Permanent Representatives of Finland, Germany and Jordan to the United Nations addressed to the Secretary-General

Nuremberg Declaration on Peace and Justice

I. Preamble

We, the Governments of Finland, Germany and the Hashemite Kingdom of Jordan, acting in our capacity as co-organizers of the International Conference "Building a Future on Peace and Justice", held in Nuremberg, Germany, from 25 to 27 June 2007,[a]

Having pledged, with the consent of Conference participants, to translate the essential findings of the Conference into a document to be called the "Nuremberg Declaration on Peace and Justice",

Acknowledging that peace, justice, human rights and development are at the heart of the international community, that they are interlinked and mutually reinforcing and that they need to be addressed in accordance with the Charter of the United Nations, the Universal Declaration of Human Rights[b] and other standards of human rights and international humanitarian law, including, where applicable, the Rome Statute of the International Criminal Court,[c]

Aware of, and *encouraged* by, the advances of the worldwide movement to fight impunity, and *reaffirming* in this context that the most serious crimes of concern to the international community as a whole must not go unpunished,

Motivated by the desire to contribute to the prevention and non-recurrence of armed conflict,

Recognizing that peace and stability are more likely to prevail when the root causes of conflict are addressed in a manner that affected societies perceive as legitimate, non-discriminatory and just, and when societies deal constructively with their past,

Stressing that the advancement of peace and justice is a long-term endeavour, requiring a comprehensive and inclusive approach that is sensitive to political, cultural and gender aspects,

---

[a] From 25 to 27 June 2007, more than 300 policymakers and practitioners gathered in Nuremberg, Germany, to attend the International Conference "Building a Future on Peace and Justice", organized by the Governments of Finland, Germany and Jordan in cooperation with the Crisis Management Initiative (CMI), Helsinki; the International Center for Transitional Justice (ICTJ), New York; the Friedrich-Ebert-Stiftung (FES), Berlin; the Centre for the Study of Violence and Reconciliation (CSVR), Johannesburg, South Africa; the Working Group on Development and Peace (FriEnt), Bonn, Germany; the Centre for Peacebuilding (KOFF) — swisspeace, Bern; and the Georg-August University, Goettingen, Germany. At the conclusion of the Conference, its participants agreed that the Conference organizers would elaborate a declaration. It was drafted, under the auspices of Óscar Arias, President of Costa Rica, by a group of international experts designated by the Conference organizers and was the subject of consultations, before its publication in June 2008, with practitioners and civil society organizations.

[b] General Assembly resolution 217 A (III).

[c] United Nations, *Treaty Series*, vol. 2187, No. 38544.

Propose that the present Declaration guide those involved at the local, national and international levels in all phases of conflict transformation, including mediation, post-conflict peacebuilding, development, and the promotion of transitional justice and the rule of law.

II. Definitions

In this Declaration,

1. **"Peace"** is understood as meaning sustainable peace.

   Sustainable peace goes beyond the signing of an agreement. While the cessation of hostilities, restoration of public security and meeting basic needs are urgent and legitimate expectations of people who have been traumatized by armed conflict, sustainable peace requires a long-term approach that addresses the structural causes of conflict, and promotes sustainable development, rule of law and governance, and respect for human rights, making the recurrence of violent conflict less likely.

2. **"Justice"** is understood as meaning accountability and fairness in the protection and vindication of rights, and the prevention and redress of wrongs.

   Justice must be administered by institutions and mechanisms that enjoy legitimacy, comply with the rule of law and are consistent with international human rights standards. Justice combines elements of criminal justice, truth-seeking, reparations and institutional reform as well as the fair distribution of, and access to, public goods, and equity within society at large.

   Justice may be delivered by local, national and international actors.

III. Principles

1. Complementarity of peace and justice

Peace and justice, if properly pursued, promote and sustain one another. The question can never be whether to pursue justice, but rather when and how.

Addressing the security and the social and economic needs of affected populations creates a favourable environment for the pursuit of peace and justice and often corresponds to the most urgent expectations of post-conflict societies. But meeting these needs is neither a precondition nor a substitute for the pursuit of justice and other efforts to deal with the past.

2. Ending impunity

The most serious crimes of concern to the international community, notably genocide, war crimes, and crimes against humanity, must not go unpunished and their effective prosecution must be ensured. The emergence of this principle as a norm under international law has changed the parameters for the pursuit of peace.

As a minimal application of this principle, amnesties must not be granted to those bearing the greatest responsibility for genocide, crimes against humanity and serious violations of international humanitarian law.

Each State has the primary responsibility to protect its population from these crimes. This responsibility entails the prevention, investigation and prosecution of such crimes.

3. A victim-centred approach

Victims are central to peacebuilding, justice and reconciliation and should play an active role in such processes. Their concerns should enjoy a high priority.

4. Legitimacy

The legitimacy of strategies for pursuing peace and justice is crucial and closely linked to local ownership and compliance with the international normative framework. These strategies need to be informed by local circumstances and expectations.

5. Reconciliation

Rebuilding relationships between formerly antagonistic groups and strengthening the capacity of societies to transform themselves and their animosities contribute to the search for peace. Reconciliation requires the restoration of trust in equitable public institutions and respect for equal rights. It entails dialogue on conflicting versions of the past and addressing justice, accountability and the interests of victims.

IV. Recommendations

1. Making peace

1.1 While recognizing the imperative to stop the fighting and end the suffering, negotiations must build the foundation for both peace and justice.

1.2 Mediators bear a responsibility to contribute creatively to the immediate ending of violence and hostilities while promoting sustainable solutions. Their commitment to the core principles of the international legal order has to be beyond doubt. They should promote knowledge among the parties about the normative framework, including international human rights standards and humanitarian law, and available options for its implementation, so that the parties can make informed choices. They should be attentive to developmental needs, so that those needs are addressed from the outset.

1.3 Consultations with a broad range of actors, in particular victims, civil society, and women, need to be held as soon as possible.

1.4 While public security and governance demands are critical in the immediate post-conflict period, the consolidation and maintenance of peace need to be bolstered by a sense that grievances are being redressed through accountability, the establishment of legitimate State structures, and the elimination of the root causes of conflict.

1.5 Parties to a conflict should agree on measures that contribute to dismantling the causes of impunity and violence, such as disbanding non-State armed groups, repealing emergency laws, and vetting officials implicated in human rights abuses, and on modalities for implementing such measures.

2. **Dealing with the past**

2.1 Dealing with the past is essential to a society's present and future. While there is no standard model for dealing with the past, there are a range of proved measures that can assist a society in this endeavour. They should be both comprehensive and inclusive, engaging all relevant actors.

2.2 These measures should help a society to transform itself through governance, structural and institutional reforms, particularly in the fields of justice, human rights, education and the security sector, and should promote a culture of peace and non-violence.

2.3 Outreach and consultation are crucial elements of legitimacy and ownership of transitional justice measures. All those involved need to understand fully the potential and limitations of available options.

2.4 Transitional justice strategies should integrate criminal justice, truth-seeking, reparations and institutional reform. The relationship between these various elements and the socio-economic dimension of justice should be given early consideration. It should take into account the principle of complementarity between national and international mechanisms.

2.5 Traditional and community justice measures, when operating within the bounds of international human rights standards, can play an important role.

2.6 Amnesties, other than for those bearing the greatest responsibility for genocide, crimes against humanity and war crimes, may be permissible in a specific context and may even be required for the release, demobilization and reintegration of conflict-related prisoners and detainees.

2.7 Justice and victim-centred approaches should be given the same level of attention and resources as security sector reform, disarmament, demobilization and reintegration, and other stabilization measures.

2.8 Particular attention should be given to the increased representation and the full and active involvement of women in transitional justice strategies. Appropriate measures should be taken to protect the dignity and privacy of victims and witnesses, in particular when the crimes involve sexual or gender violence. Post-conflict legal orders should rectify legal and social discrimination based on gender.

2.9 Reparations programmes should include restitution, compensation and rehabilitation, and should entail public recognition of victims as citizens, thus contributing to the restoration of trust in civic institutions and to social solidarity.

2.10 An effective transitional justice strategy will contribute to reconciliation. Reconciliation may include symbolic measures such as asking for forgiveness, removing compromised symbols, and searching for common identities.

3. **Promoting development**

3.1 Conflict often results from a lack of social justice. Addressing root causes of conflict and supporting access to public goods and services, economic resources and opportunities in a non-discriminatory and equitable manner are a critical part of peacebuilding and development programmes. Special attention should be given to those most affected by the conflict.

3.2 Supporting institutional reform processes, which allow for socio-economic development, participation in decision-making, the rule of law and respect for human rights are also important development goals.

3.3 Transitional justice mechanisms and development efforts have specific and distinct roles, which should complement each other and be integrated into comprehensive peacebuilding strategies.

3.4 National and international development actors should be sensitive in dealing with the past when designing post-conflict development strategies and take into account relevant recommendations of accountability mechanisms.

Annex

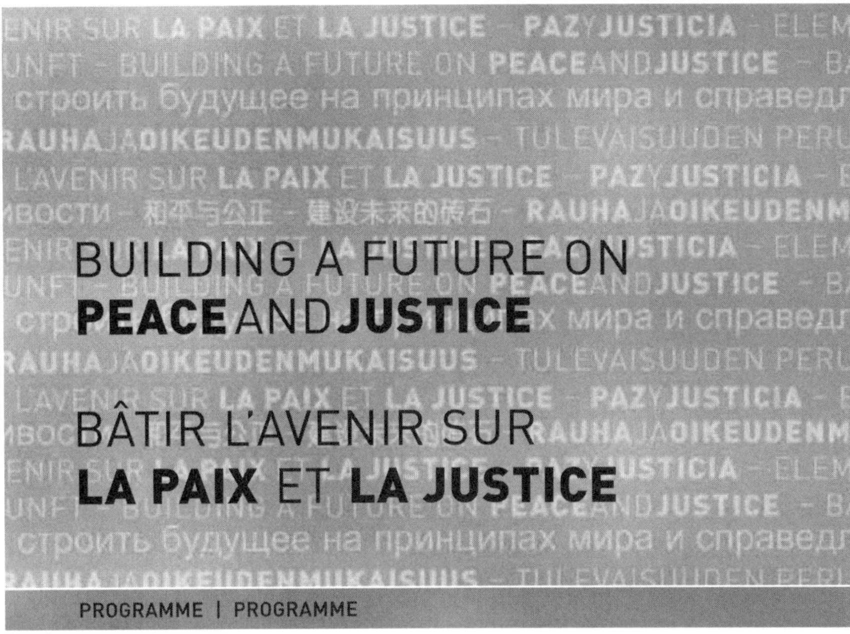

International conference
Building a Future on Peace and Justice
Nuremberg, 25 – 27 June 2007

Conférence internationale
Bâtir l'avenir sur la paix et la justice
Nuremberg, 25 – 27 juin 2007

Programme

K. Ambos et al. (eds.), *Building a Future on Peace and Justice: Studies on Transitional Justice, Peace and Development.*

FRIEDENUNDGERECHTIGKEIT
BAUSTEINE DER ZUKUNFT

2 CONTENTS | SOMMAIRE 3

PREFACE

— **Peace and justice** are key goals in the work of the United Nations and a number of regional organisations. Institutions and mechanisms designed to achieve justice are acquiring increasing importance worldwide, as the example of the International Criminal Court shows.

— **Peace and justice** are not contradictory forces. Rather, properly pursued, they promote and sustain one another. But there are situations in which peace and justice appear to compete. The question, then, can never be whether to pursue justice and accountability, but rather when and how. At the conference, some 300 invited participants, including representatives of states and international organisations, practitioners, academics and members of civil society from all over the world will endeavour to contribute to a better understanding of the tensions that may arise between peace and justice and to make proposals for dealing with them constructively and creatively. Ultimately, the conference outcomes are intended to translate into concrete recommendations for action by governments and international organisations.

PRÉFACE

— **La paix et la justice** sont des objectifs majeurs des travaux des Nations Unies et d'un certain nombre d'organisations régionales. Comme le montre l'exemple de la Cour Pénale Internationale, les institutions et les mécanismes conçus pour assurer la justice prennent de plus en plus d'importance à l'échelle mondiale.

— **La paix et la justice** ne sont pas des forces contradictoires. Au contraire, correctement appliquées, elles se privilégient et se soutiennent mutuellement. Mais il y a des situations où la paix et la justice sont apparemment en concurrence. La question, alors, ne peut jamais être de savoir s'il faut appliquer le principe de justice et de responsabilité, mais de savoir quand et comment. Lors de la conférence, quelque 300 participants invités, parmi lesquels des représentants d'états et d'organisations internationales, des professionnels, des universitaires et des membres de la société civile venus du monde entier, tenteront d'apporter leur contribution à une meilleure compréhension des tensions susceptibles d'apparaître entre justice et paix, et de faire des propositions pour aborder ces tensions de manière constructive et créative. Finalement, les conclusions de la conférence doivent se traduire en recommandations concrètes de mesures à prendre par les gouvernements et les organisations internationales.

FRIEDENUND**GERECHTIGKEIT** – BAUSTEINE
ELEMENTOS CONFORMADORES DEL FUTURO – строить бу
المستقبل بناء فى أساسيتان لبنتان - العدالة و السلام - **RAUHA**JA**OIKE**
BÂTIR L'AVENIR SUR **LA PAIX** ET **LA JU**
будущее на принципах мира и справедливости –
FRIEDENUND**GERECHTIGKEIT** – BAUSTEINE DER ZUKUNFT – BUIL

PAZY**JUSTICIA**
ELEMENTOS CONFORMADORES DEL FUTURO

4 PANEL DISCUSSION 1 | PANEL 1 5

OPENING CEREMONY

Monday, 25 June 2007
09.30 – 11.30 h | Higher Regional Court of Nuremberg, Crown Courtroom 600

HOSTED BY
- Günter Gloser, German Minister of State for Europe

KEYNOTE SPEAKERS
- Frank-Walter Steinmeier, German Foreign Minister
- Sharif Al-Zu'bi, Minister of Justice of the Hashemite Kingdom of Jordan
- Sonia Picado, former Executive Director of the Inter-American Institute of Human Rights, Personal Representative of Oscar Arias, President of Costa Rica
- Luis Moreno-Ocampo, Prosecutor of the International Criminal Court

English, Arabic, German
Interpreting service into English, French, Spanish and German

— In post-conflict situations, peace must be built on efforts to deal with a legacy of genocide, war crimes and crimes against humanity. This is an important heritage of the Nuremberg Trials, where 60 years ago the nazi crimes were tried. The site of these trials – Courtroom 600 of the Higher Regional Court of Nuremberg – is an appropriate setting for the opening ceremony that features addresses by four distinguished speakers.

CÉRÉMONIE D'OUVERTURE

Lundi, 25 Juin 2007
09.30 – 11.30 h | Tribunal Régional Supérieur de Nuremberg, Salle d'assises 600

PRÉSIDÉE PAR
- Günter Gloser, Ministre adjoint allemand, chargé des Affaires européennes

CONFÉRENCIERS PRINCIPAUX
- Frank-Walter Steinmeier, Ministre federal allemand des Affaires étrangères
- Sharif Al-Zu'bi, Ministre de la Justice du Royaume hachémite de Jordanie
- Sonia Picado, ancienne présidente de l'Institut interaméricain des droits de l'homme, représentante personnelle du président Oscar Arias du Costa Rica
- Luis Moreno-Ocampo, Procureur de la Cour Pénale Internationale

anglais, arabe, allemand
Service d'interprétation en anglais, français, espagnol et allemand

— Dans les situations post-conflit, l'instauration de la paix doit s'appuyer sur la volonté d'aborder la question de l'héritage du génocide, des crimes de guerre et des crimes contre l'humanité. C'est là un important héritage des procès de Nuremberg où, il y a 60 ans, les crimes nazis ont été jugés. Le site de ces procès – la salle d'assises 600 du Tribunal Régional Supérieur de Nuremberg – est un cadre approprié pour la cérémonie d'ouverture au cours de laquelle quatre invités de marque prendront la parole.

NEGOTIATING PEACE AND CONFLICT RESOLUTION

Monday, 25 June 2007
14.00 – 15.00 h | Congress Center Nuremberg (CCN Ost), room "Sydney"

HOSTED BY
- Antje Herrberg, Crisis Management Initiative

KEYNOTE SPEAKERS
- Martti Ahtisaari, President of the Crisis Management Initiative
- Lakhdar Brahimi, former United Nations Special Representative to Iraq, Afghanistan and Haiti
- Gareth Evans, President and Chief Executive of the International Crisis Group
- Juan Méndez, former United Nations Secretary-General Special Adviser on the Prevention of Genocide, President of the International Center for Transitional Justice
- Rangin Dadfar Spanta, Foreign Minister of Afghanistan

English
Interpreting service into French and German

— In the first of four high-level panel discussions, eminent practitioners will discuss how mediators attempt to facilitate solutions that are perceived as sustainable and legitimate by disentangling the knot of peace and justice, personal and collective interests, the immediate demands of the situation and the imperatives of often complex international norms and standards. How can the interests of conflict actors, of affected populations, of vulnerable groups and of the international community be integrated in mediation processes?

NÉGOCIATION DE LA PAIX ET RÉSOLUTION DES CONFLITS

Lundi, 25 Juin 2007
14.00 – 15.00 h | Congress Center Nuremberg (CCN Ost), salle "Sydney"

PRÉSIDÉ PAR
- Antje Herrberg, Crisis Management Initiative

CONFÉRENCIERS PRINCIPAUX
- Martti Ahtisaari, Président du Crisis Management Initiative
- Lakhdar Brahimi, ancien Représentant spécial des Nations Unies pour l'Iraq, l'Afghanistan et Haïti
- Gareth Evans, Président du International Crisis Group
- Juan Méndez, ancien Conseiller spécial du Haut Commissariat aux droits de l'homme pour la prévention des génocides du Secrétaire général des Nations Unies, Président du International Center for Transitional Justice
- Rangin Dadfar Spanta, Ministre des Affaires étrangères d'Afghanistan

anglais
Service d'interprétation en français et allemand

— Dans le premier des quatre panels de haut niveau, d'éminents intervenants discuteront de la façon dont les médiateurs tentent de faciliter l'adoption de solutions perçues comme durables et légitimes en démêlant le nœud de la paix et de la justice, des intérêts personnels et collectifs, des exigences immédiates de la situation et des impératifs de normes et de critères internationaux souvent complexes. Comment peut-on concilier les intérêts des acteurs d'un conflit, des populations touchées, des groupes vulnérables et de la communauté internationale dans le processus de médiation?

FRIEDENUND**GERECHTIGKEIT** – BAUSTEINE DI
ELEMENTOS CONFORMADORES DEL FUTURO – строить буду
السلام و العدالة - لبنتان أساسيتان في بناء المستقبل - **RAUHA**JA**OIKEU**

السلام والعدالة لبنتان أساسيتان في بناء المستقبل

6 PANEL DISCUSSION 2 | PANEL 2

JUSTICE AND HUMAN RIGHTS

Monday, 25 June 2007
15.00 – 16.00 h | Congress Center
Nuremberg (CCN Ost), room "Sydney"

HOSTED BY
- Marieke Wierda, International Center for Transitional Justice

KEYNOTE SPEAKERS
- Lord Bonomy, Judge, International Criminal Tribunal for the former Yugoslavia
- Jan Egeland, United Nations Special Adviser
- Elisabeth Rehn, former Special Representative of the United Nations Secretary-General in Bosnia and Herzegovina
- Yasmin Sooka, Foundation for Human Rights in South Africa

English
Interpreting service into French and German

— Transitional justice stems from the increased recognition that massive human rights violations occurring during a period of conflict ought to be confronted through a range of techniques such as truth-seeking, reparations, institutional reforms, criminal justice and reconciliation. A set of renowned personalities will discuss the role of human rights issues in peace negotiations and how justice issues and armed conflict have an impact on each other. These complex issues include the possibility of amnesties and the role of the International Criminal Court.

JUSTICE ET DROITS HUMAINS

Lundi, 25 Juin 2007
15.00 – 16.00 h | Congress Center
Nuremberg (CCN Ost), salle "Sydney"

PRÉSIDÉ PAR
- Marieke Wierda, International Center for Transitional Justice

CONFÉRENCIERS PRINCIPAUX
- Lord Bonomy, Juge, Tribunal Pénal International pour l'ex-Yougoslavie
- Jan Egeland, Conseiller spécial des Nations Unies
- Elisabeth Rehn, ancienne Représentante spéciale du Secrétaire général des Nations Unies en Bosnie-Herzégovine
- Yasmin Sooka, Fondation pour les droits humains en Afrique du Sud

anglais
Service d'interprétation en français et allemand

— La justice transitoire résulte de la reconnaissance accrue du fait que les violations massives des droits humains en période de conflit doivent être confrontées à un éventail de techniques telles que la recherche de la vérité, les réparations, les réformes institutionnelles, la justice pénale et la réconciliation. Plusieurs personnalités éminentes discuteront du rôle des droits humains dans les négociations de paix et de l'impact que les questions de justice et les conflits armés ont l'un sur l'autre. Ces questions complexes aborderont également la possibilité des amnisties et le rôle de la Cour Pénale Internationale.

PANEL DISCUSSION 3 | PANEL 3 7

SOCIAL, ECONOMIC AND POLITICAL DEVELOPMENT

Monday, 25 June 2007
16.30 – 17.30 h | Congress Center
Nuremberg (CCN Ost), room "Sydney"

HOSTED BY
- Chandra Sriram, University of East London

KEYNOTE SPEAKERS
- Kathleen Cravero, Director United Nations Development Programme Bureau for Crisis Prevention & Recovery
- Alvaro de Soto, former United Nations Special Coordinator for the Middle East Peace Process
- Frances Johnson Morris, Minister of Justice of Liberia
- Sadako Ogata, President of the Japan International Cooperation Agency, former United Nations High Commissioner for Refugees

English
Interpreting service into French and German

— In peace negotiations and post-conflict peace-building, immediate humanitarian needs as well as the needs of longer-term social, economic and political development must be addressed and inequalities which often lie at the root of the conflict must be overcome. Balancing measures to deal with the past and forward-looking strategies is a challenge, involving questions such as appropriate resource allocation, timing and sequencing. These issues will be discussed in the third panel, featuring again eminent practitioners.

DÉVELOPPEMENT SOCIAL, ÉCONOMIQUE ET POLITIQUE

Lundi, 25 Juin 2007
16.30 – 17.30 h | Congress Center
Nuremberg (CCN Ost), salle "Sydney"

PRÉSIDÉ PAR
- Chandra Sriram, University of East London

CONFÉRENCIERS PRINCIPAUX
- Kathleen Cravero, Directrice du Bureau du Programme des Nations Unies pour le développement de la prévention et le relèvement
- Alvaro de Soto, ancien Coordonnateur spécial pour le processus de paix des Nations Unies au Moyen-Orient
- Frances Johnson Morris, Ministre de la Justice du Liberia
- Sadako Ogata, Présidente de l'Agence de Coopération Internationale Japonaise, ancienne Haut Commissaire des Nations Unies pour les réfugiés

anglais
Service d'interprétation en français et allemand

— Dans les négociations de paix et les efforts d'instauration d'une paix post-conflit, la question des besoins humanitaires immédiats et des besoins de développement social, économique et politique à plus long terme doit être abordée et les inégalités qui sont souvent la cause profonde du conflit doivent être éliminées. Trouver un équilibre entre les mesures pour surmonter le passé et les stratégies pour aller à l'avant est un véritable défi à relever, et pose notamment la question de la bonne allocation des ressources du calendrier et des étapes à respecter. Ces questions seront abordées dans le troisième panel auquel participeront, là encore, d'éminents intervenants.

KEIT – BAUSTEINE DER ZUKUNFT – BUILDING A FUTURE ON **PEACE**AND**JUSTICE**
TURO – строить будущее на принципах мира и справедливости
السلا – **RAUHA**JA**OIKEUDENMUKAISUUS** – TULEVAISUUDEN PERUSTA

BÂTIR L'AVENIR SUR **LA PAIX** ET **LA JUSTICE**

SUSTAINABLE PEACE-BUILDING

Monday, 25 June 2007
17.30 – 18.15 h | Congress Center
Nuremberg (CCN Ost), room "Sydney"

FACILITATED BY
- Lyse Doucet, Correspondent for BBC World TV

KEYNOTE SPEAKERS
- Jan Egeland, United Nations Special Adviser
- Frances Johnson Morris, Minister of Justice of Liberia
- Ian Martin, Special Representative of the Secretary-General United Nations Mission in Nepal
- Sadako Ogata, President of the Japan International Cooperation Agency, former United Nations High Commissioner for Refugees
- Rangin Dadfar Spanta, Foreign Minister of Afghanistan
- Alvaro de Soto, former United Nations Special Coordinator for the Middle East Peace Process

English
Interpreting service into French and German

— Sustainable peace-building must flow from an integrated approach that incorporates peace, justice and development. But the international community is still struggling with integrated approaches. What have we learnt from experiences in the Balkans, West Africa, Timor-Leste, Afghanistan and elsewhere? Are there lessons that we draw from these examples? What principles and tools have emerged over the last decade? This panel, moderated by BBC journalist Lyse Doucet, will attempt to project an integrated view.

BÂTIR UNE PAIX DURABLE

Lundi, 25 Juin 2007
17.30 – 18.15 h | Congress Center
Nuremberg (CCN Ost), salle "Sydney"

MODÉRÉ PAR
- Lyse Doucet, Correspondante pour BBC World TV

CONFÉRENCIERS PRINCIPAUX
- Jan Egeland, Conseiller spécial des Nations Unies
- Frances Johnson Morris, Ministre de la Justice du Liberia
- Ian Martin, Représentant spécial du Secrétaire général de la Mission des Nations Unies au Népal
- Sadako Ogata, Présidente de l'Agence de Coopération Internationale Japonaise, ancienne Haut Commissaire des Nations Unies pour les réfugiés
- Rangin Dadfar Spanta, Ministre des Affaires étrangères d'Afghanistan
- Alvaro de Soto, ancien Coordonnateur spécial pour le processus de paix des Nations Unies au Moyen-Orient

anglais
Service d'interprétation en français et allemand

— L'instauration d'une paix durable doit découler d'une approche intégrée tenant compte de la paix, de la justice et du développement. Mais la communauté internationale ne maîtrise toujours pas cette notion d'approche intégrée. Qu'avons-nous appris des expériences des Balkans, de l'Afrique de l'Ouest, du Timor-Leste, de l'Afghanistan et ailleurs? Y a-t-il des leçons à tirer de ces exemples? Quels nouveaux principes et outils sont apparus au cours de la dernière décennie? Présidé par Lyse Doucet, journaliste pour BBC, ce panel tentera de donner un point de vue intégré.

CONCERT & RECEPTION

Monday, 25 June 2007
20.00 | Historical City Hall

HOSTED BY
- Ulrich Maly, Mayor of the City of Nuremberg

WELCOME ADDRESS by Ulrich Maly, Mayor of the City of Nuremberg and Peter Theiner for the participating foundations: Dräger Foundation and Robert Bosch Stiftung

POEM by Isabelle Balot, music performed by Sebastian Hess (cello) and Olaf Dreßler (piano) – world premiere

CONCERT by the Nuremberg Symphony Orchestra, Sebastian Hess (cello) and Olaf Dreßler (piano), including a world premiere of a composition by Mikis Theodorakis

RECEPTION hosted by the City of Nuremberg

German, English, French
Interpreting service into English

We would like to thank Sparkasse Nürnberg for its kind support of this event.

Please bring your name badge and invitation in order to gain admission.

CONCERT & RECEPTION

Lundi, 25 Juin 2007
20.00 h | Hôtel de ville historique

PRÉSIDÉS PAR
- Ulrich Maly, Maire de la Ville de Nuremberg

DISCOURS DE BIENVENUE de Ulrich Maly, maire de la ville de Nuremberg et Peter Theiner pour les fondations: Dräger Foundation et Robert Bosch Stiftung

POÈME d'Isabelle Balot, accompagnement musical de Sebastian Hess (violoncelle) et Olaf Dreßler (piano) – première mondiale

CONCERT de l'Orchestre Symphonique de Nuremberg, Sebastian Hess (violoncelle) and Olaf Dreßler (piano), avec une première mondiale d'une œuvre de Mikis Theodorakis

RÉCEPTION donnée par la Ville de Nuremberg

allemand, anglais, français
Service d'interprétation en anglais

Nous tenons à remercier la Sparkasse Nürnberg pour son aimable soutien à cette soirée.

Veuillez vous munir de votre badge et de votre invitation pour l'admission.

RAUHAJA**OIKEUDENMUKAISUUS**
TULEVAISUUDEN PERUSTA

10 | WORKSHOP 1 | ATELIER 1

FROM MEDIATION TO SUSTAINABLE PEACE

Tuesday, 26 June 2007
09.30 – 13.00 h | Congress Center
Nuremberg (CCN Ost), room "Kopenhagen"

CHAIR
- Judith Large, Crisis Management Initiative

EXPERTS
- Chandra Sriram, University of East London
- Christine Bell, University Ulster
- Lars Kirchhoff, University Viadrina

English
Interpreting service into German

— What are the connections between transitional justice and mediation? The workshop will discuss questions such as the integration of human rights elements into the design of mediation processes; matching specific mediation models with existing structures and conflict constellations; post-peace agreements, including monitoring.

WORKSHOP RESPONSIBLE
- Crisis Management Initiative

DE LA MÉDIATION À LA PAIX DURABLE

Mardi, 26 Juin 2007
09.30 – 13.00 h | Congress Center
Nuremberg (CCN Ost), salle "Kopenhagen"

PRÉSIDÉ PAR
- Judith Large, Crisis Management Initiative

EXPERTS
- Chandra Sriram, University of East London
- Christine Bell, University Ulster
- Lars Kirchhoff, University Viadrina

anglais
Service d'interprétation en allemand

— Quels sont les liens entre la justice transitionnelle et la médiation? L'atelier abordera, entre autres, l'intégration d'éléments des droits humains dans la conception des processus de médiation, la concordance de modèles de médiation spécifiques avec les structures existantes et la constellation du conflit, ainsi que les accords d'après-paix, y compris le suivi.

RESPONSABLE DE L'ATELIER
- Crisis Management Initiative

WORKSHOP 2 | ATELIER 2 | 11

JUSTICE IN SITUATIONS OF ONGOING CONFLICT

Tuesday, 26 June 2007
09.30 – 13.00 h | Congress Center
Nuremberg (CCN Ost), room "Kiew"

CHAIR
- Silvia Fernández, Ministry of Foreign Affairs Argentina

EXPERTS
- Adam O'Brien, International Crisis Group
- Michael Otim, Independent Expert, Gulu NGO Forum
- Marieke Wierda, International Center for Transitional Justice
- David Crane, Syracuse University
- Moses Chrispus Okello, Makerere University
- Patrick Vinck, University of California

English
Interpreting service into French and German

— Questions to be addressed include: Can there be sufficient rule of law and impartiality in situations of violent conflict to go ahead with justice programmes? What impact (favourable/unfavourable) do criminal proceedings have on peace processes? What considerations should guide justice institutions in times of conflict?

WORKSHOP RESPONSIBLE
- International Center for Transitional Justice

LA JUSTICE DANS LE CONTEXTE DES CONFLITS EN COURS

Mardi, 26 Juin 2007
09.30 – 13.00 h | Congress Center
Nuremberg (CCN Ost), salle "Kiew"

PRÉSIDÉ PAR
- Silvia Fernández, Ministère des affaires étrangères de l'Argentine

EXPERTS
- Adam O'Brien, International Crisis Group
- Michael Otim, Independent Expert, Gulu NGO Forum
- Marieke Wierda, International Center for Transitional Justice
- David Crane, Syracuse University
- Moses Chrispus Okello, Makerere University
- Patrick Vinck, University of California

anglais
Service d'interprétation en français et allemand

— Les questions à aborder sont les suivantes: la loi et l'impartialité sont-elles suffisantes dans les conflits violents en cours pour permettre des programmes de la justice? Quels sont les impacts (favorables/ défavorables) des procédures pénales sur les processus de la paix? Quelles considérations devraient guider les institutions judiciaires en période de conflits?

RESPONSABLE DE L'ATELIER
- International Center for Transitional Justice

ZUKUNFT – BUILDING A FUTURE ON **PEACE**AND**JUSTICE**
зе на принципах мира и справедливости
NMUKAISUUS – TULEVAISUUDEN PERUSTA
Е-строить будущее на принципах мира и справедлив
与公正 – 建设未来的[illegible]
A FUTURE ON **PEACE**AND**JUSTICE**
зе на принципах мира и справедливости
NMUKAISUUS – TULEVAISUUDEN PERUSTA

Строить будущее на принципах мира и справедливости

12 WORKSHOP 3 | ATELIER 3

LOOKING BACK AND MOVING FORWARD – THE NEXUS BETWEEN JUSTICE AND DEVELOPMENT

Tuesday, 26 June 2007
09.30 – 13.00 h | Congress Center
Nuremberg (CCN Ost), room "Istanbul"

CHAIR
- Dan Smith, International Alert

EXPERTS
- Ingrid Samset, Chr. Michelsen Institute
- Pablo de Greiff, International Center for Transitional Justice
- Rama Mani, International Center for Ethnic Studies
- Arjun Karki, Rural Reconstruction Nepal

English
Interpreting service into French and German

— Starting from a broad, multidimensional notion of sustainable peace, the workshop will discuss resource allocation, the sequencing and complementarity of actors and identify links between development cooperation/aid programmes and transitional justice mechanisms in the framework of country-specific development strategies.

WORKSHOP RESPONSIBLE
- Federal Ministry for Economic Cooperation and Development, Working Group on Development and Peace (FriEnt)

RÉTROSPECTIVE ET PERSPECTIVES – L'INTERFACE ENTRE JUSTICE ET DÉVELOPPEMENT

Mardi, 26 Juin 2007
09.30 – 13.00 h | Congress Center
Nuremberg (CCN Ost), salle "Istanbul"

PRÉSIDÉ PAR
- Dan Smith, International Alert

EXPERTS
- Ingrid Samset, Chr. Michelsen Institute
- Pablo de Greiff, International Center for Transitional Justice
- Rama Mani, International Center for Ethnic Studies
- Arjun Karki, Rural Reconstruction Nepal

anglais
Service d'interprétation en français et allemand

— Partant d'une acception large et multidimensionnelle de la notion de paix durable, cet atelier se penchera sur l'affectation des ressources, les missions et la complémentarité des acteurs, et il identifiera des liens entre la coopération du développement/les programmes d'aide et les mécanismes de la justice transitionnelle dans le cadre de stratégies nationales de développement.

RESPONSABLE DE L'ATELIER
- Ministère fédéral de la Coopération économique et du Développement, Groupe de travail Développement et Paix (FriEnt)

WORKSHOP 4 | ATELIER 4 13

THE LEGAL FRAMEWORK

Tuesday, 26 June 2007
09.30 – 13.00 h | Congress Center
Nuremberg (CCN Ost), room "Riga"

CHAIR
- Prof. Christian Tomuschat, Humboldt University Berlin

EXPERTS
- Kai Ambos, Georg-August-University Göttingen
- Diane Amann, University of California
- David Nsereko, University of Botswana
- Louise Mallinder, Queen's University Belfast

English
Interpreting service into German

— The workshop will take stock of the national and international legal framework regarding amnesties and the rights of victims (truth, participation, reparation, restitution), and will discuss legal issues arising out of the Rome Statute of the International Criminal Court.

WORKSHOP RESPONSIBLE
- Institute for Criminal Law and Criminal Justice, Department for Foreign and International Criminal Law, Georg-August-University Goettingen

LE CADRE JURIDIQUE

Mardi, 26 Juin 2007
09.30 – 13.00 h | Congress Center
Nuremberg (CCN Ost), salle "Riga"

PRÉSIDÉ PAR
- Prof. Christian Tomuschat, Humboldt University Berlin

EXPERTS
- Kai Ambos, Georg-August-University Göttingen
- Diane Amann, University of California
- David Nsereko, University of Botswana
- Louise Mallinder, Queen's University Belfast

anglais
Service d'interprétation en allemand

— Cet atelier dressera un inventaire des cadres juridiques nationaux et internationaux en ce qui concerne les amnisties et les droits des victimes (vérité, participation, réparation, restitution) et examinera les questions juridiques découlant du Statut de Rome de la Cour Pénale Internationale.

RESPONSABLE DE L'ATELIER
- Institut de criminologie, division de droit pénal étranger et international, l'Université Georg August, Göttingen

BÂTIR L'AVENIR SUR **LA PAIX** ET **L**
будущее на принципах мира и справедливост
FRIEDENUND**GERECHTIGKEIT** – BAUSTEINE DER ZUKUNFT – B
ELEMENTOS CONFORMADORES DEL FUTURO – **строить**
السلام و العدالة – لبنتان أساسيتان في بناء – **RAUHA**JAO
BÂTIR L'AVENIR
строить будущее на принципах мира и справедливост

BUILDING A FUTURE ON PEACEANDJUSTICE

14 | WORKSHOP 5 | ATELIER 5

LESSONS FROM NEGOTIATED JUSTICE OPTIONS IN SOUTH AFRICA AND COLOMBIA

Tuesday, 26 June 2007
09.30 – 13.00 h | Congress Center
Nuremberg (CCN Ost), room "Oslo"

CHAIR
- Nader Nadery, Afghanistan Independent Human Rights Commission

EXPERTS
- Paul van Zyl, International Center for Transitional Justice
- Graeme Simpson, International Center for Transitional Justice
- Roger Uprimny, Independent Expert, Colombia

English
Interpreting service into Spanish and German

— In a number of country contexts, justice options were capped during peace negotiations. How were these compromises arrived at? What impact do they have on the peace process? How are they perceived by victims? How does the continued presence of potential "spoilers" affect the situation?

WORKSHOP RESPONSIBLE
- International Center for Transitional Justice

LEÇONS TIRÉES DES OPTIONS DE JUSTICE NÉGOCIÉE EN AFRIQUE DU SUD ET EN COLOMBIE

Mardi, 26 Juin 2007
09.30 – 13.00 h | Congress Center
Nuremberg (CCN Ost), salle "Oslo"

PRÉSIDÉ PAR
- Nader Nadery, Afghanistan Independent Human Rights Commission

EXPERTS
- Paul van Zyl, International Center for Transitional Justice
- Graeme Simpson, International Center for Transitional Justice
- Roger Uprimny, Independent Expert, Colombia

anglais
Service d'interprétation en espagnol et allemand

— Dans un nombre de pays, la justice a été reléguée au second plan pendant les négociations de paix. Comment ces compromis ont-ils été possibles? Quelle est leur incidence sur le processus de paix? Comment sont-ils perçus par les victimes? En quoi la présence permanente de "fauteurs de troubles" potentiels affecte-t-elle la situation?

RESPONSABLE DE L'ATELIER
- International Center for Transitional Justice

WORKSHOP 6 | ATELIER 6 | 15

NEGOTIATING JUSTICE

Tuesday, 26 June 2007
14.30 – 18.00 h | Congress Center
Nuremberg (CCN Ost), room "Oslo"

CHAIR
- Tina Thorne, Centre for Humanitarian Dialogue

EXPERTS
- Leslie Vinjamuri, Georgetown University
- Priscilla Hayner, International Center for Transitional Justice
- Nick Grono, International Crisis Group

English
Interpreting service into Spanish and German

— Justice issues need to be dealt with as early as possible in the peace process. How have such issues been addressed in peace agreements? How do the mediators involved in negotiations view them? The workshop will draw on case studies by the Centre for Humanitarian Dialogue.

WORKSHOP RESPONSIBLE
- Crisis Management Initiative, Centre for Humanitarian Dialogue

NÉGOCIER LA JUSTICE

Mardi, 26 Juin 2007
14.30 – 18.00 h | Congress Center
Nuremberg (CCN Ost), salle "Oslo"

PRÉSIDÉ PAR
- Tina Thorne, Centre for Humanitarian Dialogue

EXPERTS
- Leslie Vinjamuri, Georgetown University
- Priscilla Hayner, International Center for Transitional Justice
- Nick Grono, International Crisis Group

anglais
Service d'interprétation en espagnol et allemand

— Il est nécessaire d'aborder la question de la justice le plus tôt possible dans le processus de paix. Comment ces questions ont-elles été prises en compte dans les accords de paix? Qu'en pensent les médiateurs impliqués dans les négociations? L'atelier prendra appui sur des études de cas du Centre for Humanitarian Dialogue.

RESPONSABLE DE L'ATELIER
- Crisis Management Initiative, Centre for Humanitarian Dialogue

– BUILDING A FUTURE ON **PEACE**AND**JUSTICE**
инципах мира и справедливости
UUS – TULEVAISUUDEN PERUSTA
ть будущее на принципах мира и справедлив
E ON **PEACE**AND**JUSTICE**

THE IMPACT OF THE INTERNATIONAL CRIMINAL COURT (ICC)

Tuesday, 26 June 2007
14.30 – 18.00 h | Congress Center
Nuremberg (CCN Ost), room "Riga"

CHAIR
- Prince Zeid Ra'ad Zeid Al-Hussein, Ambassador of the Hashemite Kingdom of Jordan to the United States of America

EXPERTS
- Paul Seils, International Criminal Court
- Suliman Baldo, International Center for Transitional Justice
- Barney Afako, Independent Expert, Uganda
- Tatiana Carayannis, Independent Expert, Democratic Republic Congo

English
Interpreting service into German

— The workshop will shed light on the complementary relationship between the International Criminal Court and national justice systems. It will discuss the risks and benefits of International Criminal Court action in areas of conflict, including its role as an actor/catalyst in promoting security, humanitarian issues and development.

WORKSHOP RESPONSIBLE
- Government of the Hashemite Kingdom of Jordan with support from the International Centre for Transitional Justice

L'IMPACT DE LA COUR PÉNALE INTERNATIONALE (CPI)

Mardi, 26 Juin 2007
14.30 – 18.00 h | Congress Center
Nuremberg (CCN Ost), salle "Riga"

PRÉSIDÉ PAR
- Ambassadeur du Royaume hachémite de Jordanie auprès des Etats-Unis

EXPERTS
- Paul Seils, Cour Pénale Internationale
- Suliman Baldo, International Center for Transitional Justice
- Barney Afako, Independent Expert, Uganda
- Tatiana Carayannis, Independent Expert, Democratic Republic Congo

anglais
Service d'interprétation en allemand

— Cet atelier élucidera la complémentarité de la Cour Pénale Internationale et des systèmes judiciaires nationaux. La discussion portera sur les risques et les bénéfices de l'action de la Cour Pénale Internationale dans les zones de conflit, et sur son rôle d'acteur/de catalyseur dans la promotion de la sécurité, de l'aide humanitaire et du développement.

RESPONSABLE DE L'ATELIER
- Gouvernement du Royaume hachémite de Jordanie avec l'appui du International Center for Transitional Justice

RECONCILIATION

Tuesday, 26 June 2007
14.30 – 18.00 h | Congress Center
Nuremberg (CCN Ost), room "Istanbul"

CHAIR
- Yasmin Sooka, Foundation for Human Rights in South Africa

EXPERTS
- Hizkias Assefa, Center for Justice and Peacebuilding, Eastern Mennonite University
- David Bloomfield, Berghof Research Center
- Mohammad Farid Hamidi, Afghanistan Independent Human Rights Commission
- Hugo van de Merwe, Centre for the Study of Violence and Reconciliation

English
Interpreting service into French and German

— The workshop will discuss the importance of reconciliation, understood as a pragmatic process of building group relationships: How does this process relate to other justice and development requirements? What is the role of civil society in building such relationships? Gender justice and reconciliation?

WORKSHOP RESPONSIBLE
- Centre for the Study of Violence and Reconciliation, Friedrich-Ebert-Stiftung

RÉCONCILIATION

Mardi, 26 Juin 2007
14.30 – 18.00 h | Congress Center
Nuremberg (CCN Ost), salle "Istanbul"

PRÉSIDÉ PAR
- Yasmin Sooka, Foundation for Human Rights in South Africa

EXPERTS
- Hizkias Assefa, Center for Justice and Peacebuilding, Eastern Mennonite University
- David Bloomfield, Berghof Research Center
- Mohammad Farid Hamidi, Afghanistan Independent Human Rights Commission
- Hugo van de Merwe, Centre for the Study of Violence and Reconciliation

anglais
Service d'interprétation en français et allemand

— L'atelier portera son attention sur l'importance de la réconciliation, comprise comme un processus pragmatique de création de liens entre les groupes. Quelle interaction existe-t-il entre ce processus et d'autres exigences pour la justice et le développement? Quel est le rôle de la société civile dans l'établissement de ces relations? Traitement équitable entre les sexes et la réconciliation?

RESPONSABLE DE L'ATELIER
- Centre for the Study of Violence and Reconciliation, Friedrich-Ebert-Stiftung

FRIEDENUND**GERECHTIGKEIT**
BAUSTEINE DER ZUKUNFT

JUSTICE MECHANISMS AND THE QUESTION OF LEGITIMACY: CONCEPTS AND CHALLENGES

Tuesday, 26 June 2007
14.30 – 18.00 h | Congress Center
Nuremberg (CCN Ost), room "Kiew"

CHAIR
- Jürg Lindenmann, Swiss Federal Department of Foreign Affairs

EXPERTS
- Pierre Hazan, City of Geneva
- Refik Hodzic, International Criminal Tribunal for the former Yugoslavia
- Barbara Oomen, Roosevelt Academy, Utrecht University
- Habib Nassar, Human Rights First

English
Interpreting service into French and German

— Based on three case studies, the workshop will seek to clarify the legitimacy of internal and external actors and justice mechanisms. To that end it will discuss concepts of the legitimacy of justice, perceptions of external and internal justice models, and challenges for the transition from external to local justice mechanisms.

WORKSHOP RESPONSIBLE
- Co-organised by the Working Group on Development and Peace (FriEnt), and the Center for Peacebuilding (KOFF) - swisspeace

LES MÉCANISMES DE JUSTICE ET LA QUESTION DE LA LÉGITIMITÉ: CONCEPTS ET DÉFIS

Mardi, 26 Juin 2007
14.30 – 18.00 h | Congress Center
Nuremberg (CCN Ost), salle "Kiew"

PRÉSIDÉ PAR
- Jürg Lindenmann, Swiss Federal Department of Foreign Affairs

EXPERTS
- Pierre Hazan, City of Geneva
- Refik Hodzic, International Criminal Tribunal for the former Yugoslavia
- Barbara Oomen, Roosevelt Academy, Utrecht University
- Habib Nassar, Human Rights First

anglais
Service d'interprétation en français et allemand

— Basé sur trois études de cas, l'atelier s'emploiera à clarifier la légitimité des acteurs et des mécanismes de la justice, internes et externes. À la fin, il examinera des conceptions de la légitimité de la justice, la perception de modèles de justice externes et internes et les défis qu'implique la transition d'une justice externe vers une justice locale.

RESPONSABLE DE L'ATELIER
- Co-organisé par le Groupe de travail Développement et Paix (FriEnt) et le Centre pour la promotion de la paix (KOFF) - swisspeace

ZUKUNFT – BUILDING A FUTURE ON **PEACE**AND**JUSTICE**
ее на принципах мира и справедливости
:NMUKAISUUS – TULEVAISUUDEN PERUSTA
CE-строить будущее на принципах мира и справедлив
与公正 – 建设未来的砖石

ALTERNATIVE APPROACHES TO DEALING WITH THE PAST

Tuesday, 26 June 2007
14.30 – 18.00 h | Congress Center
Nuremberg (CCN Ost), room "Kopenhagen"

CHAIR
- Mark Salter, International Institute for Democracy and Electoral Assistance

EXPERTS
- Paloma Aguilar, Universidad Nacional de Educación a Distancia, Spain
- Stef Vandeginste, University of Antwerp
- Victor Igreja, Leiden University

English
Interpreting service into German

— How have some countries achieved (relative) stability and human rights protection despite the absence of formal or recognised transitional justice mechanisms? The workshop will examine some of the more frequently cited examples.

WORKSHOP RESPONSIBLE
- Crisis Management Initiative

DE NOUVELLES APPROCHES POUR SURMONTER LE PASSÉ

Mardi, 26 Juin 2007
14.30 – 18.00 h | Congress Center
Nuremberg (CCN Ost), salle "Kopenhagen"

PRÉSIDÉ PAR
- Mark Salter, International Institute for Democracy and Electoral Assistance

EXPERTS
- Paloma Aguilar, Universidad Nacional de Educación a Distancia, Spain
- Stef Vandeginste, University of Antwerp
- Victor Igreja, Leiden University

anglais
Service d'interprétation en allemand

— Comment certains pays sont-ils parvenus à une stabilité (relative) et à protéger les droits humains malgré l'absence de mécanismes de justice transitionnelle formels ou reconnus? L'atelier examinera quelques-uns des exemples les plus fréquemment cités.

RESPONSABLE DE L'ATELIER
- Crisis Management Initiative

PAZ Y **JUSTICIA**
ELEMENTOS CONFORMADORES DEL FUTURO

RECEPTION HOSTED BY THE GOVERNMENT OF THE STATE OF BAVARIA

Tuesday, 26 June 2007
20.00 h | Imperial Castle

HOSTED BY
- Günther Beckstein, Deputy Bavarian Prime Minister and Bavarian Minister of the Interior

WELCOME ADDRESS by Günther Beckstein, Deputy Bavarian Prime Minister and Bavarian Minister of the Interior and Erkki Tuomioja, Member of Parliament, former Finnish Foreign Minister

VISIT of the old chapel (optional)

German, English
Interpreting service into English

Please bring your name badge and invitation in order to gain admission.

RECEPTION DONNÉE PAR LE GOUVERNEMENT DE L'ETAT LIBRE DE BAVIERE

Mardi, 26 Juin 2007
20.00 h | château impérial

PRÉSIDÉE PAR
- Günther Beckstein, Vice Premier ministre et ministre de l'Intérieur de Bavière

DISCOURS DE BIENVENUE de Günther Beckstein, Vice Premier ministre et ministre de l'Intérieur de Bavière et Erkki Tuomioja, membre du Parlement, ancien ministre finlandais des Affaires étrangères

VISITE de la vieille chapelle (facultatif)

allemand, anglais
Service d'interprétation en anglais

Veuillez vous munir de votre badge et de votre invitation pour l'admission.

WRAP-UP

Wednesday, 27 June 2007
09.30 – 11.00 h | Congress Center
Nuremberg (CCN Ost), room "Sydney"

WORKHOP SUMMARY REPORT
- Prince Zeid Ra'ad Zeid Al-Hussein, Ambassador of the Hashemite Kingdom of Jordan to the United States of America

CLOSING CEREMONY

Wednesday, 27 June 2007
11.30 – 12.00 h | Congress Center
Nuremberg (CCN Ost), room "Sydney"

HOSTED BY
- Prince Zeid Ra'ad Zeid Al-Hussein, Ambassador of the Hashemite Kingdom of Jordan to the United States of America

SPEAKERS
- Erkki Tuomioja, Member of Parliament, former Finnish Foreign Minister
- Günther Gloser, German Minister of State for Europe (farewell)

English
Interpreting service into French and German

— On the closing day of the conference, the results of the workshops will be reported back to the plenary. This will also provide a first opportunity to identify the main, recurrent insights of the conference, to draw political conclusions and to make the first steps towards condensating the conference results into political recommendations. Günther Gloser will bid farewell to conference participants.

SYNTHÈSE

Mercredi, 27 Juin 2007
09.30 – 11.00 h | Congress Center
Nuremberg (CCN Ost), salle "Sydney"

ATELIER – RAPPORT DE SYNTHÈSE
- Prince Zeid Ra'ad Zeid Al-Hussein, Ambassadeur du Royaume hachémite de Jordanie auprés des États-Unis

CÉRÉMONIE DE CLÔTURE

Mercredi, 27 Juin 2007
11.30 – 12.00 h | Congress Center
Nuremberg (CCN Ost), salle "Sydney"

PRÉSIDÉE PAR
- Prince Zeid Ra'ad Zeid Al-Hussein, Ambassadeur du Royaume hachémite de Jordanie auprés des États-Unis

CONFÉRENCIERS
- Erkki Tuomioja, membre du Parlement, ancien ministre finlandais des Affaires étrangères
- Günther Gloser, Ministre adjoint allemand, chargé des affaires européennes (adieu)

anglais
Service d'interprétation en français et allemand

— Le jour de clôture de la conférence, les résultats des ateliers seront portés à la connaissance de la plénière. Ce fournira une première occasion pour identifié les principaux enseignements de la conférence, pour tirer des conclusions politiques et pour commencer à faire la synthèse des résultats de la conférence et à les transcrire en recommendations politiques. Günther Gloser prendra congé des participants à la conférence.

BÂTIR L'AVENIR SUR **LA PAIX** ET L
будущее на принципах мира и справедливос
FRIEDENUND**GERECHTIGKEIT** – BAUSTEINE DER ZUKUNFT – I

List of Participants

Counsellor Hindi Elmahdi Abdlatif Director of International Organization Department, Ministry of Foreign Affairs Libya

Mr. Ibrahim Abdulle Director, Center for Research and Dialogue - Somalia (CRD), Canada

Mr. Ram Prasad Acharya Organization For Peace, Human Rights and Conflict Studies (OPHC), Nepal

Ms. Chadia Afkir Human Rights Officer, Integrated Office of the United Nations in Burundi, France/Morocco

Mr. Wolfgang Ahrens Head of Project, Deutsche Gesellschaft für Technische Zusammenarbeit (GTZ) GmbH, Germany

Dr. Zuhair Fahd Al Harthy Board Member, Human Rights Commission Saudi Arabia, Saudi Arabia

Mr. Turki Said Al Shehri Researcher, Organizations and International Relations, Human Rights Commission Saudi Arabia, Saudi Arabia

Ms. Safia Al Souhail Member of the Iraqi Parliament, Iraqi Parliament, Iraq

Colonel Saif Ahmad Al-Aamri Head of Legal Affairs, Ministry of Defense QA, Qatar

Staff Brigadier-General Salim Fahd Al-Hababi Ministry of Defense QA, Qatar

His Excellency Khalfia Al-Harthy Ambassador, Embassy of Oman, Oman

His Excellency Alaa Al-Hashimy Ambassador, Embassy of the Republic of Iraq, Iraq

Mr. Ali Al-Nasani Amnesty International, Germany

Mr. Moad Rashad Al-Saggaa In-charge of Training, Human Rights Commission Saudi Arabia

Mr. Abdulla Al-Suwaidi Head HR Department, Emirates Center for Strategic Studies and Research ECSSR

Ms. Gabriela Alvarez Master Student, Katholieke Universiteit Leuven, Ecuador

Mr. Gamini Amarawardena Additional Secretary, Ministry of Disaster Management and Human Rights, Sri Lanka

Mr. Bakhtiar Amin Former Minister of Human Rights, International Alliance for Justice, Iraq

Dr. Hirbod Aminlari Principal Advisor - Promotion of Rule of Law in Afghanistan, Deutsche Gesellschaft für Technische Zusammenarbeit (GTZ) GmbH, Germany

---

List of Participants

K. Ambos et al. (eds.), *Building a Future on Peace and Justice: Studies on Transitional Justice, Peace and Development*.

Ms. Rina Amiri Senior Regional Advisor, Open Society Institute, Afghanistan

Ms. Monica Andersson Senior Adviser, International Law and Human Rights Department, Ministry for Foreign Affairs SE, Sweden

Mr. Milos Antic Center for Trauma

Mr. Martin Arévalo de León Executive Director, National Reparation Program, Gutemala

Mr. Rodrigo Arrangoiz Raya Advisor to the Undersecretary for Multilateral Affairs & HR, Ministry of Foreign Affairs, Mexico

Ms. Jana Asher Statistics and Human Rights, USA

Ms. Amy Baker Director, Human Rights and Participation, Canadian International Development Agency, Canada

Mr. Pascal Balegamire Bureau por l'Observatoire de la Republique

Ms. Isabelle Balot Africa Division I Desk Officer Sudan, UN Secretariat

Mr. Ian Bannon Manager, World Bank Group, Australia

Mr. Dongmo Eric Bapfou Field Co-ordinator, Global Foundation for Peace, Justice, Human Right Democracy and Development, Cameroun

Ms. Nicole Barrett Trial Attorney, Prosecution, International Criminal Tribunal for the Former Yugoslavia ICTY, USA

Mr. Sefan Barriga Botschaftsrat LL.M, Botschaft des Fürstentums Liechtenstein

Dr. Sebastian Bartsch Administrator, OECD, Germany

Ms. Carmen A. Baugbog Gender Advisor, United Nations Volunteer-United Nations Mission in Sudan, Philippines

Ms. Gloriose Bazigaga Coordinatrice Régionale, International Alert, Rwanda

Ms. Carola Becker DED Friedensfachkraft, Center for Conflict Resolution and Reconciliation (CCRR), Germany

Ms. Karin Becker Oberlandesgericht Nürnberg, Germany

Dr. Nicolas Beger Director, European Peacebuilding Liaison Office EPLO, Germany

Mr. Ewald Behrschmidt Oberlandesgericht Nürnberg, Germany

Ms. Paula Gaviria Benatanaur

Mr. Richard Bennett Chief Human Rights Officer, United Nations Assistance Mission in Afghanistan, New Zealand

Mr. Paul Bentall Head, International Security and Global Issues Research Group, Foreign and Commonwealth Office UK, UK

Mr. Mayele Bernardin Ghyor Ebokwol Head of Department Europe, Ministry of Foreign Affairs RD Congo, RD Congo

Ms. Jessica Berns Program Manager, Coexistence International at Brandeis University, USA

Rev. Rigobert Minani Bihuzo Chef de Secteur, Réseau d'Organisations des Droits Humains, RD Congo

Ms. Mô Bleeker Chargée de programme, Ministère des Affaires Etrangères CH, Switzerland

Mr. Silas Bogati Executive Director, Caritas Nepal, Nepal

Ms. Yabah Berthe Bognini Consultante, Association Ivoirienne pour le Développement du Droit, Ivory Coast

Ms. Viola Bölscher Senior Consultant, Iber-Consult, Germany

Mr. Emmanuel Bombande Executive Director, WANEP, Ghana

Lord Iain Bonomy Judge, UN International Criminal Tribunal for the former Yugoslavia, UK

Ms. Monika Borgmann-Slim Co-Direktor, Umam Documentation & Research, Germany

Mr. Goran Božicevic Director, Miramida Center - Regional Peacebuilding Exchange, Croatia

Ms. Helga Brandstätter Menschenrechtsbildung, Stadt Nürnberg, Germany

Ms. Dunja Brede Seniorfachplanerin, Deutsche Gesellschaft für Technische Zusammenarbeit (GTZ) GmbH, Germany

Dr. Susanne Buckley- Zistel Peace Research Institute Frankfurt, Germany

Ms. Anna Buellesbach Head of Liaison Office, UNHCR, Germany

Ms. Diana Burghardt Bonn International Center for Conversion BICC, Germany

Prof. William Burke-White Professor, University of Pennsylvania Law School, USA

Ms. Maureen Burnley The Desmond Tutu Education Center

Ms. Vannath Chea Deputy Chief Commissioner, Girl Guide Association of Cambodia, Cambodia

Ms. Sofiane Chouiter Avocat, Ligue Algerienne pour la defense des droits de l'homme, Algeria

Ms. Maria Giuliana Civinini Référéndaire, Cour de Cassation - Italie, Italy

Ms. Sarah Cliffe Head, Fragile States Group, World Bank, UK

Counsellor Fernando Joao Conselho Embassy of Mozambique, Mozambique

Mr. Jesus Cuellar

Mr. Esteban Cuya Koordinator, Koalition gegen Straflosigkeit, Germany

Ms. Awa Dabo Transitional Governance Specialist, UNDP/BCPR, Gambia

Mr. Hussam Daher avocat a la cour/ doctorant en droit international, Barreau du Tripoli, LIBAN, Lebanon

Mr. Jone Dakuvula Director of Programmes, Citizens' Constitutional Forum, Fiji

Dr. Yael Danieli Past-President, Senior Representative to the United Nations, International Society for Traumatic Stress Studies, USA/Israel

Mr. Suvash Kumar Darnal Chairperson, Jagaran Media Center, Nepal

Ms. Vanita Datta Global Services, IBM, USA

Mr. Paco de Oris Producer, Skylight Pictures, USA

Ms. Franceline Delgado Ariza Becaria del DAAD, Universidad de Gottingen, Colombia

Mr. Richard Dicker director, international justice program, Human Rights Watch

Mr. Jens Dieckmann Attorney at Law, Germany, Becher&Dieckmann, Germany

Mr. Volker Dieckmann Nürnberger Menschenrechtszentrum e.V., Germany

Ms. Aleksandra Dimic Projektassistentin, Deutsche Gesellschaft für Technische Zusammenarbeit (GTZ) GmbH, Serbia

Ms. Andrea Dini Modigliani Student, Università degli studi di Trento, Italy

Mr. Kouassi Dotche-Togbe Government of Togo

Mr. Jesus Gestuveo Dureza Head of Agency, Office of the Presidential Advisor of the Peace Process, Philippines

Dr. Alistair D. Edgar Executive Director, Academic Council on the UN System, British/Canadian

Mr. Leon-Gomez Eduardo-Pizarro President, Comision Nacional de Reconciliation y Reparacion

Ms. Jihan El-Alaily Chief News Editor/UNMIS Radio, UN Mission in Sudan/UNMIS, Egypt

Christina Elich Senior Programme Officer, UNDP Guatemala, Netherlands

Mr. Steffen Emrich Referent Friedensförderung, World Vision Germany, Germany

Dr. Diane Enns Assistant Professor, McMaster University, Canada

Ms. Eysa Escobar Panama

Ms. Helga Fastrup Ervik senior adviser, Ministry of Foreign Affairs Norway, Norway

Ms. Birgit Felleisen Fachreferentin für Frieden und zivile Konfliktbearbeitung, Misereor, Germany

Dr. Martina Fischer stv. Leiterin, Berghof Forschungszentrum f. konstruktive Konfliktbearbeitung, Germany

Ms. Sylvia Fletcher Sr Advisor & Governance Portfolio Manager, UNDP Somalia, USA

Ms. Caroline Flintoft Research Manager, International Crisis Group, USA

Mr. Ekkehard Forberg Manager Advocacy and Peacebuilding, World Vision Germany, Germany

Mr. Andreas Forer Berater der kolombianischen Staatsanwaltschaft, Stiftung für internationale rechtliche Zusammenarbeit (IRZ), Germany

Dr. Stefan Franke Oberlandesgericht Nürnberg, Germany

Dr. Jörg Freiberg -Strauß Programmleiter des Friedensprogramms der GTZ in Guatemala, Deutsche Gesellschaft für Technische Zusammenarbeit (GTZ) GmbH, Germany

Mr. Ulrich Frey Plattform Zivile Konfliktbearbeitung, Germany

Dr. Emanuela Fronza University of Trento

Ms. Ann Frotscher Political Affairs Officer, UN/MINUSTAH, Germany

Ms. Ruth Fuchs Doktorandin, GIGA Hamburg, Germany

Ms. Martina Gaebler Student in, MA, Universität Manchester, Germany

Mr. Gustavo Gallón Director, Comisión Colombiana de Juristas, Colombia

Ms. Patricia Galvao Teles Consultant, Ministry of Foreign Affairs Portugal

Mr. Ronald Gamarra Professor universitario, Universidad Nacional Mayor de San Marcos, Peru

Mr. Jean-Marie Gasana SENIOR ANALYST, FEWER Africa, Rwanda

Ms. Paula Gaviria Directora Derechos Humanos y paz, Fundacion Social, Colombia

Mr. Kiflemariam Gebrewold Christian Relief and Development Association

Mr. Gerhard Geim Oberlandesgericht Nürnberg, Germany

Dr. Nils Geissler Amnesty International, Germany

Dr. Rainer Gemählich Oberlandesgericht Nürnberg, Germany

Konsul Weldeslassie Ghebremedhin Ambassador, Embassy of the State of Eritrea, Eritrea

Mr. Avner Gidron Senior Policy Adviser, Amnesty International, USA/UK

Generalkonsul Claus Gielisch Jordanischer Honorarkonsular Embassy of the Hashemite Kingdom of Jordan, Germany

Mr. Tikue B. Girmay UN Mission in Sudan

Mr. Wilfried Graf Co-Director, Institute for Conflict Transformation and Peacebuilding IICP, Austria

Mr. Igor Grexa Director General, Ministry of Foreign Affairs Slovakia

Prof. Dr. Nick Grief Steele Raymond LLP Professor of Law, Bournemouth University, UK

Ms. Huma Haider Research Fellow, GSDRC - University of Birmingham

Ms. Astrid Hake Koordination, peace brigades international, Germany

Ms. Lubna Hammad Al-Quds University

Dr. Gerd Hankel wissenschaftlicher Mitarbeiter, Hamburger Institut für Sozialforschung, Germany

Dr. Peter Hanser-Strecker Schott Musik International

Mr. Yinbiao Hao Program Officer, United Nations Association

Mr. Adnan Hasanbegovic Centre for Non-Violent Action Sarajevo

Mr. Dietmar Hasse Gesellschaft für bedrohte Völker

Ms. Ute Hegener Sprecherin German Platform for Peaceful Conflict Transformation, Germany

Mr. Wilhelm Heidrich Stadt Nürnberg

Dr. Roland Helgerth Oberlandesgericht Nürnberg, Germany

Mr. Dominik Helling Consultant, Robert Bosch Stiftung, Germany

Ambassador Ortwin Hennig Vice President & Head of Conflict Prevention Program, EastWest Institute, Germany

Mr. Yazir Henry Director, Direct Action Centre for Peace and Memory DAC, South Africa

Helmut Henseler German Jordanian Society

Ms. Ulrike Herbig Nürnberger Symphoniker

Mr. Ahmed Herzenni Conseil Consultatif des Droits de l'Homme

Ms. Kate Hess

Dr. Hans Hesselmann Head of the Human Rights Office, City of Nuremberg, Germany

Dr. Ahmed Hood Engineer, Sudan

Prof. Dr. Thomas Hoppe, Prof. für katholische Sozialethik Helmut-Schmidt-Universität Hamburg, Germany

Dr. Rainer Huhle Nürnberger Menschenrechtszentrum e.V., Germany

Mr. Mohamed Ibrahim Chairman, CRD

Mr. Niamatullah Ibrahimi Research Officer, Crisis States Research Centre, The London School of Economics and Political Science (LSE), Afghanistan

Ms. Gertrude Imbwae Permanent Secretary, Ministry of Justice Zambia

Mr. Hassan Jabareen Adalah

Mr. Shawan Jabarin General Director, Al Haq

Mr. Allan Jacobsen Deputy Head of Department, Ministry of Foreign Affairs DK, Denmark

Mr. Alpha Amadu Jalloh National Director, Youth Movement for Peace & Non-Violence, Sierra Leone

Mr. Joshi Janak

Mr. Stefan Jansen Senior Consultant, Iber-Consult, Germany

Dr. Riad Jarjour President/acting director, Forum for Development, Culture and Dialogue, Lebanese/cypriot

Dr. Radhames Jimenez Peña Procurador General, Procuraduria General de Republica Dominicana, Dominikanische Republik

Ms. Agneta Johansson Deputy Director, International Legal Assistance Consortium (ILAC), Sweden

Ms. Claudia Josi lic. iur. Graduate Assistant, Institut für Föderalismus, Fribourg, Switzerland

Mr. Jude Kagoro Project Officer, Makerere University, Uganda

Mr. Wolfgang Kaiser Ref. Entwicklungspolitischer Dialog, Evangelischer Entwicklungsdienst (EED), Germany

Mr. Tobias Kallenbach Graduate Assistant, University of Fribourg, Switzerland

Mr. Nilly Kanana First Secretary, Kenya Permanent Mission to UN, Kenya

Ms. Gesche Karrenbrock UNHCR

Dr. Klaus Kastner Oberlandesgericht Nürnberg, Germany

Mr. Kaswamu Katota Legal Officer, Ministry of Foreign Affairs Zambia

Ms. Barbara Kemper Associate Fellow, Institut für Entwicklung und Frieden - Universität Duisburg-Essen, Germany

Ms. Annie Keogh Vocational Training Advisor, Ministry of Labour and Community Reinsertion AUS, Australia

Ms. Christina Kerll Referendarin, Landgericht Köln, Germany

Dr. Sona Khan Head of the Organization, Khan Law Firm, India

Dr. Uwe Kievelitz Kompetenzfeldleiter, Deutsche Gesellschaft für Technische Zusammenarbeit (GTZ) GmbH, Germany

Mr. Ken Kinney Executive Director, Development Institute Ghana, Ghana

Dr. Riina Kionka Personal Representative for Human Rights, of Secretary-General/High Representative, Council of European Union, Estonia

Mr. Emmanuel Kisiangani PhD Candidate, University of the Witwatersrand, Kenya

Mr. Dismas Kitenge Senga Président du Groupe LOTUS et Chef de Travaux à l'Université Groupe LOTUS-Université de Kisangani, RD Congo

Mr. Michael Kläver Sparkasse Nürnberg

Ms. Jhanna Kläver Sparkasse Nürnberg

Mr. Matthias Kloth Rechtsreferent, Europarat, Germany

Mr. Nandor Knust Researcher, Max Planck Institute for Foreign and International Criminal Law, Germany

Ms. Sutheshna Kodeeswaran Program Officer, FLICT/GTZ Sri Lanka, Sri Lanka

Mr. Venance Konan journaliste, écrivain, Ivory Coast

Prof. Dr. Horst Kopp Universität Erlangen-Nürnberg

Ms. Gudrun Kramer Co-Director, Institute for Conflict Transformation and Peacebuilding IICP, Austria

Ms. Gabriele Kruk Deutsche Gesellschaft für Technische Zusammenarbeit (GTZ) GmbH, Germany

Dr. Koulsy Lamko Director, Kuljaamaopcion, Tschad

Mr. Stephen Arthur Lamony Coordinator Uganda Coalition for the ICC, Human Rights Network Uganda, Uganda

Prof. Dr. Jon-Mirena Landa Gorostiza Director de Derechos Humanos, Gobierno Vasco, Spain

Ms. Andrea Laverde Universidad de Bologna, Colombia

Dr. Young Jo Lee Standing Commissioner, Truth and Reconciliation Commission, Korea

Mr. Marcus Lenzen Conflict Programme Specialist, UNDP - Bureau for Crisis Prevention and Recovery, Germany

Mr. Kai Leonhardt Fachkonzeptionist/ Diplom-Psychologe, Deutsche Gesellschaft für Technische Zusammenarbeit (GTZ) GmbH, Germany

Mr. Salomón Lerner Febres Presidente ejecutivo, Instituto Democracia y Derechos Humanos de la Pontificia Universidad Católica del Perú, Peru

Mr. Mariusz Lewicki III Secretary, Peacekeeping/Peacebuilding Expert, Ministry of Foreign Affairs Poland, Poland

Mr. Paul Linnarz DW-Media Services GmbH, Germany

Ms. Michaela Lissowsky Nürnberger Menschenrechtszentrum e.V., Germany

Mr. Jörg Lüer Generalsekretär der Europäischen Kommission Justitia et Pax, Deutsche Kommission Justitia et Pax, Germany

Ms. Lynn Maalouf Consultant, ICTJ Consultant, Beirut, Lebanon

Ms. Holly D. Maassarani graduate student, American University

Ms. Sofia Macher Coordinadora Area de Gobernabilidad y Derechos Humanos, Instituto de Defensa Legal, Peru

Mr. Antonio Madariaga Director Ejecutivo, Corporacion Viva la Ciudadanía, Colombia

Mr. Tshepo Madlingozi Advocacy coordinator, Khulumani Support Group, South Africa

Mr. Dieter Magsam Avocat/Consultant, Republikanischer Anwältinnen und Anwaltsverein e.V., Germany

Mr. Jean Makenga Director General, Ministry of Justice Burundi

Mr. Ulrich Mans Researcher, Hague Centre for Strategic Studies

Ms. Binta Mansaray Special Court Outreach Coordinator, Special Court for Sierra Leone, Sierra Leone

Prof. Julissa Mantilla Professor, Pontificia Universidad Católica del Perú, Peru

Prof. Wolfgang Manz Hochschule für Musik

Mr. Ojara Martin Mapenduzi District Speaker, Gulu District Local Government, Uganda

Mr. Peter Mares Leiter Projekt zivik, Institut für Auslandsbeziehungen e. V., Germany

Mr. David Marshall Office of the High Commissioner for Human Rights, UN Secretariat

Mr. Percy Masigo Project Manager, Denis Hurley Peace Institute, South Africa

Mr. Rami Masri German Palestinian Friendship Association

Ms. Geraldine Mattioli International Justice Advocate, Human Rights Watch, France

Mr. Phebe Mavungu PhD STUDENT, OLIVER SCHREINER SCHOOL OF LAW, University of the Witwatersrand, RD Congo

Mr. Chris Mburu Regional Advisor on Democracy, United Nations Centre for Human Rights and Democracy, Kenya

Dr. Eamonn McKee Director Conflict Resolution Unit, Department of Foreign Affairs IE, Ireland

Ms. Claudia Medina Directora de Proyectos, Centro Internacional de Toledo para la Paz (CITpax)

Mr. Mato Meyer Programme Specialist, UNDP Serbia, USA

Mr. Nils Meyer-Abich Wiss. Mitarbeiter, Universität Göttingen, Germany

Mr. Hassan Mneimneh Iraq Memory Foundation

Dr. Eirin Mobekk Consultant, Center for International Cooperation and Security CICS, Norway

Dr. Ralf-Matthias Mohs Referatsleiter 204 (Afghanistan, Bangladesh, Pakistan), BMZ, Germany

Ms. Carolin Moje MPP Kandidatin, Hertie School of Governance, Germany

Ms. Moliehi Florence Mokoteli Deputy Director, Ministry of Justice Lesotho, Lesotho

Ms. Adriana Montenegro Master student, Katholieke Universiteit Leuven, Ecuador

Ms. Irene Morada Santiago Chair and Chief Executive Officer, Mindanao Commission on Women, Philippines

Rev. Mulbah K. Morlu Chairman, Forum for the Establishment of a War Crimes Court in Liberia, Liberia

Ms. Horia Mosadiq Afghan Civil Society

Commissaire General Marius Mouambenga Ministre Delegue, Comite de Suivi de la Convention pour la Paix CG

Ms. Khanyisela Moyo PHd Research Fellow, Transitional Justice Institute, University of Ulster, Zimbabwe

Ms. Florence Mpaayei Acting Executive Director, Nairobi Peace Initiative - Africa, Kenya

Dr. Karin Müller Coordinator, Ecumenical Network Central Africa (ÖNZ), Germany

Mr. Maxie Joseph Muwonge Executive Director, Fellowship Of Reconciliation in Uganda (Jamii Ya Kupatanisha), Uganda

Ambassador Marcin Nawrot Director of the UN Department, MFA, Ministry of Foreign Affairs Poland, Poland

Ms. Fatuma Ndangiza Unity and Reconciliation Commission, Rwanda

Mr VLR I Thomas Neisinger Head of Division International Penal Law, Auswärtiges Amt, Germany

Mr. Soth Plai Ngarm Executive Director, Alliance for Conflict Transformation (ACT), Cambodia

Mr. Arnold J. Nicholson Attorney General and Minister of Justice, Ministry of Justice Jamaica, Jamaica

Ms. Heike Niebergall Senior Legal Officer / Reparation Programmes, International Organization for Migration (IOM), Germany

Mr. Louis-Marie Nindorera Country Director, Global Rights, Burundi

Mr. Ousman Njikam Research assistant, Institute for Criminal Law and Criminal Justice - Universität Göttingen, Germany

Mr. Günter Nooke Beauftragter der Bundesregierung für Menschenrechtspolitik und Humanitäre Hilfe im Auswärtigen Amt, Auswärtiges Amt, Germany

Ms. Martine Nourry Assistante de Coordination, CSAPR Tchad, France

Fr. Emmanuel Ntakarutimana Coordinateur, Centre Ubuntu, Burundi

Rev. Daniel Ntoni-Nzinga Executive Secretary, Comite Inter-Ecclesial para Paz em Angola, Angola

Mr. Thomas Obel Hansen PhD Fellow, University of Aarhus, Denmark, Denmark

Mr. Jin Hwan Oh Commissioner, Truth and Reconciliation Commission Korea, Korea

Mr. Boniface Ojok Project Officer and Research Advisor, Justice and Reconciliation Project, Gulu District NGO Forum and Liu Institute for Global Issues, Uganda

Mr. Torsten Oltmanns Roland Berger Consultants

His Highness David Onen Acana II (RWOT), Paramount Chief, Ker Kwaro Acholi, Uganda

Mr. Lievin Ongombe Avocat/Président de la C P J asbl, Culture pour la Paix etla Justice 'C P J 'asbl, RD Congo

Dr. Henry Onoria Senior Lecturer, Makerere University, Uganda

Ms. Onyinye Onwuka Senior Research Fellow, Institute for Peace and Conflict Resolution, Nigeria

Mr. Sonny Onyegbula HUMAN RIGHTS OFFICER, UN Mission Ethopia and Eritrea, Nigeria

Mr. Seth Oppenheim Robert Bosch Stiftung, USA

Ms. Maria del Carmen Orbegoso Alvarez Estudiante, Hertie School of Governance, Peru

Mr. Alina Orosan 3rd Secretary, Ministry of Foreign Affairs Romania, Romania

Ms. Juliane Osterhaus Projektleiterin, Deutsche Gesellschaft für Technische Zusammenarbeit (GTZ) GmbH, Germany

Mr. Bruce Michael Oswald Senior Lecturer in Law, University of Melbourne, Australia

Dr. Galain Pablo Researcher, Max-Planck-Institut für ausländisches und internationales Strafrecht, Uruguay

Mr. William Pace Convenor, Coalition for the International Criminal Court, USA

Mr. Wolf-Christian Paes Senior Researcher, Bonn International Center for Conversion BICC, Germany

Ms. Anne Palm Secretary General, Civil Society Conflict Prevention Network KATU, Finland

Ms. Carol Palmer Permanent Secretary, Ministry of Justice Jamaica, Jamaica

Ms. Michelle Parlevliet Conflict Transformation Advisor

Ms. Christa Pelikan Institut für Rechts- und Kriminalsoziologie, Austria

Mr. Rinzin Penjor Judge, Judiciary of Bhutan, Bhutan

Mr. Max Pensky Senior Visiting Fellow, Department of Politics and International Relations, Oxford University, USA

Dr. Luis Peral Director, Conflict Prevention and Resolution Programme, International Center of Toledo for Peace, Spain

Ambassador Hipolito Pereira Zozimo Patricio Inspector General, Ministry of Foreign Affairs and Cooperation MZ, Mozambique

Dr. Phoung Pham Associate Director, Payson Center of Tulane University, USA

Mr. Said Pirmurat Doktorand, Universität Göttingen, Germany

Ms. Beatrice Pisani University of Trento, Italy

Dr. Michael Platzer Visiting Professor, Bond University Australia, Austria

Mr. Jagadish Chandra Pokharel Vice Chairman, National Planning Commission

Ms. Olivera Puric Team Leader, UNDP Serbia, Serbia

Ms. Tatjana Quast Direktorin für Menschenrechte, European Law Students Association, Germany

H.E. Salem A. Quateen Head of Mission, League of Arab States - Mission Berlin, Libya

Mr. Joseph Rahall Executive Director, Green Scenery, Sierra Leone

Mr. Iavor Rangelov London School of Economics, Bulgaria

Mr. Knut Rauchfuss Campaign "Justice heals", Germany

Ms. Ursula Reich freie Gutachterin, Switzerland

Ms. Gerda-Marie Reitzenstein Oberlandesgericht Nürnberg, Germany

Ms. Ursula Renner Projektkoordinator, Forum Ziviler Friedensdienst, Germany

Ms. Cornelia Richter Bereichsleiterin PuE, Deutsche Gesellschaft für Technische Zusammenarbeit (GTZ) GmbH, Germany

Dr. Matthias Ries Leiter der Fachgruppe Zivile Konfliktbearbeitung und Friedensförderung, Deutscher Entwicklungsdienst DED, Germany

Mr. Syed Rifaat Hussain Executive Director, Regional Centre for Strategic Studies, Pakistan

Dr. Susanne Riveles Convenor of the Commission on Peace and Security and Consultant with FENICC, International Alliance of Women; and Faith and Ethics Network for the ICC, American/German

Mr. Wolfram Rohde-Liebenau Director, Ökumenisches Netz Bayern, Germany

Ms. Catrin Rosquist Life and Peace Institute, Sweden

Ms. Julia Rutz Senior expert Human Rights and Governance, AGEG Consultants, Germany

Ms. Henriette Sachse Gastwissenschaftlerin/Doktorandin HU-Berlin, Stitung Wissenschaft und Politik, Germany

Mr. Choucri Sader Chef du departement de la legislation et des consultations, Ministry of Justice Libanon, Libanon

Mr. Noah Salameh Director, Center for Conflict Resolution and Reconciliation (CCRR), Palestine

Mr. Mario Schäffer Oberlandesgericht Nürnberg, Germany

Ms. Ingrid Schantora Stadt Nürnberg

Dr. Stephanie Schell-Faucon Senior Advisor, Deutsche Gesellschaft für Technische Zusammenarbeit (GTZ) GmbH, Germany

Dr. Elisabeth Scheper Fellow, Harvard Weatherhead Centre for International Affairs, Netherlands

Ms. Hildegard Scheu Project Coordinator Africa, medico international, Germany

Dr. Monika Schlicher Geschäftsführerin, Watch Indonesia! e.V., Germany

Ms. Bianca Schmolze Project Manager, Campaign "Justice heals", Germany

Ms. Martien Schotsmans International and transitional justice, Avocats Sans Frontières, Belgium

Ms. Eva Schreuder Policy Advisor, Netherlands Ministry of Foreign Affairs, Netherlands

Ms. Petra Schultz Project Coordinator, Eurient, Germany

Ms. Christiane Schulz Regionalkoordination Lateinamerika, Diakonisches Werk der EKD, Germany

Mr. Günter Schulz-Weckert Oberlandesgericht Nürnberg, Germany

Mr. Jürgen Schurr Project Coordinator, FIDH & REDRESS, Germany

Ms. Gaby Schuster Stadt Nürnberg

Mr. Nenad Sebek Executive Director, Center for Democracy and Reconciliation Southeast Europe (CDSEE), UK

Mr. Luis Serradas Tavanes Director, Ministry of Foreign Affairs Portugal, Portugal

Mr. Manhal Shaath Economic Affairs Department, Ministry of Foreign Affairs, Palestinian National Authority

Mr. Adel Shaltut Third Secretary, Foreign Affairs Libya, Libya

Ms. Rebecca Shaw Peace, Conflict and Development Manager, AusAID, Australia

Mr. Ben Shepherd Africa Research Analyst, Foreign and Commonwealth Office UK, UK

Dr. Javad Rekabi Sherbaf Managing Director, Neda Institute for Scientific Political Research, Iran

Ms. Indira Shrestha Chief-executive, Sthriishakti, Nepal

Prof. Dr. Ulrich Sieber Direktor, Max-Planck-Institut für ausländisches und internationales Strafrecht, Germany

Ms. Friederike Sieber

Mr. Jan Michael Simon Referatsleiter Lateinamerika, Max-Planck-Institut für ausländisches und internationales Strafrecht, Germany

Ms. Susanne Skoruppa Visiting Fellow, UNDP/BDP/DGG, Germany

Mr. Lokman Slim Director, Umam Documentation and Research

Counsellor Muftah Ali Smeida Head of Section, Ministry of Foreign Affairs Libya, Libya

Ms. Durga Sob President, Feminist Dalit Organisation FEDO, Nepal

Mr. Raji Sourani Director, Palestinian Centre for Human Rights, Palestine

Mr. Christoph Sperfeldt Wiss. Mitarbeiter, Friedrich-Schiller-Universität Jena, Germany

Ms. Caroline Sperling Civil Peace Servant, peace brigades international, Germany

Ms. Bea Stalenhoef Programme Officer, OxfamNovib, Netherlands

Oberkirchenrat Wilfried Steen Stellv. Vorstandsvorsitzender, Evangelischer Entwicklungsdienst (EED), Germany

Mr. Uecker Stefan Desk Officer, Federal Office for Migration and Refugees, Germany

Mr. Ignaz Stegmiller Lehrstuhl Ambos, Universität Goettingen, Germany

Ms. Margot Stroeken Country Policy Officer (Uganda), Centre for Justice and Reconciliation, Netherlands

Dr. Robert Sturm Botschafter der Republik Vanuatu, Germany

Dr. Mia Swart Senior Lecturer, University of the Witwatersrand, South Africa

Mr. Bukeni T. Waruzi Executive Director, AJEDI-Ka, RD Congo

Prof. Yukiko Takashiba Director, Institute for International Strategic Studies (ISS), Asia Pacific University (APU), Japan

Mr. Guillaume Teerling First Secretary, Netherlands Embassy Kabul, Netherlands

Ms. Marika Theros Crimes of War Project

Mr. Engelbert Theuermann Director, Federal Ministry for European and International Affairs AT

Ms. Petra Thöla Stadt Nürnberg

Ms. Nanna Thue Senior Adviser, Norwegian Ministry of Foreign Affairs, Norway

Ms. Ilona Topa PhD Candidate, University of Silesia, Poland

Ms. Susanne Treiber UNIFEM, Germany

Prof. Bakhtiyar Tuzmukhamedov Counsellor, Constitutional Court of the Russian Federation, Russian Federation

Ms. Barbara Unger Deputy Director & Senior Coordinator, Berghof Foundation for Peace Support, Germany

Ms. Marta Valiñas Researcher, Katholieke Universiteit Leuven, Portugal

Ms. Nahla Valji Project Manager, Centre for the Study of Violence and Reconciliation

Ms. Iris Van der Mark Research consultant Reconciliation, Centre for Justice and Reconciliation, Netherlands

Dr. Patrick Vinck Director, Berkeley-Tulane Initiative on Vulnerable Populations, University of California, Berkeley, Belgium

Ms. Leonie von Braun Working Group against Impunity - Speaker, Amnesty International, Germany

Ms. George Wachira Senior Research & Policy Advisor, Nairobi Peace Initiative - Africa, Kenya

Mr. Abdul Wahab Musah Programs Officer, Center for Democratic Development-Ghana, Ghana

Mr. Ndung'u Wainaina Director, International Center for Policy and Conflict

Mr. Patrick Walsh SRP-CAVR Secretariado Tecnico, Australia

Ms. Massa Washington Commissioner, Truth & Reconciliation Commission, Liberia

Mr. Horst Weise Leiter, Institut für internationale Sicherheitspolitik (ISPOL), Germany

Prof. Dr. Elmar Weitekamp Professor, Institute of Criminology, University of Tübingen, Germany

Mr. Jan Erik Wetzel Universität Bonn, Germany

Dr. Undine Whande Board Member, Weltfriedensdienst, Germany

Dr. Carsten Wieland Leiter Kolumbien, Konrad Adenauer Stiftung, Germany

Dr. Georg Witschel Director General for Legal Affairs, Auswärtiges Amt, Germany

Dr. Norbert Wühler Director, Reparation Programmes, International Organization for Migration (IOM), Germany

Ms. Pamela Yates President, Skylight Pictures , USA

Ambassador Sirajuddin Hamid Yousuf Ambassador, Ministry of Foreign Affairs SD, Sudan

Mr. Markus Johannes Zech PhD Candidate, University of Constance, Germany

Prof. Marcos A. Zilli Professor and State Criminal Judge, Instituto Brasileiro de Ciências Criminais - IBC-CRim, Brazil